The Effects of Taxation on
Capital Accumulation

A National Bureau
of Economic Research
Project Report

The Effects of Taxation on Capital Accumulation

Edited by **Martin Feldstein**

 The University of Chicago Press

Chicago and London

Martin Feldstein is the George F. Baker Professor of Economics
at Harvard University and President of the National Bureau of
Economic Research.

The University of Chicago Press, Chicago 60637
The University of Chicago Press, Ltd., London

© 1987 by the National Bureau of Economic Research
All rights reserved. Published 1987
Printed in the United States of America

96 95 94 93 92 91 90 89 88 87   5 4 3 2 1

Library of Congress Cataloging-in-Publication Data

The Effects of taxation on capital accumulation.

(A National Bureau of Economic Research project
report)
  Bibliography: p.
  Includes index.
  1. Taxation. 2. Saving and investment. I. Feldstein,
Martin S. II. Series.
HJ2305.E29 1987 332'.0415   86-25025

ISBN 0-226-24088-6

Relation of the Directors to the
Work and Publications of the
National Bureau of Economic Research

1. The object of the National Bureau of Economic Research is to ascertain and to present to the public important economic facts and their interpretation in a scientific and impartial manner. The Board of Directors is charged with the responsibility of ensuring that the work of the National Bureau is carried on in strict conformity with this object.

2. The President of the National Bureau shall submit to the Board of Directors, or to its Executive Committee, for their formal adoption all specific proposals for research to be instituted.

3. No research report shall be published by the National Bureau until the President has sent each member of the Board a notice that a manuscript is recommended for publication and that in the President's opinion it is suitable for publication in accordance with the principles of the National Bureau. Such notification will include an abstract or summary of the manuscript's content and a response form for use by those Directors who desire a copy of the manuscript for review. Each manuscript shall contain a summary drawing attention to the nature and treatment of the problem studied, the character of the data and their utilization in the report, and the main conclusions reached.

4. For each manuscript so submitted, a special committee of the Directors (including Directors Emeriti) shall be appointed by majority agreement of the President and Vice Presidents (or by the Executive Committee in case of inability to decide on the part of the President and Vice Presidents), consisting of three Directors selected as nearly as may be one from each general division of the Board. The names of the special manuscript committee shall be stated to each Director when notice of the proposed publication is submitted to him. It shall be the duty of each member of the special manuscript committee to read the manuscript. If each member of the manuscript committee signifies his approval within thirty days of the transmittal of the manuscript, the report may be published. If at the end of that period any member of the manuscript committee withholds his approval, the President shall then notify each member of the Board, requesting approval or disapproval of publication, and thirty days additional shall be granted for this purpose. The manuscript shall then not be published unless at least a majority of the entire Board who shall have voted on the proposal within the time fixed for the receipt of votes shall have approved.

5. No manuscript may be published, though approved by each member of the special manuscript committee, until forty-five days have elapsed from the transmittal of the report in manuscript form. The interval is allowed for the receipt of any memorandum of dissent or reservation, together with a brief statement of his reasons, that any member may wish to express; and such memorandum of dissent or reservation shall be published with the manuscript if he so desires. Publication does not, however, imply that each member of the Board has read the manuscript, or that either members of the Board in general or the special committee have passed on its validity in every detail.

6. Publications of the National Bureau issued for informational purposes concerning the work of the Bureau and its staff, or issued to inform the public of activities of Bureau staff, and volumes issued as a result of various conferences involving the National Bureau shall contain a specific disclaimer noting that such publication has not passed through the normal review procedures required in this resolution. The Executive Committee of the Board is charged with review of all such publications from time to time to ensure that they do not take on the character of formal research reports of the National Bureau, requiring formal Board approval.

7. Unless otherwise determined by the Board or exempted by the terms of paragraph 6, a copy of this resolution shall be printed in each National Bureau publication.

(Resolution adopted October 25, 1926, as revised through September 30, 1974)

Contents

Acknowledgments

This volume brings together fourteen papers that were prepared as part of an ongoing study of the effects of taxation on capital accumulation that is being carried out at the National Bureau of Economic Research. Taken as a whole, these studies show that current tax rules and changes in tax rules have powerful effects on business investment in plant and equipment, on personal saving, and on the realization of capital gains.

The NBER research on taxation and capital accumulation has been discussed at regular meetings of the Bureau's tax program and at special meetings focused on this project. The papers included in this volume were presented at a conference on February 13–16, 1986. The remarks of the discussants at that conference are also included in this volume.

The collaborative research presented here was made possible by continuing activities of the NBER's tax program. Several members of that program contributed to the effort even though they did not prepare papers for this volume. The volume thus benefited from the general guidance of tax program director David F. Bradford. National Bureau Directors George T. Conklin, Jr., Ann F. Friedlaender, and J. Clay LaForce have reviewed the entire manuscript. National Bureau staff members Mark Fitz-Patrick, Deborah Mankiw, Kathi Smith, Annie Spillane, Gail Swett, and Kirsten Foss Davis contributed to the overall effort.

Introduction

Martin Feldstein

Capital formation has long been a central focus of the research of the National Bureau because of the central role of capital accumulation in the process of economic growth. NBER studies in this area, including the work of Simon Kuznets, Raymond Goldsmith, and Milton Friedman, have focused on the determinants of saving as well as on the process of investment in plant and equipment.

A high saving rate leads to a high rate of investment in plant and equipment and in housing since the increased flow of saving reduces the equilibrium cost of funds to prospective borrowers. The rate of saving is, of course, influenced by many factors in addition to the tax rules emphasized in the current volume. Demographic factors, retirement arrangements, and public and private pension systems have an important independent influence. Tax rules, as the evidence in this volume indicates, are important because they affect the return that savers receive in exchange for postponing consumption.

Investment in plant and equipment is a critical aspect of economic activity, for it contributes directly to raising productivity and therefore to raising the nation's standard of living. An increase in saving does not automatically produce a rise in such investment, however; the savings can go instead into housing or foreign investment. A variety of factors influence the division of the nation's capital stock between plant and equipment, housing and foreign investment. These factors can be summarized as affecting the relative profitability and riskiness of alternative types of investments. The studies in this volume deal with the way taxes affect the profitability of different investments and the impact of those profitability differences on the allocation of the capital stock.

A finding common to several of these studies is that the process of capital formation is quite sensitive to tax rules. With respect to personal

1

saving, Steven Venti and David Wise report an analysis of new survey evidence that indicates that Individual Retirement Accounts have a powerful effect on personal wealth accumulation. They estimate, for example, that an increase in the annual IRA contribution limits would significantly raise contributions, with about half of that increased contribution coming from reduced consumption and most of the remainder coming from reduced tax liabilities. Relatively little of the increased IRA contributions would come from reductions in other types of saving. Thus a rise in the IRA contribution limits would raise national saving even though it reduced tax revenue.

A quite different type of evidence on the sensitivity of personal saving to tax rules is provided by Gregory Mankiw's analysis of the effects of the after-tax interest rate on consumer durable spending. Mankiw's analysis indicates that the after-tax interest rate is an important determinant of consumer spending, especially spending on consumer durables. This implies that tax policies that raise the after-tax return on saving, like the IRA or a partial exclusion of personal interest income, would stimulate personal saving. Similarly, the proposal to eliminate or limit the deductibility of consumer interest would reduce consumer borrowing and raise the net saving rate.

Lawrence Lindsey analyzes the long-term capital gains reported in each tax bracket in every year since 1965. This important body of aggregate data by income class has confirmed the finding of previous studies based on individual tax returns and on household survey data that the decision to realize capital gains is quite sensitive to effective tax rates on realized gains. Lindsey calculates that the sensitivity to high capital gains tax rates is such that a capital gains tax rate above 20% reduces total tax revenue.

My own study with Joosung Jun examines the relationship between tax-induced changes in the net profitability of investment during the past three decades and the share of GNP devoted to net investment in plant and equipment. The evidence indicates a powerful effect of tax rules on business investment that is consistent with past research and with the rise in net investment in the 1980s. Our analysis implies that the types of changes in tax rules that have recently been proposed by the Reagan Administration and legislated by the House of Representatives would significantly reduce business fixed investment. The eventual effect would be to reduce such investment by approximately the full amount of the additional corporate tax revenue.

The frequent changes in tax rules have sensitized businesses to the possibility that existing tax rates and tax rules are subject to change. Alan Auerbach and James Hines analyze the response of business investment to anticipated changes in tax rules and conclude that business investment responds to anticipated tax changes as well as to existing tax rules. Their paper presents estimates of the likely effects of different recent tax proposals on the timing and magnitude of business investments in equipment and structures.

A significant alternative to investment in the United States is additional direct investment in overseas production facilities. The paper by Michael Boskin and William Gale reports that tax-induced changes in the net profitability of investment in the United States has an important effect on the international location of investment, particularly on the amount of foreign direct investment financed by retained earnings. More precisely, Boskin and Gale estimate that for every dollar of increase in U.S. domestic investment induced by tax policy, there is a reduction of approximately six cents of U.S. direct investment abroad financed out of overseas retained earnings. In addition, the increase in U.S. domestic investment includes a significant inflow of direct foreign investment from abroad.

Several previous studies have indicated that existing tax rules distort the allocation of capital among different types of investments. These distortions were a primary reason advanced by the Treasury for its proposed changes in depreciation rules and for elimination of the investment tax credit. The present research confirms the existence of important distortions in investment incentives but indicates that the nature of the bias in current tax law is quite different from what has previously been asserted.

More specifically, in contrast to the common assertion that current tax law factors investment in equipment relative to investment in structures, the study by Roger Gordon, James Hines, and Lawrence Summers concludes that current tax rules favor investment in structures relative to investment in equipment because of the opportunities to redepreciate buildings that are resold, the differential ability to use debt to finance investments in structures, and the possibility of arbitrage between investors in different tax brackets.

Patric Hendershott's study emphasizes that the important investment bias in current tax law is not among different components within the category of business fixed investment but between business fixed investment as a whole and investments in inventories and in owner-occupied housing. Current tax rules impose a much higher effective tax rate on investment in inventories than on investments in business plant and equipment. Moreover, current tax rules imply a much lower effective tax rate on investments in owner-occupied housing than on all forms of business investment. As a result, current tax rules increase the share of investment going into owner-occupied housing and decrease the shares in business plant and equipment and especially in inventories.

Hendershott's analysis shows that although the Treasury's tax plan would reduce the difference in effective tax burdens among different types of corporate assets, it would increase the advantage of real estate relative to corporate assets. Hendershott's calculations indicate that the tax bill passed by the House of Representatives would actually increase the existing overall misallocation of capital and raise the efficiency loss by exacerbating the existing bias in the allocation of capital toward owner-occupied housing and away from corporate investments.

Tax reform could increase national income by achieving a more "level playing field" among different types of assets, but the work of Gordon, Hines, and Summers and that of Hendershott indicate that the critical ingredient in such reform is to reduce the tax on business capital relative to owner-occupied housing.

In a related study, Lawrence Summers reports new evidence from a survey that he conducted of major industrial corporations. The corporations were asked about their method of evaluating investment options, and those companies that used a discounted cash flow technique were asked the discount rate that they used. Summers found that the vast majority of firms used a formal capital budgeting procedure and that the discount rates used for calculating the present value of depreciation allowances (and other components of corporate cash flow) had a median of 15% and a mean of 17%. These discount rates are substantially higher than the 4% real rate assumed by the Treasury in its calculations. One important implication of a high discount rate is that the investment tax credit is a substantially more powerful incentive to invest than an increase in depreciation allowances with an equal present value when discounted at the rate assumed by the Treasury in its analysis.

An important focus of the tax reform debate has been on those companies that pay no corporate tax in a particular year. The papers by Alan Auerbach and James Poterba and by Saman Majd and Stewart Myers examine some of the reasons for and consequences of the temporary no-tax status of corporations. Since these companies in general expect to be subject to tax in the future, the temporary no-tax status has very different effects on their incentives to borrow and invest than a permanent tax exemption would have. These papers indicate the need for addition work on this subject.

Mervyn King's paper explores the implications of shifting to a "cash flow corporate income tax," in which corporations are taxed on the net cash flow received from their activities rather than on any accounting measure of income. Such a tax permits the expensing of all investment but taxes the receipts from borrowing. King discusses a number of the practical problems that would be involved in adopting such a tax.

The final two papers in the volume present calculations based on disaggregated computable general equilibrium models of alternative tax reform proposals. The analysis by Don Fullerton (an NBER Research

Associate and University of Virginia professor who was on leave and serving as Treasury Deputy Assistant Secretary for Tax Policy when this study was completed) and Yolanda Henderson evaluates the potential effect of the Treasury Tax Plan of November 1984 and the president's proposal of May 1985. Their model allows them to assess the potential gains from changes in interasset, intersectoral, interindustry, and intertemporal distortions. They present two parallel analyses corresponding to two alternative views of the effects of dividend taxation on the cost of capita. One view implies that the Treasury plan would produce a sizable increase in the cost of corporate investments while the other view implies that the Administration's tax proposals would cause a slight reduction in the overall cost of capital.

The paper by Charles Ballard, John Scholz, and John Shoven uses a general equilibrium model to evaluate the effects of a value-added tax. The paper finds that the introduction of a VAT and an equal-yield reduction in the personal income tax would improve the efficiency of the economy. The analysis shows the substantial reductions in this gain that result when different value-added tax rates are imposed on different types of goods and services.

The studies in this volume show the substantial effects of taxation on the process of capital formation and therefore on the overall operation of the economy. While some of the research confirms earlier findings, other studies show that previous conclusions must be reconsidered. The National Bureau will be continuing its tradition of research on capital formation in general and the current project on the effects of taxation on capital accumulation in particular. Although the National Bureau does not make policy recommendations, we hope that these studies will be helpful to those who are concerned with policy decisions concerning taxation.

1   IRAs and Saving

Steven F. Venti and David A. Wise

Individual retirement accounts (IRAs) were established in 1974 as part of the Employee Retirement Income Security Act to encourage employees not covered by private pension plans to save for retirement. The Economic Recovery Tax Act of 1981 extended the availability of IRAs to all employees and raised the contribution limit. The legislation emphasized the need to enhance the economic well-being of future retirees and the need to increase national saving. Now any employee with earnings above $2,000 can contribute $2,000 to an IRA account each year. An employed person and a nonworking spouse can contribute a total of $2,250, while a married couple who are both working can contribute $2,000 each. Current tax proposals contemplate substantial increases in the limits. The tax on the principal and interest is deferred until money is withdrawn from the account. There is a penalty for withdrawal before age $59\frac{1}{2}$, which is apparently intended to discourage the use of IRAs for nonretirement saving.

To determine whether IRA accounts serve as a substitute for private pension plans, it is important to know who contributes to IRAs. Whether they are an important form of saving for retirement depends on how

Steven F. Venti is an assistant professor of economics at Dartmouth College, and a faculty research fellow at the National Bureau of Economic Research. David A. Wise is a John F. Stambaugh Professor of Political Economy at the John F. Kennedy School of Government, Harvard University, and a research associate at the National Bureau of Economic Research.

The authors are grateful for discussions with Axel Boersch-Supan, Angus Deaton, Mervyn King, Jim Poterba, and Jim Stock. The research was supported by grant number 84ASPE130A from the Department of Health and Human Services. The research reported here is part of the NBER research program on the Economics of Aging and on Taxation, and projects on Government Budgets and on Capital Formation. Any opinions expressed are those of the authors and not those of the National Bureau of Economic Research.

much is contributed. In addition, the short-run tax cost of IRAs depends on their prevalence. These questions have been addressed by Venti and Wise (1985a) for the United States and by Wise (1984, 1985) for Canada. The central focus of this paper is the relationship between IRA contributions and other forms of saving. What is the net effect of IRA accounts on individual saving? In addressing this question, estimates of desired IRA contributions are also obtained, and these estimates can be compared with results based on other data sources.

Ideal data to answer this question would provide information on changes in all forms of assets over time. One could then compare annual IRA contributions with increases or decreases in other forms of saving. The set of questions that can be addressed directly with available data is limited, however. IRAs were only open to most employees beginning in 1982, and currently available data pertain only to that year. In addition, only limited information is available on changes in other asset holdings in 1982. Given the data limitations, the goal of the analysis presented in this paper is to estimate the effect that changes in the IRA contribution limit would have on other forms of saving, as well as on IRA contributions themselves. As explained below, other forms of saving probably are best thought of as liquid assets.

Two central questions arise in considering the effect of newly available IRAs on net saving: the first is the extent to which IRA contributions are made by withdrawing funds from other existing balances, and thus explicitly substituting one form of saving for another. Presumably such substitution would be made by taking funds from existing liquid asset balances, like other savings accounts. It is unlikely that, in the short run, IRA contributions would be made by reducing nonliquid asset balances like housing. A related question, although possibly more subtle and difficult to answer empirically, is whether new saving would have been placed in other accounts were it not for the availability of IRAs, independent of existing balances.

Another question is the extent to which IRA contributions may ultimately serve as a substitute for nonliquid assets. In the long run, individuals may contribute to IRAs instead of investing in housing, for example. This question is more difficult to address empirically, and no attempt is made to answer it here. Whether IRA contributions were substituted for other liquid assets in 1982 is the question that can be most directly addressed using the available data. But we believe that the estimates may also provide a reasonable indication of the trade-off between IRA contributions and liquid assets in the long run as well. The spirit of the paper is to distinguish direct evidence about which the results are likely to be relatively robust from questions about which the evidence is only indirect. An attempt is made to draw inferences based on the weight of the evidence. In short, given the available data and their limitations, what can be said about the effect of IRAs on net individual saving?

Background data on IRA contributions and other wealth holdings are presented in section 1.1. The model used for estimation is developed in section 1.2. Its key feature is constrained optimization, with the limit on IRA contributions the primary constraint. The principle goal is to obtain estimates of the effect of changes in IRA limits on other saving, as well as on IRA contributions themselves. The model addresses the allocation of current income. This approach has been chosen over a model of presumed lifetime saving behavior, although the allocation of current income could be thought of as the reduced form of a life-cycle model. In addition, estimates of the allocation of current income based on age and other personal attributes allow inferences about life-cycle saving behavior.

The results are presented in section 1.3. The emphasis is on the sensitivity of the results to model specification and to the interpretation of a key variable, "savings and reserve funds." The most important results are presented in the form of simulations of the effect of proposed limit changes on IRA contributions and other saving. Some of the results developed here can be compared with evidence based on other data sources. Comparable evidence on IRA contributions for 1982 has been developed by Venti and Wise (1985), based on Current Population Survey data. The results of the present paper are based on the 1983 Survey of Consumer Finances (SCF), which presents information on IRAs in 1982. Section 1.4 presents a summary of the findings and concluding discussion.

1.1. Descriptive Statistics

About 16% of wage earner families have IRA accounts, as shown in table 1.1.[1] Few families with incomes under $10,000 have them and only about 7% of families with incomes between $10,000 and $20,000 do. Somewhat more than half of those with incomes greater than $50,000

Table 1.1   **Proportion of Families with IRA Accounts, by Income and Age**

Income Interval ($1000's)	Age Interval						
	< 25	25–34	35–44	45–54	55–64	65+	All
0–10	.01	.00	.03	.01	.04	.01	.01
10–20	.04	.04	.04	.09	.20	.04	.07
20–30	.05	.11	.10	.21	.36	.06	.14
30–40	.15	.25	.14	.34	.43	.19	.25
40–50	.00	.21	.41	.42	.38	.31	.34
50–100	.00	.33	.51	.53	.75	.36	.51
100+		.49	.66	.79	.65	.58	.65
All	.03	.12	.19	.26	.30	.06	.16

Note: The data are weighted to be representative of all families. The total sample size for this table is 3,205.

contribute to IRAs.[2] But because there are relatively few families with incomes greater than $50,000, almost 70% of contributor families have incomes below that level. As shown in Venti and Wise (1985), about 90% of individual wage earners who contribute have incomes less than $50,000. The distribution of contributor families by income interval is as follows:

Income Interval (in $1,000's)	Percentage of Contributors
0–10	2
10–20	15
20–30	17
30–40	20
40–50	15
50–100	24
100+	8

Older persons are considerably more likely than younger ones to contribute, although the proportion drops at age 65, when a large proportion of employees retire. For example, among families in the $20,000 to $30,000 income interval, 36% of those 55 to 64 contributed but only 11% of those aged 25 to 34.

The subsequent analysis will rely in part on responses to a question that asked: "Considering all of your savings and reserve funds, *overall*, did you put more money in or take more money out in 1982?"[3] The precise interpretation that should be assigned the responses is unclear. In particular, it is not clear whether savings and reserve funds include or exclude IRA contributions. The analysis is conducted and the results are evaluated using both interpretations, although we believe it is most plausible to assume that IRAs are excluded. We presume that responses do not reflect nonliquid assets like housing. The proportion of families indicating an increase in "savings and reserve funds" is shown in table 1.2. Only 32% of respondents indicated an increase in 1982, while the remainder indicated a decrease or no change.[4] The proportion indicating an increase rises markedly with income, but shows little relationship to age.

A key consideration in our analysis is the relationship between IRA contributions and the change in "savings and reserve funds." Suppose IRA contributions were typically taken from "savings and reserve funds" balances. If savings and reserve funds included IRAs, there would be no change in overall savings and reserve funds. If the latter were interpreted to exclude IRAs, contributions to IRAs should be associated with a decline in savings and reserve funds. Apparently neither is true. Persons who contribute to IRAs are much more likely to indicate an

Table 1.2   **Proportion of Families with Increase in "Savings and Reserve Funds," by Income and Age**

Income Interval ($1000's)	Age Interval						
	< 25	25–34	35–44	45–54	55–64	65 +	All
0–10	.10	.15	.13	.05	.10	.20	.14
10–20	.33	.23	.19	.12	.32	.35	.26
20–30	.35	.37	.26	.21	.47	.56	.35
30–40	.31	.46	.40	.47	.41	.58	.44
40–50	.75	.47	.42	.56	.41	.75	.50
50–100	.00	.48	.56	.54	.57	.71	.56
100 +		.58	.53	.47	.54	.65	.54
All	.26	.32	.32	.30	.35	.33	.32

Note: The data are weighted to be representative of all families. The total sample size for this table is 3,208.

Table 1.3   **Proportion of IRA Contributors with Increase in "Savings and Reserve Funds," Divided by Proportion of Noncontributors with Increase in "Savings and Reserve Funds," by Income and Age**

Income Interval ($1000's)	Age Interval						
	< 25	25–34	35–44	45–54	55–64	65 +	All
0–10	—	—	—	—	—	—	—
10–20	—	1.83	—	—	1.60	—	1.54
20–30	—	1.61	2.41	2.16	1.41	—	1.77
30–40	—	1.45	1.92	1.48	2.38	—	1.68
40–50	—	1.60	1.56	1.24	3.10	—	1.47
50–100	—	.96	1.65	1.41	1.62	—	1.40
100 +		—	—	—	.87	—	2.19
All	—	1.78	2.37	2.22	2.00	1.86	2.10

Note: Not reported for cells in which there were fewer than 8 IRA contributors.

increase than those who don't. The ratio of the proportion of IRA contributors with an increase in "savings and reserve funds" to the proportion of noncontributors with an increase is shown in table 1.3, by income and age. Overall, contributors are more than twice as likely as noncontributors to indicate an increase, although this number reflects in part different distributions of contributors and noncontributors by income and age. The average of the cell ratios is 1.77.

Thus these numbers suggest that there are savers and nonsavers and that savers save both through IRAs and through other forms; the positive relationship reflects an individual-specific effect. The subsequent analysis provides support for an individual-specific savings effect, while also suggesting a substantial positive effect of IRAs on net individual saving.

To put IRA contributions in perspective and to help to interpret the analysis below, it is useful to have in mind the magnitude of individual wealth holdings. The median wealth of persons in the sample is $22,900, excluding pensions and Social Security wealth.[5] Even among persons 55 to 64, the median is only $55,000 (see table 1.4). Most of this wealth is nonliquid, the preponderance of which is housing. Consistent with other evidence (e.g., Hurd and Shoven [1985], Bernheim [1984], Diamond and Hausman [1984]), a large proportion of individuals have very little nonhousing wealth; they save very little. Median liquid assets, excluding stocks and bonds, are shown in table 1.5, by income and age. The median for all families is $1,200. For families earning $30,000 to $40,000 with a head 45 to 54 years it is only $4,600. While most people have some liquid assets, only about 20% have financial assets in the form of stocks or bonds.[6] Thus it is clear that most people have

Table 1.4   Median of Wealth, by Income and Age, in Thousands of Dollars

Income Interval ($1000's)	Age Interval						
	< 25	25–34	35–44	45–54	55–64	65 +	All
0–10	.3	.0	.1	.1	1.5	10.0	.5
10–20	.8	2.0	10.3	30.0	40.9	65.8	10.0
20–30	2.5	13.8	31.6	44.6	90.2	125.5	28.3
30–40	15.4	34.3	47.3	71.4	77.8	269.7	50.5
40–50	10.9	40.3	74.6	90.5	114.4	219.0	80.6
50–100	33.2	85.5	101.1	122.7	196.6	220.5	123.6
100 +	—	124.8	182.9	317.1	334.5	1308.7	279.0
All	0.6	5.9	35.6	47.1	55.0	40.1	22.9

Note: The data are weighted to be representative of all families. The total sample size for this table is 2,249.

Table 1.5   Median of Liquid Assets, by Income and Age, in Thousands of Dollars

Income Interval ($1000's)	Age Interval						
	< 25	25–34	35–44	45–54	55–64	65 +	All
0–10	.2	.0	.0	.0	.0	.5	.1
10–20	.4	.3	.5	.9	3.5	16.2	.7
20–30	.6	1.2	1.6	1.9	4.9	46.8	1.7
30–40	1.0	2.9	2.4	4.6	3.6	107.0	3.5
40–50	2.0	2.8	4.7	5.6	12.8	36.5	5.5
50–100	16.4	5.7	13.8	8.7	22.1	37.8	12.8
100 +	—	12.8	12.5	42.7	74.2	124.0	30.4
All	.4	.8	1.7	1.9	3.0	4.0	1.2

Note: Stocks and bonds are excluded. The data are weighted to be representative of all families. The total sample size for this table is 2,729.

not been accumulating financial assets at a rate close to the $2,000 per year that an IRA allows.

The median wealth of IRA contributors divided by the median wealth of noncontributors, by income and age, is shown in table 1.6. Contributors have substantially higher wealth on average. The average of the cell ratios is 1.50.[7] The analysis below, however, indicates that after controlling for other variables, total wealth is in fact negatively related to IRA contributions. The results, including detail by liquid versus nonliquid wealth, suggest that the numbers in table 1.6 also reflect individual-specific saving effects; some people are savers, others are not.

In summary: the descriptive data confirm that low-income persons are unlikely to contribute to IRAs. But they provide no direct evidence that IRA contributions are offset by reductions in other forms of saving; persons who contribute to IRAs are more likely than those who do not to indicate an overall increase in savings and reserve funds. The descriptive data, however, do not reveal whether savers save more because of the IRA option. The subsequent analysis is intended to shed light on this issue.

1.2   Allocation of Income: Individual Saving and IRA Constraints

Given the limitations of the data, the goal is to develop a statistical model that will allow inferences based on the information that is available. The approach is to consider the allocation of current income in the spirit of expenditure studies, but with concentration on what is not spent for current consumption. The key feature of the approach is to incorporate the limit on tax-deferred saving in the estimation procedure and then to infer from the parameter estimates how saving behavior

Table 1.6   Median Wealth of IRA Contributors Divided by Median Wealth of non-IRA Contributors, by Income and Age

Income Interval ($1000's)	Age Interval						
	< 25	25–34	35–44	45–54	55–64	65+	All
0–10	—	—	—	—	—	—	—
10–20	—	6.05	—	—	1.95	—	7.03
20–30	—	1.81	1.61	1.18	1.23	—	2.15
30–40	—	1.55	1.74	1.14	1.11	—	1.67
40–50	—	1.58	1.77	1.62	.73	—	1.86
50–100	—	1.66	1.17	1.03	1.03	—	1.25
100+	—	—	—	—	.25	—	2.71
All	—	7.30	3.19	1.87	2.08	3.46	5.26

Note: Not reported for cells in which there were fewer than 8 IRA contributors.

would change if the limit were changed. To assure that estimated constrained and unconstrained behavior are internally consistent, the functional forms of the estimated equations are related through an underlying decision function. The model is intended to be "structural" with respect to changes in the IRA limit although, as explained below, not necessarily with respect to the individual variables that are used to estimate choice parameters of individuals. We begin with a simple example and then present the specifications used for estimation. For expository purposes, we also discuss first a specification that implies only a limited form of substitution between IRA and other saving. We then present a model that allows more flexible substitution and that incorporates the first as a special case.

1.2.1 A Simple Example

Suppose that current income Y can be allocated to tax-deferred IRA saving S_1, to other forms of saving S_2, or to current uses, $Y - S_1 - S_2$. Assume also that were there no limit on S_1, or if persons were not constrained by the limit, observed levels of S_1 and S_2 would be fit by the functions

(1) $S_1 = b_1 Y$, and

                                 $S_2 = b_2 Y$.

For estimation, we need also to consider saving functions that are consistent with these, but for persons who are constrained by the limit on S_1. These may be obtained by considering an underlying decision function that is consistent with observed saving decisions.

The saving allocations in (1) are in accordance with the decision function

(2) $V = (Y - S_1 - S_2)^{1-b_1-b_2} S_1^{b_1} S_2^{b_2}$,

where b_1 and b_2 are parameters. Maximization of (2) with respect to S_1 and S_2 yields (1). The presumption is that the b's depend on measured personal attributes like age, income, wealth, education, marital status; unmeasured attributes that affect saving behavior in general; and unmeasured attributes like expected future liquidity needs or attitude toward risk that may affect the preferred allocation of income to S_1, versus S_2. This specification treats IRAs and other forms of saving as different "goods," thus emphasizing nonprice differences between the two forms of saving. In particular, because of the early withdrawal penalty that makes IRAs less liquid than other saving, they may tend to be more narrowly targeted to retirement consumption; much of saving in other forms may be for different and more short term purposes. The "price" difference between the two forms of saving is brought out below. Following the decision function (2), if S_1 cannot exceed the limit L, the saving functions are

$$(3) \qquad S_1 = \begin{cases} b_1 Y & \text{if } b_1 Y < L, \\ \\ L & \text{if } b_1 Y \geq L, \end{cases}$$

$$S_2 = \begin{cases} b_2 Y & \text{if } b_1 Y < L, \\ \\ \dfrac{b_2}{1 - b_1} (Y - L) & \text{if } b_1 Y \geq L. \end{cases}$$

The relationship between income and S_2 saving depends on whether the limit on the tax-deferred S_1 saving has been reached. In the subsequent discussion, we shall begin with a decision function, but it should be understood that it is chosen to be consistent with observed saving decisions. It is a construct that assures that constrained and unconstrained savings functions are consistent with each other.

It will be important to estimate the change in S_2 with a change in the limit L. In this case $dS_2/dL = -b_2/(1 - b_1)$, depending only on the b's. Thus to obtain good estimates of the effect of limit changes, it is necessary only to have good estimates of these parameters; not necessarily of the effect on the b's of the variables that will be used to estimate them. Figure 1.1 describes graphically the relationship between income and S_1 and S_2, with particular reference to the estimated specification described in section 1.2.2 below.

1.2.2 The Estimated Model: A Special Case

In practice, S_2 could be negative. "Desired" S_1 could also be negative, although not its observed value. Previous work by Venti and Wise (1985a) and by Wise (1985) indicates that IRA contributions alone can be described well by a Tobit specification with limits at zero and L.[8] In addition, the cost of one dollar of S_1 in terms of current consumption is $(1 - t)$, where t is the marginal tax rate, whereas the cost of S_2 is 1.

A decision function and implicit budget constraint that incorporates these characteristics is

$$(4) \quad V = [Y - T - S_1(1 - t) - S_2]^{1 - b_2 - b_2} [S_1 - a_1]^{b_1} [S_2 - a_2]^{b_2}.$$

The presumption is that if both S_1 and S_2 were zero, current consumption would be $Y - T$, where T is total taxes. This amount serves as the base case. If IRA contributions S_1 are made, taxes are reduced by tS_1.[9] In practice, "current consumption" includes some forms of saving like housing since the variable used to describe S_2 does not reflect all forms of non-IRA saving.[10]

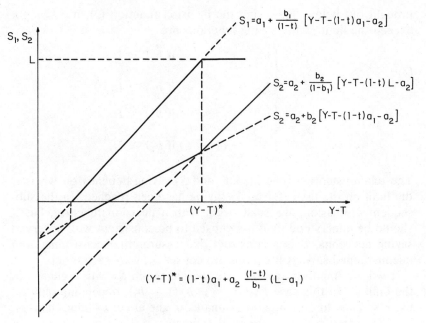

Figure 1.1   Savings versus after-tax income

Consistent with (4), the "desired" level of tax-deferred saving S_1 is given by

(5a) $$S_1 = a_1 + \frac{b_1}{(1-t)} [(Y - T) - (1 - t)a_1 - a_2],$$

and the observed level s_1 by

(5b) $$s_1 = \begin{cases} 0 \text{ if } S_1 \leq 0, \\ S_1 \text{ if } 0 < S_1 < L, \\ L \text{ if } L \leq S_1. \end{cases}$$

Non-tax-deferred saving is given by

(6)

$$S_2 = \begin{cases} a_2 + \dfrac{b_2}{1 - b_1} [(Y - T) - a_2] & \text{if } S_1 < 0, \\[2ex] a_2 + b_2 [(Y - T) - a_1 (1 - t) - a_2] & \text{if } 0 < S_1 < L, \\[2ex] a_2 + \dfrac{b_2}{1 - b_1} [(Y - T) - L(1 - t) - a_2] & \text{if } S_1 \geq L. \end{cases}$$

Stylized versions of the S_1 and S_2 functions are graphed in figure 1.1, where $(Y - T)*$ is the after-tax income level at which the limit L on S_1 is reached.

For expositional purposes, an advantage of the specification described above is that a closed-form solution to the constrained saving function can be obtained from the decision function. This is not always the case. Indeed, as shown below, it is not true with the more general specification described in section 1.2.3 below.[11] General discussions of demand with "rationing" are presented in Deaton and Muellbauer (1981) and in Deaton (1981), with the discussion often in terms of indirect utility or expenditure functions. Deaton shows that closed-form solutions to constrained demand functions can be obtained in some cases even when the utility function is not separable, the property that assures a closed-form solution in the specification above.

The parameters b_1 and b_2 are specified as functions of individual attributes by

(7)
$$b_1 = \Phi[XB_1] ,$$
$$b_2 = \Phi[XB_2] ,$$

where X is a vector of individual characteristics and the B's are vectors of parameters to be estimated. The unit normal distribution function Φ constrains b_1 and b_2 to be between 0 and 1.[12]

To allow for random preferences for saving among individuals, presumably reflecting unmeasured individual attributes, the parameters a_1 and a_2 are allowed to be stochastic, with a bivariate normal distribution

(8)
$$\begin{bmatrix} a_1 \\ a_2 \end{bmatrix} \sim BVN \left(\begin{bmatrix} \bar{a}_1 \\ \bar{a}_2 \end{bmatrix} ; \begin{bmatrix} \sigma_1^2 & \rho\sigma_1\sigma_2 \\ & \sigma_2^2 \end{bmatrix} \right) .$$

Large values of a_1 and a_2 indicate high desired S_1 and S_2 respectively; large a_1 means lower desired S_2 and large a_2 lower desired S_1.[13]

In addition, an alternative stochastic specification assumes that a_1 and a_2 are nonstochastic, but simple additive disturbance terms are added to the unconstrained S_1 and S_2 equations. Details of the stochastic structure under both specifications are presented in Venti and Wise (1985b). An important parameter is the correlation between the disturbance terms in S_1 and S_2. This correlation contributes to inference about the extent to which observed saving behavior results from unmeasured individual-specific effects or the extent to which saving in one form is offset by saving in another.

The possible outcomes and associated probability statements are listed below, under the two interpretations of "savings and reserve funds," denoted by S. If S includes IRAs, $S = S_1 + S_2$; if it does not, $S = S_2$.

Outcome	Probability:	
	If $S = S_1 + S_2$	If $S = S_2$
$s_1 = 0, S > 0$	$Pr[\, S_1 \leq 0 \text{ and } S_2 > 0]$	$Pr[\, S_1 \leq 0 \text{ and } S_2 > 0]$
$0 < s_1 < L, S > 0$	$Pr[\, S_1 = s_1 \text{ and } S_2 > -s_1]$	$Pr[\, S_1 = s_1 \text{ and } S_2 > 0]$
$s_1 = L, S > 0$	$Pr[\, S_1 \geq L \text{ and } S_2 > -L]$	$Pr[\, S_1 \geq L \text{ and } S_2 > 0]$
$s_1 = 0, S < 0$	$Pr[\, S_1 \leq 0 \text{ and } S_2 < 0]$	$Pr[\, S_1 \leq 0 \text{ and } S_2 < 0]$
$0 < s_1 < L, S < 0$	$Pr[\, S_1 = s_1 \text{ and } S_2 < -s_1]$	$Pr[\, S_1 = s_1 \text{ and } S_2 < 0]$
$s_1 = L, S < 0$	$Pr[\, S_1 \geq L \text{ and } S_2 < -L]$	$Pr[\, S_1 \geq L \text{ and } S_2 < 0]$

The latter interpretation is we believe the most likely to reflect the respondent's intent. Most of the discussion and reported simulations are based on this assumption. Nonetheless, we shall present some estimates based on the $S = S_1 + S_2$ interpretation. This interpretation should provide the most stable estimates.[14] We show that estimates based on this interpretation are rather insensitive to important assumptions. Estimates are obtained by maximum likelihood.

Implicit in the functional form described above is an "independence" assumption that restricts the implied substitution between S_1 and S_2 on the one hand and current consumption on the other. Consider the allocation of a marginal dollar of current income before and after the limit on S_1 has been reached. The marginal shares allocated to S_1, S_2, and consumption are:

	Unconstrained[15]	Constrained
S_1	$b_1/(1 - t)$	0
S_2	b_2	$b_2/(1 - b_1)$
C	$1 - b_1 - b_2$	$(1 - b_1 - b_2)/(1 - b_1)$

Thus the ratio of the marginal share that goes to S_2 versus the share that goes to consumption, $b_2/(1 - b_1 - b_2)$, is independent of whether the limit on S_1 has been reached. One might expect, however, that this ratio would increase after the limit is reached if there is greater substitution between S_1 and S_2 than between either of these and consumption.

The importance of this property is what it implies about the effect of an increase in the tax-deferred limit L on non-tax-deferred saving S_2. Only persons at the limit will be affected by increasing it. For these people, $dS_1/dL = 1$. The amount that is taken from non-tax-deferred saving to fund the dollar increase in S_1 is $dS_2/dL = -(1 - t)b_2/(1 - b_1)$, for those who are at the limit.[16] The amount from consumption is $-(1 - t)(1 - b_1 - b_2)/(1 - b_1)$. Thus the model implies a proportionate reduction in S_2 and C in accordance with the unconstrained shares.

Therefore results based on a functional form that allows more flexible substitution between S_1 and S_2 are also obtained.

1.2.3 Relaxing the Independence Assumption

To relax the restrictive substitution implications of the specification above, suppose that preferred allocations of current income are in accordance with the function

$$(9) \qquad V = [Y - T - P_1 S_1 - P_2 S_2]^{1-\beta} \{ [\alpha(S_1 - a_1)^k$$
$$+ (1 - \alpha)(S_2 - a_2)^k]^{\frac{1}{k}} \}^\beta ,$$

where the left-hand term in brackets incorporates the budget constraint. The cost of S_1 in terms of current consumption is P_1 and the cost of S_2 is P_2. This function has a tree structure with one branch consumption and the other saving. The two branches are combined in a Cobb-Douglas manner with parameter β. The two forms of saving are combined in a C.E.S. subfunction to form the saving branch. The parameter α indicates the relative "preference" for S_1 versus S_2. If they were treated as equivalent, α would equal .5.[17] The elasticity of substitution between S_1 and S_2 is $1/(1 - k)$.[18]

The limiting case of (1) as k goes to zero is given by

$$(10) \quad V = [Y - T - S_1(1 - t) - S_2]^{1-\beta}[S_1 - a_1]^{\alpha\beta}[S_2 - a_2]^{(1-\alpha)\beta},$$

with $P_1 = 1 - t$ and $P_2 = 1$. The unrestricted "desired" levels of S_1 and S_2 are given by

$$(11) \qquad S_1 = a_1 + \frac{\alpha}{(1 - t)}\beta[Y - T - (1 - t)a_1 - a_2] ,$$
$$S_2 = a_2 + (1 - \alpha)\beta[Y - T - (1 - t)a_1 - a_2] .$$

The function (10) is the same as the preference function (4) above and yields the same constrained savings functions as those in equations (5) and (6), but with $b_1 = \alpha\beta$ and $b_2 = (1 - \alpha)\beta$.

Because the parameters α and β have informative interpretations, we shall estimate them as functions of X, as an alternative to estimation of b_1 and b_2. Although if b_1, b_2, α, and β were the same for all persons in the sample—not functions of attributes X—the equalities would hold, they will not necessarily hold when each is estimated as a function of X. For example, the mean over X of $\hat{b}_1 = \Phi[X\hat{B}_1]$ will not equal the mean over X of $\hat{\alpha} \cdot \hat{\beta}$. Analogous to the parameterization of b_1 and b_2, we estimate α and β as

$$\alpha = \Phi[XA],$$
$$\beta = \Phi[XB],$$

where A and B are vectors of parameters to be estimated.

With this parameterization, it is convenient to think of β as the marginal after-tax dollar devoted to saving (S_1 and S_2) and α as the proportion of a saved dollar devoted to S_1. Define $\gamma_1 = \alpha/(1 - t)$. It is the amount of tax-deferred S_1 obtained for the proportion α, and $\gamma_2 = 1 - \gamma_1(1 - t) = 1 - \alpha$ is the proportion devoted to non-tax-deferred S_2.[19]

If $k \neq 0$, it is informative first to describe the saving functions in terms of both P_1 and P_2. In this case, the unconstrained desired levels of S_1 and S_2 are given by

$$(12) \qquad S_1 = a_1 + \gamma_1\beta(Y - T - P_1a_1 - P_2a_2) ,$$

$$S_2 = a_2 + \gamma_2\beta(Y - T - P_1a_1 - P_2a_2) .$$

From the constraint $\gamma_1P_1 + \gamma_2P_2 = 1$, $\gamma_2 = (1 - \gamma_1P_1)/P_2$. The distribution factory γ_1 is given by

$$(13) \qquad \gamma_1 = \frac{(P_1/\alpha)^{\frac{1}{k-1}}}{P_1(P_1/\alpha)^{\frac{1}{k-1}} + P_2[P_2/(1 - \alpha)]^{\frac{1}{k-1}}} .$$

With $P_2 = 1$ and $\gamma_2 = 1 - \gamma_1P_1$, γ_1 can be written as

$$(14) \qquad \gamma_1 = \frac{P_1^{\frac{1}{k-1}}}{P_1 \cdot P_1^{\frac{1}{k-1}} + [\alpha/(1 - \alpha)]^{\frac{1}{k-1}}} .$$

If $k = 0$, this expression reduces to $\alpha/P_1 = \alpha/(1 - t)$ as in equation (11).

If the S_1 constraint is binding so that $S_1 = L$, S_2 is defined only implicitly, by the relationship

$$(15) \quad \frac{P_2(1 - \beta)[\alpha(L - a_1)^k + (1 - \alpha)(S_2 - a_2)^k]}{(1 - \alpha)(S_2 - a_2)^{k-1}}$$
$$= (Y - T - P_1L - P_2S_2)$$

obtained by maximizing (9) with respect to S_2, with $S_1 = L$. This function must be evaluated at each iteration of the maximum-likelihood estimation routine. We have not attempted to do this with random a_1 and a_2. Only the additive disturbance specification has been used in this case. Estimates based on the restricted specification described in section 1.2.2, however, lead us to believe that the results are not very sensitive to which of these stochastic specifications is used.[20]

1.3 Results

1.3.1 Data

The estimates are based on the 1983 Survey of Consumer Finances. The Survey provides detailed information on asset balances of all kinds, as well as on income and other personal attributes. From data on IRA balances it is possible to infer 1982 contributions, as explained in the appendix to this chapter. Unfortunately the data do not include changes in other asset balances in 1982, as emphasized above. The absence of this data has led us to concentrate on information contained in the change in "savings and reserve funds" question.

Estimation is based on 1,068 observations. Families were deleted from the original sample if they were ineligible for an IRA (self-employed or not working). Nonresponse reduced the sample further. The data most often missing were self-reported marginal tax rates and the series of responses required to calculate housing equity. The variable means in the estimation sample (table 1.17) are very close to the means for all of those surveyed, however.[21] Estimates based on a larger sample using predicted marginal tax rates are not appreciably different from those reported below based on self-reported rates.

1.3.2 Parameter Estimates

As emphasized above, the main concern is to obtain "reliable" estimates of b_1 and b_2 (or of α and β); they are the principle determinants of the effect of a change in L on IRA and non-IRA saving. While the effect of the variables X on the b's is of interest, it is not necessary to obtain unbiased estimates of these effects to estimate the effect of changing L. The model is intended to be structural with respect to L, not necessarily with respect to the effects of the variables X that determine the b's.[22] Given the limit L, the parameters a_1 and a_2, and the parameters b_1 and b_2, S_1 and S_2 savings are given by the functions like those graphed in figure 1.1. Their amounts may be calculated given after-tax income, $Y - T$. If the limit is increased by ΔL, the constrained S_2 function is shifted downward by $-[(1 - t)b_2/(1 - b_1)] \cdot \Delta L$, using equation (6), and its intersection (the kink point in figure 1) with the unconstrained function is shifted outward. Given the new limit, new S_1 and S_2 values may be calculated. The effect of changing the limit depends only on b_1 and b_2. Thus in reporting the results we emphasize the sensitivity of the estimated values of b_1 and b_2 to model specification. To simulate the average effect of a limit change, random values of a_1 and a_2 are selected from a bivariate normal distribution using the estimated means and covariance terms. (The alternative specification assumes additive disturbances on the S_1 and S_2 equations, also with a bivariate normal distribution.)[23]

We begin with estimates based on the limited substitution model with b_1 and b_2 parameterized (equations 5 and 6). Based on this specification we shall first consider a base case with $S = S_2$. We then discuss variants of this specification, some under the assumption that $S = S_1 + S_2$. The estimates with $S = S_1 + S_2$ should in principle be the most stable. We show in particular that the estimated values of $\sigma_1 = \sigma_2$ are very close and that the hypothesis that $\sigma_1 = \sigma_2$ cannot be rejected. This is a potentially important restriction that has been imposed under the assumption that $S = S_2$.

These latter estimates may be compared with those obtained with $k = 0$ but with α and β, instead of b_1 and b_2, parameterized. To provide a summary measure that allows comparison across the specifications, we present estimated values of S_1 and S_2 saving out of the marginal dollar of after-tax income, defined by

$$\delta_1 = \frac{b_1}{(1 - t)} = \frac{\alpha}{(1 - t)} \beta \text{ , and}$$

$$\delta_2 = b_2 = (1 - \alpha)\beta \text{ ,}$$

where the equalities hold only if b_1 and b_2, α and β are not parameterized.

Finally, estimates with k set at .65 are presented. In practice, widely varying values of k cannot be distinguished by the data.[24] Within-sample predictions are essentially the same. Nonetheless the predicted effects of limit changes do depend on the assumed substitution behavior under which the data were generated. Thus we set k at a rather high level and obtain estimates for the other parameters. Indications of model fit, simulation results, and the sensitivity of the simulations to model specification follow.

Limited Substitution, b_1 and b_2 Parameterized

a. The base specification. Parameter estimates obtained under the assumption that $S = S_2$ are shown in table 1.7. The correlation between the random preference parameters a_1 and a_2 is .47 (with a standard of error of .06). The implied correlation between the S_1 and S_2 disturbance terms is .16, evaluated at the mean of the data. Although the correlation is small, it is consistent with an individual-specific savings effect (presumably due to unmeasured individual attributes) that affects both IRA and other saving in the same direction. It does not provide support for the possibility that persons who save more in one form tend to save less in the other. This substitution hypothesis would be consistent with a negative correlation.

Table 1.7   **Parameter Estimates with b_1 and b_2 Parameterized and $S = S_2$**

Variable	Estimate (Asymptotic Standard Error)	
Origin Parameters:		
Mean of a_1	15.90 (2.09)	
Mean of a_2	4.58 (.97)	
S.D. of a_1	8.89 (1.10)	
S.D. of a_2	8.89 (—)	
Correlation of a_1, a_2	.47 (.06)	
S.D. of S_1 (at mean)	6.66	
S.D. of S_2 (at mean)	7.92	
Correlation of S_1, S_2	.16	
Determinants of b_1 and b_2:	b_1	b_2
Income ($1000's)	$-.00501$ (.00070)	$-.01042$ (.00242)
Age (years)	.0112 (.0019)	.0002 (.0044)
Total wealth ($1000's)	—	—
Nonliquid	$-.00024$ (.00010)	$-.00024$ (.00048)
Liquid	.00073 (.00048)	.01131 (.00322)
Private pension (0,1)	$-.0140$ (.0401)	.9006 (.3703)
Education (years)	.0248 (.0080)	.0366 (.0228)
Unmarried woman	.0831 (.0574)	.1703 (.1413)
Unmarried man	.0486 (.0503)	.2667 (.1019)
Constant	-1.5752 (.2043)	-2.3675 (.6762)
Predicted b_1 and b_2:	b_1	b_2
Mean	.174	.102
S.D.	.037	.072
Min.	.012	.000
Max.	.310	.820
Predicted δ_1 and δ_2	δ_1	δ_2
Mean	.247	.102
S.D.	.162	.072
Min.	.012	.000
Max.	4.448	.820
LF	-1380	

The estimated coefficients on the wealth variables also seem consistent with an individual-specific savings effect. Liquid assets, which are likely to be the most readily transferred to IRA accounts, are positively related to IRAs, but they are also positively related to other saving. Indeed the relationship to the S_2 saving is much greater than the relationship to IRAs. A $1,000 increase in liquid assets is associated with a $45 increase in S_2, but only a $5 increase in S_1. Parameterization in terms of α and β shows a positive relationship of liquid assets to total saving in the two forms but a negative relationship to the proportion of the total devoted to IRAs, as shown in table 1.8 below. Nonliquid assets are negatively related to both S_1 and S_2 saving. Parameterization of α and β shows that nonliquid wealth is negatively related to total saving in these forms, but is positively related to the proportion devoted to IRAs. (As shown in appendix table 1.20, total wealth is negatively related to total saving in the S_1 and S_2 forms, and is unrelated to the allocation to S_1 versus S_2.) Thus this evidence also seems to support individual-specific saving preferences; some persons are savers and others not, some save in liquid and others in less liquid forms. But the evidence does not provide much support for the possibility that IRA funds were typically withdrawn from other liquid asset balances.[25]

It is important to keep in mind that in this specification, cumulated assets serve as a measure of individual-specific savings effects. They are not intended to serve as exogenous determinants of the b's; in this sense they would be endogenous. But their relationship to the b's also provides us with information about the hypothesis that IRA contributions are simply taken from other saving balances.

The mean estimated b_1 and b_2 parameters, .174 and .102 respectively, also suggest a strong preference for IRA versus other saving. At the margin, 17 cents of an additional dollar of after-tax income would go to IRAs—yielding about 25 cents in IRA saving—and about 10 cents would go to S_2 saving.

It is tempting to explain the difference between b_1 and b_2 by the difference in the return to tax-deferred versus non-tax-deferred saving. The revealed preference for IRAs is distinct from the lower price of tax-deferred saving in terms of current consumption, which through the current-year budget constraint of our model serves to increase the amount of IRA saving, given b_1 and b_2. For example, suppose that r is the interest rate, t' is the marginal tax rate during the time that funds are in an IRA account, t is the rate when funds are withdrawn, and the contribution is made at age j' and withdrawn at age j. A dollar invested in an IRA yields $1 \cdot (1 - t)e^{r(j-j')} \cdot [1 - p(j)]$, where $p(j)$ is a penalty for early withdrawal. The penalty is 0 if $j > 59\frac{1}{2}$ and .1 if $j < 59\frac{1}{2}$. A dollar of non-tax-deferred saving yields $(1 - t')e^{r(1-t')(j-j')}$. Thus the ratio of the tax- to non-tax-deferred yields is $[(1 - t)/(1 - t')]e^{rt(j-j')} \cdot [1 - p(j)]$. If $t = t'$ and $j > 59\frac{1}{2}$, it is simply $e^{rt(j-j')}$. Thus because of the tax-free compounding of interest in IRA accounts, as well as the possible difference between pre- and postretirement tax rates, persons in higher marginal tax brackets should have a greater incentive to save through IRAs.[26]

The penalty for early withdrawal makes the IRA less liquid and thus may detract from the desirability of IRAs, however.[27] But the liquidity consideration should be less important for people with higher marginal tax rates. Taking account of the penalty for early withdrawal, the tabulation below shows the number of years that funds must be left in an IRA account for the return to exceed the non-tax-deferred return.

Interest Rate	Marginal Tax Rate				
	10%	20%	30%	40%	50%
2%	60.0	34.0	26.1	23.2	22.6
6%	20.8	11.7	9.0	8.0	7.8
10%	12.9	7.3	5.6	4.9	4.8
14%	9.5	5.4	4.1	3.6	3.5
18%	7.7	4.3	3.3	2.9	2.8

Thus it is clear that both the interest rate and the marginal tax rate should have a substantial effect on the desirability of IRAs to the extent that short-term liquidity is an important consideration.

We are, however, unable to demonstrate convincingly an increasing preference for IRAs with increasing marginal tax rates. The coefficient on the marginal tax rate is significant in both b_1 and b_2 when it is entered as a determinant of the b's. Indeed its estimated effect is somewhat larger in b_2 (see appendix table 1.22). Results with α and β parameterized show that the marginal tax rate is positively related to total saving, β, but is negatively related to the proportion allocated to IRAs, α. These results seem to suggest that the marginal tax rate is picking up an individual-specific saving effect, but seems not related to a particular preference for IRAs. Wise (1984) was unable to identify an effect of the marginal tax rate on tax-deferred saving in Canada, using precisely measured marginal tax rates, as opposed to the self-reported rates used here.[28] While the marginal tax rate enters our budget constraint as the cost of S_1, the functional form virtually assures a positive relationship between the tax rate and IRA saving. We do not estimate a price parameter directly. Rather the price enters as a transformation to the data. Indeed the likelihood function is somewhat higher if P_1 is set to one for everyone, although the effect on the simulations reported below is not substantial.

Thus, while difficult to demonstrate, we believe that the widespread promotion of IRA accounts may be the most important reason for increased saving through their use.

In addition, the estimates do not suggest more IRA saving among persons without than with private pension plans, one of the primary goals of IRA legislation. The coefficient on the pension variable ($-.0140$) is not significantly different from zero. Furthermore, persons *with* private pensions save more in the S_2 form. Results based on the parameterization of α and β suggest that while persons without private plans save less, they devote a larger proportion of what they do save to IRAs.

The apparent variation in saving behavior among occupations or other segments of the population has been mentioned by others.[29] The strong relationship of education to IRA saving is consistent with such variation. In its relation to b_1, a year of education is equivalent to more than two years in age and more than \$30,000 in liquid wealth. The amount of the marginal dollar devoted to IRAs increases with age but decreases with income.

b. *Variants of the base specification.* A potentially important restriction in the base specification is that the error variances of a_1 and a_2 are equal. While this restriction is not necessary in principle, under the assumption that $S = S_2$ only the functional form and the limit L allow identification of the variance of a_2. Under the assumption that $S = S_1 + S_2$, direct evidence on the residual variance of S_2 is provided. Estimates based on the assumption that "savings and reserve funds" S include IRAs and allowing separate estimates of σ_1 and σ_2 are presented in appendix table 1.18. Both variances are estimated rather precisely and are close in magnitude ($\hat{\sigma}_1 = 8.84$, $\hat{\sigma}_2 = 5.45$). Comparison with estimates in appendix table 1.19 that restrict σ_1 to equal σ_2 shows that the two are not significantly different by a likelihood ratio test. The other findings discussed above are not qualitatively affected if it is assumed that $S = S_1 + S_2$, except that the residual correlation is now not significantly different from zero.[30]

Estimates like those in appendix table 1.18, but using total wealth only, instead of liquid versus nonliquid wealth, show that total wealth is in fact negatively related to total S_1 and S_2 saving and is unrelated to the proportion allocated to S_1, as mentioned above (see appendix table 1.20). Estimates comparable to appendix table 1.18, but with $P_1 = 1$ for all persons (ignoring the marginal tax effect) are presented in appendix table 1.21. The likelihood value indeed increases, but, as shown below, conclusions about the effect of IRA limit changes are not appreciably altered. Estimates with additive disturbances, instead of random a_1 and a_2, are shown in appendix table 1.23. The estimates are very close to those in table 1.7 discussed above.

More Flexible Substitution, α and β Parameterized

a. *With $k = 0$.* Estimates with $k = 0$ are shown in table 1.8. They are comparable to those in table 1.7, except that α and β, instead of b_1 and b_2, are parameterized, and additive disturbances, instead of random a_1 and a_2, are used. (Appendix table 1.23 shows results with b_1 and b_2 parameterized and using additive disturbances.) Only estimates assuming $S = S_2$ are presented with the more flexible model.[31] The basic conclusions are the same as those based on table 1.7. The mean δ_1 is .244 versus .247 in table 1.7; but the mean δ_2, .049, is somewhat smaller than its table 1.7 counterpart, .102.

Table 1.8   **Parameter Estimates with α and β Parameterized, $k = 0$**

Variable	Estimate (Asymptotic Standard Error)		
Disturbance terms:			
σ_1	6.55 (0.50)		
σ_2	6.55 (—)		
ρ_{12}	.185 (.060)		
Origin Parameters:			
a_1	15.21 (1.98)		
a_2	2.30 (0.34)		
Determinants of β and α:	β		α
Income ($1000's)	−.0060 (.0011)		−.0048 (.0028)
Age (years)	.0137 (.0024)		.0004 (.0701)
Wealth: Nonliquid ($1000's)	−.00055 (.00010)		.0014 (.0007)
Liquid ($1000's)	.01438 (.00185)		−.0164 (.0020)
Private pension (0,1)	.1606 (.0148)		−1.4510 (.3500)
Education (years)	.0361 (.0088)		−.0465 (.0075)
Unmarried woman (0,1)	.0649 (.0925)		.0246 (.1348)
Unmarried man (0,1)	.1976 (.0736)		−.3717 (.1250)
Constant	−1.8929 (.2199)		3.0904 (.3876)
Predicted β and α:	β		α
Mean	.214		.841
S.D.	.097		.141
Min.	.008		.000
Max.	.995		.999
Predicted δ_1, δ_2:	δ_1		δ_2
Mean	.244		.049
S.D.	.195		.075
Min.	.000		.000
Max.	5.332		.995
Log-likelihood		−1379	

This parameterization, however, indicates total $S_1 + S_2$ saving out of marginal income by β, and the share of the total to S_1 by α. Some of the conclusions have been discussed above. In addition, the estimates indicate that while total saving increases with age, the proportion allocated to IRAs does not. The more educated save more but allocate a smaller proportion to IRAs, according to these results. Thus it is apparently their greater propensity to save rather than a greater preference for tax-deferred saving that leads to more IRA saving among the educated. As mentioned above, while persons *without* private pension plans save less, these results indicate that they devote a *larger* proportion of saving to IRAs. Thus it is apparently their lower propensity to save, rather than the same IRA preference as that of private pension holders, that leads to comparable desired IRA contributions among those with and without private pensions.

Table 1.9   **Parameter Estimates with α and β Parameterized, $k = 65$**

Variable	Estimate (Asymptotic Standard Error)	
Disturbance terms:		
σ_1	6.61 (.542)	
σ_2	6.61 (—)	
ρ_{12}	.176 (.060)	
Origin Parameters:		
a_1	13.61 (1.88)	
a_2	1.69 (0.31)	
Determinants of β and α:	β	α
Income ($1000's)	−.0059 (.0012)	−.0026 (.0015)
Age (years)	.0159 (.0028)	.0000 (.0026)
Wealth: Nonliquid ($1000's)	−.00052 (.00011)	.00075 (.00039)
Liquid ($1000's)	.0148 (.0019)	−.0088 (.0011)
Private pension (0,1)	.0821 (.0495)	−1.7088 (.1787)
Education (years)	.0449 (.0118)	−.0372 (.0061)
Unmarried woman	.1184 (.0948)	.9392 (.1123)
Unmarried man	.1830 (.0716)	−.1918 (.0564)
Constant	−2.2095 (.3148)	2.6269 (.0011)
Predicted β and α:	β	α
Mean	.174	.727
S.D.	.096	.187
Min.	.005	.000
Max.	.996	.994
Predicted δ_1, δ_2:	δ_1	δ_2
Mean	.213	.028
S.D.	.189	.072
Min.	.000	.000
Max.	3.763	.996
Log-likelihood	−1394	

b. With $k = .65$. Estimates with k set at .65 are shown in table 1.9. The individual parameter estimates are very close to those with $k = 0$, with the exception of the constant terms in α and β. Again, differences are summarized in the δ_1 and δ_2 measures. The mean δ_1 is .213 when $k = .65$, and .244 with $k = 0$. The mean δ_2 estimates are .028 and .049 respectively.

The effect of a change in the IRA limit depends in large part on the difference between the share of marginal income allocated to S_2 by people who are not constrained by the limit and the share allocated to S_2 by those who are constrained by the limit. These shares are denoted by δ_2 and δ_2^* respectively. Their means for $k = 0$ and $k = .65$ are as follows:

	δ_2	δ_2^*
$k = 0$	.091	.117
$k = .65$	.046	.096

Thus the predicted relative shift to S_2 when the constraint is reached is greater when the data are assumed to have been generated by individual saving behavior with greater substitution between S_1 and S_2. This is reflected in greater reduction in S_2 for the $k = .65$ model when the IRA limit is raised than for the $k = 0$ model, as indicated in the simulations below.

1.3.3   The Model Fit

Although there is some variation in the model fit by specification, the differences are quite small. Thus we present comparison of predicted versus actual values for three illustrative cases. Based on the $k = 0$ model, with α and β parameterized, table 1.10 shows simulated versus actual values of the proportion of respondents with $S_1 > 0$, $S_1 > L$, and $S > 0$, by income interval. Possibly most important are

Table 1.10   Simulated Predicted vs. Actual Values, by Income Interval, $k = 0$[a]

Income Interval[b]	Number	% $s_1 > 0$ P	% $s_1 > 0$ A	% $s_1 = L$ P	% $s_1 = L$ A	% $S > 0$ P	% $S > 0$ A
0–10	169	.07	.03	.04	.02	.38	.31
10–20	305	.11	.07	.06	.02	.42	.38
20–30	260	.19	.25	.10	.13	.45	.47
30–40	170	.30	.32	.18	.21	.52	.56
40–50	77	.46	.52	.30	.35	.56	.55
50–100	77	.65	.58	.48	.46	.66	.69
100+	10	.39	.60	.36	.50	.78	.70
Total	1068	.22	.22	.13	.14	.47	.46

	% $S > 0$ Given $s_1 = L$ N	P^c	A^d	% $S > 0$ Given $s_1 = 0$ N	P^e	A^d
0–10	7	.48	.33	162	.37	.32
10–20	17	.56	.43	288	.41	.37
20–30	25	.66	.70	235	.42	.43
30–40	30	.66	.75	140	.49	.49
40–50	23	.66	.63	54	.52	.46
50–100	37	.77	.74	40	.56	.59
100+	4	.94	.60	6	.69	.75
Total	143	.68	.69	833	.42	.40

a. Based on 10 draws per sample observation.
b. Y–T, in thousands of dollars.
c. Predicted $S > 0$, given predicted $s_1 = L$.
d. Observed in the sample.
e. Predicted $S > 0$, given predicted $S_1 < 0$.

the proportions with $S > 0$ conditional on $s_1 = L$ (at the IRA limit) and with $S > 0$ conditional on $S_1 < 0$ (no IRA). Overall the fit is very close. In particular, the model seems not to underestimate the S_2 saving of persons who are at the IRA limit, as might be expected if not enough substitution of S_2 for S_1 were allowed by the model when the S_1 limit is reached. But this simulation shows some overprediction of S_2 saving for persons below the IRA limit. The simulated predictions are based on only 10 draws per person, however, so they reflect some random variation.[32] While unconditional overall proportions will match the actual values closely, nothing in the specifications assures a close fit by income interval. The model overpredicts saving of low-income persons. This is a characteristic of all of the specifications.

This overprediction is eliminated if the disturbance terms are allowed to be heteroskedastic, with the variance increasing with income, by specifying $\epsilon_1 = n_1 Y + e_1$ and $\epsilon_2 = n_2 Y + e_2$.[33] The fit based on this model with $k = 0$ is shown in table 1.11, where it can be seen that the predicted and actual proportions are very close for all income groups. Finally, illustrative predictions with $k = .65$ are shown in table 1.12. The predicted versus actual values are very similar to those in the $k = 0$ case, although if anything the predicted proportion of those at the limit with $S > 0$ is somewhat lower than in the $k = 0$ case.[34] Predictions with b_1 and b_2 parameterized are shown in appendix table 1.24, based on the estimates in table 1.7. This specification tends to predict a lower portion of those at the limit with $S > 0$ than the model with α and β parameterized.

1.3.4 Simulations of the Effect of IRA Limit Changes

To estimate the effect of IRAs on saving, we have predicted the effect of limit changes on IRA contributions and on other saving. To add content to this exercise, we have simulated the effects of several recently proposed limit changes. The first we call the Treasury Plan.[35] It would increase the limit for an employed person from $2,000 to $2,500, and would increase the limit for a nonworking spouse from $250 to $2,500. Thus, for example, the contribution limit for a husband and nonworking wife would increase from $2,250 to $5,000. A Modified Treasury Plan increases the limit for an employed person from $2,000 to $2,500, but only increases the limit for a nonworking spouse from $250 to $500. Finally, the President's Plan would leave the limit for an employed person at $2,000, but would raise the limit for a nonworking spouse from $250 to $2,000.[36] For comparison, simulated savings under the current limit are also shown.

The predicted changes should be interpreted as indications of changes in saving had the IRA limit been higher in 1982. It is important to keep

Table 1.11   **Simulated Predicted vs. Actual Values, by Income Interval, $k = 0$, and Heteroskedastic Disturbance Terms[a]**

Income Interval[b]	Number	% $s_1 > 0$		% $s_1 = L$		% $S > 0$	
		P	A	P	A	P	A
0–10	169	.03	.03	.01	.02	.32	.31
10–20	305	.08	.07	.03	.02	.41	.38
20–30	260	.21	.25	.10	.13	.50	.47
30–40	170	.33	.32	.20	.21	.53	.56
40–50	77	.48	.52	.33	.35	.62	.55
50–100	77	.56	.58	.48	.46	.60	.69
100+	10	.58	.60	.54	.50	.67	.70
Total	1068	.21	.22	.13	.14	.47	.46

	% $S > 0$ Given $s_1 = L$			% $S > 0$ Given $s_1 = 0$		
	N	P[c]	A[d]	N	P[e]	A[d]
0–10	3	.30	.33	164	.32	.32
10–20	7	.69	.43	285	.40	.37
20–30	33	.69	.70	196	.46	.43
30–40	36	.66	.75	115	.48	.49
40–50	27	.70	.63	37	.56	.46
50–100	35	.71	.74	32	.49	.59
100+	5	.72	.60	4	.60	.75
Total	146	.69	.69	833	.42	.40

a. Based on 10 draws per sample observation.
b. Y–T, in thousands of dollars.
c. Predicted $S > 0$, given predicted $s_1 = L$.
d. Observed in the sample.
e. Predicted $S > 0$, given predicted $S_1 < 0$.

in mind that S_2 saving undoubtedly excludes changes in nonliquid wealth such as housing. The possible substitution betwen IRAs and housing wealth in the long run, for example, would not be reflected in these estimates. They are intended, however, to indicate the extent to which IRA contributions in 1982 were simply a substitute for other forms of saving, other than nonliquid assets. The top portion of the table pertains to individuals who are predicted to be at the IRA limit, since it is only this group that would be affected by an increase in the limit. The bottom portion shows simulated contributions by family type. The simulations are based on the estimation sample. Those in table 1.13 are based on the estimates in table 1.7 and those in table 1.14 on the $k = .65$ estimates shown in table 1.9. The simulated values are based on 10 random draws for each observation in the estimation sample.

The predicted changes in S_1 and S_2 under the Treasury Plan for families at the IRA limit, for example, are as follows:

	ΔS_1	ΔS_2
Base model	+1138	−94
$k = .65$	+1091	−210

These values suggest that only 10–20% of the IRA increase is offset by a reduction in other financial assets. Thus, at least in the short run, tax-deferred IRA accounts have by these estimates led to a relatively large increase in total individual saving (as defined in this paper).

Possibly the best indicator of saving is change in consumption. The average change in "consumption" (as defined implicitly in this paper) under each plan is shown in table 1.15 together with changes in S_2 and

Table 1.12   **Simulated Predicted vs. Actual Values, by Income Interval, $k = .65^a$**

Income Interval[b]	Number	% $s_1 > 0$		% $s_1 = L$		% $S > 0$	
		P	*A*	*P*	*A*	*P*	*A*
0–10	169	.08	.03	.04	.02	.40	.31
10–20	305	.11	.07	.06	.02	.44	.38
20–30	260	.20	.25	.12	.13	.45	.47
30–40	170	.28	.32	.15	.21	.48	.56
40–50	77	.44	.52	.31	.35	.52	.55
50–100	77	.63	.58	.48	.46	.61	.69
100+	10	.38	.60	.33	.50	.77	.70
Total	1068	.22	.22	.14	.14	.46	.46

	% $S > 0$ Given $s_1 = L$			% $S > 0$ Given $s_1 = 0$		
	N	P^c	A^d	*N*	P^e	A^d
0–10	8	.52	.33	162	.40	.32
10–20	19	.68	.43	286	.42	.37
20–30	30	.63	.70	230	.43	.43
30–40	26	.61	.75	144	.45	.49
40–50	24	.64	.63	54	.47	.46
50–100	37	.72	.74	40	.51	.60
100+	3	.94	.60	7	.69	.75
Total	146	.66	.69	835	.42	.40

a. Based on 10 draws per sample observation.
b. $Y–T$, in thousands of dollars.
c. Predicted $S > 0$, given predicted $s_1 = L$.
d. Observed in the sample.
e. Predicted $S > 0$, given predicted $S_1 < 0$.

Table 1.13 Simulated Increases in IRA Contributions and in Other Saving, by Plan and Family Type, Table 1.7 Parameter Estimates, b_1 and b_2 Parameterized, and $k = 0$

Family Type	Current Plan (2000/250)		Treasury Plan (2500/2500)		Mod. Treas. Plan (2500/500)		President's Plan (2000/2000)	
	s_1 (Base)	s_2	s_1 (Change)	s_2	s_1 (Change)	s_2	s_1 (Change)	s_2
Observations Predicted at the Limit								
All families								
Ave. contribution	3025	−811	1138	−94	743	−65	396	−29
% change	—	—	+38	−3	+25	−2	+13	−1
All Observations								
All families								
Ave. contribution	519	−811	142	−12	93	−8	49	−3
% change	—	—	+27	−1	+18	−1	+9	0
Unmarried head								
Ave. contribution	270	−749	50	−6	50	−6	0	0
% change	—	—	+19	−1	+19	−1	0	0
Married one earner								
Ave. contribution	350	−1643	279	−21	89	−7	191	−14
% change	—	—	+80	−1	+25	0	+55	−1
Married two earners								
Ave. contribution	797	−355	127	−11	127	−11	0	0
% change	—	—	+16	−3	+16	−3	0	0

Table 1.14   Simulated Increases in IRA Contributions and in Other Saving, by Plan and Family Type, Table 1.9 Parameter Estimates, α and β Parameterized, and $k = .65$.

Family Type	Current Plan (2000/250) s_1 (Base)	Current Plan (2000/250) s_2 (Base)	Treasury Plan (2500/2500) s_1	Treasury Plan (2500/2500) s_2 (Change)	Mod. Treas. Plan (2500/500) s_1	Mod. Treas. Plan (2500/500) s_2 (Change)	President's Plan (2000/2000) s_1	President's Plan (2000/2000) s_2 (Change)
Observations Predicted at the Limit								
All families								
Ave. contribution	3069	3831	1091	−210	754	−143	351	−67
% change	—	—	+36	−5	+25	−4	+11	−2
All Observations								
All families								
Ave. contribution	522	111	143	−28	99	−19	46	−9
% change	—	—	+27	−25	+19	−17	+9	−8
Unmarried head								
Ave. contribution	265	−471	51	−10	51	−10	0	0
% change	—	—	+19	−2	+19	−2	0	0
Married one earner								
Ave. contribution	346	14	255	−49	85	−15	177	−34
% change	—	—	+74		+25		+51	
Married two earners								
Ave. contribution	811	583	141	−27	141	−27	0	0
% change	—	—	+17	−5	+17	−5	0	0

in taxes. For example, the simulated changes under the Treasury Plan for families at the limit are:

	Base Model		$k = .65$ Model	
	Amount	Percent	Amount	Percent
IRA, S_1 Saving	+1138	100.0	+1091	100.0
S_2 Saving	−94	−8.3	−210	−19.2
Consumption	−643	−56.5	−493	−45.2
Taxes	−401	−35.2	−388	−35.6

Thus possibly 50% of the IRA increase is funded by a reduction in consumption, according to these measures, and possibly 35% by reduced taxes, with a relatively small proportion coming from reduction in other saving.

Table 1.15   **Simulated Changes in Savings, Consumption, and Taxes, by Plan and by Model Specification**

	Treasury Plan (2500/2500)		Mod. Treas. Plan (2500/500)		President's Plan (2000/2000)	
	Amount	Percent	Amount	Percent	Amount	Percent
	Base Model					
Families at limit						
ΔS_1 saving	1138	(100.0)	743	(100.0)	396	(100.0)
ΔS_2 saving	−94	(8.3)	−65	(8.7)	−29	(7.3)
Δ consumption	−643	(56.5)	−421	(56.7)	−228	(57.6)
Δ taxes	−401	(35.2)	−257	(34.6)	139	(35.1)
All families						
ΔS_1 saving	142	(100.0)	93	(100.0)	49	(100.0)
ΔS_2 saving	−12	(8.5)	−8	(8.6)	−3	(6.1)
ΔS consumption	−81	(57.0)	−53	(57.0)	−29	(59.2)
Δ taxes	−49	(34.5)	−32	(34.4)	−17	(34.7)
	$k = .65$ Model					
Families at limit						
ΔS_1 saving	1091	(100.0)	754	(100.0)	351	(100.0)
ΔS_2 saving	−210	(19.2)	−143	(19.0)	−67	(19.1)
Δ consumption	−493	(45.2)	−344	(45.6)	−162	(46.2)
Δ taxes	−388	(35.6)	−267	(35.4)	−122	(34.8)
All families						
ΔS_1 saving	143	(100.0)	99	(100.0)	46	(100.0)
ΔS_2 saving	−28	(19.6)	−19	(19.2)	−9	(19.6)
Δ consumption	−65	(45.5)	−45	(45.5)	−21	(45.7)
Δ taxes	−50	(35.0)	−35	(35.4)	−16	(34.8)

The estimated IRA increases can be compared with estimates by Venti and Wise (1985) based on 1983 Current Population Survey (CPS) data. The CPS data reported actual 1982 IRA contributions by interval, while 1982 contributions had to be inferred from balances reported in the SCF. In addition, self-reported marginal tax rates were used here, while estimated rates were used in conjunction with the CPS data. Nonetheless the simulated effects of limit increases are virtually the same. For example, for all families the simulated increase under the Treasury Plan is 27% versus 30% based on the CPS data. The increase for unmarried heads is 19% versus 19% based on the CPS; it is 80% versus 79% for married one-earner families; and 16% versus 16% for married two-earner families.

1.3.5 Sensitivity of Results to Model Specification

The sensitivity of the results to selected specification changes is shown in table 1.16. Possibly the best summary indicator of the effect of these changes is the simulated change in S_2 under the Treasury Plan. In each case, the decline in S_2 is small relative to the increase in IRAs, although the magnitude of the decline in S_2 varies by a factor of 4. None of the specification changes has much effect on the simulated IRA change. If it is assumed that $S = S_1 + S_2$, the estimated reduction in S_2 tends to be larger, except where P_1 is set to 1. In the latter case, the constrained estimate δ_2^* of δ_2 is larger because $\hat{b}_2/(1 - \hat{b}_1)$ is larger.

Table 1.16   **Sensitivity of Simulations to Alternative Specifications**

Specification	LF	δ_1	δ_2	Treasury Plan Effect for Persons at the Limit	
				ΔS_1	ΔS_2
$S = S_2$					
b_1, b_2 parameterized	-1380	.247	.102	1138	-94
b_1, b_2 parameterized; stocks & bonds included with liquid assets	-1399	.268	.103	1135	-95
b_1, b_2 parameterized; additive errors	-1377	.240	.078	1144	-83
$k = 0$; α, β parameterized; additive errors	-1379	.244	.049	1111	-69
$k = .65$; α, β parameterized; additive errors	-1394	.213	.028	1091	-210
$S = S_1 + S_2$; b_1, b_2 parameterized					
$\sigma_1 \neq \sigma_2$	-1377	.287	.059	1137	-52
$\sigma_1 = \sigma_2$	-1378	.254	.085	1141	-76
Total wealth only	-1381	.294	.061	1143	-45
$P_1 = 1$	-1363	.403	.096	1130	-172

1.4 Conclusions

Increasing the IRA limits would lead to substantial increases in tax-deferred saving according to our evidence, based on the 1983 Survey of Consumer Finances. For example, the recent Treasury Plan would increase IRA contributions by about 30%. Virtually the same estimate was obtained in previous analysis based on Current Population Survey data, suggesting that this conclusion may be relatively robust. The primary focus of this paper, however, has been the effect of limit increases on other saving. How much of the IRA increase would be offset by reduction in non-tax-deferred saving? The weight of our evidence suggests that very little of the increase would be offset by reduction in other financial assets, possibly 10–20%, maybe less. Our estimates suggest that 45–55% of the IRA increase would be funded by reduction in consumption, and about 35% by reduced taxes.

The analysis rests on a preference structure recognizing the constraint that the IRA limit places on the allocation of current income. The model fits the data well and in particular distinguishes accurately the savings decisions of persons at the IRA limit versus the decisions of those who are not.

The greatest potential uncertainty about the results and the greatest statistical complication for analysis stems from the limited information on non-IRA saving and from the consequent difficulty of obtaining direct estimates of the degree of substitution between tax-deferred and non-tax-deferred saving. We have addressed these issues by considering the sensitivity of our conclusions to specification changes, including assumptions about the interpretation of key variables and the extent of substitution underlying observed saving outcomes. Although the magnitude of the estimated reduction in other saving, with increases in the IRA limit, is sensitive to specification changes, the reduction as a percentage of the IRA increase is invariably small.

In addition to these primary conclusions, our evidence suggests substantial variation in saving behavior among segments of the population. We also find that IRAs do not serve as a substitute for private pension plans, although persons without private plans devote a larger proportion of their lower total saving to IRAs. Thus the legislative goal of disproportionately increasing retirement saving among persons without pension plans is apparently not being realized. But the more general goal of increasing individual saving is.

Appendix
Imputing 1982 IRA Contributions

The Survey of Consumer Finances (SCF) asked respondents if they had any IRA accounts and the total dollar value in all of them. The SCF did not ask respondents for their 1982 contribution. Given that the Economic Recovery Tax Act liberalized eligibility beginning in 1982 (nearly three-quarters of all 1982 accounts were opened in 1982), the following criteria are used to impute 1982 contributions:

(a) If the total value of IRAs is less than the 1982 family limit then the total value is assumed to be the 1982 contribution.

(b) If the total value of IRAs exceeds the 1982 family limit then the family limit is assumed to be the 1982 contribution.

Imputed IRA contributions based on this procedure compare favorably to evidence from the CPS, which presents 1982 contributions by interval.

Table 1.17   Summary Statistics for Estimation Subsample

	All		Contributors Only	
Variable	Mean	S.D.	Mean	S.D.
Total after-tax				
income $(Y - T)^a$ ($)	26,239	22,442	41,093	30,354
Age	37.7	11.4	44.0	11.2
Wealth[b]	59,781	115,927	120,628	169,900
Liquid wealth ($)	7,796	19,109	17.974	30,156
Nonliquid wealth ($)	51,984	109,231	102,654	160,011
Private pension $(0,1)^c$	0.67	0.47	0.80	0.40
Education (years)	13.4	2.5	14.5	2.3
Unmarried woman $(0,1)$	0.17	0.38	0.10	0.30
Unmarried man $(0,1)$	0.14	0.35	0.11	0.31
Marginal tax rate	0.25	0.15	0.31	0.14
IRA ($)	533	1164	2423	1257
IRA > 0 $(0,1)$	0.22	0.41	—	—
"S" $(0,1)$	0.46	0.50	0.65	0.48
Number of observations	1068		235	

a. Total after-tax income is obtained by using the reported marginal tax rate and inferred filing status to calculate (using 1982 tax tables) the taxes paid by each family, and subtracting this amount from total income.

b. The wealth variables are defined in note 4 to this chapter.

c. For two worker families the variable is unity if either member participates in a pension plan, and zero otherwise.

Table 1.18   **Parameter Estimates with b_1 and b_2 Parameterized, Assuming that $S = S_1 + S_2$, $\sigma_1 \neq \sigma_2$**

Variable	Estimate (Asymptotic Standard Error)		
Origin parameters			
Mean of a_1	17.79 (2.52)		
Mean of a_2	3.02 (1.10)		
S.D. of a_1	8.84 (1.10)		
S.D. of a_2	5.45 (1.91)		
Correlation of a_1, a_2	.17 (.17)		
S.D. of S_1 (at mean)	6.98		
S.D. of S_2 (at mean)	5.19		
Correlation of S_1, S_2	$-.09$		
Determinants of b_1 and b_2	b_1		b_2
Income ($1000's)	$-.00557$ (.00071)		$-.01156$ (.00382)
Age (years)	.0108 (.0019)		$-.0054$ (.0049)
Total wealth ($1000's)	—		—
Nonliquid	$-.00022$ (.00010)		$-.00022$ (.00075)
Liquid	.00103 (.00047)		.01242 (.00389)
Private pension (0,1)	$-.0339$ (.0403)		.9854 (.5127)
Education (years)	.0227 (.0077)		.0233 (.0237)
Unmarried woman	.0754 (.0594)		.1911 (.1532)
Unmarried man	.0538 (.0497)		.3231 (.1100)
Predicted b_1 and b_2	b_1		b_2
Mean	.203		.059
S.D.	.040		.052
Min.	.011		.000
Max.	.340		.739
Predicted δ_1 and δ_2	δ_1		δ_2
Mean	.287		.059
S.D.	.191		.052
Min.	.011		.000
Max.	5.303		.739
LF		-1377	

Table 1.19   **Parameter Estimates with b_1 and b_2 Parameterized, Assuming that $S = S_1 + S_2$, $\sigma_1 = \sigma_2$**

Variable	Estimate (Asymptotic Standard Error)
Origin parameters	
Mean of a_1	16.15 (2.15)
Mean of a_2	4.37 (.87)
S.D. of a_1	8.48 (1.07)
S.D. of a_2	8.48 (—)
Correlation of a_1, a_2	.33 (.08)
S.D. of S_1 (at mean)	6.60
S.D. of S_2 (at mean)	7.88
Correlation of S_1, S_2	.01

Table 1.19   (continued)

Variable	Estimate (Asymptotic Standard Error)	
Determinants of b_1 and b_2	b_1	b_2
Income ($1000's)	$-.00506$ (.00068)	$-.01182$ (.00354)
Age (years)	.0111 (.0019)	$-.0030$ (.0050)
Total wealth ($1000's)	—	—
Nonliquid	$-.00024$ (.00010)	$-.00026$ (.00071)
Liquid	.00093 (.00046)	.0129 (.0039)
Private pension (0,1)	$-.0304$ (.0397)	1.1708 (.5963)
Education (years)	.0244 (.0077)	.0350 (.0253)
Unmarried woman	.0709 (.0578)	.2060 (.1593)
Unmarried man	.0505 (.0498)	.3137 (.1149)
Constant	-1.5334 (.2011)	-2.5778 (.8737)
Predicted b_1 and b_2	b_1	b_2
Mean	.179	.085
S.D.	.037	.072
Min.	.012	.000
Max.	.311	.844
Predicted δ_1 and δ_2	δ_1	δ_2
Mean	.254	.085
S.D.	.169	.072
Min.	.012	.000
Max.	4.660	.844
LF	-1378	

Table 1.20   **Parameter Estimates with b_1 and b_2 Parameterized, Assuming that $S = S_1 + S_2$, $\sigma_1 \neq \sigma_2$, using Total Wealth**

Variable	Estimate (Asymptotic Standard Error)	
Origin parameters		
Mean of a_1	18.28 (2.58)	
Mean of a_2	3.07 (1.16)	
S.D. of a_1	9.04 (1.13)	
S.D. of a_2	5.34 (1.78)	
Correlation of a_1, a_2	.19 (.16)	
S.D. of S_1 (at mean)	7.05	
S.D. of S_2 (at mean)	5.01	
Correlation of S_1, S_2	$-.08$	
Determinants of b_1 and b_2	b_1	b_2
Income ($1000's)	$-.00536$ (.00058)	$-.00704$ (.00289)
Age (years)	.0116 (.0017)	$-.0036$ (.0047)
Total wealth ($1000's)	$-.00021$ (.00010)	.000096 (.00032)
Nonliquid	—	—
Liquid	—	—
Private pension (0,1)	$-.0452$ (.0370)	.5845 (.3329)
Education (years)	.0232 (.0078)	.0249 (.0223)
Unmarried woman	.0759 (.0566)	.2055 (.1419)
Unmarried man	.0558 (.0495)	.3664 (.1131)
Constant	-1.4058 (.2024)	-2.1174 (.6683)

Table 1.20 (continued)

Variable	Estimate (Asymptotic Standard Error)	
Predicted b_1 and b_2	b_1	b_2
Mean	.208	.061
S.D.	.042	.035
Min.	.011	.000
Max.	.351	.187
Predicted δ_1 and δ_2	δ_1	δ_2
Mean	.294	.061
S.D.	.195	.035
Min.	.013	.000
Max.	5.393	.187
LF	-1381	

Table 1.21   **Parameter Estimates with b_1 and b_2 Parameterized, Assuming that $S = S_1 + S_2$, $\sigma_1 \neq \sigma_2$ and $P_1 = 1$**

Variable	Estimate (Asymptotic Standard Error)	
Origin parameters		
Mean of a_1	31.29 (6.96)	
Mean of a_2	6.24 (3.26)	
S.D. of a_1	13.23 (3.08)	
S.D. of a_2	9.65 (4.55)	
Correlation of a_1, a_2	.54 (.22)	
S.D. of S_1 (at mean)	6.66	
S.D. of S_2 (at mean)	8.26	
Correlation of S_1, S_2	$-.05$	
Determinants of b_1 and b_2	b_1	b_2
Income ($1000's)	$-.00685$ (.00077)	$-.00853$ (.00247)
Age (years)	.0078 (.0017)	$-.0042$ (.0037)
Total wealth ($1000's)	—	—
Nonliquid	$-.000093$ (.000087)	$-.00016$ (.00048)
Liquid	.00205 (.00046)	.00797 (.00293)
Private pension (0,1)	$-.0064$ (.0313)	.5626 (.2495)
Education (years)	.0213 (.0066)	.0158 (.0179)
Unmarried woman	.0670 (.0458)	.1331 (.1153)
Unmarried man	.0469 (.0392)	.2444 (.0911)
Constant	$-.6726$ (.2384)	-1.6834 (.5608)
Predicted b_1 and b_2	b_1	b_2
Mean	.403	.096
S.D.	.052	.048
Min.	.023	.000
Max.	.599	.540
Predicted δ_1 and δ_2	δ_1	δ_2
Mean	.403	.096
S.D.	.052	.048
Min.	.023	.000
Max.	.599	.540
LF	-1363	

Table 1.22 **Parameter Estimates with b_1 and b_2 Parameterized, Assuming that $S = S_1 + S_2$, $\sigma_1 \neq \sigma_2$, $P_1 = 1$, and Marginal Tax Rate in b_1 and b_2**

Variable	Estimate (Asymptotic Standard Error)			
Origin parameters				
Mean of a_1	32.73 (7.59)			
Mean of a_2	7.45 (3.45)			
S.D. of a_1	13.20 (3.13)			
S.D. of a_2	10.06 (4.16)			
Correlation of a_1, a_2	.57 (.20)			
S.D. of S_1 (at mean)	6.42			
S.D. of S_2 (at mean)	8.23			
Correlation of S_1, S_2	$-.10$			
Determinants of b_1 and b_2	b_1		b_2	
Income ($1000's)	$-.00763$	(.00077)	$-.00915$	(.00230)
Age (years)	.0076	(.0016)	$-.0051$	(.0032)
Total wealth ($1000's)	—		—	
Nonliquid	$-.000112$	(.000080)	$-.000163$	(.00041)
Liquid	.00241	(.00049)	.00777	(.00274)
Private pension (0,1)	$-.0469$	(.0315)	.3478	(.1426)
Education (years)	.0198	(.0064)	.0051	(.0151)
Unmarried woman	.0555	(.0429)	.1006	(.1012)
Unmarried man	.0385	(.0362)	.2246	(.0844)
Marginal tax rate	.3000	(.1023)	.4884	(.2556)
Constant	$-.6464$	(.2403)	-1.3149	(.4281)
Predicted b_1 and b_2	b_1		b_2	
Mean	.412		.118	
S.D.	.058		.049	
Min.	.012		.000	
Max.	.635		.557	
Predicted δ_1 and δ_2	δ_1		δ_2	
Mean	.412		.118	
S.D.	.058		.049	
Min.	.012		.000	
Max.	.635		.557	
LF	-1358			

Table 1.23 **Parameter Estimates with b_1 and b_2 Parameterized, $S = S_2$, Additive Disturbance**

Variable	Estimate (Asymptotic Standard Error)
Origin parameters	
Mean of a_1	15.43 (2.05)
Mean of a_2	3.17 (.58)
S.D. of a_1	—
S.D. of a_2	—
Correlation of a_1, a_2	—
S.D. of S_1 (at mean)	6.75 (.62)
S.D. of S_2 (at mean)	6.75 (—)
Correlation of S_1, S_2	.15 (.06)

Table 1.23 (continued)

Variable	Estimate (Asymptotic Standard Error)			
Determinants of b_1 and b_2	b_1		b_2	
Income ($1000's)	− .00510	(.00079)	− .01225	(.0028)
Age (years)	.0113	(.0019)	− .0011	(.0053)
Total wealth ($1000's)	—		—	
Nonliquid	− .00022	(.00011)	− .00023	(.00059)
Liquid	.00144	(.00051)	.0155	(.0040)
Private pension (0,1)	− .0156	(.0410)	1.0942	(.4482)
Education (years)	.0292	(.0082)	.0444	(.0269)
Unmarried woman	.0380	(.0655)	.1013	(.1837)
Unmarried man	.0466	(.0522)	.3632	(.1311)
Constant	− 1.653	(.216)	− 2.768	(.770)
Predicted b_1 and b_2	b_1		b_2	
Mean	.169		.078	
S.D.	.036		.074	
Min.	.011		.000	
Max.	.318		.933	
Predicted δ_1 and δ_2	δ_1		δ_2	
Mean	.240		.078	
Standard deviation	.162		.074	
Min.	.011		.000	
Max.	4.427		.933	
LF			− 1377	

Table 1.24   **Simulated Predicted vs. Actual Values, by Income Interval, b_1 and b_2 Parameterized**

Income Interval[b]	Number	% $s_1 > 0$		% $s_1 = L$		% $S > 0$	
		P	A	P	A	P	A
0–10	169	.07	.03	.04	.02	.34	.31
10–20	305	.11	.07	.06	.02	.41	.38
20–30	260	.19	.25	.10	.13	.47	.47
30–40	170	.31	.32	.18	.21	.53	.56
40–50	77	.45	.52	.28	.35	.56	.55
50–100	77	.63	.58	.44	.46	.61	.69
100 +	10	.70	.60	.56	.50	.60	.70
Total	1068	.22	.22	.13	.14	.46	.46

	% $S > 0$ Given $s_1 = L$			% $s_1 = 0$ Given $s_1 = 0$		
	N	P[c]	A[d]	N	P[e]	A[d]
0–10	7	.39	.33	162	.34	.32
10–20	17	.59	.43	288	.40	.37
20–30	26	.56	.70	235	.46	.43
30–40	36	.67	.75	139	.49	.49
40–50	21	.66	.63	56	.52	.46

Table 1.24   (continued)

Income Interval[b]	Number	% $s_1 > 0$		% $s_1 = L$		% $S > 0$	
		P	A	P	A	P	A
50–100	34	.69	.74	43	.54	.59	
100+	6	.75	.60	4	.41	.75	
Total	141	.63	.69	830	.41	.40	

a. Based on 10 draws per sample observation, and on the parameter estimates in text table 1.7.
b. Y–T, in thousands of dollars.
c. Predicted $S > 0$, given predicted $s_1 = L$.
d. Observed in the sample.
e. Predicted $S > 0$, given predicted $S_1 < 0$.

Notes

1. Self-employed persons have been excluded from the analysis.
2. Numbers based on CPS data (Venti and Wise [1985]) indicate a higher proportion of wage earners with IRAs. While the CPS data are weighted to represent the employed population, the SCF data reported here are weighted to represent families with a wage earner.
3. Three responses were possible: (1) Put more money in. (2) Stayed the same. (3) Took more money out.
4. This evidence is consistent with the widespread perception that individual savings rates in the United States have been unusually low in recent years and that consumer debt has been increasing. See, for example, *New York Times*, 29 October 1985; *Boston Globe*, 15 September and 22 November 1985.
5. The following breakdown of wealth is used throughout this paper:
   Liquid assets: checking accounts, certificates of deposit, savings accounts, money market accounts, savings bonds
   Other financial assets: stocks, bonds, trusts
   IRAs and Keoghs: balances
   Other assets: value of home, other property and receivables
   Debt: mortgage and consumer debt
Total wealth is the sum of the first four categories minus debt. Wealth does *not* include the cash value of life insurance, the value of motor vehicles, and pension and Social Security wealth.
6. The median for all financial assets is 1.3 when stocks and bonds are included, versus 1.2 when they are excluded. For more detail, see Venti and Wise (1986).
7. Weighted by the number of IRA contributors.
8. For most purposes it is not necessary to specify two behavioral equations: one describing contributor status and the other the amount.
9. In practice the marginal tax rate is not constant, but incorporating this nonlinearity into the budget constraint would greatly increase the complexity of the analysis and, we believe, would not appreciably affect the results, given the small potential IRA contributions relative to income.
10. While we use the decision function simply to provide consistent functional forms for the constrained and unconstrained S_2 functions, there is some precedent for including asset (saving) balances in a true utility function. See for

example Sidrauski (1967), Fischer (1979), Calvo (1979), Obstfeld (1984, 1985), and Poterba and Rotemberg (1986). With a_1 and a_2 random, as described below, annual S_1 and S_2 flows could be thought of as proxies for balances.

11. A similar situation characterizes the specification used by Hausman and Ruud (1984), for example, to describe family labor supply. Their specification yields unconstrained closed-form solutions to the labor supply functions of the husband and the wife, consistent with an indirect utility function. But constrained functions analogous to ours are only defined implicitly.

12. Thus, for example, $b_1 = \int_{-\infty}^{XB_1} v\,dv$, where v is a standard normal variable. In practice, very few predicted b_1 or b_2 values are below zero, if the constraint is not imposed.

13. $\partial S_1/\delta a_1 = 1 - b_1$, $\partial S_2/\partial a_2 = 1 - b_2$,
$\partial S_1/\delta a_2 = -b_1/(1 - t)$, $\partial S_2/\delta a_1 = -b_2(1 - t)$.

14. To determine the magnitude of S_2, not just its sign, it is necessary to identify its residual variance. In many situations similar to this, identification of both σ_2 and σ_1 would not be possible given only qualitative information on S_2, its sign. In this case, however, identification is in principle provided by three features of the model: (1) the functional form itself; (2) the limit L on S_1; and (3) by direct information on the value of S_2 in addition to its sign, if "savings and reserve funds" is interpreted to include IRAs. For more detail, see Venti and Wise (1986).

15. A dollar of current after-tax income allocated to S_1 yields $S_1/(1 - t)$ in tax-deferred saving.

16. This effect can be seen from figure 1.1. The effect of changing the limit is to shift downward the function S_2 described by the steeper-sloped segment of the S_2 function and the dashed extension of it.

17. In this case, with $P_1 = P_2$, desired S_1 would equal desired S_2, as can be seen from equation (14) below.

18. This specification is thus a slight variant of the "S-branch" utility tree of Brown and Heien (1972). See also Blackorby, Boyce, and Russell [1978].

19. The α, β parameterization essentially allows interactions between the X variables and thus the difference in the two parameterizations is more than just interpretation. Setting $\alpha = b_1/(b_1 + b_2)$, $\beta = b_1 + b_2$, and parameterizing b_1 and b_2 would yield results the same as the section 1.2.2 specification.

20. Similar evidence for the $k = 0$ case is presented in Venti and Wise (1986), but with α and β, instead of b_1 and b_2, parameterized.

21. For example; mean wealth is $59,781 in the estimation sample and is $59,090 in the total sample, mean age is 37.7 versus 39.4, mean education is 13.4 versus 12.2, and the mean self-reported marginal tax rate is 0.25 versus 0.27.

22. Using the regression analogy, it is equivalent to obtaining an unbiased estimate of $E(Y|X)$, where $Y = Xb + \epsilon$, rather than unbiased estimates of each component of b.

23. A potentially important assumption is the presumed distribution of the random terms. The results below show that the model fits the observed data well by income interval, and this provides some support for the distributional assumptions. A better test would be to use the model to predict the effect of a limit change. While this is not possible for the United States, such predictions have been made for Canadian tax-deferred saving contributions using a specification similar to the one used here for IRA contributions. The model estimated using data from one year predicted very accurately the contributions in a later year with a 60% lower contribution limit, and vice versa. See Wise (1984, 1985). The results are also summarized in Venti and Wise (1985).

24. Similar findings are reported by Mundlak (1975) and by Griliches and Ringstad (1971) with respect to production data. In our case, the likelihood function is very flat around $k = 0$.

25. It is not possible to reach strong conclusions based on this evidence because the asset balances are reported after an IRA contribution and because it is not clear what the relationship should be if liquid assets, say, are larger than the IRA limit. But if liquid assets were relatively large at the end of the period, one might suppose that they were large when the IRA decision was made. One might also suppose that the larger the liquid asset balances, the easier it would be to forgo liquidity and to put money in an IRA.

26. It is also informative to consider the cost, in terms of current consumption, of providing retirement income. Suppose, thinking in a manner roughly consistent with statements of some pension planners, an individual wants to accumulate a given retirement fund by age $j > 59\frac{1}{2}$. If the amount accumulated through S_1 saving is to be equivalent to that accumulated through S_2 saving, $S_1(1 - t)e^{r(j-j')} = S_2(1 - t')e^{r(1-t')(j-j')}$. The amount of required S_2 relative to S_1 would be $S_2/S_1 = [(1 - t)/(1 - t')]e^{rt'(j-j')}$. The cost in terms of current consumption is given by $(S_2/S_1) = [C_2/C_1(1 - t')]$, where C represents current consumption cost. Thus

$$C_2/C_1 = [1 - t)/(1 - t')^2]e^{rt'(j-j')}. \text{ If } t = t',$$

$$C_2/C_1 = [1/(1 - t')]e^{rt'(j-j')}.$$

This is of course another way of emphasizing the IRA advantage. But it also suggests that the income effect created by the lower IRA cost could in theory lead to greater consumption, although the parameter estimates themselves, together with the simulations presented below, are inconsistent with this conceptual possibility.

27. We say "may" because the nonliquid aspect of the IRA may well be a positive attribute for some individuals, in spite of standard presumptions about "rational" behavior.

28. Wise (1984) contains analysis of Canadian tax-deferred Registered Retirement Saving Plans. In general, we have found that the estimated effect of the marginal tax rate is very sensitive to functional form. See also Wise (1985) and Venti and Wise (1985). King and Leape (1984) also mention the difficulty of isolating the effect of the marginal tax rate, and they conclude, "contrary to much of the recent literature, that taxes do not play a decisive role in explaining the difference in portfolio composition across households."

29. See, for example, the survey by King (1985).

30. It can be shown that if $S = S_2$ but it is assumed that $S = S_1 + S_2$, the estimated variance of S_2 will be biased downward. In addition, the estimated residual correlation between S_1 and S_2 will be biased downward.

31. Results with $S = S_1 + S_2$ are presented in Venti and Wise (1986).

32. In eight different simulations with 10 draws per person in each, the average of the predicted proportion of those with $S > 0$, given $S_1 = L$, was .676.

33. Similar results were obtained by Wise (1984, 1985) using Canadian data, and by Venti and Wise (1985) using Current Population Survey data.

34. The average over 8 simulations with 10 draws per person in each was .656, versus .676 in the $k = 0$ case. The average over 3 simulations with 50 draws per person in each was .652.

35. See U.S. Department of Treasury (1984).

36. See U.S. President (1985).

References

Bernheim, B. Douglas, 1984. Dissaving after retirement: Testing the pure life cycle hypothesis. NBER Working Paper no. 1409 (July).

Blackorby, Charles, Richard Boyce, and R. Robert Russell. 1978. Estimation of demand systems generated by the Gorman polar form; A generalization of the S-branch utility tree. *Econometrica* 46, no. 2 (March): 345–63.

Brown, Murray, and Dale Heien. 1972. The S-branch utility tree: A generalization of the linear expenditure system. *Econometrica* 40, no. 4 (July): 737–47.

Calvo, G. A. 1979. On models of money and perfect foresight. *International Economic Review* 20:83–103.

Deaton, Angus. 1981. Theoretical and empirical approaches to consumer demand under rationing. In A. Deaton (ed.), *Essays in the theory and measurement of consumer behavior.* Cambridge: Cambridge University Press.

Deaton, Angus, and John Muellbauer. 1981. Functional forms for labor supply and commodity demands with and without quantity constraints. *Econometrica* 49, no. 6 (November): 1521–32.

Diamond, Peter, and Jerry Hausman. 1984. Individual retirement and savings behavior. *Journal of Public Economics* 23 (June): 81–114.

Fischer, Stanley. 1979. Capital accumulation on the transition path in a monetary optimizing economy. *Econometrica* 47:1433–39.

Griliches, Zvi, and Vidar Ringstad. 1971. *Economies of scale and the form of the production function.* New York: North-Holland.

Hausman, Jerry, and Paul Ruud. 1984. Family labor supply with taxes. *American Economic Review* 74, no 2 (May): 242–48.

Hurd, Michael, and John Shoven. 1985. The Distributional Impact of Social Security. In D. Wise (ed.), *Pensions, labor, and individual choice.* Chicago: University of Chicago Press.

King, Mervyn A. 1985. The economics of saving: A survey of recent contributions. In K. Arrow and S. Honkapohja (eds), *Frontiers of economics.* Oxford: Basil Blackwell.

King, Mervyn A., and Jonathan I. Leape. 1984. Wealth and portfolio composition: Theory and evidence. NBER Working Paper no. 1468 (September).

Mundlak, Yair. 1975. Production functions—A survey of some open problems. manuscript, Hebrew University of Jerusalem.

Obstfeld, Maurice. 1984. Multiple stable equilibria in an optimizing perfect-foresight model. *Econometrica* 52:223–28.

Obstfeld, Maurice. 1985. The capital inflows problem revisited: A stylized model of southern cone disinflation. *Review of Economic Studies* 52:605–24.

Poterba, James M., and Julio J. Rotemberg. 1986. Money in the utility function: An empirical implementation. Massachusetts Institute of Technology Working Paper no. 408 (January).

Sidrauski, Miguel. 1967. Inflation and economic growth. *Journal of Political Economy* 75:796–810.

U.S. President. 1985. *The president's tax proposals to the Congress for fairness, growth, and simplicity.* Washington, D.C.: USGPO (May).

U.S. Department of Treasury. 1984. *Tax reform for fairness, simplicity, and economic growth.* Washington, D.C.: USGPO.

Venti, Steven F., and David A. Wise, 1985. The determinants of IRA contributions and the effect of limit changes. NBER Working Paper no. 1731

(October). Forthcoming in Z. Bodie, J. Shoven, and D. Wise (eds.), *Pensions in the U.S. Economy.* Chicago: University of Chicago Press.

———. 1986. Tax-deferred accounts, constrained choice, and estimation of individual saving. *Review of Economic Studies,* Econometrics Special Issue (August).

Wise, David A. 1984. The effects of policy changes on RRSP contribution. Prepared for the Tax Policy and Legislation Branch of the Canadian Department of Finance (March 1984). Manuscript.

———. 1985. Contributors and contributions to Registered Retirement Savings Plans. Prepared for the Tax Policy and Legislation Branch of the Canadian Department of Finance (April 1985). Manuscript.

Comment   Angus Deaton

I must begin by congratulating the authors on a very brave attempt to do what is probably impossible, to estimate the effects on total saving of increasing the ceiling on IRA contributions, and to do so using only a single cross section of data. Moreover, the data are far from ideal in other respects, particularly in that there is no information on the amounts saved other than in IRAs, but only on whether individuals put money in or took money out of their total savings and reserve funds. All the more remarkable then that Venti and Wise manage to estimate the fraction of IRA contributions that come from a reduction in consumption, i.e., from "new" saving, and the fraction that come from a decline in other assets. The results suggest that a large fraction of IRAs are at the expense of current consumption, so that any increase in the maximum contribution allowed would exert very powerful effects on the total amount of saving. For example, Venti and Wise calculate (table 1.13, and sec. 1.3.4) that the adoption of the Treasury Plan with an extension of the current limits of $2,000 for a working and $250 for a nonworking spouse to $2,500 for both would generate $1,138 per household of additional IRA contributions, of which only $94 would come from a reduction in other saving. The princely sum of $643 would come from a reduction in consumption, with the federal government making up the rest through a reduction in taxes of $401. Are these numbers plausible? Quite possibly, particularly if we believe that IRAs appeal to individuals who would not otherwise save, and who are persuaded to adopt IRA plans by the very intensive advertising and commercial pressures that seem to accompany the schemes. However, this is not the story that is given in the paper, which adopts a much more standard

Angus Deaton is a professor of economics and international affairs at the Woodrow Wilson School, Princeton University, and a research associate of the National Bureau of Economic Research.

approach whereby IRAs provide limited access to a very high yield form of saving. If this is the way things work, and it is the natural first approach for an economist to adopt, then I think that the results are extremely implausible, given the other things that we know about saving behavior. Venti and Wise adopt a straightforward model in which utility is linked to consumption on the one hand and to savings on the other, the latter modeled as a CES composite of IRA saving and saving in other assets. Since such a model allows two-stage separable budgeting; changes in the IRA limitations act only through the savings branch of the utility function. I find it helpful to think of the effects on consumption in terms of price effects; an increase in the amount permitted to be saved in an IRA, which carries a very attractive rate of return, effectively raises the rate of return on saving as a whole. The increase in the effective rate will depend positively on the tax bracket of the household, and will be very small for households that pay little or no tax. Since my reading of the literature is that consumption is not very sensitive to the real interest rate, I find it difficult to believe that the modest increase in rates provided by raising the IRA ceiling could possibly generate the very large falls in consumption found in the paper. Indeed, the authors find themselves "unable to demonstrate convincingly an increasing preference for IRAs with increasing marginal tax rates." Hence, if IRA saving is generated by the same forces that generate other saving, I would expect that an increase in the ceiling on IRA contributions would leave consumption more or less unchanged or would *increase* it, since individuals can now attain the same standard of living after retirement at less cost in terms of present consumption forgone. I would expect IRA saving to increase quite considerably, but I would expect most of the increase to be financed by a decline in other assets. The quite different conclusions of the paper may well be correct as estimates of what would actually happen, but they are not consistent with the general framework that is used in the paper.

How then did the results come about, and in what way do they implicitly contradict the standard results on saving, consumption, and income? One possibility is the old problem of what happens when saving is regressed on income in a single cross section, and what it tells us, or better does *not* tell us, about the effects over time of income growth on savings rates. In spite of its utility formulation, and largely because of the limitations of a single cross-sectional survey, the model of this paper is essentially an old-fashioned Keynesian model in which saving is a linear function of income. Because a great deal of saving, including IRA saving, is done by people with relatively high incomes, a regression of saving on income yields a high marginal propensity to save, and so it is here. Although what is being estimated is far from being a simple linear regression, we still get, in table 1.7, an estimated marginal propensity to save on IRAs and other saving together of 0.65, i.e. $(1 - \delta_1 - \delta_2)$ in the table. Almost no modern work on the consumption function would support an estimate this low, and there are many standard reasons why we would expect the cross-sectional correlation to be misleading (permanent and transitory income effects, individual fixed effects, and so on). Recent econometric work may have cast some shadows on parts of permanent income and life-cycle theory, but I doubt that a return to the textbook Keynesian consumption function is a real step forward.

The high estimated marginal propensity to save is part of the story. Also important is the elasticity of substitution between IRAs and other forms of saving. Unfortunately, the data are not capable of providing a precise estimate of this important quantity, and the conclusions are sensitive to the value that is assumed. If more substitution is allowed than in the baseline case, more of the increase in IRAs comes out of other assets (see the righthand panel of the table on page 00), and presumably the data are consistent with even larger effects.

There are two more econometric issues that should perhaps be put in the record. First, I am unhappy about the precise status of the explanatory variables in the analysis. The authors (rightly) make much of the existence of unobservable fixed effects that determine each household's attitudes to saving—the "Protestant ethic" effects—and the estimated positive influence of wealth on saving is ascribed to the correlation between wealth and these omitted effects. However, wealth will only be an imperfect proxy, and it is hard to believe that the other variables, and in particular income, are independent of the fixed effects. If so, the explanatory variables are not exogenous and there will be a complicated pattern of biases. The authors are aware of this and tell us that "it is not necessary to obtain unbiased estimates . . . to estimate the effect of changing L. The model is intended to be structural with respect to L, not necessarily with respect to the effects of the variables X that determine the b's." I find it difficult to interpret the second sentence, and, while the first is clearly true, I should have welcomed some proof that the effects of changing the limit are consistently estimated in view of these acknowledged econometric problems. Second, I should like to register a mild protest at the way most of the variables have been entered into the analysis. Parameterization is generally restricted to the marginal propensities to consume, and this has the effect that a whole group of variables (wealth, age, education, etc.) appear only through their interactions with income. I see no reason to restrict the analysis to what would normally be considered second-order effects, ignoring the first-order effects of the levels of the variables.

I should like to conclude by summarizing what I think are the substantive achievements of the paper. First, on a methodological level, this is a very clever piece of applied econometrics. Great subtlety is required to extract the relevant magnitudes from a rather unpromising data set, and the authors have provided exactly that in a clean and elegant piece of econometric analysis. Second, and more substantively, they have produced a stylized "fact" that raising the IRA contribution ceiling would generate a substantial volume of new saving, not just a rearrangement of existing assets. I suspect that this fact is right, especially if it is true that many households save *only* through IRA accounts. Why this should be so is still very much an open question, and I find it hard to reconcile the explanation in the paper with the other things that we know about household saving. But there are many such phenomena that do not seem to be easily explained by conventional theory. And even at a very simple level, table 1.2 tells us that only 54% of families with annual income above $100,000 have IRA accounts, a fact that in itself is not easily explained.

2 Consumer Spending and the After-Tax Real Interest Rate

N. Gregory Mankiw

2.1 Introduction

The responsiveness of consumer spending to the after-tax real interest rate has important implications for a variety of policy questions.[1] The more highly interest elastic consumer spending is, the smaller is the impact of persistent government deficits on the capital stock and the more effective are savings incentives such as Individual Retirement Accounts. Despite its importance, there is little agreement among economists regarding the interest elasticity of consumer spending. This paper examines two issues relevant to the theoretical and empirical debate.

The paper first examines the interaction between consumer durable goods and consumer nondurable goods in determining the responsiveness of total expenditure to the after-tax interest rate. I show how the introduction of durables into the consumer's decision affects the interest elasticity of total spending. The channel highlighted here might be called the "user cost effect," in that the after-tax interest rate enters the implicit user cost of consumer durable goods.

This user cost effect may be one of the most important ways in which interest rates affect consumer spending. Previous studies of this interest elasticity, such as Summers (1981), examine nondurable consumption in life cycle models. Such analyses thus emphasize intertemporal substitution and human wealth effects. Some recent empirical work, how-

N. Gregory Mankiw is assistant professor of economics at Harvard University and a faculty research fellow of the National Bureau of Economic Research.

I am grateful to Martin Feldstein, James Hines, and Laurence Kotlikoff for helpful comments. This paper was prepared for the NBER Conference on "The Effects of Taxation on Capital Formation."

ever, has cast doubt on the life cycle (permanent income) hypothesis and has suggested that borrowing constraints play an important role in determining consumer spending.[2] A borrowing constraint effectively makes a consumer face a one-period planning problem and thus reduces the importance of the intertemporal substitution and human wealth effects. In contrast, I show that even if an individual has a one-period planning horizon, the user cost effect nonetheless makes his spending highly interest sensitive.

The second goal of this paper is to examine the response of various categories of consumer spending to the events of the 1980s. The 1980s provide a natural test of the responsiveness of saving to the after-tax interest rate. I show that these events are consistent with the view that the interest elasticity of consumer spending is substantial. In particular, the evidence is consistent with the view that, because of the user cost effect, spending on consumer durables and residential construction is more highly interest sensitive than spending on nondurables and services.

2.2   Durables, Nondurables, and the Rate of Interest

In this section I examine the decision of a consumer that must choose in each period both an amount of a nondurable good to consume and an amount of a durable good to purchase. My goal in particular is to examine the long-run response of consumption decisions to the interest rate. Of course, the relevant interest rate for the consumer is the after-tax real interest rate.

The analysis here is partial equilibrium in nature. I consider an individual facing a given path of labor income and a given constant after-tax real interest rate that chooses a path of spending on the two goods. I examine how his optimal levels of spending are affected by a permanent change in the after-tax interest rate he faces. In particular, the effect of the after-tax real interest on the user cost of durable goods is highlighted.

2.2.1   A Simple Model

Let us begin with the consumer's budget constraint. Each period he spends C on the non-durable good, which equals his consumption of it, and he spends X on the durable good, which is added to his stock. The present value of his purchases must equal his "wealth." That is,

$$(1) \qquad W = \sum_{t=0}^{T} \left(\frac{1}{1 + r}\right)^{t} (C_t + X_t).$$

where "wealth" is defined as the present value of labor income, his initial non-human wealth A_0, and the value of the terminal stock of durables K_T. That is, if δ is the depreciation rate for the durable,

$$(2) \qquad W = \sum_{t=0}^{T} \left(\frac{1}{1+r}\right)^t Y_t + A_0 + \frac{(1-\delta)K_T}{(1+r)^{T+1}}$$

The third term ensures that the consumer can borrow against the terminal value of his stock of the durable good.

I assume that the durable depreciates at a constant rate, that is, exponentially. The relation between the stock K and the flow X is

$$(3) \qquad K_t = X_t + (1-\delta)K_{t-1}$$

Using the stock-flow identity we can rewrite the budget constraint in terms of the stock rather than the flow. It becomes

$$(4) \qquad \tilde{W} = \sum_{t=0}^{T} \left(\frac{1}{1+r}\right)^t [C_t + ((r+\delta)/(1+r)) K_t]$$

where the now relevant notion of wealth[3] is

$$(5) \qquad \tilde{W} = \sum_{t=0}^{T} \left(\frac{1}{1+r}\right)^t Y_t + A_0 + (1-\delta)K_{-1}$$

Equation (4) is useful because it expresses the budget constraint in terms of the stock of the durable K rather than the flow X.

The consumer maximizes an additively separable utility function:

$$(6) \qquad V = \sum_{t=0}^{T} \beta^t U(C_t, K_t).$$

The consumer receives utility in each period from his consumption of the nondurable good and his stock of the durable good.

It is a common claim that spending on consumer durables is a form of saving. While it is true that (like saving) buying durables today increases future utility, it is not accurate to view durables in this model as merely one form of saving. The "durables as savings" model suggests that transitory income should affect spending on durables. This conclusion, however, does not arise from this formulation of the consumer's decision. Consider an increase in current income and a decrease in future income that does not change the present value of income in (4). Such a change alters neither the objective nor the constraint of the consumer. Hence, it affects neither the optimal level of nondurable consumption nor the optimal stock of the consumer durable. Such an increase in current income does, however, increase saving. In this natural model of the consumer, spending on both the nondurable and the durable depends on permanent income and is unaffected by transitory income. The decision to save and the decision to buy durables are conceptually distinct.

We can see from the budget constraint (4) that the consumption decision here is analogous to a consumption decision with two nondurable goods in which $(r + \delta)/(1 + r)$ plays the role of the relative price. The first-order condition necessary for an optimum is therefore

(7)
$$\frac{U_K(C,K)}{U_C(C,K)} = \frac{r + \delta}{1 + r}.$$

The marginal rate of substitution between durables and nondurables must equal the marginal rate of transformation, which depends on the real interest rate.

Suppose $U(C,K)$ has a constant elasticity of substitution:

(8)
$$U(C,K) = \frac{1}{1 - (1/\Theta)} [C^{1-(1/\epsilon)} + \phi K^{1-(1/\epsilon)}]^{\frac{1-(1/\Theta)}{1-(1/\epsilon)}}$$

where ϵ is the elasticity of substitution between durables and nondurables, and Θ is the intertemporal elasticity of substitution. The first-order condition (7) becomes

(9)
$$\phi \left(\frac{K}{C}\right)^{-1/\epsilon} = \frac{r + \delta}{1 + r}$$

which implies

(10)
$$\log K = \log C - \epsilon \log\left(\frac{r + \delta}{1 + r}\right) + \epsilon \log\phi.$$

Differentiating equation (10) with respect to the interest rate yields

(11)
$$\frac{d \log K}{d r} = \frac{d \log C}{d r} - \epsilon \left(\frac{1 - \delta}{(r + \delta)(1 + r)}\right)$$

The responsiveness of the durable stock to the interest rate equals the responsiveness of the nondurable minus a term that depends on the depreciation rate and, most important, on the elasticity of substitution between the durable and the nondurable. Note that the intertemporal elasticity of substitution Θ, which Hall (1985) argues is very small, does not enter this first-order condition.

The relation between the durable and the nondurable expressed in equation (9) is very general. First, it holds for all planning horizons T. That is, it holds for both young and old consumers. It also holds for consumers that have long horizons because they are linked to some future generations through intergenerational altruism (Barro 1974).

Second, the utility function can be complicated in a variety of ways without affecting equation (9). Other arguments, such as leisure or public goods, can be entered additively separably, multiplicatively separably, or additively within the brackets in (8). None of these changes would affect the first-order condition (9).

Third, expression (9) also holds for consumers who cannot borrow on future labor income because of some capital market imperfection. A person facing a binding borrowing constraint is like a person with a one-period planning horizon ($T = 0$). Because the intertemporal Kuhn-Tucker conditions hold with strict inequality, the trade-off between utility today and utility tomorrow is not relevant at the margin; because he is at a corner with regard to borrowing on future labor income, the existence of that income is not relevant for today's budget constraint. Hence, positing a binding borrowing constraint is equivalent to setting $T = 0$.

It is important to realize that even if $T = 0$, the interest rate plays a role in the consumption decision. In this case the budget constraint, equations (1) and (2), becomes

$$(12) \qquad C_0 + X_0 = Y_0 + \frac{(1 - \delta)K_0}{(1 + r)} .$$

The interest rate affects the present value of terminal stock of the durable. The interest rate can affect consumer spending through this channel. In the case of a borrowing-constrained consumer, I am assuming he can borrow to the extent that the depreciated value of his durables can cover the debt; that is, his net wealth, including his stock of durables but not including his future labor income, cannot be negative. Given that consumer durable goods are commonly used as collateral for consumer loans, this assumption about borrowing constraints seems the most plausible.

2.2.2   Redefining the Consumer's Problem

It is instructive to reexpress the consumer's optimization problem given the relation between the durable and the nondurable in equation (9). By solving out for the durable stock, the consumer's problem becomes:

$$\text{Max } V = \Psi(r) \sum_{t=0}^{T} \beta^t \frac{C^{1-(1/\Theta)}}{1 - (1/\Theta)}$$

subject to

$$\tilde{W} \left[1 + \phi^{\epsilon} \left(\frac{r + \delta}{1 + r} \right)^{1-\epsilon} \right]^{-1} = \sum_{t=0}^{T} \left(\frac{1}{1 + r} \right)^t C_t$$

where $\Psi(r) = \left[1 + \phi^{\epsilon} \left(\frac{r + \delta}{1 + r} \right)^{1-\epsilon} \right]^{\frac{1-(1/\Theta)}{1-(1/\epsilon)}}$ does not affect the consumer's decision.

With one difference, the consumer's problem expressed above is identical to the standard problem without durable goods. In addition to the standard effects, a change in the real interest rate changes the factor multiplying wealth in the budget constraint. Depending on the elasticity of substitution between the durable and the nondurable, an increase in the interest rate could be effectively either wealth-diminishing or wealth-augmenting. For example, if the elasticity of substitution is less than 1, then an increase in the interest rate reduces the factor multiplying wealth; thus, nondurable spending will fall more in response to the higher interest rate than a model that ignores durables would predict.

In the special case in which the elasticity of substitution is unity, this additional factor becomes a constant. Hence, in this case, the responsiveness of nondurables to the interest rate is not affected by the presence of durable goods. The response of nondurables spending to the interest rate can therefore be taken from standard models without durables, and the response of durables spending can be inferred from equation (11).

2.2.3   Evidence on the Elasticity of Substitution Between Durables and Nondurables

In Mankiw (1985), I provide some evidence on the elasticity of substitution between consumer durables and consumer nondurables. Since this elasticity plays a key role in the interest elasticity of consumer spending, I briefly summarize that evidence here.

The technique of the previous paper, used similarly in Hansen and Singleton (1983) and Mankiw, Rotemberg, and Summers (1985), is to estimate the first-order condition, equation (10). Equation (10) states that

(13) $\log(\text{user cost}) = \text{constant} - (1/\epsilon) \log (K_t/C_t)$

where the relative price is the implicit rental price of the durable, which depends on the real interest rate and (although suppressed in the previous discussion) on the relative purchase price of the durable good. The model implies a simple bivariate relation between the relative price and the relative quantity K/C.[4] I use expenditure on nondurables and services as C and the net stock of consumer durables as K.[5]

Estimation of equation (13) yields

$$\log(\text{user cost}) = -1.95 \ -0.81 \log(K_t/C_t)$$
$$(0.06) \quad (0.11)$$
$$s.e.e. = 0.10 \quad D.W. = 1.39 \quad \bar{R}^2 = 0.62$$

Standard errors are in parentheses.

Thus, the data yields the predicted negative relation between the relative price and K/C. The coefficient implies that ϵ is about 1.

Although this result supports the model, it is possibly spurious. One might suspect that the regression is only picking up a trend in both variables. Alternatively, one might suspect that we have found merely a business cycle correlation without any deeper structural interpretation. To test these possibilities, I include a time trend and the rate of unemployment (RU_t) in the above regression. If the correlation found above is indeed spurious, then we might expect the significant relation to disappear when these additional variables are included. In fact, I find

$$\log(\text{user cost}) = -2.11 \ -1.00 \ \log(K_t/C_t)$$
$$(0.41) \quad (0.43)$$
$$+ \ 0.004 \ \text{Time} \ - \ 0.0007 \ RU_t$$
$$(0.007) \qquad\qquad (0.0182)$$

$$s.e.e. = 0.11 \qquad D.W. = 1.40 \qquad \bar{R}^2 = 0.59$$

The time trend and the unemployment rate are insignificant; I cannot reject the null hypothesis that both coefficients are zero at even the 10% level. Perhaps more striking, the relation between the relative price and K/C remains statistically and substantively significant.

The analysis so far has assumed that the only error in the relation is an expectation error. If there are shocks to tastes, however, then the error includes these taste shocks and identification requires more careful attention. In particular, ordinary least squares does not produce consistent estimates, as K/C is likely to be correlated with these taste shocks. To investigate whether taste shocks are important here, I estimate equation (13) using instrumental variables. The instruments must be orthogonal to the shocks to consumer tastes. One variable that may be exogenous is federal government purchases of durable goods per capita. Fluctuations in government purchases are largely attributable to wars, making it an almost ideal instrumental variable for many purposes. This variable is a valid instrument here if it shifts the supply curve of consumer durables but not the demand curve. It shifts the supply curve if, for example, the production of military equipment takes resources away from the production of consumer durables. Using $\log(G_t)$ and $\log(G_{t-1})$ as the instruments, I obtain

$$\log(\text{user cost}) = -2.21 \ -1.30 \ \log(K_t/C_t)$$
$$(0.15) \quad (0.28)$$

$$s.e.e. = 0.13$$

The relation found using IV is similar to that found using OLS. Both estimation methods yield a negative and significant relation. In addition, both estimates suggest ϵ is about one.

2.2.4 Some Implications of the Evidence

The evidence above suggests that the elasticity of substitution between durables and nondurables is approximately unity. This finding has important implications for the interest elasticity of consumer spending. As indicated above, a unit elasticity of substitution implies that the interest elasticity of nondurables spending is not affected by the presence of durable goods. Hence, the responsiveness of nondurables spending to the interest rate can be taken from simulations that ignore durable goods, and the responsiveness of durables spending can be inferred using equation (11).

I highlight here the implications of this finding for the case in which the planning horizon for the consumer is only one period ($T = 0$), either because of myopia or because of a binding borrowing constraint. This extreme case provides perhaps the worst circumstances to find interest sensitivity, since the human wealth and intertemporal substitution effects emphasized in previous work are absent.

The consumer's optimization problem outlined above becomes

$$(14) \qquad \text{Max } V = \log(C) + \phi \log(K)$$

subject to

$$(15) \qquad Y = C + \left(\frac{r + \delta}{1 + r}\right) K$$

I am assuming here that the initial wealth and the initial stock of the durable is zero. In subsequent periods, this consumer will carry forward both a depreciated stock of the durable and a debt; since these are equal, the problem will remain essentially the same.

The solution to the consumer's optimization is:

$$(16) \qquad C = (1/(1 + \phi)) Y$$

and

$$(17) \qquad K = \frac{(\phi/(1 + \phi)) Y}{(r + \delta)/(1 + r)}$$

In steady state, spending on the durable X is δK.

The responsiveness of spending to the interest rate should be apparent. Nondurable spending is a constant fraction of income and is not affected by the interest rate. (This is an implication of the unit elasticity of substitution.) Durable spending, however, is responsive to the interest rate. A higher interest rate raises the user cost of the durable and thus reduces K.

To gauge the magnitude of this user cost effect, it is necessary to calibrate the model. The after-tax real interest rate has historically averaged about zero, and durable goods as defined in the National Income Accounts depreciate at about 20% per year. I therefore use $r = 0.0$ and $\delta = 0.2$, as well as the estimated value of ϵ of 1.0. From equation (11) (or 17), we see that the interest semi-elasticity of durables is 4.0. That is, a one percentage point increase in the real interest rate reduces the stock of durables (and thus in steady state durables spending) by 4%.

The responsiveness of total spending, $C + X$, to the after-tax real interest rate depends on the relative importance of durables and non-durables. Since durable spending is approximately one-eighth of the total, a one-percentage-point increase in the interest rate reduces total spending of the consumer by 0.5%.

2.3 The Evidence from the 1980s

The events of the early 1980s provide a natural test of the proposition that consumer spending is sensitive to the after-tax real interest rate. In this section I present an analysis of this episode. I find that the level and composition of consumer spending during the 1980s is consistent with a high degree of interest sensitivity.

2.3.1 The After-Tax Real Interest Rate

Three related developments starting in approximately 1980 make the past half decade a useful period in which to examine the response of consumers to the after-tax real interest rate. First, monetary and fiscal policy combined to make interest rates skyrocket. In October 1979, the Federal Reserve announced a new disinflationary stance and a greater emphasis on targeting monetary aggregates over stabilizing interest rates. In November 1980, Ronald Reagan was elected committed to large-scale tax reduction. This tax reduction occurred in 1981, and was followed by deficits that were unprecedented in peacetime. As one might have expected from these changes in macroeconomic policy, interest rates rose.

The second development increasing after-tax real interest rates was a reduction in marginal tax rates on capital income. The 1981 tax cut lowered marginal tax rates across the board, reducing the top rate from 70% to 50%. (While some of the tax reduction was offset by already-scheduled Social Security tax increases, these increases are not relevant here because the Social Security tax falls only on labor income.) In addition, the introduction of Individual Retirement Accounts reduced the marginal tax rate on capital income to zero for those individuals not at the maximum contribution level. Both of these changes in the tax law raise the after-tax real interest rate.

The third development was the increased availability of market interest rates to consumers. The spread of money market mutual funds
and the deregulation of banking has allowed small savers to earn rates
much higher than those on passbook savings accounts. To the extent
that marginal saving is now earning the Treasury bill rate rather than
the passbook rate, this financial development increases the real interest
rate relevant for saving decisions.

While it is difficult to measure the importance of these latter two
developments, the increase in market interest rates is easy to document.
Table 2.1 shows that the nominal three-month Treasury bill rate averaged 6.3% in the 1970s and rose to 10.9% in the early 1980s. Mean-
while, inflation as measured by the consumer price index fell from 7.2%
to 6.1%.

To compute the after-tax real interest rate, I use a marginal tax rate
of 0.3. Since there is ample reason to believe that the marginal rate on
interest income fell during this period, using a constant marginal rate
underestimates the increase in after-tax real interest rates. Table 2.1
shows that the ex post after-tax rate measured this way rose from
-2.8% in the 1970s to 1.6% in the early 1980s.

Of course, consumer decisions are based not on ex post rates but
on ex ante rates. Since the 1970s was a period of positive inflation
surprises and the early 1980s was a period of negative inflation surprises, the increase in the ex post rate of 4.4 percentage points is
overstated. A rough measure of ex ante rates can be found using the
technique pioneered by Mishkin (1980) of regressing ex post rates on
lagged information and using the fitted values as ex ante rates. A regression of the ex post real rate (*eprr*) on its own lag for the period 1970:1
to 1984:4 yields:

$$eprr_t = -0.39 + 0.66 \, eprr_{t-1}$$
$$(0.38) \quad (0.10)$$

$$s.e.e. = 2.67 \; D.W. = 2.46 \qquad \bar{R}^2 = 0.41$$

Table 2.1   Interest Rates in the 1970s and 1980s

	Nominal Three-Month Treasury Bill Rate	Inflation	After-Tax Real Interest Rates	
			Ex post	Ex ante
1970:1–1979:4	6.3	7.2	-2.8	-2.2
1980:1–1984:4	10.9	6.1	1.6	0.3

Note: After-tax rate is computed assuming a marginal tax rate of 0.3. Ex ante real rates
are computed as the fitted value from the first-order autoregression of ex post real rates
estimated 1970:1 to 1984:4.

This equation implies an increase in the ex ante rate from -2.2% in the 1970s to 0.3% in the early 1980s.

One problem with using this equation is that consumers have more information than the lagged ex post rate when forming their expectations implicit in the ex ante rate. If this additional information is useful, then this equation underestimates the variation in the ex ante rate, since forecasts based on greater information vary more than forecasts based on more limited information. Hence, the increase in the ex ante rate of 2.5 percentage points implied by this equation is likely to understate the true increase.

2.3.2   Consumer Spending in the 1980s

For a variety of reasons, the after-tax real interest rate rose substantially from the 1970s to the 1980s. If consumer spending is sensitive to this interest rate, consumer spending in the 1980s should be lower than it otherwise would have been. My purpose in this section is to examine whether consumer spending responded to the dramatic increase in the after-tax real interest rate.

Rather than attempt to estimate a structural model relating consumer decisions to interest rates, as has been done elsewhere (Hansen and Singleton 1983; Mankiw 1985; Hall 1985), I examine the following relation

$$(18) \qquad C_t = \text{constant} + A(L)\,C_{t-1} + B(L)\,Y_t$$

where C is the log of some category of consumer spending,
$\qquad Y$ is the log of personal disposable income, and
$\qquad A(L)$ and $B(L)$ are distributed lags.
This equation is not intended to be structural. Its purpose is merely to summarize the time series co-movements of income and consumer spending.

The equation is estimated for the period 1970:1 to 1979:4, during which real interest rates were very low. The equation is then used to forecast consumer spending from 1980:1 to 1984:4 *using the actual path of disposable income*. Since the forecast is conditional on disposable income, it controls for the effect of the deep recession in 1982 and the subsequent rapid recovery. If consumer spending is not sensitive to the interest rate and instead obeys a simple Keynesian consumption function, then this equation should forecast accurately.

In contrast, if consumer spending is sensitive to the real interest rate, a major change in the interest rate should cause this equation to forecast badly. Since the equation is estimated under a low interest rate regime, it should overpredict consumer spending in the 1980s. The forecast error can be viewed as a rough guide to the effect of omitted variables on consumer spending during this period. Since interest rates are prob-

Table 2.2   Conditional Forecast Errors for Consumption

Category of Consumer Spending	Actual Level Relative to Predicted (percent)						
	80:1	80:4	81:4	82:4	83:4	84:4	Average
Total Consumer Expenditure	−0.8	−2.4	−5.3	−5.0	−4.2	−5.3	−4.0
Nondurables	−1.0	−2.5	−3.0	−3.1	−1.5	−2.0	−2.2
Services	−0.6	−1.2	−4.0	−5.3	−6.6	−7.4	−4.6
Durables	−2.2	−7.5	−16.9	−9.7	−5.4	−5.7	−8.4
Residential Construction	−3.1	−2.4	−31.6	−25.9	+2.0	−6.1	−13.1

Note: A reduced-form equation is estimated by regressing consumption on its own two lags, current personal disposable income, and two lags of income using data from 1970:1 to 1979:4. This equation is used dynamically to forecast consumption given the observed path of disposable income. The figure reported is the difference in log of actual spending and the log of predicted spending, times 100, which is approximately the percentage difference.

ably the most important of the omitted variables, it seems reasonable to attribute the forecast error to the effects of interest rates.[6]

Table 2.2 summarizes the results from this experiment. Total consumer spending was on average 4.0% lower than one would have expected from the experience of the 1970s.[7] The breakdown into the various categories is plausible. Nondurables are 2.2% lower than forecast and services 4.6% lower. The largest forecast error is for durables spending, which is 8.4% lower than forecast. This differential impact is consistent with the hypothesis that the forecast error is attributable to the high real interest rates.[8]

While the National Income Accounts treat residential construction as investment, it seems conceptually most similar to spending on consumer durables. If one performs the same experiment as above with residential construction, the results confirm the above findings. In particular, residential construction was 13.1% below the conditional forecast.

2.4 Summary

The major conclusions of this paper are as follows:

1. Spending on durables should be substantially more sensitive to the after-tax real interest rate than spending on nondurables and services. The reason is that the interest rate affects the implicit user cost of durables. The difference in interest sensitivity can be simply expressed in terms of the interest rate, the depreciation rate, and the elasticity of substitution between durables and nondurables.

2. The elasticity of substitution between durables and nondurables can be easily estimated by examining the first-order condition of the consumer. This method avoids the problems of solving for the consumer's decision rule and of obtaining proxies for future income and relative prices that would enter that decision rule. Aggregate data for the United States suggest an elasticity of substitution of about unity with a very small standard error.

3. Even if a consumer faces a one-period planning horizon, possibly because of a binding borrowing constraint, his spending should be highly interest sensitive. With an elasticity of substitution of unity, a 1% increase in the after-tax real interest rate reduces his spending on durables by 4% while not affecting his spending on nondurables.

4. After-tax real interest rates were substantially higher in the early 1980s than in the 1970s, suggesting that this episode is an ideal natural experiment to examine the interest sensitivity of consumer spending. It appears that spending on all categories of consumer spending was substantially lower in the early 1980s than one would have forecast conditional on the path of disposable income. Moreover, the forecast

error is greater for durable goods than for nondurable goods. This experience thus appears consistent with the hypothesis that real interest rates have an important impact on the level and composition of consumer spending.

Notes

1. For a discussion of the importance of this issue, see Boskin (1978).
2. See, for example, Hall and Mishkin (1982) and Zeldes (1985).
3. This concept probably corresponds best to what is normally meant by the term "wealth."
4. The error term in this equation is an expectation error attributable to the fact that the real interest rate in the relative price is not known at time t when the consumption decisions are made. Since K/C is known at time t, it is orthogonal to the error, implying that OLS leads to consistent estimates of $1/\epsilon$.
5. Consumer durables as defined in the National Income and Product Accounts excludes residential housing. In Mankiw (1985) I examined only the NIPA's category of consumer durables, which includes primarily motor vehicles, furniture, and household equipment. The technique could be extended to residential housing, however.
6. Alternatively, one could attribute any conditional forecast error to the direct effect of deficits on saving through anticipated future tax liabilities (Barro 1974). Note that this Ricardian view implicitly assumes that the long-run interest elasticity of saving is infinite, since in steady state the after-tax real interest rate must equal the subjective rate of time preference. It therefore appears inconsistent to maintain both (1) consumption is interest insensitive, and (2) consumers effectively have infinite horizons and thus foresee their future tax liabilities.
7. This result stands in contrast to the conclusion one would reach by a simple comparison of savings rates through time. That is, the dynamic comparison in table 2.2 gives a very different picture of the 1980s than would a static comparison. Reconciling these results would appear to require a structural model of some sort.
8. While these results are broadly consistent with the model, it is difficult to judge whether the magnitudes are comparable to what theory would predict. The theory discussed above applies to steady states, while the experience of the past few years is necessarily temporary or one of transition. To examine this period in detail using a structural model, the adjustment process, possibly including adjustment costs, should be modeled explicitly.

References

Barro, Robert. 1974. Are government bonds net wealth? *Journal of Political Economy* 82:1095–1117.
Boskin, M. J. 1978. Taxation, saving, and the rate of interest. *Journal of Political Economy* 86:S3–S27.

Hall, Robert E. 1985. Consumption and real interest, NBER Working Paper No. 1694.

Hall, Robert E., and Frederic S. Mishkin. 1982. The sensitivity of consumption to transitory income: Estimates from panel datas on households. *Econometrica* 50:461–81.

Hansen, Lars Peter, and Kenneth J. Singleton. 1983. Stochastic consumption, risk aversion, and the temporal behavior of asset returns. *Journal of Political Economy* 91:249–65.

Mankiw, N. Gregory. 1985. Consumer durables and the real interest rate. *Review of Economics and Statistics* 67:353–62.

Mankiw, N. Gregory; Julio J. Rotemberg; and Lawrence H. Summers. 1985. Intertemporal substitution in macroeconomics. *Quarterly Journal of Economics* 100:225–51.

Mishkin, Frederic. 1980. The real interest rate: An empirical investigation. *Carnegie-Rochester Conference on Public Policy* 15:151–200.

Summers, Lawrence H. 1981. Capital taxation and accumulation in a life cycle growth model. *American Economic Review* 71:533–44.

Zeldes, Stephen. 1985. Consumption and liquidity constraints: An empirical investigation. Mimeograph. Wharton School.

Comment   Laurence J. Kotlikoff

Greg Mankiw's paper usefully redraws attention to the fact that the after-tax interest rate determines not only intertemporal relative prices, but also the relative price of durables and nondurables at a point in time. With the exception of the recent work of Poterba (1980) and Gahvari (1985) on housing, relatively little attention has been given to the affect of changes in capital income taxation on the ratio of durables to nondurables expenditures.

Mankiw's chief point is that even if nondurable expenditures do not respond to interest rate changes, durables expenditures most likely will. While I accept this point, I'm not sure why this should alter my view of the effectiveness of government policy for changing national saving or for the elasticity of saving with respect to the interest rate. If one properly defines consumption to include imputed rent on durables, rather than expenditures on durables, and properly defines national income to include imputed rent on durables, then in the unitary elasticity case he is considering, the effect on total national wealth of changing the tax on capital income is zero.

To see this, consider the two period utility function, $U_t = \log C_{y,t} + \log C_{o,t} + \log D_{t+1}$, where D_{t+1} is the durables stock at time $t + 1$, $C_{y,t}$ is consumption when young at time t, and $C_{o,t}$ is consumption when

Laurence J. Kotlikoff is professor of economics at Boston University and research associate of the National Bureau of Economic Research.

old at time $t + 1$. Assume individuals are retired when old, but work full time when young, earning $W_t(1 - \tau_{wt})$, where τ_{wt} is the wage tax rate at time t. Let K_{t+1} stand for nondurable assets at time $t + 1$. It is easy to show that total assets at $t + 1$, $K_{t+1} + D_{t+1}$ are given by:

$$K_{t+1} + D_{t+1} = \frac{W_t(1 - \tau_{wt})}{3}$$

From this equation it is clear that the elasticity of savings as well as saving to the tax rate on capital income is zero. Total wealth is, however, very sensitive to the after tax wage. Indeed, the elasticity of savings with respect to $(1 - \tau_{w,t})$ is unity. Parenthetically, I've always been puzzled about the strong professional interest in the interest elasticity of saving and the entire lack of interest in the wage elasticity of saving.

Now including durables in this way in the model, while not altering one's views about the interest elasticity of saving, does influence one's view about the elasticity of the ratio of K_{t+1} to D_{t+1} with respect to the rate of capital income taxation. As Mankiw points out, and as Gahvari's simulation studies strongly demonstrate, the composition of national wealth as between durables and other assets can be highly sensitive to the rate of capital income taxation.

Another bit of grumbling involves Mankiw's estimation of the first order condition relating the marginal utility of durables to the marginal utility of nondurables consumption. While Mankiw states that the error term in his regression is on expectation error, I believe this is incorrect. At the point when spending occurs the two marginal utilities are known with certainty. Hence, it is not clear that a regression, rather than a calculation, is appropriate.

Finally, while I believe that the interest rate increases in the early 1980s may have played some role in reduced expenditures, I don't find convincing the procedure of running a vector autoregression, leaving out the interest rate, and then attributing the residual to the interest rate. I would find a structural model much more persuasive.

References

Gahvari, Firouz. 1985. Taxation of housing, capital accumulation, and welfare: A study in dynamic tax reform. *Public Finance Quarterly* 13, no. 2 (April).
Poterba, James. 1980. Inflation, income taxes, and owner occupied housing. NBER Working Paper no. 553 (September).

3 Capital Gains Rates, Realizations, and Revenues

Lawrence B. Lindsey

The effect of the capital gains tax on the sale of capital assets and the realization of gains on these assets have been a matter of substantial academic and political controversy. Capital gains are only taxed when an asset is sold, and so inclusion of gains in taxable income is largely discretionary from the point of view of the taxpayer. As a result, sensitivity to tax rates is probably greater for capital gains income than for other kinds of income.

This sensitivity may take a number of forms. Capital gains and losses on assets held for less than a specified time period, currently 6 months, are taxed as ordinary income while gains and losses on assets held for longer periods of time are taxed at lower rates. Within limits specified by the tax law, taxpayers have an incentive to realize losses in the short term and gains in the long term. Planning of sales around this capital gains holding period was studied by Kaplan (1981), who concluded that eliminating the distinction between long-term and short-term gains, and taxing all assets under current long-term rules, would enhance capital gains tax revenue. Fredland, Gray, and Sunley (1968) also found that the length of the holding period had a significant effect on the timing of asset sales.

The deferral of taxes on capital gains until realization enhances the incentive to postpone selling assets. A taxpayer might defer selling one asset and purchasing another with a higher pretax return because capital gains tax on the sale makes the transaction unprofitable. This is known as the "lock-in" effect. Feldstein, Slemrod, and Yitzhaki (1980) esti-

Lawrence B. Lindsey is assistant professor of economics, Harvard University and faculty research fellow, National Bureau of Economic Research.

I wish to thank Martin Feldstein and Emil Sunley for their thoughtful insights and Andrew Mitrusi and Alex Wong for their assistance in this research.

mated that the effect of lock-in was substantial enough to suggest that a reduction in tax rates from their 1978 levels would increase tax revenue. Their study focused on sales of common stock using 1973 tax return data. The results mirrored those of an earlier work by Feldstein and Yitzhaki (1977) which relied on data from the 1963–64 Federal Reserve Board Survey of the Financial Characteristics of Consumers.

Brannon (1974) found evidence of reduced realizations of capital gains as a result of tax rate increases in 1970 and 1971. A lock-in effect was also identified by Auten (1979). Later Auten and Clotfelter (1979) found a substantially greater sensitivity of capital gains realizations to short-term fluctuations in the tax rate than to long-term, average tax rate levels. Minarik (1981) studied the lock-in effect and concluded that a 1% reduction in the capital gains tax rate would increase realizations, but by substantially less than 1%. The U.S. Department of the Treasury (1985) released a report to the Congress which presented substantially higher estimates of the elasticity of capital gains realizations to tax rates and concluded that the tax rate reductions of 1978 had the effect of increasing capital gains tax revenue.

Some work has also been done on incentives to lock in capital gains for very long periods of time. Assets held until death or contributed to charity escape capital gains taxation under the income tax. In the case of death, capital gains are taxed by the estate tax since estates are subject to estate taxes on the full fair market value of the assets they contain. Bailey (1969) and David (1968) have argued that eliminating these provisions would be an efficient means of reducing the lock-in effect by eliminating the possibility of escaping capital gains tax.

The objective of the present paper is to examine the relationship among capital gains tax rates, the level of realizations of long-term gains subject to tax, and revenues from capital gains taxation over an extended period of time. The Tax Reform Act of 1969 began an era of high variability in the capital gains tax rate which had been relatively constant for the preceding 15 years. Further changes in the tax reform bills of 1976, 1978, and 1981 continued this variability.

The changes in the effective capital gains tax rate which resulted from these laws were quite complex and often involved the interaction of several provisions. This paper makes careful estimates of the effective marginal tax rate on capital gains for various income groups over the period 1965–82. These detailed estimates suggest smaller variability in rates than suggested by the maximum effective rates cited in other studies. The first section describes the computation of the effective capital gains tax rates and describes the impact of the various provisions on the capital gains tax rate. The effect of these provisions is combined using detailed tabulation data from *Statistics of Income* to estimate average marginal effective tax rates for various income groups.

The second section analyzes data from the sector balance sheets and reconciliation statements of the Federal Reserve Board's *Flow of Funds* series. These data provide estimates of the level and composition of wealth of the household sector. They also estimate the change in value of these holdings due to movements in asset prices. This section also describes the method used to allocate these wealth values among the various income classes studied.

The final section combines the data on the level and distribution of wealth with the marginal tax rate series to estimate the effect of marginal tax rates on the rate of realization. These parameter estimates are then placed in the context of a revenue-maximizing objective function to calculate the capital gains tax rate that produces the maximum revenue for the government. The sensitivity of these estimates to econometric specification is also examined in the final section.

3.1 Capital Gains Tax Rates

The Internal Revenue Code of 1954 distinguished between gains on assets held at least 6 months and those held longer. The former were taxed as ordinary income while the latter, termed long-term gains, were given a 50% exclusion from taxable income. However, this exclusion was limited to net capital gains, long-term gains in excess of short-term losses. Therefore, to the extent that long-term gains simply cancelled short-term losses, the long-term marginal tax rate equalled the short-term rate, which was the same as the tax rate on ordinary income. (There were some exceptions to this tax treatment including S.1231 gains. These gains received capital gains treatment if positive but ordinary income treatment if negative.)

There remains some debate regarding the proper measure of capital gains for analysis. Minarik (1983) has argued that long-term gains in excess of any short-term loss is the only relevant measure of gains for considering the effect of tax rates and revenue implications. On the other hand, some analyses of capital gains, such as that by Feldstein and Slemrod (1982) have included net long-term capital losses in their calculation. These net losses are permitted only limited deductibility in the year taken, although they may be carried forward to offset future tax liability. In general, their inclusion would tend to decrease the apparent effectiveness of capital gains taxation in generating revenue and raise the apparent sensitivity of taxpayers to capital gains tax rates.

Poterba (1985) examined 1982 tax return data and found that taxpayers with net long-term gains comprised the majority of all returns reporting capital gains or losses. He noted, however, that a sizable fraction of taxpayers were subject to the capital loss limitation and therefore could realize additional long-term gains without incurring any additional current tax liability. These taxpayers are unaffected by the marginal tax rate on capital gains, generate no capital gains tax liability, and are therefore neglected in the present study.

The present study examines only long-term gains in excess of short-term losses. The relevant marginal tax rate for most taxpayers is therefore half the tax rate on ordinary income as only half of such gains are included in taxable income. (After 31 October 1978 this inclusion rate was reduced to 40%.) The higher tax rate on inframarginal long-term gains used to offset short-term losses is neglected. We consider only the tax rate on marginal realizations of long-term gains for taxpayers with long-term gains in excess of short-term losses.

Although the general rule for tax rates on long-term gains is that they are half the ordinary rates (40% of ordinary rates after 31 October 1978), there are a number of other provisions of the tax code which affected the capital gains tax rate. These include the Alternative Tax Computation, the Additional Tax for Tax Preferences, the Maximum Tax on Personal Service Income, and the Alternative Minimum Tax. We consider each in turn, using detailed tabulation data from *Statistics of Income* to calculate its effect on capital gains tax rates.

3.1.1 The Alternative Tax Computation

Tax rates on ordinary income over most of the period of this study ranged up to 70%. Thus, taxation of long-term gains at half the ordinary rate would produce a maximum tax rate of 35%. However, a special provision, the Alternative Tax Computation, permitted the taxpayer to limit the marginal tax rate on at least some capital gains to 25%. Although generally described as having "effectively truncated the tax rate schedule,"[1] careful analysis of the data suggests that this was not the case. This section describes the operation and limitations of the alternative tax computation.

Prior to 1970, taxpayers were allowed to choose one of two tax computation methods. The first, called the regular method, involved using the ordinary tax rate schedule to compute tax on the taxpayer's total amount of taxable income including taxable capital gains. The second, the alternative tax computation method, involved using the ordinary tax rate schedule to compute the tax on non–capital gains income plus paying tax equal to 50% of the taxable portion of capital gains. As only half of long-term gains are taxable, the effective tax rate becomes 25%.

Figure 3.1 shows how the alternative tax computation should work. The figure plots taxable income along the horizontal axis and marginal tax rate along the vertical axis. The tax code exhibits the upward sloping form shown with the normal tax liability represented by the area of the triangle. In this case, the taxpayer's other income is sufficient to get him over the 50% bracket amount, and he pays tax liability

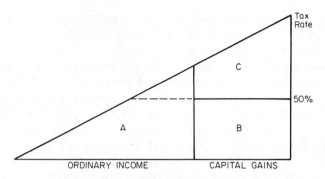

Fig. 3.1   Alternative tax computation limits capital gains tax
rate to 50%.

indicated by area A on his ordinary income. In addition, the taxpayer
pays 50% on the included portion of capital gains. This is indicated by
area B. The total tax saving to this taxpayer from the alternative tax
computation is area C, and his marginal tax rate on capital gains is
limited to 25%.

Now consider the case shown in figure 3.2. Here, the taxpayer's total
taxable income is enough to be taxed at a rate over 50%, but his non-
capital gains income is not. The taxpayer has a choice. He can elect
to be taxed under the regular tax rate schedule, in which case his tax
liability is the large triangle, or he can elect the alternative tax computation. If he chooses the alternative tax computation, tax is levied
by the ordinary schedule on his non-capital gains income, equal to area
D. In addition, he pays tax at a 50% rate on the included portion of
capital gains, indicated by areas E and F. As area E indicates, a portion
of the taxpayer's long-term gains are taxed at a rate higher than they

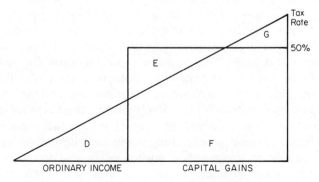

Fig. 3.2   Alternative tax computation fails to limit capital gains tax
rate to 50%.

would be under the normal tax rate schedule. This taxpayer elects the alternative tax computation only if it results in a tax savings. In this case, such a situation results only if area E is less than area G.

Consider a taxpayer situation where this is the case. The taxpayer realizes long-term gains of $200,000 and has other income of $50,000. In addition, he has itemized deductions of $40,000. The taxpayer excludes half of the long-term gains from tax, leaving an adjusted gross income (AGI) of $150,000, and then subtracts itemized deductions to produce a taxable income of $110,000. Under the tax schedule of the era (1965–69), the ordinary tax computation would produce a tax liability of $51,380. Using the alternative tax computation, he would pay ordinary tax on the first $10,000, equal to $1,820, plus a 50% tax on the $100,000 of included gains, producing a total tax liability of $51,820.

This taxpayer would elect to be taxed under the ordinary schedule as it produces a lower tax liability. However, the marginal tax rate under this schedule is 62%, producing a marginal tax rate on capital gains of 31%. In this case, the alternative tax computation did not effectively limit the tax rate on long-term gains to 25%. An effective tax rate limit of 25% would require that the last $25,000 of included capital gains be taxed at 50%, rather than the first $25,000.

Although a majority of taxpayers in upper-income brackets who realized long-term gains did avail themselves of the alternative tax computation method, a significant fraction did not. For example, in 1966, of 27,766 taxpayers with adjusted gross incomes between $100,000 and $200,000, more than one quarter did not elect the alternative tax computation. The same was true for 16% of taxpayers with adjusted gross incomes between $200,000 and $500,000 with net long-term capital gains, and for 7.5% of taxpayers in the same situation with adjusted gross income over $500,000.[2]

The data are not sufficient to indicate the reason why these taxpayers elected the ordinary tax computation. It should be noted, however, that taxpayers are less likely to choose the alternative tax computation as long-term gains rise as a share of income. An extreme example would be a taxpayer with negative ordinary taxable income but large amounts of positive capital gains. This could be due to net operating losses in a business or partnership or to itemized deductions such as state taxes, interest, and charitable contributions, exceeding his ordinary income. The ordinary tax computation effectively permits this taxpayer to shelter that portion of his long-term gain which offsets the negative part of his ordinary taxable income. But, under the alternative tax computation, the tax on this negative portion of income would be zero, while the tax on the included portion of capital gains would be at the full 50% rate.

Thus, in certain situations, taxpayers with a substantial capital gain may still find themselves excluded from the alternative tax computation. The effect of this on the average marginal tax rate on taxpayers with net long-term gains was an increase of 1.5 percentage points above the 25% theoretical maximum for taxpayers in the $100,000 to $500,000 income range.

The Tax Reform Act of 1969 changed the alternative tax computation by limiting the 25% rate to a maximum of $50,000 in net long-term gains. Thus, only $25,000 of the included half of long-term gains qualified for the "special" 50% rate. In 1970, the excess over this amount was taxed at a maximum rate of 59%. This maximum tax rate was raised to 65% in 1971 and the limit was removed completely in 1972 and later years.

The actual alternative tax computation was constructed to minimize the potential benefits to the taxpayer. Figure 3.3 shows the method of computation for a taxpayer who would receive some benefit from the computation. The tax owed was comprised of three parts. The first part, denoted as area H, was the tax owed on the taxpayer's ordinary taxable income. This corresponds to area A in figure 3.1. The second part, denoted as area I, was a 50% tax on the first $25,000 of the included portion of capital gains. If the included portion of the taxpayer's gains was less than $25,000, then the effective marginal tax rate on these gains was 25%, and no further computation is necessary. If capital gains exceeded $25,000, then the tax computation included a third part, denoted as area J. This was the difference between (a) the tax calculated using the ordinary computation on the taxpayer's total taxable income and (b) the tax calculated using the ordinary computation on the sum of $25,000 plus the taxpayer's non–capital gains taxable income.

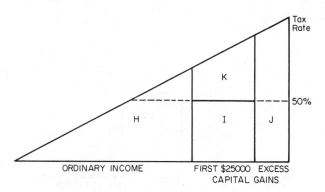

Fig. 3.3   Modified alternative minimum tax limits tax rate on some capital gains.

Table 3.1   **Revenue Loss on Inframarginal Taxpayers Using Alternative Tax Computation**

Year	Loss (in millions)
1970	$ 39.6
1971	39.4
1972	48.6
1973	53.5
1974	40.4
1975	48.1
1976	70.3
1977	88.7
1978	104.3

If the taxpayer did not elect the alternative tax computation, his tax would have been the total area under the ordinary tax schedule, denoted as areas H, I, J, and K. The net tax savings to the taxpayer was therefore area K. Note that for any taxpayer with more than $25,000 of included capital gains, the marginal tax rate on gains was the same as it would have been had there been no alternative tax computation. Thus, to the extent that capital gains realizations are based on marginal incentives, the alternative tax computation had no effect on a substantial number of taxpayers. Table 3.1 provides estimates of the revenue loss from this provision of an inframarginal tax reduction to recipients of capital gains.

The change in the alternative tax computation to limit special treatment to only $25,000 of included gains also had the effect of lowering the fraction of taxpayers electing the alternative computation, even among taxpayers with more than $25,000 of capital gains. Figure 3.4

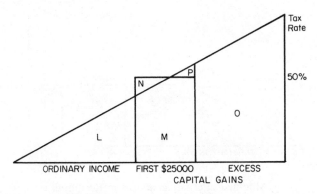

Fig. 3.4   Modified alternative minimum tax fails to lower taxes on capital gains.

shows a taxpayer situation in which it may not be in the interest of the taxpayer to elect the alternative tax computation. The taxpayer must pay tax above the statutory rate on a portion of his gains in the hope that this will offset a lower rate on some of the rest of his gains. This taxpayer would owe tax equal to areas L, M, N, and O. Under the ordinary tax computation he would owe taxes on L, M, O, and P. The taxpayer thus elects the alternative tax computation only if area N is smaller than area P.

The effect of this change in the alternative computation was to limit the marginal incentive to a minority of taxpayers in income groups with high marginal rates. Table 3.2 shows the fraction of taxpayers in high-income groups with net long-term capital gains who did not receive a marginal benefit from the alternative tax computation and the reason why. In only one income group in one year did a majority receive a marginal rate reduction.

There are two reasons for this ineffectiveness. First, it was impossible for any taxpayer with more than $25,000 in gains to benefit at the margin. Second, taxpayers with relatively small amounts of non–capital gains taxable income would also not benefit regardless of the size of their capital gains income. This limited alternative tax computation was therefore of marginal benefit only to taxpayers with relatively small amounts of capital gains income and relatively large amounts of other income. However, as noted above, much of the effect was inframarginal with regard to a taxpayer's decision making, while costing significant amounts of revenue.

3.1.2   The Additional Minimum Tax

The Tax Reform Act of 1969 began the Additional Tax for Tax Preferences, also known as the minimum tax. The excluded portion of

Table 3.2	Percent of Capital Gains Taxpayers with AGI over $100,000		
	Using Alternative Tax Computation		Alternative Computation Not Used
Year	Reduced Capital Gains Tax Rate at Margin	No Effect on Marginal Rate	
1970	22.2%	41.2%	36.6%
1971	40.3	19.0	40.7
1972	45.0	13.7	41.3
1973	45.0	13.7	41.3
1974	41.3	11.3	47.3
1975	44.5	12.3	43.2
1976	47.2	12.8	40.0
1977	51.9	13.0	35.1
1978	47.9	12.4	39.7

capital gains was among a list of 9 types of income, termed preferences, which came under the minimum tax. The additional minimum tax was levied in two forms, one from 1970 through 1975 and one from 1976 through 1978. We consider each in turn.

The early form of the tax was levied at a 10% rate on the items of tax preference reduced by an exclusion of $30,000 plus the taxpayer's ordinary tax liability and some other deductions discussed later. The effect of this was to make the taxpayer's additional tax rate negatively related to his ordinary tax rate. In the case of the capital gains tax preference, the additional tax rate was negatively related to the effective capital gains tax rate. This was true whether the taxpayer elected the alternative or the regular method of tax computation.

Consider a taxpayer with substantial preference income who realizes an additional dollar of net long-term capital gains. The excluded portion of the gains, 50 cents, enters the minimum tax base as a tax preference. This 50 cents is offset by the amount the taxpayer's ordinary tax liability increased. This ordinary tax liability is increased by the remaining part of the capital gain, which is taxed either at the ordinary rate, or at 50% if the alternative tax computation is effective. Thus, the higher ordinary tax liability is either half the taxpayer's ordinary tax rate or 25 cents for the alternative tax. So, the 50 cent increase in capital gains preference could be offset by a 25% ordinary capital gains tax rate, raising the additional tax base by 25 cents on net. The 10% additional tax rate is applied to the net increase in the tax base, raising his marginal tax rate on the added dollar of capital gain by 2.5 cents.

If, on the other hand, the effective tax rate on capital gains is 35%, the minimum tax base would only rise by 15 cents for every dollar of long-term gains realized. The additional minimum tax in this situation would only be 1.5 percentage points. Figure 3.5 shows the relationship between the marginal tax rate on the included portion of capital gains and the additional tax rate.

The additional minimum tax had a feature which reduced its effectiveness over time. Taxpayers were allowed to carry forward from any year after 1970 the excess of ordinary tax over net preferences and apply the amount carried forward against the current year's net tax preferences. For example, suppose a taxpayer had ordinary tax liability of $50,000 in 1971 and tax preferences in the same year, after the $30,000 exclusion, of $40,000. He owed no minimum tax because his ordinary tax liability exceeded his preferences by $10,000. That $10,000 could be carried forward to 1972 to offset his tax preferences in that year. So, if he had a $30,000 ordinary tax liability in 1972 and $40,000 in preferences after the exclusion, he would owe no minimum tax in 1972 either. Taxes in excess of preferences could be carried forward for up to 7 years to reduce the future effect of the minimum tax.

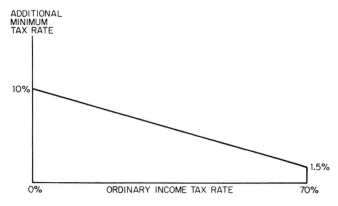

Fig. 3.5   Effect of pre-1976 additional minimum tax on capital gains tax rate.

Table 3.3 shows the effect of the additional minimum tax on the marginal tax rate on capital gains. The effect of carrying forward is clearly evident. In 1970, taxpayers in the $200,000–$500,000 income class faced an increased marginal tax rate on capital gains of 1.18 percentage points as a result of the additional minimum tax. By 1975, the effect of the additional minimum tax on the average marginal tax rate on capital gains was only 0.24 percentage points, or about 80% less. The reason for this was that substantial numbers of taxpayers had amassed amounts carried forward sufficient to exempt them from the minimum tax. In 1970, some 62% of all recipients of net capital gains with AGI between $200,000 and $500,000 paid some additional tax. By

Table 3.3   **Percentage Point Increase in Capital Gains Rate Due to the Additional Minimum Tax**

	Income Class				
Year	$50,000–$100,000	$100,000–$200,000	$200,000–$500,000	$500,000–$1,000,000	Over $1,000,000
1970	0.28	0.75	1.18	1.47	1.65
1971	0.08	0.26	0.58	0.98	1.27
1972	0.07	0.22	0.51	0.80	1.15
1973	0.06	0.20	0.42	0.72	1.02
1974	0.04	0.15	0.30	0.54	0.75
1975	0.04	0.11	0.24	0.45	1.08
1976	1.04	1.56	1.96	2.70	3.08
1977	1.37	1.72	2.21	3.75	4.62
1978	1.35	1.69	1.87	2.34	2.66

1975, only 13% of capital gains recipients in the same income category paid the additional tax.

The Tax Reform Act of 1976 made substantial changes in the minimum tax which greatly increased its scope. The sums carried forward from previous years was ended altogether. Two preferences were added, one for intangible drilling costs and one for itemized deductions in excess of 60% of adjusted gross income. The tax rate was raised to 15% and the exclusion lowered to the greater of $10,000 or one half of ordinary tax liability. The IRS estimates that this resulted in an elevenfold increase in the number of taxpayers paying the minimum tax and a sixfold increase in minimum tax revenues.[3]

The 1976 changes in the minimum tax raised the average effective tax rate on capital gains in two ways. First, it increased the number of taxpayers subject to the additional levy of the minimum tax, as the above figures indicate. Second, it increased the addition to the effective tax rate caused by the minimum tax for each minimum taxpayer. Figure 3.6 illustrates how this new minimum tax affected the marginal tax rate on capital gains.

If a taxpayer received an additional dollar of net long-term capital gains, the 50 cents excluded from the ordinary tax was treated as a tax preference. The remaining 50 cents raised the ordinary tax the taxpayer paid. Half of the increase in ordinary tax was used as an offset against preference income rather than the full amount of ordinary tax as in the 1969 law. So, if the taxpayer were in the 50% tax bracket, the additional dollar of capital gains would raise his ordinary taxes by 25 cents and his offset by 12.5 cents. In this case, the taxpayer's additional minimum tax base would rise by 37.5 cents. This base is taxed at a 15% rate,

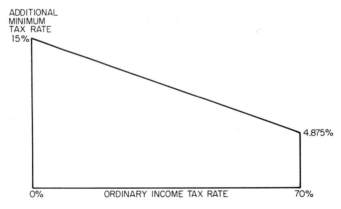

Fig. 3.6   Effect of post-1976 additional minimum tax on capital gains tax rate.

meaning that the taxes paid on the additional dollar of capital gains is increased by 5.625 cents.

As was the case before 1976, the additional taxes paid fall as the taxpayer's ordinary marginal tax rate rises. If a taxpayer's ordinary tax rate was 70% and the alternative tax computation was not effective at the margin, the ordinary tax would rise by 35 cents for every dollar of capital gains realized. This would mean a 17.5 cent offset against the additional 50 cents in tax preferences. The resulting 32.5 cent increase in the minimum tax base means that the minimum tax raised the effective tax rate on capital gains by 4.875 cents.

The additional tax had its greatest effect on the marginal tax rate on capital gains in 1977. In that year it raised the average capital gains rate in the top bracket by 4.6 percentage points. Some 92% of capital gains recipients with AGI over $1,000,000 were subject to the additional minimum tax in that year. The effect of the additional tax was much less in the top brackets in 1978. In that year only 52% of the recipients of capital gains in the over $1,000,000 income group paid additional tax. The reason for this is probably the tax legislation which moved through Congress that year. The additional minimum tax was eliminated beginning in January 1979. Tax-conscious investors may well have postponed their realizations to take account of this (and other) changes in the tax law which had the effect of lowering the capital gains tax rate.

The additional minimum tax interacted with other provisions of the tax code. As already noted, taxpayers electing the alternative tax computation would face higher additional minimum taxes on their capital gains than taxpayers who computed their tax according to the regular tax rate schedule. The additional minimum tax also interacted with the maximum tax on personal service income in a manner which increased the effective tax rate on capital gains income.

3.1.3   Maximum Tax on Personal Service Income

The Maximum Tax on Personal Service Income, otherwise known as the "maximum tax" was enacted as part of the Tax Reform Act of 1969. Its objective was to reduce the effective tax rate on wage, salary, and professional income below that on other types of income. Instead of the statutory 70% top rate, the top rate on personal service income was set at 60% in 1971 and 50% thereafter. As Lindsey (1981) showed, the maximum tax was ineffective at achieving these objectives for the vast majority of high-income taxpayers. However, a complex interaction between the maximum tax and other provisions of the tax law had the effect of raising the effective capital gains tax rate for many taxpayers.

Between 1971 and 1976, every dollar of preference income in excess of the additional tax exclusion (see above sec. 3.1.2) reduced the amount of earned income eligible for the lower rate by one dollar. In effect, every dollar of capital gains received over a certain threshold converted 50 cents of earned income into unearned income for purposes of the maximum tax. As the tax rate on earned income could be as low as 50% and the tax rate on unearned income as high as 70%, this had the effect of adding as much as 10% to the effective capital gains tax rate. This interaction between capital gains and the maximum tax is known as "poisoning."

During this era there were two types of maximum tax poisoning caused by the receipt of capital gains. The first type, described above, involved the receipt of preference income above a threshold. The second involved an absolute limit on the amount of income eligible for treatment as earned income. This limit equalled taxable income minus the included portion of capital gains. Consider an example. A taxpayer has $200,000 in earned income and a total capital gain of $300,000 of which 50%, or $150,000, is included in income, making AGI a total of $350,000. The taxpayer has itemized deductions of $100,000. Therefore, the taxpayer's taxable income is $250,000. This second type of poisoning would limit the amount of income eligible for earned income treatment to $100,000, or taxable income less the included portion of capital gains.

The actual interaction of capital gains and the maximum tax is quite complex. This complexity would generally produce a rate of poisoning slightly lower than that described above. The amount of income eligible for treatment as earned income, known as earned taxable income (ETI), is given by the following formula:

(1)   ETI = (PSINC/AGI) × TAXINC − PREFERENCES.

In this equation PSINC, or personal service income, equals income from wages, salaries, and professional income. TAXINC, or taxable income, is apportioned between earned and unearned portions according to the share of AGI contributed by PSINC. Earned taxable income is then reduced by the amount of preference income, including the excluded portion of capital gains. This latter subtraction represents the "poisoning" effect described above.

However, the derivative of ETI with respect to a change in capital gains shows that there is an offset to this poisoning as well:

$$(2)\qquad \frac{d\text{ETI}}{d\text{CAPGN}} = \frac{0.5\ \text{PSINC}(\text{AGI} - \text{TAXINC})}{\text{AGI}^2} - 0.5.$$

Using the chain rule and the fact that an additional dollar of capital gains realizations increases AGI, TAXINC, and PREFERENCES by 50 cents each, we find that the change in ETI for a change in capital gains depends on the ratios of ETI—TAXINC and PSINC to AGI. Most important is the fact that TAXINC is less than AGI. Therefore, the term in parentheses is positive. This in turn implies that ETI falls by less than the 50 cent change in preferences when capital gains increase. So, the interaction of the maximum tax and capital gains realizations means that the taxpayer was poisoned but also received a partial antidote.

The effect described by (2) was designed to allocate personal exemptions and itemized deductions between earned and other income. Moving a dollar of earned income into the unearned category will shift this allocation of personal exemptions and itemized deductions, providing the partially offsetting effect. However, this partial antidote was only effective if the taxpayer had preference income in excess of the preference exclusion. It was not effective in cases where the taxpayer's ETI was more than his TAXINC less included capital gains.

In 1977 the scope of poisoning was increased. Beginning in that year, all preference income regardless of source was used to offset ETI whether or not it exceeded the preference exclusion of the additional tax. Thus, although this change had no effect on the marginal capital gains tax rate of a poisoned taxpayer, the number of taxpayers who were poisoned was increased.

Table 3.4 presents calculations of the percentage point increase in the effective tax rate on capital gains due to the poisoning effect of the maximum tax. The effect of the 1977 changes is clear. In 1976, taxpayers in the $100,000–$200,000 income group had average marginal tax rates raised 0.34 percentage points by the maximum tax. In 1977, this jumped sixfold to 2.25 percentage points. Poisoning of the maximum tax was eliminated beginning in 1979 as a part of the Tax Reform Act of 1978.

Table 3.4   **Percentage Point Increase in Capital Gains Tax Rate Due to the Effect of the Maximum Tax**

	Income Class		
Year	$50,000–$100,000	$100,000–$200,000	Over $200,000
1971	0.01	0.07	0.18
1972	0.04	0.28	0.66
1973	0.07	0.34	0.75
1974	0.04	0.34	0.89
1975	0.04	0.32	1.02
1976	0.03	0.34	1.25
1977	0.27	2.25	3.70
1978	0.30	2.45	4.10

3.1.4   Alternative Minimum Tax

The Tax Reform Act of 1978 removed capital gains from the list of preferences subject to the additional minimum tax beginning in 1979. Instead, an alternative minimum tax was established which combined the excluded portion of capital gains, itemized deductions in excess of 60% of AGI, and the taxpayer's regular taxable income in its base. Taxes were levied at graduated rates of 10%, 20%, and 25% on this alternative tax base. The taxpayer paid the greater of his regular tax liability or his alternative tax liability.

Since the full amount of capital gains was in the alternative tax base, these three rates became the effective tax rate on capital gains for taxpayers who paid the alternative tax. These tax rates are generally lower than the ordinary capital gains rates, which could be as high as 28%, and so the alternative minimum tax had the effect of lowering the marginal tax rate on capital gains, even though the average tax rate paid by alternative minimum taxpayers was increased by the provision.

Nearly all alternative minimum taxpayers with AGI over $200,000 paid taxes at the 25% effective tax rate. In the $100,000–$200,000 income class this fell to about three-fourths of taxpayers paying the alternative minimum tax, with the average alternative minimum rate in this group at 23.6%. The average rate was only 17.6% in the $50,000–$100,000 income group.

The net result of the alternative minimum tax was to reduce the average marginal tax rate on capital gains in the top income groups by about 1.0 percentage point in 1979, and about 0.4 percentage points in 1980. But, because the top regular capital gains rate averaged 24% in 1981, the effect of the minimum tax was to increase the average marginal tax rate by about 0.2 percentage points that year. Other income groups had tax rate changes of about 0.2 percentage points as a result of the alternative minimum tax.

The Economic Recovery Tax Act of 1981 eliminated the 25% tax bracket on the alternative minimum tax. This meant that, beginning in 1982, alternative minimum taxpayers faced the same effective tax rate on capital gains as ordinary taxpayers—20%.

3.1.5   Combined Effects

Table 3.5 presents calculations of the average effective tax rate faced by taxpayers with net long-term gains in excess of short-term losses. The calculations were based on the tax computation status of taxpayers with such gains as reported in the *Statistics of Income*. The calculations weighted all taxpayers equally within a given income class in order to minimize the simultaneity between the tax rate and the level of realizations. The tax rate estimates include the effects of the interactions between the various types of taxation described in this section.

Table 3.5   **Average Effective Marginal Tax Rate on Capital Gains**

	Income Class					
Year	Under $50,000	$50,000–$100,000	$100,000–$200,000	$200,000–$500,000	$500,000–$1,000,000	Over $1,000,000
1965	11.1	25.5	26.5	26.6	26.0	25.3
1966	11.1	25.5	26.5	26.6	26.0	25.3
1967	12.5	25.5	26.5	26.6	26.0	25.3
1968	13.4	27.4	28.4	28.5	27.9	27.1
1969	13.8	28.0	29.0	29.1	28.5	27.7
1970	12.9	27.8	30.5	32.2	32.1	32.0
1971	12.5	26.3	29.1	32.0	33.3	33.9
1972	12.5	26.6	28.7	32.5	33.9	34.6
1973	12.5	26.6	28.9	32.8	34.3	35.0
1974	12.0	26.3	28.9	32.6	33.6	34.4
1975	11.6	26.3	28.8	32.5	33.5	34.7
1976	11.5	27.2	29.9	34.0	36.1	37.3
1977	10.8	27.8	31.7	36.3	39.2	41.2
1978	10.6	27.8	32.2	36.3	37.9	39.1
1979	10.6	19.4	25.3	27.3	27.0	26.9
1980	10.6	19.5	25.4	27.6	27.6	27.6
1981	10.8	19.1	22.9	24.1	24.2	24.2
1982	11.2	17.6	20.0	20.0	20.0	20.0

Also included in the tax rate estimates are the effects of the changes in the exclusion rate in the 1978 tax bill and the maximum capital gains rate in the 1981 tax bill. The 1978 act increased the rate of exclusion of net long-term gains from 50% to 60% for all assets sold after 31 October 1978. The figures for 1978 therefore take a weighted average of tax rates implied by the two exclusion rates in proportion to the fraction of the year each exclusion rate was in effect. In other words, a weight of .833 was attached to the rates applicable to a 50% exclusion and a weight of .167 was attached to the rates applicable to a 60% exclusion.

The Economic Recovery Tax Act of 1981 reduced the maximum tax rate on capital gains to 20% for all assets sold after 9 June 1981. The 1981 rates therefore reflect a weighted average of rates which ranged up to the old maximum of 28% for half the year and 20% for the other half of the year. In this case, equal weights were attached to the two tax rate scenarios.

The data show that the maximum capital gains tax rate increased rapidly between 1967 and 1977 and decreased rapidly thereafter. These data provide a significant amount of variance in the tax rate term. The next section describes how these data were combined with data on wealth to estimate the sensitivity of taxpayers to changes in the capital gains tax rate.

3.2   Capital Gains and the Value of Personal Assets

The level of capital gains realizations has been going up throughout the period of this study, 1965–82. Table 3.6 presents the nominal value of net long-term capital gains realizations in each of the 18 years encompassed by this study. Net long-term realizations in 1982 were more than 4 times their 1965 level. Of the 18 years listed, 12 were higher than the preceding year. This includes 1965, which was higher than (unlisted) 1964.

This general upward trend was marked by a number of discontinuities. Capital gains in 1969 and 1970 were well below the values of 1968. Net realizations were also lower in 1974 and 1975 than in 1973. The years 1969 and 1970 were associated with higher tax rates than preceding years due to the Vietnam War surtax. The year 1970 was associated with a decline in the stock market, as were 1974 and 1975.

On the other hand, very rapid growth in capital gains realizations occurred between 1978 and 1979. Net long-term gains in 1979 were 45% greater than in 1978. However, 1979 was associated with only a very modest advance in stock prices. The sharp decline in capital gains tax rates appears to be a primary factor in this advance in realizations. Capital gains realizations in 1978 may also have been depressed in anticipation of the cuts in 1979, increasing the apparent percentage rise in realizations.

Table 3.6	Net Long-Term Capital Gains	
	Year	Gains (in billions)
	1965	$20.8
	1966	20.8
	1967	25.9
	1968	33.5
	1969	30.7
	1970	20.4
	1971	27.6
	1972	34.9
	1973	35.7
	1974	30.9
	1975	30.4
	1976	38.6
	1977	44.0
	1978	48.6
	1979	70.5
	1980	69.9
	1981	77.1
	1982	86.1

The debate over the importance of capital gains rates in determining realizations is complicated by changes in the value of personal wealth including accrued but unrealized capital gains. The objective of this section is to estimate values for personal wealth holdings in order to control for this factor in determining the role that capital gains tax rates play in realizations.

The Federal Reserve Board issues a quarterly *Flow of Funds* report on the holdings of various sectors of the U.S. economy. These figures contain detailed balance sheets and reconciliation statements for the asset holdings of households, government, and corporations. The present study uses the values of wealth holdings by households.

The components of household wealth include many elements on which households either cannot or probably will not realize capital gains. For example, holdings of cash and checking and savings deposits do not include the possibility of capital gains. Capital gains accruing to households via financial intermediaries such as life insurance and pension funds are also not reported as capital gains when the taxpayer files his tax return. Capital gains in pension funds, including IRA and Keogh accounts, are reported as pension income when the funds are dispersed after retirement.

We therefore chose to divide household wealth into two components: those readily tradable and subject to potential capital gains realizations and those unlikely to be subject to such realizations. This section considers each in turn.

3.2.1 Tradable Wealth

Tradable wealth is comprised of those assets on which capital gains are regularly realized. The IRS has tabulated the distribution of capital gains by type of asset. Table 3.7 provides the percentage breakdown of sales of capital assets by the number of transactions and the value of net gains. The data show that sales of corporate stock, real estate, and capital gains income which passes through to the individual taxpayer from small business corporations, proprietorships, and partnerships comprise some 97% of the value of net capital gains.

In the context of the data in the *Flow of Funds*, these categories include land, residential structures, corporate equities, and equity in noncorporate businesses. This latter category includes the value of nonresidential real estate held by households. Tangible assets such as consumer durables, on which capital gains are rarely reported, were excluded from this study.

These traded assets have tended to comprise about two-thirds of all household wealth over the period studied. This share varied from a high of 69% in 1968 to a low of 65% in 1975. The most variable component of this traded wealth is household holdings of corporate equities,

Table 3.7   Realizations by Asset Type, 1977

Assets	Percent of Transaction	Percent of Gains
Included		
Corporate stock	42.1	14.7
Distributions from		
partnerships, etc.	10.7	14.1
Business real estate	2.6	9.2
Business non–real estate	8.8	10.4
Personal residence	6.5	14.9
Nonbusiness real estate	3.2	9.5
Installment sales	3.3	8.5
Excluded		
Commodities	1.3	0.1
Retirement distribution	0.4	0.7
Indeterminant	21.1	17.9

Note: This table was calculated from table 1.9 of the Department of Treasury's report to the Congress on the capital gains tax reductions of 1978, pp. 18–19.

which fell from nearly 23% of total wealth in 1968 to only 9.5% in 1979. The rapid decline in the holding of corporate equity was offset by increased holding of real estate. Nonresidential real estate peaked at 39.4% of household wealth in 1979, up from a low of 28% at the beginning of the period being studied.

Because of this variation in the components of personal wealth over time, we apportioned household wealth among the six income groups studied on a component-by-component basis. Each component was allocated according to the distribution of income reported on tax returns likely to flow from that component of household wealth. For example, the distribution of corporate equities in a given year was assumed to be the same as the distribution of dividends in that year. The sum of net rental income and net rental loss was used to apportion real estate wealth. Noncorporate business wealth was apportioned by combining net profits and net losses from proprietorships, partnerships, and small business corporations.

The key advantage of this apportioning technique was that the shares of wealth were determined from the same data base as the data on the level and distribution of capital gains realizations. Observations on individual income classes in each year were therefore independent of observations from other years. Capital gains income was excluded from the apportionment process to avoid simultaneity. At the same time, the aggregate level of wealth was determined independently of the data on capital gains realizations. Table 3.8 presents the level of tradable wealth for each income class in each year of the period studied.

Table 3.8   **Tradable Wealth by Income Class**

			Income Class			
Year	Under $50,000	$50,000– $100,000	$100,000– $200,000	$200,000– $500,000	$500,000– $1,000,000	Over $1,000,000
1965	1493	162	72	42	14	20
1966	1545	178	80	46	16	20
1967	1619	200	93	54	20	23
1968	1766	242	120	69	25	29
1969	1864	266	130	72	25	30
1970	1907	280	127	68	23	28
1971	2036	313	140	75	25	29
1972	2196	358	167	89	30	33
1973	2307	395	186	95	30	31
1974	2403	419	194	93	28	25
1975	2555	471	219	105	31	29
1976	2806	557	264	129	38	36
1977	3090	654	310	155	45	42
1978	3459	791	381	193	56	47
1979	3877	977	485	255	75	67
1980	4271	1204	617	338	106	108
1981	4659	1378	714	397	127	131
1982	4958	1455	771	455	155	161

One potential criticism of this approach is the allocation of corporate equity on the basis of dividends received. If there are clientele effects based on tax rates, this approach would tend to underestimate the value of corporate equities held by upper-income groups since these groups keep a smaller portion of their dividends after tax relative to capital gains than do other groups. However, an upward revaluation of wealth in upper-income groups to reflect this possibility would put downward pressure on the realizations-to-wealth ratio among taxpayer groups with high marginal tax rates. This would in turn suggest a greater impact of capital gains tax rates on realizations. We elected to ignore possible clientele effects in order to err on the side of conservatism in estimating the effects of capital gains tax rates.

The *Flow of Funds* data also includes reconciliation statements which explain the change in sectoral asset holdings from year to year. Holdings of a particular asset could vary for one of two reasons: net purchases or sales of the asset by the household sector or a change in the price of the existing stock of holdings. This latter effect is termed "revaluation" and for purposes of this study was used as a measure of unrealized capital gains on assets held by households.

We allocated the revaluation of each asset in the same manner as the stock of wealth held in that asset. Revaluation values were computed for holding periods up to 7 years. These were converted into inflation-adjusted terms by increasing the nominal value of the asset held at the beginning of the revaluation period to reflect prices at the end of the revaluation period. A real value was obtained by subtracting this from what the value of the assets held at the end of the revaluation would have been if no net purchases had been made. In practice, revaluation periods over one year turned out not to be significant in estimating the level of capital gains. The data suggested that much of these multiyear revaluations was picked up in the value of wealth.

3.2.2 Nontraded Wealth

Nontraded wealth was comprised mainly of cash, interest-bearing financial assets, and life insurance and pension fund reserves. Over the period being studied, pension and life insurance reserves remained a roughly constant share of household wealth at about 11%. Cash and checking accounts declined from a bit over 3% of wealth to a bit under 3%. Interest-bearing financial assets tended to absorb any fluctuations in the share of nontraded wealth in total wealth.

As in the case of traded assets, we allocated these nontradable assets on a component-by-component basis as well. Cash and checking accounts were allocated in proportion to adjusted gross income. Interest-bearing financial assets were allocated in proportion to interest income. Pension and life insurance reserves were allocated in proportion to the sum of interest and dividend income.

Again, the key advantage of this apportioning technique was that the shares of wealth were determined from the same data base as the level and distribution of capital gains. Independence of observations for individual income classes in each year was maintained. And the aggregate level of wealth was determined independently of the data on capital gains realizations.

No revaluations of nontraded assets were necessary. Revaluation of cash, checking accounts, and saving deposits is impossible. The *Flow of Funds* accounts do not provide revaluations for any interest-bearing assets, maintaining each priced at par. Although some degree of revaluation may actually have occurred as a result of fluctuating interest rates, it is likely to have been quite small. All credit market instruments comprised only 9% of total financial assets in 1982. This included short-duration assets such as commercial paper on which no capital gain or loss was likely.

The next section uses this data on the level and distribution of household wealth in estimating the determinants of capital gains realizations. Wealth and revaluation values for given years were obtained by averaging the values at the beginning and at the end of the year. All of the values for wealth and revaluations were converted into real terms using the average value of the GNP deflator for the year in question.

3.3 Capital Gains Rates, Realizations, and Revenues

The preceding two sections described the derivation of data on capital gains tax rates, realizations, and the level and distribution of personal wealth. The objective of this section is to estimate the effect of tax rates on capital gains realizations and therefore on capital gains revenues.

The basic regression equation we estimate is:

$$(3) \qquad ln\ \text{LTG}_{ij} = \beta_0 + \beta_1\ \text{MTR}_{ij} + \beta_2\ ln\ \text{TRD}_{ij}$$
$$+ \beta_3\ ln\ \text{NTRD}_{ij} + \beta_4\ ln\ \text{REV}_{ij} + \epsilon_{ij}.$$

In each case the subscript j represents one of the 6 income classes and the subscript i represents one of the 18 years being studied. LTG represents net long-term gains deflated by the GNP deflator where 1972 is valued at 100. MTR is the average marginal tax rate on net long-term gains. TRD represents the real value of tradable wealth. NTRD is the real value of wealth which is not readily traded. REV represents the revaluation of assets during the year i expressed in terms of 1972 prices. In the case of the wealth variables, midyear values were used. These were obtained by taking an average of end-of-year and beginning-of-year values.

The results of ordinary least squares regression of the data on the model described by (3) were:

Parameter	Estimate	Standard Error
β_0	-0.385	0.517
β_1	-6.199	0.787
β_2	1.100	0.107
β_3	-0.869	0.089
β_4	0.298	0.084

All four coefficients were significant except for the intercept term, which was not significantly different from zero. The adjusted R-square value for the regression was 0.8825.

The value for the tax rate parameter should be interpreted as saying that a 1.0 percentage point increase in the marginal tax rate produces a 6.2% decline in the level of long-term capital gains realizations. This represents a semielasticity format, not a pure elasticity one.

The parameter for tradable wealth should be interpreted as an elasticity. A 1% higher level of tradable wealth implies a 1.1% higher level of long-term gains realizations. The parameter estimate is within one standard error of a value of unity. In the absence of tax effects, and short-term market fluctuations, a value of unity would be expected.

The parameter for nontraded wealth should also be interpreted as an elasticity. In this case, a 1% increase in nontraded wealth decreases net long-term capital gains realizations by 0.87%. A negative value on this parameter can be understood in the context of what comprises nontraded wealth. A substantial portion of this wealth represents highly liquid assets such as cash, savings and checking deposits, and government securities. If long-term capital gains realizations are designed to raise cash for consumption purposes, we would expect to see realizations negatively correlated with the existing level of these liquid assets.

The final parameter value also represents an elasticity. A 1% increase in the revaluation of traded assets in a given year increases net capital gains realizations by 0.3%. This parameter suggests that increases in stock, business, or real estate prices prompt increased realizations. Note that this is in addition to the increase in realizations due to a higher level of wealth. So, for example, in a year in which there is a 20% rise in the value of traded assets we could expect capital gains realizations to be higher by a total of about 28%, 22% due to the higher level of wealth and 6% due to the price increases in that year. If prices remained stable in later years, capital gains realizations would fall 6% in the following year to maintain a new, permanent level of gains 22% higher than the initial level.

Before exploring the robustness of these results, consider an additional interpretation for the tax rate parameter. In the case of a single tax rate, capital gains tax receipts are the product of the capital gains tax rate and capital gains realizations. Capital gains tax revenues are maximized when a given percent increase in the capital gains tax rate just offsets an equal percentage decline in realizations resulting from the highest rate.

In the context of the parameters estimated in (3), revenue maximization occurs when the capital gains tax rate times the tax rate parameter, β_1, equals negative unity. The revenue-maximizing capital gains tax rate implied by the results of the regression is 16.1%. The range of revenue-maximizing tax rates within one standard error of the estimate goes from 14.3% to 18.5%. This range is below the current top capital gains tax rate of 20%. Other specifications presented below support this general conclusion.

It should be noted that there is nothing "optimal" about a tax rate at a revenue-maximizing level. All tax rates above this level are simply counterproductive from the point of view of raising revenue. Stated differently, the shadow price of raising additional revenue at this top tax rate is infinite. Only tax rates below this revenue-maximizing point are within the possible range of optimality.

The robustness of this result can be examined by considering the effect of changing the specification of the regression equation. Tests of alternatives were therefore carried out. Equation (4) drops the variable representing revaluations of traded assets:

(4) ln LTG $= 0.874 - 7.394$ MTR
           (0.397) (0.750)
           $+ 1.246 \, ln$ TRD $- 0.971 \, ln$ NTRD .
           (0.104)   (0.088)

Standard errors are in parentheses below the parameter estimates. The adjusted R-square for this regression is 0.8693. The standard errors show that each coefficient is statistically significant.

In this case, the parameter value for the marginal tax rate term is increased to 7.39. This implies a revenue-maximizing marginal tax rate on capital gains of 13.5%. Much of the effect of dropping the gains parameter appears to have been picked up in the traded-wealth parameter, as we would expect.

The effect of dropping the non-traded-wealth term moves the tax rate parameter in the opposite direction, as (5) shows:

(5) ln LTG $= -0.282 - 5.076$ MTR $+ 0.124$ TRD $+ 0.564$ REV .
          (0.715)   (1.077)   (0.053)   (0.110)

All parameter estimates except for the intercept remain significant, but the R-square value for this regression drops to 0.775. This suggests that nontraded wealth contributes to the regression specification. The parameter on the tax rate variable implies a revenue-maximizing capital gains tax rate almost exactly equal to the current 20% level.

Dropping both the non-traded-assets variable and the revaluation variable produces a result indicated by (6):

(6) ln LTG $= 2.468 - 7.326$ MTR $+ 0.191$ TRD .
             (0.543) (1.097)   (0.058)

Again, the parameter estimates are significant, but the R-square term falls to 0.720. The parameter estimate for the tax rate term resembles that for (4) when the revaluation term was also dropped. This reinforces the relationship between declines in capital gains tax rates and upward revaluations of the prices of stocks, real estate, and noncorporate businesses.

A further specification was run which did not differentiate the forms of wealth held. The results, shown in (7), reinforce the usefulness of separating wealth into traded and nontraded components.

(7) ln LTG $= -0.267 - 5.133$ MTR
           (0.724)   (1.092)
           $+ 0.115$ WEALTH $+ 0.565$ REV.
           (0.054)   (0.111)

The R-square for this specification was 0.773. The parameters remain significant although the wealth term shows a lower t-statistic than in the specifications where traded and nontraded wealth are run separately. Again, the MTR parameter implies a revenue-maximizing capital gains rate of about 20%.

When revaluations are dropped from the specification shown in (7), the parameter estimate on the tax rate term again rises to a value in excess of 7.

$$(8) \quad ln \text{ LTG} = 2.369 - 7.302 \text{ MTR} + 0.186 \text{ WEALTH}.$$
$$\quad\quad\quad (0.566) \quad (1.120) \quad\quad\quad (0.057)$$

The R-square value for this regression is 0.719. Again, the parameter estimate for the tax rate coefficient resembles that in other cases where the revaluation term is dropped. The MTR parameter is little affected by the specification of the wealth term, as long as all of the values for wealth are included in the regression in some fashion.

A further check on the specification involves running dummy variables for each year in the period 1966–82 to see if any particular years are causing the results. The results of the basic specification (equation 1) run with annual dummy variables is:

$$(9) \quad ln \text{ LTG} = 2.252 - 6.849 \text{ MTR} + 0.033 \text{ TRD} + 0.228 \text{ NTRD}$$
$$\quad\quad\quad (0.585) \quad (0.890) \quad\quad\quad (0.116) \quad\quad\quad (0.118)$$
$$\quad\quad\quad - 0.231 \text{ REV} + \text{ DUMMIES}.$$
$$\quad\quad\quad (0.093)$$

The coefficients on the dummy variables were significant and illustrated an underlying time trend reflecting the rising levels of long-term gains over the period. Inclusion of these annual data reduced the significance of the wealth and revaluation coefficients as variations in these terms were captured on a year-by-year basis. However, the MTR coefficient remained highly significant and increased in value relative to the basic specification.

Another specification of the regression is obtained by changing the tax rate coefficient into an elasticity format. In this case, the natural log of the portion of the gain which the taxpayer is allowed to keep becomes the tax parameter. This specification presumes that a given percentage point reduction in the tax rate, or a given percent reduction in the same value, will have an effect which varies with the level of the tax rate.

For example, a reduction in the capital gains tax rate from 25% to 24% implies an increase in the share of the gain the taxpayer keeps from 75% to 76%. That represents a 1.33% increase in the share kept by the taxpayer. The same 1 percentage point reduction in tax rate from 50% to 49% would increase the taxpayer's share from 50% to 51% of the gain, or by 2%. Similarly, a 4% reduction in the tax rate, from 25% to 24%, and from 50% to 48%, would imply a percent change in the after-tax share far greater at the higher tax rate (3 times as much) as at the lower tax rate.

The results of such a specification are:

(10) $\ln$ LTG $= -20.510 + 4.253 \ln (1 - $ MTR$) + 1.084 \ln$ TRD
             (2.301)   (0.587)   (0.110)
             $- 0.843 \ln$ NTRD $+ 0.346 \ln$ REV.
                (0.091)   (0.085)

Again, all of the parameter values are significant at a high level of confidence. The *R*-square value for this regression is 0.875, suggesting a nearly equal degree of explanation as the original specification in (3). The parameter values for the wealth and revaluation terms are also quite similar to those of (3). The addition of annual dummies raises the *R*-square term to 0.951.

The parameter estimate for the tax rate term requires reinterpretation. In this case, lower marginal tax rates increase the after-tax share. So, the positive coefficient again suggests a higher level of realizations when tax rates are reduced. The revenue-maximizing capital gains tax rate can be obtained by dividing unity by unity plus the tax rate coefficient. In this case, a revenue-maximizing capital gains tax rate of 19% is implied.

We would expect a higher revenue-maximizing rate to be implied by this specification, for a given percentage point reduction has a greater effect on the tax rate variable in high tax rate observations than in low tax rate observations. Still, the revenue-maximizing rate is slightly below the current 20% level.

A final specification of these equations was performed which included a variable for the change in the capital gains tax rate from the preceding year. If capital gains tax rates are suddenly reduced, we might expect a rush to realize gains which were not profitable to realize in earlier years with higher rates. This is known as the temporary unlocking phenomenon.

The term DMTR represents the difference between the current year's marginal tax rate and the preceding year's marginal tax rate. If the tax rate was lower in the current year, a negative value would result for DMTR. As we would expect a lower tax rate to increase realizations, a negative coefficient for DMTR is implied. Equation 11 indicates that this is the case:

(11) $\ln$ LTG $-0.713 - 5.391$ MTR $+ 1.030$ TRD $- 0.781$ NTRD
             (0.533)   (0.868)   (0.110)   (0.097)
             $+ 0.327$ REV $- 3.027$ DMTR.
                (0.084)   (1.469)

The results suggest that temporary unlocking contributes to the behavioral response to lower tax rates, thus enhancing revenue at lower rates. This implies that the permanent revenue-maximizing rate is higher than that implied by the earlier equations. The coefficient of 5.39 implies a revenue-maximizing marginal tax rate of 18.5%, higher than implied by the initial specification but lower than the current rate of 20%.

In conclusion, these data suggest a high degree of sensitivity of capital gains realizations to the tax rate imposed on such gains. The revenue-maximizing tax rate implied by these findings is at or below the current 20% level. This result is robust to the specification of the regression equation.

It is important to bear in mind the plausibility of this result in contrast to most findings about revenue-maximizing tax rates. Taxed commodities such as labor supply will show relatively little response to marginal tax rate reductions because a relatively high proportion of the maximum possible level of supply is in the market. By contrast, only a very small fraction of existing capital gains are realized in a given year.

For example, total capital gains realized in 1982 amounted to a record $86.1 billion. But, the revaluation in personally held traded assets during that year alone was $305.7 billion, implying that only 28.2% of that year's gains were realized. By contrast, in the high-tax year of 1978, total realized gains were $48.6 billion out of revaluations during that year of $693.9 billion. Only 7% of the increase in value in traded assets in that year was represented by realized gains. (Of course, in both years the stock of accumulated capital gains was enormous compared to realizations.)

Clearly the potential for increased capital gains realizations and revenues was substantial in 1978. The taxation of gains at the time of realization rather than at the time of receipt makes capital gains far more tax-rate-sensitive than other forms of income.

Notes

1. See, for example, the Department of Treasury's report to the Congress on the capital gains tax reductions of 1978, p. 35. A similar statement appears in the description of the alternative tax computation in the *Statistics of Income 1966*, p. 164: "The effect of this computation was a maximum tax of 25 percent on net long-term capital gain."
2. This data was derived from the *Statistics of Income 1966*, p. 94.
3. This data is presented in table 3B of the *Statistics of Income 1976*, p. 83.

References

Auten, G. 1979. *Empirical evidence on capital gains taxes and realizations.* Washington: Office of Tax Analysis.

Auten, G., and C. Clotfelter. 1979. *Permanent vs. transitory effects and the realization of capital gains.* Washington: Office of Tax Analysis.

Bailey, M. 1969. Capital gains and income taxation. In A. C. Harberger and M. J. Bailey (eds.), *The taxation of income from capital.* Washington: Brookings Institution.

Brame, B., and K. Gilmour. 1982. Sales of capital assets, 1973–1980. *Statistics of Income Bulletin* 2:28–39.

Brannon, G. 1974. The lock-in problem for capital gains: An analysis of the 1970–71 experience. In *The effect of tax deductibility on the level of charitable contributions and variations on the theme.* Washington: Fund for Policy Research.

David, M. 1968. *Alternative approaches to capital gains taxation.* Washington: Brookings Institution.

Feldstein, M., and J. Slemrod. 1978. The lockin effect of the capital gains tax: Some time series evidence. *Tax Notes* 8, no. 6:134–35.

Feldstein, M., J. Slemrod, and S. Yitzhaki. 1980. The effects of taxation on the selling of corporate stock and the realization of capital gains. *Quarterly Journal of Economics* 94, no. 4:777–91.

———. 1984. The effects of taxation on the selling of corporate stock and the realization of capital gains: Reply. *Quarterly Journal of Economics.*

Feldstein, M., and S. Yitzhaki. 1977. The effect of the capital gains tax on the selling and switching of common stock. *Journal of Public Economics* (February).

Fredland, E., J. Gray, and E. Sunley. 1968. The six month holding period for capital gains: An empirical analysis of its effect on the timing of gains. *National Tax Journal* 21:467–78.

Kaplan, S. 1981. The holding period distinction of the capital gains tax. NBER Working Paper no. 762.

King, M., and D. Fullerton. 1984. *The taxation of income from capital.* Chicago: University of Chicago Press.

Lindsey, L. 1981. Is the maximum tax on earned income effective? *National Tax Journal* 34:249–55.

Miller, M., and M. Scholes. 1978. Dividends and taxes. *Journal of Financial Economics* 6:333–64.

Minarik, J. 1981. Capital gains. In H. J. Aaron and J. A. Pechman (eds.), *How taxes affect economic behavior.* Washington: Brookings Institution.

———. 1983. Professor Feldstein on capital gains—again. *Tax Notes* (9 May).

Poterba, J. 1985. How burdensome are capital gains taxes? MIT Working Paper no. 410 (rev. February 1986).

Stiglitz, J. 1969. The effects of income, wealth, and capital gains taxation on risk taking. *Quarterly Journal of Economics* 83:262–83.

U.S. Department of the Treasury. 1968–85. *Statistics of Income* [1965–82, individual income tax returns]. Washington: Office of Tax Analysis.

———. 1985. *Capital Gains Tax Reductions of 1978.* Washington: Office of Tax Analysis.

Comment   John H. Makin

Lindsey examines the effects of changes in the average marginal tax rate on capital gains on the sale of tradable capital assets and consequent realization of capital gains or losses. Lindsey finds that the revenue-maximizing tax rate on capital gains is quite low, in the vicinity of 16% to 20%.

Before evaluating Lindsey's final result, it is useful to discuss an important finding that follows directly from the first two major sections of his chapter. What emerges from Lindsey's conscientious effort to measure accurately the average marginal tax rate on capital gains is a clear idea that over the sample period considered by Lindsey, 1965–82, no forward-looking investor could possibly have calculated in advance the tax rate he would have to pay upon realizing a capital gain on his investment. The alternative tax computation, the additional minimum tax, and the maximum tax on personal service income together with numerous changes in the statutory tax rate levied on nominal capital gains all combined to make calculation of the actual tax rate on realization of nominal gains a very difficult task ex post, and an impossible one ex ante.

Unfortunately, despite painstaking efforts to measure accurately the tax rate on marginal realization of net long-term gains, Lindsey overlooks what is perhaps the major problem in the tax treatment of capital gains: a failure to index the cost basis for inflation. Therefore, it is important to realize that even though Lindsey's capital gains realizations are measured in 1972 dollars, they are not "real capital gains," for there is no way to tell whether those realizing gains are selling at prices that compensate sufficiently for the effects of inflation on real gains. Another way to make the same point is simply to observe that it is nominal gains that are taxed, and it makes little difference whether the nominal gains that are taxed are measured in current dollars or 1972 dollars. Lindsey's analysis still treats identically the investor who bought an asset at a price of 100 in 1970 and sold it at 200 in 1980 for zero real gain and the investor who bought the asset at 50 in 1970 and sold it at 200 in 1980 for a positive real gain.

One interesting question is whether it is possible to determine a bias in Lindsey's estimate of the revenue-maximizing tax rate on capital gains. I am inclined to think that it may be biased downward. To see why, suppose that during Lindsey's sample period the cost basis for capital gains tax purposes had been indexed. As a result, the rapid inflation of the 1970s would have produced less "lock-in" on capital

John H. Makin is the director of fiscal policy studies at the American Enterprise Institute for Public Policy Research in Washington, D.C.

assets. Thus, realizations would have proceeded steadily over time rather than accumulating in anticipation of a possible opening such as occurred in 1981, when the maximum tax rate on nominal capital gains was adjusted downward to 20%. In other words, investors in both real and financial assets have in the presence of a poorly indexed tax system come to anticipate ad hoc corrections for mismeasurement of income from capital or capital gains that result from accelerated rates of inflation.

The same phenomenon appears with respect to measures that affect the user cost of capital, such as investment tax credits or accelerated cost recovery schedules. Inflation results in an overstatement of profits for tax purposes and thereby discourages investment until some ex post correction is made in the form of front-loaded depreciation measures like those enacted in 1981. As a result, investment and capital gains realizations tend to display a choppy pattern in response to the ebb and flow of ex post corrections made necessary by an absence of adequate indexing provisions in the area of the tax code that deals with capital gains and income from capital.

Lindsey's analysis would probably benefit from raising the question of why capital gains ought to be treated differently from ordinary income. It is sometimes suggested that an adjustment is necessary to compensate for (a) the likelihood that not all of the nominal gains which are taxed are not real or (b) the income surge phenomenon that arises because capital gains are taxed on realization rather than on an accrual basis.

The corollary to this reasoning is that if only real capital gains were taxed on an accrual basis in a neutral tax system with a top marginal rate of 30% or below, there would be no need to treat capital gains any differently than ordinary income.

A little reflection provides some interesting extensions for Lindsey's analysis. The most useful question to analyze would be whether his estimates are sensitive to the level of the inflation rate. That rate is inversely related to the real gains underlying the nominal gains measured in 1972 dollars that constitute Lindsey's dependent variable. Were Lindsey to examine a period of lower inflation or deflation either in the United States or in some other country, since nominal gains would represent less of an overstatement of real gains or even an understatement in a period of deflation, the hypothesis would be that the measured response of capital gains realizations to a reduction in the tax rate on nominal gains would be reduced. As a result, Lindsey's estimate of the revenue-maximizing tax rate on capital gains would be reduced.

A stylized representation of the situation confronting investors with capital gains or losses during the 1970s makes clearer the possible downward bias just referred to in Lindsey's estimate of the revenue-maximizing tax rate on capital gains. Investors with positive nominal capital gains, those whose sales of assets will yield tax revenue, may have positive, zero, or negative real gains depending upon the percentage appreciation in the asset relative to the percentage increase in the price level during the holding period. Reductions in the tax rate on capital gains tend to be anticipated by those following the discussion of changes in the tax code. Those with positive nominal gains that are also positive when measured in real terms will postpone realization in anticipation of a cut in the capital gains tax rate. Part of the lock-in effect results from the fact that nominal gains overstate real gains, and a cut in the tax rate on nominal gains can only mitigate the negative effect on realization of mismeasurement of real gains. At the margin, the incentive is to increase realizations promptly after the tax rate on nominal gains is reduced in cases where the lower tax makes it profitable to realize gains and purchase another asset with a higher pretax return.

The negative effect of inflation on capital gains realizations prior to ex post adjustments in the tax code is exacerbated not only by the overstatement of real gains that inflation produces but also by the bracket creep induced by high rates of inflation in the late 1970s. Here again there is a tendency to accumulate gains in anticipation of adjustment, as the congressional habit of periodically reversing the effects of bracket creep is well known. Bracket creep, like mismeasurement of real gains, tends to produce a surge of capital gains realizations immediately after an ex post adjustment in the tax code which lowers tax rates on nominal capital gains.

In sum, one should not conclude that in a comprehensive reform of the tax system, wherein real capital gains are taxed as accrued, Lindsey's work suggests that a top marginal rate would be too high. Rather, what Lindsey's estimates imply is that during inflationary periods when the mismeasurement of real gains and bracket creep combine seriously to distort the measurement of capital gains for tax purposes, a very low tax rate on nominal capital gains is required to carry forward realizations to a revenue-maximizing level.

4 The Effects of Tax Rules on Nonresidential Fixed Investment: Some Preliminary Evidence from the 1980s

Martin Feldstein and Joosung Jun

By the end of the 1970s there was widespread agreement that the rate of capital accumulation in the United States was too low and that the tax system was an important reason for that low rate of investment. Net fixed nonresidential investment had fallen to only 2.7% of GNP in the second half of the 1970s, one-third less than it had been a decade earlier. The tax system depressed the return to saving and to investing in business plant and equipment by a combination of corporate and personal taxes that took 67% of the pretax return to capital in the nonfinancial corporate sector during the years 1975 to 1979.[1] The sharp increase in this effective tax rate during the 1960s and 1970s was due in large part to the interaction between the rising rate of inflation and the persistence of tax rules that base depreciation on the nominal value of capital assets and that tax artificial nominal inventory profits and nominal capital gains.[2]

Congress and the new Reagan administration responded to this problem by enacting the Economic Recovery Tax Act (ERTA) of 1981. For individual taxpayers, this legislation stimulated saving by reducing all statutory tax rates by 25% and extending eligibility for Individual Retirement Accounts to all employees in a way that permits the majority of individuals to be taxed on a consumption tax basis with all of their saving done out of pretax income. For corporations, ERTA replaced the previous system of depreciation allowances with a simplified "Accelerated Cost Recovery System" that substantially increased the pres-

Martin Feldstein is the George F. Baker Professor of Economics at Harvard University and president of the National Bureau of Economic Research. Joosung Jun is a graduate student at Harvard University and a research assistant at the National Bureau of Economic Research.

ent value of depreciation allowances. Most purchases of equipment could be depreciated over an accelerated 5-year schedule while structures could be depreciated over 15 years using a 175% declining balance schedule. ERTA also provided for further accelerations in depreciation schedules in 1985 and 1986. According to calculations presented in *The Budget of the United States for Fiscal Year 1986,* the original ERTA provisions would have reduced 1988 corporate tax receipts by $55 billion, or 56% of currently projected corporate tax receipts for that year.[3]

The reduction in the rate of inflation also reduced the effective rate of tax on corporate sector capital income. The rate of increase of the GNP deflator reached a peak of 9.6% in 1981 and then fell to 6% in 1982 and to less than 4% for each of the next 3 years. Under the ERTA tax rules, a decline in the inflation rate from 10% to 4% raises the present value of depreciation deductions and investment tax credits per dollar of equipment investment from 45.2 cents to 49.2 cents.[4] In addition, the combination of lower inflation and the voluntary shift from FIFO to LIFO inventory accounting reduced the inventory valuation adjustment from $43 billion a year in 1979 and 1980 to only $6 billion by 1984.

In short, the 1981 tax legislation and the reduction in inflation provided a very substantial increase in the incentive to invest in plant and equipment. But within a year there was enough concern about the prospective deficits that Congress and the Administration passed a new tax bill aimed at raising substantial revenue. The Tax Equity and Fiscal Responsibility Act (TEFRA) of 1982 introduced a half-basis adjustment for the investment tax credit and repealed the prospective further accelerations in the depreciation schedule. These changes implied a $43 billion rise in 1988 corporate tax receipts, effectively canceling 78% of the reduction granted in ERTA.[5] Two years later, the Deficit Reduction Act (DEFRA) of 1984 raised projected 1988 taxes by an additional $10 billion, leaving the net 1988 corporate tax reduction from all the 1980s tax legislation at only $4 billion.

Although the 1982 and 1984 tax bills eliminated essentially all the previously enacted reduction in corporate tax liabilities, some improvement in the incentive to invest remained for most corporations. For example, 5-year property has depreciation deductions and an investment tax credit with a combined present value of 45.2 cents per dollar of investment under TEFRA (with 4% inflation and a 7% real discount rate), down from 47.1 cents under ERTA but up from 43.5 cents under the pre–ERTA rules. The decline in inflation was also important in reducing the overall effective tax rate. With a 10% inflation, the present value of the depreciation and investment tax credits was 39.0% under pre–ERTA rules and 41.8 cents under TEFRA rules. Thus the shift from an environment with 10% inflation and pre-ERTA rules to 4% inflation and TEFRA rules raised the present value of depreciation and the investment tax credit from 39.0 cents to 45.2 cents, with 1.7 cents of the increase due to the change in tax rules and the remaining 4.5 cents due to the fall in inflation. Finally, the reductions in personal tax rates and in the artificial inflation tax on capital gains reduced the personal part of the overall tax wedge between the pretax return to corporate capital and the net return received by the providers of debt and equity capital.

Any analysis of the effects of these tax changes on investment must recognize that other potentially important determinants of investment were also changing during the same period. The economy slipped into 2 back-to-back recessions beginning in the second quarter of 1980 from which it did not begin to emerge until the final quarter of 1982. The tight monetary policy in 1981 and the sharp increase in projected structural deficits in the federal budget caused an unprecedented rise in real interest rates that began in 1981. Investment in particular industries and assets was substantially affected by the dramatic surge in the U.S. merchandise trade deficit which sharply reduced output in particular industries even while the overall economy was expanding. A surge of technical change in computers and related office equipment boosted the demand for those products even among firms that were not doing any investment to expand capacity.

All of these changes mean that the research presented here must be regarded as preliminary. Additional years of data will help to reduce the remaining uncertainty, especially if the fall in real interest rates and in the cost of equity capital continues. Disaggregated data can also help to resolve questions about the special factors that raise or reduce investments in particular industries and types of assets.

The simplest and most direct interpretation of the evidence developed in the present paper is that net fixed nonresidential investment increased substantially in the first half of the 1980s as a result of the improved tax climate for investment that resulted from the 1981 tax legislation and from the reduced rate of inflation. The ratio of net fixed nonresidential investment to GNP rose from 0.027 in the second half of the 1970s and 0.030 in 1980 to 0.037 in 1984 and 0.040 in the first 3 quarters of 1985. The investment–GNP ratio for these 2 years was exceeded in only 5 years in the preceding 3 decades (1965–69).

The rise in investment is consistent with the implications of 2 previously formulated simple models of investment behavior that were developed and estimated in Feldstein (1982). The first model relates the ratio of net investment to GNP to lagged values of the capacity utilization rate and of the real net-of-tax return to the providers of debt and equity capital. In the second model, the real net return is replaced by the rate of return over cost (i.e., the difference between the maximum return that firms can afford to pay to providers of debt and equity capital and the actual cost of funds). The latter model also implies that the increase in investment in recent years would have been significantly greater if the rise in the level of the real interest rates had not substantially increased the cost of funds to corporate borrowers.

The estimation of two very different models of investment behavior deserves an extra word of comment. As Feldstein (1982) pointed out, all models are "false" in the sense that they involve substantial simplifications that could in principle cause significant biases in the estimated coefficients. The only way to draw reliable inferences is to make alternative estimates that are likely to be subject to different biases. These different estimates may involve different types of data (the biases in time series analysis are different from the biases in cross-section analysis) or different model specifications. If the different analyses have similar implications, the conclusions can be held with greater confidence and we are spared the difficult problem of choosing among false models. Fortunately, that is the case in the current study.

The econometric evidence presented in sections 4.3 and 4.4 of this paper incorporates data for 1979 through 1984 as well as revised data for earlier years to reestimate the two models of investment behavior that were previously estimated with data through 1978 (Feldstein 1982). The new estimates confirm the previous findings, showing that the parameter estimates are quite stable and robust to data revisions and to changes in the sample period.

The present paper also estimates several modifications of these 2 basic investment models. The first alternative replaces the return net of all taxes with the return net of only those taxes collected at the corporate level. This return net of corporate taxes measures the return available to pension funds and other tax-exempt shareholders. It is also plausibly a better determinant of investment behavior because changes in taxes at the level of the portfolio investor affect the net return to alternative investments in a comparable way. The statistical evidence shows that this model explains past variations in investment about as well as or perhaps slightly better than the original net-of-all-taxes rate of return.

Section 4.1 of this paper presents a brief discussion of the behavior of investment during the past 3 decades with particular attention to the period since 1979. Section 4.2 then provides summary data on the basic determinants of investment, including variations in capacity utilization and in the various rate of return and cost of funds variables. It also presents an overview of the results and implications of the econometric estimates of the basic investment models. The third section then discusses the net return model in more detail and presents the estimated regression equations. Section 4.4 presents parallel evidence for the return over cost model. There is a brief concluding section that points to several directions for additional research.

4.1 Variations in Net Nonresidential Fixed Investment

The analysis of this paper focuses on the ratio of net nonresidential fixed investment to GNP. Table 4.1 presents averages of this ratio for 5-year periods between 1955–59 and 1980–84 and annual data for the years 1979 through 1985.[6]

The distinction between net and gross investment is an important one. A comparison of columns 1 and 2 of table 4.1 shows that the ratio of gross investment to net investment has been rising since the mid-1960s. Feldstein (1983) showed that capital consumption absorbed a growing share of gross investment over this period for 3 reasons: the ratio of the capital stock to GNP increased; the share of equipment in the capital stock rose (which raises capital consumption because equipment depreciates more rapidly than structures); and the nature of the equipment shifted to more rapidly depreciating types of assets. These forces were powerful enough to maintain gross investment at a constant share of GNP from the mid-1960s through the late 1970s even though the net investment ratio declined by nearly one-third.

Net investment is the economically important concept because it is net investment that determines the growth of the nation's capital stock. From a behavioral point of view, however, specifying investment behavior in terms of net investment is clearly a simplification since it

Table 4.1	Ratios of Investment to GNP	
Years	Net Investment (1)	Gross Investment (2)
1955–59	0.026	0.093
1960–64	0.025	0.091
1965–69	0.042	0.106
1970–74	0.034	0.105
1975–79	0.027	0.104
1980–84	0.029	0.115
1979	0.037	0.115
1980	0.030	0.112
1981	0.032	0.116
1982	0.023	0.113
1983	0.022	0.111
1984	0.037	0.125
1985*	0.040	0.130

*Data for 1985 refer to the first 3 quarters only at a seasonally adjusted annual rate.

assumes that firms invest only in order to achieve a desired capital stock and ignores the special character of investments made for modernization and cost reduction.[7]

The data in table 4.1 show that net nonresidential fixed investment has averaged only 3.0% of GNP during the 3 decades from 1960 through 1984. The period began with investment at an even lower level, only about 2.5% of GNP, a condition that contributed to the Kennedy tax bill and the introduction of the investment tax credit. Net investment rose to over 4% of GNP in the second half of the 1960s and then declined to 3.4% of GNP in the first half of the 1970s and only 2.7% of GNP in the second half of the decade. In the 1980s, investment was initially just slightly above 3% of GNP, then declined during 1982 and 1983 to only 2.2% before rising to 3.7% of GNP in 1984 and 4.1% of GNP in 1985. At 4.0% of GNP, the 1985 level of net investment was only exceeded or equaled in 4 other years during the past 3 decades and always at a time when the level of capacity utilization was substantially higher than it was in 1985.

The models estimated and discussed in this paper relate the net investment ratio to lagged capacity utilization and to alternative measures of the profitability of investing in nonresidential fixed capital. As we noted above, there are of course a great many other specific factors that can influence the rate of investment in any period. Bosworth (1984) has emphasized that the growth of automobile leasing companies and rapid technological progress in computers caused a rapid rise in both types of investments in the 1980s and that when both of these are eliminated there is no increase in gross investment relative to GNP.[8]

Although this statistical fact is arithmetically correct, it is difficult to know what economic importance it has. Just as there were special exogenous reasons for a surge of investments in autos and computers in these years, there were also reasons for unusually low rates of investment in certain other industries. The early 1980s were characterized by an unprecedented 70% rise in the real value of the dollar and a sharp increase in real long-term interest rates to levels that had not been seen for a half-century. The result was a lopsided recovery in which industries exposed to international competition and interest-sensitive industries actually contracted while the economy as a whole was expanding. By the end of 1983, many of those industries had still not reached the level of output that they had experienced 5 years earlier. Even at the end of 1984, there were still a number of industries producing at less than their 1978 levels of output. For such industries, there was clearly far less reason to expand capacity.

More specifically, although real GNP rose 3.7% between 1979 and 1983, almost all the increase was in the production of services. The output of services rose $52.5 billion (in 1972 dollars) while the output of goods rose only $10.9 billion and the output of structures actually fell by $8.1 billion. Thus services rose 9.2% while the output of goods rose only 1.6%. Since the services sector is less capital intensive than the goods-producing sector, this very substantial shift in the composition of GNP would in itself tend to reduce the rate of investment.

Similarly, although overall industrial production rose by 3.3% during those years, production in the primary metals industries in December 1983 was 25% below the 1978 level. Production of iron and steel was 35% below the level in 1978. Production of fabricated metal products was 13% below its 1979 peak level, and auto production was down 11%. Other industries with less output in December 1983 than 5 years earlier included mining, construction, apparel, consumer home goods, and agriculture. Of these, only autos and consumer home goods had passed their 1978–79 output levels by the end of 1984.

In short, although unusual technical progress in the computer industry may have stimulated aggregate investment in the first half of the 1980s, the unusual character of the recovery caused by the unprecedented rise in the dollar and in real long-term interest rates may have depressed overall investment. The failure to extend the statistical models of investment behavior to include variables that adequately measure these influences may cause the resulting estimates of the rate of return variables to be biased. The magnitude of the potential bias depends on the relative importance for investment of the omitted factors and the extent to which they are correlated with the rate of return variables. A priori, it is not possible to determine whether the net effect of omitting both types of variables is to overstate or understate the effect of the rate of return variable. Bosworth's (1984) procedure of excluding the computer investments of the last few years without making a parallel adjustment for the adverse effects of the unbalanced recovery is clearly misleading and inappropriate. Its net effect is to understate any positive effect on investment of the recent changes in tax rules and the increase in net profitability.

4.2 An Overview of the Results

The next 2 sections of this paper and the appendixes will describe the data and econometric estimates in detail. Before turning to that analysis, we shall provide an overview of the results.

Five-year averages for the past 3 decades are presented for each of the alternative measures of net return as well as for capacity utilization and for the investment–GNP ratio. Annual data are also presented for the years 1979 through 1985. Inspection of these data shows the empirical relationships that the regression equations subsequently estimate with annual observations.

We also combine these data with the regression coefficients estimated later in the paper to answer three questions: (1) How well do the regression coefficients estimated on the basis of data for the past 3 decades explain the behavior of investment in the 1980s? (2) More specifically, how has the change in tax rules affected the rate of investment? (3) How would prospective investment be affected by the tax changes implied by the Administration's May 1985 plan and by the tax bill that passed the House of Representatives in December 1985?

The analysis begins with the net return models and then examines the return over cost models.

4.2.1   Investment and the Net Rate of Return

The basic data summarizing the relation between net investment and the net rate of return on corporate sector capital are presented in table 4.2. Column 1 repeats the investment–GNP ratios previously shown in table 4.1. The second column presents the capacity utilization rate, a fundamental determinant of fluctuations in investment.[9] Since studies generally indicate a lag that peaks at 12 to 18 months between changes in the determinants of investment and subsequent changes in investment, the capacity utilization variable and the other variables in table 4.2 are shown with a 1-year lag; thus capacity utilization for 1955–59 actually refers to the average capacity utilization rate in the period 1954–58. It is clear that periods of high capacity utilization tended to be periods of high net investment. But even with the 1-year lag there is a problem of simultaneity in interpreting this association; anything that raises the investment–GNP ratio during a period of several years will also raise the capacity utilization rate during that period. This causes the estimated investment equations to understate the importance of profitability and tax variables relative to capacity utilization.

The starting point for calculating the net-of-tax rate of return variable is the pretax return on nonfinancial corporate capital. We construct this as the ratio of profits (with economic depreciation and an inventory evaluation adjustment) before all state and local taxes plus net interest payments to the value of the corresponding corporate capital stock at replacement cost.[10]

To obtain the net rate of return (RN), we subtract from this the ratio of the taxes paid by the corporations, their shareholders, and their creditors to the capital stock. The calculation of the tax liabilities of shareholders and creditors takes into account the distribution of debt and equity income among different types of taxpayers (individuals by income class, pensions, and other tax-exempt institutions, insurance

Table 4.2   **The Rate of Investment and the Net Rate of Return**

Year*	Investment–GNP Ratio (I_n/Y) (1)	Capacity Utilization (UCAP) (2)	Pretax Rate of Return (R) (3)	Net Rate of Return		Cyclically Adjusted Return		Cyclically Adjusted Differential Returns	
				After All Taxes (RN) (4)	After Corporate Taxes (RNC) (5)	After All Taxes (RNA) (6)	After Corporate Taxes (RNCA) (7)	After All Taxes $(RNA - r_n)$ (8)	After Corporate Taxes $(RNCA - r)$ (9)
1955–59	0.026	0.824	0.107	0.033	0.046	0.033	0.046	—	—
1960–64	0.025	0.808	0.111	0.042	0.055	0.043	0.056	0.038	0.040
1965–69	0.042	0.880	0.137	0.060	0.077	0.056	0.071	0.041	0.042
1970–74	0.034	0.826	0.105	0.037	0.055	0.036	0.055	0.030	0.028
1975–79	0.027	0.796	0.091	0.028	0.048	0.029	0.050	0.048	0.045
1980–84	0.029	0.773	0.075	0.029	0.045	0.033	0.051	0.025	0.003
1979	0.037	0.842	0.095	0.032	0.052	0.031	0.050	0.038	0.031
1980	0.030	0.846	0.082	0.026	0.044	0.025	0.042	0.030	0.016
1981	0.032	0.793	0.070	0.019	0.037	0.021	0.040	0.021	0.001
1982	0.023	0.783	0.077	0.029	0.048	0.032	0.052	0.020	−0.011
1983	0.022	0.703	0.067	0.030	0.045	0.040	0.059	0.025	−0.002
1984	0.037	0.740	0.080	0.041	0.054	0.048	0.064	0.031	0.012
1985†	0.040	0.808	0.099	0.054	0.070	0.056	0.071	0.029	0.004

*All variables in columns 2 through 9 are lagged 1 year. Thus, capacity utilization 1965–69 refers to average capacity utilization in 1964–68.

†Investment for 1985 refers to the first 3 quarters at a seasonally adjusted rate.

companies, banks, etc.); details of the calculation are presented in Appendix A.

A high value of the net return on nonfinancial corporate capital should make this type of investment more attractive relative to other uses of funds like owner-occupied housing, government debt, real estate partnerships, and overseas investment. A comparison of columns 4 and 1 shows that there has been a strong association between the variations in this net return and the concurrent variations in the investment–GNP ratio. The net return was highest in the second half of the 1960s (6.0%) when the investment–GNP ratio was highest and lowest in the second half of the 1970s (2.8%) when the investment–GNP ratio was lowest. During the first half of the 1980s, the annual values of RN rose to a quite strong 5.4%, roughly paralleling the rise in the investment–GNP ratio.[11]

The fluctuations in the net rate of return reflect not only tax rules but also movements in pretax profitability over the business cycle and more generally. Column 6 presents a cyclically adjusted net rate of return (RNA) obtained by multiplying 1 minus the effective tax rate by a cyclically adjusted pretax return calculated by regressing the pretax return on the rate of capacity utilization and then evaluating the return that would prevail at a constant capacity utilization rate. For the 5-year periods, there is little difference between the cyclically adjusted returns of column 6 and the unadjusted returns of column 4 although cyclical adjustment does lower the 1965–69 return and raise the 1980–84 return. Cyclical adjustment is more important with the annual data and shows that the cyclically adjusted net return rose steadily from 2.1% for 1981 to 5.6% for 1985. The important implication of these figures is that they indicate that the close association between the investment–GNP ratio and the real net rate of return does not merely reflect cyclical fluctuations in profitability but is based on changes in effective tax rates and persistent changes in pretax profitability.

Column 5 presents an alternative measure of net profitability that subtracts only those taxes paid by corporations to the federal government and to state and local governments. We label the resulting variable RNC to denote that it is the return net of corporate taxes. Taxes paid by individuals and other portfolio investors are ignored. There are 2 possible reasons for preferring this RNC variable to the return net of all taxes (RN). First, for a very important class of investors, including pension funds and foreign investors, only the corporate tax is relevant. The return after corporate taxes governs the net return that they can earn as portfolio investors and therefore their willingness to direct their assets into nonfinancial corporate capital. Second, for taxable individual investors, the changes in personal tax rates that affect the ultimate net return on corporate capital (RN) also affect the net return on competing investments. The link is not complete because the RN variable reflects the specific ownership of debt and equity securities, the taxation of real and nominal capital gains, and other features that are specific to the return on nonfinancial corporate capital. But fluctuations in RN induced by the changes in taxes paid by shareholders and creditors probably exaggerate the changes in the relative desirability of investing in nonfinancial corporate capital.

The variations in the real return net of corporate taxes (RNC) generally parallel the shifts in the real return net of all taxes (RN) with the highest value in the second half of the 1960s (RNC = 0.077) and the lowest values in the first half of the 1980s (RNC = 0.045). The difference between the 2 measures does vary from time to time, depending on the tax rules for individuals and the rate of inflation. From 1955 through 1969, personal taxes and other taxes paid by portfolio investors (including banks and insurance companies) took approximately 24% of the return after corporate taxes (i.e., the final net return RN was 76% of the return net of corporate taxes RNC), but this rose to 33% in the first half of the 1970s and 42% in the second half of the 1970s as inflation created high levels of artificial nominal interest income and nominal capital gains that were taxed to portfolio investors. By 1984, the combination of personal tax changes and reduced inflation lowered the effective tax on portfolio investors to about 23% of the return after corporate taxes.

A cyclically adjusted net return after corporate taxes (RNCA) is shown in column 7. The 5-year averages of this measure show greater stability than the other measures of net return in columns 4 through 6. Nevertheless, the period 1965–69 continues to stand out as a time when the net return was high and the period from 1975 through the early 1980s remains a period of low net profitability. This measure also shows a sharp rise in net real return from 4.0% for 1981 to 7.1% for 1985 (i.e., 4.0% in 1980 and 7.1% in 1984). Although this increase is not as great as the rise in the full net return (RNA), there was clearly a very substantial rise in net profitability in these years that did not reflect either cyclical fluctuations in pretax profitability or changes in personal tax rates.

Estimated Effects of Changes in the Net Return

Section 4.3 presents estimated equations relating the investment–GNP ratio to the capacity utilization rate and to each of these 4 measures of the net return. That analysis confirms that there is a strong and statistically significant relationship between investment and the net return in the previous year. The current estimates for the sample period 1954–84 (and for subperiods within these 3 decades) are very similar to the results obtained in Feldstein (1982) with data for 1954 through

1978. The similarity of the coefficient estimates persists even though there was a major revision of the national income accounts in 1980 that changed much of the earlier data and despite a number of small improvements in the method that we have used to calculate the net rate of return variables. The earlier analysis did not consider the return net of corporate tax variables (RNC and RNCA), but these are now found to explain variations in the investment ratio as well as or better than the full net return variables (RN and RNA).

A typical example of the estimated equations implies that each percentage point increase in the real net rate of return increases the investment–GNP ratio by about 0.4 percentage points. The actual equation relates the investment–GNP ratio to the net rate of return (RN) in the immediate past year and to the capacity utilization rate (UCAP) in that same past year. When this equation is estimated with data for 1954 through 1984, the coefficient of the net return variable is 0.41 (with a standard error of 0.12). That same equation implies that each percentage point increase in capacity utilization raises the investment–GNP ratio by about 0.02 percentage points.

Although these coefficients can only approximate an average relationship over the 30-year sample period, it is interesting to see how well they explain major shifts in the investment ratio between particular dates. Consider first the sharp fall in investment between the high of 4.2% of GNP in the 1965–69 period and the 2.7% of GNP a decade later, a decline of 1.5% of GNP. Between these same periods the net return fell from 6.0% to 2.8%. This 3.2 percentage point decline and the estimated coefficient of 0.4 imply a fall of 1.3 percentage points in the investment–GNP ratio. The concurrent 8 percentage point decline in capacity utilization (from 88.0% in 1965–69 to 79.6% in 1975–79) and the estimated coefficient of 0.02 imply a fall of 0.2 percentage points in the investment–GNP ratio. Thus the decline in the net return and in capacity utilization together imply a fall of 1.5 percentage points in the investment–GNP ratio, exactly what was observed. More than 85% of this fall was attributable to the decline in the net return.

Of course, not all movements in investment can be explained as satisfactorily by the simple models used here. For example, investment rose between the early 1960s and the early 1970s even though the equation would have predicted a decline of 0.2% in the investment–GNP ratio. What matters for the purpose of this study is not the ability to provide a perfect explanation of year-to-year variations of investments (although $\bar{R}^2 = 0.60$ indicates a quite good explanation of the volatile investment–GNP ratio without the use of long distributed lags or lagged dependent variables) but the ability to measure the impact of tax changes on the level of investment.

The predictions of the simple net return model also fit well with the experience of the 1980s. The investment–GNP ratio rose from 3.3% in the years 1979–81 to 3.9% in 1984–85. The corresponding (lagged) measures of the real net return rose from 2.6% to 4.8%, implying a 0.9 percentage point rise in the investment–GNP ratio while the 5 percentage point decline in capacity utilization implies a 0.1 percentage point fall in the investment–GNP ratio. Thus the equation predicts a 0.8 percentage point increase in the investment–GNP ratio while the actual investment ratio increased 0.6 percentage points. In short, investment increased slightly less than predicted on the basis of the stronger investment incentive as measured in this way.[12]

It is interesting to decompose the effect of the change in the net return during these years into the effect of the change in tax rules and the effect of the change in the pretax rate of return. The effective tax rate declined from 69.0% in the years 1978–80 (i.e., the years relevant for investment in 1979–81) to 47.0% in years 1983–84. The pretax rate of return rose from 8.2% for the early years to 9.0% for the later years. If the tax rate had remained at the 1978–80 value while the pretax return rose, the net of tax return (RN) would have increased by 0.25 percentage points. The implied increase in the investment–GNP ratio would then be 0.1 percentage points. In contrast, if the pretax return had remained at 8.2% while the effective tax rate fell from 69.0% to 47.0%, the after-tax return would have increased by 1.8 percentage points. The implied increase in the investment would be 0.7 percentage points. Thus the fall in the effective tax rate was about 7 times as important in stimulating a rise in investment as the increase in the pretax rate of return. The capacity utilization rate actually fell slightly during this period, decreasing by just about enough (5.3 percentage points) to offset the rise in the pretax rate of return.[13] The decline in the effective tax rate is thus responsible for all the predicted rise in investment.

Of the initial 69.0% effective tax rate, 30.6 percentage points represented the federal corporate tax rate, 15.8 percentage points were state and local profits and property taxes paid by corporations, and 22.6 percentage points were federal and state income taxes paid by individuals and other providers of debt and equity capital. By 1983–84, these percentages had declined to 17.0%, 14.0%, and 16.0%. These figures imply that the taxes paid by the corporations to the federal, state, and local governments fell from 46.4% of the real pretax return to 31.0% of that return, a decline of one-third in the effective tax rate at the corporate level. The taxes paid by portfolio investors were initially 22.6% of the pretax return, or 42.2% of the return that remained after the taxes paid by corporations. By 1983–84, this declined to 16.0%

of the pretax return, or 23.2% of the return that remained after the taxes paid by corporations, a decline of nearly one-half.

To calculate what these effective tax rate declines contributed to the predicted rise in the investment–GNP ratio, we assume that the initial 8.2% pretax return remains fixed for all years. As we already noted, the decline in the overall effective tax rate implied a 1.8 percentage point rise in the real after-tax return and therefore a 0.7 percentage point increase in the investment–GNP ratio. Slightly less than two-thirds of this was accounted for by the decline in the effective federal corporate tax rate: the 13.6 percentage point decline in that effective tax rate represented a 1.1 percentage point rise in the real after-tax return and therefore an investment–GNP rise of 0.45 percentage points.

The model also provides a basis for making a very rough calculation of how investment would respond to future changes in tax rules like those proposed by the Administration in May 1985 or the ones enacted by the House in December 1985. The Administration's proposal would raise corporate tax liabilities by approximately 25% while cutting personal taxes by about 7%. It is difficult to translate the personal tax changes into a change in the effective tax rate on the interest, dividends, and capital gains arising from the earnings of nonfinancial corporations. Much of the interest and dividend income is received by pension funds and other portfolio investors that are not currently taxed and that would not be affected by the change in personal tax rates. Although the maximum marginal tax rate on interest and dividends received by individuals would be reduced from 50% to 35%, much of the overall reduction in personal taxes would take the form of an increase in the personal exemption that left the tax rate on capital income unchanged. In addition, special provisions would limit the use of 401k saving plans and would impose heavier taxes on financial institutions. Fortunately, the calculation is not very sensitive to alternative assumptions about the change in the effective tax on individuals and other portfolio investors.

For the purpose of this calculation, we assume that the pretax rate of return and the rate of capacity utilization would remain unchanged. Federal corporate taxes in 1984 took 16.6% of the total real pretax return on nonfinancial corporate capital. A 25% increase in federal corporate liabilities would raise this to 20.8%. The combined federal, state, and local taxes paid by corporations would rise from 29.6% to 33.8% of pretax capital income. The return net of corporate taxes would therefore fall from 70.4% of pretax income to 66.2%. Taxes on individuals and other portfolio investors in 1984 took 21.7% of the net capital income after corporate taxes. If this fraction remained unchanged, the effect of the modified corporate tax rates would be to reduce the final net share of pretax capital income received by portfolio investors from 55.1% (i.e., 78.3% of 70.4%) to 51.8% (i.e., 78.3% of 66.2%).

If the pretax rate of return is unchanged, the after-tax rate of return (RN) would fall from the 5.5% observed in 1984 to 5.1%. Since each percentage point decline in the real net return causes a 0.4 percentage point decline in the investment–GNP ratio, this projected decline in the net return (from 5.4% to 5.1%) would reduce the investment–GNP ratio by about 0.12 percentage points. This represents about 3% of the investment level in 1984–85 and about one-fifth of the increase in investment between 1979–81 and 1984–85.

A 5% increase or decrease in the tax paid by individual and institutional portfolio investors would alter this change in investment by about one-fifth of its value. Thus an average decline of 5% in the effective tax on portfolio investors (from 21.7% of the after-corporate-tax return to 20.6%) would imply a decline in the investment–GNP ratio that was about 3% of the 1984–85 level, or one-sixth of the increase since 1979–81. Conversely, a rise of 5% in the effective tax rate on portfolio investors (from 21.7% of the after-corporate-tax return to 22.8%) would imply a decline in the investment–GNP ratio that was about 5% of the 1984–85 level, or one-third of the increase since 1979–81.

The bill passed by the House of Representatives in December 1985 would depress investment by substantially more than the Administration proposal. A critical difference between the two plans is that the Administration plan calls for full indexing of the base for depreciation while the House version would index the depreciation base only to the extent of half of the inflation in excess of 5%. At a 5% inflation rate, indexing raises the present value of depreciation allowances in the Administration's plan by 15% for most types of equipment (the class 4 assets under the Administration's plan). At a 10% inflation rate, fully indexed depreciation would have a present value 22% higher than the "half indexed over 5 percent" depreciation provided by the House bill.

The difference in indexing rules is even more important for structures. At a 5% inflation rate, indexing raises the present value of depreciation allowances for most structures by 60%. At a 10% inflation rate, the fully indexed depreciation would have a present value that is 84% higher than the half indexed over 5% depreciation provided by the House bill.

The House bill is also more harmful to investment in a variety of other ways. It would depreciate the typical equipment investment over 10 years instead of the 7 years provided by the Administration, although at a double-declining balance rate instead of the approximately 1.5 times declining balance rate prescribed in the Administration plan. The House also enacted a slightly higher corporate tax rate than the Administration proposed.

Because of the lack of indexing and the difference in the timing of depreciation, the House bill eventually raises corporate taxes by much more than the Administration bill. Although both bills would raise corporate taxes by about 25% in 1987 and 1988, by 1990 the Administration bill would increase the corporate tax by 23% and the House would increase it by 37%. Under the House bill, corporate taxes would rise by about 50% in the first half of the 1990s, twice the increase that we have assumed in evaluating the potential impact of the Administration plan.

To evaluate the impact on investment, we again assume that the pretax rate of return and the rate of capacity utilization are unaffected. Since federal corporate taxes in 1984 took 16.6% of the total real pretax return on nonfinancial corporate capital, the 50% increase implied by the House bill would raise that to 24.9%. The combined federal, state, and local taxes paid by corporations would rise from 29.6% to 37.9%. Taxes on individuals and other portfolio investors in 1984 took 21.7% of the net capital income after all corporate taxes. If this fraction remained unchanged, the effect of the House plan would be to reduce the final net share of real pretax capital income received by portfolio investors from 55.1% (i.e., 78.3% of 70.4%) to 48.6% (78.3% of 62.1%).

With the pretax return unchanged at 9.9%, the after-tax return (RN) would fall from the 5.4% actual value in 1984 to 4.8%. This projected decline would reduce the investment–GNP ratio by 0.24%, or twice the decline implied by the Administration bill. This represents about 6% of the investment level in 1984–85 and about 40 percent of the increase in the investment–GNP ratio between 1979–81 and 1984–85.

The Return Net of Corporate Taxes

These particular numerical conclusions depend on the specification of the net return after all taxes as the key determinant of the investment–GNP ratio. The alternative equation relating net investment to the return after corporate taxes (RNC) implies a somewhat larger effect of the Administration's proposed tax changes. Section 4.3 shows that estimates of the RNC equation imply that each percentage point change in the net return at the corporate level shifts the investment–GNP ratio by 0.45 percentage points. More important than the slight increase in this coefficient is the fact that the change in the net return at the corporate level is not diluted by subsequent portfolio taxation.

Consider the implications of this specification for the change in effective tax rates and investment between 1979–81 and 1984–85. The effective tax rate at the corporate level fell from 46.4% of the 8.2% pretax return to 31.0% of the 9.0% pretax return. The return net of the corporate tax thus rose from 4.4% to 6.2%. Multiplying the 1.8 percentage point rise by the 0.45 investment sensitivity figure implies a rise in the investment–GNP ratio of 0.8 percentage points. Since the decline in the capacity utilization rate implied a 0.1 percentage point fall in the investment–GNP ratio and the actual investment–GNP ratio rose 0.6 percentage points, the rise in the net return after the corporate tax explains the actual movement in the investment–GNP ratio quite well.

To isolate the impact of the change in tax rates, note that if the pretax return had remained constant at 8.2%, the decline in the effective tax rate at the corporate level would have raised the return net of corporate taxes by 1.2 percentage points and therefore increased the investment–GNP ratio by 0.54 percentage points, almost the entire observed rise.

The estimated sensitivity of the investment–GNP ratio to the return net of the corporate tax implies that a relatively modest increase in the effective corporate tax rate would have a substantial impact on the investment–GNP ratio. Thus a fall in the return net of corporate taxes from 70.4% of pretax income to 66.2% (as implied by the Administration's tax proposal) would reduce the 1984 value of the return net of corporate taxes from 7.0% (RNC = 0.070) to 6.5%. This 0.5% fall in the net rate of profit would translate into a 0.22 percentage point decline in the investment–GNP ratio. This is a decline of nearly 6% of the 1984–85 investment–GNP ratio and more than one-third of the rise in the investment–GNP ratio from the level of 1979–81.

The fall in the return net of corporate taxes from 70.4% to 62.1%, as implied by the House bill, would reduce the 1984 value of the return net of all corporate taxes from 7.0% to 6.1%. This 0.9% fall in the net rate of profit would translate into a 0.41 percentage point decline in the investment–GNP ratio. This is a decline of 11% of the 1984–85 investment–GNP ratio and three-quarters of the rise in the investment–GNP ratio of 1979–81.

Relative Rates of Return

Increases in the real net return on corporate capital raise the investment–GNP ratio by attracting funds away from alternative uses. This suggests that the behavior of investment might be better explained and predicted if the statistical model explicitly included the real return on alternative assets as well as the return on investments in nonfinancial corporate capital. The problem with doing this in practice is that there are a wide range of alternatives to investment in corporate capital including government debt, real estate, oil drilling and other natural resource investments, overseas investments, owner-occupied housing, consumer durables, and other forms of consumer spending.

Moreover, as the experience of the early 1980s dramatically demonstrated, a substantial amount of U.S. investment can be financed by an inflow of capital from the rest of the world. The U.S. current account deficit in 1984 was $101 billion, or 2.8% of GNP, implying that the capital inflow was equivalent to approximately two-thirds of all net fixed nonresidential investment. By contrast, the United States had a current account surplus in 1980 and invested more abroad than foreigners invested in the United States.

The present paper makes a first step in analyzing the sensitivity of investment to other rates of return by explicitly including the real net return on government bonds. For this purpose, we measure the nominal return on government bonds by the yield on 5-year Treasury bonds and calculate the real interest rate by subtracting an estimate of the expected rate of increase of the GNP deflator during the same 10 year period.[14] The difference between the real cyclically adjusted net return to corporations (RNCA) and the expected rate of inflation is presented in column 9 of table 4.2. For the real return on corporate capital net of all taxes (RNA), the analogous comparison is to the real net-of-tax interest rate, that is, the net of tax nominal interest rate minus the expected rate of inflation. For this purpose, we use the same effective tax rate on nominal interest income that is used for the interest component of the portfolio income generated by the nonfinancial corporate capital. This is a weighted average of the marginal tax rates of individuals in different tax brackets and of different types of taxable and nontaxable financial institutions.[15] The difference between the real net return on corporate capital and the real net interest rate is shown in column 8 of table 4.2.

It is clear that neither measure of the relative return on corporate capital has moved closely with the variations in the investment–GNP ratio. Both measures showed the greatest differential in favor of corporate capital in the 1975–79 period when the investment–GNP level was actually very low. This occurred because the very high level of actual and expected inflation during these years caused the real return on Treasury bonds to drop to only 1% and the real net-of-tax return on those bonds to become negative. Moreover, the investment–GNP ratio rose significantly in the 1980s even though the differential between the return to corporate capital and to government bonds declined because of the rise in the real return on government bonds.

These observations indicate that the yield differential between corporate capital and government bonds is not a good measure of the attractiveness of corporate investment. As we noted above, investors face a wide range of alternative investments. Moreover, whatever the yield on Treasury bonds, they can only displace saving to the extent that the government deficit increases the stock of bonds. And recent experience shows that a combination of high yields on government bonds and on corporate capital can at least temporarily attract substantial funds from the rest of the world. Until a far more complete model of the alternative to corporate capital investment is implemented, it seems better to focus on the real net return to corporate capital rather than on a differential rate of return.

4.2.2 Investment and the Rate of Return over Cost

The analysis relating investment to the net rate of return is the simplest possible model of investment behavior. The economy is treated like a black box in which the mechanism is obscure but which produces the plausible result that more capital flows into nonfinancial corporate capital when the rate of return on that type of asset is high.[16]

We now turn to a more explicit model of investment behavior in which corporate demand to invest reflects the difference between the profitability of new additions to the stock of plant and equipment and the cost of funds with which to finance that investment. This approach, labeled the return over cost model of investment, differs from the previous analysis in two fundamental ways. First, the investment decision is explicitly made by the corporation. Second, the decision reflects a comparison of the cost of funds and the prospective yield on new marginal investments rather than the yield on existing capital.

The return over cost model is the empirical implementation in a world of taxes and mixed debt-equity finance of the simple textbook model in which the rate of investment depends on the rate of interest and the marginal efficiency of investment. To make that operational, the location of the investment demand schedule is represented by the rate of return that the firm can afford to pay for funds used to finance a "typical" project. This return, which we label the "maximum potential net return",[17] is analogous to the internal rate of return of a project in an economy without taxes. Changes in tax rules, inflation, and pretax profitability all alter the maximum potential net return and therefore the incentive to invest.

More specifically, the maximum potential real net return (MPRNR) is the maximum real return that a corporation can pay to the providers of debt and equity capital on a project that consists of both equipment and structures in a ratio that matches the equipment-structure ratio of the nonfinancial corporate capital stock. Two sets of calculations are presented: in one the pretax real rate of return is fixed at 10.3%, the average pretax return during the period 1961 to 1984. In the other, the calculation assumes that the pretax return varies from year to year and is equal to the then current *ex post* return on nonfinancial corporate capital.

The calculations described in more detail in section 4.4 show that, for example, with a pretax return of 10.3%, the tax rules of 1984, and an expected inflation rate of 5.5%, the maximum potential real net return that the firm could pay to the providers of capital would be 7.3%. The maximum potential net return measure is "net" in the sense that it represents the net cost that the firm can afford to pay after taking the tax deduction for interest expenses. In 1984, the nominal interest rate on high grade corporate debt was 12.3%, implying that the net-of-tax cost of debt was 6.6% and the real net cost of debt was 1.1%. The required real return on equity capital (i.e., the ratio of economic earnings to the share price) was, however, 8.4%. We assume that firms are forced by risk considerations to use a mixture of two-thirds equity and one-third debt (approximately the average ratio during the sample period) to finance their investments. The weighted average real net cost of funds in 1984 was therefore 0.33 (1.1) + 0.67 (8.4) = 6.0 percent.[18]

Table 4.3 presents summary data on the maximum potential real net return (MPRNR) and the real net cost of funds (RCOF). For reference, the investment–GNP ratio is presented in column 1 and the capacity utilization rate in column 2. Column 3 shows that the changes in tax rules raised the MPRNR between the early 1960s and the second half of that decade and that the 1981–82 changes in tax rules and the sharp fall in inflation have caused a very substantial increase in the MPRNR since 1980.

Column 4 shows the effect of dropping the assumption of constant pretax profitability and assuming instead that firms adjust their projected future pretax profitability in proportion to the annual variations in observed pretax profitability. This calculation, which obviously exaggerates the extent to which firms react to year-to-year variations in profits, shows a much stronger increase in the MPRNR in the second half of the 1960s but much lower values in the 1980s.

The real net cost of funds is shown in column 5 and the difference between the maximum potential return and the cost of funds in columns 6 and 7. The real cost of funds was relatively high in the late 1960s, was high again in the late 1970s (when the high cost of equity outweighed the very low cost of debt), and rose again in the 1980s because of the combination of high real interest rates, low inflation, and relatively high equity costs.

Although the effect of the variations in the real cost of funds has been to leave the 5-year average difference between the maximum potential return and the cost of funds almost constant, the individual annual values show substantial variation. Column 6 shows that the difference (MPRNR − RCOF) rose from 0.7% for 1979 to 2.9% for 1984, implying a substantial increase in the incentive to invest.

Table 4.3   The Rate of Investment and the Rate of Return over Cost

Year*	Investment–GNP Ratio (I_n/Y) (1)	Capacity Utilization (UCAP) (2)	Maximum Potential Real Return		Real Cost of Funds (RCOF) (5)	Maximum Potential Return Minus Cost of Funds	
			Fixed Profitability (MPRNR) (3)	Varying Profitability (MPRNRVP) (4)		Fixed Profitability (MPRNR − RCOF) (6)	Varying Profitability (MPRNRVP − RCOF) (7)
1961–64	0.026	0.806	0.050	0.057	0.033	0.017	0.024
1965–69	0.042	0.880	0.059	0.074	0.041	0.018	0.033
1970–74	0.034	0.826	0.051	0.052	0.036	0.015	0.016
1975–79	0.027	0.796	0.056	0.050	0.040	0.016	0.010
1980–84	0.029	0.773	0.068	0.052	0.050	0.018	0.002
1979	0.037	0.842	0.059	0.049	0.052	0.007	−0.003
1980	0.030	0.846	0.061	0.040	0.053	0.008	−0.013
1981	0.032	0.793	0.059	0.036	0.047	0.012	−0.011
1982	0.023	0.783	0.072	0.055	0.053	0.019	0.002
1983	0.022	0.703	0.075	0.061	0.053	0.022	0.008
1984	0.037	0.740	0.075	0.068	0.046	0.029	0.022
1985†	0.040	0.808	0.073	0.072	0.060	0.013	0.012

*All variables in columns 2 through 7 are lagged 1 year. Thus, capacity utilization 1965–69 refers to average capacity utilization in 1964–68.
†Investment for 1985 refers to the first 3 quarters at a seasonally adjusted rate.

Estimated Effects of Changes in the Return over Cost

The regression equations presented in section 4.4 relate the investment–GNP ratio to the rate of return over cost (MPRNR – RCOF) in the immediate previous year and to the capacity utilization rate in that year. The estimated coefficient of the rate of return over cost variable implies that each 1 percentage point increase in that differential raises the investment–GNP ratio by 0.3 percentage points. The estimated equation also implies that each percentage point increase in capacity utilization raises the investment–GNP ratio by 0.09 percentage points.

Although these values cannot be expected to explain each short-run fluctuation in the investment–GNP ratio, it is interesting to see what their implications are for the recent shifts in tax policy and in the cost of funds and to speculate about the likely effects of future changes in tax rules. The rate of return over cost relevant for 1979–81 averaged 0.009 and rose to 0.021 for 1984–85. The rise of 0.012 implies an increase in the investment–GNP ratio of 0.36%, thereby accounting for 60% of the observed rise in the investment–GNP ratio between the 3.3% average for 1979–81 and the 3.9% average for 1984–85. However, the fall in capacity utilization between these two same dates (from 0.827 for 1979–81 to 0.774 for 1984–85) outweighed the improvement in the rate of return over cost and, according to the statistically estimated equation, implied that the investment–GNP ratio should have declined over the period. One possible reason for this forecast error is that businesses in 1979 and 1980 recognized that the high level of capacity utilization at that time was transitory because the shift toward a tight monetary policy that began in October 1979 would inevitably bring about a substantial recession.

The experience for the 1980s as a whole also shows the offsetting effects of an improved tax environment and the increasing cost of funds. The maximum potential real net return rose from 6.0% for 1979–81 (i.e., in 1978–80) to 7.3% for 1985; the increase of 1.3 percentage points implies an increase in the investment–GNP ratio of 0.4 percentage points. But during these same years, the real cost of funds rose from 5.1% to 6.0%, offsetting two-thirds of the increased incentive to invest. It is interesting to note that the cost of equity funds was the same for 1985 as it had been for 1979–81, implying that the entire increase in the cost of funds was due to the rise in the cost of debt (from a real 3.4% for 1979–81 to 6.0% for 1985). To the extent that the increase in the deficit in the federal budget was responsible for this rise in the rate of interest, it had the effect of offsetting a large part of the increased incentive to invest that resulted from the change in tax rules and the reduction in inflation.[19]

The relation between the investment–GNP ratio and the rate of return over cost gives some hint of how future fiscal policies might affect the future investment level. According to the estimates in Feldstein (1986), a decline of the projected budget deficit from the 4% of GNP prevailing in 1984 to 1% of GNP would reduce the real interest rate by approximately 3 percentage points (and therefore back to its historic norm). This in turn would lower the cost of capital by 1 percentage point if it left the cost of equity capital unchanged and by 3 percentage points if the returns on debt and equity declined by equal amounts. The estimated relation between the investment–GNP ratio and the rate of return over cost implies that this fall in the cost of capital would raise the investment–GNP ratio by between 0.3 percentage points and 0.9 percentage points, an increase equal to between 10% and 30% of the average investment–GNP ratio of the past quarter-century.

The changes in the tax law that the Administration proposed in May 1985 would reduce the MPRNR by only about 0.2 percentage points at the 1984 rate of inflation, from 7.3% to 7.1%. This decline reflects a sharper decline for equipment and an actual increase for structures. This decline in the rate of return over cost (assuming that the real cost of funds remained unchanged) would reduce the investment–GNP ratio by only about 0.06 percentage points, or about 2% of the investment–GNP level in 1984–85. The MPNR–COF framework thus implies only about half of the reduction in the overall investment–GNP ratio in response to the Administration's bill as the reduction implied by the RN and RNC calculations. In considering this relatively small total reduction, it should be recalled that the fall in the MPRNR for equipment is much more substantial so that the composition of the overall investment would change in the direction of structures and away from equipment. The magnitude of this shift will be examined in a later paper using the MPRNR data disaggregated into structures and equipment.

In contrast to the small effect of the president's plan on aggregate investment, the House bill implies that the MPRNR for 1984 would fall from 7.3% to 5.9%. If the cost of funds remained unchanged, the resulting 1.4 percentage point decline in the rate of return over cost would reduce the investment–GNP ratio by approximately 0.42 percentage points. This decline is 7 times larger than the decline implied by the Administration's plan. The fall in the investment–GNP ratio would be approximately 11% of the 1984–85 level of that ratio and three-quarters of the rise in the investment–GNP ratio from 1979–81 to 1984–85. This agrees almost exactly with the decline in the investment–GNP ratio implied by the model that relates that investment ratio to the rate of return net of taxes at the corporate level.

4.3 The Net Return and the Rate of Investment: Statistical Evidence

This section presents the estimated equations relating the investment–GNP ratio to the net rate of return on the capital of nonfinancial corporations. Appendix A describes the calculation of the pretax rate of return on that capital and of the tax rates paid by corporations and portfolio investors that provide debt and equity capital. Appendix A also presents the annual time series of the basic regression variables (that were summarized in table 4.2) and of the components of the tax rate.

Equation (1) reproduces the basic specification estimated in Feldstein (1982) relating the ratio of net investment to GNP (I_t^n/Y_t) to the real net rate of return in the previous year (RN_{t-1}) and the rate of capacity utilization ($UCAP_{t-1}$). The equation is estimated with a first-order autocorrelation correction, and the simultaneously estimated autocorrelation coefficient is presented as the coefficient of the variable u_{t-1}.

(1) $$I_t^n/Y_t = -0.014 + 0.459\ RN_{t-1} + 0.028\ UCAP_{t-1} + 0.29\ u_{t-1}$$
$$(0.095)\phantom{\ RN_{t-1}}(0.025)\phantom{\ UCAP_{t-1}}(0.25)$$

$$\bar{R}^2 = 0.754,\ DWS = 2.04,\ 1954\text{--}78$$

After this equation was estimated in the summer of 1980, the Commerce Department prepared a major data revision that substantially modified a number of the series used to calculate each of the variables. In addition, in preparing to reestimate this and other equations, we have introduced a number of improvements in the procedure used to calculate the real net return to capital. Nevertheless, when this equation is reestimated with the new data for the same period, the resulting parameter estimates are very similar to those presented in Feldstein (1982):

(2) $$I_t^n/Y_t = -0.004 + 0.453\ RN_{t-1} + 0.020\ UCAP_{t-1} + 0.445\ u_{t-1}$$
$$(0.114)\phantom{\ RN_{t-1}}(0.025)\phantom{\ UCAP_{t-1}}(0.230)$$

$$\bar{R}^2 = 0.698,\ DWS = 1.99,\ 1954\text{--}78$$

Extending the sample through 1984 has very little effect on the estimated coefficients:

(3) $$I_t^n/Y_t = -0.003 + 0.412\ RN_{t-1} + 0.021\ UCAP_{t-1} + 0.431\ u_{t-1}$$
$$(0.116)\phantom{\ RN_{t-1}}(0.024)\phantom{\ UCAP_{t-1}}(0.206)$$

$$\bar{R} = 0.598,\ DWS = 1.92,\ 1954\text{--}84$$

The coefficient of the net return variable is 0.412, implying that each 1 percentage point rise in RN causes the investment–GNP ratio to rise by 0.412 percentage points. The associated elasticity at the mean values of RN (0.038) and of the investment–GNP ratio (0.030) is 0.52.

The persistently strong effect of the real net return does not reflect the dominant effect of the early years or of any other part of the sample. When the sample is divided in half, the effect of the real net return is quite strong in both halves. For the period from 1954 through 1969 we obtain

$$(4a) I_t^n/Y_t = -0.055 + 0.433 \, RN_{t-1} + 0.079 \, UCAP_{t-1} - 0.565 \, u_{t-1}$$
$$ (0.067) \qquad\qquad (0.023) \qquad\qquad (0.253)$$

$$\bar{R}^2 = 0.808, \, DWS = 2.17, \, 1954\text{--}69$$

The results for the second half of the sample are

$$(4b) I_t^n/Y_t = -0.040 + 0.576 \, RN_{t-1} + 0.065 \, UCAP_{t-1} + 0.166 \, u_{t-1}$$
$$ (0.136) \qquad\qquad (0.022) \qquad\qquad (0.347)$$

$$\bar{R}^2 = 0.611, \, DWS = 1.79, \, 1970\text{--}84$$

The coefficient of RN is actually higher in each of the sample periods than it is for the overall period. In particular, the evidence for the most recent 15 years implies an effect that is nearly 40% stronger than for the entire sample.

The estimated coefficients are also quite insensitive to the use of the autocorrelation correction. When the equation is reestimated for the entire period by ordinary least squares, the coefficient of RN shifts only from the 0.41 value presented in equation (3) to 0.37. Even more reassuring are the estimates obtained when the basic specification is first-differenced:

$$(5) \quad \frac{I_t^n}{Y_t} - \frac{I_{t-1}^n}{Y_{t-1}} = 0.0004 + 0.422 \, (R_{t-1} - R_{t-2})$$
$$(0.126)$$

$$+ \, 0.022 \, (UCAP_{t-1} - UCAP_{t-2})$$
$$(0.022)$$

$$\bar{R}^2 = 0.317, \, DWS = 2.45, \, 1955\text{--}84$$

The stability of these parameter estimates is certainly very impressive, indicating that the investment–GNP ratio does respond to year-to-year variations in RN and UCAP and not just to the broad shifts in these variables.

We have also tested the simple lag structure of the basic specification and found that the implications about the effects of RN and UCAP are unchanged when more general lag structures are estimated. Equation

(6) shows that a second lagged value of RN is not statistically significant and that the sum of the 2 coefficients is increased only modestly above the coefficient of a single RN variable:

$$(6) \quad I^n_t/Y_t = -0.0002 + 0.351 \, RN_{t-1} + 0.156 \, RN_{t-2}$$
$$(0.126) \qquad\qquad (0.143)$$
$$+ \, 0.014 \, UCAP_{t-1} + 0.488 \, u_{t-1}$$
$$(0.033) \qquad\qquad (0.233)$$

$$\bar{R}^2 = 0.616, \ DWS = 1.84, \ 1955\text{–}84$$

This conclusion is confirmed when the lagged values of RN are replaced by a second-order polynomial distributed lag over 4 lagged values with no restriction on the final distributed lag coefficient. The sum of the lag coefficients is 0.419 with a standard error of 0.229. The lagged UCAP variable has a coefficient of 0.022 with a standard error of 0.037, and the $\bar{R}^2$ value is 0.624.

Additional lagged values of the capacity utilization variable are also insignificant and leave the coefficient of the RN variable essentially unchanged:

$$(7) \quad I^n_t/Y_t = -0.006 + 0.361 \, RN_{t-1} + 0.037 \, UCAP_{t-1}$$
$$(0.124) \qquad\qquad (0.028)$$
$$- \, 0.009 \, UCAP_{t-2} + 0.413 \, u_{t-1}$$
$$(0.022) \qquad\qquad (0.218)$$

$$\bar{R}^2 = 0.598, \ DWS = 1.96, \ 1955\text{–}84$$

More complex lag structures for UCAP, including polynomial distributed lags, confirmed this conclusion.

We also considered a variety of alternatives to capacity utilization. Substituting the unemployment rate among adult males left the coefficient of RN essentially unchanged (at 0.445 with a standard error of 0.112) but was itself insignificant (a coefficient of -0.020 with a standard error of 0.075). Substituting a distributed lag in the percentage change in real nonfarm business product (PCNFBP), as suggested by the traditional accelerator model, leaves the coefficient of RN essentially unchanged.

$$(8) \quad I_t/Y_t = 0.011 + 0.400 \, RN_{t-1} + 0.026 \, (PCNFBP)_{-1}$$
$$(0.126) \qquad\qquad (0.027)$$
$$+ \, 0.046 \, (PCNFBP)_{-2} + 0.034 \, (PCNFBP)_{-3}$$
$$(0.031) \qquad\qquad\qquad (0.028)$$
$$+ \, 0.011 \, (PCNFBP)_{-4} + 0.47 \, u_{-1}$$
$$(0.021) \qquad\qquad\quad (0.18)$$

$$\bar{R}^2 = 0.590, \ DWS = 1.97, \ 1954\text{–}84$$

Finally, we experimented with a number of possible additional variables including the ratio of cash flow to GNP, the rate of inflation, and a time trend. The coefficients of these variables were not significant, and the coefficient of the RN variable remained essentially unchanged. A typical example of this specification is presented in equation (9):

$$(9) \quad I_t^n/Y_t = -0.043 + 0.372 RN_{t-1} + 0.054\ UCAP_{t-1}$$
$$ (0.074) \qquad\qquad (0.028)$$
$$+ 0.106\ (\text{cash flow/GNP})_{t-1}$$
$$(0.194)$$
$$+ 0.00028\ \text{time} - 0.042\ u_{t-1}$$
$$(0.00021) \qquad\qquad (0.248)$$
$$\bar{R}^2 = 0.693\ \text{DWS} = 1.96,\ 1954\text{–}84$$

We have also reestimated the basic equation using the cyclically adjusted net return, RNA. This variable is constructed by calculating a regression equation relating the pretax profitability to the concurrent rate of capacity utilization and then calculating the pretax return that would have prevailed at a constant rate of capacity utilization. The effective tax rate is then applied to this cyclically adjusted pretax rate of return to obtain the cyclically adjusted net rate of return, RNA. The regression coefficient of this variable is essentially identical to the coefficient of RN in the basic estimate of equation (3):

$$(10) \quad I_t^n/Y_t = -0.025 + 0.416\ RNA_{t-1} + 0.048\ UCAP_{t-1}$$
$$ (0.118) \qquad\qquad (0.021)$$
$$+ 0.422\ u_{t-1}$$
$$(0.205)$$
$$\bar{R}^2 = 0.595,\ \text{DWS} = 1.95,\ 1954\text{–}84$$

Although our analysis focused on the net return after all taxes, we also estimated the basic equations using the rate of return after corporate taxes only. As we explained in section 4.2.1, the return after corporate taxes is the appropriate measure of the attractiveness of investing in nonfinancial corporate capital for tax-exempt investors like pension funds and for foreign investors. Looking at the return after the corporate tax is also appropriate to the extent that changes in personal tax rates have an equal effect on the net return to the competing investments. Equation (11) shows that variations in the rate of return after corporate taxes (RNC) have a slightly stronger effect on the investment–GNP ratio than the RN measure of the net return:

(11) $I_t^n/Y_t = -0.008 + 0.455 \text{ RNC}_{t-1} + 0.016 \text{ UCAP}_{t-1}$
           (0.104)   (0.024)
           $+ 0.276 u_{t-1}$
           (0.221)

$\bar{R}^2 = 0.632$, DWS $= 1.85$, 1954–84

The results with the cyclically adjusted measure of the real return net of corporate tax have almost the same coefficient of the net return variable but a stronger effect of the capacity utilization variable:

(12) $I_t^n/Y_t = -0.044 + 0.455 \text{ RNCA}_{t-1} + 0.061 \text{ UCAP}_{t-1}$
           (0.103)   (0.020)
           $+ 0.240 u_{t-1}$
           (0.222)

$\bar{R}^2 = 0.626$, DWS $= 1.87$, 1954–84

In both equations, the explanatory power ($\bar{R}^2$) is greater with the RNC variable than with the RN variable. Moreover, since the RNC and RNCA variables are about 40% larger on average than the corresponding RN variables, the elasticity of the investment–GNP ratio with respect to RNC is approximately 0.80.

Finally, we have estimated equations describing the rate of growth of the net capital stock, that is, replacing the ratio of investment to GNP with the ratio of investment to the net capital stock at the end of the preceding year. The results, shown in equation (13), are qualitatively very similar to the basic investment–GNP estimates of equation (3):

(13) $\dfrac{I_t^n}{K_{t-1}^n} = -0.21 + 0.608 \text{ RN}_{t-1} + 0.045 \text{ UCAP}_{t-1}$

           (0.121)   (0.032)

           $+ 0.138 u_{t-1}$

           (0.241)

$\bar{R}^2 = 0.682$, DWS $= 1.91$, 1954–84

The coefficient of RN is nearly 50% larger than the corresponding coefficient in the equations for the investment GNP ratio while the investment-capital ratio averages only about 30% larger than the investment–GNP ratio. Thus the elasticity of the investment-capital ratio with respect to RN, calculated at the mean investment-capital ratio (0.039) and the mean value of RN (0.038), is 0.59, or somewhat greater than the previously calculated elasticity of 0.52 of the investment–GNP ratio with respect to RN.

4.4   The Rate of Return over Cost and the Rate of Investment: Statistical Evidence

The second basic model that we discussed above and that was developed in Feldstein (1982) relates the investment–GNP ratio to the difference between the maximum potential net return on a standard investment project and the net cost of funds that firms face. This model is the operational extension to an economy with taxes of Irving Fisher's (1896, 1930) notion that investment depends on the difference between the marginal efficiency of capital (or the internal rate of return on an incremental investment) and the rate of interest.

In the standard textbook version of this theory, the firm faces a downward sloping marginal-efficiency-of-capital schedule and a horizontal rate-of-interest line. At the point where the two intersect, the firm has an optimal stock of capital. If, however, the marginal efficiency of capital exceeds the rate of interest, the firm has an incentive to invest. Adjustment costs limit the speed with which the firm closes the gap, but the volume of investment can be assumed to be an increasing function of the difference between the marginal efficiency of capital and the rate of interest.

In an economy with complex tax rules, the analog to the marginal efficiency of capital schedule depends on the tax rate, the depreciation rules and investment tax credits, and the rate of inflation, as well as on the pretax profitability of the available investment projects. Each point on the schedule represents the maximum net cost of funds that the firm can afford to pay to support that incremental project. We represent shifts in the level of this entire schedule by the maximum net cost of funds that the firm can afford to pay on a hypothetical "standard" project.

More explicitly, we derive the maximum potential net return (MPNR) on the assumption that the basic investment project is a "sandwich" of equipment and structures that lasts for 30 years and replicates the average mixture of equipment and structures in the capital stock of the nonfinancial corporate sector. The sandwich consists of an initial investment of $.33 of structures and $.33 of equipment. The output associated with the structures is assumed to decay exponentially at a rate of 3% a year; at the end of 34 years, the remaining structure is scrapped without value. The output associated with the equipment decays more rapidly, at 13% per year, and the equipment is scrapped without value at the end of 17 years. After 17 years, a new equipment investment is made with real value (in the prices of year 1) of $.33. This then decays in the same way as the initial equipment investment and is scrapped at the same time as the structure.

The net output values of the structure and equipment components are set for the first year of each project to satisfy 2 conditions. First, the overall pretax return on the investment sandwich is 10.3%, the average pretax return for the period from 1961 to 1984 (or at the pretax return of the current year in the varying profitability model). Second, the after-tax rates of return on the 2 types of capital are equal under the tax rules prevailing in the base period (chosen to be 1960). These conditions uniquely determine a path of net output that we shall denote x_t.

The MPNR is defined as the net rate of return that the firm can pay on the funds "borrowed" (as a loan or an infusion of equity capital) to finance an investment sandwich and can have "paid off" the initially invested funds by the end of the life of the project. More specifically, we consider a project that has annual pretax real net output of x_t per dollar of plant and equipment initially invested and nominal pretax net receipts of $p_t x_t$. The price level of the firm's net output is assumed to vary in proportion to the price level of the economy as a whole. The firm is allowed depreciation deductions for tax purposes of a_t and pays tax on nominal output less interest expenses and depreciation allowances at rate τ. The firm needs initial cash per dollar of the equipment investment equal to $1 minus the investment tax credit. Thereafter, the "loan" balance (L_t) is reduced by the project's after-tax income but grows by an annual amount equal to the product of the net cost of funds and the previous year's "loan" liability. The value of the rate of return on the "borrowed" funds that permits the "loan" to be just repaid when the project ends defines the maximum potential net return.[20]

The nominal MPNR is thus the value that satisfies the equation

$$(14) \qquad L_t = (1 + \text{MPNR})L_{t-1} - (1 - \tau)p_t x_t - \tau a_t$$

subject to the condition that $L_0 = 0.66$ minus the investment tax credit per dollar of equipment investment, that L_{1T} is increased by the net cost of the new equipment investment, and that the loan is repaid when the project is scrapped ($L_T = 0$).

An alternative measure of the MPNR is also calculated on the assumption that firms assume that the real pretax return on prospective investment projects varies from year to year and is equal to the average pretax return actually earned in that year on all nonfinancial corporate capital. This measure is denoted MPNRVP (where the last 2 letters denote varying profitability).

The net cost of funds is taken to be a weighted average of the costs of debt and equity funds. The cost of equity funds (e) is the ratio of adjusted economic earnings per share to the price per share.[21]

The gross cost of debt is the yield on newly issued high grade corporate bonds (i). The net cost of funds is thus

$$(15) \qquad \text{COF} = b(1 - \tau)i + (1 - b)e$$

where b is the proportion of investment financed by debt. We take b to be one-third, approximately the average value of the ratio of the market value of debt to the replacement value of the capital stock during the period 1960 to 1984. The annual values of the cost of funds and of its components are presented in table 4.8 (see Appendix B).

An estimated relation of the net investment–GNP ratio to the rate of return over cost (MPNR $-$ COF) and the rate of capacity utilization was presented in Feldstein (1982):

$$(16) \qquad I_t^n/Y_t = -0.040 + 0.316 \, (\text{MPRN} - \text{COF})_{t-1}$$
$$(0.066)$$
$$+ \, 0.073 \, \text{UCAP}_{t-1} + 0.70 \, u_{t-1}$$
$$(0.020) \qquad\qquad (0.17)$$
$$\bar{R}^2 = \; = 0.784, \, \text{DWS} = 1.79, \, 1955{-}77$$

It should be noted that MPNR $-$ COF $=$ MPRNR $-$ RCOF since MPRNR equals the MPNR minus the rate of inflation and RCOF equals the COF minus the rate of inflation.

Although there were substantial revisions in the national income account data and a number of significant improvements in the process of calculating the MPNR and COF variables, the reestimation of this equation with data for the quarter-century beginning in 1961 produced remarkably similar parameter estimates:

$$(17) \qquad I_t^n/Y_t = -0.044 + 0.313 \, (\text{MPNR} - \text{COF})_{t-1}$$
$$(0.169)$$
$$+ \, 0.086 \, \text{UCAP}_{t-1} + 0.350 \, u_{t-1}$$
$$(0.033) \qquad\qquad (0.286)$$
$$\bar{R}^2 = 0.510, \, \text{DWS} = 1.74, \, 1961{-}84$$

A strong test of this specification is obtained by splitting the return over cost variable into its 2 components. Equation (18) shows that the coefficients of the 2 components do have quite similar absolute values, as implied by the initial specification.

$$(18) \qquad I_t^n/Y_t = -0.012 + 0.294 \, \text{MPNR}_{t-1} - 0.394 \, \text{COF}_{t-1}$$
$$(0.172) \qquad\qquad (0.185)$$
$$+ \, 0.058 \, \text{UCAP}_{t-1} + 0.565 \, u_{t-1}$$
$$(0.033) \qquad\qquad (0.236)$$
$$\bar{R}^2 = 0.514, \, \text{DWS} = 1.78, \, 1961{-}84$$

A second type of evidence that indicates the robustness of the parameter estimates is the fact that very similar coefficients are obtained when the basic specification is estimated by ordinary least squares (i.e., without the first-order autoregressive transformation) or by first-differencing the data before estimation. In the ordinary least squares regression, the coefficient of the return over cost variable is 0.27 with a standard error of 0.15. When the data are first-differenced, the estimates are

$$(19) \quad \frac{I_t^n}{Y_t} - \frac{I_{t-1}^n}{Y_{t-1}} = 0.0005 + 0.333 \, [(MPNR - COF)_{t-1}$$

$$(0.175)$$

$$- (MPNR - COF)_{t-2}] + 0.072 \, [UCAP_{t-1}$$

$$(0.044)$$

$$- UCAP_{t-2}] - 0.177 \, u_{t-1}$$

$$(0.363)$$

$$\bar{R}^2 = 0.202, \, DWS = 1.94, \, 1962–84$$

Splitting the sample produced less satisfactory results, with too little information in each 12-year subperiod to permit accurate estimation of the key parameter values:

$$(20a) \quad I_t^n/Y_t = -0.083 + 0.035 \, (MPNR - COF)_{t-1}$$
$$(0.200)$$
$$+ 0.139 \, UCAP_{t-1} - 0.004 \, u_{t-1}$$
$$(0.042) \qquad\qquad (0.472)$$

$$\bar{R}^2 = 0.567, \, DWS = 1.56, \, 1961–72$$
$$SSR = 0.000222$$

and

$$(20b) \quad I_t^n/Y_t = -0.056 + 0.575 \, (MPNR - COF)_{t-1}$$
$$(0.325)$$
$$+ 0.094 \, UCAP_{t-1} + 0.280 \, u_{t-1}$$
$$(0.053) \qquad\qquad (0.458)$$

$$\bar{R}^2 = 0.248, \, DWS = 1.74, \, 1973–84$$
$$SSR = 0.000329$$

The point estimates imply that the rate of return over cost had a very small and insignificant effect in the first subperiod but a quite powerful effect in the second half of the sample. The coefficients of the capacity utilization variables are much closer to each other. However, a standard F-test shows that the coefficients in the 2 separate subsamples are not significantly different from each other. The sum of squared residuals for the single overall sample in 1961 through 1984 is 0.000609 while the sum of the 2 subsample sums of squared residuals is 0.000551; the resulting F-statistic is only 0.42 while the critical value at the 5% level with 16 and 4 degrees of freedom is 4.49. The difference in the coefficients in equations (20a) and (20b) should therefore only be interpreted as indicating that there is insufficient evidence in the separate subsamples to estimate separate coefficient values.

Different lag distributions did not alter the basic estimates or improve the explanatory power of the equation. Thus a second-order polynomial distributed lag on the coefficients of 4 lagged values of MPNR $-$ COF had coefficients that summed to 0.49 with a standard error of 0.42. Only the first of the coefficients was larger than its standard error; it had a value of 0.33 with a standard error of 0.17. With 2 lagged values for MPNR $-$ COF the estimated equation is

$$
(21) \quad I_t^n/Y_t = -0.047 + 0.291 \, (\text{MPNR} - \text{COF})_{t-1}
$$
$$
(0.178)
$$
$$
- 0.052 \, (\text{MPNR} - \text{COF})_{t-2}
$$
$$
(0.221)
$$
$$
+ 0.092 \, \text{UCAP}_{t-1} + 0.290 \, u_{t-1}
$$
$$
(0.039)
$$

$$
\bar{R}^2 = 0.480, \text{DWS} = 1.69, \, 1962\text{--}84
$$

The coefficient of the second MPNR $-$ COF variable is completely insignificant, and the coefficient of the first MPNR $-$ COF variable is very close to the value of 0.313 in the basic equation (17).

Several alternatives to the capacity utilization variable were also considered as different ways of measuring the impact of economic activity on investment. The unemployment rate for adult males (RUM 20 +) worked reasonably well as an alternative to capacity utilization but provided less overall explanatory power:

$$
(22) \quad I_t^n/Y_t = 0.034 + 0.443 \, (\text{MPNR} - \text{COF})_{t-1}
$$
$$
(0.190)
$$
$$
- 0.211 \, \text{RUM20}_{t-1} + 0.447 \, u_{t-1}
$$
$$
(0.115) \qquad\qquad (0.258)
$$

$$
\bar{R}^2 = 0.427, \text{DWS} = 1.66, \, 1961\text{--}84
$$

When a third-degree polynomial distributed lag over 4 annual values of the percentage change in nonfarm business output (with the final value unconstrained) is added to the basic specification, the capacity utilization variable continues to have a coefficient of 0.085 (with a standard error of 0.038) while none of the distributed lag coefficients is as large as its standard error; the sum of the distributed lag coefficients is 0.0010 with a standard error of 0.0014.

Including a variety of additional plausible variables in the equation has little effect on the coefficient of the return over cost variable. For example, the coefficients of the ratio of corporate cash flow to GNP and of a time trend are both insignificant:

$$(23) \quad I_t^n/Y_t = -0.056 + 0.293 \, (\text{MPNR} - \text{COF})_{t-1}$$
$$(0.181)$$
$$+ \, 0.091 \, \text{UCAP}_{t-1} + 0.00014 \, \text{time}$$
$$(0.075) \qquad\qquad (0.00056)$$
$$+ \, 0.051 \, (\text{cash flow/GNP})_{t-1} + 0.306 \, u_{t-1}$$
$$(0.457) \qquad\qquad\qquad (0.380)$$
$$\bar{R}_2 = 0.463, \, \text{DWS} = 1.82, \, 1961\text{--}84$$

In contrast to the MPNR variable that has been used in all the above equations, the MPNRVP variable assumes that firms adjust their assumed pretax rate of return from year to year in proportion to that year's actual pretax profitability of capital in the nonfinancial corporate sector. The standard deviation of the rather volatile MPNRVP − COF variable is twice as high for the period 1960 through 1984 as the standard deviation of the MPNR − COF variable. Moreover, as equation (24) shows, it is statistically insignificant and, when combined with the capacity utilization rate, provides a much less satisfactory explanation of the behavior of the investment–GNP ratio:

$$(24) \quad I_t^n/Y_t = -0.051 + 0.0005(\text{MPNRVP} - \text{COF})_{t-1}$$
$$(0.0008)$$
$$+ \, 0.095\text{UCAP}_{t-1} + 0.272 \, u_{t-1}$$
$$(0.046) \qquad\qquad (0.389)$$
$$\bar{R}^2 = 0.425, \, \text{DWS} = 1.63, \, 1961\text{--}84$$

Finally, we present an equation relating the growth of the net capital stock (i.e., the ratio of net investment to the net capital stock at the end of the previous year) to the basic rate-of-return-over-cost and capacity-utilization variables:

$$(25) \quad \frac{I_t^n}{K_{t-1}^n} = -0.068 + 0.482 \, (\text{MPNR} - \text{COF})_{t-1}$$
$$(0.234)$$
$$+ \, 0.122 \, \text{UCAP}_{t-1} + 0.351 \, u_{t-1}$$
$$(0.054) \qquad\qquad (0.323)$$
$$\bar{R}^2 = 0.555, \, \text{DWS} = 1.80, \, 1961\text{--}84$$

The coefficient of MPNR $-$ COF is some 60% larger than the corresponding coefficient in the equation for the investment–GNP ratio. Since the investment-capital ratio is about 30% greater than the investment–GNP ratio, the coefficient implies a more powerful effect of MPNR $-$ COF on the capital growth rate than on the investment–GNP ratio. Since a similar result was obtained with the real net return model, this method of specifying investment behavior deserves more careful examination in a future study.

4.5   Concluding Comments

The evidence presented in this paper confirms that tax-induced changes in the profitability of investment have had a powerful effect on the share of GNP devoted to net investment in nonresidential fixed capital and on the rate of growth of that net capital stock. More specifically, we have reestimated 2 very simple models of aggregate investment that were previously studied in Feldstein (1982). The present study extends the previous analysis by incorporating revised national income account estimates, by improving the estimation of the effective tax rate and the profitability of new investments, and by extending the sample to include the years 1978 through 1984, a period of very substantial changes in tax rules and sharp shifts in inflation and in the business cycle. Despite all these changes, the new statistical estimates are remarkably close to the previous results.

The statistical estimates imply that each percentage point increase in the real after-tax net return on capital in the nonfinancial corporate sector raises the ratio of net fixed nonresidential investment to GNP by 0.4 percentage points. Since the 22 percentage point decline in the effective tax rate paid by corporations and their shareholders and creditors between 1978–80 (just before the passage of the 1981 tax act) and 1983–84 (the most recent years for which data are available) implies a 1.8 percentage point rise in the real net return, the implied increase in the investment–GNP ratio is approximately 0.7 percentage points. Although it is inappropriate to treat the specific implications of these models as precise predictors of the impact of taxes in any particular short period, the predicted rise in the investment–GNP ratio accords quite well with the observed 0.6 percentage point increase. After taking into account the fall in capacity utilization over this same period, the analysis shows that virtually all the rise in the investment–GNP ratio appears to have been due to the reduction in effective tax rates that occurred because of the decline in inflation and in personal tax rates and to the accelerated depreciation of investment in plant and equipment.

A separate analysis that relates the investment–GNP ratio to the difference between the potential return on new investment and the cost of funds also shows the importance of changes in taxes as a cause of changes in the investment–GNP ratio over the past quarter-century. Each percentage point rise in the difference between the potential return on new investment and the cost of funds raises the predicted investment–GNP ratio by 0.3 percentage points. Between 1979–81 and 1984–85, the maximum potential real return on new investment rose by 1.3 percentage points, implying a 0.4% of GNP rise in investment.

Although this model is not as successful as the net return model in explaining year-to-year variations in the investment–GNP ratio in general, and the experience between 1980 and 1985 in particular, it does imply that changes in the return on new investment and in the cost of funds do have powerful effects on the investment–GNP ratio. It also shows that about two-thirds of the increase in investment that might have resulted from the improved after-tax profitability between 1978–80 and 1984 was offset by the rise in the cost of funds during the same period. All of this increase in the cost of funds was in the cost of debt. Therefore, to the extent that the increase in expected budget deficits caused the rise in interest rates, it had the effect of offsetting a large part of the increased incentive to invest that resulted from the change in tax rules.

The 3 alternative models of investment behavior all imply that the types of tax changes proposed by the Reagan administration or passed by the House of Representatives would significantly depress the ratio of investment to GNP. Depending on the particular statistical specification, the Administration proposal would reduce the investment–GNP ratio by between 20% and 40% of the increase experienced between 1979–81 (before the 1981 change in tax rules) and 1984–85. The bill passed by the House of Representatives would reduce investment by substantially more.

A high priority now is to reestimate the analysis of this paper with the revised national income and product account data released in December 1985. It is also possible to extend the present analysis in a number of ways. The relation between investment and the net return after corporate taxes but before personal and other portfolio taxes should be analyzed further. Additional attention should also be given to analyzing the rate of growth of the net capital stock as well as or instead of the investment–GNP ratio. The process of replacement and modernization investment also deserves more explicit analysis in this framework. The flexible accelerator models of Jorgenson (1963) and Hall and Jorgenson (1967) and the marginal -q models of Abel (1984), Summers (1981), and Hayashi (1982) should also be estimated.[22] Finally, a disaggregation of investment by types of assets and by industry may also improve our understanding of the investment process and of the impact of changes in tax rules.

Appendix A
The Pretax Rate of Return and Effective Tax Rates

This appendix presents annual data for 1953 through 1984 on the investment rate, capacity utilization, pretax and net-of-tax rates of return, and effective tax rates. Our procedures for estimating these magnitudes from data published by the Commerce Department, the Federal Reserve Board, and the Internal Revenue Service are described.

Our method follows the procedure used in Feldstein, Poterba, and Dicks-Mireaux (1983) but makes some modifications that we believe provide better estimates of both the pretax return and effective tax rates. The calculations use the most recent data available in the fall of 1985. This means that the December 1985 benchmark revisions of the national income and product accounts and the subsequent changes adopted by the Federal Reserve Board for the flow of funds accounts are not incorporated.

All of our estimates of the pretax rate of return and of the effective tax rates are for nonfinancial corporations. Nonresidential fixed investment includes all sectors of the economy. The capacity utilization measure is the Federal Reserve Board's estimate for the manufacturing industries.

The columns of table 4.4 present the following annual values: column 1, the ratio of net investment in nonresidential fixed capital to gross national product; column 2, the ratio of net investment in nonresidential fixed capital to the net stock of nonresidential fixed capital at the end of the previous year; column 3, the capacity utilization rate in manufacturing industry; column 4, the pretax real rate of return on capital in the nonfinancial corporate sector; column 5, the real rate of return on capital in the nonfinancial corporate sector after all taxes paid by corporations, their shareholders, and their creditors; column 6, the real rate of return on capital in the nonfinancial corporate sector after all taxes paid by corporations; column 7, the cyclically adjusted real rate of return on capital in the nonfinancial corporate sector after all taxes; and column 8, the cyclically adjusted real rate of return on capital in the nonfinancial corporate sector after all corporate taxes. The first 2 series are calculated directly from data published by the Commerce Department. The data in column 3 are published by the Federal Reserve

Table 4.4   Investment and the Real Net Rate of Return

Year	Investment–GNP Ratio (I_n/Y) (1)	Growth of Capital Stock (I_n/K^r_{t-1}) (2)	Capacity Utilization (UCAP) (3)	Pretax Real Return (R) (4)	Net Rate of Return		Cyclically Adjusted Return	
					After All Taxes (RN) (5)	After Corporate Taxes (RNC) (6)	After All Taxes (RNA) (7)	After Corporate Taxes (RNCA) (8)
1953	0.028	0.041	0.893	0.114	0.031	0.043	0.027	0.038
1954	0.024	0.033	0.801	0.105	0.032	0.045	0.033	0.046
1955	0.029	0.041	0.870	0.129	0.043	0.058	0.040	0.054
1956	0.031	0.044	0.862	0.110	0.030	0.045	0.028	0.042
1957	0.030	0.041	0.836	0.102	0.031	0.044	0.030	0.042
1958	0.018	0.023	0.750	0.089	0.028	0.040	0.032	0.045
1959	0.021	0.029	0.817	0.102	0.038	0.051	0.038	0.051
1960	0.024	0.032	0.802	0.102	0.036	0.048	0.037	0.049
1961	0.021	0.028	0.773	0.103	0.037	0.049	0.040	0.053
1962	0.025	0.034	0.814	0.116	0.047	0.061	0.047	0.061
1963	0.026	0.035	0.835	0.125	0.052	0.067	0.051	0.065

1964	0.031	0.043	0.857	0.134	0.060	0.075	0.057	0.071
1965	0.042	0.059	0.896	0.146	0.068	0.084	0.062	0.076
1966	0.047	0.066	0.911	0.144	0.065	0.082	0.057	0.072
1967	0.040	0.054	0.868	0.131	0.059	0.075	0.055	0.070
1968	0.039	0.051	0.870	0.130	0.050	0.069	0.047	0.064
1969	0.041	0.053	0.867	0.116	0.039	0.059	0.036	0.055
1970	0.035	0.043	0.792	0.095	0.031	0.049	0.032	0.051
1971	0.029	0.036	0.774	0.102	0.036	0.054	0.039	0.059
1972	0.031	0.039	0.828	0.108	0.041	0.059	0.040	0.058
1973	0.040	0.051	0.870	0.105	0.036	0.055	0.033	0.050
1974	0.035	0.042	0.826	0.080	0.012	0.035	0.012	0.035
1975	0.019	0.021	0.723	0.086	0.027	0.047	0.033	0.056
1976	0.020	0.023	0.774	0.095	0.033	0.050	0.036	0.054
1977	0.027	0.032	0.815	0.099	0.035	0.055	0.035	0.055
1978	0.034	0.042	0.842	0.095	0.032	0.052	0.031	0.050
1979	0.037	0.045	0.846	0.082	0.026	0.044	0.025	0.042
1980	0.030	0.035	0.793	0.070	0.019	0.037	0.021	0.040
1981	0.032	0.036	0.783	0.077	0.029	0.047	0.032	0.052
1982	0.023	0.025	0.703	0.067	0.030	0.045	0.040	0.059
1983	0.022	0.025	0.740	0.080	0.041	0.054	0.048	0.064
1984	0.037	0.046	0.808	0.099	0.054	0.070	0.056	0.071

Board. The method of calculating the remaining columns is discussed in the remainder of this appendix.

The Pretax Rate of Return

The pretax rate of return is calculated as the ratio of the total pretax capital income of the nonfinancial corporate sector to the replacement value of that capital stock including fixed capital, land, and inventories. The Federal Reserve Board's *Balance Sheets for the United States, 1945–84* presents year-end values for these components. We average values for the end of the previous year and the end of the current year to obtain an average value of the capital stock during the year. These capital stock values are reported in column 1 of table 4.5.

The pretax capital income of the nonfinancial corporate sector consists of four basic components: (1) corporate profits with the capital consumption adjustment and inventory valuation adjustment; (2) net interest paid by the corporations; (3) the property taxes paid to state and local governments; and (4) the inflation-induced changes in the value of the net financial liabilities of the nonfinancial corporations other than the liabilities to those who are providers of capital to the corporations. Each of these components will now be explained and the time series presented in table 4.5.

Corporate profits with the capital consumption adjustment and inventory valuation adjustment are the basic data provided by the Department of Commerce as their national income account measure of the inflation-adjusted pretax profits. This series is presented in column 2 of table 4.5.

Since we want the return to all providers of capital, we must add to these profits the net interest payments of nonfinancial corporations. These data are also from the national income accounts. Note that these are nominal interest payments since any inflation-induced loss to the creditors is a gain to the equity owners and leaves total real capital income unchanged. The net interest payments are shown in column 3 of table 4.5.

The Commerce Department treats state and local property taxes as a cost of production rather than a tax on capital. We therefore add this tax to the other components of capital income to obtain a more correct estimate of the return to capital. Since data are not available on the state and local property tax paid by nonfinancial corporations, we estimate that the ratio of these taxes to all state and local property taxes is the same as the ratio of the fixed capital of nonfinancial corporations to the total fixed capital of the private sector other than the nonprofit sector. This method is subject to a variety of potential biases since it (1) assumes that nonfinancial corporate capital and other capital are

Table 4.5		The Pretax Rate of Return on Nonfinancial Corporate Capital (in billions of dollars)				
Year	Capital Stock (1)	Corporate Profits with CCA and IVA (2)	Net Interest Paid (3)	State and Local Property Taxes (4)	Inflation Gain on Miscellaneous Net Liabilities (5)	Total Capital Income (6)	Real Pretax Rate of Return (7)
1953	299.427	—	1.275	2.823	−0.084	34.063	0.114
1954	310.174	—	1.550	2.994	−0.509	32.585	0.105
1955	328.526	—	1.600	3.216	−0.826	42.440	0.129
1956	362.339	—	1.750	3.568	−1.175	39.892	0.110
1957	393.023	—	2.175	3.970	−0.780	40.215	0.102
1958	409.466	—	2.700	4.286	−0.534	36.577	0.089
1959	425.132	40.125	3.125	4.506	−0.832	46.924	0.110
1960	442.201	37.350	3.475	4.843	−0.524	45.143	0.102
1961	455.687	38.250	3.925	5.143	−0.059	46.959	0.103
1962	472.839	45.575	4.525	5.527	−0.755	54.873	0.116
1963	491.374	51.250	4.775	5.955	−0.556	61.425	0.125
1964	512.545	57.700	5.275	6.395	−0.536	68.834	0.134
1965	546.146	67.700	6.050	6.921	−0.952	79.719	0.146
1966	595.641	72.150	7.375	7.488	−1.380	85.633	0.144
1967	650.105	68.825	8.750	8.414	−1.100	84.889	0.131
1968	701.417	73.225	10.075	9.387	−1.723	90.964	0.130
1969	765.263	67.475	13.100	10.342	−1.989	88.928	0.116

(continued)

Table 4.5 (continued)

Year	Capital Stock (1)	Corporate Profits with CCA and IVA (2)	Net Interest Paid (3)	State and Local Property Taxes (4)	Inflation Gain on Miscellaneous Net Liabilities (5)	Total Capital Income (6)	Real Pretax Rate of Return (7)
1970	837.431	52.675	16.975	11.826	−1.749	79.727	0.095
1971	898.534	62.150	18.000	13.118	−1.747	91.521	0.102
1972	963.715	72.700	19.075	13.781	−1.750	103.807	0.108
1973	1,075.446	78.625	23.025	14.431	−2.845	113.236	0.105
1974	1,289.332	63.575	29.650	15.528	−5.818	102.935	0.080
1975	1,481.256	86.075	30.800	17.340	−6.151	128.064	0.086
1976	1,597.678	107.275	29.550	18.622	−4.158	151.289	0.095
1977	1,761.203	129.475	32.125	19.472	−5.919	175.154	0.099
1978	1,984.841	142.050	36.875	18.726	−8.788	188.864	0.095
1979	2,276.362	134.700	43.900	18.412	−9.339	187.673	0.082
1980	2,611.250	120.275	56.275	19.566	−12.919	183.197	0.070
1981	2,937.722	147.450	67.375	22.071	−11.546	225.350	0.077
1982	3,152.104	118.075	72.300	24.730	−5.448	209.657	0.067
1983	3,262.572	170.950	69.00	26.669	−4.991	261.628	0.080
1984	3,417.042	234.700	79.500	28.895	−5.207	337.888	0.099

taxed at the same effective rates, probably causing an understatement of the tax on nonfinancial corporations; (2) ignores the tax on inventories, causing a further understatement; but (3) ignores the tax that some states levy on consumer durables, which offsets some of the downward bias. The estimated tax is shown in column 4 of table 4.5.

The final adjustment is for the corporations' inflation-induced gains and losses on financial assets and liabilities which are appropriately excluded from the net capital provided to the nonfinancial corporate sector by individuals and other portfolio investors. The net loss of the nonfinancial corporations is equal to the inflation rate multiplied by the sum of (1) the outstanding net trade credit (a nominal asset of the nonfinancial corporations), (2) federal government securities less net amounts owed to the federal government; and (3) state and local government securities less net amounts owed to these governments. Unfortunately, currency is not reported and therefore cannot be included. The inflation rate is computed as the fourth quarter to fourth quarter change in the GNP deflator, and the financial assets and liabilities are estimated as the average of the values for the end of the year and the end of the previous year. The net gain is shown in column 5 of table 4.5.

Adding all these together gives the total income produced by the capital of the nonfinancial corporate sector. This is shown in column 6 of table 4.5.

Dividing the total capital income by the capital stock of column 1 yields the pretax real return shown in column 7 of table 4.5.

The Effective Tax Rates

The tax on the capital income of the nonfinancial corporate sector includes the taxes paid by the corporations themselves (to the federal government and to state and local governments) and the taxes paid by those who receive dividend income, interest income, and capital gains. Since we are interested in deriving the overall effective tax rate on this capital income rather than tax rates on each component, we shall express each component of the overall tax rate as a proportion of the pretax capital income shown in column 6 of table 4.5. Some intermediate effective tax rates used in the calculation are shown in table 4.5.

The federal corporate tax payments as a proportion of pretax capital income are shown in column 1 of table 4.6. The corresponding state and local corporate tax payments are shown in column 2. The state and local property taxes discussed above and presented in column 4 of table 4.4 are expressed as a fraction of the pretax capital income in column 3 of table 4.5. Adding together these 3 columns gives the total taxes paid by the corporations themselves as a fraction of their pretax capital income. This figure is presented in column 4 of table 4.6.

Table 4.6   Components of the Effective Tax Rate on the Capital Income of Nonfinancial Corporations

Year	Federal Corporate Tax (1)	State and Local Corporate Tax (2)	State and Local Property Tax (3)	Total Tax at Corporate Level (4)	Tax on Dividends (5)	Tax on Real Capital Gains (6)	Tax on Nominal Capital Gains (7)	Tax on Interest (8)	Total Effective Tax Rate (9)
1953	0.521	0.022	0.083	0.626	0.086	0.006	0.003	0.010	0.732
1954	0.459	0.021	0.092	0.572	0.090	0.009	0.008	0.013	0.692
1955	0.457	0.021	0.076	0.554	0.080	0.013	0.011	0.010	0.668
1956	0.478	0.024	0.089	0.591	0.091	0.010	0.025	0.012	0.729
1957	0.452	0.023	0.099	0.573	0.091	0.009	0.011	0.016	0.700
1958	0.417	0.023	0.117	0.557	0.099	0.007	0.001	0.021	0.686
1959	0.420	0.022	0.096	0.538	0.082	0.011	0.003	0.019	0.654
1960	0.401	0.023	0.107	0.532	0.088	0.009	0.001	0.022	0.651
1961	0.390	0.023	0.110	0.523	0.086	0.009	0.001	0.024	0.643
1962	0.353	0.024	0.101	0.477	0.077	0.013	0.003	0.024	0.594
1963	0.347	0.023	0.097	0.468	0.077	0.013	0.001	0.022	0.581
1964	0.325	0.023	0.093	0.441	0.068	0.015	0.005	0.021	0.550
1965	0.319	0.022	0.087	0.428	0.064	0.016	0.005	0.020	0.533

1966	0.322	0.023	0.087	0.432	0.065	0.017	0.014	0.024	0.551
1967	0.302	0.025	0.099	0.425	0.070	0.015	0.010	0.029	0.550
1968	0.338	0.029	0.103	0.470	0.074	0.014	0.018	0.035	0.611
1969	0.341	0.032	0.116	0.489	0.074	0.018	0.034	0.048	0.662
1970	0.304	0.035	0.148	0.487	0.079	0.013	0.030	0.069	0.678
1971	0.290	0.035	0.143	0.468	0.068	0.016	0.033	0.061	0.647
1972	0.284	0.039	0.133	0.456	0.063	0.017	0.026	0.056	0.619
1973	0.311	0.042	0.127	0.480	0.059	0.019	0.037	0.062	0.658
1974	0.357	0.051	0.151	0.559	0.067	0.015	0.117	0.092	0.850
1975	0.277	0.045	0.135	0.458	0.065	0.018	0.065	0.079	0.684
1976	0.298	0.051	0.123	0.471	0.066	0.015	0.036	0.063	0.652
1977	0.288	0.052	0.111	0.451	0.063	0.020	0.057	0.058	0.648
1978	0.304	0.051	0.099	0.453	0.069	0.022	0.057	0.062	0.663
1979	0.312	0.056	0.098	0.467	0.076	0.013	0.051	0.074	0.682
1980	0.303	0.062	0.107	0.473	0.086	0.011	0.052	0.105	0.726
1981	0.230	0.054	0.098	0.381	0.085	0.011	0.037	0.107	0.622
1982	0.162	0.049	0.118	0.329	0.082	0.006	0.008	0.121	0.547
1983	0.175	0.047	0.102	0.324	0.068	0.010	0.005	0.086	0.492
1984	0.166	0.043	0.086	0.296	0.058	0.012	0.005	0.077	0.449

To estimate the tax on dividend income, we begin by using the Flow of Funds data on equity ownership to distribute dividends among classes of investors: individuals, nonprofit organizations, insurance companies, banks, pensions, and so forth. The largest class of investors is individuals, whom we assume account for 93% of the dividends received by the household sector. To obtain an effective tax rate on the dividends received by individuals, we have updated the series originally prepared by Brinner and Brooks (1981). The effective federal dividend tax is constructed as a weighted average of individual tax rates, using the fraction of dividends received each year by each income class and the corresponding statutory marginal tax rate. A state dividend tax series is calculated using the assumption that the net marginal tax rate on dividends is 1.5 times the average state personal tax rate implied by the national income account aggregates. Columns 1 and 2 of table 4.7 show the effective federal and state taxes on individual dividend income; these tax rates are expressed as percentages of dividend income. We further assume that dividends received by nonprofit organizations, pension funds, foreign equity owners, and other miscellaneous investors are untaxed. Insurance companies and banks pay a tax equal to 15% of the corporate tax rate. The appropriate weighted average of these tax rates is the effective tax rate on dividend income and is shown in column 3 of table 4.7. Multiplying this number by the total dividends paid by nonfinancial corporations and dividing by the pretax capital income of those corporations yields the tax on dividends as a proportion of pretax capital income; this component of the overall effective tax rate on pretax capital income is shown in column 5 of table 4.6.

The effective tax on capital gains also reflects the distribution of the ownership of corporate equity and the further fact that capital gains are only taxed when assets are sold. The distribution of equity ownership is again based on the Flow of Funds data on the distribution of dividends among different classes of investors and the Internal Revenue Service data on the distribution of dividend income among different income classes. For the sample years before 1969, individual capital gains were taxed when realized at half the individual's statutory rate on dividends but subject to an "alternative" maximum rate of 25%. For the years between 1969 and 1978, the effective tax rate on capital gains was raised in a number of ways: the use of the alternative tax was limited, the value of the loss-offset was reduced, the "untaxed" portion of capital gains was subject to a minimum tax, and the amount of ordinary income eligible for the maximum tax on personal services income was reduced in relation to the amount of the "untaxed" portion of realized capital gains. In 1978 legislation was passed that substantially reduced the effective tax on realized capital gains, and this happened again in 1985. Throughout all of the period, the principle was

Table 4.7   Effective Tax Rates on Selected Components of Capital Income

Year	Federal Tax on Dividends (1)	State Tax on Dividends (2)	Tax on Dividends (3)	Total Capital Gains (4)	Tax on Interest (5)	Tax Rate on Equity Capital Income	
						Corporate Taxes Not Imputed (6)	Corporate Taxes Imputed (7)
1953	0.437	0.018	0.398	0.050	0.279	0.749	0.675
1954	0.436	0.019	0.398	0.050	0.277	0.713	0.645
1955	0.444	0.020	0.404	0.049	0.278	0.683	0.615
1956	0.441	0.022	0.401	0.049	0.281	0.750	0.674
1957	0.431	0.023	0.392	0.049	0.289	0.724	0.650
1958	0.428	0.024	0.389	0.048	0.289	0.717	0.645
1959	0.425	0.026	0.386	0.048	0.292	0.680	0.606
1960	0.415	0.027	0.375	0.048	0.292	0.681	0.593
1961	0.424	0.029	0.382	0.048	0.292	0.676	0.589
1962	0.415	0.030	0.373	0.048	0.290	0.622	0.539
1963	0.417	0.031	0.374	0.048	0.288	0.606	0.517
1964	0.380	0.033	0.342	0.048	0.278	0.573	0.481
1965	0.364	0.033	0.327	0.047	0.270	0.555	0.460
1966	0.369	0.035	0.331	0.047	0.278	0.577	0.486
1967	0.378	0.038	0.339	0.047	0.285	0.580	0.491
1968	0.392	0.042	0.352	0.047	0.312	0.648	0.540

(continued)

Table 4.7 (continued)

Year	Federal Tax on Dividends (1)	State Tax on Dividends (2)	Tax on Dividends (3)	Total Capital Gains (4)	Tax on Interest (5)	Tax Rate on Equity Capital Income	
						Corporate Taxes Not Imputed (6)	Corporate Taxes Imputed (7)
1969	0.385	0.045	0.345	0.067	0.324	0.721	0.608
1970	0.383	0.048	0.339	0.067	0.323	0.773	0.653
1971	0.386	0.052	0.338	0.066	0.311	0.729	0.610
1972	0.378	0.059	0.327	0.065	0.306	0.690	0.572
1973	0.379	0.057	0.319	0.065	0.305	0.748	0.623
1974	0.393	0.057	0.323	0.064	0.319	1.066	0.940
1975	0.394	0.060	0.322	0.064	0.329	0.797	0.708
1976	0.407	0.063	0.333	0.064	0.321	0.732	0.638
1977	0.423	0.065	0.343	0.064	0.314	0.723	0.633
1978	0.431	0.065	0.346	0.064	0.316	0.747	0.655
1979	0.455	0.063	0.360	0.046	0.316	0.793	0.700
1980	0.453	0.065	0.359	0.045	0.342	0.897	0.810
1981	0.453	0.065	0.358	0.037	0.359	0.734	0.662
1982	0.373	0.068	0.301	0.037	0.352	0.649	0.572
1983	0.357	0.072	0.285	0.037	0.324	0.552	0.484
1984	0.339	0.071	0.275	0.037	0.329	0.486	0.416

maintained of taxing capital gains only when assets were sold and permitting a step-up in basis when assets were transferred at death.

It is not possible to provide an accurate evaluation of the appropriate weighted average tax rate on capital gains for every year in our sample. Instead, we make the conservative assumption that households paid an effective tax of only 5% on accruing capital gains for the years through 1968, 7.5% in 1969 through 1978, 5% in 1979 and 1980, and then 4% in 1981 through 1984. Banks and insurance companies are taxed at a 30% statutory rate on capital gains realizations. Because of the effect of deferral, we assume that this is equivalent to an effective 15% rate. We assume that all other equity holders pay no capital gains taxes. The overall effective tax rate on capital gains is shown in column 4 of table 4.7.

To translate this capital gains tax rate into taxes as a share of the total pretax income, we must estimate the annual value of capital gains. It is convenient to estimate 2 kinds of capital gains separately: the real gains and the nominal gains that result from inflation. To calculate the real capital gains, we combine the real retained earnings of nonfinancial corporations and the real inflation-induced gain that equity owners make at the expense of creditors. This inflation-induced gain is calculated as the product of the rise in the price level (the increase in the GNP deflator from the fourth quarter of the preceding year to the fourth quarter of the year in question) and the market value of the debt of nonfinancial corporations.[23] Multiplying this amount of real capital gains by the effective tax rate on capital gains and dividing the product by the total capital income of the nonfinancial corporate sector yields the real capital gains component of the overall effective tax rate shown in column 6 of table 4.6.

To calculate the additional nominal capital gain associated with the nominal increase in the value of corporate assets that results from a general rise in the price level, we abstract from the year-to-year fluctuations in stock market values and calculate the nominal rise in the replacement value of the capital stock.[24] To measure changes in the nominal value of the capital stock, we have constructed a price index for the tangible assets of nonfinancial corporations as a weighted average of the nonfarm business price deflator (for inventories) and the price deflator for gross domestic fixed investment. The fourth quarter to fourth quarter change in this price index is multiplied by the nominal value of the tangible assets to get the nominal increase in the value of the capital stock of the nonfinancial corporations. This nominal capital gain is multiplied by the effective tax rate on capital gains (column 4 of table 4.7) to obtain the nominal capital gains component of the overall effective tax rate shown in column 7 of table 4.6.

The final component of the effective tax rate is the tax paid on the interest received by the creditors of the nonfinancial corporations. We understate this tax rate by ignoring the state and local taxes on interest income. To obtain the federal effective tax rate on interest income, we calculate a weighted average of the tax rates of the different providers of debt capital to the nonfinancial corporations, using the fixed weights for 1976 derived from the Flow of Funds data by Feldstein and Summers (1979).[25] We follow the Feldstein-Summers procedure of setting the household tax rate on interest income at 35%, the mutual savings bank rate at 24%, and the rate for private pensions, government accounts, and "miscellaneous creditors" at zero. In computing the marginal tax rate for life insurance companies, we have followed Warshawsky (1982) in approximating the Menge formula by the product of the federal corporate statutory rate and the factor $0.15 + 8.5$ times the difference between the Baa corporate bond rate and the average interest rate assumed for life insurance reserves. Finally, for commercial banks we assume that two-thirds of the interest received is taxed at the statutory corporate tax rate while the remaining one-third avoids all corporate tax; the income net of corporate tax is then taxed at a weighted average of the dividend tax rate and the capital gains tax rate with weights reflecting the dividend payout rate of the banks. The combined effective tax rate on interest income is shown in column 5 of table 4.7. The product of this rate and the interest payments of the nonfinancial corporations divided by the total capital income of the nonfinancial corporations gives the interest component of the overall effective tax rate shown in column 8 of table 4.6. All of these numbers are combined in the final effective tax rate shown in column 9 of table 4.6.

As a matter of interest, we also calculate two alternative estimates of the effective tax rate on the equity income of nonfinancial corporations. The first of these is calculated on the assumption that the providers of debt capital bear only the tax that is levied on interest income, that is, the tax shown in column 8 of table 4.6. The second alternative assumes that the taxes paid by the corporations fall equally on debt and equity capital.

The first effective tax rate on equity capital income is therefore defined as the ratio of all taxes paid other than the tax on interest income to all capital income other than interest payments. Operationally, the numerator is the product of the total capital income (column 6 of table 4.5) and the difference between the total effective tax rate (column 9 of table 4.6) and the interest component of that tax rate (column 8 of table 4.5). The denominator is the difference between the total capital income (column 6 of table 4.5) and the interest paid to creditors (column 3 of table 4.5). The resulting effective tax rate on equity income is shown in column 6 of table 4.7.

The alternative procedure is to impute to the providers of debt capital a share of the taxes paid by the corporations (columns 1 through 3 of table 4.6) equal to the ratio of the market value of the debt to the replacement value of the capital stock. The numerator of the equity tax rate is then equal to the numerator described in the previous paragraph minus the imputed tax paid by creditors. The denominator is the same as before. The resulting effective tax rate on equity income with imputed corporate taxes is shown in column 7 of table 4.7.

Appendix B
The Maximum Potential Net Return and the Cost of Funds

Table 4.8 presents annual values of the basic variables used in the rate of return over cost models of section 4.4 and summarized and discussed in section 4.2.

Column 1 shows the maximum potential net return calculated according to the method described in section 4.4. The expected inflation series used in this calculation are derived by a "rolling" estimation of an ARIMA process (using only those data available as of each date), using the estimated coefficients to project inflation for the next 10 years, and calculating the weighted average of those inflation rates. These expected inflation rates are shown in column 2 of table 4.8.

The maximum potential real net return (MPRNR) is the difference between the MPNR value of column 1 and the expected inflation value of column 2. It is shown in column 3.

The MPNR value is calculated assuming a constant 10.3% real pretax return on capital of the nonfinancial corporations. The "varying profitability" alternative, MPNRVP, for each year is calculated with the assumption that the future pretax profitability will be the real pretax return on capital observed that year and shown in column 7 of table 4.5. Subtracting expected inflation from the MPNRVP yields the maximum potential real net return with varying profitability (MPRNRVP) series shown in column 4 of table 4.8.

The cost of funds to which the MPNR series is compared in evaluating the incentive to invest is a weighted average of the cost of equity capital and the net-of-tax cost of debt capital. We calculate the cost of equity capital as the ratio of adjusted earnings to the share price. The starting point of this calculation is the Standard and Poor's price-earnings ratio for industrial companies. We then multiply this by the ratio of estimated aggregate net-of-tax book earnings to estimated net aggregate

Table 4.8   The Maximum Potential Net Return and the Cost of Funds

Year	MPNR (1)	Expected Inflation (2)	MPRNR (3)	MPRNRVP (4)	Adjusted Earnings-Price Variable (5)	Interest Rate (6)	Corporate Tax Rate (7)	Cost of Funds (8)
1960	0.065	0.022	0.043	0.044	0.048	0.047	0.520	0.054
1961	0.064	0.021	0.043	0.048	0.044	0.044	0.520	0.050
1962	0.078	0.021	0.057	0.066	0.048	0.042	0.520	0.053
1963	0.077	0.020	0.057	0.069	0.055	0.052	0.520	0.057
1964	0.082	0.017	0.065	0.080	0.053	0.044	0.500	0.055
1965	0.083	0.016	0.067	0.087	0.055	0.045	0.480	0.055
1966	0.085	0.018	0.067	0.083	0.063	0.054	0.480	0.064
1967	0.073	0.021	0.052	0.064	0.062	0.058	0.480	0.066
1968	0.071	0.027	0.044	0.054	0.055	0.065	0.528	0.065
1969	0.085	0.033	0.052	0.055	0.058	0.077	0.528	0.072
1970	0.081	0.037	0.044	0.042	0.056	0.085	0.492	0.076
1971	0.084	0.040	0.044	0.049	0.052	0.074	0.480	0.074
1972	0.100	0.041	0.059	0.061	0.050	0.072	0.480	0.073
1973	0.103	0.045	0.058	0.053	0.057	0.077	0.480	0.081
1974	0.125	0.075	0.050	0.031	0.072	0.090	0.480	0.114
1975	0.148	0.097	0.051	0.052	0.072	0.090	0.480	0.128
1976	0.118	0.058	0.060	0.060	0.063	0.083	0.480	0.095
1977	0.120	0.060	0.060	0.057	0.071	0.081	0.480	0.101
1978	0.123	0.064	0.059	0.049	0.087	0.089	0.480	0.116
1979	0.131	0.070	0.061	0.040	0.089	0.099	0.460	0.123
1980	0.135	0.076	0.059	0.036	0.076	0.125	0.460	0.123
1981	0.152	0.080	0.072	0.055	0.080	0.150	0.460	0.133
1982	0.145	0.070	0.075	0.061	0.077	0.139	0.460	0.123
1983	0.131	0.056	0.075	0.068	0.066	0.116	0.460	0.102
1984	0.128	0.055	0.073	0.072	0.084	0.123	0.460	0.115

economic earnings. Net aggregate book earnings are derived from the national income account estimate of the net profits of nonfinancial corporations before the capital consumption adjustment and inventory valuation adjustment by adding the sum of (1) the tax rate times the acceleration component of the capital consumption allowance, plus (2) the difference between the investment tax credit and an average of the ITC of the past 10 years. Aggregate economic earnings are derived from the national income account estimate of the profits of nonfinancial corporations after the capital consumption adjustment and inventory valuation adjustment by adding an estimate of the gain that equity owners make at the expense of creditors (referred to in connection with column 6 of table 4.6) and the gain made on miscellaneous net liabilities (column 5 of table 4.5). The resulting adjusted earnings price ratio is presented in column 5 of table 4.8.

The gross cost of debt funds is represented by the interest rate on high grade corporate bonds calculated by Data Resources, Inc. This is shown in column 6 of table 4.8.

Because the MPNR and MPRNR variables are net concepts, the cost of funds must also be measured as a net of the corporate tax deduction for interest expenses. Column 7 is the statutory corporate tax rate against which interest expenses are deducted.

The nominal cost of funds is defined as a weighted average of the nominal cost of equity capital (the earnings price ratio of column 5 plus the expected inflation rate of column 2) and the nominal net cost of debt capital (the product of the interest rate of column 6 and the 1 minus the corporate tax rate of column 7) with a weight of one-third on debt and two-thirds on equity. The resulting cost of funds variable is presented in column 8 of table 4.8.

Notes

1. A similar measure of the combined corporate-personal tax burden was first derived by Feldstein and Summers (1979) and is updated in Appendix A on the basis of revised data and an improved procedure.

2. Feldstein (1983) contains several papers that discuss this interaction of inflation, tax rules, and capital formation.

3. *The Budget of the United States for Fiscal Year 1986* projected corporate tax receipts of $99 billion in 1988 under current law and indicated that the original ERTA provisions would, on the basis of 1985 economic projections, have reduced 1988 corporate receipts by $55 billion. See pages 4-2 and 4-7 of Office of Management and Budget (1985).

4. This assumes a 4% real discount rate. With a 10% real discount rate, the corresponding present value rises from 41.8 cents to 45.2 cents. With the slower depreciation rules of the pre–ERTA tax law, the increases are greater: from

41.2 cents to 46.2 cents with a 4% real discount rate and from 37.2 cents to 41.2 cents with a 10% real discount rate. These figures are taken from *The Economic Report of the President for 1983*.

5. By contrast, the 1988 personal tax increases in TEFRA were only $19 billion, or 8% of the original ERTA personal tax reductions. These figures are from *The Budget of the United States for Fiscal Year 1986*.

6. The data in table 4.1 and all other data presented and used in this paper are based on the national income and product accounts (NIPA) that became available in the fall of 1985. The December 1985 benchmark revisions of the NIPA are not reflected in any of the current analysis since information on the net capital stock, net investment, and other key variables was not available by the end of 1985. The data for 1985 refer to only the first 3 quarters of the year since data for the fourth quarter is not available on the old NIPA basis.

7. There is substantial literature on replacement and modernization investment (see Feldstein and Rothschild 1974, Feldstein and Foot 1971, and the work cited therein). This specification of investment in terms of achieving a desired net capital stock has, of course, been characteristic of most modern econometric research on investment; see, for example, Jorgenson (1963), Hall and Jorgenson (1967), Nickell (1978), Abel (1980, 1984), and Summers (1981).

8. Bosworth's analysis must be done in terms of gross investment because the Department of Commerce does not produce data on net investment in autos and computers.

9. The variable in column 2 is the Federal Reserve Board's measure of the capacity utilization rate in manufacturing industry. The more general total industry capacity utilization rate would in principle be a better variable for the present purpose but was never constructed for the years before 1967. Feldstein (1982) showed that additional variables measuring fluctuations in demand (e.g., past changes in sales, available retained earnings or cash flow, or the rate of unemployment) do not increase the explanatory power of investment equations of the type studied here when the manufacturing capacity utilization rate is already included. Similar evidence for the more recent sample is presented below.

10. Our calculation of the pretax return to capital follows the basic procedure of Feldstein, Poterba, and Dicks-Mireaux (1983), but several improvements have been made. More details are presented in Appendix A.

11. Recall that all variables in column 2 through 9 refer to 1 year earlier; thus the real net return reached 0.054 in 1984.

12. Note that comparing 1985 with 1979–81 shows a similar result. The investment–GNP ratio rose 0.8 percentage points while the equation predicts a rise of 1.0 percentage points.

13. The 5.3 percentage point decline and the estimated investment sensitivity of 0.02 together imply a decline of 0.1 percentage points in the investment–GNP ratio.

14. The projected increases in inflation are taken from Feldstein (1986) and are only available from 1960. The projected increases in inflation were calculated by estimating a first-order autoregressive moving average process, using it to project annual inflation for 10 future years, and then taking an average of those inflation rates.

15. This series of effective tax rates on interest income is presented in table 4.6 (see Appendix A).

16. On the case for studying such a simple model and for examining several alternative models rather than looking for the "true" model, see Feldstein (1982).

17. The maximum potential net return was introduced in Feldstein and Summers (1978) and used in Feldstein (1982) to explain investment behavior. A more formal description of the maximum potential net return is presented in section 4.4.

18. Note that the maximum potential net return that a firm can afford to pay is independent of its debt-equity ratio. In contrast, the returns the firm can afford to pay on debt and equity capital separately depend very much on the debt-equity mix.

19. The evidence in Feldstein (1986) indicates that the rise in anticipated budget deficits was the primary reason for the increase in real medium-term interest rates between 1979–81 and 1984. In particular, there is no evidence that the increase in the MPRNR raised interest rates.

20. Note that if the project were financed by debt, the MPNR would be the interest rate net of the tax deduction. If there are no taxes, the MPNR is the traditional internal rate of return. The maximum potential real net return is obtained by subtracting the expected inflation rate from the nominal MPNR value. Annual values of MPNR and MPRNR are presented in table 4.8 (see Appendix B).

21. The method of doing this adjustment and the adjusted data are presented in Appendix B.

22. We have done some preliminary analysis with a variety of alternative marginal q-models and find that a specification of marginal -q based on the potential profitability of investment provides a better explanation of past investment experience than the method used by Summers (1981).

23. This debt series has been estimated for the nonfinancial corporate sector and the total corporate sector and will be discussed in Feldstein and Jun (1986).

24. Because of nonneutral tax rules, a change in the rate of inflation changes the ratio of the stock market value to the nominal replacement value of the underlying assets but, with a persistent constant rate of inflation, the nominal stock market value should rise at the same rate as the nominal value of the underlying assets. See Feldstein (1980).

25. These weights are individuals, 0.082; mutual savings banks, 0.055; life insurance companies, 0.255; commercial banks, 0.427; all others, 0.181.

References

Abel, A. 1980. Empirical investment equations: An interpretive framework. Carnegie-Rochester Series on Public Policy. *Journal of Monetary Economics.*

———. 1984. A stochastic model of investment, marginal q, and the market value of the firm. NBER Working Paper no. 1484.

Bosworth, B. 1984. Taxes and the investment recovery. *Brookings Papers on Economic Activity.*

Brinner, R., and S. Brooks. 1981. Stock prices. In *How taxes affect economic behavior,* ed. H. Aaron and J. Pechman, 121–98. Washington: Brookings Institution.

Feldstein, M. 1980. Inflation and the stock market. *American Economic Review* 70, no. 5.

———. 1982. Inflation, tax rules and investment: Some econometric evidence. The 1980 Fischer-Schultz Lecture of the Econometric Society. *Econometrica* 50, no. 4.

————. 1983a. *Inflation, tax rules, and capital formation.* Chicago: University of Chicago Press.

————. 1983b. Has the rate of investment fallen? *Review of Economics and Statistics* 65, no. 1.

————. 1986. Budget deficits, tax rules and real interest rates. Forthcoming.

Feldstein, M., and D. Foot. 1971. The other half of gross investment: Replacement and modernization expenditures. *Review of Economics and Statistics* 53, no. 1.

Feldstein, M., and Joosung Jun. 1986. The market value of corporate debt and the changing debt-capital ratio. Forthcoming.

Feldstein, M., J. Poterba, and L. Dicks-Mireaux. 1983. The effective tax rate and the pretax rate of return. *Journal of Public Economics* 21, no. 2.

Feldstein, M., and M. Rothschild. 1974. Toward an economic theory of replacement investment. *Econometrica* 42, no. 3.

Feldstein, M., and L. Summers. 1978. Inflation tax rules and the long-term interest rate. *Brookings Papers on Economic Activity.*

————. 1979. Inflation and the taxation of capital income in the corporate sector. *National Tax Journal* 32, no. 4.

Fisher, I. 1896. Appreciation and interest. *Publications for the American Economic Association 2.*

————. 1930. *The theory of interest.* London: Macmillan.

Hall, R. E., and D. W. Jorgenson. 1967. Tax policy and investment behavior. *American Economic Review* 57:391–414.

Hayashi, F. 1982. Tobin's marginal q and average q: A neoclassical interpretation. *Econometrica.*

Jorgenson, D. 1963. Capital theory and investment behavior. *American Economic Review,* no. 53. pp. 247–59.

Nickell, S. 1978. *The investment decision of firms.* Cambridge Economic Handbooks. Cambridge: Cambridge University Press, and Welwyn: James Nisbet & Company.

Office of Management and Budget. 1985. *The budget of the United States for fiscal year 1986.* Washington: Government Printing Office.

Summers, L. 1981. Taxation and corporate investment: A q-theory approach. *Brookings Papers on Economic Activity.*

Warshawsky, M. 1982. Life insurance savings and the after-tax life insurance rate of return. NBER Working Paper no. 1040.

Comment   Roger H. Gordon

The objective of the Feldstein and Jun paper is to estimate the effect the Reagan tax changes had on the rate of corporate investment and to forecast what effect currently proposed tax changes might have on future rates of corporate investment. To do this, they use 2 alternative models of corporate investment, first presented in Feldstein (1982),

Roger H. Gordon is professor of economics at the University of Michigan in Ann Arbor and a research associate of the National Bureau of Economic Research.

which they reestimate using more recent data and a slightly different construction of the variables.

Attempting to estimate the numerical size of the effect of these recent tax changes on corporate investment is no simple task. Both the 1981 and 1982 tax changes were complex pieces of legislation. Together, they accelerated dramatically the schedule of depreciation deductions for both structures and equipment, though they also reduced the basis for depreciation of equipment by 5%. These changes should by themselves have increased the incentive to invest. However, this legislation also reduced personal tax rates substantially. For a given market interest rate, this reduction would have increased the rate of return available on alternative assets, thereby discouraging corporate investment. In fact, nominal market interest rates rose considerably at about the same time while the inflation rate dropped, thereby further increasing the required rate of return on corporate investment. The problem of measuring the net effect of these various changes on corporate investment rates is further complicated by the presence of a major recession during this period.

In order to estimate the effect of these tax changes on the rate of investment, Feldstein and Jun use 2 alternative empirical models of corporate investment. Each model has its strengths and weaknesses, and I will discuss each in turn.

The story underlying the first model is that the growth rate of corporate capital should depend positively on the net rate of return available on new investment in corporate capital. This net rate of return on new investment is approximated by the net of tax net of depreciation rate of return recently earned on existing corporate capital. The effect of the tax law is therefore summarized by the average tax rate on existing capital. Use of the average tax rate rather than a calculated marginal tax rate has some clear advantages. There are many special provisions in the tax law, and in the recent tax legislation, which affect particular industries or particular types of capital, but which are not taken into account in any of the standard measures of the marginal tax rate on capital. These special provisions would show up in the average tax rate. In addition, the lack of full loss offset in the tax law would show up in the average tax rate but is normally ignored in measures of the marginal tax rate.

Use of the average tax rate also has clear disadvantages, however. Consider how the incentive effects of the recent tax legislation would show up in the model. In the first year that the new depreciation and tax credit provisions are available, the average tax rate should not be affected since it is based on data from the previous year. In subsequent years, the average tax rate clearly would be affected by the new legislation but in proportion to the amount of new investment undertaken.

Given the strong autocorrelation in the time pattern of investment, this leads to a simultaneity bias and an overestimate of the effect of the new tax provisions.

In addition, even if this simultaneity were controlled for, the effects of the tax changes on the average tax rate should not necessarily approximate well their effects on the marginal tax rate. Consider 2 examples. The original Treasury I tax reform proposal recommended that depreciation deductions be based on much longer lifetimes but also be indexed to inflation. The present value of these deductions, depending on the discount rate used, would be close to comparable to those allowed under existing law. Yet the average tax rate in the years immediately following the new legislation should rise since the depreciation deductions taken then would be smaller than under the previous law. As a second example, consider the effects of reducing the statutory corporate tax rate as proposed in the House bill. Such a reduction would lead to a clear rise in the net of tax return earned on existing capital but may have quite different effects on the incentive to invest in new capital.[1]

While this first model may not adequately capture the effects of the new depreciation and tax credit provisions, it makes no attempt at all to capture the effects of the cut in personal tax rates and the changes in market interest rates and inflation rates on the rate of return required by investors on new corporate investments. There is no reason to presume these effects are small, so it is hard to place confidence in the forecasts of a model that ignores them.

Their second model is in many ways much more interesting. In this model, they assume that the rate of net investment depends on the difference between the marginal after-tax rate of return available on new capital investments and the rate of return, net of corporate taxes, required by investors in the firm.[2] Here, they explicitly attempt to calculate the required rate of return and so should be able to capture the effects of personal tax rate changes and the effects of changes in market interest rates. In addition, in this second model they focus on the marginal tax rate rather than the average tax rate and thereby avoid the various problems with the average tax rate described above.

This approach, although it is closely analogous to that used by Hall and Jorgenson (1967), differs in two key respects. First, Feldstein and Jun go to much greater effort to measure the required rate of return.

---

1. For example, if new investment in equipment is subsidized, then a cut in the statutory corporate tax rate should discourage such investment.

2. In a closed economy, one would need to worry as well about the determinants of the amount of savings being divided between alternative investments. If the economy is open, however, focusing just on relative rates of return would be appropriate.

While Hall and Jorgenson (1967) assumed that the required rate of return was 10% in all years, Feldstein and Jun attempt to measure explicitly the rate of return required on both the debt and equity issued to finance new investment. Also, while Hall and Jorgenson assume that the marginal product of capital depends on the existing capital-output ratio in the economy, Feldstein and Jun assume that the pretax marginal product of corporate capital is fixed and focus on the effects of the tax law. This assumption of a fixed pretax marginal product may have important implications if the model is used to forecast the long-run effect of tax changes on investment. However, it has a key advantage in that the estimated effects of the tax law on investment are not tied directly in the estimation to the effects of output changes on investment, as in Hall and Jorgenson (1967).

There are a variety of questions that can be raised about their implementation of this model, however. They approximate the required rate of return on corporate investments by a weighted average of the rates of return required on bonds and on equity. The key difficulty is measuring the rate of return required on equity. In principle, this rate of return should equal the after-tax risk-free rate of return that equity holders can earn elsewhere, plus a suitable risk premium, divided by 1 minus the effective personal tax rate on the return to equity. The problem is that the required risk premium cannot be measured with any accuracy.[3] The simplest procedure would be to assume that this risk premium is constant during the sample period, so that any movements in the required rate of return on investment arise from movements in the after-tax interest rate. Feldstein and Jun in fact attempt this in section 4.2.1 and find that with this specification taxes no longer have much relation to the investment rate.

Given the difficulties in measuring the risk premium directly, Feldstein and Jun instead approximate the required rate of return on equity by the earnings-price ratio then prevailing for corporate equity. The earnings-price ratio certainly should include a risk premium in it. The trouble is that it also should include a variety of additional factors. For example, as discussed above, after-tax earnings are affected by the investment rate and so are endogenous to the model. In addition, stock prices are a very good indicator of market expectations of future profitability. When expectations are optimistic, prices are high and the earnings-price ratio therefore is low. This low value does not result from a low required rate of return on new investment, however, and the close association between the investment rate and the cost of capital therefore may result from extraneous factors. Much more work is needed

3. For a discussion of the problems, see Merton (1980).

to judge whether the statistical success of this second model relative to one assuming a fixed risk premium results from these various biases rather than from the inclusion of an implicit measure of the risk premium.

An additional problem with their measure of the required rate of return is that they assume a fixed debt-equity ratio when constructing this measure rather than using the prevailing debt-equity ratio. To see how this can be a problem, consider a change in a firm's debt-equity ratio in a setting without taxes or bankruptcy. In this setting, an increase in a firm's debt-equity ratio means that the risk in the return to corporate capital is divided among fewer shares of equity, making each share riskier. Given the assumptions, the required return on corporate capital should not change, even though the observed earnings-price ratio would have increased. However, Feldstein and Jun would estimate an increase in the required rate of return. Therefore, they would overestimate the required return during periods when debt-equity ratios are high, as in the 1970s, which was also a period when investment rates were low.

I also have a few questions about the procedure they use to calculate the rate of return that could be earned on new corporate investment. To begin with, they implicitly calculate the present value of depreciation deductions allowed by the tax law using as a discount rate the calculated nominal rate of return on new corporate investment. However, the stream of income from depreciation deductions has essentially no nominal risk and so ought to be discounted at the rate of return available to the corporation on nominally risk-free investments—the after-corporate-tax interest rate. With this change, the estimated available rate of return on corporate investments should be much less sensitive to changes in the depreciation schedule in the tax law, and it should also be less sensitive to changes in the inflation rate.

The final part of the paper I would like to discuss is the procedure they use to forecast the effects of recently proposed tax changes. In forecasting the effects of enacting the Administration's proposals or enacting the House bill, Feldstein and Jun assume that the required rate of return would be unaffected. However, there are a variety of reasons to expect that this required rate of return would increase as a result of these tax changes. To begin with, the drop in personal tax rates should lead to an increase in the rate of return that equity holders can get elsewhere and so an increase in the rate of return that they would require on new equity investments. In addition, the proposed drop in the corporate tax rate implies that a larger fraction of the random fluctuations in the return to corporate investments would be borne by equity holders rather than passed on to the government. Since equity holders would be bearing a larger fraction of the risk, the risk premium per dollar invested ought to increase, again raising the required rate of return on new investments. Taking into account these increases in the required rate of return would strengthen Feldstein's and Jun's forecast that these tax changes would reduce the rate of corporate investment.

One further problem in forecasting the effects of tax changes on future investment rates is taking into account market expectations of future changes in the tax law. As Lucas (1976) argued, if tax changes are viewed to be temporary, the investment rate should react much more quickly to tax changes.[4] Forecasting the long-run changes in the capital stock based on observed or estimated short-run responses is very difficult. Since these long-run effects are of much more interest for tax analysis than the size of the short-run response, these complications cannot be avoided.

In summary, Feldstein and Jun have provided intriguing and dramatic evidence on the possible effects of recent and proposed tax changes on the rate of corporate investment. However, it seems premature to conclude anything with confidence about the empirical size of the effects of these tax changes on the rate of investment.

References

Auerbach, A. and J. R. Hines, Jr. 1986. Anticipated tax changes and the timing of investment. Mimeo.

Feldstein, M. 1982. Inflation, tax rules and investment: Some econometric evidence. *Econometrica* 50.

Hall, R. E., and D. W. Jorgenson. 1967. Tax policy and investment behavior. *American Economic Review* 57:391–414.

Lucas, R. E. 1976. Econometric policy evaluation: A critique. *Journal of Monetary Economics*.

Merton, R. C. 1980. On estimating the expected return on the market: An exploratory investigation. *Journal of Financial Economics* 8:323–61.

4. For estimates of the effects of these expectations on effective tax rates, see Auerbach and Hines (1986).

5 Anticipated Tax Changes and the Timing of Investment

Alan J. Auerbach and James R. Hines, Jr.

Since 1981, important changes in the federal tax provisions affecting investment in business plant and equipment have occurred in every year except 1983. There is no reason to believe that 1986 will be another exception. Yet the methods economists commonly use to measure the impacts of tax law changes not only generally assume that such changes will be permanent but also ignore problems of transition. Such analysis can be valuable for understanding the underlying differences among alternative tax systems, but may be unhelpful, even misleading, if one is attempting to understand the short-run impact on investment of a tax change that may have been anticipated and may be foreseen as temporary.

The purpose of this chapter is to present and use a framework for tax analysis that is closely related to previous approaches but capable of assessing the short-run impact on investment of very complicated combinations of tax policies undertaken at specified dates with different degrees of anticipation on the part of investors. At the same time, the model generates predictions about the impact of these changes on the market value of corporate securities that are consistent with the predicted path of investment.

Because the model's parameters are based on empirical evidence for the United States, its predictions are not simply illustrative, but should convey an impression of the actual quantitative effects of tax policy

Alan J. Auerbach is professor of economics at the University of Pennsylvania and a research associate of the National Bureau of Economic Research. James R. Hines, Jr., is assistant professor of economics and public affairs at the Woodrow Wilson School, Princeton University and a faculty research fellow at the National Bureau of Economic Research.

We are grateful to Andrew Abel for helpful comments and to the Sloan Foundation for financial support.

163

changes. Because it is a historical model, based on data beginning in 1953, it also allows us to perform counterfactual experiments to estimate the effects of historical policies. Thus, we can (and do) evaluate the performance of the activist tax policy of the last three decades in altering the level and stability of investment over that period.

Another primary objective, however, concerns the future. In the past couple of years, numerous tax reform plans have surfaced that would make important changes in the incentives for business fixed investment. Most would rationalize the treatment of depreciation for different types of assets, remove the investment tax credit, and compensate, at least in part, for the reduction in these investment incentives through reductions in the statuary corporate tax rate. Among the most influential such plans have been the Bradley-Gephardt "Fair Tax" (originally formulated in 1983), the first and second Treasury plans (introduced in November 1984 and May 1985), and the Rostenkowski plan formulated by the House Ways and Means Committee and passed by the full House in January 1986.

Each of these plans has been greeted with mixed but predominantly negative responses from the business community, the primary criticism being that they would reduce investment. The analysis below evaluates these criticisms by estimating the marginal effects of several of the proposals on the level and distribution of investment and on the value of the stock market. An interesting point that surfaces in this analysis is that, even to the extent that such plans may harm investment, they should be very beneficial for the value of corporate equity. It is thus somewhat ironic that they should be so vehemently opposed by many of those who would appear to benefit.

Before turning to these results we describe the model used in this paper, based on that developed in Auerbach and Hines (1986), and the choice of parameter values used for the simulations.

5.1 Modeling Investment Behavior

The model of investment used in this chapter assumes that there are two types of fixed investment (structures and equipment) and costs to adjusting the capital stock. These costs may be separate or mutual and may differ between structures and equipment. It is, in other words, a q investment model with two types of capital. We choose this level of aggregation to allow comparability with previous work, and because the greatest variation in tax treatment has historically been between these two broad classes of assets.

Consistent with the data, ours is a discrete time model with one-year intervals. Each capital good is assumed to decay exponentially, and the representative competitive firm produces its output using labor and the two types of capital subject to a constant returns to scale, Cobb-Douglas production function, with α_1 and α_2 representing the gross shares (including depreciation) of the equipment and structures, respectively, in production. The adjustment cost function is assumed to have the following form:[1]

(1) $$A(I_t) = \tfrac{1}{2}[\beta_0(I_t/K_{t-1})^2 K_{t-1}$$
$$+ \beta_1(I_{1t}/K_{1t-1})^2 K_{1t-1} + \beta_2(I_{2t}/K_{2t-1})^2 K_{2t-1}]$$

where I_{it} and K_{it} are net investment and capital of type i in year t, I_t and K_t are sums over both types of investment and capital, and β_0, β_1, and β_2 are adjustment cost terms reflecting joint costs and costs specific to the two types of capital, respectively.

Given the homogeneity of the production function and adjustment cost function with respect to the scale of the firm, the value of the firm will be proportional to the size of its capital stock and the behavior of all firms can be represented by a single, aggregate representative firm.

The quadratic adjustment cost function in (1) is a two-capital-good version of the one used by Summers (1981) in his empirical analysis. It also differs in two other respects. First, it is based on net rather than gross investment. Second, there is no constant subtracted from the ratio I/K in each quadratic term. However, one may equivalently view the current model as being based on gross investment, with a constant equal to the rate, δ, of economic depreciation being subtracted. Either way, the notion is that minimum average adjustment costs (in this case, zero) occur when net investment is zero. This makes sense if one views the costs as general ones involving changing the scale of operations rather than bolting down the new machines. Summers's preferred estimate of the constant term (.088) is quite consistent with this interpretation.

We ignore changes in relative prices between capital goods and output and between different types of capital, and assume that all new investment goods have a real price of unity in every year. The adjustment costs are assumed to be "internal," in that they relate not to an upward sloping supply schedule for capital goods but to the costs of absorption at the firm level. This is consistent with the observation that historical fluctuations in capital goods prices are relatively minor compared to estimated costs of adjustment.

The firm's optimization problem consists of choosing equipment, structures, and labor at each time t, taking account of current and (to the extent of the assumed planning horizon) future economic conditions. There is no risk from the firm's point of view; whatever it expects about the future (right or wrong) is expected with certainty. If we let the production function in the three factor inputs be $F(\cdot)$, then the firm seeks to maximize its value at time t, equal to the discounted value of its real, after-tax cash flows:

$$(2) \quad V_t = \sum_{s=t}^{\infty} (1 + r)^{-(s+1-t)} \{(1 - \tau_{s+1})(F(K_{1s}, K_{2s}, N_s) - w_s N_s)$$

$$- (1 + r)(1 - \tau_s)A(I_s) + (1 + r) \sum_{i=1}^{2} [-(1 - k_{is}) G_{is}$$

$$+ \tau_s \sum_{x=-\infty}^{s} ((1 + r)/(1 + r + \pi))^{(s-x)}D_i(s,x)G_{ix}]\}$$

where N_s is the labor input in period s; r is the real, after-tax required return; w_s is the real wage rate paid at the end of year s; $D_i(s, x)$ is the depreciation allowance at the beginning of year s for assets of type i purchased at the beginning of year x; k_{it} is the investment tax credit received on investment of type i at the beginning of year t; π is the rate of inflation; δ_i is the rate at which capital of type i depreciates; G_{it} is gross investment of type i at the beginning of year t; and τ_t is the tax rate at the beginning of year t.[2] Depreciation allowances decay at the inflation rate because they are not indexed.

We use the convention that year t investment occurs at the beginning of the period, while quasirents occur at the end, with period t investment yielding its first return at the end of the same period. We also assume that adjustment costs are immediately expensed, as would be the case for internal adjustment costs that require extra factors or reduce productivity. Gross and net investment of type i are related by the identity:

$$(3) \qquad\qquad G_{it} = I_{it} + \delta_i K_{it-1}$$

For labor, the optimal condition derived by differentiating (2) with respect to N calls for the firm to set the marginal product of labor equal to the real wage. As usual in models of this sort with constant returns to scale, the labor demand equation is omitted from explicit analysis. For each type of capital good i, it is most convenient to derive the first-order condition with respect to gross investment at each date t, G_{it}. Assuming, for the moment, an infinite horizon and perfect foresight, this yields:

$$(4) \qquad \rho_{it} = [(1 + r)/(1 - \tau_{t+1})] [q_{it} - k_{it}$$

$$- \sum_{s=t}^{\infty} (1 + r + \pi)^{-(s-t)} \tau_s D_i(s - t)$$

$$- \sum_{s=t+1}^{\infty} (1 - \delta_i)^{(s-t)}(1 + r)^{-(s-t+1)}(1 - \tau_{s+1})\rho_{is}]$$

where (using (1) and (3))

(5) $\rho_{it} = dF_t/dK_{it} - dA_{t+1}/dK_{it}$
        $= dF_t/dK_{it} + \frac{1}{2}\beta_0[(I_{t+1}/K_t)^2 + 2\delta_i(I_{t+1}/K_{it})]$
        $+ \frac{1}{2}\beta_i[(I_{it+1}/K_{it})^2 + 2\delta_i(I_{it+1}/K_{it})]$

is the "total" marginal product of capital at the end of period t, taking account of reduced concurrent costs of adjustment, and q_{it} is the marginal cost of a unit of capital, less tax savings associated with costs of adjustment:

(6) $q_{it} = 1 + (1 - \tau_t)[\beta_0(I_t/K_{t-1}) + \beta_i(I_{it}/K_{it-1})]$

Equation (5) reminds the reader that there are two components to the firm's marginal value of an additional piece of capital this year: the marginal product of capital (dF_t/dK_{it}) and the reduction in next year's adjustment costs (dA_{t+1}/dK_{it}). Expression (4) says that firms should invest in capital of type i at date t until its marginal product, after tax, equals its after-tax cost (multiplied by $(1 + r)$ because costs are borne at the beginning of the period) less the present value of investment credits, depreciation allowances, and future quasirents. Thus, the expression is the result of the optimal backward solution for firm behavior. When expectations are static, as is commonly assumed, (4) reduces to the standard user cost of capital formula:

(7) $\rho_{it} = q'_{it}(r + \delta_i)(1 - k_{it} - \tau_t z_{it})/(1 - \tau_t)$

where z_{it} equals the present value of depreciation allowances $D_i(s, t)$ and

(8) $q'_{it} = (q_{it} - k_{it} - \tau_t z_{it})/(1 - k_{it} - \tau_t z_{it})$

is a tax-adjusted price of new capital goods that we will interpret below.

Because of the assumption that production is governed by a Cobb-Douglas production function, the direct marginal product of capital of type i in period t is:

(9) $F_{it} = a_t N_t^{(1-\alpha_1-\alpha_2)} \alpha_i K_{it}^{-(1-\alpha_i)} K_{jt}^{\alpha_j}$ $j = 3 - i$

where a_t is the production function constant. Thus, given the optimal choice of labor input, expressions (4) and (5) for i and j give us two equations in the capital stocks K_{1t} and K_{2t}. Without adjustment costs, this would permit a closed-form, backward solution for these capital stocks in each period.[3] However, since q_t depends on lagged capital stocks, this solution method is no longer possible, and we must resort to simulation analysis.

5.1.1   Parameterization

Three types of parameters appear in the model just described, relating to production (a, α_1, α_2, δ_1, δ_2, β_0, β_1, and β_2) taxation (τ, k_1, k_2, $D_1(\cdot)$ and $D_2(\cdot)$) and financial markets (r and π). For π, we use the realized values of the GNP deflator (year on year), while τ is set equal to the statutory corporate tax rate that prevailed for the majority of the year.[4] Firms' required rate of return, r, is set equal to after-tax real rate on 4- to 6-month commercial paper which prevailed in the year of investment, plus a risk premium that is taken to be constant. This series on adjusted interest rates was calculated by (10):

(10) $$r_a = 0.06 + (1 - \tau)PR - INFL$$

where r_a is the adjusted rate, PR is the nominal (annualized) return on 4- to 6-month paper, and $INFL$ is the contemporaneous inflation rate. The after-tax risk premium in (10) is 6%, which roughly corresponds to the historical difference between after-tax risk-free interest rates and after-tax profit rates.

In order to calculate the production parameters α and δ and the tax terms k and $D(\cdot)$, it is necessary to aggregate data on 34 classes of assets for which we have data (20 equipment and 14 structures) into corresponding values for aggregate equipment and structures. This turns out to be a very complex problem. The method used is described in the appendix.

Once values of δ_1 and δ_2 are known, it is possible to estimate the capital share parameters α_1 and α_2 from production and capital stock data. We begin by calculating the net-of-depreciation, before-tax return to capital in the corporate sector in 1977 by dividing the difference between value added and labor compensation in the corporate sector, taken from the 1977 Census of Manufactures, by the total corporate capital stock, equal to equipment and structures plus inventories and land. We then assume that all forms of capital earned this before-tax rate of return, R_g.[5] Next, we assume that the Cobb-Douglas production function specified above refers to gross output net of returns to inventories and land,[6] calculated as follows:

(11) $$G = Y + \delta_1 K_1 + \delta_2 K_2 - R_g(K_3 + K_4)$$

where Y is value added and K_3 and K_4 are stocks of inventories and land.

Once we have obtained this value of G, we note that, since output is observed net of adjustment costs, the production function $F(\cdot)$ must satisfy:

(12) $$F(K_1, K_2, N) = G + A(I)$$

Finally, we define the net return to capital of type i ($i = 1, 2$) in the current period as being the derivative of G with respect to K_i, holding constant the capital stock *growth rates* (I_1/K_1), (I_2/K_2) and (I/K), less depreciation δ_i.[7] This yields (using (1) and (9)):

(13) $R_g = \alpha_i F/K_i - \frac{1}{2}\beta_0(I/K)^2 - \frac{1}{2}\beta_i(I_i/K_i)^2 - \delta_i$ $\quad i = 1, 2$

which can immediately be solved for α_i.[8]

The resulting parameter values are:

$$\alpha_1 = .166$$

$$\alpha_2 = .181$$

$$\delta_1 = .137$$

$$\delta_2 = .033$$

with the estimated value of R_g equal to 10.4%. This estimate of the marginal product of capital (which is used only in the calculation of α_1 and α_2) is consistent with previous findings. In interpreting the sizes of the two share coefficients, it should be remembered that these are shares in *gross* output, *less* estimated returns to land and inventories. Relative to usual calculations of the capital share of net output, the first of these factors (the use of gross output) would lead to a larger total share (since depreciation is included in both numerator and denominator) while the second (excluding part of the capital stock) would lead to a smaller total share (since returns to excluded capital are subtracted from both numerator and denominator.)

The production function constant a is obtained for 1977 by dividing $F(\cdot)$ by the product of its component factors raised to the power of their respective factor shares. We then assume that the labor input, in efficiency units, grows at a constant rate of 3% over the entire sample period.[9] This imparts a trend rate of growth to the steady state of the model. That it is slightly below the historical capital stock growth rate of about 4% may be because part of that growth is attributable to the historical decline in effective tax rates on investment.

In order to obtain a historical series for a that would be consistent with observed fluctuations in the profitability of capital, we use data on after-tax corporate rates of return from Feldstein, Poterba, and Dicks-Mireaux (1983), updated to include 1984. We took the 1984 value to prevail for all subsequent years. Assuming capital market equilibrium and constant returns technology, this rate of return will be equal to the marginal gross return to capital, R_g in (13). Note that this methodology implicitly assumes that yearly variation in the return to capital is attributable to shocks to the production function and not to changes in the capital/labor ratio. Then, using (9) and (13), the technical and labor-related component of the production function can be computed:

$$(14) \qquad a_t = \frac{(C + R_g^t)}{D} \left(\frac{K_t}{N_t}\right)^{(1-\alpha_1-\alpha_2)}$$

where the left side of (14) is the value to be calculated, and C and D are constants, with C equal to:

$$(15) \qquad C = \tfrac{1}{2}(0.03)^2(\beta_0 + \beta_1 s_1 + \beta_2 s_2) + \delta_1 s_1 + \delta_2 s_2$$

where s_i is the share of capital of type i in the capital stock ($s_1 + s_2 \equiv 1$).

Since (14) is a relationship which holds for all years, it must hold for 1977, the year from which values are calibrated. Marginal products of capital for all other years were calculated using α_1 and α_2 and the assumption that K_t/N_t is constant: to solve for a_t relative to its value in 1977,

$$(16) \qquad \frac{a_t}{a_{77}} = \frac{C + R_g^t}{C + R_g^{77}}$$

The only parameters that remain to be chosen are the adjustment costs terms β_0, β_1, and β_2, which are quite crucial to our analysis. Previous studies have inferred these parameters from regressions of investment on "tax-adjusted q." The authors of these studies have derived "tax-adjusted q" by correcting the ratio of the market value of the firm to its capital stock (presumed to be average q) for tax factors such as the investment tax credit, accelerated depreciation, and the deductibility of adjustment costs that would cause marginal and average q to differ. In one case (Abel and Blanchard 1986), average q is explicitly estimated from projected future profits and interest rates. A regression of I on adjusted q can then be interpreted as estimating the inverted marginal cost function.

In a model with one capital stock, the coefficient on adjusted q would be an estimate of $1/\beta$, the inverted marginal adjustment cost. Although such regressions cannot be done if there is more than one capital stock, one can still interpret the coefficient as the inverse of the sum of marginal adjustment costs associated with investment of type i, or $[\beta_0 + \beta_i]^{-1}$ in the current model.

Empirical investigations have found this coefficient to be quite small. However, for many reasons usually pointed out by authors of the previous studies, these coefficients (which are not always even statistically significant) may be prone to serious downward bias because of an inexact measure of q being used.[10]

Given the uncertainty of what the "true" values of β_0, β_1, and β_2 should be, we choose values that, given the other parameters of the model, make the variances of the growth rates of investment in equipment, structures, and the two categories together that are generated by a historical simulation with perfect foresight roughly equal to their historical values for the period 1954–84. While this methodology is somewhat arbitrary, it derives from the observation that, in the simulations, fluctuations in investment are particularly sensitive to the configuration of adjustment costs.

Postwar investment history suggests that adjustment costs are substantial and not symmetric between equipment and structures. The net stock of equipment grew at a mean annual rate of 5.0% between 1954 and 1984, while structures grew 3.1% annually and total capital grew at a 3.9% rate. The historical variances of equipment, structures, and total net investment rates were .041%, .0070%, and .012% respectively. Adjustment cost parameters for the simulations were chosen to approximate as closely as possible these variances with those generated by the perfect foresight simulation when investors expect the 1985 tax law to stay unchanged forever. Choosing β_0, β_1, and β_2 to equal the common value of 6, as in Auerbach and Hines (1986), produces investment variability that does not conform well with the historical evidence: structures investment is too variable in these runs and equipment investment not variable enough. On the basis of experiments with several parameterizations, we found that the values $\beta_0 = 15$, $\beta_1 = 0$, $\beta_2 = 20$ produced results which most closely mirrored actual investment. This specification of adjustment costs yields equipment, structures, and total investment variances equal to .035%, .0067%, and .012% respectively.[11]

To compare these chosen values of β_0, β_1, and β_2 to those found in the previous literature on aggregate investment, note that the value of β corresponding to a dollar increase in net investment proportional to the weights of equipment and structures in the capital stock is $\beta = \beta_0 + k_1\beta_1 + k_2\beta_2$, where k_i is the fraction of the capital stock represented by capital of type i. Given typical values of k_1 and k_2, this yields a value of β approximately equal to 28, which is quite reasonable given previous research.[12]

5.1.2   Solution of the Model

In the presence of adjustment costs, the model as specified can only be solved numerically. There exist different techniques to obtain such solutions. The one used here is described in great detail in Auerbach and Hines (1986).

All simulations begin with the assumption that, prior to 1954, the economy was in a steady state: that economic conditions had been stable for sufficiently long that the stocks of both kinds of capital had completely adjusted, and no change in these conditions was anticipated. Though this is undoubtedly inaccurate, some such assumption is required to fix the initial values of capital stocks in a way that is consistent with the assumed production technology.

This solution for the steady state in 1953 does not depend on any future variables. Indeed, when expectations are assumed to be completely myopic throughout, the model can then be solved forward without iteration, with each year's solution beginning with K_{t-1} and solving for K_t. At the other extreme is the assumption of perfect foresight. By this we mean that all tax and inflation rates are correctly anticipated until the present. It is hard to implement this assumption for future dates, so we make assumptions about the values of these variables and suppose that firms' expectations match them. We then solve the model into the twenty-first century to guarantee convergence to a new steady state.

5.1.3 Measuring the Effects of Policies

In addition to the two capital stocks, we calculate three variables of interest. One is the *average q* of the representative firm, its value relative to the replacement cost of its capital stock. This starts with the marginal q obtained directly from the adjustment cost function, and then takes account of the variety of tax provisions that make old and new capital differ in value. The second is the *effective tax rate*, which summarizes the incentive to invest in a particular asset in a given year. The third is the *net investment flows* of equipment and structures which the simulation generates.

5.1.4 Estimating Average q

It is this variable that tells us what the overall impact of a tax change will be on market value. Generally, there will be two effects. To the extent that the incentive to invest increases, marginal q, defined to be the basic price of a unit of capital capital plus the derivative of the adjustment cost function with respect to investment, will rise. In the absence of taxes, the homogeneity of production and adjustment cost functions would imply that this would also be the firm's value per unit of capital.

But to the extent that the new incentive magnifies the distinction between new and old capital, the difference between marginal q and average q will also rise. The net effect on average q can be either positive or negative for expansionary or contractionary policies. Holding marginal q constant, an increase in average q may be viewed as a lump sum transfer to the owners of corporate capital.

The formula for average q is based on an arbitrage condition between old and new capital. Since new capital goods must generate after-tax cash flows equal to marginal q, it follows that

(17) $\bar{q}_{it} = \tau_t[\beta_0(I_t/K_{t-1}) + \beta_i(I_{it}/K_{it-1})] + PV_{it} + k_{it}$

$$+ \sum_{s=t}^{\infty} \tau_s((1 + r)/(1 + r + \pi))^{(s-t)}D_i(s, t)$$

where $\bar{q}_{it}$ is marginal q and PV_{it} is the present value of the after-tax quasirents accruing to an new asset purchased for one dollar at date t. Since capital purchased at $t' < t$ has a present value of quasirents of $(1 - \delta_i)^{t-t'}PV_{it}$, it follows that its value at date t, per efficiency unit of capital, is

(18) $\bar{q}_{it, t'} = PV_{it} + [\sum_{s=t}^{\infty} \tau_s((1 + r)/(1 + r$

$$+ \pi))^{(s-t)}D_i(s, t')]/(1 - \delta_i)^{t-t'}$$

Solution of (17) for PV_{it} and substitution of this expression into (18) gives a solution for the value of capital of type i and cohort t' at time t, in terms of $\bar{q}_{it}$. From (1) and the definition of marginal q, we also have:

(19) $$\bar{q}_{it} = 1 + \beta_0(I_t/K_t) + \beta_i(I_{it}/K_{it})$$

Combining (18) and (19) to get each cohort's value, we then aggregate these values of average q over all vintages and both types of capital to obtain an overall value for the firm at date t.

Note that this expression for average q is consistent with the assumption of perfect foresight. When myopic expectations are assumed, we change (17) and (18) correspondingly.

5.1.5 Calculating Effective Tax Rates

In models based on myopic expectations, it is common to define the effective tax rate to be the percentage difference between the net (of depreciation) marginal products of capital before and after taxes. Given a fixed after-tax return, this calculation also tells us what the before-tax, or social return to capital must be for the firm to earn zero profits. Unless the economy actually is in a steady state, however, this will be correct only in the year the calculation is made. Hence, the effective tax rate as commonly used measures the required before-tax return to capital in the same year, assuming myopia.

When firms are not myopic, the formula for the user cost of capital is different, but we can still answer the same question, namely, What rate of return on capital must the firm earn in the current year, taking account of future changes in taxes, inflation, and the firm's marginal product of capital? As before, this will tell us what the firm's rate of return on investment must be, before taxes, in the current year. Dropping subscripts, the effective tax rate is defined to be:

$$(20) \qquad \theta = [(\rho/q - \delta) - r]/(\rho/q - \delta)$$

where ρ is the marginal product of capital defined in (5).

It is not clear which value of q should be used in (20). The most obvious candidate is marginal q, as defined in expression (19). However, use of this value has the effect of incorporating the tax deduction for adjustment costs in the effective tax rate. This is perfectly acceptable; it reflects the fact that part of the cost of investment is expensed. However, it makes more difficult a comparison with previous results, since even when there is economic depreciation of direct capital costs, the effective tax rate will be less than τ. By using the tax adjusted value, q', defined in (8),[13] one "undoes" the differential tax treatment of adjustment costs, and obtains the usual results for expensing, economic depreciation, and other special cases. Hence, for the sake of comparability with other studies in which adjustment costs were ignored, we take this latter approach.

5.2 Simulation Results

This section presents the results of simulations, chosen to provide answers to some of the questions raised above. We begin by contrasting the historical patterns of net investment in equipment and structures with net investment series produced by simulation runs using myopic and perfect foresight assumptions about investor expectations of future tax laws and macroeconomic conditions.

Table 5.1 presents net corporate investment, expressed as a fraction of the capital stock, in equipment and structures for the period 1953–84. These investment rates are not derived from the published BEA net investment series; they are calculated by applying the BEA gross investment data and Hulten-Wykoff depreciation rates to form a perpetual inventory of corporate capital assuming the published 1925 net capital stock to be accurate. The investment series produced by this method are then measured consistently with net investment calculations from the simulation runs.

Table 5.1 illustrates several sharp features of the postwar investment experience. Equipment investment strongly accelerates in the mid-1960s, possibly in part in response to the introduction of the investment tax credit and repeal of the Long amendment. Both equipment and structures appear to be affected by business cycle downturns in 1970–71 and 1975–76. Structures never recover from the latter shock. Investment in every year of the post-1975 period fails to equal any of its previous values.

Table 5.1   **U.S. Corporate Net Investment, 1954–84**

Year	Equipment	Structures	Total
1953	5.1%	3.7%	4.2%
1954	3.6	3.5	3.5
1955	4.7	4.1	4.3
1956	5.0	4.3	4.5
1957	4.9	3.9	4.3
1958	0.5	3.1	2.1
1959	2.3	2.8	2.6
1960	3.0	3.2	3.1
1961	2.0	3.2	2.8
1962	3.5	3.3	3.4
1963	4.1	3.1	3.4
1964	6.0	3.4	4.3
1965	8.1	4.4	5.7
1966	9.6	4.5	6.4
1967	7.0	4.1	5.2
1968	7.0	4.1	5.2
1969	7.3	4.1	5.4
1970	5.2	3.6	4.2
1971	3.6	3.0	3.2
1972	5.3	3.1	4.0
1973	7.6	3.3	5.1
1974	6.6	3.0	4.5
1975	2.8	2.1	2.4
1976	3.4	2.0	2.6
1977	5.4	1.8	3.4
1978	6.2	2.2	4.0
1979	6.2	2.7	4.3
1980	5.4	2.4	3.8
1981	5.2	2.3	3.6
1982	2.9	2.1	2.4
1983	3.6	1.4	2.4
1984	6.7	2.7	4.6
Mean growth rate	5.0%	3.1%	3.9%
Variance of investment	0.041%	0.0070%	0.012%

Tables 5.2a–c and 5.3a–c present results from simulations in which investors have myopic expectations and perfect expectations respectively. The main point is to illustrate the effects of expectations on the smoothing of investment and the impact that movements in marginal q have on average q when adjustment costs are present. Both simulations are performed for the period 1953–90, under the assumption that Congress passes no post-1985 tax reform proposals and investors (in the perfect foresight simulation) correctly anticipate that there will be no changes.

Table 5.2a   Effective Tax Rates: Myopic Expectations

Year	Equipment	Structures
1953	59%	48%
1954	53	46
1955	56	48
1956	59	50
1957	60	50
1958	54	47
1959	56	48
1960	54	47
1961	52	46
1962	38	43
1963	37	43
1964	28	40
1965	28	39
1966	31	41
1967	45	42
1968	41	48
1969	43	49
1970	53	48
1971	53	48
1972	10	42
1973	19	44
1974	33	53
1975	104	101
1976	11	42
1977	13	44
1978	22	47
1979	25	45
1980	27	44
1981	4	35
1982	−2	30
1983	2	28
1984	4	30
1985	4	31

Table 5.2a and 5.3a present effective tax rates for these two simulations. For each year there are two numbers: the effective tax rates
for equipment and structures, respectively. These results are quite consistent with those of the previous literature. Since effective tax rates
depend not only on the tax treatment of new investment but also on
macroeconomic conditions and investment adjustment costs, a casual
examination of effective tax rates does not reveal all the incentives
built into the tax code. Effective tax rates may be useful for purposes
of comparison, however.

Table 5.2b   **Investment: Myopic Expectations**

Year	Equipment	Structures	Total
1953	3.0%	3.0%	3.0%
1954	3.6	3.2	3.3
1955	5.4	4.4	4.8
1956	3.3	4.6	4.1
1957	2.6	4.2	3.6
1958	1.9	2.7	2.4
1959	3.7	3.0	3.3
1960	2.7	2.3	2.4
1961	2.9	2.1	2.4
1962	6.8	2.9	4.4
1963	6.3	2.8	4.2
1964	6.9	3.0	4.5
1965	6.8	3.9	5.0
1966	5.8	4.4	5.0
1967	2.7	4.4	3.7
1968	4.4	5.3	4.9
1969	3.3	4.5	4.0
1970	0.4	4.2	2.7
1971	1.6	5.4	3.9
1972	6.5	4.0	4.9
1973	5.3	3.7	4.4
1974	1.7	6.7	4.7
1975	−3.3	15.3	8.2
1976	8.4	3.4	5.1
1977	7.1	4.5	5.4
1978	5.5	5.0	5.2
1979	4.4	3.9	4.1
1980	3.2	3.3	3.3
1981	4.6	2.6	3.3
1982	3.4	1.0	1.8
1983	3.6	1.1	2.0
1984	3.2	0.7	1.6
1985	3.0	0.7	1.6
Mean growth rate	4.0%	3.9%	4.0%
Variance of investment	0.055%	0.0062%	0.018%

Beginning from effective tax rates in 1953 well above the statutory rate of 52% for equipment, and somewhat lower for structures, effective tax rates for the myopic simulation in table 5.2a move lower with the tax changes introduced in 1954, and again in 1962 with the introduction of the investment tax credit. Tax rates on equipment go down again in 1972 with the reintroduction of the investment tax credit and the introduction of the Asset Depreciation Range (ADR) System. Effective tax rates for equipment and structures move strongly in 1975 for reasons

Table 5.2c   Average q: Myopic Expectations

Year	Equipment	Structures	Total
1954	1.37	1.50	1.45
1955	1.48	1.73	1.65
1956	1.43	1.70	1.61
1957	1.38	1.63	1.55
1958	1.29	1.40	1.36
1959	1.35	1.49	1.44
1960	1.28	1.36	1.34
1961	1.27	1.34	1.32
1962	1.32	1.52	1.45
1963	1.29	1.49	1.42
1964	1.31	1.56	1.47
1965	1.35	1.72	1.58
1966	1.34	1.77	1.61
1967	1.30	1.68	1.53
1968	1.29	1.76	1.58
1969	1.22	1.63	1.47
1970	1.19	1.58	1.44
1971	1.29	1.81	1.62
1972	1.25	1.71	1.55
1973	1.21	1.65	1.49
1974	1.24	1.98	1.71
1975	1.49	3.15	2.56
1976	1.23	1.64	1.51
1977	1.25	1.77	1.60
1978	1.24	1.82	1.63
1979	1.17	1.65	1.49
1980	1.10	1.52	1.38
1981	1.07	1.39	1.28
1982	0.94	1.08	1.04
1983	0.96	1.11	1.06
1984	0.93	1.05	1.01
1985	0.92	1.06	1.01

to be discussed shortly. By 1980, higher rates of inflation have pushed effective tax rates back up to earlier levels, particularly on equipment. The introduction of ACRS in 1981 brought effective tax rates on equipment essentially to zero, also lowering tax rates on structures to a postwar low. Reduced inflation in 1982 brought tax rates down still further. Rates went up in 1983 on equipment and 1984 on structures because of the 1982 and 1984 tax acts, which introduced a 50% basis adjustment for the investment tax credit and an 18-year (instead of 15-year) tax life for structures, respectively.

The net investment rates for equipment, structures, and aggregate capital are displayed in table 5.2b, expressed as a percentage of the respective capital stocks. The substantial adjustment costs built into

Table 5.3a   **Effective Tax Rates: Perfect Foresight**

Year	Equipment	Structures
1953	58%	49%
1954	54	48
1955	65	58
1956	65	59
1957	62	57
1958	49	44
1959	56	49
1960	48	40
1961	54	40
1962	47	46
1963	44	43
1964	38	42
1965	45	48
1966	41	51
1967	57	52
1968	57	61
1969	40	55
1970	45	52
1971	67	63
1972	42	57
1973	39	55
1974	54	74
1975	100	100
1976	42	63
1977	54	70
1978	59	73
1979	48	67
1980	46	64
1981	25	52
1982	−38	25
1983	−1	27
1984	−8	22
1985	−7	23

the model have the effect of raising marginal q when investment tax incentives are strong, thereby encouraging firms to smooth their investment. Despite this effect, the investment series in table 5.2b is highly erratic. The variance of structures investment is almost ten times its historical value, and episodes such as the introduction of the investment tax credit in 1962 and its removal at the end of the 1960s produce unrealistically sharp investment changes.

Years such as 1975 illustrate some of the hazards of modeling investment behavior under myopic expectations. Net structures investment in the model is 15% that year, and equipment investment is −3%. These incongruous results are produced by the economy's deep reces-

Table 5.3b   Investment: Perfect Foresight

Year	Equipment	Structures	Total
1953	3.0%	3.0%	3.0%
1954	4.2	3.9	4.0
1955	4.2	3.9	4.0
1956	3.5	3.9	3.8
1957	3.2	3.9	3.6
1958	3.0	3.8	3.5
1959	3.6	3.8	3.7
1960	3.5	3.7	3.7
1961	3.9	3.8	3.8
1962	7.6	3.5	5.0
1963	6.9	3.6	4.9
1964	6.7	3.4	4.7
1965	5.7	3.4	4.3
1966	4.9	3.4	4.0
1967	2.0	3.8	3.1
1968	4.7	3.7	4.1
1969	4.0	3.7	3.8
1970	1.3	3.6	2.7
1971	1.5	3.4	2.6
1972	5.3	2.6	3.7
1973	4.6	2.6	3.4
1974	4.3	2.6	3.3
1975	3.9	2.4	3.0
1976	2.7	2.4	2.5
1977	2.2	2.2	2.2
1978	1.6	2.1	1.9
1979	0.9	1.9	1.5
1980	0.7	1.7	1.3
1981	1.5	1.8	1.7
1982	1.4	1.8	1.6
1983	1.0	1.8	1.5
1984	1.3	1.7	1.5
1985	1.6	1.6	1.6
Mean growth rate	3.4%	3.0%	3.2%
Variance of investment	0.035%	0.0067%	0.012%

sion that year and the accompanying low real interest rates and marginal products of capital. The enormous decline in real interest rates leads to a desired shift to longer-lived investment. Since myopic investors expect the cost of capital never to change in the future, they find themselves desperately short of structures when costs fall in 1975. Their one-period time horizon prevents them from delaying enough of their investment to minimize adjustment costs efficiently, and leads to unrealistically sensitive investment demands. That is, they are assumed not to anticipate a decline in marginal q from its current high level.

Values of average q, as reported in table 5.2c, reflect the pattern of investment as well as tax law changes. Average q has generally declined over the years as the distinction made by the tax system between old and new capital has widened. Under a system of economic depreciation, average q would equal marginal q net of the tax deduction of adjustment costs, as defined in (6) (averaged over the two types of capital). At a steady state growth rate of 3%, a corporate tax rate of about 50%, and with structures comprising about 60% of total capital, the steady state value of average q would be 1.14. In the short run, average q is determined both by the distinction between new and old capital (the difference between average q and marginal q) and by the value of marginal q itself. A change in the incentive to invest will typically affect both of these terms, sometimes in different directions.

Though the estimated time series given in table 5.2c suggest that average q for total capital was above one throughout the postwar period, it exceeded 1.14 only for the period before 1982. After the acceleration of depreciation allowances in 1954, and throughout the 1950s and until 1981, average q remained quite high. The mid-1960s investment boom in particular contributed to marginal q and therefore average q. Adverse macroeconomic conditions discourage investment in the 1980s, thereby lowering marginal q. Combined with the increased gap between new and old capital brought about by ERTA, this moves average q closer to one.

Table 5.3a presents effective tax rates for the perfect foresight simulation. The results are qualitatively similar to those in table 5.2a, with the exception that investment is steadier and so effective tax rates are jostled less by movements in marginal q.

Table 5.3b contains the perfect foresight investment series. Structures investment is very smooth over the whole time period, generally declining from 1954 until the late 1960s, rising then and declining thereafter. The presence of substantial joint adjustment costs raises the cost of structures investment when firms are investing heavily in equipment, and this effect is reflected in downward movements in structures investment rates for 1962 and 1972, years in which the investment tax credit was introduced. Similarly, structures investment recovers in 1967, when the investment tax credit was removed. Equipment investment follows the opposite pattern over these years, and is subject to much wider investment swings generally. The persistence of very high historical equipment investment over the period 1965–69 as reported in table 5.1 is not reproduced in the equipment investment series in table 5.3b; simulated investment responds quickly to incentives in 1962 and 1964, but dies out much more quickly in subsequent years.

Table 5.3c reports average q's for this perfect foresight simulation. As in the simulation with myopic expectations, average q follows a

Table 5.3c	Average q: Perfect Foresight		
Year	Equipment	Structures	Total
1954	1.42	1.63	1.56
1955	1.42	1.63	1.56
1956	1.40	1.62	1.54
1957	1.39	1.60	1.53
1958	1.37	1.59	1.51
1959	1.38	1.60	1.52
1960	1.37	1.60	1.52
1961	1.37	1.61	1.53
1962	1.37	1.62	1.53
1963	1.35	1.62	1.52
1964	1.32	1.62	1.51
1965	1.30	1.61	1.49
1966	1.27	1.60	1.47
1967	1.25	1.57	1.45
1968	1.23	1.57	1.44
1969	1.21	1.54	1.42
1970	1.19	1.52	1.40
1971	1.19	1.51	1.39
1972	1.16	1.48	1.36
1973	1.14	1.46	1.34
1974	1.12	1.44	1.32
1975	1.10	1.40	1.28
1976	1.05	1.33	1.22
1977	1.02	1.30	1.19
1978	0.99	1.26	1.16
1979	0.96	1.22	1.12
1980	0.94	1.18	1.09
1981	0.92	1.16	1.07
1982	0.91	1.14	1.05
1983	0.93	1.14	1.06
1984	0.92	1.15	1.06
1985	0.85	1.11	1.01

strong secular drift downward over the whole time period. Other than for the effects of strong investment and consequent high marginal q's in the mid-1960s, changes in the tax system have over time progressively increased the distinction between old and new capital in these runs.

The salient features of the historical investment pattern seem to be best captured by the perfect foresight simulation. Besides the generally less variable investment behavior it produces, its results for equipment in the mid-1970s and structures at the end of the 1970s are much closer to the actual investment pattern than is the case for the myopic simulation. Historical equipment and structures investment remained strong through 1974 and then declined in response to the recession. Investment in the myopic simulation responds too quickly to the macroeconomic and tax law changes, while the perfect foresight investors can see ahead to the next tax reform or phase in the business cycle and so their investments show the same kind of smooth transitions one finds in the historical series. Of course, the perfect foresight investment series do not always match historical investment: at the end of the 1970s, for example, perfect foresight investors would have known that ACRS was coming and would have reduced equipment investment much more than was the case in reality. And neither simulation run can explain the recent boom in equipment investment.[14]

5.3 Effects of Historical Investment Policies

One of the most important investment incentives of the period under consideration is the investment tax credit. While the investment tax credit reduces the partial-equilibrium user cost of equipment, some authors have suggested that the destabilizing effects of the credit over the business cycle mitigated its investment incentive for equipment and reduced incentives for structures investment.[15]

Table 5.4 presents investment series from a simulation in which it is assumed that the government never instituted an investment tax credit. The tax law is otherwise unchanged, and this run assumes that investors have perfect foresight. Some of the results are predictable: equipment investment rises much less quickly in 1962 and 1972 than it does in table 5.3b. In addition, equipment investment dies at the end of the 1970s when the investment tax credit is not present to mitigate the effects of adverse macroeconomic conditions.

The variance of equipment investment in this simulation is 0.024%, which is less than the 0.035% variance of investment reported in the perfect foresight run (table 5.3b) when the investment tax credit is present. While one might be tempted to conclude that the investment tax credit was destabilizing, such an interpretation depends on the sense in which stability is understood. Mean equipment growth for the simulation reported in table 5.4 is 2.86%, which is substantially less than the 3.4% growth rate reported in table 5.3b. The coefficient of variation for investment in the simulation with the tax credit removed is 0.54, which is very close to the 0.55 coefficient of variation for investment in the historical law perfect foresight (table 5.3b) simulation. It appears, then, that in raising both the mean and variance of investment the investment tax credit has not substantially changed its relative stability. Of course, it is hard to know in a model like this one whether absolute or relative stability is more appropriate in making welfare comparisons.

Table 5.4   Investment: Perfect Foresight and No Investment Tax Credit

Year	Equipment	Structures	Total
1953	3.0%	3.0%	3.0%
1954	4.2	3.8	4.0
1955	4.2	3.8	4.0
1956	3.5	3.8	3.7
1957	3.2	3.7	3.5
1958	3.0	3.7	3.4
1959	3.6	3.6	3.6
1960	3.6	3.6	3.6
1961	4.0	3.6	3.7
1962	6.2	3.5	4.5
1963	5.8	3.6	4.4
1964	5.1	3.5	4.1
1965	4.4	3.4	3.8
1966	3.8	3.4	3.6
1967	3.2	3.4	3.3
1968	3.5	3.7	3.6
1969	3.0	3.6	3.4
1970	2.6	3.2	3.0
1971	2.6	3.0	2.9
1972	3.1	2.8	2.9
1973	2.8	2.7	2.8
1974	2.8	2.6	2.7
1975	2.7	2.5	2.6
1976	1.8	2.5	2.0
1977	1.5	2.0	1.8
1978	0.9	1.9	1.5
1979	0.2	1.7	1.1
1980	0.1	1.5	1.0
1981	0.7	1.7	1.3
1982	0.6	1.6	1.2
1983	1.0	1.6	1.3
1984	1.3	1.4	1.4
1985	1.6	1.4	1.5
Mean growth rate	2.9%	2.9%	2.9%
Variance of investment	0.024%	0.0072%	0.012%

Table 5.5 presents investment series from simulations in which the investment tax credit was never introduced and firms have myopic expectations about future conditions. The mean growth rate of equipment is 3.54%, which is higher than in the perfect foresight simulation but still smaller than the 4.0% growth rate when investors receive the investment tax credit. The variance of equipment investment is 0.047%, and the coefficient of variation is 0.61. Thus the relative stability of equipment investment in the absence of an investment tax credit seems to be affected little by the nature of expectations of future tax policies.

Table 5.5   **Investment: Myopic Expectations and No Investment Tax Credit**

Year	Equipment	Structures	Total
1953	3.0%	3.0%	3.0%
1954	3.6	3.2	3.3
1955	5.4	4.4	4.8
1956	3.3	4.6	4.1
1957	2.6	4.2	3.6
1958	1.9	2.7	2.4
1959	3.7	3.0	3.3
1960	2.7	2.1	2.4
1961	2.8	2.1	2.4
1962	5.5	3.1	4.0
1963	5.4	2.9	3.9
1964	5.5	3.1	4.0
1965	5.9	3.9	4.7
1966	5.1	4.4	4.7
1967	3.9	4.1	4.0
1968	3.3	5.3	4.5
1969	2.4	4.5	3.7
1970	1.6	3.9	3.0
1971	2.7	5.2	4.2
1972	4.3	4.2	4.3
1973	3.7	3.9	3.8
1974	0.4	6.6	4.3
1975	−4.2	15.0	8.1
1976	8.0	3.1	4.7
1977	6.8	4.2	5.0
1978	5.1	4.7	4.9
1979	3.9	3.6	3.7
1980	2.5	3.1	2.9
1981	3.8	2.5	2.9
1982	2.3	0.9	1.4
1983	3.6	0.9	1.8
1984	3.1	0.4	1.4
1985	2.8	0.5	1.3
Mean growth rate	3.5%	3.8%	3.7%
Variance of investment	0.047%	0.0061%	0.017%

The introduction of ACRS in 1981 made new investment significantly more attractive than it would have been under the prevailing ADR system. Table 5.6 presents simulation results which illustrate the effects of this legislative change while holding the rest of the economic environment constant. In this simulation investors have perfect foresight and ACRS is never introduced.

Equipment investment in table 5.6 is significantly lower than corresponding perfect-foresight equipment investment in table 5.3b for the ACRS years, in particular 1981 and 1982. Because perfect-foresight

Table 5.6   **Investment: Perfect Foresight and ACRS Never Introduced**

Year	Equipment	Structures	Total
1953	3.0%	3.0%	3.0%
1954	4.2	3.9	4.0
1955	4.2	3.9	4.0
1956	3.5	3.9	3.7
1957	3.2	3.9	3.6
1958	3.0	3.8	3.5
1959	3.6	3.7	3.7
1960	3.5	3.7	3.7
1961	3.9	3.7	3.8
1962	7.6	3.5	5.0
1963	6.9	3.5	4.8
1964	6.7	3.4	4.7
1965	5.7	3.3	4.3
1966	4.8	3.4	4.0
1967	2.0	3.8	3.0
1968	4.6	3.7	4.1
1969	3.9	3.7	3.8
1970	1.2	3.6	2.6
1971	1.4	3.4	2.6
1972	5.3	2.6	3.7
1973	4.6	2.6	3.4
1974	4.2	2.6	3.2
1975	3.8	2.4	3.0
1976	2.6	2.3	2.5
1977	2.1	2.2	2.2
1978	1.5	2.1	1.8
1979	0.8	1.9	1.4
1980	0.5	1.7	1.2
1981	0.7	1.6	1.2
1982	0.6	1.5	1.1
1983	1.0	1.4	1.2
1984	1.1	1.4	1.3
1985	1.3	1.4	1.4
Mean growth rate	3.3%	3.0%	3.1%
Variance of investment	0.038%	0.0082%	0.014%

investors correctly anticipate and wish to smooth future adjustment costs, equipment investment in this run falls off slightly from investment in table 5.3b as early as 1966. In the absence of ACRS, average annual equipment investment is somewhat lower and its variance marginally higher (since ACRS was introduced at a time when macroeconomic conditions were unfavorable to investment). The coefficient of variation for equipment investment in this run is 0.59. Structures investment is less sharply affected by the absence of ACRS. Structures investment in table 5.6 is slightly lower than that in table 5.3b starting in 1959, and experiences a small drop in 1981.

High rates of inflation may discourage investment by lowering the present value of nominal depreciation allowances.[16] Table 5.7 illustrates the effects of rising inflation in the late 1960s and 1970s, by presenting results from a perfect-foresight simulation in which depreciation allowances are indexed to inflation starting in 1954. Equipment investment in table 5.7 is substantially higher over the period 1965–74 than it is in the perfect-foresight simulation without indexing (table 5.3b). Despite more generous depreciation allowances under indexing, equipment investment in table 5.7 is lower in the 1980s than is the investment series in table 5.3b. This feature of table 5.7 reflects the process of

Table 5.7   **Investment: Perfect Foresight and Indexing Introduced in 1954**

Year	Equipment	Structures	Total
1953	3.0%	3.0%	3.0%
1954	4.3	4.0	4.1
1955	4.3	3.9	4.1
1956	3.5	4.0	3.8
1957	3.1	3.9	3.6
1958	3.0	3.9	3.5
1959	3.6	3.8	3.7
1960	3.6	3.8	3.7
1961	4.2	3.8	4.0
1962	7.5	3.6	5.1
1963	7.0	3.7	5.0
1964	7.1	3.5	4.9
1965	6.1	3.5	4.5
1966	5.4	3.5	4.3
1967	2.7	3.9	3.4
1968	5.4	3.8	4.5
1969	4.6	3.8	4.1
1970	1.9	3.7	3.0
1971	2.1	3.5	2.9
1972	5.7	2.8	4.0
1973	5.2	2.7	3.7
1974	4.6	2.7	3.5
1975	3.8	2.6	3.1
1976	2.9	2.4	2.6
1977	2.4	2.3	2.4
1978	1.8	2.2	2.0
1979	1.0	1.9	1.5
1980	0.6	1.8	1.3
1981	0.9	2.0	1.5
1982	0.7	1.8	1.4
1983	0.3	1.9	1.2
1984	0.8	1.7	1.3
1985	1.1	1.6	1.4
Mean growth rate	3.5%	3.1%	3.3%
Variance of investment	0.041%	0.0068%	0.014%

adjustment from a higher capital stock, and is a further reminder of how misleading static cost-of-capital calculations can be in explaining investment. Equipment investment and its variance in table 5.7 are somewhat higher than those in table 5.3b, and have a coefficient of variation of 0.58. Structures investment in table 5.7 is slightly higher than investment in table 5.3b, but does not diverge from the other series very much over any ranges.

5.4   The Economic Effects of Tax Reform

In this section, we consider the impact on investment and firm value of three tax reform proposals that have been seriously considered by the Congress during the past year. The proposals share certain attributes but also have their differences.

All three plans would repeal the investment tax credit. The first plan, the Bradley-Gephardt "Fair Tax," would reduce the corporate tax rate to 30% and provide assets with 250% declining balance depreciation over lifetimes similar to those of the asset depreciation range of the 1970s. The second plan, proposed by President Reagan in May 1985 and generally referred to as Treasury II, would provide specified write-off patterns with comparable lifetimes, fully indexed for inflation, and reduce the corporate tax rate to 33%.[17] The third plan, passed by the House of Representatives and often called the Rostenkowski plan after the chairman of the House Ways and Means Committee, would reduce the corporate tax rate to 36% and provide 200% declining balance depreciation with a switchover to straight-line, indexed for half of all price level changes in excess of 5% per year.

Because all plans would remove the investment tax credit, one would expect a shift in the mix of investment toward structures. The statutory rate reductions should contribute to increases in the value of corporate equity, though the total impact on value of these plans will also depend on the as yet undetermined effects on the overall incentive to invest.

In order to compare the effects of the plans, we simulate each starting from the same initial conditions, and assuming that 1985 economic conditions (e.g., profitability and inflation) will prevail in each subsequent year. The particular assumptions made about previous behavior affect only the equipment and structures capital stocks with which we begin. We assume that investors behaved from 1954 through 1985 with perfect foresight, but expected the tax law and economic conditions of 1985 to last forever.

In considering the effects of the plans, we must also make an assumption about the behavior of interest rates. Since both corporate and personal tax rates would fall under each plan, it is reasonable to expect that some decline in before-tax interest rates would occur; how much is difficult to know without a more complete model of interest rate determination. Thus we consider two polar assumptions: that the real interest rate *after-tax* remains constant, and that the real interest rate *before-tax* remains constant.

Tables 5.8a and 5.8b show the effects on investment of the plans. For comparison, we present in the first column the investment figures predicted for the case in which no change in policy occurs. Tables 5.9a and 5.9b present the corresponding values for average *q*.

Table 5.8a, which presents results for the constant after-tax real interest rate assumption, shows that, without any change in the tax law, investment would be predicted to grow slowly over the next five years as a fraction of the capital stock but remain low. This is a continuation of the investment pattern that should have occurred in recent years in response to the very high prevailing real interest rates and low returns to capital. The growth simply reflects the gradual approach back to the steady state investment level of 3%.

A switch to Bradley-Gephardt would increase the tax burden on equipment and decrease that on structures. In the long run, the effective tax rate on equipment would be 23%, that on structures 26%, compared

Table 5.8a   **Tax Reform and Investment (Constant After-Tax Real Interest Rate): Percentage Growth Rates of Capital under Different Plans**

| | Tax Regime | | | | | |
| | Current Law | | | Rostenkowski | | |
	Equip.	Struc.	Total	Equip.	Struc.	Total
1985	1.6	1.6	1.6	1.6	1.6	1.6
1986	1.7	1.7	1.7	−0.8	2.0	0.8
1987	1.9	1.7	1.8	−0.3	1.9	1.0
1988	2.0	1.7	1.8	0.2	1.9	1.2
1989	2.1	1.8	1.9	0.6	1.8	1.4
1990	2.1	1.8	2.0	0.9	1.8	1.5

| | Bradley-Gephardt | | | Treasury II | | |
	Equip.	Struc.	Total	Equip.	Struc.	Total
1985	1.6	1.6	1.6	1.6	1.6	1.6
1986	0.0	2.1	1.3	0.3	2.2	1.5
1987	0.4	2.1	1.4	0.7	2.2	1.6
1988	0.8	2.1	1.5	1.1	2.2	1.7
1989	1.1	2.0	1.7	1.3	2.2	1.8
1990	1.3	2.0	1.8	1.6	2.2	1.9

Table 5.8b **Tax Reform and Investment (Variable After-Tax Real Interest Rate): Percentage Growth Rates of Capital under Different Plans**

	Tax Regime					
	Current Law			Rostenkowski		
	Equip.	Struc.	Total	Equip.	Struc.	Total
1985	1.6	1.6	1.6	1.6	1.6	1.6
1986	1.7	1.7	1.7	−1.7	1.5	0.2
1987	1.9	1.7	1.8	−1.1	1.4	0.4
1988	2.0	1.7	1.8	−0.5	1.4	0.6
1989	2.1	1.8	1.9	0.0	1.3	0.8
1990	2.1	1.8	2.0	0.4	1.3	1.0

	Bradley-Gephardt			Treasury II		
	Equip.	Struc.	Total	Equip.	Struc.	Total
1985	1.6	1.6	1.6	1.6	1.6	1.6
1986	−1.3	1.4	0.3	−0.7	1.6	0.6
1987	−0.8	1.3	0.5	−0.2	1.5	0.8
1988	−0.3	1.3	0.7	0.2	1.5	1.0
1989	0.2	1.3	0.8	0.6	1.5	1.1
1990	0.5	1.3	1.0	0.9	1.5	1.3

Table 5.9a **Tax Reform and Market Replacement Cost (Constant After-Tax Real Interest Rates): Ratio of Market Value of Capital to Replacement Cost**

	Tax Regime					
	Current Law			Rostenkowski		
	Equip.	Struc.	Total	Equip.	Struc.	Total
1985	0.85	1.11	1.01	0.85	1.11	1.01
1986	0.85	1.12	1.02	1.00	1.28	1.17
1987	0.85	1.12	1.02	0.97	1.28	1.17
1988	0.85	1.13	1.02	0.96	1.28	1.16
1989	0.85	1.14	1.03	0.95	1.28	1.16
1990	0.86	1.14	1.03	0.95	1.29	1.17

	Bradley-Gephardt			Treasury II		
	Equip.	Struc.	Total	Equip.	Struc.	Total
1985	0.85	1.11	1.01	0.85	1.11	1.01
1986	1.07	1.39	1.27	1.05	1.36	1.24
1987	1.08	1.40	1.28	1.06	1.36	1.25
1988	1.08	1.41	1.29	1.06	1.36	1.25
1989	1.09	1.41	1.29	1.07	1.37	1.26
1990	1.10	1.42	1.30	1.08	1.38	1.27

Table 5.9b   **Tax Reform and Market Replacement Cost (Variable After-Tax Real Interest Rates): Ratio of Market Value of Capital to Replacement Cost**

	Tax Regime					
	Current Law			Rostenkowski		
	Equip.	Struc.	Total	Equip.	Struc.	Total
1985	0.85	1.11	1.01	0.85	1.11	1.01
1986	0.85	1.12	1.02	0.94	1.16	1.08
1987	0.85	1.12	1.02	0.92	1.16	1.07
1988	0.85	1.13	1.02	0.91	1.17	1.07
1989	0.85	1.14	1.03	0.91	1.17	1.08
1990	0.86	1.14	1.03	0.91	1.18	1.08
	Bradley-Gephardt			Treasury II		
	Equip.	Struc.	Total	Equip.	Struc.	Total
1985	0.85	1.11	1.01	0.85	1.11	1.01
1986	0.98	1.19	1.11	1.00	1.18	1.11
1987	0.98	1.20	1.12	0.98	1.18	1.11
1988	0.99	1.21	1.13	0.97	1.19	1.11
1989	1.00	1.23	1.14	0.96	1.20	1.11
1990	1.02	1.24	1.16	0.96	1.20	1.11

to 4% and 31%, respectively, under present law. This results in a predicted drop in equipment investment of 1.6% of the equipment capital stock, and an increase of .5% in structures investment. By 1990, the aggregate capital stock is predicted to be about 1.5% lower because of the change. At the same time, the proposal is predicted to cause a jump in the stock market. The average q for both equipment and structures rises substantially, with an aggregate increase in market value of 26%! Over time, it continues to increase as the level of aggregate investment recovers.

Under Treasury II, investment in both equipment and structures would fare better than under the Bradley-Gephardt plan. Overall, investment would fall very little, with long-run effective tax rates of 18% on equipment and 23% on structures. Because of the higher corporate tax rate imposed, Treasury II would also result in lower windfalls than under Bradley-Gephardt, despite its more favorable impact on investment and marginal q.

The Rostenkowski plan would be less favorable for investment than either of the other two proposals, imposing, in the long run, an effective tax rate of 31% on both equipment and structures. The larger rise in the equipment tax burden, combined with the much lower adjustment costs associated with equipment, leads to a sharp decline in equipment investment in 1986, with structures investment behaving much as it did in the previous two simulations. Aggregate fixed investment is predicted to drop by .9 percentage points in 1986 because of adoption of the plan. Given the size of the fixed corporate capital stock relative to GNP, this translates into a drop in investment of just under six-tenths of a percent of GNP and about 5% of gross nonresidential fixed investment. By 1990, the capital stock would be about 3.3% lower than under current law.

Because it would lower the statutory tax rate the least, to 36%, and because it decreases marginal q the most through reduced investment, this plan would provide the smallest windfall to existing capital of the three plans. The aggregate value of average q would rise by 16%, compared to 26% under Bradley-Gephardt and 23% under Treasury II. Thus the Rostenkowski plan would raise more revenue from both new and old assets than would either of the other plans.

The simulations presented in tables 5.8b and 5.9b correspond to the assumption of a fixed before-tax interest rate. The associated increase in after-tax interest rates under the reform plans leads to further reductions in investment and windfalls to old capital. Nevertheless, in no simulation does the windfall fall below 7% of the market value of the capital stock, despite the quite large declines in investment and marginal q that are predicted.

5.5 Conclusion

The analysis in this chapter illustrates the importance of anticipated changes in taxes and other economic variables on investment behavior and firm valuation. Simulation results suggest that postwar U.S. corporate investment behavior can be understood as the outcome of a process in which investors anticipate the general direction of future tax changes. To be sure, our simple model of perfect foresight corporate investment does not explain all the major movements in investment over this period. Yet the simulation runs which explore the consequences of myopic investor expectations reveal how poorly this modeling approach, which is standard in static models, performs in a dynamic context.

The simulation experiments presented in this chapter describe the likely consequences of several alternatives to the historical pattern of corporate taxation. We examine the effects of the investment tax credit by simulating the last 25 years of firm behavior in its absence, and find that although the tax credit increased the variance of equipment investment, it increased mean equipment investment by even more. Of more pertinence to current policy discussions, we also simulate the effects of three of the proposed tax reform proposals. We find that the Treasury II, Bradley-Gephardt and Rostenkowski corporate tax plans all would discourage investment and reduce the size of the corporate capital stock relative to the effects of the current law. One of the advantages of the model described in this chapter is that we can use it to measure the extent of the windfall gains enjoyed by old capital upon introduction of these plans.

Several important aspects of the determinants of corporate investment and firm valuation remain poorly understood. The results in this chapter make us suspect that more attention needs to be devoted to the process by which investors form expectations about future tax policy and macroeconomic conditions.

Appendix
Aggregation of Depreciation Rates and Tax Parameters

What we seek are parameters for aggregate capital goods that, by some measure, accurately reflect those of their components. One criterion that seems reasonable is to require that, for a particular tax system, both net and gross rates of return to capital before tax be the same for the aggregate assets as for the sums of their components. A particular motivation for using this approach is that it results in the effective tax rate, as usually measured, being invariant to the aggregation procedure.

To see what weights this criterion dictates, consider first the special case in which adjustment costs are zero and expectations are myopic. Let Ω_{ij} be the fraction of capital stock j of the total in its class i (equipment or structures) at a particular date. (We suppress the time subscript but emphasize that these capital stock weights are not time invariant.) The gross before tax return to capital of type i is then

(A1) $$\rho_i = \sum_j \Omega_{ij}\rho_j = \sum_j \Omega_{ij}(r + \delta_j)(1 - k_j - \tau z_j)/(1 - \tau)$$

where δ_j, k_j and z_j correspond to asset j. The net return is:

(A2) $$r_i^n = \rho_i - \sum_j \Omega_j \delta_j$$

Thus, the criterion would be satisfied by weighting the individual values of δ by capital stock weights Ω and the tax parameters k and z by $\Omega(r + \delta)$; the tax parameters of short-lived assets should be more heavily weighted. This is an important choice, since the values of $k + \tau z$ generally increase monotonically with δ.[18]

Since capital stock weights change over time, this formula would require recomputation every year. However, this presents an index number problem, and it is unclear that we should prefer a measure with varying weights. Even after this issue is resolved, one must deal with the problem of adjustment costs and varying values of asset-specific q's, about which there is little information. Finally, there is the problem of expectations. When the marginal product of capital is dictated by expression (4), there are no simple weights (that we can think of!) that satisfy the criterion. One would generally have to determine the weights simultaneously with the solution for the marginal product itself, which would make the problem intractable.

In light of the situation, we choose to weight δ by Ω and tax parameters by $\Omega(r + \delta)$, using fixed values for r and the capital stock weights Ω over time. The capital stock weights used are for the year 1977, as described in Auerbach (1983). The rates of economic depreciation come from calculations by Hulten and Wykoff (1981). The fixed value used for r is .04.

Notes

1. For ease of notation, we write $A(\cdot)$ as a function of I_t alone rather than all its arguments.
2. The constancy of π is not assumed in our analysis, and is used here only for the sake of simplicity. Some of the later simulations examine the effect of allowing r to vary.
3. Note that net investment is simply the first difference of the capital stock.
4. This and other tax data used are described in appendix A of Auerbach (1983).
5. This would be true only if, among other things, the effective tax rates on all forms of capital were equal, which they were not.
6. This assumption is required if we are to consider the investment decisions separately for structures and equipment.
7. This marginal product definition is required for G to be homogeneous of degree one with respect to its inputs.
8. The internal consistency of this procedure can be verified by noting that, given this solution for α_1 and α_2, $R_g(K_1 + K_2)$ equals $[(\alpha_1 + \alpha_2)F - A(I) - \delta_1 K_1 - \delta_2 K_2]$ which, by (11) and (12), equals $[Y - R_g(K_3 + K_4) - (1 - \alpha_1 - \alpha_2)F]$. Thus the net returns to capital equal value added less the competitive return to labor.
9. Denison (1979, 92) finds all factors and productivity changes other than capital growth to contribute exactly 3.00% annually to the growth of U.S. nonresidential business output over the period 1948–73. While this figure includes noncorporate businesses and would presumably be lower over the period of the 1970s, it suggests that 3% is the most reasonable choice for the exogenous growth rate of noncapital inputs.

10. These include the presence of returns to other factors in the firm's market value, heterogeneity of the capital stock, and the standard use of a tax adjustments based on myopia of expectations about future changes in the tax law. Some evidence in support of this comes from the finding by Abel and Blanchard (1986) that the coefficient of investment on adjusted q rises substantially when the variable is purged of that part of its variation estimated to have come from fluctuations in the cost of capital (as opposed to profitability). In addition, there has been very little work done which estimates separate adjustment cost parameters for different types of capital; for an exploratory effort, see Chirinko (1984).

11. As Andrew Abel has pointed out, if actual investment series are measured with noise then our calibration method will in general lead to adjustment cost parameters which are smaller than the true parameters. However, our resulting estimates are similar to those obtained from q investment equations, which we believe to yield estimates that are biased upward.

12. See the discussion in Auerbach and Hines (1986).

13. When expectations are nonmyopic, q' is defined consistently, with future changes in π taken into account.

14. Nor is it easily explained by the assumption that investors know that one of the favorable tax reform proposals is imminent. In a perfect foresight run (not reported here) in which it was known all along that the House Ways and Means Committee proposal was to be adopted in 1986, equipment investment in 1985 would be only 1.3%. This conclusion could be reversed, however, if investors only recently learned of a forthcoming tax law change.

15. See, for example, Auerbach and Summers (1979).

16. Of course, inflation affects the incentive to invest through other channels as well. See, for example, the discussions in Auerbach (1979), Bradford (1981), and Hall (1981).

17. Also proposed as part of Treasury II was a recapture of "excess depreciation" attributable to investors being able to take into the tax base at a 33% rate income deferred through accelerated depreciation under the current 46% tax rate. The provision would have raised an estimated $56.1 billion between fiscal years 1986 and 1989, equal to about 2% of the value of the fixed corporate capital stock in present value. This provision is not included in our calculations. If truly unanticipated, however, its inclusion in our model would simply lead to a reduction in the 1986 value of average q under Treasury II of about 2%, with no other impact. As the results below suggest, this lump sum tax is quite small compared to the windfall gains that Treasury II would produce overall for owners of existing assets.

18. We note in passing that if the rate of growth of the capital stock, say g, equals the interest rate, then this latter set of weights corresponds to using investment *flow* weights rather than capital *stock* weights.

References

Abel, A., and O. Blanchard. 1986. The present value of profits and cyclical movements in investment. *Econometrica* 54, no. 2:249–73.

Auerbach, A. 1979. Inflation and the choice of asset life. *Journal of Political Economy* 87, no. 3:621–38.

————. 1983. Corporate taxation in the United States. *Brookings Papers on Economic Activity* 14, no. 2:451–505.

Auerbach, A., and J. Hines. 1986. Tax reform, investment, and the value of the firm. NBER Working Paper no. 1803 (January).

Auerbach, A., and L. Summers. 1979. The investment tax credit: An evaluation. NBER Working Paper no. 404 (November).

Bradford, D. 1981. Issues in the design of savings and investment incentives. In *Depreciation, inflation, and the taxation of income from capital,* ed. C. Hulten, 13–47. Washington, D.C.: The Urban Institute Press.

Chirinko, R. 1984. Investment, Tobin's Q, and multiple capital inputs. Cornell University, mimeograph.

Denison, E. 1979. Accounting for slower economic growth: The United States in the 1970s. Washington, D.C.: Brookings Institute.

Feldstein, M., J. Poterba, and L. Dicks-Mireaux. 1983. The effective tax rate and the pretax rate of return. *Journal of Public Economics* 21:129–58.

Hall, R. 1981. Tax treatment of depreciation, capital gains, and interest in an inflationary economy. In *Depreciation, inflation, and the taxation of income from capital,* ed. C. Hulten, 149–66. Washington, D.C.: The Urban Institute Press.

Hulten, C., and F. Wykoff. 1981. The measurement of economic depreciation. In *Depreciation, inflation, and the taxation of income from capital,* ed. C. Hulten, 81–125. Washington, D.C.: The Urban Institute Press.

Summers, L. 1981. Taxation and corporate investment: A q theory approach. *Brookings Papers on Economic Activity* 12, no. 1:67–127.

Comment   Andrew B. Abel

Alan Auerbach and James Hines have skillfully built, calibrated, and simulated a model to analyze the effects of tax policy on U.S. capital investment. Their simulation model produces time series for investment in equipment and structures, effective tax rates, and market valuations of firms. I will address three major issues in my comments: (1) the usefulness of a q-theoretic simulation model to examine the dynamic response of investment to tax policy changes; (2) calibration versus estimation as a method for choosing parameter values; and (3) the stabilizing or destabilizing effects of the investment tax credit.

1. The q theory of investment provides a simple and logically coherent framework for analyzing the dynamic response of investment to changes in tax policy. The theory depends quite heavily on the existence of convex adjustment costs—the notion that the marginal cost of investment is an increasing function of the rate of investment.

Andrew B. Abel is Amoco Foundation Term Professor of Finance at the Wharton School of the University of Pennsylvania and a research associate of the National Bureau of Economic Research. This comment was prepared while he was John L. Loeb Associate Professor of the Social Sciences at Harvard University.

Increasing marginal adjustment costs imply that investment will respond smoothly to changes in tax policies, and the q theory has proved to be extremely useful in analyzing the responses to temporary as well as permanent tax changes and the responses to anticipated as well as unanticipated tax changes. The phase diagrams used in the q model are simple and powerful tools which probably lead some of us to put more faith in the ability of q models to predict the short-run dynamic behavior of investment than is warranted.

Although there is some empirical support for the q model of investment, there are three major problems when the q theory is confronted with actual data. The theory predicts that investment will be a function only of the contemporaneous value of marginal q. In particular, neither contemporaneous output or profits nor lagged q should affect investment. However, empirical investment equations typically find that, on quarterly data, both lagged q and some measure of output or profits have significant effects on investment. Furthermore, these equations usually leave unexplained a large serially correlated portion of the variation in investment. Of these three departures from the simple theory, the most crucial for the issue of the *timing* of investment is the finding that lagged q and twice lagged q have significant effects on investment. If lagged q as well as contemporaneous q is a determinant of investment. then the dynamic structure of investment and, in particular, the short-run response of investment to tax policy is dramatically altered. Although the econometric evidence to date cannot definitively conclude that the significance of lagged q is due to delivery lags, it does at least remind us of the fact that it often takes several months for new equipment to be ordered, acquired, and installed. The delivery lag for structures is more appropriately measured in quarters or even in years.

The Auerbach-Hines model is based on annual data and one may argue that for equipment, at least, delivery lags are not important. However, the lags for new structures probably are quite substantial and, to the extent that the time paths of equipment and structures are linked (both through each component's effects on the marginal product of the other component and through interrelated adjustment costs), the lags in structures investment will spill over into equipment investment.

2. After specifying the structure of their simulation model, Auerbach and Hines had to choose values for the parameters of the model. I will focus on their method for choosing the parameters of the adjustment cost function β_0, β_1, and β_2. Previous authors have estimated these cost parameters from regressions of investment on q. In a model with only one type of capital good, the adjustment cost parameter β is equal to the inverse of the coefficient of investment on q. Auerbach and Hines decided against using available econometric estimates for the

adjustment cost parameters because, in their judgment as well as the judgment of some the people who produced these estimates, the estimated adjustment costs are too large; equivalently, the coefficient on q is considered to be too small. The reason for the alleged downward bias in the coefficient on q is that q is measured with error.

In order to avoid the downward bias in the response of investment to changes in q, Auerbach and Hines chose values of the adjustment cost parameters β_0, β_1, and β_2 which produced simulations in which the variance of investment is equal to the historical variance of investment. A complete analysis of the properties of the Auerbach-Hines procedure for choosing values for β is quite complex and certainly beyond the scope of this comment. To examine their procedure in a simple special case, suppose that y_t is investment and that we want to estimate θ in the regression

$$(1) \qquad\qquad y_t = \theta q^*_t + \epsilon_t$$

where q^*_t is the true value of marginal q at time t. However, the true value of marginal q is unobservable but we can observe q_t which is a noisy measure of marginal q

$$(2) \qquad\qquad q_t = q^*_t + \eta_t$$

For simplicity, we assume that ϵ_t and η_t are each serially uncorrelated and are uncorrelated with each other. Substituting (2) into (1) yields a relation between investment y_t and the observable variable q_t

$$(3) \qquad\qquad y_t = \theta q_t + \epsilon_t - \theta \eta_t$$

The Auerbach-Hines procedure chooses an estimate θ_{AH} to equate the variance of the predicted series $\theta_{AH}^2 \text{var}(q_t)$ with the variance of y_t. Letting θ_{OLS} be the ordinary least-squares estimate of θ, we have

$$(4) \qquad\qquad \text{plim } \theta_{OLS} = \text{cov}(y, q)/\text{var}(q) = \rho \sigma_y/\sigma_q$$

$$(5) \qquad\qquad \text{plim } \theta_{AH} = [\text{var}(y)/\text{var}(q)]^{1/2} = \sigma_y/\sigma_q$$

where σ_x denotes the standard deviation of x and ρ is the contemporaneous correlation between q_t and y_t. It is clear from (4) and (5) that θ_{AH} is greater than θ_{OLS} which is biased downward because of measurement error. However, θ_{AH} is not in general a consistent estimate of θ since

$$(6) \qquad\qquad \text{plim } \theta_{AH}^2 = \theta^2 + [\sigma_\epsilon^2 - \theta^2 \sigma_\eta^2]/\sigma_q^2$$

As a measure of how well the simulated investment series tracks the expected value of the investment series over the historical sample, we can calculate the correlation of the predicted series, $\theta_{AH} q_t$, and the expected value of y_t, θq^*_t. It can be shown that asymptotically

$$(7) \qquad\qquad \text{correlation }(\theta_{AH} q_t, \theta q^*_t) = [\sigma_{q^*}^2/(\sigma_{q^*}^2 + \sigma_\eta^2)]^{1/2}$$

Observe from (7) that the correlation of the simulated series and the expected value of y_t approaches one as σ_η^2 approaches zero. However, as σ_η^2 approaches zero, the estimate θ_{AH} becomes increasingly biased upward. The implication of this upward bias is that if the measurement error is unaffected by the simulated changes in policy, then the simulated effects of tax policy on investment will be overstated.

3. In order to address the question of whether the investment tax credit (ITC) is stabilizing or destabilizing, Auerbach and Hines present simulation results both with and without the ITC. They find that the presence of the ITC leads to a higher mean rate of investment and a higher variance of the rate of investment; the coefficient of variation of the rate of investment is hardly affected by the presence or absence of the ITC. In addressing the question of whether or not the ITC is stabilizing, Auerbach and Hines come to different conclusions depending on whether they measure stability by the variance or by the coefficient of variation of investment. The authors do not take a stand on which measure is more appropriate. It is worth noting that in the absence of population growth, the stochastic steady state of the economy would have an average growth rate near zero (the average value of I/K may not be literally zero), and in this case the coefficient of variation would be undefined.

If one is ultimately interested in social welfare, then the focus on the stability of investment is, of course, misplaced. Ideally, the model could be closed by including consumers who save and consume in order to maximize an intertemporal utility function. Specifying individual utility functions would then allow for a direct comparison of utility in the cases with and without the ITC.

In the absence of a general equilibrium model, it would appear that focusing on the stability of GNP would be more appropriate than focusing on the stability of the rate of investment. To get a handle on the question of the stability of GNP, note that under myopic expectations $q = F_K/[(1 - k - \tau z)r]$ where F_K is the marginal product of capital, r is the real rate of interest, k is the rate of the ITC, τ is the corporate tax rate, and z is the present value of depreciation deductions. Now consider a simple IS/LM model in which $Y = c(Y) + I(q) + G$ where Y is national income, $c(Y)$ is a Keynesian consumption function, $I(q)$ is the investment equation, and G is government purchases of goods and services. In comparing the cases with and without the ITC, note that the interest sensitivity of q is greater in the presence of the ITC. Therefore, the presence of the ITC causes the IS curve to be flatter than in the absence of the ITC. Finally we assume that the rate of inflation π is fixed and that there is a standard upward-sloping LM schedule $m = L(Y, r + \pi)$ where m is real money balances and $L(,)$ is the real demand for money.

Now consider the case in which the IS curve is fixed but the LM schedule is subject to random shocks. In this case, an outward shift of the LM schedule reduces the interest rate and increases both investment and output. In the presence of the ITC, the increases in both output and investment are greater than in the absence of ITC (see fig. 5.1). A symmetric argument for leftward shifts of the LM schedule suggests that the ITC destabilizes both output and investment.

Alternatively, suppose that the LM schedule is fixed but that G is stochastic. An increase in G shifts the IS curve to the right, leading to higher output, higher interest rate, and lower investment. In the presence of the ITC, the drop in investment is larger and increase in output is smaller than in the absence of the ITC (see fig. 5.2). A symmetric argument for a decrease in G suggests that under this stochastic specification the ITC again destabilizes investment. However, contrary to the case with a stochastic LM schedule, the ITC stabilizes output.

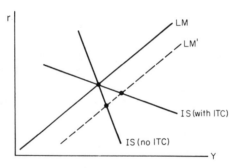

Fig. 5.1   Stochastic LM curve

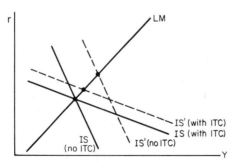

Fig. 5.2   Stochastic government spending

6 New Results on the Effects of Tax Policy on the International Location of Investment

Michael J. Boskin and William G. Gale

6.1 Introduction

Foreign direct investment (FDI) in the United States and U.S. direct investment abroad (DIA) are important economic phenomena as well as a source of political controversy. In 1980, FDI reached $17 billion, about 22% as large as net domestic fixed investment. Correspondingly, DIA reached $19 billion, about 25% as large as net domestic investment in plant and equipment. Since 1980, substantial FDI has continued, whereas DIA has fallen precipitously. Further, the sources of finance for FDI and the uses of earnings on DIA have changed dramatically in the past few years.

These flows—in both directions—have become a concern of tax policy. For example, the adoption of the Accelerated Cost Recovery System (ACRS) in 1981, as amended in 1982, was expressly limited to investment in the United States. While the primary motivation behind ACRS was to increase U.S. domestic capital formation, a secondary concern, evidenced in the hearings preceding its adoption, was to stem the flow of U.S. investment abroad. Further, FDI is often seen as an important justification for continuing the U.S. corporate income tax, even by those who favor corporate and personal tax integration. Another example of revenue (and perhaps location of investment) concern is the per country limitation to the foreign tax credit in the administration's tax reform proposal.

Michael J. Boskin is professor of economics at Stanford University and research associate in the Taxation Program of the National Bureau of Economic Research, Inc. William G. Gale is currently a John M. Olin Graduate Research Fellow at Stanford University.

The authors wish to thank Steve Tomlinson for valuable advice, David Hartman for suggestions, and Martin Feldstein and Joosung Jun for generously sharing their data with us.

Multinational firms undoubtedly invest outside their home country for a wide variety of reasons: access to markets, political considerations, labor costs, proximity to suppliers, and expected economic conditions, to name a few. Often, the reasons may be industry-, firm-, or even product-specific. Given these other forces shaping the international location of investment, however, tax laws potentially affect the attractiveness of U.S. direct investment abroad and foreign direct investment in the U.S., as well as the repatriation of earnings and/or capital. The major changes in U.S. domestic investment incentives enacted in 1981 and 1982 (ERTA and TEFRA, respectively) combined with the trends in FDI and DIA, as well as current tax reform proposals which might affect tax rates on DIA and FDI substantially, lead us to reexamine the question of the extent to which tax policy appears to influence the international location of investment.

We begin in section 6.2 with a brief literature review, focusing on the differing effects on the location of investment of tax policy toward domestic investment and toward foreign source income. The argument in Hartman (1981,1984, 1985)—that foreign investment financed by retained earnings should not be influenced by the (deferred) home country tax on foreign source income—is presented and some caveats suggested.

Section 6.3 presents a description of recent trends in FDI and DIA, their sources of finance and their uses, as well as their industrial composition and origin or location, respectively. It also describes the data used in our study.

Section 6.4 presents our empirical results. First, for the period 1965–79, we compare our results using revised data to those of Hartman. The results are fairly robust to the data revisions. Next, for both FDI and DIA we use revised data on extended sample periods and several alternative functional forms and combinations of variables to test the impact of tax policy on FDI and DIA. We conclude that tax policy can have significant effects on the international location of investment. Our results are similar to the quantitative estimates in Hartman's several studies for some of the effects, but they are only about one-third to one-half as large for others, for example, the impact of U.S. domestic tax policy on U.S. direct investment abroad.

Section 6.5 presents a brief summary and conclusion, including rough estimates of the likely impacts of recent tax policy and current proposals on the international location of investment, and an analysis of the welfare effects of taxation of FDI and DIA.

6.2 A Brief Review of the Literature

The effects of domestic tax policy on the international location of investment occur primarily through two channels: home country tax policy toward investment in the home country and home country tax policy toward foreign source income.[1]

Domestic tax policy toward investments made in the home country affects both FDI in the home country and DIA by home country firms. This occurs because tax policy alters the relative rates of return available at home and abroad. Entrepreneurs investing capital will naturally be attracted to locations where the (risk-adjusted) rate of return is highest.[2] Of course, this channel hinges on the substitutability of foreign and domestic investment for a firm. However, the common conception of foreign and domestic investment as alternative methods of producing the same good and/or serving the same (geographic) market suggests that there is some substitution between locations of investment. Moreover, as discussed in Hartman (1981), if there are financial constraints on firms, there will be a clear tradeoff between foreign and domestic operations. Thus, there are good theoretical reasons for domestic tax policy to affect both FDI and DIA through its effects on relative rates of return. Empirically, this view has been supported by results in Hartman (1981, 1984) and below.

The importance of taxes on foreign source income has long been a subject of debate. There are two major approaches to taxation of foreign source income. In the "territorial" approach, the company pays no home country taxes on foreign income. In the "residence" approach, the company does pay home country taxes, but often a credit or deduction is allowed for taxes paid in the host country. The United States taxes with the residence approach, but allows a credit for taxes paid to other countries.

Research in the 1960s and 1970s focused largely on the issue of "capital export neutrality," the equivalent tax treatment of the foreign and domestic returns of multinational companies. In this regard, it was argued that, under a residential system with a credit for foreign taxes, the ability to defer taxation on foreign source income conferred a tax advantage toward investment abroad.[3]

This view has been challenged by Hartman (1981, 1984, 1985). Hartman properly draws attention to the distinction between investment financed out of retained earnings abroad and investment financed by transfers from home. If the subsidiary is investing out of retained earnings, the home country tax on foreign source income does not affect the marginal investment decision, because the repatriation of earnings, not the earnings themselves, are the tax base. The home country tax on foreign source income is unavoidable, and its present value does not depend on the length of deferral. Thus, the marginal investment decision for investment out of retained earnings should depend only on net returns available in the home country or the host country. Hartman calls this "capital import neutrality," that is, the same tax rates influence the decisions of both U.S. firms in the U.S. and foreign firms in the U.S. that finance investment by retained earnings.[4]

For firms that finance foreign investment by transfers from home, the home country tax on foreign source income does matter because no foreign earnings have accrued and thus the tax on foreign source income is avoidable. One implication of this theory is that a foreign affiliate should never simultaneously repatriate earnings and draw funds from home, since this creates a completely avoidable tax liability. Hartman defines firms that finance foreign investment by retention of earnings as "mature" firms, those that finance investment by transfers from home as "immature." He argues that a large part of U.S. DIA is undertaken by mature firms, since approximately 70% of DIA in 1975–79 was financed by retained earnings. Thus, he concludes, "the size of the U.S. tax burden on foreign source income should be irrelevant for investment decisions" (1985, p. 119).

Several caveats apply to this conclusion. First, it should be noted that neither we nor Hartman test this proposition. Second, in recent years DIA financed by retained earnings has risen while DIA has fallen, suggesting a reexamination of the issues. Third, domestic treatment of foreign source income will not matter for timing of repatriation only if the domestic tax rate is known and thought to be permanent. If major tax policy revisions occur frequently (as in fact they have), then a firm will have an incentive to wait for lower rates.

6.3 Data

6.3.1 Introduction

Foreign direct investment refers to the infusion of funds into a U.S. subsidiary by the foreign parent or the retention of earnings by that subsidiary. The Bureau of Economic Analysis defines a U.S. affiliate as "a U.S. business enterprise in which a foreign person owns or controls, directly or indirectly, at least 10% of the voting securities if an incorporated U.S. business enterprise or an equivalent interest if an unincorporated business enterprise."[5] U.S. direct investment abroad is defined equivalently for the foreign subsidiaries of U.S. parent companies.[6]

Two aspects of this definition merit comment. First, foreign direct investment and direct investment abroad are not necessarily the dominant aspects of international capital flows. As of the end of year 1984, foreign direct investment in the United States accounted for approximately 18% of all foreign assets in the United States, while U.S. direct investment abroad represented 25% of U.S. assets abroad (Scholl 1985).

Second, foreign direct investment is not the exact counterpart to domestic net investment figures. For example, inflows of funds (or retention of earnings) are not necessarily used to purchase real capital assets, so FDI may overstate real foreign net investment. On the other hand, U.S. borrowing by the U.S. subsidiary is not part of the calculation of FDI. Hartman (1984) suggests that it is reasonable to use FDI figures as net foreign investment. Hartman (1981) shows that an equivalent proposition also holds for U.S. direct investment abroad.

6.3.2 Trends

Summary data for foreign direct investment in the United States and U.S. direct investment abroad are presented in tables 6.1, 6.2, and 6.3.

As shown in table 6.1, foreign direct investment has grown 2000% in real terms from 1950 to 1984. Large swings characterize the last

Table 6.1 Selected Data on Foreign Direct Investment in the United States, 1950–84

Year	FDI (current $ millions)	FDI as a % of Non-residential Net Investment	% of FDI Financed by Retained Earnings[a]	Reinvestment Ratio for FDI Income[b]
1950	$270	2.8%	70.4%	52.9%
1960	315	2.6	55.2	44.2
1970	1,464	4.3	29.6	49.6
1971	367	1.2	147.7	46.6
1972	949	2.5	60.0	44.3
1973	2,800	5.3	32.5	56.6
1974	4,760	9.6	22.4	80.0
1975	2,603	8.5	45.7	53.3
1976	4,346	12.6	38.2	53.3
1977	3,728	7.3	42.5	55.9
1978	7,896	10.7	32.7	61.3
1979	11,876	13.3	33.3	62.2
1980	16,918	21.9	30.6	60.0
1981	25,195	27.8	11.7	43.8
1982	13,792	22.5	− 17.2	− 75.4
1983	11,946	24.0	0.7	1.6
1984	22,514	21.0	16.5	36.5

Source: Foreign direct investment and its components: *U.S. Department of Commerce, Bureau of Economic Analysis, 1984,* and various issues of *Survey of Current Business.* Nonresidential net investment: *Economic Report of the President, 1985,* table B-15, p. 250. Values of GNP deflator are 1950:53.56, 1960:68.70, 1970:91.45, 1980:178.42, 1984:223.38.

[a]Foreign direct investment is financed either by retention of earnings or by intercompany flows of equity or debt. Retained earnings are negative when divident payments to equity holders are larger than earnings. Intercompany flows are net figures and are negative when more funds flow out of the U.S. subsidiary than into it. Thus, the ratio listed above may be greater than 100% or less than 0. In 1982, retained earnings were negative.

[b]This ratio measures FDI financed by retained earnings divided by FDI income. It can be negative for the reasons stated in note a.

third of this period, with tremendous growth from 1977 to 1981, a collapse of 50% in 1982 and 1983, and a doubling in 1984. FDI figures are also large in relative terms. In every year since 1980, FDI has been more than 20% of U.S. nonresidential net investment in plant and equipment. This is especially noteworthy for 1984, because net investment in the U.S. rose by over 100% of its 1983 level. The composition of the sources of FDI has changed over time. Since 1977, the percentage of FDI financed by retained earnings has fallen substantially. This has occurred contemporaneously with the large rise in FDI documented in column 1, thus suggesting that investment financed by intercompany debt and equity flows has dominated FDI in recent years. Finally, column 4 shows that the reinvestment ratio for FDI income has also fallen since 1982, though it was relatively stable in earlier periods.

U.S. direct investment abroad, shown in table 6.2, grew steadily through 1979 but has since collapsed, representing a large and continuing repatriation of funds to the U.S. Real DIA in 1984 is only 2% higher than it was in 1950. These notions are reinforced by examination of DIA as a percentage of U.S. nonresidential net investment. DIA was consistently 20% or more of net investment in the 1960s and 1970s but has collapsed to 11% or less since 1981. The composition of DIA finance, shown in column 3, has undergone extreme gyrations in recent years. Nevertheless, the reinvestment ratio for DIA income has remained relatively stable.

Table 6.3 provides a snapshot of the level and composition of the U.S. positions in FDI and DIA as of the end of 1984. Both FDI and DIA have accumulated substantial positions. Approximately one-third of the FDI position is in manufacturing and one-sixth in petroleum. These two industries also account for 40% and 25% of the DIA position, respectively. Not surprisingly, European countries account for the largest share of both positions. Although Japan accounts for only 9.3% of the FDI position, it should be noted that this figure has risen from 2.1% in 1975 and 6.4% in 1979. Moreover, as noted above, capital inflows may occur predominantly in forms other than FDI.

Thus, even a cursory examination of the data suggests that both FDI and DIA can be substantial. The wide swings suggest further that international investment flows may be very sensitive to current or anticipated conditions. Before proceeding to a more formal analysis, however, issues concerning the data should be noted.

6.3.3 Sources

All data on FDI and DIA have been obtained from either *Selected Data on Foreign Direct Investment in the United States, 1950–79; Selected Data on U.S. Direct Investment Abroad, 1950–76;* or the

Table 6.2   Selected Data on Direct Investment Abroad by U.S. Firms, 1950–84

Year	DIA (current $ millions)	DIA as a % of Non-residential Net Investment	% of DIA Financed by Retained Earnings[a]	Reinvestment Ratios for DIA Income[b]
1950	$1,096	11.4%	43.3%	26.8%
1960	2,941	23.9	43.0	35.0
1970	7,589	22.3	41.8	38.9
1971	7,617	24.4	41.7	34.7
1972	7,746	20.9	58.5	41.4
1973	11,353	21.8	71.8	49.3
1974	9,052	18.4	85.9	40.6
1975	14,244	47.0	56.5	48.5
1976	11,949	34.8	64.4	40.5
1977	11,893	23.5	53.8	32.5
1978	16,056	21.8	70.6	44.6
1979	25,222	28.4	75.2	49.7
1980	19,222	24.9	88.5	45.8
1981	9,624	10.6	140.1	41.6
1982	− 4,424	− 7.2	− 151.6	29.7
1983	5,394	10.8	178.0	45.1
1984	4,503	4.2	243.5	47.5

Source: Direct investment abroad and its components: U.S. Department of Commerce, Bureau of Economic Analysis, (1983b), and various issues of *Survey of Current Business.*
[a]See note a table 6.1. In 1982, DIA financed by retained earnings was positive, but DIA financed by transfers was negative and larger in absolute value.
[b]See note b, table 6.1.

Table 6.3   U.S. Direct Investment Positions, 1984

Position	Foreign Direct Investment (millions)	Direct Investment Abroad (millions)
Total	$159,571	$233,412
By Industry		
Petroleum	24,916	63,319
Manufacturing	50,664	93,012
Wholesale Trade	24,042	—
Other	59,949	77,081
By Political Unit		
Canada	14,001	50,467
Europe	106,567	103,663
Japan	14,817	8,374
Other	24,187	70,908

Source: Survey of Current Business, August 1985, pp. 30, 36, 47.

annual surveys of these topics in the *Survey of Current Business,* all of which are publications of the Bureau of Economic Analysis (BEA).

BEA develops these series by conducting occasional benchmark surveys of virtually all firms involved in FDI or DIA. They construct between year data by conducting annual sample surveys and extrapolating the total figures based on the firms in the sample surveys and the previous benchmark survey. Thus, as the time since the latest benchmark survey increases, the chance of misestimation would seem to increase. BEA conducted DIA benchmark surveys in 1966, 1977, and 1982. FDI surveys were undertaken in 1974 and 1980.

The 1980 FDI survey in particular generated substantial revisions in data for 1980 and later dates. For example, the direct investment position in FDI was revised upward by 21%, capital inflows (i.e., foreign direct investment) were revised upward by 24%, and FDI income was revised downward by 9% (Belli 1984). With these revised data for 1980, the direct investment position rose 52% from its 1979 value, and FDI was 42% higher than in 1979. Note that BEA did not revise the data from the 1970s based on the 1980 benchmark survey.

There is reason to believe that a substantial part of the abrupt jumps in these series is due to underreporting during the 1970s. Specifically, BEA estimates that about 75% of the revision in the capital inflows figure was accounted for by affiliates that *should have reported* in the annual sample surveys but did not.[7]

One additional concern is that through 1979 BEA collected retained earnings for incorporated affiliates only. In 1980, unincorporated affiliates began to report retained earnings too. Thus, the series "investment financed by retained earnings" (I_{re} below) refers to incorporated affiliates only through 1979, and all affiliates in 1980 and thereafter. BEA presented separate data for incorporated and unincorporated affiliates for 1980–83, but has since discontinued the practice.

To account for the problems with the data discussed above, we have conducted a variety of alternative specifications. The alternatives are discussed with other regression results in section 6.4.

All tax rate and rate-of-return data have been generously supplied by Martin Feldstein and Joosung Jun (1986). Data on U.S. gross national product, actual and middle cycle expansion path, have been taken from the *Economic Report of the President, 1985* and de Leeuw and Holloway (1983). Data concerning gross domestic product in OECD countries were obtained from *National Accounts of OECD Countries, 1950–68* and *1950–78,* and *OECD Main Economic Indicators* in recent years.

6.4   Results

Table 6.4A presents FDI equations for 1965–79 estimated by us and Hartman (1984). The data that Hartman used were presented in an

Table 6.4A   Comparison of Basic Results for Foreign Direct Investment, 1965–79

Dependent Variable	$\ln(I_{re}/Y)$[a]		$\ln(I_{re}/E)$[b]		$\ln(I_f/Y)$[c]	
	Hartman	Boskin & Gale[d]	Hartman	Boskin & Gale	Hartman	Boskin & Gale
Coefficient (s.e.) on						
constant	-6.573	5.217	2.386	1.932	8.535	4.698
	(.679)	(1.102)	(.679)	(.751)	(1.635)	(2.604)
$\ln$ (return on FDI)[e]	1.436	1.443	.275	.306	.552	.536
	(.118)	(.113)	(.087)	(.091)	(.284)	(.314)
$\ln$ (Foreigners' net return in U.S.)[f]	1.232	.879	1.045	.810	1.674	1.096
	(.376)	(.341)	(.277)	(.232)	(.905)	(.806)
$\ln$ (relative tax term)[g]	-1.720	-1.382	-1.602	-1.397	-2.329	-1.763
	(.415)	(.393)	(.306)	(.267)	(.998)	(.928)
Standard error of regression	.096	.117	.071	.070	.590	.244
Adjusted R^2	.940	.931	.750	.753	.286	.205
Durbin-Watson	1.67	1.54	2.26	2.32	1.92	1.87

Source: All data are provided in Hartman (1984). A revised series for tax rates and rates of return have been supplied by Martin Feldstein and Joosung Jun (1986).

[a] I_{re} is foreign direct investment financed by retained earnings.

[b] E represents income from foreign direct investment. Income = earnings + interest (net of withholding taxes) − withholding taxes on distributed earnings.

[c] I_f refers to investment financed by transfers of funds into the country. This series is also multiplied by 1000 and divided by GNP. Moreover, since I_f is negative in 1971, Hartman adds 1.676 billion to I_f before transforming. To allow comparability, we add this constant too.

[d] Our results use the updated series provided by Feldstein and Jun. Our estimates using the data presented in Hartman (1984) are very close to our results in this table.

[e] Return on FDI is calculated as income from foreign direct investment divided by end-of-year direct investment position (in FDI) for the previous year.

[f] Foreigners' return in the United States is defined as the overall gross rate of return × one − the tax rate paid at the corporate level.

[g] The relative tax term = $(1 - t')/(1 - t)$, where t' = the total effective tax rate, t = tax rate paid at the corporate level.

appendix to that article. Our results use a revised tax rate and rate-of-return series presented in Feldstein and Jun (1986). Our results with the original data are very close to Hartman's. With the revised data, our estimates of the effects of taxes and rates of return are still similar to Hartman's, especially for the retained earnings equations. For the equations examining I_{re}, our estimates show a decline in the elasticities with respect to foreigners' net return in the U.S., to 0.9 from 1.2 in the I_{re}/Y equation, and to 0.8 from 1.0 in the retention ratio equation. We also find a lower elasticity for the relative tax term.[8] None of the point estimates changes by more than one standard deviation. We are thus heartened by the stability of the major qualitative conclusions and quantitative results for the I_{re} equations. The results hold up well with either the original or revised data. The I_t/Y equations seem to be slightly more sensitive to the data revisions. The t-statistics and relative magnitudes of the coefficients do remain stable, though.

In table 6.4B, we present basic results for DIA in the 1965–79 period. Here, the data revisions have no effect on the sensitivity of DIA to its

Table 6.4B   **Comparison of Basic Results for Direct Investment Abroad, 1965–79**

Dependent Variable	(I_{re}/Y)[a]			
	Hartman	Boskin & Gale	Hartman	Boskin & Gale
Coefficient (s.e.) on				
constant	.003736	− .000994	.003681	− .001257
	(.000489)	(.000898)	(.001758)	(.002060)
Net return[b]	− .0671	− .0207	—	—
in U.S.	(.0080)	(.0102)		
Return on DIA[c]	.0412	.0404	.0411	.0407
	(.0045)	(.0039)	(.0048)	(.0045)
Gross return	—	—	− .0674	− .0224
in U.S.	—	—	(.0138)	(.0157)
Gross return ×	—	—	.0684	.0267
effective tax	—	—	(.0420)	(.0431)
rate				
Dummy for 1974	− .00186	.000991	− .00188	− .00105
	(.00049)	(.000475)	(.00064)	(.00064)
Standard error	.000405	.000399	.000424	.000418
of regression				
Adjusted R^2	.937	.941	.931	.954
Durbin-Watson	2.15	1.82	2.15	1.82

Source: Hartman (1981).

[a]Defined as direct investment abroad financed by retained earnings divided by U.S. GNP.

[b]Defined as overall gross rate of return × (one − the total effective tax rate.)

[c]Defined as income from direct investment abroad divided by the end-of-year direct investment position (in DIA) for the previous year.

own rate of return. The effect is quite strong (the elasticity calculated at mean values is approximately 1.4) and statistically significant. Our estimates of the response of DIA to the net return in the United States, however, are approximately one-third the size of Hartman's. (We estimate an elasticity of 0.2, compared to Hartman's 0.66.) Our estimates, like Hartman's, found that the after-tax return is the relevant measure; the coefficients on gross return are equal and opposite in sign to the coefficients on gross return times the total effective tax rate. As with the net return, Hartman's coefficients are three times as large as ours. These basic equations appear to fit the data well. Nevertheless, the data revisions seem to have an important effect on the sensitivity of DIA to variations in the net-of-tax return in the United States.

In summary, except for the I_t/Y equation for FDI and the elasticity of DIA with respect to net return in the United States, we obtain results very similar to Hartman's (1981, 1984), even with revised tax rate and rate-of-return data.

6.4.1 New Results for Foreign Direct Investment

Tables 6.5A and 6.5B present new results for FDI. In these equations we extend the sample forward to 1984, and in some cases backward to 1956, use the revised series mentioned above, and experiment with a variety of alternative explanatory variables and functional forms. Estimates can vary substantially depending on the assumptions made.

Table 6.5A presents regressions explaining the log of various foreign direct investment rates. The second equation shows typical results for the addition of alternative explanatory variables. In short, the basic rate-of-return and tax variables seem to contain most of the explanatory power.

For 1965–84, the elasticity of (I_{re}/Y) is estimated to be 1.0 with respect to its own rate of return, 1.9 with respect to the average foreigners' net return in the United States, and -2.9 with respect to the relative tax term. Compared to results for 1965–79, the estimates in column 2 show a smaller response to return on FDI, and a much larger response to foreigners' net return in the United States and relative taxes.

Results are presented for the 1956–84 period, too, in order to demonstrate the sensitivity to sample period. These results imply smaller elasticities than the results for 1965–79 or 1965–84.

The retention ratio is modeled in columns 3 and 4. We found elasticities for 1956–84 and 1965–84 that bracket the 1965–79 estimates for foreigners' net return in the United States and relative tax rates. In each case the elasticity for 1965–84 is largest. The estimates show a considerable degree of variation. For the return on FDI, the 1965–79 estimates show the largest elasticity.

Table 6.5A   New Results for Foreign Direct Investment

DEPENDENT VARIABLE	$ln(I_{re}/Y)$[a]		$ln(I_{re}/E)$[a]		$ln(I_t/Y)$[b]
Sample Period	1956–84	1965–84	1956–84	1965–84	1956–84
Coefficient (s.e.) on					
constant	4.894	11.848	2.644	3.968	.533
	(1.082)	(3.764)	(1.535)	(1.330)	(1.175)
ln (return on FDI)	.978	1.039	.193	.228	0.41
	(.130)	(.185)	(.133)	(.135)	(.179)
ln (Foreigners'	.400	1.906	.475	1.121	− .214
net return in U.S.)	(.323)	(.643)	(.331)	(.415)	(.435)
ln(relative	− .979	− 2.895	− 1.107	− 1.633	− .537
tax term)	(.353)	(1.265)	(.361)	(.411)	(.486)
Dummy for 1980s	—	.242	—	—	—
	—	(.237)	—	—	—
Adjusted U.S.	—	− 2.713	—	—	—
GNP[c]	—	(2.806)	—	—	—
Adjusted OECD	—	− .903	—	—	—
GDP[d]	—	(.879)	—	—	—
Dummy for 1974	—	− .509	—	—	—
	—	(.629)	—	—	—
Standard Error	.202	.192	.209	.205	.262
of Regression					
Adjusted R^2	.727)	.831	.345	.542	.218
Durbin-Watson	2.26	2.36	1.98	1.90	2.00

Sources: Middle expansion trend GNP: de Leeuw and Holloway (1983), and subsequent issues of Survey of Current Business. OECD data: National Accounts of OECD Countries, 1950–68 and 1950–78, and OECD Main Economic Indicators in subsequent years.

[a]Because I_{re} is negative in 1982, a constant was added to $(I_{re} \times 1000)$/GNP before taking logarithms. The constant = 3,880, chosen such that the minimum (transformed) observation was roughly equivalent to the minimum (transformed) observation for I_t.

[b]This variable is as defined on table 6.4A.

[c]Measured as U.S. GNP divided by middle expansion trend U.S. GNP.

[d]Measured (GDP of all OECD countries − U.S. GDP), divided by its linear trend value.

The equations modeling investment financed by transfers fit poorly, as was the case in the 1965–79 sample period. Various modifications, including the addition of output variables, dummies for various periods, and alternative functional forms do not alter this result.

Turning to other functional forms, table 6.5B presents results for linear equations in the rate and level of the variables used in table 6.5A. In general, these equations do not perform as well as the logarithmic equations. The coefficients have the correct signs and take on reasonable values. Using mean values over the sample period, the elasticity of I_{re}/Y with respect to the return on FDI is 2.0, with respect to foreigners' net return in the United States is 0.8, and with respect to the

Table 6.5B   **New Results for Foreign Direct Investment**

Dependent Variable	(I_{re}/Y)	(I_{re}/E)	(I_{re}/E)	(I_{re}/E)	(I_{re})
Sample Period	1956–84	1965–84	1956–84	1965–84	1956–84
Coefficient (s.e.) on					
constant	.119	.764	.512	.867	−371
	(.441)	(.384)	(.339)	(.220)	(1762)
Return on FDI	14.506	4.026	3.495	4.960	10151
	(1.891)	(1.659)	(1.320)	(.865)	(5334)
Foreigners' net return	9.106	13.029	4.730	18.646	25035
in U.S.	(6.237)	(5.178)	(3.633)	(2.339)	(14754)
Relative tax term	−1.737	−1.879	−.754	−2.747	−4809
	(.717)	(.645)	(.542)	(.349)	(1536)
Dummy for 1980s	.287	—	−.329	—	—
	(.165)	—	(.094)	—	—
Income from FDI	—	—	—	—	.718
					(.089)
Standard Error of	.224	.196	.183	.136	449
Regression					
	.714	.362	.566	.884	.904
Adjusted R^2	1.85	2.18	2.01	2.30	2.18
Durbin-Watson					

Note: All variables have been defined in table 6.4A.

relative tax term is −2.0. Correspondingly, for the retention ratio, the elasticities for the 1965–84 period are 1.0, 2.3, −4.2, respectively. Columns 2 and 3 show that, again, regressions extending backward to 1956 do not perform as well. These coefficients imply elasticities ranging from 0.5 to 1.5 for foreigners' net return in the United States, 0.6 to 0.7 for return on FDI, and −1.4 to −2.9 for relative taxes.

We also employed several alternative specifications including a dummy variable to capture the negative I_{re} in 1982, instrumental variables to account for potential endogeneity of the return on FDI, expanding the values of FDI (by 20%) in the late 1970s to proxy for the underreporting discussed in section 6.3, and alternative output terms. The overriding result of these alternative specifications is, as the tables above would suggest, that the estimates are fairly sensitive to the specifications made.

6.4.2   New Results for Direct Investment Abroad

Table 6.6 presents some basic extensions of the DIA results given in table 6.4B. The results are presented only for I^*_{re}/Y as the other two equations fit poorly over the entire period. The I^*_{re} equations, in rates and level, tend to confirm strongly our earlier estimates, from table 6.4B. In particular, the net return in the United States enters with an

Table 6.6   New Results for Direct Investment Abroad

DEPENDENT VARIABLE	$ln(I^*_{re}/Y)$[a]	(Γ_{re}/Y)
Sample Period	1965–84	1965–84
Coefficient (s.e.) on		
constant	3.070	−.670
	(.619)	(.730)
Net return in U.S. [b]	−.196	−15.95
	(.103)	(8.71)
Return on DIA[b]	1.219	37.11
	(.163)	(3.33)
Standard error of regression	.146	.047
Adjusted R^2	.900	.938
Durbin-Watson	1.62	1.76

[a](I^*_{re}/Y) is DIA financed by retained earnings × 1000 divided by GNP.
[b]See table 6.4B for definition.

elasticity of approximately −0.2 in each specification, while the net return abroad has an elasticity estimated at 1.2 to 1.3. Alternative specifications led to varying results and are not reported here.

In summary, our empirical research supports the notion that domestic tax policy can have a significant impact on DIA and FDI. Our results are similar to Hartman's for 1965–79, although our elasticity estimates are somewhat smaller for the response of DIA to a change in net returns in the United States and for the response of FDI to changes in the return on FDI.

6.5 Summary and Implications

We have presented above new evidence that U.S. domestic tax policy affects the international location of investment. While the results are somewhat sensitive to sample period, functional form, and other considerations, the qualitative conclusions tend to hold up well. Of particular interest are two empirical issues—the likely impact of the 1981–82 corporate tax changes on FDI and DIA and the corresponding potential effects of any corporate tax reform. Also important are the welfare aspects of international location of investment.

Our estimates of the impact on DIA of changes in the after-tax rate of return in the United States suggest that a reduction of approximately 4 cents of DIA occurs for every dollar of increased U.S. domestic investment. This estimate derives from a comparison of analogous coefficients on domestic investment equations estimated by Feldstein and Jun (1986).[9] This refers only to investment out of retained earnings.

It is likely that transfers from domestic parent companies to foreign subsidiaries, or the establishment of such subsidiaries, is also responsive to domestic tax policy, but the data are insufficient to reach any specific conclusions on the matter.

We estimate that a tax policy which raises the after-tax rate of return enough to lead to a dollar of increased domestic investment in the U.S. brings with it between 8 and 27 cents of FDI.[10] These results are consistent with those found by Hartman (1981, 1984).

Several studies have attempted to analyze the effect of the 1981–82 investment incentives on effective marginal tax rates (e.g., see Auerbach 1983, Feldstein and Jun 1986, Gravelle 1983, and Hulten and Robertson 1983). These studies generally find that the effective corporate tax rate was reduced by about 20% to 35%.[11] With a constant before-tax rate of return and a pre-ERTA effective tax rate of about 33%, the tax changes increased foreigners' average net return in the United States by 10% to 17%. Other things equal, our estimates suggest that this change in net return would bring about approximately a 2% to 4% decline in DIA and an 11% to 20% rise in FDI. This would imply capital inflows of about $0.5 billion to $1.0 billion from smaller DIA and $2 billion to $4 billion in increased FDI. Of course, these figures refer to FDI and DIA out of retained earnings only. Likewise, a tax reform such as H.R.3838, which raises (except perhaps at very high inflation rates) the effective tax rate on U.S. corporate investment, would result in an increase in direct investment abroad by U.S. firms and a decrease in foreign direct investment in the United States. However, because these results contain no long-term dynamic theory of the optimal international location of investment, they should not be taken as any final guide to the impact of these tax changes on investment patterns.

Finally, the welfare economics of the international location of investment, described in Caves (1982), Goulder, Shoven, and Whalley (1983), and Hartman (1984) should be addressed. Domestic economic welfare rises with FDI because the United States receives a claim on the rate of return to foreign capital through the taxation of FDI income. Conversely, domestic economic welfare falls when U.S. firms substitute DIA for investment at home,[12] because the nation then receives only the net-of-foreign-tax return (and that only when it is repatriated) rather than the gross return. These welfare effects are augmented by the beneficial effects on labor productivity of greater investment— foreign or domestic—in the United States. Thus, a reduction in taxation of new corporate investment improves welfare through three channels: the standard mechanism, through which lowering the effective marginal tax rate generates new domestic investment opportunities for U.S. firms; a reallocation of the location of investment by U.S. firms toward home and away from abroad; and an increase in FDI. In this paper, we have presented some new evidence that these last two effects are quantitatively important and therefore that it is necessary to consider them in any evaluation of domestic investment incentives.

The welfare effects of tax policy clearly depend on the responsiveness of FDI and DIA to net-of-tax returns. The welfare gains to a tax reduction confined to new corporate investment are positively linked to the responsiveness of DIA and of FDI with respect to net-of-tax returns in the United States.

Our results suggest that accelerated depreciation or tax credits for *new* investment which decrease the effective marginal tax rate paid at the corporate level by 10% would, through its effect on the net-of-tax return available to FDI, raise FDI by 9%. Corporate tax revenues from taxation of FDI could be expected to rise correspondingly. Similar, though smaller, revenue effects would occur for DIA. These results refer to investment financed by retained earnings only. Note, however, that tax revenue is greater per dollar of potential DIA diverted to domestic investment than per dollar of FDI, because foreign owners of U.S. capital pay taxes only at the corporate level, while domestic owners are also responsible for state, local, and personal taxes.

Our results suggest that the tax effects on the international location of investment are important. Tax policies, such as ACRS and ITC, which raise the after-tax rate of return on new investment without losing revenue from previous investment, not only stimulate domestic fixed investment, but also attract additional investment from abroad. The additional investment supplements the domestic investment impact on productivity and raises corporate tax revenue. However, our results should be taken as preliminary estimates, not as definitive statements about the long-run impacts of tax policy.

Notes

1. The home country is where the parent company is based.
2. Issues concerning risk adjustment are not addressed in this paper.
3. See Bergsten, Horst, and Moran (1978) or Caves (1982) for a review of this position.
4. However, even when the tax on foreign source income is not a concern, it is not the case that foreign firms in the U.S. respond to the same tax rates as do U.S. firms. Foreign firms care about the tax rate paid at the corporate level. U.S. firms should respond to the total effective tax rate. These rates are developed in Feldstein, Dicks-Mireaux, and Poterba (1983) and Feldstein and Jun (1986). They do not always move in tandem. Moreover, it would be easy

to design policies that affect the rates differently, e.g., the current tax reform bill H.R.3838.

5. U.S. Department of Commerce, Bureau of Economic Analysis (1983a), p. 1. A person is defined to include any individual, associated group, estate, trust, corporation, or any government.

6. U.S. Department of Commerce, Bureau of Economic Analysis (1981), p. 2.

7. Belli (1984), p. 34. BEA estimates that all of the revision in capital inflows was due to underreporting, but 25% of the underreporting was by exempt affiliates. For the direct investment position, two-thirds of the upward revision was due to underreporting, one-third due to revision or correction in the sample data. BEA does not state what part of the underreporting of direct investment position should have been reported, but if (as for capital inflows) 75% of the underreporting should have been reported, then one-half (2/3 × 3/4) of the upward revision in direct investment position should have been reported in the sample survey. This suggests that the position in FDI was also substantially underreported in the 1970s.

8. The relative tax term is meant to capture differences between domestic saving incentives and investment incentives. Thus, a savings incentive that lowered t' but not t would then increase savings, lower the pretax rate of return and thus lead to a fall in FDI.

9. This estimate is obtained as follows. Feldstein and Jun (1986) regress net investment divided by GNP on several variables, including the (lagged) overall net rate of return. Their coefficient on the rate-of-return variable is .459. When our equations are transformed into the appropriate units (i.e., when coefficients are divided by 1000; see note in table 6.6), our estimate of the effect of net rate of return in the United States on U.S. direct investment abroad is $-.016$, which is about 4% as large (in absolute value) as .459.

10. This is obtained by multiplying the elasticity of I_{re}/Y with respect to foreigners' net return in the United States (shown in cols. 1 and 2, table 6.5A) by the average value of foreigners' net return in the United States (.054) and dividing by the average of the (transformed) I_{re}/Y (.00355).

11. Studies differ in their estimates because of differing assumptions about expected inflation, discount rates, debt/equity ratios, and hurdle rates, among other things.

12. Of course, not all DIA comes at the expense of domestic investment.

References

Auerbach, Alan J. 1983. Corporate taxation in the United States. *Brookings Papers on Economic Activity,* pp. 451–505.

Belli, David R. 1984. Foreign direct investment in the United States in 1983. *Survey of Current Business,* October, p. 34.

Bergsten, C. Fred, Thomas Horst, and Theodore H. Moran. 1978. *American multinationals and American interests.* Washington: Brookings Institution.

Brownlee, Oswald H. 1979. *Taxing the income from U.S. corporations investments abroad.* Washington: American Enterprise Institute.

Caves, Richard. 1982. Multinational enterprise and economic analysis. *Cambridge Surveys of Economic Literature*. Cambridge: Cambridge University Press.

de Leeuw, Frank, and Thomas M. Holloway. 1983. Measuring and analyzing the cyclically adjusted budget. Prepared for the Federal Reserve Bank of Boston Conference on the Trend and Measurement of the Structural Deficit.

Feldstein, Martin. 1982. Inflation, tax rules, and investment. *Econometrica* 50:825–62.

Feldstein, Martin, Louis Dicks-Mireaux, and James Poterba. 1983. The effective tax rate and the pretax rate of return. *Journal of Public Economics* 21: 129–58.

Feldstein, Martin, and Joosung Jun. 1986. The effects of tax rates on nonresidential fixed investment: Some preliminary evidence from the 1980s. Chapter 4 in this volume.

Frisch, Daniel J., and David G. Hartman. 1983. Taxation and the location of U.S. investment abroad. NBER Working Paper no. 1241, November.

Goldsbrough, David. 1979. The role of foreign direct investment in the external adjustment process. *IMF Staff Papers* 26, no. 4 (Nov.): 725–54.

Goulder, Lawrence H., John B. Shoven, and John Whalley. 1983. Domestic tax policy and the foreign sector: The importance of alternative foreign sector formulations to results from a general equilibrium tax analysis model. In Martin Feldstein, ed., *Behavioral simulations in tax policy analysis*, pp. 333–67. Chicago: University of Chicago Press.

Gravelle, Jane G. 1983. Capital income taxation and efficiency in the allocation of investment. *National Tax Journal* 36:297–306.

Hartman, David G. 1980. The effects of taxing foreign investment income. *Journal of Public Economics* 13:213–30.

———. 1981. Domestic tax policy and foreign investment: Some evidence. NBER Working Paper no. 784, October.

———. 1984. Tax policy and foreign direct investment in the United States. *National Tax Journal* 37:475–87.

———. 1985. Tax policy and foreign direct investment. *Journal of Public Economics* 26:107–21.

Hulten, C., and J. Robertson. 1983. Corporate tax policy and economic growth: An analysis of the 1981 and 1982 tax acts. Urban Institute. Mimeographed.

Kwack, Sung Y. 1972. A model of U.S. direct investment abroad: A neoclassical approach. *Western Economic Journal* 10, no. 4, pp. 376–83.

National Accounts of OECD Countries, 1950–1968. Vol. 1. Organization for Economic Community and Development. Paris.

National Accounts of OECD Countries, 1950–1978. Vol. 1. Organization for Economic Community and Development. Paris.

OECD Main Economic Indicators. OECD, Department of Economics and Statistics, selected issues. Paris.

Scholl, Russell B. 1985. The international investment position of the United States in 1984. *Survey of Current Business* 65, no. 6 (June): 25–33.

Stevens, Guy V. B. 1972. Capital mobility and the international firm. in F. Machlup, W. S. Salant, and L. Tarshis, eds., *International mobility and movement of capital*, pp. 323–53. New York: National Bureau of Economic Research.

U.S. Department of Commerce, Department of Economic Analysis. 1981. *U.S. direct investment abroad, 1977*. Washington: Government Printing Office.

———. 1983a. *Foreign direct investment in the U.S., 1980*. Washington: Government Printing Office.

————. 1983b. *Selected data on U.S. direct investment abroad, 1950–76.* Washington: Government Printing Office.

————. 1984. *Selected data on foreign direct investment in the United States, 1950–79.* Washington: Government Printing Office.

Comment   David G. Hartman

Being one of the few researchers active in what I regard as an extremely important field—tax policy and foreign investment—I can only applaud this effort by Boskin and Gale. At the same time, I feel as if I should express sympathy for them, upon their entry into an area in which evidence is sparse, the available information is often unreliable, and the reliable statistics are often unrelated to the concepts one would expect and hope to be measuring.

That said, let me also indicate that the nature of this paper makes a critical review very difficult. Boskin and Gale, as they have indicated, set out to replicate and then extend several pieces of empirical work I have published over the past several years. Given the severe data problems to which I have alluded, it is particularly appropriate to have other researchers test the same basic model, using "a variety of alternative explanatory variables, functional forms, and sample periods." I can hardly be critical of the authors' methodology without dragging skeletons out of my own closet; and, since "the qualitative conclusions tend to hold up well" under this scrutiny, I likewise have little disagreement with the conclusions.

It is highly encouraging that my somewhat tentative conclusions on the effects of tax policy on U.S. investment abroad and foreign investment in the United States are confirmed when information from the 1980s is combined with the evidence I examined. In a way it is also surprising to me. Indeed, there were several reasons for my having ended my period of study of these phenomena with 1979.

First, foreign direct investment in the United States has surged in this decade, as table 6.1 indicates. Increasing integration of the world's capital markets, in general, is a feature of the 1980s which is apparent to all. We also know, as a number of the other chapters in this book make explicit, that the 1981 tax reforms in the United States provided a basic structural change in the incentives for investment. My reluctance to use data from the 1980s was based on the fear that these two factors would conspire to produce inflated estimates of tax effects.

David G. Hartman is chief international economist at Data Resources, and a research affiliate of the National Bureau of Economic Research.

Furthermore, record inflows of foreign investment in 1981 and 1984 were associated with a few huge corporate takeovers. Shell's purchase of the publicly held shares of the U.S. subsidiary was, for instance, probably not closely related to the phenomena we are interested in isolating here. The fact that this paper confirms evidence drawn entirely from the pre-1980s period is, while encouraging, quite a surprise.

In the analysis of U.S. direct investment abroad, several features of the data should make one more cautious. First, as the authors indicate, there are some definitional changes which are of uncertain impact.

More importantly, the nature of what is being measured may be quite different from the fundamental decision to expand or contract foreign operations, which I have emphasized in my previous work. One reason is the growth and later decline in Netherlands Antilles financing affiliates. The U.S. withholding tax on capital returns paid to foreigners, from which payments to the Netherlands Antilles were exempt by treaty, resulted in the 1980s in subsidiaries in that region borrowing at attractive Eurodollar rates and transferring funds to U.S. parent firms. Such transfers, which appear in the U.S. international accounts as negative investment in foreign subsidiaries, would be a mere curiosity, except for their magnitude, which reached nearly $14 billion in 1982. As table 6.2 indicates, this explains virtually the entire plunge in foreign direct investment (DIA). While these flows are undoubtedly of importance, they are conceptually quite different from what we typically think of as direct investment. With the repeal of the withholding tax in 1984, borrowing abroad could be done directly, without showing up in the direct investment figures. At this time, we are left with only a return flow of interest payments through foreign subsidiaries, which will continue to appear as positive direct investment until the loans are repaid.

Of even more significance in research relating foreign investment to foreign investment returns is the manner in which exchange rates are reflected in the accounts. Table 6.7 indicates the magnitude of the problem. Reinvested earnings are calculated by subtracting capital gains and losses, as well as interest and dividend payments, from the income of foreign affiliates. The reported income of foreign affiliates, likewise excludes capital gains and losses, which mainly reflect the effects of changes in the value of the dollar on the dollar value of foreign assets. How (and even whether) exchange rate changes truly affect the value of a firm's foreign operations is not a settled issue, and the magnitudes of the accounting adjustments shown in table 6.7 are clearly disturbing. As the value of the dollar surged, the negative foreign income and the negative foreign reinvestment flows that were "created" became very large relative to the "real flows." Thus, for instance, exchange rate adjustments alone transformed a foreign income series from one which

Table 6.7   U.S. Direct Investment Abroad (Some Simple Arithmetic)

	1980	1981	1982	1983	1984	1985:1	1985:2	1985:3
Earnings	$36.5b	$32.2b	$24.4b	$24.5b	$27.5b	$5.7b	$9.7b	$10.3b
Distributed	19.5	18.8	17.7	14.9	16.5	4.4	2.7	3.8
Retained	17.0	13.5	6.7	9.6	11.0	1.3	7.1	6.5
Interest	.6	.2	-1.8	-3.2	-4.4	-1.0	-1.1	-1.1
Income	37.1	32.4	22.6	21.3	23.1	4.7	8.6	9.2
Capital gains/losses	-1.6	.5	-2.1	-6.5	-8.4	-2.6	1.0	3.1
Income before capital gains/losses	38.8	32.0	24.7	27.8	31.5	7.3	7.6	6.1
Income before capital gains/losses	38.8	32.0	24.7	27.8	31.5	7.3	7.6	6.1
Reported income	37.1	32.4	22.6	21.3	23.1	4.7	8.6	9.2
Reinvested earnings before capital gains/losses	18.6	13.0	8.8	16.1	19.4	3.9	6.1	3.4
Reported reinvestment	17.0	13.5	6.7	9.6	11.0	1.3	7.1	6.5
Reinvestment ratio before capital gains/losses	48.9%	40.6	35.6	57.9	61.6	53.4	80.3	55.7
Reported reinvestment ratio	45.8	41.7	29.6	45.1	47.6	27.7	82.6	70.7

Source: Survey of Current Business, U.S. Department of Commerce, various issues.

would have shown a robust recovery after the 1982 recession, into an indicator of continuing stagnation abroad. Reported reinvested earnings, on the other hand, did exhibit strong recovery after 1982, but naturally not as strong as without the subtraction of dollar-related capital losses. More recent data, reflecting the plunge in the dollar, show corresponding boosts in both investment abroad and earnings. A regression of reinvestment on rates of return during this unsettled period is potentially quite problematic.

These difficulties again highlight the importance of my eclectic approach, which Boskin and Gale have followed, of fitting a variety of equations: for foreign investment as a function of rates of return; for the reinvestment ratio (with the currency effect incorporated in both the numerator and denominator) as a function of rates of return; and for foreign investment as a function of lagged rates of return.

While this litany of the limitations on our ability to reach concrete conclusions seems discouraging, the fact of the matter is that the Boskin and Gale results are quite consistent with the results I obtained using data largely immune to these difficulties. The message that the data seem intent on telling us is that U.S. taxes matter for the international allocation of investment. The precise coefficients are of less importance than this basic conclusion, given the long-standing tendency of policymakers to ignore the international implications of their decisions.

The domestic welfare effects of tax policy changes can easily be overwhelmed by the international reallocation of capital, as we have learned from a number of previous NBER studies. For this reason, it is particularly important that we learn more about the nature of the international flows of capital and their responsiveness to U.S. policy changes. The success of future work will hinge on the availability of better data. One possibility would be to focus on particular episodes of major tax changes and investment flows between the United States and a specific country, such as Canada or the U.K. Since tax policy changes in both countries could easily be taken into account, a sharper analysis of tax effects could be performed.

In any event, the issues are crucial, but the data problems are severe. Nonetheless, the results reported here are a useful addition to our knowledge on the topic.

7 Notes on the Tax Treatment of Structures

Roger H. Gordon, James R. Hines, Jr., and
Lawrence H. Summers

More than three-quarters of the United States' tangible capital stock represents structures. Despite their relatively low rates of depreciation, structures account for more than half of all gross fixed investment in most years. Tax policies potentially have a major impact on both the level and composition of investment in structures. This point is explicitly recognized in most discussions of the effects of capital income taxation. Two aspects of the taxation of structures—the relative burden placed on structures as opposed to equipment investment and the non-taxation of owner-occupied housing under the income tax—have attracted substantial attention in recent years. This paper explores these two aspects of the taxation of structure investments.

The Treasury (1984), in its recent tax reform proposal, pointed to the extra tax burdens placed on structures relative to equipment as a major defect of the current accelerated cost recovery system. The 1985 *Economic Report of the President* echoes this sentiment, concluding that, "The effective tax rate . . . is lower for equipment than for structures. Because different industries utilize different mixes of capital goods, differential taxation of assets results in differential taxation of

Roger H. Gordon is professor of economics at the University of Michigan and a research associate of the National Bureau of Economic Research. James R. Hines Jr. is assistant professor of economics and public affairs at the Woodrow Wilson School, Princeton University and a faculty research fellow of the National Bureau of Economic Research. Lawrence H. Summers is professor of economics at Harvard University and a research associate of the National Bureau of Economic Research.

We are indebted to the Harvard-MIT Joint Center for Housing Studies for partial support of this research. We thank Patric Hendershott, Jack Mintz, Anthony Pellechio, James Poterba, and Emil Sunley for helpful comments on an earlier draft. Mary Joyce and John Musgrave of the Bureau of Economic Analysis and Karen Cys, Gail Moglen, Thomas Petska, and Alan Zemple of the Internal Revenue Service kindly provided us with unpublished data.

capital income by industry. The average effective Federal corporate tax rate on fixed investment varies widely by industry." The decision of the Congress in 1984 and 1985 to scale back the depreciation benefits to structures but not to equipment is perhaps surprising in light of these conclusions.

The allegedly favorable treatment of owner-occupied housing has long been a target of academic critics of the tax system although suggestions for reform have generated little if any political support. The failure to include imputed rent is often treated as a tax subsidy. A large literature summarized in Rosen (1985) has estimated the welfare loss thought to come from tax-induced changes in tenure choice. And the corporate income tax is often opposed on the ground that it exacerbates the distortions caused by the nontaxation of owner-occupied housing.

While the tax system may well have a potent impact on the level and composition of structure investment, this paper argues that conventional analyses of these effects are very misleading. We reach two main conclusions. First, under current tax law, certain types of structure investment are very highly tax-favored. Overall, it is unlikely that a significant bias toward equipment and against structures exists under current law. Second, the conventional view that the tax system is biased in favor of homeownership is wrong. Because of the possibility of tax arbitrage between high-bracket landlords and low-bracket tenants, the tax system has long favored rental over ownership for most households. The 1981 reforms, by reducing the top marginal tax rate, reduced this bias somewhat.

Many earlier analyses have reached different conclusions because of their failure to take account of several aspects of the behavior of real world investors which serve to reduce the effective tax burden on structure investment. First, structures may be depreciated more than once ("churned") for tax purposes. Particularly where devices can be found to reduce the effective rate of capital gains tax below the statutory rate, the effective purchase price of a structure may be reduced substantially by the knowledge that it can be depreciated several times. Second, some types of structures, particularly commercial buildings, are very easy to borrow against because they are quite liquid assets. To the extent that the tax system favors the use of debt finance they too will be favored. Third, certain types of investments, especially residential rental capital, facilitate tax arbitrage.

The paper is organized as follows. Section 7.1 reviews trends in structure investment over the past few years and highlights the dramatic increase in the rate of investment in commercial buildings that has occurred in recent years. Some information on the ownership of different types of structure investments is also presented. Section 7.2 describes the tax rules governing the churning of capital assets and considers the circumstances under which the churning of assets will be tax-advantaged. Section 7.3 considers the role of leverage and raises the possibility that structure investments are favored under current tax law because of their ability to carry debt. Section 7.4 examines the tax advantages to homeownership and shows that the tax law actually provides incentives for most households to rent their homes. Section 7.5 concludes the paper by discussing the implications of our results for tax reform and future research.

7.1   Patterns of Structure Ownership and Investment

A number of studies, notably Auerbach (1983) and Fullerton and Henderson (1984), have made rather elaborate calculations of the dead-weight losses arising from the failure of the tax system to impose equal burdens on different types of corporate investment. In large part it is the assumed differential taxation of equipment and structures that drives the results of these studies. This differential taxation creates production inefficiencies within industries and also favors some industries at the expense of others. Despite the results of many academic experts and the results of staff analyses suggesting that the then current law was heavily biased in favor of equipment, the Congress in 1984 chose to scale back the depreciation benefits associated with structure investments while not altering the tax treatment of equipment investments. Tax legislation in 1982 had reduced somewhat the value of depreciation allowances for equipment, but standard calculations still showed equipment to be strongly tax-favored over structures. The 1984 action was taken at least in part because of a widespread perception that the 1981 acceleration of depreciation allowances had led to the rapid growth of tax shelters based on investments in structures. Additional tax law changes in 1984 and 1985 further reduced the value of depreciation allowances for structures while leaving equipment allowances intact.

7.1.1   Ownership of Structures

How can one square the perception that structures are a common tax shelter with the calculations suggesting that they are among the most heavily taxed assets? Part of the answer may be found in table 7.1, which examines the composition of the stock of structures in 1983, the most recent year for which data are available. The first row of the table shows that corporate structures represented less than a quarter of all structures in 1983 and that they accounted for less than half of all depreciable structures.

While detailed data are not available on the ownership of different types of structures, it is clear from the data in the table that the vast majority of residential capital represents owner-occupied housing with the bulk of the remaining residential capital representing partnerships

Table 7.1   The Ownership of Structures in 1983

	Corporate	Other Business	Owner-occupied Housing
Total Structures	1075.6	1124.4	2269.5
	(24.1%)	(25.2%)	(50.8%)
Nonresidential Structures	1005.8	628.1	—
	(61.6%)	(38.4%)	
Residential Structures	69.8	496.3	2269.5
	(2.5%)	(17.5%)	(80.0%)

Source: Musgrave (1984).

Note: Figures in the table refer to current dollar net capital stocks. Numbers in parentheses are percentages of row totals. It is assumed that all corporate residential structures are rental properties.

and proprietorships. Only a negligible fraction of residential capital is held in corporate form. The ownership of nonresidential structures is more complex. It appears likely to us that most of the noncorporate structures are commercial buildings owned by partnerships or proprietors. The other main categories of nonresidential structures—industrial buildings, mines, and public utility structures—are probably largely owned by corporations.

7.1.2   Patterns of Structures Investment

Table 7.2 presents some information on the composition of structure investment in 1980, before the introduction of ACRS, and in 1985. The table highlights a number of aspects of structure investment that seem critical in assessing neutrality arguments suggesting a tax bias against structure investment. First, a substantial share of structure investment takes place in forms where the effects of taxes cannot sensibly be analyzed in isolation. In 1985, for example, public utilities accounted for about 20% of all investment in structures. The profit rate of most public utilities is regulated and in many cases the benefits associated with tax incentives, especially the investment tax credit, are passed on to consumers. Public utility firms may have objectives more complicated than simple unconstrained profit maximization. About 40% of structure investment takes place in forms where other public microeconomic policies are intimately involved in guiding the allocation of resources—educational and hospital buildings, mining and petroleum, and farming. As with public utilities examining the effects of tax benefits in isolation is likely to be very misleading. The remaining 40% of structure investment takes place in industrial and commercial buildings where tax considerations are presumably of primary importance. What is perhaps surprising is that industrial buildings (plants) represent only

Table 7.2   Structures Investment in 1980 and 1985 (billions of constant
                   1982 dollars)

	1980	1985
Total Structures Investment	273.8	338.9
Nonresidential Structures	136.2	165.8
Industrial Buildings	16.0	14.2
Commercial Buildings	34.7	54.2
Office Buildings	15.3	28.3
Other	19.4	25.9
Education, Religious & Hospital	7.9	8.6
Mining & Petroleum	31.7	39.8
Public Utilities	30.3	31.8
Farm Structures	6.1	3.4
Other	9.5	13.8
Residential Structures	137.6	173.1
Owner-occupied	60.7	95.3
Rental	76.9	77.8

Source: Unpublished data, Bureau of Economic Analysis, U.S. Department of Commerce.

about 10% of all nonresidential structure investment. Commercial buildings account for the remaining 30% of nonresidential structure investment.

Second, the information in the table indicates that there has been a fairly dramatic shift in nonresidential structure investment toward commercial buildings and in particular office buildings over the last 5 years. The dollar volume of investment in commercial buildings more than doubled between 1980 and 1985 compared to an increase of less than 50% in overall structure investment. The industrial building category has been particularly weak over the same period, so commercial building investment is now 4 times as great as industrial building investment compared with a ratio of 2 to 1 in 1980. It is perhaps ironic that the 1981 tax cut, which had as a major objective spurring corporate investment, has been followed by a dramatic spurt in commercial building investment—a large part of which occurs outside the corporate sector. Between 1980 and 1985, real investment in commercial structures increased by 56%, of which office building investment rose 85%, compared to 22% increase in overall nonresidential construction and a 26% increase in equipment investment. As we discuss in detail below, the dramatic divergence between patterns of investment in commercial buildings and other structures raises the suspicion that despite their identical depreciation schedules the tax system affects them very differently.

We resist the temptation to analyze closely the evolution of investment in different types of assets over the last few years because of the problem stressed by Auerbach and Hines (1986) among others of gauging the effects of anticipated changes in tax policy. In 1984 and 1985 the depreciation incentives for investment in structures were reduced. In addition, rules limiting investors' ability to utilize structure investments as a tax shelter were introduced. More changes in the same direction are currently under discussion. It is at least conceivable that some of the strength in commercial building investment, and perhaps other types of investment as well, comes from a desire to accelerate investments so that they will receive favorable tax treatment. Given the common political view that real estate investments are a major tax shelter, it is possible that these effects are most important in the case of commercial buildings.

Table 7.2 also indicates that residential investment has been surprisingly strong over the last five years. The dollar volume of residential investment has increased by more than 50% over the past 5 years, and real investment in residential structures has increased by 26%, the same rate of growth exhibited by equipment investment. Virtually all of the real growth in residential investment is attributable to owner-occupied housing, which has risen 57% despite the fact that alone among structures it received no new tax incentives in 1981. Hendershott (1986) provides some evidence suggesting that at the same time that residential investment has been strong the homeownership rate has increased substantially.

The patterns of structure investment documented in this section suggest that conventional analyses of the effects of taxation may be seriously misleading. Such analyses do not distinguish between tax effects on different types of nonresidential structures and so cannot account for the great strength of commercial building investment relative to other types of structure investment. Many conventional analyses emphasize an alleged tax bias toward owner-occupied housing. These analyses cannot account for the observation that owner-occupied housing investment rose more rapidly than that of any other major category following the 1981 tax change which conferred substantial depreciation benefits on rental housing. These apparent anomalies may just reflect nontax factors which exert a substantial influence on investment. Alternatively, it is possible that important aspects of the effects of the tax system on structures have been neglected. We consider the latter possibility below.

7.2 Tax Churning of Nonresidential Real Property

As is now well understood, the present value of the depreciation allowances permitted on a capital asset has an important impact on the incentive to invest in it. Indeed, differences in the treatment of depreciation between assets is often regarded as a major source of nonneutrality in the tax system. Unfortunately, calculation of the present value of the depreciation allowances on a given capital asset is not straightforward because of the possibility of the assets being transferred and depreciated more than once for tax purposes. Particularly in an inflationary environment, there may be large advantages to turning assets over so their depreciable bases will be increased. Even with no inflation, asset sales raise the value of prospective depreciation allowances as long as depreciation allowances are more accelerated than economic depreciation. However, the incentive to churn assets is mitigated by the capital gains taxes and recapture taxes which must be paid when depreciable assets are sold.

This section examines the effects on investment incentives of the possibility that assets can be depreciated more than once.[1] After a review of the legal treatment of depreciation allowances and recapture, we analyze the desirability of churning different classes of assets. We find that the incentive to churn and the related incentive to invest is rather sensitive to both tax rates and assumed discount rates.

7.2.1 Depreciation and Recapture Rules

The Economic Recovery Tax Act of 1981 established shorter and faster write-offs of capital costs for new investment in equipment and structures. The accelerated cost recovery system (ACRS) included a provision for depreciation of most classes of structures by a 175% declining balance method over 15 years. ACRS replaced the asset depreciation range (ADR) system, which was by comparison far less generous in its treatment of capital depreciation allowances.

The ACRS significantly reduced corporations' costs of investing in structures and equipment. Other than the named goal of economic recovery, one of the purposes of the law was to rectify the effect of rising inflation on incentives to invest. Since the favorable depreciation provisions were designed to undo by themselves the effects of inflation, the law contained features which made it more costly than before to sell assets in order to permit the purchaser to get depreciation allowances on the higher, inflated basis.

The 1981 tax law permits investors to choose from a variety of options for depreciating most classes of real property. Besides using 175% declining balance with switch-over to straight-line over an asset life of 15 years, investors could select a straight-line depreciation method for an asset life of 15, 35, or 45 years as they chose. Under normal business circumstances, of course, an investor who planned never to sell his assets would always choose the shortest and most accelerated depreciation method.[2] However, the recapture provisions of the law depend on the chosen method of asset depreciation.

For investors who choose straight-line depreciation and who sell their assets, the difference between the sales price and the tax basis is treated as a capital gain and is taxed at the capital gain rate. However, for investors in nonresidential structures who choose the 175% declining balance depreciation scheme and who sell their assets at a gain, the value of all depreciation allowances taken to date are recaptured as ordinary income (rather than as capital gains). This recapture of all past depreciation deductions is normally sufficiently costly that an investor would be better off using straight-line depreciation if he intended to sell the asset at any point.

Congress has modified the tax treatment of structures since passage of the 1981 act, although not substantially. The 1984 Deficit Reduction Act (DEFRA) lengthened the tax life of most structures to 18 years and changed slightly the tax treatment of installment sales. Structures' tax life was further extended to 19 years in 1985. Depreciation and recapture provisions were otherwise unaffected by these laws.[3]

7.2.2 Evaluating the Incentive to Churn

The feasibility of churning an asset depends on its characteristics. A specialized industrial structure is likely to be difficult to sell because its functional specificity limits the range of potential buyers. And it may be difficult to sell and lease back because of the moral hazard and other problems associated with rental contracts. Most commercial real estate, on the other hand, is not highly specialized and is therefore easily leased. Indeed Pan Am rents space in the Pan Am Building and Exxon rents its space in Rockefeller Center. A natural conjecture then is that if the tax benefits of churning are substantial, a significant tax distortion may be created in favor of liquid assets. We explore this possibility by considering the magnitude of the tax incentive for the churning of commercial buildings.

Consider an investor, corporate or noncorporate, which invests in a commercial building in 1985, expecting the tax law, inflation, and the interest rate not to change in the future. There are three possible depreciation strategies that must be considered. First, the investor can use accelerated depreciation (with straight-line switch-over) and never churn the asset. Second, the investor can use accelerated depreciation and churn at the optimal point. Third, the firm can use straight-line depreciation and churn at the optimal point. We consider the attractiveness of each of these alternatives in turn.

Depreciation allowances can be easily calculated for scenarios in which firms do not churn their assets. For the current 19-year tax lifetime, it is optimal for firms to use 175% declining balance for the

first 10 years of asset life, switching to straight-line depreciation thereafter. The value to the firm of these allowances is:

(1) $$PV = \tau \sum_{j=1}^{19} D_a(j) \cdot [1 + i(1 - \tau)]^{-j},$$

where $D_a(j)$ is the depreciation allowance in the jth year using ACRS
acceleration and i is the required nominal before-tax rate of return.[4]
Here τ is the investor's ordinary tax rate, and so equals 46% for a
corporation and can be as high as 50% for an individual.

If instead the firm chooses the second option of depreciating its
structure using the straight-line method and selling the asset after k
years, then the present value of the firm's depreciation allowances
minus capital gains liability is:

(2) $$NET(k) = \tau \sum_{j=1}^{k} D_s(j)[1 + i(1 - \tau)]^{-j}$$
$$- CG\{Q(k) - [1 - \sum_{j=1}^{k} D_s(j)]\}[1 + i(1 - \tau)]^{-k},$$

where $D_s(j)$ is the straight-line depreciation allowance in the jth year
and $Q(k)$ is the market value of the asset after k years. In this case,
$D_s(j) = 1/19$ for all j. CG in (2) is the capital gains rate, which normally
equals 28% for a corporation and is at most 20% for an individual. With
the further assumption that structures depreciate exponentially at an
annual rate δ, $Q(k)$ simplifies to:

(3) $$Q(k) = [(1 - \delta)(1 + \pi)]^k,$$

where π is the inflation rate. To calculate the tax benefits from churning,
assume that k represents the optimal choice of waiting time between
asset purchase and sale. Then the second-round optimal tax treatment
of the used asset will also include churning after k more years. Assume
for simplicity that the firm sells the asset to itself at a market price,
incurring a transaction cost in the process. Then the present value of
all net depreciation benefits minus costs is:

(4) $$PV = \sum_{j=0}^{\infty} \{NET\,(k) - TC \cdot Q(k)[1 + i(1 - \tau)]^{-k}\}$$
$$\cdot \{[(1 + \pi)(1 - \delta)]/[1 + i(1 - \tau)]\}^{kj},$$

where TC is the fraction of sales price the firm pays as a transaction
cost. This expression simplifies to:

(5) $$PV = \{NET_s(k) - TC \cdot Q(k)[1 + i(1 - \tau)]^{-k}\}/$$
$$\{1 - [(1 + \pi)(1 - \delta)/(1 + i(1 - \tau))]^k\}.$$

The third option the firm faces is somewhat more complicated. Assuming that the rate of inflation exceeds the asset's exponential depreciation rate, so that the seller realizes a capital gain over purchase price, net depreciation benefits after churning in the kth year are:

(6)
$$NET_a = \tau \sum_{j=1}^{k} D_a(j)[1 + i(1 - \tau)]^{-j} - \{CG[Q(k) - 1]$$
$$+ \tau \sum_{j=1}^{k} D_a(j)\}[1 + i(1 - \tau)]^{-k}.$$

The potential tax benefits of churning are sensitive to the choice of capital gains tax rate. Previous calculations of the tax effects of asset sales have assumed that capital gains are all taxed upon realization at the statutory rate. Particularly for individuals but to some extent for corporations as well there are devices available which permit capital gains taxes to be avoided or deferred. This makes the churning of assets much more attractive. The features of the tax system that permit capital gains taxes to be avoided or reduced in present value include installment sales, variations in marginal tax rates, artificially generated losses, steps up in basis, and outright cheating.

The main device that both corporations and individuals can use to defer capital gains taxes is the installment sale. Rules governing installment sales were actually liberalized in 1980 but have been tightened more recently.[5] In an installment sale the seller accepts a sequence of installment payments for his property. The buyer is permitted to use the present value of these payments, the sale price, as his depreciation basis. However the seller must pay capital gains tax on the principal component of installment payments only as they are received. The net effect is to defer the seller's capital gains tax liability. The advantage can be quite substantial since at current interest rates deferral for 7 years halves a tax liability. The advantage is magnified if for some reason the seller's tax rate is expected to decline. While the installment sale is a commonly discussed tax avoidance device, we are not aware of quantitative information on the frequency of its use.

For individuals with temporarily low income or corporations with negative or very small taxable profits, progressivity of the tax code makes the effective marginal capital gains tax rate lower than its normal (statutory) value. Since taxpayers have some freedom to realize capital gains during advantageous (low tax rate) years, there is an option value attached to an anticipated future capital gains liability that reduces the effective rate. The results of Auerbach and Poterba (1986) suggest that this may be more important for individuals than corporations.

The possibilities for avoiding capital gains taxes are broadened considerably when the possibility of generating artificial losses is recognized. Stiglitz (1983) among others has discussed a variety of tax-timing strategies that allow taxpayers to generate capital losses without taking on substantial risks.[6] The law limits the ability of individuals and corporations to deduct capital losses against ordinary income. To the extent that these limits bind, the marginal tax rate on additional capital gains income is zero. Poterba (1986) presents evidence suggesting that about 20% of household dividends were received by taxpayers for whom marginal capital gains were untaxed because they were in this situation. It seems plausible that the fraction is higher for the sophisticated investors who hold commercial real estate.

The tax code provides for a tax-free step up in the basis on an asset if the taxpayer dies and bequeaths the asset or if the asset is given to charity. To the extent that taxpayers anticipate that they may die in the period in which they plan to hold an asset, the expected tax rate is reduced. The step up in basis on some kinds of charitable gifts means that individuals who plan to donate to charity an amount greater than their capital gains income can avoid capital gains taxes entirely. These two provisions mean that even naive and honest taxpayers can avoid capital gains tax burdens.

Finally there is the possibility of failing to report capital gains. Overall, Poterba estimates that about 40% of capital gains are not reported. This figure refers to capital gains on all types of assets. Unfortunately, separate figures are not available for real estate.[7]

The combination of these factors suggests that capital gains arising when structure investments are churned are effectively taxed at much less than the statutory rate. We therefore consider also the incentives for churning that arise when individuals' capital gains are completely untaxed and when they are taxed at half the statutory rate, as well as corporations' incentives when their capital gains are taxed at half and three-quarters the statutory rate.

7.2.3 Results

Table 7.3 reports values of net before-tax corporate depreciation allowances and effective tax rates for representative parameter values. These calculations employ the 2.47% annual exponential depreciation rate Hulten and Wykoff (1981) report for commercial structures and assume that transaction costs when assets are sold equal 5% of the sales price. The table presents results with required rates of return of 2% and 4%. As Summers (chap. 9) argues, these rates are if anything higher than those suggested by theory but are rather lower than those actually used by corporations. The 4% figure is standard in the effective tax rate literature.

For the churning scenarios it is assumed that the firm chooses the depreciation method and interval between asset sales so as to maximize

Table 7.3   Depreciation Benefits and Effective Tax Rates for Corporations

| | Depreciation Method | | | |
| | Accelerated Depreciation | Churning: Effective Capital Gains Rate | | |
Inflation Rate		0.14	0.21	0.28
	Required Rate of Return = 0.02			
3%	0.69	0.81	0.71	0.59
	(37%)	(26%)	(36%)	(44%)
6%	0.58	0.60	0.48	0.36
	(44%)	(43%)	(50%)	(55%)
10%	0.47	0.41	0.33	0.24
	(50%)	(53%)	(58%)	(59%)
	Required Rate of Return = 0.04			
3%	0.61	0.62	0.55	0.48
	(35%)	(35%)	(38%)	(42%)
6%	0.58	0.47	0.40	0.36
	(37%)	(42%)	(45%)	(47%)
10%	0.43	0.38	0.33	0.27
	(44%)	(46%)	(48%)	(50%)

Note: Top entry is the present value of depreciation benefits; bottom entry in parentheses is the corresponding effective tax rate.

profits. As this table makes clear, under current law corporations will seldom want to churn structures for tax reasons. This is hardly surprising, since the recapture provisions of the tax law were designed to prevent such transactions. If the marginal corporate investor faces less than the statutory capital gains rate, then it may become slightly preferrable to churn its structures.

Table 7.4 presents similar calculations for top-bracket individuals who invest in structures through such devices as partnerships or proprietorships. As the table suggests, individuals have much stronger incentives to churn structures than do corporations. The top individual tax rate for ordinary income is 50%, and the top capital gains rate is 20%. Even ignoring the likely ability of individuals to avoid more of their capital gains liability than corporations can theirs, the 30% spread between the ordinary income and statutory capital gains rate is a much stronger churning incentive than the 18% spread faced by corporations.

At a 3% rate of inflation and 2% required rate of return individuals always choose to churn their assets, and if they can avoid capital gains taxes, may face negative effective tax rates. Even at higher inflation rates churning is a tax-preferred activity for individuals. Whether at a particular inflation rate corporations or individuals face higher effective

Table 7.4   **Depreciation Benefits and Effective Tax Rates for Individuals**

| | | Depreciation Method | | |
| | | Churning: Effective Capital Gains Rate | | |
Inflation Rate	Accelerated Depreciation	0.00	0.10	0.20
	Required Rate of Return = 0.02			
3%	0.69	1.06	0.90	0.75
	(41%)	(−14%)	(18%)	(35%)
6%	0.58	0.85	0.68	0.53
	(48%)	(26%)	(42%)	(51%)
10%	0.47	0.69	0.48	0.36
	(54%)	(41%)	(54%)	(59%)
	Required Rate of Return = 0.04			
3%	0.61	0.75	0.66	0.57
	(38%)	(29%)	(35%)	(41%)
6%	0.52	0.61	0.52	0.43
	(44%)	(39%)	(44%)	(48%)
10%	0.43	0.50	0.41	0.34
	(48%)	(45%)	(49%)	(51%)

Note: Top entry is the present value of depreciation benefits; bottom entry in parentheses is the corresponding effective tax rate.

tax rates may depend on their marginal capital gains rates. The source of funds matters as well, since the double taxation of corporate earnings may make the required corporate rate of return for new savings capital substantially higher than the rate for, say, partnership investors. Section 7.3 treats this issue in more depth, but it is sufficient at this point to note that individuals may face strong incentives to invest in structures and sell them later.[8] In particular, these results suggest that the tax code favors individual rather than corporate ownership of structures.

The preceding analysis is subject to two qualifications. Our calculations understate the potential importance of the resale of assets because they ignore the option value associated with uncertainty in asset values. If an asset appreciates rapidly, there will be tax advantages to turning it over. For a careful treatment of tax churning in a model where depreciation is stochastic, see Williams (1981). He finds that introducing uncertainty significantly increases the effect of the churning on the effective purchase price of new capital goods. For example, parameter values which most closely approximate the current tax treatment of structures produce the following result: doubling the variance of future asset prices raises the expected present value of depreciation allowances by about 15%.[9] Uncertainty in the tax law and the possibility of favorable future tax law changes may contribute to this effect. The second qualification is that our results may overstate the gains from churning by ignoring the capital gains taxes which often must be paid on land sales that accompany the transfer of structures. It is not clear to what degree these two qualifications offset each other.

7.2.4   The Extent of Churning

The limited available empirical evidence suggests that churning is an important part of the depreciation strategy for investors in structures.[10] Table 7.5 presents data on the depreciation methods chosen by corporations and partnerships for their structure investments in 1981 and 1982. Corporations used straight-line depreciation for 38% of the value of their structure investments in 1981 and for 33% in 1982. Except in

Table 7.5   **Choice of Depreciation Method under ACRS (millions of current dollars)**

	Corporations	
	1981	1982
Total allocable 15-year real property other than low-income housing and public utility property	24,836	25,276
Accelerated depreciation	15,474	16,923
(%)	(62.3%)	(67.0%)
Straight-line	9,362	8,353
(%)	(37.7%)	(33.0%)
Unallocable property, foreign property, and tax-exempt organizations	6,171	5,294

	Partnerships	
	1981	1982
Total allocable 15-year real property other than low-income housing and public utility property	29,044	46,553
Accelerated depreciation	11,700	18,344
(%)	(40.3%)	(39.4%)
Straight-line	17,344	28,209
(%)	(59.7%)	(60.6%)
Unallocable property, foreign property, and tax-exempt organizations	1,879	1,492

Source: Unpublished preliminary data, Statistics of Income Division, Internal Revenue Service.

Note: Entries correspond to dollar values of 15-year real property (other than low-income housing and public utility structures) put in place and depreciated by the indicated method in these years. Unallocable property could not reliably be assigned to either the accelerated or straight-line depreciation category. These data exclude investments for which the IRS was unable to determine from the tax form which type of capital was being depreciated.

very unusual circumstances, use of straight-line depreciation makes sense only when firms plan to sell their assets at some date. In addition, under the generous pre-1984 recapture rules for installment sales, some firms may have used accelerated depreciation even if they wanted to churn their assets later. By such extensive use of straight-line depreciation, the corporate sector gives up the substantial tax benefits of acceleration in order, presumably, to avoid costly recapture when the structures are sold later.[11]

The bottom panel of table 7.5 presents far more striking information on partnerships. Fully 60% of the value of structures put in place by partnerships since the introduction of ACRS was depreciated straight-line. This is, of course, quite consistent with our findings that churning can be very attractive for individual investors and that individuals are more likely than corporations to take advantage of churning possibilities. The 60% figure in table 7.5 is likely to understate the extent of straight-line use for nonresidential investment, since the entry includes residential investment other than low-income housing. The absence of a special recapture penalty makes it very likely that partnerships use accelerated depreciation for their residential investments, so the fraction of nonresidential structures depreciated straight-line is probably well above 60%. While the data on partnership and corporate depreciation methods are preliminary and subject to reporting error, it seems clear that they support the hypothesis that investors often plan to sell their assets. At the very least, this information casts doubt on the relevance of standard effective tax rate calculations that assume all investors use accelerated depreciation methods.

The results in this section suggest that taking account of the possibility of tax churning may help to explain the recent boom in commercial building. If individuals use low discount rates and can avoid capital gains taxes, the tax burden on commercial structures may now be small or even negative. This reflects both the 1981 tax reforms and the reduction in inflation since 1980. It probably represents a substantial reduction in the tax burden from the situation that prevailed prior to 1981.

7.3 Corporate Financial Policy and the Effective Tax Rates on Structures Investment

Our analysis so far has concerned features of the tax treatment of investments in structures which are common to individual investors, partnerships, and corporations. The conventional wisdom that current tax law favors equipment over structures is derived from studies which have focused on corporate investment rather than overall investment.[12] The calculations underlying these claims are almost always based on a variant of the formula for the user cost of capital derived by Hall and Jorgenson (1967). This formula, however, ignores a variety of factors, among them personal taxes and corporate financial policy. In this section, we argue that when the effects of personal taxes and corporate financial policy are taken into account, there is a much smaller difference between the calculated effective tax rates on structures and equipment, and perhaps even a tax advantage to investments in structures.

The intuitive point is very simple. The tax law seems to treat debt-financed investments more favorably. Therefore, to the degree that a project can be financed with debt, it becomes more attractive. Investments in structures should be much more easily financed with debt than investments in equipment. Structures are easily used as collateral for a loan, there is a dense secondary market for most types of buildings that a creditor can go to if the collateral must be liquidated, and the market value of a building used as collateral is normally much more predictable than the values of many other assets. A firm should therefore be able to obtain a much larger loan on a building than on many other assets without imposing any effective default risk on the lender.[13]

The difficulty with examining the implications of the tax incentive to use debt is that there is no consensus in the literature concerning the determinants of corporate debt-equity ratios. Most of this section will focus on what we will call the traditional model of debt-equity decisions, though we will explore at the end the implications of some alternative models.

7.3.1 The Incentive to Use Debt Finance

In this traditional model, corporations have at the margin a tax incentive to favor debt finance. Income accruing within a corporation is taxed at a higher rate than income accruing directly to shareholders. Corporate income is taxable both under the corporate tax and again, either as dividends or as capital gains, under the shareholders' personal income tax, while income accruing directly to shareholders is taxable only under the personal tax. This difference in tax rates creates an opportunity for tax arbitrage. A firm and its shareholders can shift taxable income from the firm to the shareholders simply by having the firm borrow from the shareholders, using the proceeds to repurchase equity from the shareholders. The direct effects of this transaction are to lower the taxable income of the corporation by the amount of the interest payments made on the debt and to raise the individuals' taxable income by this amount less the change in income from equity.

In spite of this tax incentive to use debt finance, firms do not use debt exclusively because the possibility of bankruptcy leads to conflicts of interest between debt and equity holders, with associated real costs.[14] These real costs could take the form of direct legal and administrative costs in bankruptcy, monitoring costs of lenders as they try to protect themselves, and agency costs created by the incentive on the firm to change its behavior to aid equity holders at the expense of bond holders.[15]

In deriving an explicit expression for the size of the tax incentive to use debt, it is important to take account of the degree to which the income that shareholders receive from equity takes the form of dividends rather than capital gains. While there is no convincing explanation for why firms pay dividends, we presume that shareholders prefer to have at least some of the return from equity take the form of dividends, perhaps for liquidity reasons or perhaps because of the signal conveyed about the solvency of the firm. Our approach to dividends is very similar to that of Poterba and Summers (1985).

Except for the changes described above, we continue to follow the approach developed by Hall and Jorgenson (1967). When will an investment just break even? Assume that the value of the marginal product of the investment equals ρ and that the asset depreciates exponentially at a rate δ. The construction cost of the project is q. However, the out-of-pocket cost of the project to the firm is only $q(1 - k - uz)$, where k is the investment tax credit rate, u is the corporate tax rate, and z represents the present value of the depreciation deductions allowed under the tax law. We assume that the firm finances this amount by borrowing $bq(1 - k - uz)$, raising the rest of the funds from equity holders. Let i represent the nominal coupon rate on this debt, and let π represent the inflation rate. By using debt, the firm incurs some real costs due to the possibility of bankruptcy. Denote these real costs by $C(b)$. We assume that $C(0) = 0$, that $C' > 0$, and that these costs are deductible from taxable corporate income. Then the after-corporate-tax real return, R, to equity holders from this project, net of depreciation, will equal $R = [\rho - C(b)](1 - u) - q(1 - k - uz)\{\delta + b[i(1 - u) - \pi]\}$.

This real return is taxable under the personal income tax as either dividends or capital gains. Assume that a fraction p of this return is paid out as dividends and that the personal tax rate on dividends is m, while that on accruing capital gains is c. The effective tax rate, e, on the real return therefore equals $e = pm + (1 - p)c$.[16] Not only is the real return taxable, however, but the inflationary increase in nominal value is also taxable. We assume that this inflationary capital gain is taxable only at the capital gains tax rate. Shareholders therefore receive a net of personal tax return from this investment equal to $R(1 - e) - c\pi(1 - b)q(1 - k - uz)$. They receive this return on an initial investment of $(1 - b)q(1 - k - uz)$. Had they invested these funds in bonds instead, they could have received a net of tax return per dollar invested of $i(1 - m) - \pi$. However, due to the illiquidity of income received as capital gains rather than as coupon payments or dividends, they would require that their return on an investment in equity be higher by an amount $D(p)$, where we assume that $D(1) = 0$ and $D' < 0$.

Given these assumptions, shareholders are indifferent to the choice between investing in bonds or investing in this corporate project if

$$(7) \quad R(1 - e) - c\pi(1 - b)q(1 - k - uz)$$
$$= (1 - b)q(1 - k - uz)[i(1 - m) - \pi + D].$$

This equation implicitly determines not only the required rate of return, ρ, on an investment project, but also the firm's optimal dividend pay-out rate, p^*, and optimal debt-value ratio, b^*. The firm would set b and p to minimize the required ρ^* that it must earn on capital. Simple algebra shows that the first-order conditions for the optimal b^* and p^* imply

$$(8) \quad C'(b^*) = (q(1 - k - uz)/[(1 - u)(1 - e)])\{i[u$$
$$+ e(1 - u) - m] - p(m - c)\pi + D\}.$$

$$(9) \quad -D'(p^*) = (m - c)[i(1 - m) - \pi(1 - c) + D]/(1 - e).$$

Equation (8) shows that the debt-equity ratio would be increased until the rise in bankruptcy costs from extra debt just equals the extra tax savings from further use of debt plus the gain from the greater liquidity of income from debt. Similarly, equation (9) shows that the dividend pay-out rate would be increased to the point where the tax loss from paying more dividends just equals the gain to the individual from the extra liquidity.

Given these values for b^* and p^*, equation (7) then implies that

$$(10) \quad \rho = C + q(1 - k - uz)$$
$$\cdot \{(1 - b^*)[i(1 - m) - \pi(1 - c) + D]$$
$$+ (1 - e)(\delta + b^*[i(1 - u) - \pi]\}/[(1 - u)(1 - e)].$$

This equation corresponds to the expression for the user cost of capital in Hall and Jorgenson (1967), corrected for the effects of corporate financial decisions and personal taxes.

As long as the expression in braces in equation (10) is the same for all projects, conditional on the value of δ, these extra complications make little difference. The numerical value of this expression is difficult to estimate, even without the complications added here, and so past authors have chosen to assign some arbitrary value for the expression as a whole rather than to make an attempt to estimate each parameter.[17] However, to the extent that the optimal values of b^* or p^* differ by project, these differences ought to be taken into account when comparing the effects of the corporate tax on different types of investments.

There is every reason to expect the optimal value of b^* to vary by type of capital, for the reasons described above. It should also vary by industry, if only because the variability of the profits of a firm vary systematically by industry. Certainly the observed debt-value ratios differ substantially by industry. According to the figures reported in Fullerton and Gordon (1983) for the debt-value ratio in a select group of industries in 1973, the observed ratios ranged from 0.08 in construction to 0.787 in real estate. The average in the economy was 0.399.[18]

Unfortunately, there are no good data on the differing degrees to which debt is used to finance different types of capital within an industry. Auerbach (1985) attempted to explain differences in the debt-value ratios of different firms in part by differences in their use of structures versus equipment and found no systematic relation—coefficient estimates differed wildly across specifications. However, the use of structures versus equipment by industry can easily be correlated with other omitted factors which differ by industry and affect desired debt-value ratios. Given the lack of any good evidence on differences in the use of debt to finance different types of capital, the modest objective of this section is to demonstrate the importance of plausible differences in debt-value ratios for different projects to calculated effective tax rates for these different projects.

7.3.2   Effective Tax Rates

The effective tax rate, τ, on a project, as Auerbach (1983) defines it, would satisfy the equation

$$(11) \quad \rho_n = \rho^* - C - (1 - b)Dq(1 - k - uz)$$
$$= q[(i(1 - m) - \pi)/(1 - \tau) + \delta].$$

In our context ρ_n is the value of the net marginal product, since a new investment generates incentive and agency costs due to the tax-induced incentive to favor debt and avoid dividends. Here $\tau = 0$ only if the value of the marginal return to new capital, net of depreciation, equals the individual's marginal time preference rate.

To indicate the potential importance of differences in debt-value ratios between assets, assume that we have calculated various effective tax rates assuming no differences in the use of debt finance. If, for example, the value of b for structures in fact exceeds that for equipment by 0.4, what effect does this have on the estimated tax rate? If τ_0 is the previously estimated effective tax rate on structures and τ_1 is the revised estimate, then it follows easily from equations (10) and (11) that

$$(12) \quad [i(1 - m) - \pi][1/(1 - \tau_0) - 1/(1 - \tau_1)]$$
$$= 0.4(1 - k - uz)\{i[u(1 - e) - (1 - p)(m - c)]$$
$$- p\pi(m - c) + D[u + e(1 - u)]\}/[(1 - u)(1 - e)].$$

In evaluating this expression, we attempt to follow the parameter assumptions made in Auerbach (1983) wherever possible. In particular, we assume that the initial estimate of the effective tax rate on structures is 0.421, as Auerbach calculated for 1982, that $u = 0.46$ and $k = 0$ by statute,[19] that $i(1 - m) = \pi + 0.04$, again as in Auerbach,[20] that $p = 0.4$, and that i equals the AAA corporate bond yield in 1982 of 0.138. We approximated z by 0.5.[21] For the personal tax rates m and c, we initially set $m = 0.35$ and $c = 0.05$.

Choosing a value for D is more arbitrary. However, equation (9) gives an equilibrium condition for D', and if we assume a functional form for D, we can calculate its value. We therefore assumed that $D(p) = a(1 - p)$, for some value a, implying that $D(p) = -(1 - p)D'$, with D' given by equation (9). This specification implies that in equilibrium the optimal dividend pay-out rate for any given firm is indeterminate, though the average pay-out rate for all firms together may be explicitly determined. We note below how our estimates change if we assume instead that $D(p) = a(1 - p)^2$, which leads to a unique optimal pay-out rate for each firm.

Given these parameter values, the new estimate of the effective tax rate on structures drops dramatically from 0.421 to 0.193. In contrast, the estimated effective tax rate on equipment reported by Auerbach for 1982 was 0.084. At least with these parameter values, the difference becomes minor. Given these parameter values, the calculated value of D equaled 0.0118, implying that a rather modest value of liquidity is sufficient to offset the tax disadvantage to dividends.

The key parameters in this calculation are the estimate of the difference in the value of b between equipment and structures, the estimates of m and c, and the value of the real after-tax interest rate. If, for example, the debt-value ratio for structures exceeds the value for equipment by only 0.3, then the effective tax rate on structures drops to only 0.265.

Similarly, let us maintain our previous assumption about the difference in the debt-value ratios, but now consider two alternative assumptions about the values of m and c. First, assume that $m = 0.46$ and $c = 0$.[22] With these values, the tax advantage to using debt is much reduced, since capital gains from equity are untaxed while interest income is taxed more heavily under the personal tax. Under these assumptions, the effective tax rate on structures drops to only 0.285. However, if we make the alternative assumption that $m = 0.225$, following the results in Gordon and Malkiel (1981), and set $c = 0.05$, then the effective tax rate on structures drops to 0.076.

Let us now return to our initial assumptions that the difference in the debt-value ratio used in funding structures and equipment is 0.4, and continue to assume that $m = 0.35$ and that $c = 0.05$, but assume that the real after-tax interest rate is only 0.03, changing the estimate of the inflation rate accordingly. With these assumptions, the effective tax rate on structures drops to 0.071.

Finally, if we again maintain our initial assumptions, but assume that the functional form for D is $D(p) = a(1 - p)^2$, implying a smaller value for D in equilibrium, then the effective tax rate on structures drops to only 0.232.

Therefore, at least using the traditional model of corporate financial decisions, differences in the optimal debt-value ratio for different types of capital can make a substantial difference when calculating effective tax rates. For most of the cases explored, the remaining difference in the effective tax rates on equipment and structures is minor and can be of either sign.

This traditional model of corporate financial decisions is far from the only one discussed seriously in the finance literature. For example, the papers by Miller (1977) and by DeAngelo and Masulis (1980) each argue, on different grounds, that firms may have increased their use of debt to the point where the tax advantage of using debt is eliminated. Miller considers the effect of the increased personal interest income on the marginal personal tax rate, while DeAngelo and Masulis consider the drop in corporate taxable income due to interest deductions on the marginal corporate tax rate. Under either model, differences in debt-value ratios by project have no impact on the effective tax rates on different projects. Each of these arguments depends critically on the marginal corporate or personal tax rate evolving enough before the debt-value ratio becomes so high as to lead to non-negligible agency or bankruptcy costs.

A quite different model of corporate financial policy was developed recently in Myers and Majluf (1984). They argue that when market investors see a firm issue new equity or new risky bonds, they will infer from this that the firm's managers view the current prices of equity or bonds as too high and are trying to take advantage of it. As a result, market prices fall when new securities are issued, and managers must take this into account when considering going to the market for new funds. They argue, as a result, that the firm will prefer to use internal sources of funds and will require a higher rate of return on a new project if it must raise the funds by issuing risky securities to outside investors.

Their argument does not consider the implications of the tax incentive to use debt finance. As long as bonds issued by the corporation remain riskless, then this favorable tax treatment would make debt finance cheaper than internal finance. If new debt issues are risky, then there is a trade-off between the tax advantage of new debt issues and the disadvantage of outside finance on which their model focuses. But the ability to finance a project with riskless bonds will vary by project, since projects differ in their suitability as collateral for a loan. If, as we argued above, structures make good collateral and can be financed heavily with debt before that debt becomes risky, then the required rate of return for structures should normally be lower than that for other projects, even ignoring tax effects, and would be lowered further by the tax advantage to debt finance. In this context, however, a simple comparison of effective tax rates is no longer sufficient to judge the effect of the tax law on the efficiency of the composition of the capital stock, since capital may be allocated inefficiently even without tax distortions.

The analysis in this section suggests that effective tax rate calculations are extremely sensitive to assumptions about marginal debt-equity ratios. To the extent that different types of capital assets have different abilities to carry debt, this means that standard calculations which assume constant (often zero) marginal debt-equity ratios are likely to be misleading. The vast disparities in debt-equity ratios across industries suggest that the error introduced by ignoring variations in the leverageability of assets is probably large. These results also help to resolve the empirical puzzle raised at the beginning of this chapter. Commercial buildings, especially office buildings, can probably carry much more debt than other more specialized structures. They may therefore be burdened much less by taxes than conventional analyses suggest.

7.4 Taxation and Tenure Choice

It is widely believed that the tax system favors owner-occupied housing. This conclusion is repeated in many textbooks and forms the basis for a significant amount of research on the effects of taxation on tenure choice. The standard argument is straightforward. The services of owner-occupied housing are untaxed while rental payments are treated as taxable income. While landlords are permitted tax deductions not permitted to homeowners, as long as there is some positive effective tax rate on rental income, homeownership is nonetheless thought to be tax-favored. As a number of authors including Litzenberger and Sosin (1977), Titman (1982), and Hendershott (1986) have recognized, there is an important defect in this argument. It ignores the possibility of tax arbitrage between high-bracket landlords and low-bracket tenants. High-bracket taxpayers have a comparative advantage over low-bracket taxpayers in making use of interest deductions which they can exploit by borrowing in order to buy real estate which they then rent to low-bracket taxpayers.

When this effect is recognized, it turns out that homeownership is tax-favored for only a very small number of taxpayers. In this section we demonstrate this conclusion by considering the effects of home-ownership in a setting where people would be indifferent to the choice of owning and renting their homes but for tax incentives. In reality, of course, other considerations such as transaction costs, desire to own one's own place of residence, and the differing incentive effects of rental and ownership contracts influence tenure choice. But in order to study the incentives provided by the tax system, we abstract from these effects.

Before turning to a calculation of the tax incentive for different households to own their own home, it is useful to begin by illustrating the potential tax advantage of tenancy. The user cost of owner-occupied housing for a taxpayer in the t_p percent tax bracket is:

$$(13) \qquad c_o = (1 - t_p)(i + p_t) - \pi + n + \delta,$$

where c_o represents the user cost, i is the nominal interest rate, p_t is the property tax rate, π is the inflation rate, n represents maintenance costs expressed as a fraction of house value, and δ is the sum of the depreciation rate and risk premium.

Calculation of the cost of rental housing is more complex. We assume that competition forces rents down to the point where landlords earn the same risk-adjusted return on rental property as they could on bonds. This assumption is warranted as long as landlords can, at the margin, borrow or lend. It will become apparent that top-bracket landlords will be able to charge the lowest rents and so represent the marginal supplier of rental housing. The break-even condition for top-bracket landlords requires that:

$$(14) \qquad R = \frac{[(1 - t^*)i - \pi + \delta](1 - t^*z)}{(1 - t^*)} + p_t + n,$$

where t^* is the top-bracket tax rate, and z represents the present value of depreciation allowances permitted for tax purposes.[23] It follows that taxpayers will prefer to rent rather than own their homes as long as $c_o > R$, which occurs as long as the following condition is satisfied:

$$(15) \qquad t_p < \frac{t^*zi + [(\pi - \delta)t^*(1 - z)/(1 - t^*)]}{(i + p_t)}.$$

It is clear from (15) that if real after-tax interest rates are assumed to be positive, the break-even tax rate at which investors are just indifferent to owning their homes is an increasing function of z and of the top tax rate t^*. It is also an increasing function of the rate of inflation, assuming that the real interest rate remains constant. This is because increases in nominal interest raise the advantage to structuring transactions so as to allocate interest deductions to high-bracket taxpayers. These considerations suggest that the effects of the 1981 tax reform on tenure choice cannot be evaluated on an a priori basis. On the one hand, the introduction of ACRS tends to promote rental housing, while the reduction in the top tax rate from 70% to 50% tends to reduce the incentives for renting housing. Therefore, we turn to a quantitative calculation of the break-even tax rate under alternative tax regimes.

Under ACRS, residential property was permitted 175% declining-balance depreciation over a useful life of 15 years (now 19 years). In addition, residential property has the desirable feature that upon sale accelerated depreciation is recaptured at ordinary income rates only to the extent that it has exceeded straight-line depreciation. The 1981 act also permits purchasers of used assets to use the 175% declining-balance depreciation method. Prior to 1981, asset lives were substantially longer but investors in new residential structures were allowed 200% declining-balance (or sum-of-the-years-digits) depreciation. Purchasers of used assets were required to use 125% declining-balance depreciation, thereby lowering the prices of used structures relative to new structures and reducing the value of tax churning. High individual marginal tax rates provided ample incentive for investment in rental housing, however. The appendix describes the method used to determine the value of depreciation allowances with churning under pre-ACRS tax rules.

Table 7.6 presents values of marginal tax rates for individuals who were indifferent between homeownership and renting for the years 1965–85. To solve equation (15), we follow DeLeeuw and Ozanne (1979) in assuming that $\delta = 0.014$ and $p_t = 0.02$. In performing the user-cost calculations (7), we add a 0.04 premium to δ in order to adjust the cost of asset depreciation for risk. Individuals' expectations of future inflation are represented by a distributed lag on past inflation, and the before-tax interest rate is the historical Baa corporate bond rate. In each year owners of residential rental property are assumed to optimize over the choice of depreciation method and potential churning period.[24]

The results in table 7.6 describe four scenarios. We examine cases in which individuals who own rental housing avoid half their capital gains liability at the margin and also cases in which they pay the full statutory rate on capital gains. In addition, we report separately specifications in which investors treat depreciation allowances as risky (and so add 0.04 to the annual discount rate in calculating their present value) and in which they are viewed as riskless.

The striking implication of the findings reported in table 7.6 is that homeownership has not until recently been favored by the tax code.[25] High individual tax rates before 1982 encouraged most taxpayers to rent their dwellings from top-bracket individuals. While the results in table 7.6 reflect changing inflation and interest rates as well as statutory tax changes, it is hard to escape the conclusion that falling personal taxes have undone changes in the depreciation provisions to make

Table 7.6   **Tenure Choice and Tax Status, 1965–85 (percentages)**

| | | Minimum Tax Bracket for Owner-Occupiers | | | |
| | | Full Capital Gains Liability | | One-Half Capital Gains Liability | |
Year	Maximum Personal Tax Bracket	Risky Returns	Riskless Returns	Risky Returns	Riskless Returns
1965	70	0	64	0	70+
1970	73	24	62	27	69
1975	70	59	59	59	59
1980	70	55	63	56	64
1981	69	53	56	53	56
1982	50	32	50+	41	50+
1983	50	28	50	38	50+
1984	50	19	34	37	44
1985	50	11	23	13	29

Note: Entries correspond to break-even tax rates for tenure choice. Taxpayers with lower marginal tax rates will be renters, and those with higher marginal rates will be owner-occupiers.

homeownership much more attractive in recent years. From this perspective, it is perhaps not surprising that homeownership and residential investment have been strong in recent years.

7.5 Conclusions

The analysis in this paper highlights the difficulty of predicting the effects of tax rules on the level and composition of investment. The incentives for investment provided by the tax law turn out to depend on a number of quite specific features of the law, rather than just on tax rates and depreciation schedules. They also depend on how the tax law interacts with the liquidity characteristics of different types of assets. Analyses that omit these factors are likely to have little predictive power for the effects of tax changes on the composition of investment. And normative conclusions based on models that omit them are likely to be very misleading.

Our findings imply that there are at most minimal allocative losses resulting from the differential treatment of equipment and structures under current depreciation schedules. There are substantial reasons to believe that residential and nonresidential real estate investments made by partnerships are substantially favored under current law, because of the tax advantages associated with churning assets, arbitrage between taxpayers in different brackets, and leverage. Movements to equalize effective tax rates on structure and equipment investments as these rates are normally measured would be likely to exacerbate these distortions.

Changes in the tax rules governing recapture, limited partnerships, and the use of nonrecourse debt have the potential for reducing the tax benefits accruing to investments in rental properties and commercial buildings. Alternatively the possible tax bias in favor of these assets could be mitigated by providing them with depreciation schedules different from those afforded other structure investments. More generally, the incentive to churn assets and the tax advantages of those assets which can be churned would be reduced if depreciation allowances were indexed for inflation rather than accelerated. Similarly, the tax advantages of debt-financed investments would be reduced if firms were permitted to deduct only real rather than nominal interest payments.

The conclusion that the tax system discriminates strongly in favor of rental housing and against owner-occupied housing raises important issues for subsequent research. Given tax incentives, some other explanation must be given for the predominance of homeownership. A natural candidate is the moral hazard problem associated with rental contracts. Tenants have little incentive to care for properties which they do not own. Landlords have strong incentives to deny tenants the right to alter properties in ways that tenants may prefer but which may ultimately reduce market value. These problems are solved when people rent from themselves as with owner-occupied housing. In the presence of moral hazard problems, the market is unlikely to attain an optimal solution even in the absence of taxes. The imposition of taxes which discourage home ownership may result in very substantial deadweight losses given the presence of pre-existing distortions.

A similar point applies to the question of debt-financed investments in structures. To the extent that there are important information problems bearing on types of capital which are not liquid, too little investment in these types of capital is likely to take place even in the absence of taxes. These biases may be exacerbated by tax rules which favor liquid investments. If so, the social costs of nonneutral taxation may be much greater than the losses associated with distortionary taxation in environments without preexisting distortions. Consideration of structure investments highlights the need for the development of models considering the effects of taxes in markets already distorted by information problems. It seems likely that the welfare consequences of the interaction of tax rules and information problems are likely to be far greater than those found in typical neutrality calculations. We plan to pursue these issues in future research.

Appendix
Calculation of Depreciation Allowances with Churning

This appendix describes the solution method used to evaluate the present value of depreciation allowances when firms or individuals churn their assets. The procedure is slightly more complicated than standard present-value calculations because the value of future tax benefits is a function of the prices of used assets, which are functions of those tax benefits, and so on. Consistency requires that anticipated prices of used assets take churning possibilities into account.

These calculations assume that investors expect inflation rates, interest rates, and the tax law not to change in the future. In addition, our results employ the assumption that assets depreciate at constant exponential rates. These assumptions are standard in the effective tax rate literature when computing the value of depreciation allowances. Hendershott and Ling (1984) assume a different, reverse-sum-of-the-years depreciation schedule, which permits a direct numerical evaluation of churning benefits. Assets that depreciate exponentially have no terminal dates, thus making it impossible to use the solution technique Hendershott and Ling describe to evaluate churning of these assets. Pellechio (1985) employs a solution method that can accommodate exponential depreciation but is different from the one used here.

Equations (2)–(6) in the text describe the value of depreciation allowances when firms churn their assets after k years. These equations include terms for $Q(k)$, the market price of a used asset k years after its initial purchase (the price of new capital in the first year is normalized to 1). Under the assumption that the tax treatment of old assets is the same as that accorded new assets, $Q(k)$ is as given in (3):

$$(16) \qquad Q(k) = [(1 - \delta)(1 + \pi)]^k.$$

Unfortunately, this assumption of symmetric treatment of old and new assets is valid only under ACRS. Before the introduction of ACRS, used nonresidential structures had to be depreciated straight-line. Pre-ACRS residential structures were depreciated at declining balance rates of 200% when new and 125% when used. These features make old assets less valuable than (16) indicates. Of course, these rules do not change the *relative* prices of used assets of different ages, since their tax treatment if sold is identical; it will, for example, always be the case that

$$(17) \qquad Q(k + n) = [(1 - \delta)(1 + \pi)]^n \, Q(k).$$

In calculating the present value of depreciation allowances, we used (17) and prevailing depreciation rules to solve numerically for the optimal treatment of used assets. Denote by z_{iu} the present value of all depreciation allowances (including those obtained after churning), net of transaction costs and capital gain taxes, for an investor in asset i when it is used. If z_{in} represents the present value of all (churning inclusive) depreciation allowances net of costs for a new asset, then it will be the case that:

$$(18) \qquad Q(k) = [(1 - \delta_i)(1 + \pi)]^k (1 - \tau z_{in})/(1 - \tau z_{iu}).$$

Given the depreciation and recapture rules of equations (2)–(6), the maximized present value of depreciation benefits for a new asset which the investor plans to sell in year k will be:

$$(19) \qquad\qquad\qquad z_{in} = \alpha_{ik} + \beta_{ik} Q(k)$$

where α_{ik} and β_{ik} depend on tax rules, inflation, depreciation rates, and other parameters. Substituting (17) into (18) produces

$$(20) \quad z_{in} = \{\alpha_{ik} + \beta_{ik}[(1 - \delta_i)(1 + \pi)]^k\}/$$
$$\{1 + \beta_{ik}\tau[(1 - \delta_i)(1 + \pi)]^k - \tau z_{iu}\}$$

The optimal churning program maximizes the value of z_{in} in (20), and we use that value of z_{in} for the calculations in the tables.

Notes

1. Hendershott and Ling (1984) and Pellechio (1985) have examined the incentives for churning assets. Our treatment generalizes their work by allowing for the important possibility that effective capital gains rates are below statutory rates. This accounts for our more positive view of churning as a device for reducing tax liabilities.

2. Limitations on loss carried forward may induce some small number of firms in special circumstances to choose the longer depreciation lives and the associated straight-line method. See Auerbach and Poterba (1986).

3. We do not consider the churning of equipment; however, in general it is never desirable to churn equipment for tax reasons alone. The investment tax credit (ITC) constitutes a substantial part of cost recovery for equipment investment, and the tax law includes harsh recapture provisions for the ITC upon early sale of equipment. Since used equipment is ineligible for the ITC, the combined effect is to make asset sales unattractive from a tax standpoint. Auerbach and Kotlikoff (1983) find that not even equipment put into place before the introduction of ACRS could be profitably churned after 1981.

4. The formula actually requires a minor correction for discounting of depreciation allowances within each year and the mid-month convention; the calculations in the tables embody these subtleties.

5. Tax changes in 1984 required that investors pay recapture taxes immediately upon sale of an asset, even if the buyer pays in installments. As Gilson, Scholes, and Wolfson (1986) illustrate, however, an installment sale can still significantly reduce the seller's effective capital gains tax rate.

6. Recent law changes have limited but by no means eliminated investors' abilities to use these strategies.

7. We are agnostic on the question of whether sophisticated real estate investors are more likely than other investors to underreport their gains. It may be particularly difficult to avoid declaring capital gains on an asset for which a taxpayer has received depreciation allowances for years.

8. Note that the incentive to churn is strongest at low inflation rates. Under current recapture rules, churning serves less to undo the effects of inflation than it does to exploit the difference between economic depreciation and tax depreciation.

9. This calculation comes from table 2 of Williams (1981) and assumes a 50% tax rate, 6% transactions cost for asset sales, capital gains taxed at 40% of the ordinary income rate, 10% interest rate, 3% annual risk-adjusted growth of asset prices, and a declining balance depreciation method which provides allowances equal to 9% of the basis each year. When, in this scenario, the annual variance of asset prices is 10% of value, the present value of depreciation allowances is .516; if the variance were 20%, the present value would be .599.

10. The ability to churn assets affects other aspects of firm strategy as well. Firms can sell assets as an alternative to using such devices as leases and takeovers in order to keep taxable status every year.

11. These fractions of depreciation taken using acceleration are substantially lower than fractions Wales (1966) reports for most industries in 1960. Running his learning functions forward to 1982 predicts rates of use of accelerated depreciation even more at variance with firms' practices, despite changes which have made accelerated depreciation more generous than before.

12. For a recent example, see Auerbach (1983).

13. Buildings are not unique in this regard. Our argument applies as well to any asset where there is a good secondary market and a relatively stable price. Other examples might include motor vehicles, airplanes, or mainframe computers. Most types of equipment, however, tend to be specialized to the activities of a particular firm and so have little value to a creditor if they are seized in lieu of repayment of the debt. Conversely, not all types of buildings are equally liquid or have an equally stable value. Office buildings, for example, are probably far more liquid than factory buildings.

14. For a recent exposition of this view, see Modigliani (1982) or Gordon (1982).

15. For an exposition on these points, see Gordon and Malkiel (1981), Myers (1977), Jensen and Meckling (1976), or White (1983).

16. In this section c refers to the effective capital gains tax rate on *accruing* gains rather than on realized gains as in the last section.

17. Hall and Jorgenson (1967) set this expression equal to $\delta + 0.1$. Auerbach (1983), while also deriving a related formula involving the effects of debt finance, set the resulting expression equal to $\delta + 0.4$.

18. These figures represent the average use of debt for all the capital in the firm and not necessarily the marginal debt-value ratio. However, there is no systematic reason in the above model why the desired value of b^* ought to change as a firm expands.

19. We ignore here the possibility that the firm may have taxable losses that cannot be carried back to previous tax years or at least carried forward and

used up quickly. For further discussion, see Auerbach (1983) and Auerbach and Poterba (1986).

20. Bradford and Fullerton (1981) demonstrated the sensitivity of estimated tax rates to this estimate of the individual's opportunity cost of funds. By following Auerbach (1983) in assuming such a high after-tax real interest rate, we reduce the effects of debt finance on the estimated effective tax rate.

21. See Summers (1986) for a discussion of the discounting of depreciation allowances.

22. In order to keep the real after-tax interest rate at 0.04, we adjust the estimate for the inflation rate as needed.

23. In deriving (14), we follow Bulow and Summers (1984) in assuming that the tax system does not share in the risks associated with owning structures.

24. Calculations for the pre-ACRS period ignore potential complications involving interactions of depreciation allowances and the maximum tax on earned income, as described by Hite and Sanders (1981). For our purposes it is enough to assume that for marginal investors the bulk of their income is unearned. In addition, these calculations ignore the cost of land and the capital gains tax liability that may be generated when a residence is churned and land is sold. We assume implicitly that owner-occupiers and renters rent the land for their residences at equal rates.

25. These results differ substantially from more standard calculations of authors such as Diamond (1980) and Hendershott and Shilling (1982) that find homeownership to have become progressively more attractive over the 1970s. Our model incorporates tax arbitrage and also differs from theirs in assuming that investors expect house prices to be in equilibrium, and therefore rising at the general rate of inflation.

References

Auerbach, Alan J. 1985. Real determinants of corporate leverage. In Benjamin M. Friedman, ed., *Corporate capital structures in the United States.* Chicago: University of Chicago Press.

——. 1983. Corporate taxation in the United States. *Brookings Papers on Economic Activity* 2:451–506.

Auerbach, Alan J., and James R. Hines, Jr. 1986. Tax reform, investment, and the value of the firm. NBER Working Paper no. 1803, January.

Auerbach, Alan J., and Laurence Kotlikoff. 1983. Investment versus savings incentives: The size of the "bang for the buck" and the potential for self-financing business tax cuts. In L. Meyer, ed., *The economic consequences of government deficits.* Boston: Kluwer-Nijhoff.

Auerbach, Alan J., and James Poterba. 1986. Tax loss carryforwards and corporate tax incentives. Chapter 10 in this volume.

Bradford, David F., and Don Fullerton. 1981. Pitfalls in the construction and use of effective tax rates. In Charles R. Hulten, ed., *Depreciation, inflation, and the taxation of income from capital.* Washington: Urban Institute Press.

Bulow, Jeremy I., and Lawrence H. Summers. 1984. The taxation of risky assets. *Journal of Political Economy* 92:1, 20–39.

Constantinides, George M. 1983. Capital market equilibrium with personal tax. *Econometrica* 51:611–36.

Constantinides, George M., and Jonathan E. Ingersoll, Jr. 1984. Optimal bond trading with personal taxes. *Journal of Financial Economics* 13:299–335.

DeAngelo, Harry, and Ronald W. Masulis. 1980. Optimal capital structure under corporate and personal taxation. *Journal of Financial Economics* 8:3–29.

DeLeeuw, Frank, and Larry Ozanne. 1979. The impact of the federal income tax on investment in housing. *Survey of Current Business* 59:12, 50–61.

Diamond, Douglas B., Jr. 1980. Taxes, inflation, speculation and the cost of homeownership. *Journal of the American Real Estate and Urban Economics Association* 8:3, 281–98.

Economic Report of the President. 1985. Washington: U.S. Government Printing Office.

Fullerton, Don, and Roger H. Gordon. 1983. A reexamination of tax distortions in general equilibrium models. In Martin Feldstein, ed., *Behavioral simulation methods in tax policy analysis.* Chicago: University of Chicago Press.

Fullerton, Don, and Yolanda Henderson. 1984. Incentive effects of taxes on income from capital: Alternative policies in the 1980s. In Charles R. Hulton and Isabel V. Sawhill, eds., *The legacy of Reaganomics: Prospects for long term growth.* Washington: Urban Institute Press.

Gilson, Ronald J., Myron S. Scholes, and Mark A. Wolfson. 1986. Taxation and the dynamics of corporate control: The uncertain case for tax motivated acquisitions. Stanford Law School, Law and Economics Program, Working Paper no. 873, February.

Gordon, Roger H. 1982. Interest rates, inflation, and corporate financial policy. *Brookings Papers on Economic Activity* 2:461–88.

Gordon, Roger H., and Burton G. Malkiel. 1981. Corporation finance. In Henry J. Aaron and Joseph A. Pechman, eds., *How taxes affect economic behavior.* Washington: Brookings Institution.

Hall, Robert E., and Dale W. Jorgenson. 1967. Tax policy and investment behavior. *American Economic Review* 57:391–414.

Hendershott, Patric H. 1986. Tax changes and capital allocation in the 1980's. Chapter 8 in this volume.

Hendershott, Patric H., and David C. Ling. 1984. Trading and the tax shelter value of depreciable real estate. *National Tax Journal* 37:2, 213–23.

Hendershott, Patric H., and James D. Shilling. 1982. The economics of tenure choice, 1955–1979. In C. Sirmans, ed., *Research in real estate,* Vol. 1. Greenwich, Conn.: JAI Press.

Hite, Gailen L., and Anthony B. Sanders. 1981. Excess depreciation and the maximum tax. *Journal of the American Real Estate and Urban Economics Association* 9:2, 134–47.

Hulten, Charles, and Frank Wykoff. 1981. The measurement of economic depreciation. In Charles R. Hulten, ed., *Depreciation, inflation, and the taxation of income from capital.* Washington: Urban Institute Press.

Jensen, Michael C., and William H. Meckling. 1976. Theory of the firm: Managerial behavior, agency costs and ownership structure. *Journal of Financial Economics* 3:305–60.

Litzenberger, Robert, and Howard Sosin. 1977. Taxation and the incidence of home ownership across income groups. *Journal of Finance* 32:261–75.

McCulloch, J. Houston. 1975. The tax adjusted yield curve. *Journal of Finance* 30:811–30.

Miller, Merton. 1977. Debt and taxes. *Journal of Finance* 32:261–75.

Modigliani, Franco. 1982. Debt, dividend policy, taxes, inflation and market valuation. *Journal of Finance* 37:255–73.

Musgrave, John C. 1984. Fixed reproducible tangible wealth in the United States, 1980–83, *Survey of Current Business* 64, no. 8 (August): 54–59.

Myers, Stewart C. 1977. Determinants of corporate borrowing. *Journal of Financial Economics* 5:147–75.

Myers, Stewart, and N. Majluf. 1984. Corporate financing and investment decisions when firms have information investors do not have. *Journal of Financial Economics* 13:187–221.

Pellechio, Anthony J. 1985. Taxation, real property value, and optimal holding periods: An analytic solution and application to tax reform. Mimeo. August.

Poterba, James M. 1986. How burdensome are capital gains taxes? NBER Working Paper 1871, March.

Poterba, James M., and Lawrence H. Summers. 1985. The economic effects of dividend taxation. In Edward I. Altman and Marti G. Subrahmanyam, eds., *Recent advances in corporate finance*. Homewood, Ill.: Richard D. Irwin.

Rosen, Harvey. 1985. Housing subsidies: Effects on housing decisions, efficiency, and equity. In Alan J. Auerbach and Martin S.Feldstein, eds., *Handbook of Public Economics,* Vol. 1. Amsterdam: North-Holland.

Stiglitz, Joseph E. 1983. Some aspects of the taxation of capital gains. *Journal of Public Economics* 21:257–94.

Summers, Lawrence H. 1986. Investment Incentives and the Discounting of Depreciation Allowances. Chapter 9 in this volume.

Titman, Sheridan D. 1982. The effect of anticipated inflation on housing market equilibrium. *Journal of the American Real Estate and Urban Economics Association* 37:827–42.

U.S. Department of the Treasury. 1984. *Tax reform for fairness, simplicity, and economic growth: The Treasury Department report to the President.* Washington: U.S. Department of the Treasury. November.

Wales, Terence J. 1966. Estimation of an accelerated depreciation learning function. *Journal of the American Statistical Association* 61:995–1009.

White, Michelle J. 1983. Bankruptcy costs and the new bankruptcy code. *Journal of Finance* 38:477–88.

Williams, Joseph. 1981. Trading depreciable assets. Mimeo. New York: New York University School of Business, October.

Comment   Emil M. Sunley

Are equipment or structures more tax-favored? The capital recovery rules suggest that equipment is more tax-favored: the investment tax credit and 5-year ACRS depreciation together are about equivalent to expensing, and expensing results in a zero effective tax rate.[1] Buildings

Emil M. Sunley is director of tax analysis at Deloitte Haskins and Sells, Washington, D.C.

1. Assuming a 10% discount rate and discounting the first year's tax savings one-half year and the second year's tax savings one and one-half years, etc., the current capital recovery rules for equipment are about equivalent to expensing. That expensing is equivalent to a zero effective tax rate, see Musgrave (1959).

generally are not eligible for the investment tax credit and the allowable depreciation is not as accelerated as that for equipment. Therefore, the effective tax rate on investments in buildings must be higher than for investments in equipment, or so the argument goes.

It is also often alleged that homeownership is favored over renting because the homeowner is not taxed on imputed rental income and is allowed to deduct mortgage interest and property taxes in determining taxable income.

Gordon, Hines, and Summers explore three issues relating to the tax treatment of structures (1) the churning of depreciable buildings, (2) leverage, and (3) the tenure choice between homeownership and renting. They conclude that structures are not tax-disadvantaged and that until very recently homeownership has not been favored by the tax law.

Churning

Repeated sales of buildings may lead to significant tax advantages for investors and a corresponding drain on the Treasury. Gordon, Hines, and Summers set up a fairly straightforward model to measure the benefits from churning buildings. They conclude that if the gain on sale is taxed at full capital gains rate, it generally does not pay to churn. However, if the capital gains tax can be avoided or reduced, for example, through installment sales, churning can reduce the tax burden on buildings.

When a building is sold, according to Brannon and Sunley (1976), three things happen and two of them are bad. First, gain is recognized and this gain is taxed as ordinary income or capital gains depending on the recapture rules. This is a minus for the investors and a plus for the Treasury. Second, there is a step up of basis. The new owner gets to claim depreciation deductions based on the price paid for the building. This is a plus for the investors and a minus for the Treasury. Third, the depreciation allowed with respect to the seller's remaining basis in the building will be stretched out. For example, if the seller had continued to hold the building, the cost might be fully recovered over the next 10 years. The buyer will recover cost over the next 19 years. This is a minus for the investors and a plus for the Treasury.

The Gordon, Hines, and Summers model of churning captures most of the essentials of the question to sell or not to sell. Unlike Pellechio (1985), they do not make the selling price of the building a function of the tax treatment of the subsequent owners. Instead the market value of the building is assumed to decline at a constant annual rate. Also the model ignores the fact that land and buildings are usually sold together. Any gain on the land generates tax today but no depreciation deductions tomorrow. This is clearly a minus for the investors and can easily offset the other benefits from churning.

An alternative to selling a building is a like-kind exchange which for tax purposes does not result in recognition of any gain. Instead the gain is deferred until the building is later sold and gain is recognized. The taxpayer in a like-kind exchange carries over the basis from the first building to the second one. In short, no gain is recognized, the basis is not stepped up, and remaining basis continues to be written off as it would have been if no trade had taken place.[2]

Leverage

Increasing the amount of debt, with one exception, neither creates nor destroys income in the system. The interest paid on the debt is deductible by the payor and taxable to the recipient. The one exception is when a corporation increases its leverage because the double tax on corporate income may be avoided if the loanable funds are supplied by individuals.

Though increasing leverage does not destroy income in the system, there may still be significant tax advantages of debt if the borrowers are in higher tax brackets than the lenders. The tax savings from the interest deduction will exceed the tax paid on the interest income. Gordon, Hines, and Summers focus on the tax arbitrage between borrowers and lenders and build a model to suggest that buildings will be more heavily leveraged. Unfortunately, they present no evidence that buildings are, in fact, more heavily leveraged than other investments.

Renting versus Homeownership

The traditional view is that homeownership is favored because imputed rental income is not taxed and mortgage interest and property taxes are deductible. The tax benefits of homeownership increase with the marginal tax rate of the owner. Gordon, Hines, and Summers accept the traditional analysis of the tax benefits of homeownership but also consider the tax benefits associated with rental properties. These tax benefits may be passed through to tenants in the form of reduced rent.

The Gordon, Hines, and Summers model of the tax benefits of rental properties is similar to the one developed by Sunley (1970). Unlike Sunley, however, they assume that top-bracket landlords represent the marginal supplier of rental housing. This critical assumption is wrong.

---

2. This simplified description of a like-kind exchange assumes that both buildings are of equal value. Where "boot," that is, money or other nonqualifying property,—is transferred from one party to the other in order to equalize the contributions of each party, the taxpayer will recognize gain to the extent of any boot received. The transferred basis in the new property is decreased by any money received and increased by any gain recognized.

There are not enough top-bracket investors to hold all the depreciable rental estate. As lower-bracket investors are induced to hold real estate, the tax benefits that can be passed through to tenants will be reduced. This reasoning is similar to the argument that the yield differential between taxable and tax-exempt bonds depends on the tax bracket of the marginal investor in tax exempts. The yield differential must narrow to induce lower-bracket investors to hold tax exempts. If Gordon, Hines, and Summers had used a more reasonable tax rate for the marginal investor in rental housing, they would not have concluded that "homeownership has not until recently been favored by the tax code."

Their conclusion also appears to contradict the facts. According to Hendershott (chap. 8), in recent years the homeownership rate has increased only for the oldest married couples. For younger couples homeownership has declined. The rapid increase in homeownership rates occurred in just those years when renting, Gordon, Hines, and Summers concluded, was more tax-favored than homeownership.

References

Brannon, Gerald M., and Sunley, Emil M. 1976. The "recapture" of excess tax depreciation on the sale of real estate. *National Tax Journal* 24:4, 413–21.

Musgrave, Richard A. 1959. *The theory of public finance.* New York: McGraw-Hill.

Pellechio, Anthony J. 1985. Taxation, real property value, and optional holding periods: An analytic solution and application to tax reform. Mimeo. August.

Sunley, Emil M. 1970. Tax advantages of homeownership versus renting: A cause of suburban migration? *Proceedings of the Sixty-Third Annual Conference on Taxation of the National Tax Association,* 377–92. Columbus, Ohio.

8   Tax Changes and Capital Allocation in the 1980s

Patric H. Hendershott

Three tax bills were enacted in the first half of the 1980s: the Economic Recovery Tax Act of 1981, the Tax Equity and Fiscal Responsibility Act of 1982, and the Deficit Reduction Act of 1984. Moreover, major tax reform proposals, most notably the November 1984 Treasury plan and the May 1985 Administration plan, have been advanced for implementation in the second half of this decade, and the U.S. House of Representatives passed a reform bill in December 1985. The passed or proposed tax changes have altered or would significantly affect both the overall taxation of capital and taxation in different uses. As a result, changes in interest rates, homeownership, and investment in various types of capital have been or would probably be induced. The nature and extent of these changes are the subjects of this paper.

The method of analysis is the construction and manipulation of a relatively small simulation model. The principal features of the model are the dependencies of the demands for various types of capital on their gross (of depreciation) user costs of capital and of the user costs on tax parameters and interest rates. Special emphasis is placed on the housing sector where households at six different income levels make tenure and quantity-demanded decisions. Finally, the level of taxable interest rates is determined by equality between the total demand for capital and the existing capital stock.

The model is first used to simulate the 1981–82 tax changes.[1] The implied effects of the tax legislation on interest rates, homeownership, and capital allocation are then compared with observed changes in the 1981–84 period. The model implications are at least roughly consistent

Patric H. Hendershott is a professor of finance at The Ohio State University and is a research associate at the National Bureau of Economic Research.

259

with observed events. The model is then employed to simulate the impacts of the Treasury and Administration tax proposals and the House bill. The proposals are analyzed in a 5% inflation world; the inflation neutrality of current law and the reform proposals are compared; and efficiency losses due to misallocation of capital are computed for the various tax regimes.

8.1 Investment Hurdle Rates or User Costs

8.1.1 General Considerations

As is well known (Hall and Jorgenson 1967), the decision to invest depends on whether the present value of the expected revenue from investment exceeds the supply price of capital, and on marginal investments the two will be equal. After allowance for taxation, the equilibrium condition for investment is

$$(1) \qquad \rho = \frac{(r + d + \tau_\pi \pi)(l - k - \tau z)}{1 - \tau},$$

where τ is the business tax rate, ρ is the gross marginal product of capital, r is the real after-tax financing rate, d is the economic depreciation rate, τ_π is the concurrent equivalent tax rate on inflationary gains, π is the expected inflation rate, and k is the investment tax credit.[2] In general, z is the present value of the stream of tax depreciation allowances, $TAXDEP_t$, obtained by discounting the stream of depreciation allowances by the required nominal after-tax financing rate; taking into account the reduction in depreciable basis if the investment tax credit is claimed:

$$(2) \qquad z = (1 - k/2) \sum_{t=1}^{N} \frac{TAXDEP_t}{[(1 + r)(1 + \pi)]^t},$$

where N is the depreciation period of the asset. The right side of equation (1) is the "investment hurdle rate" or rental user cost for a particular asset. The lower the user cost, the greater will be production of the asset, and the lower will be the productivity of the marginal investment (ρ).

In a "neutral" tax system, the net user and thus net marginal productivities ($\rho - d$) would be the same for all equally-risky assets. This can be achieved in a variety of ways. For example, with $k = 0, \tau_\pi = 0$ and either $z = 1$—expensing—or $\tau = 0$, then $\rho - d = r$. If the r's were equal for all assets, the tax system would be neutral across them. Alternatively, with $k = 0, \tau_\pi = 0$ and $z = d/(r + d)$—tax depreciation equal to economic depreciation, then $\rho - d = r/(1-\tau)$. If the r's and the τ's were the same for all assets, then the system would also be neutral. Because the τ's are zero for owner-occupied housing, expensing for depreciable assets (and the nondeductibility of property taxes on owner-occupied housing) would lead to tax neutrality—assuming equal r's—but setting tax depreciation equal to economic depreciation would not.[3]

Assuming that firms use a fixed fraction of debt, b, for financing all investments, the real after-tax financing rate can be expressed as

$$(3) \qquad r = [b(1 - \beta\tau)i + (1 - b)(1 - \gamma\tau)e - \pi]/(1 + \pi),$$

where β and γ, respectively, are the portions of interest and equity returns that are deductible at the business level, and e is the required nominal return to investors. (Currently $\beta = 1$ and $\gamma = 0$.) Firms will choose the b at which the *marginal* costs of debt and equity, including contracting and bankruptcy costs, are equal. (Because this marginal cost is unknown, average values of i and e are used in the calculation of r.)

Portfolio equilibrium of investors requires that

$$(4) \qquad\qquad (1 - \tau_e)e = (1 - x)i + \delta,$$

where τ_e is the rate at which equity returns are taxed at the personal level, x is the relevant tax rate for taxable interest (the lower of the personal tax rate and that implicit in tax-exempt yields), and δ is the risk premium required on equity investments. For all investments except owner-occupied housing of low- and middle-income households, x is the tax rate implicit in tax-exempt yields x_e. Substituting (4) into (3), the real after-tax financing rate for capital other than owner-occupied housing is:

$$(3') \qquad r = [b(1 - \beta\tau)i$$
$$+ (1 - b)(1 - \gamma\tau)\frac{(1 - x_e)i + \delta}{1 - \tau_e} - \pi]/(1 + \pi).$$

If $\tau\gamma$ were equal to τ_e (which would be true if $\gamma = \tau_e = 0$) and $x_e = \beta\tau$, r would equal $[(1 - \beta\tau)i - \pi + \delta(1 - b)]/(1 + \pi)$ for all assets. Further, if all interest expense were deductible at the same rate and all investments were equally risky, all r's would be equal.

For corporations, τ_e depends on the taxation of dividends and capital gains and the division of equity raised between new issues and retained earnings (Auerbach 1979). More generally,

$$(5) \qquad\qquad \tau_e = n\tau_{div} + (1 - n)\tau_{cg},$$

where n is the proportion of equity funds raised by new issues, and τ_{div} and τ_{cg}, respectively, are the effective tax rates on dividends and equity capital gains. In general, $\tau_{div} = \tau_{im}/2$ and $\tau_{cg} = (1 - exclu)\tau_{im}/4$, where τ_{im} is the effective maximum tax rate on personal interest and *exclu* is the statutory capital gains exclusion. The divisions by 2 and 4 allow for tax deferral and avoidance activities. An n of 0.1 is assumed; as a result, τ_e is relatively low ($0.14\tau_{im}$ under current law). For noncorporate businesses (including households investing in owner-occupied housing), τ_e equals 0.

Empirically, the tax rate implicit in tax-exempt yields varies with the maturity of the security. For short-term tax exempts, the ratio of prime grade tax-exempt to risk-free taxable yields has not deviated far from unity less the corporate tax rate or roughly 0.5. For 10-year bonds, which are more relevant for the long-term investments being analyzed, the ratio has been closer to 0.7. The implicit tax rate of 0.3, rather than the federal tax rate of 0.46 (the state and local tax rate is not relevant if corporations invest in their own jurisdictions), reflects a number of factors, but the most important is likely the tax saving from optimally trading bonds (e.g., taking capital losses and deferring capital gains).[4] This is especially important because high transactions costs virtually eliminate any gains from trading municipal bonds. The tax rate implicit in long-term tax-exempt yields is assumed to be given by:

(6) $$x_e = (\beta - 0.3)\tau_f,$$

where τ_f is the federal corporate tax rate and the 0.3 measures the gains from optimal trading.

All interest expense is not deductible at the same rate, the clearest example being owner-occupied housing. Because this asset is held by households with a wide range of income subject to the full array of marginal personal tax rates, the tax rates at which interest is deductible (and at which equity the owner has in the house would have been taxed had the household rented) vary across households.[5] More generally, the real after-tax financing rate for the jth household is

(7) $$r_j = [b_j(1 - \tau_j)i + (1 - b_j)(1 - x_j)i - \pi + \delta_j]/(1 + \pi).$$

The tax rate applicable to own equity investment, x_j, is defined as the minimum of the tax rate paid on the last dollar of taxable interest earned, $\beta\tau_j$, or that implicit in tax-exempt yields, x_e.

For all investments other than real estate, $b = 1/3$. For real estate investments other than owner-occupied housing, $b = 2/3$. This assumption is consistent with available data on large-scale (over 50-unit) rental projects, which probably accounted for over two-thirds of the rental units constructed in the 1970s.[6] The data in table 8.1 indicate that ownership of these properties has shifted sharply from corporations to partnerships over the past two decades (the vast majority of additions to the stock have certainly been owned by partnerships), most of these properties have mortgages (97% of those owned by partnerships in 1980), and the initial loan-to-value ratio on the 81% of

Table 8.1   **Data on Ownership and Debt for Stock of Over-50 Unit Rental Properties**

	1960	1970	1980
% Ownership			
Individuals	21	22	18
Partnerships	14	36	56
Rental Corporations	49	29	12
Other	6	3	4
Mortgaged Properties			
% of Total Properties	90	93	92
Median Loan-to-Value Ratio	54	67	53
Properties with First Mortgage			
(new or assumed) at Time of Purchase			
% of Mortgaged Properties	57	71	81
Median Loan-to-Value Ratio	83	87	87

Sources: U.S. Department of Commerce, Bureau of the Census, Residential Finance Sections of 1960, 1970, and 1980 Census of Housing.

properties with a first mortgage at time of purchase is 87%. In 1970, the median loan-to-value ratio was 67%. The median was only 53% in early 1981, when mortgage rates were at historic highs and terms had been quite unfavorable for refinancing for 3 years. The two-thirds ratio is a reasonable approximation for a present-value, weighted average loan-to-value ratio in normal times.

For owner-occupied housing, we vary b_j depending on the relative attractiveness of debt and equity financing. More specifically,

$$(8) \qquad b_j = \begin{cases} 0.667 \text{ if } x_j = \tau_j \\ 0.85 \text{ if } x_j < \tau_j. \end{cases}$$

By our definitions, x_j cannot exceed τ_j. While these ratios far exceed the 0.33 to 0.4 average economy-wide ratio observed for owner-occupied housing, the observed ratio is heavily influenced by older owning households who have repaid their mortgages and are relatively insensitive to housing rental costs (see below).[7] Households under 40 use far more debt (the average loan-to-value ratio for first-time homebuyers in 1984 was 87%) and often make quite long-term housing decisions. It is the decisions of such households that we are attempting to model, and their present-value, weighted-average, loan-to-value ratio is probably near two-thirds.

Based upon Ibbotson-Sinquefield calculations, we assume δ for corporate equities is 0.075, and thus the risk premium for corporate assets, which have a one-third loan-to-value ratio, is $(1 - b)\delta = 0.05$. The risk premium for depreciable real estate investors in properties with roughly 0.80 *initial* loan-to-value ratios is also about 0.075.[8] Because these real-estate assets have a mean loan-to-value ratio of two-thirds (initial ratio of near 80%), their risk premium is only 0.025. For owner-occupied housing, a premium of 0.01 is assumed. This relatively low premium is consistent with owners having certainty with regard to their "vacancy" and "breakage" rates and thus greater certainty with respect to their net operating incomes than is the case with rental properties.

8.1.2   Tax Parameters

Tables 8.2 and 8.3 list the important business tax parameters under the laws existing in 1980 and 1981–85, in the proposed Treasury and Administration tax plans and in H.R. 3838 passed in December 1985. The 1981 Tax Act roughly halved depreciation tax lives and lowered the percentage of straight line for equipment and utility and residential

Table 8.2   **Depreciation and Tax Credit Parameters**

	Equipment	Public Util.	Industrial	Commercial	Residential
1980					
%SL	2.0	2.0	1.5	1.0	2.0
Tax Life	11	21/31	37	37	32
Tax Credit	.096	.10	0	0	0
1981-85					
%SL	1.5	1.5	1.75	1.0	1.75
Tax Life	5	10/15	15[b]	15[b]	15[b]
Tax Credit	.10[a]	.10	0	0	0
Treasury					
Depr. Rate	.15 (aver.)	.08/.05	.03	.03	.03
Tax Life	5 to 24	24/38	63	63	63
Tax Credit	0	0	0	0	0
Administration					
%SL	1.62	1.54/1.7	1.12	1.12	1.12
Tax Life	6 (aver.)	7/10	28	28	28
Tax Credit	0	0	0	0	0
House Bill					
%SL	2.0	2.0	1.0	1.0	1.0
Tax Life	8 (aver.)	20/30	30	30	30
Tax Credit	0	0	0	0	0

[a]The 1982 Tax Act reduced the depreciable base by one-half the tax credit.
[b]The 1984 Tax Act raised the life from 15 to 18 years, and the 1985 Act raised it to 19.

Table 8.3   Tax Rates and Deductibility Provisions

	1980	1981–85	Treasury	Admin.	House
Corporate Tax Rate					
Federal (τ_f)	.48	.46	.33	.33	.36
Total (τ)	.512	.4924	.37	.37	.3984
Personal Tax Rates					
Interest Income (τ_{im})[a]	.568	.53	.41	.41	.4172
Equity Income (τ_e)	.0795	.0742	.1128	.0662	.0753
Tax Exempts (x_e)	.336	.322	.081[b]	.231	.252
Tax on Inventory Gains	70% of regular rate	70% of regular rate	0	70% of regular rate[c]	70% of regular rate
Interest Indexation	No	No	Yes[d]	No	No
Dividend Exclusion	0	0	0.5	0.1	No
Deductibility of Property Taxes	Full	Full	No	No	Full

[a]These are the rates at which interest income is taxed (real interest under the Treasury plan). The rate at which business (noncorporate) interest expense would be deducted is lower under the Treasury and Administration plans, 0.389, owing to the state and local offset at the Federal level.

[b]This rate varies with the expected inflation rate because $x_e = (\beta - 0.3)\tau_f$ and $\beta = .06/(.06 + \pi)$. The value shown is for $\pi = 0.05$. For $\pi = 0.0$, $x_e = 0.231$; for $\pi = 0.1$, $x_e = 0.025$.

[c]Tax was removed in original version but added later to achieve revenue neutrality.

[d]Home mortgage interest expense is not indexed.

structures, raised the percentage for industrial structures, and maintained straight-line for commercial real estate (straight-line is preferred over accelerated methods due to more onerous recapture provisions upon sale).[9] The 1981 Act promised more accelerated methods in 1985, but the 1982 Tax Act reneged on the promise and reduced the depreciable base for equipment by one-half the investment tax credit. The 1984 Act raised the tax life for structures, other than public utilities, back to 18 years and this was raised further to 19 years in late 1985.

The 1981 Tax Act also cut the maximum federal tax rates from 0.48 to 0.46 for corporations, and from 0.7 to 0.5 for households. We assume that the marginal noncorporate investor was in the 54% bracket in 1980 (at roughly the same real income level at which the 49% tax rate applied in 1985). The income tax rates in table 8.3 presume a 0.06 state and local tax rate deductible at the federal level.

The personal tax rates on real corporate equity returns follow from equation (5) and the surrounding discussion, given a capital gains exclusion of 0.6 (0.0 under the Treasury plan, 0.5 under the Administration plan and 0.42 in the House bill). The tax rate implicit in tax-exempt yields follows from equation (6). Finally, the inflation tax, τ_m, is 0.7τ on inventories because FIFO accounting is used for 70% of inventories and is effectively zero for other assets.

The Treasury plan attempted to neutralize the tax system for inflation by indexing everything. Only real capital gains, including those on inventories, would be taxed ($\tau_\pi = 0$); depreciation would be on a replacement, rather than historic, cost basis; and only the "real" part of interest expense would be taxed and could be deducted.[10] The Treasury plan also attempted to tax all assets and business forms (except owner-occupied housing) equally. To this end, tax depreciation for each depreciable asset would equal the Treasury's best estimate of true economic depreciation; the investment tax credit would be dropped; real capital gains would be taxed at the regular income tax rate; and half of corporate dividends would be deductible at the corporate level. The indexation of inventory gains, the removal of the tax credit, and the proposed tax depreciation treatment would result in $\rho - d$ equaling $r/(1 - \tau)$ for all properties except owner-occupied housing, and the partial dividend exclusion would reduce discrepancies between the r's for corporate and noncorporate investments.

The Administration plan retreated from these principles in significant respects: all interest would continue to be deductible; investors in nondepreciable assets would have the option of paying taxes on nominal capital gains at one-half of the regular income tax rate; tax depreciation would exceed economic depreciation; only one-tenth of dividends would be deductible; and, in order to make the plan revenue neutral, the indexation of inventory gains would be dropped. Tax depreciation would be especially generous for equipment that continues to be classified as

3 or 5 years and for public utility structures; allowable depreciation would exceed that under current law even at zero inflation. However, most 5-year equipment would be reclassified as 6- , 7- , and even 10-year equipment. For industrial structures, tax depreciation would be more favorable only at inflation rates of roughly 5% or greater. The House bill has double declining balance depreciation for equipment and public utility structures, but longer depreciation tax lives than the Administration plan and only partial indexation of the depreciable base (half of the inflation above 5%) results in significantly less favorable overall depreciation.

The partial dividend exclusion is of little import in our model because only 10% of equity financing is assumed to be from new share issues on which dividends are paid. (Dividends are saved initially by the retention of earnings, offsetting the future payment of dividends.) Thus γ in the model is only 0.05 under the Treasury plan and 0.01 under the Administration plan, 10% of the 50 and 10% exclusions, respectively.

In our analysis of owner-occupied housing, we consider households at five different income levels in order to deduce the tax rates that are representative of households in five income ranges. The ranges for 1980 are listed in the top panel of table 8.4; the 1985 ranges, which exceed those from 1980 by a third to two-fifths to reflect the growth in nominal incomes per household, are listed in the lower panel. (The exact income levels for which the tax rate calculations were performed are listed in parentheses.) The state-and-local and federal tax rates relevant to the quantity-demanded decision in 1980 are listed in the next two columns in the top panel, and the total tax rate—the federal plus the state times one minus the federal—is shown in the fourth column. For the highest income class, $x_j = x_e$. For the other classes, the x_j equals β (equals 1 except in the Treasury plan) times the τ_j shown in the table. The interest indexation feature of the Treasury plan ($\beta < 1$) has a major impact on the opportunity cost of own equity financing of owner-occupied housing (as well as on tax-exempt yields—see note a to table 8.3).[11] The last column is the tax rate relevant to tenure choice (a weighted average of the average tax rates applied to debt and equity).[12] The lower panel lists similar calculations for 1985 incomes under current law and the tax reforms, the Treasury and Administration proposals reflecting the nondeductibility of state and local taxes.

8.2   The Capital Allocation Model[13]

8.2.1   An Overview

The basic model allocates a fixed private capital stock among various classes of nonresidential and residential capital. The allocation depends on the rental or user costs for the capital components, the price elas-

Table 8.4   Tax Rates Relevant to Housing Decisions

1980 Income (thousands)	State and Local	Federal	Quantity-Demanded Total	Tenure Choice Total
9–18½ (12½)	.03	.16	.185	.132
18–22½ (20)	.035	.18	.209	.201
22½–37½ (30)	.04	.24	.270	.306
37½–75 (50)	.05	.37	.402	.435
over 75 (97½)	.06	.49	.521	.565

1985 Income (thousands)	Federal			Quantity-Demanded			Tenure Choice			
	Current	Treas. & Admin.	House	Current	Treas. & Admin.	House	Current	Treas.	Admin.	House
12½–25 (17½)	.14	.15	.15	.166	.180	.176	.147	.119	.092	.071
25–30 (27½)	.16	.15	.15	.189	.185	.180	.210	.146	.130	.097
30–50 (35 & 40)	.18/.22	.15	.15/.25	.232	.190	.232	.279	.178	.198	.208
50–100 (70)	.33	.25	.35	.364	.300	.383	.402	.300	.300	.383
over 100 (130)	.42	.35	.35	.455	.410	.389	.476	.410	.410	.404

ticities of demand with respect to the rental costs, and the elasticities of homeownership with respect to the cost of owning versus renting. The interest rate adjusts in response to tax changes so as to maintain the aggregate demand for capital at its initial level. The fixed capital stock assumption implies zero interest elasticity of saving.

Table 8.5 lists the distribution of the U.S. capital stock at the end of 1984 by type. A number of simplifying assumptions are made in the construction of the model. Because well over 90% of inventories are held by corporations and nearly 90% of rental housing is held by non-corporate business, we assume that each of these assets is held totally by corporate and noncorporate business, respectively. While equipment is depreciable over 3 or 5 years, about 95% of it is classified as 5-year. We treat all equipment as 5-year. Because public utility structures (which are virtually all corporate) are depreciated over a shorter life than other structures and are eligible for the investment tax credit, they are treated separately. With these assumptions and distinctions,

Table 8.5   **Private Capital Stock in the U.S.**

	End 1983 Dollar Value (in billions)	Percent Share of Real Stock		
		1980	1984	%
Inventories	814	12.79	12.43	−2.8
Corporate	769			
Noncorporate	45			
Equipment	1451			
Corporate	1183	18.95	20.10	6.0
Noncorporate	269	4.26	4.40	3.0
Nonresidential Structures	1634			
10-Year Public Utilities	138	6.86 ⎰ 2.29	6.54 ⎰ 2.18	−4.7
15-Year Public Utilities	322	⎱ 4.57	⎱ 4.36	
Industrial (corporate)	546	7.85	7.92	0.9
Commercial (noncorporate)	628	8.31	8.64	4.0
Residential Structures	2893	40.96	39.97	−2.4
Corporate Rental	70			
Noncorporate Rental	553			
Owner-Occupied	2270			
	6793	100.00	100.00	

Sources: Data for all assets except inventories and public utilities are from Musgrave (1984). The inventory data are from the Federal Reserve (1984); the aggregate public utility data are from unpublished data supplied by John Musgrave; and the 1/3, 2/3 division between 10 and 15 years are based on the fraction given in Gravelle (1982).

the capital shares in 1980 and 1984 are those listed in the percent share columns. The last column indicates that a reallocation of capital toward equipment and commercial real estate occurred between 1980 and 1984.

Current law treats owner-occupied housing differently depending upon the tax position of the owner, with higher-income households paying a lower rental cost owing to their lower after-tax financing rate. Thus it is necessary to distribute the housing stock across households at different income levels. The distribution depends upon the number of owners within each income range as well as the income range and the rental costs for each of the ranges.

For all assets except rental housing, the demand for the asset is determined by the investor in the asset, be it a corporation, unincorporated business or a household. For rental housing, demand is determined by renters, based upon their incomes and the market rent level. Thus, the total quantity of rental housing, like the total quantity of owner housing, is built up as the sum of the demands by households in different income brackets.

Table 8.6 indicates divisions of the demand for housing across the same five income classes listed in table 8.4, with a lower-income class of all renters added. The first three columns contain the income classes selected, the division of 80 million households across these classes, and the assumed ownership rates for these classes. Columns 4 and 5 give the distribution of the income of owners and renters across these

Table 8.6   **Assumed Distribution of Owner and Rental Housing Across Six Income Classes**

Income Range (thousands)	Households (in millions)	Fraction that own	% of Income		% of Housing Stock	
			of owners	of renters	Owner-Occupied	Rental
1980						
less than 9	9.6	0	0	11	—	2.7
9–18½	24	.577	12	22	7.6	4.9
18½–22½	12	.625	11	15	7.1	3.6
22½–37½	22.4	.707	34	34	24.3	7.9
37½–75	9.6	.813	28	15	23.9	3.6
over 75	2.4	.889	15	4	13.5	0.9
	80		100	100	76.4	23.6
1985						
less than 12½	9.6	0	0	11	—	2.6
12½–25	24	.631	14	17	9.4	4.6
25–30	12	.664	12	14	8.0	3.3
30–50	22.4	.703	33	33	23.9	8.0
50–100	9.6	.781	28	18	22.2	4.4
over 100	2.4	.819	13	7	12.1	1.7
	80		100	100	75.5	24.5

classes. Column 4 is the product of the first three columns divided by the sum of the products. In the column 5 calculation, the fraction of households owning is replaced by the fraction renting. Columns 6 and 7 give the distribution of the owned and rented stocks. These distributions and the ownership rates were calculated from model equations described below. Based upon 1980 data, the equations imply an aggregate ownership rate of 0.59, slightly below that existing then.

8.2.2   Model Equations

The model explains 13 rental costs: seven for the different types of nonresidential capital, five for owner-occupied housing of households in our five income ranges, and one for rental housing. As discussed in the previous section, these costs depend on numerous provisions of the tax law, the depreciation rate of the asset, the expected inflation rate and the level of interest rates in the economy. Moreover, rental costs for household tenure choice decisions ($\hat{\rho}_j$) differ from those for quantity demanded decisions (ρ_j) because the tax rates relevant to the after-tax financing rates differ (see table 8.4). We summarize the rental cost equations as

(1)–(7) $\rho_k = \rho_k(tax_k, d_k, \pi, i)$

(8)–(12) $\rho_j = \rho_j(tax_j, d_j, \pi, i)$

(13) $\rho = \rho(tax, d, \pi, i)$

(14)–(18) $\hat{\rho}_j = \hat{\rho}_j(ta\hat{x}_j, d_j, \pi, i)$.

There are seven demand equations for nonresidential capital (NK): corporate inventories, corporate and noncorporate 5-year equipment, 10- and 15-year public utility structures, and other corporate (industrial) and noncorporate (commercial) structures. Assuming that production functions are Cobb-Douglass (Berndt 1976), these demand equations can be written as

(19)–(25) $NK_k = Z_k/\rho_k,$

where the Z_k are constants (depending on given outputs) and the ρ_k are the rental costs.

The housing demand and tenure choice equations come from the specification of a translog indirect utility function for households (King 1980) and the empirical application of it to the ownership decision (Hendershott and Shilling 1982). The estimated odds-of-owning equation was

$$log\ \frac{o_j}{1 - o_j} = -3.846log[\hat{\rho}_j/(\rho/.9)] - .383[(log\hat{\rho}_j)^2 - (log\ \rho/.9)^2].$$

The division by 0.9 reflects the fact that those renting have to pay more than the user cost to offset the revenues lost from vacancies. Taking antilogs and solving, the ownership rates for the five highest income classes are

$$(26)–(30) \qquad o_j = e^{L_j}/(1 - e^{L_j}),$$

where the L_j equals the right-hand side of the log $[o_j/(1 - o_j)]$ expression. The ownership rate for the lowest-income class is assumed to be zero.

There are also five demand equations for owner housing and six for rental housing based on our six income classes, the lowest of which consists solely of renters. These demands are the products of the demands per owning/renting household and the number of owning/renting households. The specific form of the equations comes from application of Roy's identity to the indirect utility function and substitution from the estimated odds of owning equation. For owner housing (OH), the demand equations are

$$(31)–(35) \qquad OH_j = o_j HH_j Z_j (3.846 + .766 \, log \, \rho_j)/\rho_j,$$

where o_j is the ownership rate for the jth class, HH_j is the number of households in the jth class, and the Z_j are constants which are proportional to the incomes of representative households in the classes. For rental households *(RH)*, the equations are

$$(36)–(41) \quad RH_j = (1 - o_j) HH_j Z_j (3.846 + .766 \, log \, \rho/.9)/(\rho/.9),$$

where $\rho/.9$ is the rental price facing all renting households.

Lastly, equality between the sum of the demands and the existing capital stock determines the level of interest rates in the economy:

$$(42) \qquad \Sigma NK_k + \Sigma OH_j + \Sigma RH_j = K.$$

Given a specific tax regime and assumed levels of the interest and expected inflation rates, the ρ_k, ρ_j, $\hat{\rho}_j$, and ρ can be computed. The NK_k were listed in table 8.5, and the OH_j and RH_j are products of the total residential structures share reported in table 8.5 and the fractions of those shares listed in table 8.6. The o_j and HH_j were also listed in table 8.6. The Z_k can be calculated from equations (19)–(25); the Z_j are proportional to the incomes of the representative households in the classes and are scaled such that the sum of the demands for owner and rental housing (as proportions of the total capital stock) equals the existing housing stock (as a proportion of total capital).

A number of simplifying assumptions of the model should be noted. These include, but are not limited to, constant risk premia and infinite real supply price elasticities (zero transactions costs) and thus constant real asset prices. Simulated changes in the allocation of capital are thus meant to indicate how the composition of net investment would be altered by tax (and inflation) changes, not precisely what the new capital allocation will be 5 or 10 years following a change in tax regime or inflation rate.

8.3   The Changing Tax and Inflation Environment, 1980–85

In this section we deduce the impact of the Economic Recovery Tax Act of 1981 on interest rates, the homeownership rate, and the allocation of real capital. Because over 4 years have now passed since the passage of ERTA, we can also "test" the underlying simulation model by comparing the simulated impact of the Act with observed events. This requires analyzing all major disturbances that have occurred since early 1981, not just the passage of ERTA. The first part of this section simulates the impacts of ERTA alone and of ERTA combined with a decline in the inflation rate. The second part compares the simulated impacts with observed changes in recent years.

8.3.1   ERTA and Disinflation

The disturbance of major interest to us is the passage of the Economic Recovery Tax Act of 1981. As documented in Section 8.1, this Act substantially enhanced tax depreciation allowances and lowered personal tax rates. A second major phenomenon in the early 1980s was a reduction in the inflation rate. In 1980, inflation was proceeding at a 10% rate; by 1984 and 1985, the rate was slightly below 4%. We presume that the decline in the long-run expected inflation rate was a smaller drop from 8 to 5%, the 10% reflecting temporarily surging energy prices and declining value of the dollar and the 4% rate reflecting the reverse.

The first column of table 8.7 lists the assumed 1980 interest and inflation rates, the model simulated homeownership rate, and the 1980 distribution of the capital stock listed in table 8.5. The second column contains the model simulation results for these variables (except for the assumed constant inflation rate) based upon enactment of ERTA. The third column reflects ERTA (and the 1982 reduction in the depreciation base by half of the investment tax credit) plus a decline in the inflation rate to 5%. These simulations are discussed in turn.

Comparing the second and first columns, the more favorable tax treatment of depreciable property provided by ERTA raises the demand for such capital at pre-ERTA interest rates. While the cut in personal tax rates lowers the demand for owner-occupied housing—the after-tax financing rate and opportunity cost of owner equity rise—the decline is not nearly sufficient to offset the increased demand for other

Table 8.7   ERTA and Disinflation

	1980	ERTA	% Δ	ERTA plus Inflation Decline	% Δ
Inflation Rate	.08	.08		.05	
Interest Rate	.13	.1406		.0944	
Real Capital					
Inventories	12.79	12.68	−0.9	12.77	−0.2
Equipment	23.21	25.83	11.2	25.61	10.4
Nonresidential					
Structures					
Industrial	7.85	8.61	9.7	8.83	12.5
Public Util.	6.86	7.21	5.1	7.31	6.5
Commercial	8.31	8.56	3.0	8.19	−1.5
Residential					
Structures	40.96	37.11	−9.5	37.28	−9.2
	100.00	100.00		100.00	
Homeownership					
Rate	.589	.544		.585	

capital, so interest rates rise.[14] The computed increase is just over a percentage point.

In spite of this increase, the hurdle rates for equipment, industrial structures and public utilities decline by 2½, 1½ and 1 percentage points, respectively. Those for depreciable real estate are roughly unchanged (the interest rate increase and more generous depreciation roughly offsetting), while those for inventories and owner-occupied housing increase by just over a percentage point. The homeownership rate declines by 4½ percentage points. On net, the capital stock is shifted sharply from residential to nonresidential uses, with the aggregate housing stock declining by 9½%. Of the nonresidential components, the increases are roughly 10% for equipment and industrial structures and about 5% for public utilities and commercial real estate. Inventories decline by 1%.

Incorporating a 3 percentage point decline in the inflation rate sharply alters the results. Because the interest rate declines by roughly a point and a half for each point decline in inflation, disinflation is good for owner-occupied housing; the real after-tax financing rate will decline for households in tax brackets below 33%. Thus we see a 4 percentage point increase in the homeownership rate relative to the case of no decline in inflation. The total housing stock is roughly unchanged, however; the increase in owner-occupied housing is about offset by the decline in rental housing. The disinflation also induces a shift in the composition of structures, with corporate structures rising and highly-levered noncorporate structures declining (the advantages of debt are reduced at lower interest rates).

8.3.2   A Comparison with Observed Changes

Model simulations should not be expected to track observed economic changes closely. Simulations provide an estimate of where an economy in full equilibrium at the initial parameter values will eventually move in response to a specified disturbance (change in model parameters, structure or state of the world). However, even if the model accurately characterizes the economy, the observed economic changes may differ from those implied by the model for two reasons. First, the economy may have been far from full equilibrium when the disturbance occurred. If the tendency toward this equilibrium differs significantly from the tendency created by the specified disturbance, the observed changes in the economy may not resemble the simulated changes. Second, disturbances other than those specified may have occurred. If these have impacts that correlate negatively in some respects from the specified disturbances, again the simulated changes may differ significantly from the actual changes. Nonetheless, simulations of the major disturbances to an economy should trace out the broad contours of subsequent economic events.

The principal phenomena that the model simulations would lead us to expect are:

a. an increase in long-term interest rates until the decline in long-run expected inflation sets in,
b. a shift from owning to renting, until the impact of the decline in long-run expected inflation is felt, and
c. a shift from residential (and inventory) to nonresidential uses, especially equipment investment early on.

The correspondence of observed events with each of these expectations is discussed in turn.

Table 8.8 contains data on the corporate bond rate and two measures of the December-to-December changes in the CPI: all items less food, energy, and home purchase and finance and the new CPI X–I, which became the official CPI after 1982. The major difference between the inflation series is the exclusion of food and energy from the former; these components rose particularly rapidly in the late 1970s and 1980 and slowly in the 1982–84 period. The bond rate certainly jumped in 1981 and 1982. The rate exceeded 14% for the entire July 1981–July 1982 period (was over 15% in September–October 1981 and January–February 1982) before plummeting by year end 1982. The 1-year inflation rate also plummeted in 1982 and has continued to drift downward since then. A lagged response of long-run expected inflation to short-run observed inflation would suggest a gradual decline in the former throughout the 1983–85 period. In general, we would anticipate that the 1981–84 data changes would largely reflect the ERTA simulation,

Table 8.8   Interest Rates and Inflation

	Corporate Aaa Bond Rate		%ΔCPI, Dec. to Dec.	
	Average	December	Basic*	X-I
1980	11.94	13.21	9.9	10.8
1981	14.17	14.23	9.4	8.5
1982	13.79	11.83	6.1	5.0
1983	12.04	12.57	5.0	3.8
1984	12.71	12.13	4.4	4.0
1985	11.6	10.2	4.0	3.3

Sources: Economic Report of the President, Tables B–55 and B–66, 1985 (and earlier years).
*CPI excluding food, energy, and shelter.

with post-1984 data gradually reflecting the ERTA plus disinflation simulation.

The correspondence between simulations of the homeownership rate and observed changes is especially tenuous because the changes are quite sensitive to shifts in the age composition of the population. To illustrate, the aggregate rate rose by only 3½ percentage points between 1960 and 1979, even though ownership rates of every age cohort rose by close to 10 percentage points. The reason for this discrepancy was a surge in young households (under 25) who tend to rent and a relative decline in older households (over 34) who predominantly own. The data in table 8.8 illustrate the dependency of ownership on age. Old households tend to be less mobile, have higher incomes, and be wealthier, characteristics that lower the effective cost of owning.

The data in table 8.9 refer to married couples only in order to abstract from other demographic effects, but the results would be roughly com-

Table 8.9   Homeownership Rate for Married Couples

	1974	1980	1983	Change, 1980 to 83
20–24	33.5	36.1	31.9	−4.2
25–29	54.9	58.6	52.2	−6.6
30–34	72.3	75.2	69.7	−5.5
35–39	78.7	82.6	78.6	−4.0
40–44	82.9	85.2	85.2	0.0
45–54	85.6	87.3	87.1	−0.2
55–64	85.0	88.6	89.6	1.0
65–74	83.0	86.9	88.7	0.8
75+	79.4	81.1	84.1	3.0

Source: Annual Housing Survey and Housing Vacancy Survey.

parable for all households. As can be seen, a shift to homeownership occurred for all age groups between 1974 and 1980 and even continued after 1980 for households over age 54. For younger more mobile households that are more likely to be making tenure decisions based upon current economic conditions, 1980 was a watershed for ownership. In just 3 years, the ownership rate for those under 40 declined by 4 to 6½ percentage points, just as would be anticipated under the ERTA scenario. Whether the offsetting disinflation impact will be observed in later data is uncertain.

The ERTA simulation suggests a large decline in residential structures and an increase in equipment. These shifts are reflected in the 1984 data (see table 8.4) with the equipment share already up by half the predicted 11% increase and residential structures down by one-quarter of the estimated 9½% decline. Much of the observed decline is certainly due to the changed behavior of younger households. If this change were allowed to work its way through to older households in a long-run adjustment, the decline in residential structures would approach the large simulated decline.

The observed reallocation of nonresidential structures does not correspond nearly as well with the hypothesized partial movement to the simulated new equilibrium. Commercial structures have already increased in share by more than the simulated amount, while public utility structures have declined significantly as a share of the total capital stock (not increased as the simulation predicts) and industrial structures have risen little. Even here, plausible explanations are available. The expansion of the rehabilitation tax credit in ERTA, which is not reflected in the simulations, must have significantly increased the value of commercial structures; moreover, high vacancy rates suggest that commercial structures have been overbuilt—the new equilibrium could entail a less than 4% increase in this share. As for the relative decline in public utility structures, energy conservation in response to the sharp run up in real energy prices in the 1979–81 period and the well-publicized problems of the nuclear power industry are likely causes. Dwelling on such explanations is probably not worthwhile; the important fact is that observed data, on the whole, are not inconsistent with the ERTA model simulation.[15] Thus, the simulation model appears to be a reasonable vehicle for analyzing the impact of proposed tax reforms.

8.4 Capital Allocation Under Current Law and Proposed Tax Reforms

The likely impacts of the Treasury and Administration tax reform proposals and the House bill on the level of interest rates, rental user costs, capital shares, and the homeownership rate are calculated in this section. We begin with a comparison of the risk-adjusted net user costs and interest rates under current law and the reforms and then turn to the capital stock effects. The analysis presumes 5% inflation. The sensitivity to inflation of various tax regimes is then examined, and efficiency losses from the misallocation of capital under the regimes are calculated.

8.4.1   Five Percent Inflation: Net Rental Costs

The risk-adjusted net (of depreciation) rental costs for alternative investments are reported in table 8.10 for current law and three reforms. (The risk adjustment is 0.04 for nonreal estate assets and 0.015 for depreciable real estate.) The interest rate (risk-free) under current law is presumed to be 10% (slightly above the 9½% model simulation of a 5% inflation world with ERTA tax law). The first numbers (those not in parentheses) given for the reforms are based upon the listed model-computed interest rates; the numbers in parentheses presume an unchanged 10% interest rate.

Under a neutral tax system, the risk-adjusted net hurdle rates would be the same for all assets. As can be seen, this is far from true under current law. The tax-favored assets are housing of high-income owners and noncorporate equipment. The tax-penalized assets are corporate structures, especially industrial structures that receive no tax credit, and inventories, whose inflationary gains are not indexed (with $\tau_\pi = 0.7\tau$, $\tau = 0.5$ and $\pi = 0.05$, the inflation tax raises the user cost by 0.035). More generally, corporate investments are penalized relative to noncorporate; less-leveraged investments are penalized relative to more-leveraged investments; and risky assets are penalized relatively to less risky assets (Bulow and Summers 1984). The over 3½ percentage point difference in net hurdle rates for industrial and rental structures reflects all three penalties. The largest penalty is the difference in asset risk, 0.05 for nonreal estate versus 0.025 for real estate, which accounts for 2 of the 3½ points. The corporate (double taxation) penalty is the smallest, accounting for only ½ of the 3½ points because the taxation of corporate equity at the personal level is relatively light under the new view of corporate financing.

The Treasury plan greatly reduces the difference in risk-adjusted net hurdle rates among corporate assets by eliminating the inventory tax and the investment tax credit. All hurdle rates move toward that for industrial structures. The gross hurdle rate (net plus depreciation rate plus 0.04) for equipment rises by 14% and that for public utility structures rises by 8%, while that for inventories (with their 100% depreciation) falls by 3%. However, the plan increases the advantages of real estate. While the hurdle rates for depreciable properties are roughly unchanged (at 3 points below those for corporate assets), those for owner-occupied housing decline significantly; the 2.6 percentage point fall in the level of interest rates swamps the loss of the property tax deduction and the reduction in rates at which interest is deductible.

The increased advantage of owner-occupied housing stems from two factors: removal of tax advantages for business capital (especially the investment tax credit), and the introduction of an additional advantage for owner-occupied housing (the nonindexation of mortgage interest expense). The data in the third column of table 8.10 are calculations assuming the Treasury plan were amended to include indexation of home mortgage interest expense. As can be seen, full indexation lowers the interest rate by another 30 basis points and the hurdle rates for business investments by 40 basis points. In contrast, the declines in the hurdle rates for middle-income owner-occupied housing are reduced by 25 basis points, and high-income owner-occupied housing faces a 50 basis point rise in hurdle rate.

The Administration plan drops interest indexation (and thus the new advantage for owner-occupied housing), deletes inventory indexation (in the revisions needed to achieve revenue neutrality), and "gives back" part of the investment tax credit by accelerating depreciation deductions for equipment and public utilities relative to economic depreciation; the present value of a dollar of depreciation on 5-year equipment increases from 76 to 85 cents, while that for 15-year public utilities rises from 50 to 76 cents or by over 50%. The latter change is so generous that the investment hurdle rate actually declines in spite of the loss of the ITC. With these changes, the level of interest rates falls by only 60 basis points, and the net result is a tax system that is less tilted toward high-income owner-occupied housing than current law.

The House bill postpones depreciation deductions, except on equipment, even more than the Treasury plan and does not index depreciation deductions unless inflation exceeds 5%. As a result of these changes and the removal of the investment tax credit, the aggregate demand for capital falls sharply and a 125 basis point decline in the level of interest rates occurs, a decline which significantly lowers the cost of owner-occupied housing at all except the very highest income levels. Like the Treasury plan, the House bill would tend to equalize net user costs across corporate investments.

As discussed, the model computes the level of interest rates that would maintain the aggregate demand for capital (net investment in a growth context) at its prereform level. However, a decline in U.S. interest rates would represent a decline in after-tax returns to foreigners unless foreign countries cut their marginal tax rates on interest income or move their interest rates *pari passu* with those in the U.S. As a result capital would flow out of the U.S. and domestic interest rates would not need to fall as much to bring the demand and supply of capital in the U.S. into balance. In the extreme case of no adjustment in foreign taxes or interest rates and perfectly elastic international capital flows, U.S. interest rates would not fall at all but the U.S. capital stock would, the fall being greater the larger is the decline in interest rates computed from the fixed-capital stock model.[16] A more balanced view would incorporate less than perfectly elastic capital flows and significant changes in foreign interest rates in response to movements in U.S. rates. Thus a fall in foreign demand for U.S. capital would tend to dampen the decline in U.S. rates, but not eliminate it.

To indicate the sensitivity of the relationships among the adjusted net rental costs to the computed interest rate declines, rental costs

Table 8.10   **Interest Rates and Risk-Adjusted Net Rental User Costs (Expected Inflation Rate of 5%)**

	Current Law	Treasury Plan	Fully-Indexed Treasury Plan	Administration Plan	House Bill
Level of Interest Rates	.10	.0742	.0712	.0941	.0873
		(.10)	(.10)	(.10)	(.10)
Inventories	.1092	.0739	.0696	.0862	.0832
		(.1108)	(.1108)	(.0930)	(.0982)
Equipment					
Corporate	.0361	.0684	.0642	.0510	.0630
		(.1041)	(.1041)	(.0567)	(.0758)
Noncorporate	.0293	.0558	.0518	.0435	.0548
		(.0898)	(.0898)	(.0489)	(.0670)
Structures					
Utility	.0605	.0724	.0681	.0479	.0722
		(.1091)	(.1091)	(.0536)	(.0863)
Industrial	.0750	.0732	.0689	.0638	.0704
		(.1099)	(.1099)	(.0704)	(.0849)
Commercial	.0430	.0414	.0375	.0357	.0401
		(.0749)	(.0749)	(.0414)	(.0525)
Rental	.0391	.0414	.0375	.0357	.0401
		(.0749)	(.0749)	(.0414)	(.0525)
Owner-Occupied Housing					
17,500[a]	.0394	.0209	.0232	.0354	.0283
		(.0414)	(.0480)	(.0400)	(.0404)
27,500	.0368	.0206	.0230	.0349	.0279
		(.0410)	(.0478)	(.0395)	(.0400)
40,000	.0323	.0203	.0229	.0345	.0233
		(.0406)	(.0476)	(.0391)	(.0355)
70,000	.0187	.0137	.0194	.0256	.0102
		(.0317)	(.0427)	(.0296)	(.0225)
130,000	.0103	.0071	.0160	.0172	.0097
		(.0228)	(.0379)	(.0207)	(.0221)

[a]1985 income ($).

based upon no rate decline have been computed and are listed in parentheses in table 8.10. With higher (than the model-computed) interest rates, the rental costs are higher. For the Administration and House reforms, the relationships among the costs are little affected. For the Treasury plan, the already strong bias toward owner-occupied housing is magnified because all home mortgage interest is deductible, whereas only the real component of interest financing other investments is.

8.4.2   Five Percent Inflation: Capital Stock Impacts

The data in table 8.11 suggest how the capital stock would be reallocated under the various reforms. These reallocations follow fairly directly from the realignment of investment hurdle rates just discussed. Removal of the inflation tax raises inventories, while the loss of the investment tax credit tends to shrink equipment and utilities, although utilities would actually rise in response to the far more generous depreciation allowances of the Administration plan. The Treasury and Administration reforms have sharply different impacts on the three types of structures. Under the Treasury plan, residential structures rise by 8%, while industrial and commercial structures are unaffected. Under the Administration plan, the reverse is true; residential structures are roughly unchanged while industrial and commercial structures rise by 8%. Moreover, the homeownership rate rises by 6 percentage points under the Treasury plan, but falls by 4 points under the Administration plan. The reallocations under the House bill are close to those of the Treasury plan, although the increase in the homeownership rate is only 2½ percentage points.

In general, an across-the-board cut in tax rates would be expected to have a negative impact on owner-occupied housing, the income from which is not taxed. This impact would be reinforced by a loss of the deductibility of property taxes on primary residences. Thus, the homeownership rate would decline, as would the share of structures in

Table 8.11	Reallocation of Capital Under Tax Reforms When Inflation is 5 Percent (Percentage Change)		
	Treasury Plan	Administration Plan	House Bill
Inventories	3	2	2
Equipment	−12	−6	−11
Utility Structures	−8	8	−8
Industrial Structures	1	8	3
Commercial Structures	2	9	3
Residential Structures	7	−2	6
Change in Home Ownership Rate	.063	−.037	.025

residential use. The simulated effect of the Administration plan corresponds to these expectations. The inverted effect of the Treasury plan follows from its interest indexation provision and the sharp decline in interest rates (largely in response to the indexation). A decline in interest rates is more beneficial to investors in low tax brackets than to those in high brackets because the investor receives more of the rate decline (and the Treasury receives less). Thus a sharp decline in interest rates is particularly beneficial to housing demanded by low- and middle-income owners. This factor is exaggerated in the Treasury plan by the exemption of home mortgage interest expense from the interest indexation feature. Thus housing of owners at all income levels (but especially at lower incomes) increases, and the homeownership rate jumps. The demand for owner-occupied housing would also rise under the House bill. This reflects the absence of a cut in the tax rates relevant to the quantity-demanded decision of owners with incomes under $100,000 (see table 8.4), the continued deductibility of property taxes, and the sharp 125 basis point decline in interest rates.

8.4.3 Inflation Neutrality

Next we consider the impact of inflation under the various tax regimes by simulating an increase in inflation from zero to 10%. Inflation is quite negative for owner-occupied housing under current law because the average tax rate at which expenses are deductible is significantly less for owner housing (except for owners with very high incomes) than for other capital. Thus, the real after-tax interest rate paid by owners tends to rise, while that for other capital falls (see Titman 1982 and Follain 1986).[17] On the other hand, inflation is very positive for depreciable real estate because the advantages of debt are magnified at higher interest rate levels. Thus the increase in inflation lowers the homeownership rate by 11 percentage points (the first column of table 8.12), and raises the demand for both rental and commercial structures, the latter by 19%. The total housing stock increases because the stimulus to renter housing outweighs the negative impact on owner housing. With real estate expanding, the other capital components must decline. As can be seen, $di/d\pi = 1.46$, midway between the nontax (unity) and tax $[di/d\pi = 1/(1 - \tau) \sim 2]$ Fisherian values.

The Treasury plan makes a serious attempt at achieving inflation neutrality by setting tax depreciation equal to economic depreciation and indexing capital gains, depreciation allowances, and interest. Unfortunately, the plan fails badly. To understand the failure, it is best to consider first the impact of an increase in inflation in a fully-indexed variant of the Treasury plan, i.e., one in which home mortgage interest expense is also indexed. The data in the second column of table 8.12 show this impact. Increases in inflation are generally favorable for the

Table 8.12   **Percentage Changes in Capital in Response to an Increase in Expected Inflation from Zero to Ten Percent**

	Current Law	Fully-Indexed Treasury Plan	Treasury Plan	Aministration Plan	House Bill
Inventories	−1	−1	−2	−3	−2
Equipment	−7	−3	−7	−1	−5
Utility Structures	−7	−4	−10	−2	−5
Industrial Structures	−4	−5	−12	−2	−6
Commercial Structures	19	7	−5	15	9
Residential Structures	3	2	9	−1	3
$di/d\pi$	1.46	1.08	1.15	1.45	1.39
Change in Home Ownership Rate	−.111	−.029	−.032	−.131	−.083

sector with the highest tax rate (noncorporate business has a tax rate of 0.41 versus 0.37 for the corporate sector) because the after-tax interest rate rises least. The aggregate homeownership rate declines because the negative impact on lower-income (tax) households outweighs the positive impact on high-income households. The interest rate rises by more than the increase in inflation because of imperfect indexation; under our assumptions, only a third of interest is real at 5% inflation $[(7.42 − 5)/7.42]$, but the Treasury indexation formula would treat six-elevenths as real (see note 10). With some inflationary interest being taxed, the interest rate responds more than one-for-one to inflation. Nonetheless, the fully-indexed variant of the Treasury plan is significantly less sensitive to inflation than current law; more specifically the sharp tilt toward depreciable real estate is greatly dampened.

Exclusion of home mortgage interest from the indexation provision changes the impact of inflation enormously. Homeownership and the demand for owner-occupied housing are greatly stimulated by inflation because the real-after tax financing rate for even our lowest-income owning households declines. The surge in housing is matched by declines in all other capital types. The actual Treasury plan proposed is even less inflation neutral than current law.

The next to the last column in table 8.12 shows the impact of inflation on capital allocation under the Administration tax plan. Just as under current law, the homeownership rate would be significantly lowered by inflation. However, the stimulation for depreciable real estate and constriction of nonresidential capital would be far less. The Administration plan is thus significantly more inflation neutral than current law. The last column suggests that the House bill would be marginally more neutral than current law.

8.4.4   Efficiency Losses

The differences in the risk-adjusted net rental costs in table 8.10 provide a general indication of the misallocation of capital under the various tax laws. A single efficiency loss number for each tax regime is computed from the Harberger equation:

$$LOSS = \frac{1}{2}\sum_{j}(EFFADJ\rho - ADJ\rho_j)(CAP_j - EFFCAP_j),$$

where the $ADJ\rho_j$'s are the risk-adjusted net user costs listed in table 8.10, $EFFADJ\rho$ is the single risk-adjusted net user cost (0.0406) that when used to obtain gross user costs equates the sum of the demands for capital to the aggregate stock, the CAP_j are the likely percentage capital stocks under a given tax law (listed in table 8.13), and the $EFFCAP_j$ are the percentage allocations when the gross user costs are based on $EFFADJ\rho$. The efficient allocation of capital is listed in the first column of table 8.13.

The efficiency loss under current law, listed at the bottom of table 8.13, is roughly 0.12% of the capital stock or about 0.25% of GNP.[18] The major source of the loss is 10% too much residential capital (largely offset by 24% too few industrial structures and 12% too few utility structures).[19] The widely-cited overinvestment in equipment is only 3%; while substantial overinvestment in equipment exists relative to corporate structures, overinvestment relative to capital generally is minor. Of the three reforms, only the Administration plan reduces the efficiency loss, and the reduction is a sharp 50%. This is achieved by both a better allocation between residential and nonresidential capital (the overinvestment in residential capital is reduced from 10 to 8%)

Table 8.13   **Efficient and Likely Allocations of Capital under Various Tax Regimes**

	Efficient	Current	Treasury	Admin.	House
Residential	36.23	39.97	42.82	39.30	42.25
Nonresidential					
Inventories	13.23	12.43	12.82	12.68	12.72
Equipment	23.89	24.50	21.51	22.98	21.90
Public Utility	7.39	6.54	6.03	7.03	6.01
Industrials	10.38	7.92	8.02	8.58	8.18
Commercial	8.89	8.64	8.80	9.43	8.94
Efficiency Loss					
(% of Capital Stock)		.1185	.1815	.0611	.1614
% Change in Loss			53	−48	36

and better allocations within the residential and nonresidential sectors. The difference between the net user costs for the highest- and lowest-income owning households is reduced from 0.029 to 0.018, and the large underinvestment in corporate structures is reduced significantly.

The Treasury plan and the House bill would increase the efficiency loss by 53 and 36%, respectively, the principal reason being the further overinvestment in residential capital (18 and 17% versus the current 10%). Not only do these bills remove the investment tax credit for equipment and utilities, but they reduce the value of depreciation deductions. The greater efficiency loss under the Treasury plan relative to the House bill is attributable to a substantial increase in the existing bias in favor of owning over renting. This, in turn, is due to the great advantage of debt financing of owner-occupied housing given by the partial taxation of interest income but full deduction of home mortgage interest expense. The fully-indexed Treasury variant (only real mortgage interest expense is deductible) leads to a smaller increase in residential capital, a better allocation within residential, and thus a negligible 6% increase in the efficiency loss.

Efficiency losses have also been calculated at different inflation rates. The losses under all tax regimes are lower at a zero inflation rate and greater at 10% inflation. For current law, the loss is 12% less at zero inflation and 37% greater at 10% inflation. The efficiency loss under the Administration plan is roughly half that of current law over the entire inflation range examined. At zero inflation, the losses under the Treasury plan and House bill are virtually identical to those under current law. At higher inflation rates the losses, especially under the Treasury plan, increase relative to current law; at 10% inflation the loss under the Treasury plan is nearly double that under current law. Such is not the case with the fully-indexed Treasury variant; its loss at 10% inflation is slightly less than that of current law.

8.5 Summary

The paper begins with presentation of a methodology for computing annual rental costs of capital or investment hurdle rates under any tax regime. Tax law over the 1980–84 period is specified and the provisions of the Treasury and Administration tax reform proposals and H.R. 3838 are described. A model is then constructed to allow calculation of the impact of changes in tax regimes and/or expected inflation on interest rates and the allocation of real capital. The model allocates a fixed private capital stock among various classes of nonresidential and residential capital, depending upon the rental costs for the capital components, the price elasticities of demand with respect to the rental costs, and the elasticities of homeownership with respect to the cost of owning versus renting. The interest rate adjusts in response to tax/inflation changes so as to maintain the aggregate demand for capital at this initial level.

Simulation of the Economic Recovery Tax Act of 1981 suggests an increase in interest rates, a decrease in homeownership, and a shift in capital from residential to nonresidential uses, especially equipment. Data since 1980 are consistent with these "forecasts" when one abstracts from the impact of the decline in inflation on interest rates after the middle of 1982. The decline in ownership is restricted to younger (under 40) households who are likely to be making tenure decisions based upon current economic conditions. The general correspondence between these simulations and recent economic events suggests that the simulation model is appropriate for analyzing the impact of proposed tax reforms.

Under a neutral tax system, the risk-adjusted net (of depreciation) investment hurdle rates would be the same for all assets. This is far from true under current law. The tax-favored assets are housing of high-income owners and noncorporate equipment. The most tax-penalized asset is inventories, whose inflationary gains are not indexed. Corporate structures are also penalized, especially industrial structures that receive no tax credit. More generally, corporate investments are penalized relative to noncorporate; less-leveraged investments are penalized relative to more-leveraged investments; and risky assets are penalized relative to less risky assets.

The Treasury plan greatly reduces the difference in risk-adjusted net hurdle rates among corporate assets by eliminating the inventory tax and the investment tax credit. However, the plan increases the advantages of real estate. While the hurdle rates for equipment and utilities rise to that for industrial structures, those for owner-occupied housing decline significantly in response to a 2.6 percentage point decline in interest rates (and the nonindexation of home mortgage interest expense). The Administration plan drops interest indexation and accelerates depreciation deductions for equipment and, especially, public utilities relative to economic depreciation. With these changes, the level of interest rates falls by only 0.6 percentage points, and the demand for owner-occupied housing by middle- and high-income households declines. In contrast, the House bill has even less general depreciation allowances than current law. Consequently, hurdle rates for equipment and utilities rise sharply, while the 125 basis point decline in interest rates lowers hurdle rates for owner-occupied housing. The basic results are the same in the absence of interest-rate declines; hurdle rates decline *relatively* for owner-occupied housing under the Treasury plan and House bill, but not under the Administration plan. That is, whether rates decline or not, the former two proposals would tilt the playing field toward owner-occupied housing, the most tax-favored asset under current law.

Reallocation of the capital stock follows fairly directly from the realignment of investment hurdle rates. Removal of the inflation tax raises inventories, while the loss of the investment tax credit tends to shrink equipment and utilities, although utilities would actually rise in response to the far more generous depreciation allowances of the Administration plan. While the specific provisions of the Treasury plan and the House bill differ widely, these two reforms should be expected to have remarkably similar impacts on capital allocation. In contrast, the Administration plan would have a sharply different impact on the three types of structures. Under the Treasury and House plans, residential structures rise by 8%, while industrial and commercial structures are largely unaffected. Under the Administration plan, the reverse is true. Moreover, the homeownership rate rises significantly under the Treasury and House plans, but falls by 4 points under the Administration plan.

Inflation is quite negative for owner-occupied housing under current law because the average tax rate at which expenses are deductible is significantly less for owner housing than for other capital. Thus, the real after-tax interest rate paid by owners tends to rise with an increase in inflation, while that for other capital falls. On the other hand, inflation is very positive for depreciable real estate because the advantages of debt are magnified at higher interest rate levels. While an increase in inflation lowers the homeownership rate, commercial structures increase sharply. Moreover, total housing increases because the stimulus to renter housing outweighs the negative impact on owner housing. With real estate expanding, the other capital components decline.

The Treasury plan makes a serious attempt at achieving inflation neutrality by setting tax depreciation equal to economic depreciation and indexing capital gains, depreciation allowances, and interest. Unfortunately, the plan fails badly. While a fully-indexed variant of the Treasury plan would be less sensitive to inflation than is current law, exclusion of home mortgage interest expense from the indexation provision of the Treasury plan reverses this result. Homeownership and the demand for owner-occupied housing are strongly stimulated because the real-after tax financing rate for even low-income owning households declines. The surge in housing is matched by declines in all other capital types.

Just as under current law, the homeownership rate would be significantly lowered by inflation if the Administration plan or House bill were in place. However, the stimulation of depreciable real estate and the constriction of nonresidential capital would be far less under the Administration plan. The Administration plan is thus significantly more inflation neutral than current law; the House bill would be mildly more neutral.

Of the three plans, only that proposed by the Administration would lead to a more efficient allocation of capital, i.e., one that is less biased toward high-income housing and away from corporate structures. The current efficiency loss would be roughly halved. The Treasury plan, while equating hurdle rates across corporate assets, would greatly increase the current efficiency loss at positive inflation rates by stimulating additional overinvestment in housing. The increases in the loss would be roughly 50% at 5% inflation and nearly 100% at 10% inflation. The House bill, too, would increase the efficiency loss, and for the same reason, but the increase would be a smaller 25 to 40% at inflation rates between 3 and 10%.

Notes

1. Earlier simulation analyses of ERTA include Gravelle (1982) and Hendershott and Shilling (1982).

2. We do not consider the impact of imperfect loss offsets. For an analysis of these and other details of corporate taxation, see Auerbach (1983).

3. Because property taxes on owner-occupied housing are deductible, the tax saving from these taxes on a dollar of housing (assuming a property tax rate of 0.012) is subtracted from the right side of (1).

4. Optimal bond trading is discussed in Constantinides and Ingersoll (1984). Other sources of the low implicit yield in longer-term tax exempts are the greater risk of losses due to default and call on municipals relative to Treasuries and the 80% limitation of the portion of interest on indebtedness used to carry tax exempts that commercial banks can deduct.

5. While the explicit and implicit tax rates relevant to the quantity-demanded decision are marginal rates, those relevant to the decision of whether to own or rent depend on the average rates at which interest for the entire house purchase is deducted and on which the entire owner-equity investment would have been taxed (Hendershott and Slemrod 1983).

6. One million of the 1–4 unit properties in 1980 were no more than a decade old, as were 77,500 of the 5–49 unit properties and 22,700 of the over-50 unit properties. With 1.3, 11, and 160, respectively, as the average number of units in each of these three classes of properties, 63% of the total units no more than a decade old were in properties with 50 or more units. Because a significant number of the 1–4 unit properties were originally built for ownership, two-thirds to three-quarters of the newly-constructed rental units were probably in properties with 50 or more units.

7. 60% of owning households with incomes under $15,000 in 1983 had house-to-income ratios exceeding 4, suggesting that the households were retired and did not have a mortgage. In contrast, 80% of owning households with incomes over $25,000 had mortgages and only 5% with incomes above $25,000 had house-to-income ratios above 4.

8. The National Association of Homebuilders (1985, p. 51) assumes a 14% value for e when π is 6%. This inflation rate translates into a tax-exempt rate

just above 8% in our model and thus a risk premium of about 6%. Price-Waterhouse has used an e of 16% in their calculations.

9. The 1981 act also expanded the investment tax credit slightly. Both this expansion and the more generous depreciation deductions were effective 1 January 1981.

10. The Treasury would assume a real interest rate of 6% and allow the deduction of (or would tax) only $6/(6 + \pi)$ of interest paid (or earned), where π is the actual inflation rate in a tax year. Thus if inflation were 5%, only 55% of interest would be taxed and deducted. With zero inflation, all interest would be taxed and deducted; with 10% inflation only 38% would. (However, mortgage interest outlays on one's principal residence would be fully deductible.)

11. Because only 55%/38% of nominal interest income would be taxed in a 5/10% inflation world, the tax rate relevant to own equity financing would be 55%/38% of the marginal rates shown in table 8.2 or the tax-exempt rate, whichever is less.

12. The methodology for computing these tax rates is discussed in Hendershott and Ling (1986).

13. The model is both an extension and simplification of that used by Hendershott and Shilling (1982) to analyze the Economic Recovery Tax Act of 1981. The extension is a more detailed treatment of nonresidential capital; the simplification is an exogenous specification of risk premia. Gravelle (1985) uses a somewhat similar model to analyze the Treasury plan. Fullerton (1985) analyzes the impact of the Treasury plan on effective tax rates.

14. Higher interest rates pulled in foreign capital, but the dampening effect of this inflow on rising interest rates is assumed to have been offset by increased Federal deficits.

15. Bosworth (1985) makes the somewhat contrary argument that business investment in recent years is not consistent with the passage of ERTA.

16. In simulations where the aggregate capital stock was determined endogenously as that consistent with the imposed 10% interest rate, the total capital stock falls by 15% in the Treasury simulation, 8% in the House bill simulation, and 3% for the Administration plan.

17. This statement would seem to be at variance with the sharp shift to homeownership in the 1970s. The latter occurred because interest rates did not fully reflect expected general inflation and expected house price inflation likely exceeded expected general inflation by 2 to 3 percentage points.

18. This is an understatement of the loss because it does not take into account inefficiencies created by industry specific tax provisions or by tax-exempt financing of private purpose activities. Moreover, the gains from removing such inefficiencies by, say, the Treasury plan are understated.

19. The loss is independent of the presumed risk premium associated with owner-occupied housing ($\rho - d - \delta$ is independent of δ) and is largely independent of its presumed loan-to-value ratio (under current law an advantage of debt financing exists only for high-income owners).

References

Auerbach, A. J. 1979. Wealth maximization and the cost of capital. *Quarterly Journal of Economics* 93 (August): 433–46.

———. 1983. Corporate taxation in the United States. *Brookings Papers on Economic Activity* 2: 451–505.

Berndt, E. R. 1976. Reconciling alternative estimates of the elasticity of substitution. *Review of Economics and Statistics* (February): 59–68.

Board of Governors of the Federal Reserve System. 1984. *Balance Sheets for the U.S. Economy* (April).

Bosworth, B. P. 1985. Taxes and the investment recovery. *Brookings Papers on Economic Activity* 1: 1–38.

Bulow, J. I., and L. H. Summers. 1984. The taxation of risky assets. *Journal of Political Economy* 92: 20–39.

Constantinides, G. M., and J. E. Ingersoll, Jr. 1984. Optimal bond trading with personal taxes. *Journal of Financial Economics* 13 (September): 299–335.

Follain, J. R. 1986. Another look at tenure choice, inflation and taxes. Office of Real Estate Research Working Paper no. 24, University of Illinois (January).

Fullerton, D. 1985. The indexation of interest, depreciation, and capital gains: A model of investment incentives. NBER Working Paper no. 1655 (June).

Gravelle, J. G. 1982. Effects of the 1981 depreciation revisions on the taxation of income from business capital. *National Tax Journal* 35 (March): 1–20.

———. 1985. Assessing structural tax revision with economic models: The treasury tax proposals and the allocation of investment. Congressional Research Service, The Library of Congress (April 8).

Hall, R. E., and D. W. Jorgenson. 1967. Tax policy and investment behavior. *American Economic Review* 57 (June): 391–414.

Hendershott, P. H., and D. C. Ling. 1986. Likely impacts of the Administration proposal and the House Bill. In *Tax Reform and Real Estate*, ed. J. Follain. The Urban Institute.

Hendershott, P. H., and J. D. Shilling. 1982. The impacts on capital allocation of some aspects of the Economic Recovery Tax Act of 1981. *Public Finance Quarterly* (April): 242–73.

Hendershott, P. H., and J. Slemrod. 1983. Taxes and the user cost of capital for owner-occupied housing. *Journal of the American Real Estate and Urban Economics Association* (Winter): 375–93.

King, M. A. 1980. An econometric model of tenure choice and the demand for housing as a joint decision. *Journal of Public Economics* 14: 137–59.

Musgrave, J. C. 1984. Fixed reproducible tangible wealth in the United States, 1980–83. *Survey of Current Business* (August): 54–59.

National Association of Home Builders. 1985. Impacts of the President's tax proposal on housing (July).

Titman, S. D. 1982. The effect of anticipated inflation on housing market equilibrium. *Journal of Finance* 37: 827–42.

Comment   Harvey S. Rosen

Summary

Hendershott's paper uses a relatively small simulation model to analyze the effects of tax law changes on the allocation of capital. He specifies the model, plugs in parameter estimates, and simulates the

Harvey S. Rosen is a professor of economics at Princeton University and a research associate at the National Bureau of Economic Research.

effects of 1981–82 tax law changes. The simulation results are then compared with the actual pattern of changes in 1981–84. Even given Hendershott's caveat that simulation results are not intended to mimic real world changes, it is very brave indeed to submit one's results to this kind of test.

Standard user costs of the Jorgensonian type form the backbone of the model. One interesting aside in the discussion of user costs is worth special note. This concerns the necessary conditions for achieving neutrality (in the sense of equal net marginal productivities for all assets). Typically, either expensing depreciable assets or setting tax depreciation equal to economic depreciation will do the trick. However, things change when owner-occupied housing is included in the set of assets. As long as the imputed rent from owner occupation is not subject to tax, only expensing will secure neutrality.

The various user costs are inserted into a capital allocation model, which allocates a fixed private capital stock among various classes of nonresidential and residential capital. The interest rate equilibrates the demand with the (fixed) supply of capital. An important feature of the model is the fact that there are five components to the demand for owner-occupied housing, one for each of five income brackets. The demands for the various types of capital are generated by assuming cost minimization subject to a Cobb-Douglas technology, and the demand for housing is based on a translog indirect utility function suggested by King (1980).

When it comes to doing the tax simulations, Hendershott makes the important point that if one hopes to replicate the actual course of events, then not only must tax law changes be analyzed, but other important changes in the economic environment must be as well. In this case, the key event is the reduction in the inflation rate. Hendershott finds that ERTA by itself would have shifted the capital stock sharply from residential to nonresidential uses, but incorporating a 3 percentage point decline in the inflation rate sharply alters this result— the total housing stock is roughly unchanged.

How well do the simulation results mimic actual changes? As far as housing goes, Hendershott argues that the model does pretty well, especially if one is careful to disaggregate housing demand by age. The results for nonresidential structures are not as good, but Hendershott argues that the model's predictions are still close enough to use the simulation model to analyze the impact of tax reform with some confidence. The impacts of various reforms are then analyzed; the results include estimates of the changes in capital allocation that each reform would generate, and the associated welfare loss. The welfare losses for both the status quo and the various proposals are generally less than 1% of GNP.

Comments

This is a medium-sized model. I think that this is a nice size. It is complicated enough to surprise, but sufficiently small so that once you have been surprised, it is possible to figure out why. For example, some have argued that under the current tax regime, inflation tends to stimulate owner-occupation relative to investment capital, because the capital gains from owner-occupation are for all intents and purposes exempt from taxation (see the papers summarized by Rosen 1985, pp. 400–401). In Hendershott's model, however, owner-occupation is hurt by inflation because the average rate at which expenses are deductible is significantly less for owner-occupied housing than for other capital.

As I now proceed to list some possible deficiencies of the model, I will try to distinguish between problems that could be remedied, still maintaining the basic simple character of the model, and those that would require major increases in its complexity. It turns out that most of the changes that one might desire really would require substantial increases in the complexity of the model.

Uncertainty. Beyond the inclusion of (exogenous) risk premia for certain assets, there really is not much consideration of uncertainty in this model. There are several ways in which uncertainty might influence capital allocation decisions: (a) capital income uncertainty of the sort discussed by Bulow and Summers (1984) might lead to different rates of economic depreciation than those posited in the model. Further, these rates might be endogenous to changes in the tax system; (b) the tax system might be serving a risk-sharing function as suggested by Tobin (1958); in this case the allocational effects might be smaller than those estimated in the paper; and (c) uncertainty about the tax laws themselves may affect investment decisions. To see the potential seriousness of this consideration we need only reread the first paragraph of Hendershott's paper, which reminds us of the many statutory changes that have been made in the space of a few years. Indeed, it is still far from clear what the tax law will look like a year from now. However, the user costs in this paper implicitly assume that investors believe that the current law will last forever. Having pointed this out, however, I cannot think of a way to incorporate it that would be both simple and compelling.

No other distortions. In general, the welfare losses from the distortionary tax treatment of capital depend on other distortions in the economy. In this model, there are no other wedges. The leisure-income decision is not considered. Similarly, intertemporal consumption trade-offs are ignored. (For the most part, the model assumes that saving is perfectly fixed; even where this assumption is relaxed, no serious choice theoretic model of saving is proposed.) Finally, given the emphasis on housing in this paper, it is important to contemplate the existence of housing market distortions. Mills (1986) argues that housing is perhaps the most heavily regulated of all important sectors of the economy; just think of the rules regarding financing, sales, land use, construction, etc. To the extent that such regulations lead to less housing than otherwise would be the case, one could argue that favorable tax provisions for housing in the federal tax code are an improving distortion. But it is hard to think of a way in which such considerations could be introduced without complicating the model greatly.

No disequilibrium. In evaluating his model's predictions, Hendershott notes that "even if the model accurately characterizes the economy, the observed economic changes may differ from those implied by the model" if the economy was "a significant distance from full equilibrium when the disturbances occurred." This statement, while true, is potentially devastating to the paper. If a disequilibrium was possible when a disturbance occurred, then a disequilibrium could have generated the data used to calibrate the model. If this is the case, it is not clear what to make of the underlying parameter estimates. That this is a real danger seems to be implied by the econometric literature on investment functions, which indicates the presence of long adjustment lags to changes in the cost of capital. However, no one yet has provided a generally accepted way for modeling disequilibria; it would surely be unfair to require this analysis to do so.

Model of housing behavior. One of the unique features of this model is the very close attention given to the housing sector. Housing demand functions are allowed to vary by income class, and both the tenure choice and the quantity demanded decisions are examined. As noted above, the housing demand and tenure choice equations come from a translog indirect utility function suggested originally by King. Regarding this specification, it is important to note the following: (a) it imposes homotheticity; (b) it assumes that the same utility function generates the tenure choice and quantity demanded decisions. From a theoretical point of view this is entirely desirable. However, when King tests that hypothesis (conditional on the translog specification), it is rejected by the data; (c) it assumes that the same parameters apply to each income class; and (d) it is a bit hard to interpret, in the sense that it is not obvious what the parameters imply for price elasticities of demand for each of the income groups.

The purpose of King's paper was to estimate housing demand functions in the presence of rationing. It was therefore necessary to have an explicit utility function, and the translog form was perfectly suitable. However, it seems to me that given Hendershott's desire to provide a relatively rich model of housing demand, an alternative research strategy could have been selected. Use cross-sectional data to estimate simple tenure choice and quantity demanded functions separately for each income group, and use these instead of the indirect translog function. The inability to exhibit an explicit utility function is unimportant in the current context. I expect that implementing this suggestion would make the predictions more reliable and the model easier to understand. And it could be done without increasing substantially the complexity of the exercise of the whole.

I have another comment related to the treatment of housing. Obviously, things could be simplified considerably if there were only one representative owner-occupier instead of five of them. Hendershott argues strongly that disaggregation by income group is really important. He could strengthen that case if he actually did some simulations assuming only one type of owner, and showing that this assumption leads to very erroneous conclusions.

Finally, I would like to give some attention to the paper's estimates of the welfare loss of the system of capital taxation. Hendershott estimates that the efficiency cost of the status quo is one quarter of 1% of GNP. Is this big or small? Certainly, there are a lot of dollars involved. But compared to the political costs of "reforming" the tax law, and the economic costs created by uncertainty over what the future law will be, the cost of distortionary capital taxation may not be all that huge. If we take Hendershott's results seriously, perhaps the tax law we should endorse is one which promises not to make any changes in the next five years.

References

Bulow, Jeremy I., and Lawrence H. Summers. 1984. The taxation of risky awards. *Journal of Political Economy* 92 (February): 20–39.
King, Mervyn A. 1980. An econometric model of tenure choice and demand for housing as a joint decision. *Journal of Public Economics* (October): 137–60.
Mills, Edwin S. 1986. Has the United States overinvested in housing? Princeton Univ., mimeo.
Rosen, Harvey S. 1985. Housing subsidies: Effects on housing decisions, efficiency, and equity. In *Handbook of Public Economics,* ed. Alan J. Auerbach and Martin Feldstein, 376–420. Amsterdam: Elsevier Science Publishers.
Tobin, James. 1958. Liquidity preference as attitude toward risk. *Review of Economic Studies* (February): 65–86.

9 Investment Incentives and the Discounting of Depreciation Allowances

Lawrence H. Summers

The importance of depreciation and investment tax credit provisions in determining the level and composition of investment is widely recognized. Economists have long understood that the present value of depreciation tax shields along with the investment tax credit determines the effective purchase price of new capital goods, which in turn determines the cost of capital. Measures of the cost of capital are widely used in evaluating the likely effect of proposed tax reforms on the total level of investment and in assessing the distortions across capital goods caused by tax rules.

The cost of capital depends on the present value of depreciation allowances permitted by the tax system. This raises the question of what discount rate should be used in calculating this present value and determining the cost of capital. The choice of a discount rate is of considerable importance in assessing investment incentives. For example, the much-discussed adverse effect of inflation in conjunction with historic cost depreciation on investment results from the increased discount rate that must be applied to future nominal depreciation allowances. At a zero discount rate all depreciation schedules that permitted assets to be fully depreciated would be equivalent. It is only because of discounting that depreciation schedules affect investment decisions, and their effects depend critically on the assumed discount rate.

Lawrence H. Summers is professor of economics at Harvard University and a research associate of the National Bureau of Economic Research.

This paper was prepared for the NBER Conference on Capital Taxation in Palm Beach, Florida, February 14–15, 1986. Deborah Mankiw helped in the design and dissemination of the survey reported in this paper as well as providing valuable comments. Jim Hines, Jim Poterba, and Andrei Shleifer provided helpful comments.

Tax reform proposals often change the extent to which depreciation tax benefits are "backloaded." For example, the proposal of Auerbach and Jorgenson (1980) would have given firms all of their depreciation benefits in the year that investments were made. On the other hand, the recent proposal of the president (1985) stretches out the tax benefits associated with investment outlays by indexing depreciation allowances and abolishing the investment tax credit. A comparison of either of these proposals with current law will depend critically on the discount rate applied to future tax benefits in computing the cost of capital.

Despite its importance, the choice of an appropriate discount rate for depreciation allowances has received relatively little attention from tax analysts. This chapter examines both theoretically and empirically the discounting of depreciation allowances and its implications for tax policy. I conclude that economic theory suggests that a very low and possibly negative real discount rate is appropriate for calculating the present value of future tax benefits. But empirical evidence from a survey of 200 major corporations suggests that most companies in fact use very high real discount rates for prospective depreciation allowances. This conflict makes the analysis of alternative tax policies difficult. It surely suggests that there is little basis for confidence in tax policy assessments based on specific assumed discount rates that are constant across companies.

The chapter is organized as follows. Section 9.1 argues that, given the risk characteristic of depreciation tax shields, a very low or negative real discount rate should be applied. Section 9.2 reports survey results on the actual capital budgeting practice of firms and discusses possible reasons for the apparent conflict between the recommendation of theory and firms' reported behavior. Section 9.3 concludes the chapter by discussing the implications of the analysis for the assessment of alternative tax policies.

9.1 How Should Depreciation Allowances Be Discounted?

This section begins by reviewing the theory of capital budgeting and its application to the discounting of depreciation allowances. The theory has clear implications. Because prospective depreciation allowances are very nearly riskless, they are more valuable than other prospective sources of cash flow. The appropriate discount rate for safe cash flows, like the stream of future depreciation deductions, is lower than the rates applicable to risky physical investments. An argument is made that the appropriate discount rate for depreciation deductions is the same rate applied to the after-tax coupon payments on a safe bond. The present value of depreciation deductions so computed can then be used in assessing potential investment projects. At current levels of inflation and interest rates, it appears that only a negligible real interest rate is appropriate for assessing alternative tax policies.

In theory (and in practice as demonstrated below), firms decide whether or not to undertake investments by computing the present value of the net cash flows they generate, using a discount rate corresponding to their cost of funds.[1] In a frictionless world of certainty, this process is completely straightforward. There is only one available rate of return and firms invest to the point where the marginal project earns just this rate of return. Or put more precisely, the net present value of the marginal project evaluated at the required rate of return is zero.

Once it is recognized that a project may be risky, the problem of capital budgeting becomes much more difficult. The theoretically appropriate procedure is to find the certainty equivalent of each period's cash flow and then to discount the certainty equivalents at the return paid by riskless assets. In reality it is difficult to assess certainty equivalents because the certainty equivalent of the cash flow payable in a given period generally depends on the distribution of cash flows in preceding and subsequent periods. Hence the normal procedure is to use a "risk-adjusted discount rate" appropriate to the project under consideration. This rate in general will depend on the covariance of its returns with aggregate returns in the economy. In the special case where a given project's returns will mirror the returns of the entire firm, it is often suggested that the appropriate discount rate be inferred from the firm's stock market beta.

A fundamental principle in finance is that of superposition. The valuation of a stream of cash flows is the same regardless of how it is broken up into components. This insight makes it clear how depreciation allowances should be treated at least to a first approximation. Consider an arbitrary investment project. The project will, after an initial outlay, generate a stream of uncertain future operating profits that will then be taxed. It will also generate a stream of future depreciation deductions that can be subtracted from the firm's income to reduce its tax liabilities. These two streams can be valued separately for analytic purposes. The valuation of the profit stream is difficult in the absence of a satisfactory way to gauge its riskiness. But the valuation of future depreciation tax shields is much easier since they are close to being riskless.[2] They therefore should be evaluated by discounting at a riskless rate. Since depreciation tax shields represent after-tax cash flows, they should be discounted at an after-tax rate of return. Their present value can then be added to the present value of the profit stream evaluated at an appropriate risk adjusted discount rate to evaluate the total return on an asset.

The same conclusion may be reached using an arbitrage argument as in Ruback (1986). Consider a set of prospective depreciation deductions that a firm is entitled to utilize. Imagine that the firm instead possesses a portfolio of Treasury bills designed so that the after-tax coupon payments in each period equal exactly the value of the tax deductions. It should be obvious that the firm has an equally valuable asset in either case. It follows that the appropriate discount rate for valuing depreciation deductions is the same as that for the Treasury bill portfolio—the after-tax nominal interest rate on safe assets. Note that the after-tax nominal interest rate is likely to be much lower than the appropriate discount rate for a project's operating cash flows.

At present nominal interest rates on safe assets are less than 10%. With a 46% corporate tax rate, it follows that the appropriate discount rate for future depreciation allowances is no more than a 5% nominal rate. This means a real rate very close to zero, contrary to the 4% real rate assumed in many calculations of the effects of tax incentives.

The assumption that prospective depreciation deductions represent a riskless asset has been maintained so far. In fact future depreciation deductions are subject to some risks. Depreciation deductions will be useless for firms that make losses and become nontaxable and are unable to make use of carryback and carryforward provisions. The results of Auerbach and Poterba (chap. 10 of this volume) suggest that this is not an important factor for most large firms. There is also the possibility of changes in tax rules. Since depreciation deductions represent a hedge against changes in tax rates, this source of uncertainty may drive the appropriate discount rate down rather than up. Finally there is always the possibility that the depreciation rules will be changed with respect to assets already in place. This has never occurred in the United States. On balance, it seems fair to conclude that depreciation tax shields represent an essentially riskless asset.

The arguments made so far indicate that firms should separately discount at different rates expected operating profits and depreciation deductions. It might be thought that firms could use a common discount rate for all the components of cash flow on a given project that reflected their average degree of riskiness in some way. But this is not correct because there is no way to know how much weight to give each component of cash flow until its value is determined, which in turn requires the choice of a discount rate. Even if an appropriate rate could be found, it would vary across projects depending on the value of prospective depreciation deductions. Moreover, a weighted average rate is unlikely to be varied when tax rules change and alter the share of a project's value represented by depreciation tax shields.

Before turning to an examination of tax policies, the next section reports evidence on firms' actual capital budgeting practices. They do not in general conform to those recommended in this section.

9.2   How Are Depreciation Deductions Discounted?

In order to learn how depreciation deductions are discounted by actual major corporations in making their investment decisions, a brief questionnaire was sent to the chief financial officers of the top 200 corporations in the Fortune 500. A copy of the questionnaire and covering letter are provided in the appendix to this chapter. Usable replies were received from 95 corporations. No effort was made to raise the response rate by following up on the initial mailing but there is little reason to suspect systematic differences in capital budgeting procedures between responding and nonresponding firms. The questionnaire was designed to find out whether capital budgeting procedures embodied the principles suggested in the preceding section and to find out what discount rates firms actually apply to depreciation deductions.

The survey results are reported in table 9.1. As the table indicates, the vast majority of corporate respondents stated that they had capital budgeting procedures and that these procedures were of "considerable" but not "overriding" importance in corporate investment decisions. Only 6% of the companies responding indicated that they discounted different components of cash flow on a given project at different rates, and even several of these companies did not distinguish operating profits and depreciation allowances. Many of the responding companies indicated that they dealt with risk issues by discounting projects emanating from different divisions or locations at different rates, but that they discounted all the cash flows from a given project at the same rate. It is clear that the practice of separately discounting safe and unsafe components of a project's return as suggested by theory is rare in American industry.

The lower part of the table indicates the distribution of the rates used by companies to discount depreciation allowances. In most cases

Table 9.1   **Survey Results on the Discounting of Depreciation Allowances**

1. Capital budgeting procedure is of:		
overriding importance		6%
considerable importance		91%
little importance		3%
2. Cash flow components discounted at different rates:	Yes	6%
	No	94%
3. Discount rate applied to depreciation allowances:	< 12%	13%
	13–15%	48%
	16–18%	16%
	19–21%	13%
	22%+	10%

the figure refers to the common nominal discount rate applied to all cash flows. The reported discount rates for depreciation allowances were surprisingly high, with a median of 15% and a mean of 17%—far in excess of the after-tax nominal interest rate. Given that depreciation tax shields have very similar risk characteristics across firms, it is also noteworthy that the rate at which they are discounted varies widely. The discount rates reported by firms varied from 8% to 30%. This variability is almost certainly the result of firms applying a common discount rate to all cash flows.

It is not easy to account for the level and variability of depreciation discount rates. One possibility is that managers do not understand the financial theory outlined in the preceding section or find it too complex to implement. Another possibility is that shareowners represent the locus of irrationality. If they apply a common discount rate to all components of cash flow, value-maximizing managers will do so as well. It is also conceivable that some of the variations in discount rates across firms result from different conceptual definitions of the required rate of return.

Before turning in the next section to the implications of these results for tax policy, there is an important methodological question to be addressed.[3] Economists continue to assume that consumers maximize utility even though it is clear that they never actually solve explicit optimization problems and indeed would reject the idea that they are maximizing anything. Firms rarely admit to knowing their marginal costs yet economists frequently assume they equate price to marginal cost. The reason is the power of "as if" modeling. There is a great deal of evidence that firms and consumers behave "as if" they were maximizing profits or utility functions, even if they do not do so consciously. Can a similar point be made with respect to evidence that firms use inappropriate discount rates in making investment decisions?

In a case like the discounting of depreciation allowances, the usual arguments for "as if" reasoning do not seem compelling. Evolutionary pressures against firms who do not optimize are likely to be weak. And the linkages between what managers say they are doing and what they actually do seem reasonably straightforward. Capital budgeting is a tool developed to help managers make more rational investment decisions than their unaided intuitions would permit. When it yields the "wrong" answer it seems excessively Panglossian to assert that managers are unconsciously doing what is right anyway. The next section therefore focuses on the implications of these survey results for tax reform.

9.3 Tax Policy Implications

This section treats two aspects of the relationship between the discounting of depreciation allowances and tax policy. First, I illustrate the sensitivity of judgments about the effects of alternative tax policies on incentives to the discount rate applied to future depreciation allowances. Second, I argue that the high and variable depreciation discount rates used by firms may themselves create important distortions, which the tax structure may either mitigate or exacerbate.

Table 9.2 presents estimates of the sum of the present value of depreciation allowances and the deduction value of the investment tax credit under current tax law, the president's proposal of May 1985, and the House of Representatives' 1985 tax bill using alternative discount rates for depreciation. The possibility of churning assets discussed by Gordon, Hines, and Summers (chap. 7 of this volume) is ignored.

Calculations indicate that the effects of alternative tax rules are quite sensitive to the assumed discount rate for depreciation allowances. At the theoretically appropriate zero real discount rate, only the House bill is less generous than a policy of immediate expensing of investment outlays. Current law provides a substantial subsidy to the purchase of new equipment because of the availability of the investment tax credit. On the other hand, with a 10% real discount rate applied to depreciation allowance, as the survey results suggest, all three tax laws provide benefits significantly less generous than expensing. Especially for long-lived equipment in asset class IV, both the Treasury bill and the House proposal would lead to a substantial increase in the effective purchase price.

The choice of a discount rate is especially important in evaluating the incentives provided for long-lived structures investments. At a zero discount rate the president's proposal provides far more incentives to structures investment than does current law. On the other hand, at a 10% rate current law is much more generous than the president's proposal.

Table 9.2   **Effects of Alternative Discount Rates on the Present Value of Depreciation Deductions under Alternative Proposals[a]**

ACRS asset class	I	II	III	IV	V	VI
$d = 0$						
Current law	1.06	1.08	1.08	1.08	.939	.736
President's proposal	1.00	1.00	1.00	1.00	1.00	1.00
House bill	.916	.890	.853	.807	.654	.624
$d = .1$						
Current law	.972	.938	.938	.938	.709	.487
President's proposal	.891	.862	.820	.759	.694	.351
House bill	.794	.741	.667	.583	.396	.366

[a]The present value of depreciation includes the value of the investment tax credit. A value of 1.0 corresponds to expensing. All calculations assume a 5% inflation rate. The discount rate is denoted by d.

The fact that firms use very high discount rates in evaluating projects suggests that the investment tax credit is likely to be a very potent tax incentive per dollar of government revenue foregone. The government will presumably want to trade off tax revenue at present and in the future using its borrowing rate. If firms discount future tax benefits at a rate higher than the government borrowing rate, tax incentives can be enhanced with no increase in the government's permanent cost by restructuring tax incentives to move the benefits forward, without changing the present value of the revenue foregone. The investment tax credit is frontloaded in this way. Still greater frontloading of tax incentives is possible through accelerating depreciation allowances, since this policy keeps the sum of the deductions that can be taken on an investment constant while increasing their present value. On the other hand, indexation of depreciation allowances tends to increase the duration of tax benefits.

The fact that firms use widely varying and inappropriate discount rates for depreciation allowances suggests that patterns of investment may be very substantially distorted in ways not considered in standard analyses of the effects of tax incentives. Certainly the returns demanded on marginal projects vary by much more across firms than do conventional measures of the cost of capital.

The reasons for these patterns are a potential subject for future research. One possible clue is that corporations and individuals seem to apply very different discount rates to depreciation allowances. The frequency with which individuals churn structures suggests that they apply a much lower (and more appropriate) discount rate than do corporations. This raises the possibility that agency issues may help to explain observed patterns of corporate capital budgeting. If this turns out to be the case, they may have an important bearing on the linkage between tax policies and investment decisions.

Appendix

September 20, 1985

Dear ———:

As part of its ongoing program of research on the economics of capital formation, the National Bureau of Economic Research is studying the effects of proposed reforms in the investment tax credit and tax depreciation schedules. The effects of alternative proposals depend critically on how taxes are factored into companies' capital budgeting procedures. I am therefore attempting to systematically gather information on major corporations' capital budgeting techniques.

I would be very grateful if you could fill in the enclosed questionnaire regarding your company's capital budgeting procedure, and return it in the enclosed envelope. Information identifying individual companies will not be presented in any of our research reports. I will of course furnish you with the results of the study when it is completed.

Thank you for your consideration.

Sincerely,

Lawrence H. Summers
Professor of Economics
Harvard University

Questionnaire

1. Does your company use a capital budgeting procedure based on evaluations of the discounted cash flows from proposed projects? _____yes _____no

2. If yes, would you say that the present value of the cash flows from proposed projects is of _____ overriding importance
_____ considerable importance
_____ some consequence
_____ little consequence
in determining whether they are undertaken?

3. What is the hurdle rate of return you apply to new projects? Specifically in your capital budgeting procedure, what discount rate do you apply to the after tax nominal cash generated by the typical project? _____
(Alternatively, please provide the real discount rate which you use and the expected inflation rate which enters your calculations.)

4. In evaluating projects some companies discount different components of cash flow at different rates because of their different risk characteristics. For example, some companies discount prospective depreciation tax shields at a low rate because there is not much uncertainty associated with them. Does your company treat different components of cash flow differently? _____ yes _____ no.

5. If so, what discount rate do you apply to each of the following types of cash flow: _____ operating profits
_____ scrap value
_____ depreciation tax benefits
_____ investment tax credits
_____ rental income

Comments:

Notes

1. For a general discussion of capital budgeting principles, see Brealey and Myers (1984).

2. The risk characteristics of depreciation tax shields are considered below.

3. I am grateful to Greg Mankiw for impressing on me the possible importance of this issue.

References

Auerbach, A., and D. Jorgenson. 1980. Inflation-proof depreciation of assets. *Harvard Business Review* 58:113–18.

Auerbach, A., and J. Poterba. Tax loss carryforwards and corporate tax incentives. Chapter 10 of this volume.

Brealey, R., and S. Myers. 1984. *Principles of corporate finance*. New York: McGraw Hill.

Gordon, R., J. Hines, and L. Summers. Notes on the tax treatment of structures. Chapter 7 of this volume.

Jorgenson, D., and R. Hall. 1967. Tax policy and investment behavior. *American Economic Review* 57:391–414.

The president's tax proposals to the Congress for fairness, growth and simplicity. 1985. Washington, D.C.: Government Printing Office.

Ruback, R. S. 1986. Calculating the market value of riskless cash flows. *Journal of Financial Economics*, pp. 610–620.

10 Tax-Loss Carryforwards and Corporate Tax Incentives

Alan J. Auerbach and James M. Poterba

The corporate income tax in the United States provides only limited tax relief to firms that report tax losses. Firms that have paid positive taxes during the three years prior to the loss year may "carry back" their losses and receive a tax refund, provided it does not exceed their total taxes in those three years. For some firms, however, current losses exceed potential carrybacks. This may happen when a firm experiences losses in several consecutive years, or when it incurs an especially large loss in a single year. Firms that exhaust their potential carrybacks must carry losses forward, using them to offset future taxable earnings. For these firms, the marginal tax rate on current earnings, as well as the value of tax deductions, depends critically upon when, and if, they regain their taxable status. Firms that anticipate persistent loss carryforwards will in effect face very low marginal tax rates.

Imperfect loss-offset provisions may substantially alter the incentive effects of the corporate income tax. Two features of the tax, the incentive to undertake new investment and the incentive to use debt as opposed to equity finance, are particularly sensitive because loss-carryforward firms may be unable to claim the benefits of depreciation or of interest tax shields.

Alan J. Auerbach is professor of economics at the University of Pennsylvania and a research associate at the National Bureau of Economic Research. James M. Poterba is associate professor of economics at the Massachusetts Institute of Technology and a research associate at the National Bureau of Economic Research.

This research is part of the NBER Program on Taxation. We are indebted to Lars Bespolka, Sandi Fine, William Gentry, and Julie Harrold for help in gathering data, and to Kevin Hassett for excellent research assistance. David Bradford, Paul Healy, and Lawrence Summers made valuable comments on an earlier draft. We thank the NBER, NSF, and the Sloan Foundation for financial support.

Standard analyses of corporate investment incentives assume that firms claim depreciation allowances and investment tax credits as they accrue. For firms with loss carryforwards, however, accrual and realization occur at different dates. This timing difference can change both the relative tax incentives for investments in plant and equipment, and the overall investment incentive facing the firm. For assets with high tax burdens, typically those with long depreciation lives, such as structures, a loss-carryforward firm may have a greater incentive to invest than a currently taxable firm. This occurs because the gain from postponing the tax payments on the asset's earnings exceeds the loss from postponing its tax depreciation benefits. The opposite result may obtain for assets with highly accelerated depreciation allowances, such as equipment. For these assets, the cost of delayed realization of the depreciation benefits may exceed the gain from deferring taxes on the project's profits, and loss-carryforward firms may therefore face smaller investment incentives than taxable firms.

Loss-offset provisions may also exert an important influence on corporate financing choices. Interest deductions are worth less to a loss-carryforward firm than to a currently taxable firm, so a firm with a tax-loss carryforward has less incentive to use debt finance than does a currently taxable firm. In addition, a firm's probability of experiencing future loss carryforwards may depend upon its financial policy, since higher interest deductions lower taxable profits and raise the chance of realizing losses. This has led some to propose a theory of corporate capital structure based on the proposition that firms borrow until the expected marginal cost of additional debt due to the increased probability of becoming nontaxable and losing preexisting tax shields equals the expected marginal benefit of additional deductions when taxable. This theory implies that tax systems with more generous loss-offset provisions provide a greater incentive for corporate borrowing.

Several recent studies have suggested that the loss-carryforward provisions of corporate tax codes are of more than academic interest. Cordes and Sheffrin (1983) analyzed the distribution of corporate marginal tax rates on additional interest deductions, and estimated that only 56% of corporate receipts accrued to firms that paid the maximum statutory corporate tax rate on marginal earnings. This is due to the combined effect of tax-loss carryforwards and binding income-linked constraints on the use of investment and foreign tax credits.[1] In Canada, Mintz (1985) reports that only half of the investment in manufacturing is undertaken by currently taxable firms, and the incidence of loss-carryforward firms is much higher in some other sectors, such as mining. For Great Britain, Mayer (1986) cites evidence that, during the early 1980s, only 40% of British companies were paying corporation tax on marginal profits. The stock of tax-loss carryforwards in the United Kingdom was nearly three times as large as the annual revenue yield of the corporation tax.

This paper presents new evidence on the importance of tax-loss carryforwards in the United States. It uses a new data set gathered from corporate annual reports and 10-K forms to investigate the incidence of loss carryforwards, and then examines how effective tax rates on different assets are affected by loss-offset constraints. The most important finding is that tax-loss carryforwards are highly persistent and significantly affect investment incentives for some firms. Nearly 15% of the firms in our sample had tax-loss carryforwards in 1984, and the fraction is much higher in some industries. Analyzing the effect of the corporate income tax on tax-loss firms is therefore essential to understanding investment and financing incentives in these industries. We estimate the persistence of loss carryforwards and use the results to calculate effective tax rates on new investments in structures and industrial equipment for both currently taxable and loss-carryforward firms. We find that the presence of a tax-loss carryforward has a dramatic effect on a firm's incentive to invest in equipment but relatively little impact on the incentive to invest in structures.

The paper is divided into five sections. The first outlines the tax rules governing loss carryforwards and carrybacks. It also explains the difficulties that arise in using standard data sources to measure tax-loss carryforwards, and describes our new data set. The second section presents our basic findings on the importance of firms with tax-loss carryforwards and examines the persistence of loss carryforwards for the firms that experience them. The third section outlines how loss-offset constraints alter the effective tax rates on various assets and describes our numerical procedures. The fourth section presents our calculations of the effective tax rates on plant and equipment investment for both currently taxable and loss-carryforward firms. A concluding section discusses the implications of our results for understanding the allocative effects of the corporate income tax and suggests a number of directions for future work.

10.1 The Definition and Measurement of Tax-Loss Carryforwards

Loss-offset constraints restrict a firm's ability to obtain tax refunds when it generates negative taxable profits. A firm that realizes a tax loss may carry the loss back against tax payments in the previous three years, provided it does not claim current refunds in excess of total tax payments in those years. Firms that have exhausted their carrybacks may carry unused losses forward for a maximum of fifteen years, after which the losses expire and can no longer be used to reduce tax liability. Prior to 1981, loss carryforwards expired in five years. For firms with loss carryforwards, an additional dollar of taxable income has no effect on current tax liability. The marginal tax burden on an additional dollar of taxable earnings depends upon when the firm becomes taxable again in the future.

It is important to distinguish between firms with loss carryforwards and "firms that pay no taxes."[2] A firm with a tax-loss carryforward in a given year pays no tax, but it may receive a refund if it can carry part of the loss back against previous tax payments. A marginal change in the firm's taxable earnings, however, will have no effect on its current tax liability. Its current marginal tax rate is zero, although if it expects to exhaust its loss carryforwards in the near future it will face an effective marginal tax rate that differs from the statutory tax rate only by the price of an interest-free loan for the duration of its remaining tax-loss period.

Not all firms with negative current tax payments have loss carryforwards, however. Some firms that are carrying back current losses may not have exhausted their carryback potential. For these firms, the marginal tax rate on additional income is the statutory tax rate, because an additional dollar of earned income will reduce the amount of their carryback. These firms face the statutory marginal rate even though their current tax payments are negative.

Loss carryforwards are not the only factor that may cause a firm's marginal tax rate to differ from the statutory rate. Cordes and Sheffrin (1983) explain how constraints on the use of tax credits and the corporate minimum tax also affect the distribution of marginal corporate tax rates.[3] Unfortunately, publicly available information is not detailed enough to enable us to measure the marginal tax rates facing individual corporations. To calculate a firm's carryback potential, we would need information on its current tax credits, its credit and loss carryforwards, and even its previous tax payments. These data can only be obtained from a firm's past and present tax returns, which are confidential.[4] One type of tax data which can be gathered from published sources is the identity of firms with tax-loss carryforwards. Corporate annual reports and 10-K filings typically contain some information on carryforwards, so we focus on this source of variation in marginal corporate tax rates.

Data limitations prevent us from assessing the significance of firms with tax-credit carryforwards. Most of the firms that we identified as having tax-loss carryforwards also reported credit carryforwards. There may be other firms, however, with credit carryforwards but no loss carryforwards; Cordes and Sheffrin (1983) suggest that these credit-carryforward firms account for a substantial fraction of the firms facing marginal corporate tax rates below the statutory levels. We implicitly assume that firms either encounter loss and credit carryforwards simultaneously or that they encounter neither. Preliminary results, based on IRS data and incorporating both loss and credit carryforwards, are reported in Altshuler and Auerbach (1987).

The standard source of machine-readable information on corporate accounts is the COMPUSTAT data base compiled by Standard and Poor. Although the data set contains a company's tax-loss carryforward if the annual report includes one, there are several serious problems with these data. First, there are two distinct ways of calculating a firm's tax-loss carryforward. One is for *tax* purposes, the other is for *financial reporting* purposes. In computing financial-reporting loss carryforwards, firms exclude depreciation allowances in excess of straight-line depreciation. Financial-loss carryforwards may therefore be smaller than tax-loss carryforwards, because accounting profits are larger than taxable profits. The two measures also differ in the treatment of discontinued operations, write-offs, and many other activities. A firm that decides to write down its investment in an unprofitable subsidiary may book a substantial loss but receive no tax benefits for the transaction, thereby leading financial-reporting losses to exceed tax-purpose losses. The relevant measure for analyzing corporate incentives is the tax-purpose loss; unfortunately, if a firm reports both tax and financial-loss carryforwards, COMPUSTAT records the financial-purpose carryforward. This may lead to spurious classification of firms. Second, COMPUSTAT aggregates foreign tax-loss carryforwards along with U.S. carryforwards. For multinational firms, the data may therefore provide an unreliable description of current tax status.

Firms with loss carryforwards typically report both financial and tax-purpose data in their annual reports or 10-K statements. These published data, although not available in machine-readable form, provide the basis for our study. We began with the list of COMPUSTAT firms reporting loss carryforwards for any of the fiscal years from 1981 to 1984. We then consulted the annual reports for each of these firms; when it was available, we recorded the tax-purpose carryforward. We also investigated all of the firms on COMPUSTAT with either negative federal tax payments or zero investment tax credits. In some cases, we found that firms with COMPUSTAT carryforwards did not have U.S. tax-basis carryforwards; these were reclassified as loss-free firms. In other cases, the firms reported only one measure of their loss carryforward and did not indicate whether it was a tax or financial number. These firms (of which there were very few) were deleted from our sample. We also deleted all foreign-based firms before investigating the pattern of loss carryforwards.[5] Our data set includes 1,425 firms, 228 of which experienced tax-loss carryforwards at some point between

1981 and 1984. The total market value of the firms in our sample is roughly three-quarters of the total market value of the nonfinancial corporate sector.

There are several potential biases in our data sample that should be recognized at the outset. First, COMPUSTAT does not include all of the corporations which file tax returns; there were over three million such firms in 1982! The firms on COMPUSTAT are large, publicly traded firms. If losses tend to be more prevalent among smaller or start-up firms, then we may understate the number of firms with tax-loss carryforwards. Second, the data set follows COMPUSTAT in including only firms that were active in 1984. Some corporations that encountered tax-loss carryforwards in earlier years may either have been taken over or gone bankrupt, and the end-of-sample sampling rule imparts a clear selection bias. This may cause us to understate the number of loss-carryforward firms in 1981 through 1983, although the bias is likely to be small given the relatively low rate of both bankruptcy and takeover for firms on the COMPUSTAT tape. A third source of bias arises because not all firms with losses may report them. Firms are required to report loss carryforwards only if they are "material"; since some firms with small carryforwards may not appear as carryforward firms on COMPUSTAT, we may understate their importance.

A final problem with loss-carryforward data gathered from annual reports and 10-K filings is the divergence between the divisions of the firm included on its consolidated tax return and those included on the financial statements. For example, as Dworin (1985) explains, some firms do not include their finance subsidiaries in their financial statements although for tax purposes these subsidiaries are consolidated with the parent corporation.[6] We may therefore classify a parent firm as having a tax-loss carryforward even though the total taxpaying entity has no carryforward. This problem is impossible to overcome when using data published in annual reports.[7]

It is difficult to evaluate the impact of these biases. One simple check involves comparison of our aggregate estimate of loss carryforwards with aggregate IRS data. A lower bound for loss carryforwards by nonfinancial corporations can be calculated as the current deficit reported by firms with current losses, less total losses carried back. This lower bound was $57.1 billion in 1981 and $75.2 billion in 1982, roughly five times as large as our aggregate estimates. While the source of this discrepancy is unclear, we believe it is due primarily to small firms not included in our data and some large firms which do not report loss carryforwards on their accounting statements. This is likely to contaminate our estimates of the incidence of tax losses much more than our estimates of transition probabilities and effective tax rates.

10.2   The Importance and Persistence of Loss Carryforwards

This section uses our annual-report data set for the post-1981 period, as well as accounting-purpose loss-carryforward data available on COMPUSTAT for a longer sample period, to explore the economic significance of tax-loss carryforwards. We ask how many firms have carryforwards, and then examine the persistence of these losses.

10.2.1   The Importance of Loss-Carryforward Firms

Table 10.1 presents summary evidence on the importance of firms with tax-loss carryforwards in the years since 1981. It considers the total population of nonfinancial firms, as well as some particular industries. The table shows that about 15% of all firms are in the loss-carryforward regime. We also weighted firms by their 1984 net book assets, and found that 5.9% of all assets were held by loss-carryforward firms.

Table 10.1 also shows that there is substantial concentration of carryforward firms in some industries. In the oil industry (SIC codes 1311 and 2911), for example, nearly a quarter of the firms (accounting for 2% of the common stock) had loss carryforwards in 1984. In 1982 and 1983, 40% of the firms (accounting for about 10% of the value of outstanding common stock) in motor vehicles and car bodies reported tax loss carryforwards. In the steel industry, the findings suggest a third of the firms have losses, and, they account for half of the industry's outstanding equity value. Finally, for airlines we also find a high in-

Table 10.1   **Tax-Loss Carryforward Firms, 1981–1984**

Industry	Sample Firms (N)	% of Firms with Loss Carryforwards			
		1981	1982	1983	1984
All Nonfinancial corporations	1,425	7.58	12.00	13.96	14.67
Oil (SIC 1311 & 2911)	69	13.04	23.19	24.64	24.64
Autos (SIC 3711)	7	42.86	42.86	42.86	28.57
Steel (SIC 3310)	25	12.00	32.00	32.00	36.00
Airlines (SIC 4511)	20	30.00	35.00	35.00	40.00

Note: All calculations are based on the authors' data set, which is described in the text.

cidence of loss carryforwards: forty percent of the firms (accounting for roughly one-tenth of the industry's equity value).

Table 10.2 shows the total value of the loss carryforwards for the firms in our sample. These carryforwards aggregated to 5.1 billion dollars in 1981, 10.0 billion in 1982, 15.1 billion in 1983, and 12.8 billion in 1984. As noted above, the aggregate number for the nonfinancial corporate sector is probably substantially larger. The center panel in table 10.2 relates the value of the tax-loss carryforwards to the market value of the affected firms. In 1984, the nominal value of the carry-forwards equalled 48% of the equity of the firms with these carryfor-wards. In some industries, notably steel, autos, and airlines, tax-loss carryforwards actually exceed the equity value of the loss-carryforward firms.

To provide additional perspective on the problem of loss-carryforward firms, table 10.3 displays the twenty largest loss-carryforward firms in our sample, measured by equity value, with their tax-loss carryfor-wards for 1983. The table depicts the same industry concentrations described above: the twenty firms include three railroads, four auto or heavy machinery manufacturers, four steel companies, and two copper companies. Although most firms on the list experienced tax losses because of poor profit performance, some firms (Storer Communica-

Table 10.2   **Estimates of Tax-Loss Carryforwards, 1981–1984**

Tax-Loss Carryforwards, Millions of Current Dollars				
Industry	1981	1982	1983	1984
All nonfinancial				
corporations	5,070.1	10,000.8	15,083.6	12,841.7*
Oil	45.7	129.4	1,353.3	1,291.3
Autos	2,278.7	2,407.0	2,853.0	1,262.0
Steel	96.8	1,274.0	2,389.1	3,808.3
Airlines	568.5	1,054.1	2,197.8	2,171.5
Tax-Loss Carryforwards as % of Affected Firms' Equity Value				
Industry	1981	1982	1983	1984
All nonfinancial				
corporations	38.5	44.3	37.2	47.6*
Oil	2.0	9.5	29.2	36.3
Autos	371.9	125.0	65.6	147.4
Steel	10.1	51.7	64.4	148.8
Airlines	127.8	141.1	279.8	204.6

Note: Calculations are based on the authors' data set consisting of 1,425 firms.

*Tabulations for 1984 exclude the Penn Central Company, for which no data were available. See text for further details.

Table 10.3   **The Tax-Loss Carryforward Top Twenty, 1983**

Firm	Equity Value ($ million)	Tax-Loss Carryforward
1. Burlington Northern	3,677.8	405.1
2. Chrysler Corporation	3,365.0	1,600.0
3. U.S. Steel	3,178.4	1,200.0
4. General Dynamics	3,064.4	137.3
5. Syntex Corporation	1,799.7	110.0
6. Bethlehem Steel	1,318.1	682.3
7. Penn Central	1,164.0	2,097.4
8. LTV Corporation	1,017.6	630.0
9. IC Industries	799.1	126.3
10. Asarco Inc.	775.6	12.4
11. Inland Steel	771.8	466.1
12. Phelps Dodge Corp.	622.2	380.0
13. Storer Communication	612.7	39.8
14. Clark Equipment	560,2	44.0
15. Datapoint Corporation	552.8	4.2
16. Alleghany Corporation	524.9	unknown
17. American Motors	514.0	257.0
18. Turner Broadcasting	484.2	17.3
19. Best Products	478.1	1.0
20. International Harvester	466.7	996.0

Note: Firms are ranked by outstanding equity value at the end of 1983. The Alleghany Corporation reported the presence of tax-purpose loss carryforwards, but it did not report their amount.

tions and Turner Broadcasting, for example) appear because substantial investment programs generated depreciation allowances significantly greater than taxable earnings from current operations.

10.2.2   The Persistence of Tax-Loss Carryforwards

The extent to which the restricted loss-offset provisions in the corporation tax affect investment and financing incentives depends upon the duration of nontaxable spells. If firms with loss carryforwards can expect to recover their taxable status within a year or two, then the absence of loss-offset provisions will have relatively little effect on incentives. If firms with carryforwards tend to be constrained for many years, however, then they may face incentive effects which are substantially different from those of taxable firms.

We adopt two different approaches to analyzing the persistence of tax-loss carryforwards. First, we use our data for the last four years to fit simple Markov models for transitions into and out of the loss-carryforward state. This provides the basis for our analysis of effective tax rates in later sections, but it is limited by the fact that our data span a period of only four years. Moreover, since these years include a very deep recession, transition probabilities from the recent period may be unrepresentative of those confronting firms over a longer horizon. To obtain information on long-term persistence of loss carryforwards, we therefore perform the same calculations using a second data source, the partially contaminated accounting loss-carryforward data from COMPUSTAT, for the period 1968–84. These data are also used to construct empirical distributions of the number of firms with losses that persisted for one year, two years, three years, etc. Although the differences between tax and book loss-carryforwards make these tabulations an imperfect source of information on persistence, they do permit us to compare the recent experience with that in prior years.

Table 10.4 reports summary statistics, based on our post-1981 data sample, for transitions into and out of loss-carryforward status. The top panel shows probabilities based on the first-order Markov assumption, i.e., treating a firm's current status as containing all relevant information about its transition prospects. These estimates show that for the 1983–84 period, the probability of a firm without a loss carryforward in period t experiencing one in period $t + 1$ is .026. For a

Table 10.4   **Tax-Status Transition Probabilities**

First-Order Markov Model		
Probability of Moving to State of		
Previous State	No Loss Carryforward	Loss Carryforward
No loss carryforward	.974	.026
Loss carryforward	.087	.913
Second-Order Markov Model		
State in Period $t + 1$:		
Previous State	No Loss Carryforward	Loss Carryforward
No loss carryforward ($t - 1$) No loss carryforward (t)	.977	.023
No loss carryforward ($t - 1$) Loss carryforward (t)	.099	.901
Loss carryforward ($t - 1$) No loss carryforward (t)	.680	.320
Loss carryforward ($t - 1$) Loss carryforward (t)	.083	.917

Note: All calculations are based on the authors' data set, described in the text, which yields 2,849 firm years of data. The estimates are for transitions observed in 1983 and 1984.

firm with a loss carryforward in period t, the probability of remaining in the loss-carryforward state at $t + 1$ is .913.

In calculating simple Markov probabilities, we are implicitly assuming that all firms have identical transition probabilities and that these probabilities did not vary between 1983 and 1984. Neither assumption is realistic, and these results should therefore be regarded as a simple way of summarizing the data rather than as parameters of a structural model of transition behavior.

There are two significant reasons why the transition probabilities are likely to vary across firms: different firms have loss carryforwards of different sizes, and there are probably differences in the stochastic processes driving their taxable income streams. Auerbach (1983) estimates a model for tax status in which the firm's tax-loss carryforward was modeled as a continuous variable. This requires imputing potential carrybacks to firms with no loss carryforwards, and it also necessitates complicated numerical integration in evaluating effective tax rates. The Markov model used here yields great simplification in computing tax incentives. Both procedures may be sensitive to missing information about the vintages of carryforwards, since two firms with loss carryforwards of identical size, one with losses generated fifteen years ago and the other with losses generated last year, have radically different probabilities of escaping from the loss-carryforward state.

The second source of heterogeneity, potential differences in profit processes, is more difficult to treat because it invalidates our assumption of a simple Markov process. A firm's characteristics, including lagged values of its loss-carryforward status, may affect its transition probability.[8] We introduce some additional flexibility in our transition matrix by estimating a second-order Markov process.

The results of estimating the second-order process are shown in the second panel of table 10.4. We tested the assumption of a first-order Markov process against the alternative of a second-order process (see Anderson and Goodman [1957]) and rejected the first-order assumption at the .10 level but not the .05 level. The $\chi^2(2)$ statistic was 5.02, with a .05 critical value of 5.99. We use the second-order process in later sections to calculate effective tax rates.

Two important conclusions emerge from table 10.4. First, it is very unlikely for a firm without a tax-loss carryforward to incur one. Second, it is also unlikely for a firm with a tax-loss carryforward to "escape" and become taxable again. These findings are important, because they suggest that the burden of the tax code's asymmetry is not borne uniformly, but rather falls heavily on the relatively few firms with tax-loss carryforwards. This also implies that standard calculations of effective tax rates which neglect the role of loss carryforwards may conceal important interfirm variations in tax incentives.

The most significant drawback of our post-1981 data is that we cannot examine the long-term persistence of tax-loss carryforwards. We can address this issue using the data on accounting tax-loss carryforwards drawn from the COMPUSTAT tape, however. To evaluate the potential biases associated with these data, we compared their second-order Markov transition probabilities for the 1983–84 period with those obtained from our annual reports data. The probability that a firm with two previous years of loss carryforward would remain in the loss-carryforward state was .928 in the COMPUSTAT data, compared with .917 in the annual reports data. The probability of remaining carryforward-free after two years of being currently taxable was .966 rather than .977. The COMPUSTAT data therefore probably overstate the persistence of tax losses because the chances of experiencing a tax loss in a given year, for firms that have as well as those that have not experienced them in the past, are higher in these data. This is consistent with our finding that financial-purpose loss carryforwards, because they include asset write-offs and other losses, may appear more significant than the comparable tax-purpose losses. Nonetheless, the close agreement between the COMPUSTAT and annual report-based data suggest that valuable information can be obtained by studying COMPUSTAT transition probabilities over time.

Table 10.5 presents the pattern of transition probabilities from the COMPUSTAT sample. It reports our estimates of the four basic transition rates for each year between 1968 and 1984, as well as the probabilities for the full sample period and two subsamples. Two conclusions emerge. First, the probability that a firm with loss carryforwards in the two previous years will experience another year of tax loss increased substantially in 1981. We denote this probability as p_{LLL}, where the subscripts refer to the tax status in periods $t-2$, $t-1$, and t, respectively. The subscript takes the value L for loss carryforward, and T for currently taxable. The probability p_{LLL}, which never exceeded .90 in the years prior to 1980 and which was frequently below .80, averages .928 since 1981. The probability of remaining in the loss position rises between 1981 and 1983, then declines in 1984, reflecting in part changing business-cycle conditions. There is also a discontinuity in 1981 in the probability that a firm which has experienced a taxable year followed by a loss year will remain in the loss state, p_{TLL} in our notation. From a pre-1981 average of .787, p_{TLL} changes to a post-1981 value of .909.

The table also shows a substantial post-1981 increase in the probability that a taxable firm will experience a loss carryforward. From .024 before 1981, p_{TLL} increased by nearly 40% to .034. There is a smaller increase in the chance that a firm which has experienced a loss-carryforward year followed by a taxable year will reenter loss status.

Table 10.5   **Tax-Status Transition Probabilities Estimated from Compustat Sample**

Year	P_{TTL}	P_{TLL}	P_{LTL}	P_{LLL}
1968	.034	.533	.000	.758
1969	.024	.840	.067	.800
1970	.030	.700	.267	.702
1971	.045	.889	.129	.895
1972	.021	.800	.000	.822
1973	.022	.773	.133	.778
1974	.035	.760	.108	.802
1975	.020	.900	.069	.798
1976	.018	.696	.033	.734
1977	.026	.850	.087	.786
1978	.015	.849	.036	.793
1979	.016	.647	.167	.709
1980	.015	.696	.119	.894
1981	.020	.727	.050	.921
1982	.047	.963	.167	.920
1983	.034	.923	.000	.941
1984	.036	.950	.231	.926
Means				
1968–84	.027	.825	.103	.830
1968–80	.024	.787	.102	.789
1981–84	.034	.909	.113	.928

Note: Each column reports the transition probabilities calculated from the COMPUSTAT data set of financial purpose tax-loss carryforwards.

These movements in the Markov transition probabilities correspond to changes in the steady-state distribution of firms with respect to tax status. The pre-1981 probabilities imply that in the steady state 10.9% of all firms have tax-loss carryforwards. The comparable steady-state value for the post-1981 probabilities is 33.5%, a striking increase.[9] This undoubtedly overstates the long-run effect of the 1981 tax reform, since it is difficult to disentangle the effects of the 1981 tax reform from the post-1981 recession.

Our estimates of second-order Markov transition rates are incomplete because they shed no light on the behavior of firms that have experienced losses for many periods. One way to study this long-term persistence is by calculating the probability that a firm with a loss in a particular year will experience losses for one more year, two more years, etc. Table 10.6 presents calculations of these long-term transition rates from the COMPUSTAT data sample for the period 1974–83.[10] The table shows that a significant fraction of firms that experience tax losses in a given year will continue to have such losses for at least four more years. The probability of this much persistence has also risen

Table 10.6   **Persistence of Tax-Loss Carryforwards, 1974–1983**

Year of Initial Loss	Fraction of Firms with Loss Carryforwards for:									
	1 Year	2 Years	3 Years	4 Years	5 Years	6 Years	7 Years	8 Years	9 Years	10 Years
1974	.801	.588	.432	.319	.226	.179	.152	.125	.117	.105
1975	.734	.548	.411	.302	.246	.210	.181	.153	.133	
1976	.760	.591	.436	.364	.316	.267	.231	.187		
1977	.782	.559	.472	.418	.355	.314	.259			
1978	.705	.589	.521	.430	.377	.309				
1979	.784	.668	.558	.484	.394					
1980	.813	.696	.601	.500						
1981	.836	.717	.594							
1982	.849	.709								
1983	.818									

Note: Tabulations are based on the financial-purpose loss carryforwards reported by firms on the 1984 COMPUSTAT industrial data file. See text for further details.

over time, from .32 in 1974 to .50 in 1980, the last year for which it is possible to calculate the four-year-later transition rate.

The estimates presented in this section are at best a rough characterization of the transition probabilities confronting firms. In the next two sections, we calculate effective tax rates for hypothetical firms whose movements into and out of the tax-loss state are given by our estimates. This analysis, which is primarily illustrative, demonstrates the potentially important effect of loss-offset provisions on effective tax rates.

10.3   The Incentive to Invest in the Presence of Tax Losses

Unlike more direct forms of investment subsidy, tax-loss carryforwards are not likely to have uniform effects on different firms and asset types. A firm with substantial unused tax benefits may appropriately view itself as temporarily "tax exempt," while a firm with a small carryforward which it expects to utilize during the next year regardless of its current decisions should take no account of it in making investment decisions. The differences across asset types stem from differences in the timing of taxable income. Many assets, such as equipment under current law, may be expected to generate negative taxable income in their initial years. If a firm has unused tax benefits when the project begins, this will *decrease* the asset's after-tax income. Since the accruing losses must be carried forward until the firm achieves a positive tax liability, some investments may actually be discouraged by the presence of unused tax benefits.[11] This section describes our methodology for quantifying these incentive effects.

There are a number of approaches to measuring the impact of tax-law asymmetries on investment incentives. Ideally, one would specify a dynamic model of firm value maximization in which risky investment would be affected by, and in turn would affect, the magnitude of unused tax benefits present at different dates in different states of nature. This problem is complicated by the joint endogeneity of investment and the firm's tax status.[12] To make the problem more tractable, if less general, one may restrict the endogeneity of either the firm's investment behavior or its tax status. The former approach is taken by Majd and Myers (1985, 1986). They value the tax payments associated with risky projects, taking account of the project's impact on the firm's future tax status. Their approach highlights the interaction between the project's risk and the risk of other random changes in the firm's tax status, but it ignores potential changes in corporate behavior which may result from variation in tax status.

An alternative approach, the one taken here, assumes that the probability distribution of future tax status is determined by the firm's history alone. This can be interpreted as treating the marginal investment project as small relative to the rest of the firm, so that the firm's tax status is determined by the stochastic returns on its prior investments. The assumption that the probability distribution of tax status is invariant with respect to marginal decisions is justified if this distribution is the direct result of firm optimization decisions. This interpretation highlights a shortcoming of this approach, however, in that it is necessarily restricted to partial equilibrium analysis of changes in tax rules or other components of the economic environment. We cannot predict how a change in tax regime would affect the incentive to invest, since it could both change the firm's statutory tax benefits holding its investment decisions fixed and alter the probability distribution of its future tax status.

10.3.1   Effective Tax Rates with Loss-Offset Limits

The summary statistic used throughout our analysis is the effective tax rate on a marginal investment project, calculated as the percentage difference between the internal rates of return on expected cash flows before and after tax. We assume that these marginal investments are inherently risk-free, and that the only source of uncertainty is the time profile of future tax payments. We designate the project's before-tax rate of return as ρ, which is set equal to .06 in all calculations. The asset depreciates at a constant rate, δ, so an investment made at the beginning of period O yields a gross return in period t of $(\rho + \delta)(1 - \delta)^{t-1}$ per dollar of initial investment.

We assume that the investment tax credit and the first half-year depreciation allowance accrue at date O. Thus, the firm's project-specific accrued tax liability (B_t) at date t is:

$$(1) \qquad B_t = \begin{cases} \tau[(\rho + \delta)(1 - \delta)^{t-1} - D_t(1 - i)^t] & t > 0 \\ - k - \tau D_0 & t = 0 \end{cases}$$

where τ is the corporate tax rate, k the investment tax credit, D_t is the nominal date t depreciation allowance, and i is the inflation rate. These expressions describe an equity-financed project; with debt finance, interest deductions would also enter the formula for B_t.

Under a symmetric tax system with full loss offset, equation (1) would describe actual tax payments. The project's after-tax internal rate of return, r, would be defined implicitly by the expression:

$$(2) \quad -B_0 + \sum_{t=1}^{\infty} (1 + r)^{-t}[(\rho + \delta)(1 - \delta)^{t-1} - B_t]$$

$$= \sum_{t=1}^{\infty} (1 + r)^{-t}[(\rho + \delta)(1 - \delta)^{t-1}] - T(r) = 1$$

where $T(r)$ denotes the present value of tax payments computed using discount rate r. After simplification, equation (2) yields the more familiar user cost of capital expression:

(3) $$\rho + \delta = (r + \delta)(1 - k - \tau z)/(1 - \tau).$$

We use z to denote the present value of depreciation allowances discounted at r. The value of r which solves (2) is used to define the effective tax rate:

(4) $$ETR = (\rho - r)/\rho$$

which is just the difference between the pretax and posttax rate of return, measured as a fraction of the pretax return.

When the tax system imposes limitations on the deduction of losses, actual tax payments may differ from B_t. This requires us to amend equation (2) before r and the effective tax rate can be calculated. Each accrued tax liability gives rise to a *distribution* of expected tax payments, since the firm may not be taxable when the tax liability or benefit accrues. In some states of nature, the firm will be taxable in period t and the accruing tax, B_t, can then be realized immediately. If the firm has a tax-loss carryforward and B_t is positive, its loss carryforward will be reduced and the firm will experience an increase in its tax payments in the year when it exhausts its carryforward and becomes taxable. If B_t is negative, loss carryforwards will increase and there will be a reduction in the firm's tax payments in the (future) year when the firm begins paying taxes again.

To describe the distribution of tax payments corresponding to a tax accrual in period t, we need some notation. We define $\pi^t_{L^sT}$ to be the probability that a firm with a loss carryforward in year t returns to being taxable in year $t + s$. The subscripts denote the firm's tax status in the years beginning in year t, and a T subscript indicates a taxable year while an L indicates a year with a loss carryforward.[13] Thus, π^t_{LT} is the probability that a firm with a loss carryforward in year t will become taxable in the next year. Both π^t_{LLT} and $\pi^t_{L^2T}$ represent the probability that a firm with a loss carryforward in period t will remain nontaxable for one more period, and then return to current taxable status two periods in the future. These probabilities, which we will ultimately derive from our Markov transition parameters, enable us to compute the expected tax payments corresponding to a tax accrual in period t.

Our analysis so far has omitted two important features of the tax system. First, since there are limits on the number of years (N) an accrued tax payment can be carried forward, the distribution of tax payments from an accrual at t will be truncated after $t + N$. Second, we have ignored the role of loss carrybacks. Once carrybacks are permitted, each expected tax payment increases the firm's potential ability to subsequently carry back future tax losses. We will use v_{ts} to denote the shadow value of additional tax payments in year $t + s$, viewed from the perspective of year t. With these complications, the present expected value of tax payments, T, becomes

$$(5) \quad T(r) = \sum_{t=0}^{\infty} B_t \left(\frac{1-i}{1+r} \right)^t \left[\sum_{s=0}^{\infty} \left(\frac{1-i}{1+r} \right)^s \pi_{L^s T}^t (1 - v_{ts}) \right].$$

The term in brackets is the expected present value of a one-dollar tax accrual in period t. Equation (5) defines $T(r)$, which can in turn be substituted into (2) to compute effective tax rates based on expected tax payments.[14]

10.3.2 Computing the Time Distribution of Tax Payments

To implement these effective tax-rate calculations, we need the probability distribution of tax payment dates for each accrued tax liability. We compute these distributions from the second-order transition probabilities in tables 10.5 and 10.6. These calculations are facilitated if we introduce new variables corresponding to the probability that a firm is in each of the four possible states, TT, TL, LT, and LL, in a given period. We use q_{ij}^t to represent these probabilities. For a firm which is known to have a tax loss in the period before, and period of, a new investment, $q_{LL}^0 = 1$ and $q_{LT}^0 = q_{TL}^0 = q_{TT}^0 = 0$. In general, the probability that a firm will be taxable in period one is

$$(6) \quad \pi_T^1 = q_{LT}^1 + q_{TT}^1 = (q_{LL}^0 p_{LLT} + q_{TL}^0 p_{TLT}) + (q_{TT}^0 p_{TTT} + q_{LT}^0 p_{LTT}).$$

The second part of the equation shows how the year-one probabilities can be built up recursively from the starting conditions, the q_{ij}^0, and the transition probabilities that were discussed in the last section. Similar calculations permit us to derive the probabilities of finding the firm in other tax states in period one.

The probability that the firm will carry its taxes from the investment year forward exactly one period is $\pi_{LT}^0 = q_{TL}^0 p_{TLT} + q_{LL}^0 p_{LLT}$. Parallel calculations show that the unconditional probability of carrying taxes forward for two years or more is $\pi_{LL}^0 = q_{TL}^0 p_{TLL} + q_{LL}^0 p_{LLL}$, and the probability of carrying a loss forward for exactly two years is $\pi_{LLT}^0 = p_{LLT} \pi_{LL}^0$. Probabilities corresponding to longer carryforwards can also be calculated recursively.

While these calculations have considered the distribution of tax accruals from period zero, it is straightforward to apply this approach to compute the distribution of tax payments corresponding to accruals later in the project's life. The initial conditions are just the $\{q_{ij}^t\}$ corresponding to the firm's probabilities of being in each tax state at the beginning of period t. These can be calculated recursively from the

$\{q_{ij}^0\}$ and the transition probabilities as in equation (6). As we iterate forward, however, the firm's tax status in year zero becomes less important as a predictor of its period t status, and the π vector converges to a steady-state value. In practice, we truncate our calculated π vector after twenty elements and let the twenty-first element capture all of the remaining probability.[15]

We incorporate loss carryforwards by assuming that all deferred tax payments may be carried forward N years, where N is the statutory maximum for carrying losses forward.[16] Incorporating carrybacks is more complicated, since the opportunity to carry losses back has the effect of making every tax payment potentially valuable in facilitating the accelerated deduction of future tax losses. This imparts a shadow value to tax payments; we calculate this shadow value in two stages. First, we compute a distribution of expected tax payments under the assumption that there are no carrybacks. Then, we account for carrybacks by reducing each dollar of estimated tax payments by a shadow value which depends upon the firm's current tax status and the estimated transition probabilities. The calculation of the carryback shadow value is described in greater detail in the Appendix.

10.3.3   Qualifications

All of the analysis in this section presumes that the effective tax rates which apply to a firm's investment choices are a function of its own tax status. This need not be the case. Leasing arrangements are one example of a channel through which the effective tax rates of the firms using and owning an asset can be separated. These institutions have been particularly popular in some of the industries with a significant incidence of tax losses, such as airlines. It is important to realize, however, that although leasing can reduce the present value of tax payments for a constrained firm, its impact on the firm's incentive to invest in new capital is less clear. A firm that has a loss carryforward would be better off if it could utilize this tax benefit right away, since the tax benefit loses value over time and may expire. Given that the firm cannot use this tax benefit, however, it may be encouraged to invest more, since additional taxable income generated by new investment will enable it to offset part of the loss carryforward.

A second limitation inherent to our analysis is its exclusive focus on tax policies. For some of the large firms that have tax-loss carryforwards, taxation is just one of the many ways in which the government and the firm interact. Examples of other policies that clearly affect the performance of the firms and the welfare of their shareholders include direct loan guarantees, regulation (especially for airlines and railroads), tariff policy, and in some cases government purchasing policy. Analyzing changes in tax rules without considering the offsetting changes which might occur in the other policy instruments is necessarily incomplete.

10.4   Empirical Results

This section presents numerical calculations illustrating how tax losses affect investment incentives. We consider general industrial equipment and industrial buildings, and estimate the effective tax rates associated with each under the tax regimes of 1965, 1975, and 1985. We then explore the sensitivity of these tax rates under current law to changes in both the tax code and the economic environment.

10.4.1   Changes in Effective Tax Rates over Time

In 1965, the corporate tax rate was .48 and the investment tax credit, which was available only on equipment, was 0.07 with no basis adjustment. The equipment class could be written off over twelve years using the double-declining balance method with an optimal switch to straight-line, while structures received the same treatment over twenty-nine years. Tax losses could be carried forward for five years and back for three.

By 1975, the ITC on equipment had been raised to 0.10 and, due to the introduction of the Asset Depreciation Range System, equipment could be written off in ten years. In addition, structures had been restricted to using the 150% declining-balance method. The corporate tax rate was still .48, and the carryforward and carryback provisions were the same as those in 1965.

Through tax changes in 1978, 1981, 1982, 1984, and 1985, equipment in 1985 received a 10% ITC with 50% basis adjustment and depreciation over five years following the pattern established by the Accelerated Cost Recovery System (ACRS). Structures could be written off over nineteen years through the use of the 175% declining-balance method with switchover to straight-line. In 1981, the carryforward period for losses was increased to fifteen years. The statutory corporate tax rate in 1985 was .46.[17]

We estimate the pattern of before-tax cash flows for each asset, assuming that the before-tax rate of return, net of depreciation, is 6% and that the asset depreciates at the rate estimated by Hulten and Wykoff (1981): 3.61% per year for buildings, 12.25% per year for equipment. We set the inflation rate at 4% throughout our calculations, and use a real discount rate of .03 to compute the shadow values of potential carrybacks.[18]

A firm's tax burden is critically dependent on the vector of probabilities describing the number of years that will elapse before its first passage into currently taxable status. Using the transition probabilities estimated for the COMPUSTAT sample in the 1968–84 period, we calculate this vector for two hypothetical firms. The first has just experienced its second consecutive year of tax losses ($q_{LL} = 1$), while the second is "the representative firm" in the sense that it has probabilities of being in states *LL, LT, TL,* and *TT* corresponding to the steady state of the Markov process.

Table 10.7 shows the π vectors for each of these firms. The π vector reports the probability that each firm will experience tax-loss spells of different lengths. The low probability of switching states leads very little of the representative firm's weight to be in states *TL* or *LT*. In the steady state, 83.2% of firms are taxable in both the current and the previous year, while 12.1% of firms have had tax-loss carryforwards in both years. Alternatively, roughly 85% of all accrued tax payments

Table 10.7   **Distributions of Years until First Passage into Taxable Status**

Number of Years Until Taxable	Firm with Loss Carryforward in Periods t and $t - 1$	Representative Firm
Currently Taxable	0.000	0.854
1	0.170	0.025
2	0.141	0.021
3	0.117	0.017
4	0.097	0.014
5	0.081	0.012
6	0.067	0.010
7	0.056	0.008
8	0.046	0.007
9	0.038	0.006
10	0.032	0.005
11	0.026	0.004
12	0.022	0.003
13	0.018	0.003
14	0.015	0.002
15	0.013	0.002
16	0.010	0.002
17	0.009	0.001
18	0.007	0.001
19	0.006	0.001
20 +	0.029	0.005

Note: All calculations are based on average transition probabilities from the full-sample 1968–84 COMPUSTAT data file. The first column reports the π^t vector for a firm that reports a tax-loss carryforward in periods t and $t - 1$. The second column shows the analogous π^t vector for a firm which has the steady-state probabilities of being in each state: *TT* with 82.9% probability, *TL* and *LT* each with 2.5% probability, and *LL* with 12.1% probability. See text for further details.

will accrue to firms that can deduct them immediately.[19] Firms that are nontaxable remain nontaxable for long periods, however. A firm with tax losses in the previous two years is more likely than not to wait at least four years until paying a currently accruing tax liability.

Table 10.8 presents our effective tax-rate calculations for the years 1965, 1975, and 1985 based on the assumption that each asset is entirely equity-financed. The table shows the general trend toward reduced effective tax rates on equipment over this time period, with the ETR for a taxable firm falling from 27.5% in 1965 to −5.0% in 1985. The dramatic reductions in the ETRs for taxable firms are, however, not reflected in the ETRs for tax-loss carryforward firms, where the reduction is from 30.8% in 1965 to 15.0% in 1985. For structures, the differences between taxable firms and loss-carryforward firms are much smaller. This is of course due to the much longer lifetime of these assets, and the consequent tendency for initial differences in tax status to be damped out over the project horizon.[20]

The effect of asymmetric treatment of gains and losses on effective tax rates is ambiguous, as noted in Auerbach (1983). Having a loss

Table 10.8   **Investment Incentives Measured by Effective Tax Rates**

General Industrial Equipment			
Firm Type	1965 Law	1975 Law	1985 Law
Loss carry-forwards at t and $t - 1$	30.8	24.2	15.0
Taxable at t and $t - 1$	27.5	9.2	−5.0
Firm facing perfect loss-offset code	34.2	15.8	0.8

Industrial Buildings			
Firm Type	1965 Law	1975 Law	1985 Law
Loss carry-forwards at t and $t - 1$	42.5	45.0	39.2
Taxable at t and $t - 1$	49.2	53.3	42.5
Firm facing perfect loss-offset code	56.7	60.8	48.8

Note: All calculations assume an inflation rate of .04 and a pretax return to capital of .06. For equipment, $\delta = .1225$ and for structures, $\delta = .0361$. We employ the 1968–84 transition probabilities from table 10.5.

postpones all tax liabilities, but especially the earliest ones, which may be negative. The latter effect is most important for equipment, where the currently taxable firm faces a much lower effective tax rate than the loss-carryforward firm. The impact on structures, for which immediate tax benefits are smaller, is in the opposite direction.

The results also confirm the common view that tax losses prevent firms from receiving the full incentive to invest intended by increases in accelerated depreciation and the investment tax credit over recent years. While holding inflation at 4%, the hypothetical firm under symmetric taxation had its effective tax rate on equipment reduced by 33.4 percentage points in the last two decades. The taxable firm enjoyed a similar decline of 32.5 percentage points, but the reduction was just 15.8 percentage points for the nontaxable firm. It therefore received less than half of the full statutory benefit.

Our earlier results suggesting the high concentration of tax-loss firms in a few industries also indicate that previous estimates of effective tax rates by industry may be misleading.[21] For steel, airlines, and automobiles, for example, it is essential to recognize that a substantial fraction of firms have tax-loss carryforwards and therefore face effective tax rates different from those facing taxable firms. In these industries, there are also likely to be important interfirm differences in effective tax rates due to variation in corporate histories and tax status.

Our algorithm also computes the shadow value of carrybacks and the value of a dollar of accruing tax losses for a firm that has just entered the untaxed state. For 1965 and 1975, when the carryforward period was five years, the shadow value of a carryback to a firm that had been taxable for two years was .040; for a firm that had been nontaxable in the previous year and was taxable in the current year, this value was .072. The expected present value of a dollar of currently accruing losses to a firm that had just incurred a tax-loss carryforward for the first time was .479 dollars. In 1985, with the longer period for carrying losses forward, these three parameters were respectively .026, .044, and .661.

The magnitude of the carryback shadow values suggest the limited usefulness of current carryback provisions. This is because most losses accrue to firms that experience several years of losses, and because most future losses will be recovered through the carryforward provision. Allowing firms the option of carrying losses back typically accelerates the recognition of tax benefits but does not enable the firm to claim tax benefits that would otherwise have expired unused. By contrast, the length of carryforward provision does appear to have a substantial effect on the expected value of a dollar of accruing tax losses. The longer carryforward period in 1985 both raises the value of a marginal dollar of carryforwards and lowers the value of the carrybacks, since accelerating the recovery of a tax loss is less critical with the expiration constraint relaxed.

10.4.2 Sensitivity of Effective Tax Rates

Our results in table 10.8 may actually underestimate the dispersion of effective tax rates facing corporations. Table 10.9 presents calculations for a number of alternative assumptions about economic conditions, corporate behavior, and tax policy. The second row of each panel shows the effect of an inflation shock that raises the inflation rate from .04 to .10. This causes a large jump in all of the calculated effective tax rates, the largest for taxable firms investing in equipment. The effective tax rate rises by more in each case for currently taxable than for nontaxable firms. This is because loss-carryforward firms are

Table 10.9	Sensitivity of Effective Tax Rates to Alternative Assumptions (Estimates Using Transition Probabilities from COMPUSTAT Data Sample)		
Assumption	Firm with Loss Carryforward in Periods t & $t - 1$	Firm Taxable in Periods t & $t - 1$	Hypothetical Firm Facing Perfect Loss-Offset
General Industrial Equipment			
Base case	15.0	−5.0	0.8
Inflation = .10	26.7	9.2	19.2
Real interest payments = .10 (pretax returns)	5.0	−20.0	−15.8
Unlimited carryforwards	14.2	−5.0	0.8
Elimination of carrybacks	15.8	−5.8	0.8
Industrial Buildings			
Base case	39.2	42.5	48.3
Inflation = .10	44.2	51.7	60.8
Real interest payments = .10 (pretax returns)	28.3	30.0	34.2
Unlimited carryforwards	39.2	42.5	48.3
Elimination of carrybacks	40.8	43.3	48.3

Note: The baseline case corresponds to the 1985 law in table 10.8. Maintained assumptions are the same as those in table 10.8.

already receiving their depreciation allowances at later dates than currently taxable firms. This reduces the contribution of the depreciation allowances to the project's present value, and hence lowers the sensitivity of the effective tax rate to inflation shocks, which further erode the value of these allowances.

The third row of each panel shows the effective corporate tax rate, net of interest deductions, when investments support real interest payments equal to a historically typical 10% of before-tax investment returns. With the addition of interest deductions, the value of being taxable increases, particularly as inflation rises. The use of partial debt-finance lowers the expected corporate tax bill, although its effect on total corporate and individual tax payments is probably smaller given the individual tax advantage to holding equity. It is of greatest benefit for taxable firms. The effective tax rate reductions for equipment and structures are 15.0 and 12.5 percentage points for the firm with no losses in the last two years, compared to 10.0 and 10.9 points for the firm with two consecutive loss years and 16.6 and 14.1 points for the firm facing perfect loss-offsets. Overall, the addition of this moderate level of interest expense amplifies the advantage of being taxable. The effective tax rates on structures are very close, while taxable firms enjoy a substantial advantage in equipment. If interest deductions are taken into account, being nontaxable probably discourages marginal investment and induces a shift away from equipment investment.

The last two sets of calculations in table 10.9 consider the impact of altering the tax provisions regarding the loss carryforwards themselves. The first set estimates the effect of permitting unlimited carryforwards, while the second examines the impact of eliminating the ability to carry losses back. Our earlier calculations suggested that increasing the time limit on the use of tax losses from five to fifteen years in 1981 substantially increased the expected present value of a dollar of loss carryforwards. Extending the limit beyond fifteen years appears to be less important. For taxable firms, the effective tax rates on both equipment and structures are only changed in the second decimal place, and for equipment there is a small (0.8 percentage point) change in the effective tax rate for nontaxable firms as a result of allowing unlimited carryforwards. Similarly, disallowing carrybacks has a relatively small impact. The largest change in an effective tax rate is for structures, where the ETR on a nontaxable firm rises 1.6 percentage points and that for a taxable firm increases 1.2 points. Both types of firms experience smaller effects on the effective tax rate for equipment. Structures are more affected because the chance of a firm having an opportunity to use a loss-carryback provision is substantially greater due to the asset's longer life.

The pattern of ETR changes associated with carryback and carry-forward reforms underscores the interaction between these provisions. Eliminating carrybacks raises the effective tax rate on all assets except equipment investment by taxable firms, where the ETR declines. Equipment investments initially had a negative effective tax rate, and the ETR becomes more negative. All of the other asset/firm status combinations had positive ETRs, and they become more positive. This is because eliminating carrybacks raises the shadow cost of tax payments and lowers the shadow value of tax benefits. When carrybacks are permitted, the firm's shadow cost of a tax payment is less than the actual payment because it may be used to carry back future losses. Eliminating carrybacks removes this option, and thereby raises the present value of the tax payments for all assets with initial positive tax rates. Since tax payments are now more costly, those assets with mostly positive tax payments are reduced in value. By comparison, the value of those assets with net tax benefits (i.e., equipment purchased by a currently taxable firm) increases, because the shadow value of receiving a tax deduction has also increased. This reduces still further the negative effective tax rates.

Allowing for unlimited carryforwards has no noticeable effect on any effective tax rate except that for nontaxable firms investing in equipment, where the effective tax rate rises. This occurs even though the firm carrying losses forward will be better off with an extension of the time limit, because positive marginal tax payments that otherwise might have been entirely avoided may now have to be made.

The results in this section have all been derived using the average transition probabilities estimated over the 1968–84 period. These suffer from several drawbacks, as suggested in the second section. Table 10.10 reports the baseline current-law effective tax rate and sensitivity calculations using the second-order transition probabilities estimated for the 1981–84 period. The results are strikingly similar to those in table 10.9, with the one significant exception being the effective tax rate on structures for firms with tax-loss carryforwards. Using the full-sample probabilities, this effective tax rate was 39.2%. In table 10.10, it is only 24.2%. The difference arises because, using the post-1981 transition probabilities, a firm with two years of loss carryforwards has a greater chance (.913) of remaining in the untaxed state than under the full-sample probabilities (.830). This increases the persistence of tax-loss carryforwards and raises the probability that a loss firm will defer the tax payments on the structure's earnings, as well as the (less important) depreciation allowances. This deferral reduces the effective tax rate.

There are other minor differences between the results in tables 10.9 and 10.10. When the post-1981 probabilities are used, the equipment

Table 10.10   **Sensitivity of Effective Tax Rates to Alternative Assumptions** (Estimates Using Transition Probabilities from 1981–1984 Annual Report Data)

Assumption	Firm with Loss Carryforward in Periods t & $t-1$	Firm Taxable in Periods t & $t-1$	Hypothetical Firm Facing Perfect Loss Offset
General Industrial Equipment			
Base case	8.3	−6.7	0.8
Inflation = .10	12.5	8.3	19.2
Real-interest payments = .10 (pretax returns)	3.3	−20.8	−15.8
Unlimited carryforwards	7.5	−6.7	0.8
Elimination of carrybacks	10.8	−8.3	0.8
Industrial Buildings			
Base case	24.2	40.0	48.3
Inflation = .10	25.0	50.0	60.8
Real-interest payments = .10 (pretax returns)	18.3	28.3	34.2
Unlimited carryforwards	25.0	40.0	48.3
Elimination of carrybacks	30.0	40.0	48.3

Note: Maintained assumptions are the same as those in table 10.9 except that we use the transition probabilities from table 10.4 rather than those from table 10.5.

ETR for a firm with tax-loss carryforwards is 8.3%, compared with 15.0% if the full-sample probabilities describe the transition matrix. The loss-carryforward firms are also much less sensitive to the inflation rate under the post-1981 probabilities, primarily because the chance that these firms will ever return to taxable status is lower, and so the present value of the tax allowances, the part of the calculation which is sensitive to the inflation rate, is much reduced.

10.5 Conclusions

This paper has explored the recent incidence of tax-loss carryforwards amongst nonfinancial corporations. Fifteen percent of all firms report loss carryforwards. There are, however, some industries in which losses are being carried forward by a significant fraction of firms, and where current loss-offset restrictions significantly affect corporate tax incentives.

A firm's tax status is a key determinant of its investment incentives. For firms with tax-loss carryforwards, effective tax rates on plant and equipment may be significantly different from those for taxable firms that are able to utilize tax deductions as they accrue. For equipment investments under 1985 law, taxable firms face lower effective tax rates than do firms with loss carryforwards. The opposite is true for structures. These findings, coupled with the concentration of losses in some industries, suggest that previous attempts to estimate interindustry differences in effective tax rates neglect an important source of tax-rate variation. The differences between firms in the same industry, depending on their current tax status, may be even more substantial.

Our calculations may understate the economic importance of tax-loss carryforwards for several reasons. First, as we emphasize in the text, aggregate evidence suggests that tax losses are substantially more prevalent than our estimates imply. Second, we have modeled the incentive effects assuming that all firms face the economy-wide probabilities of transiting between taxable and nontaxable states. If some firms have precise knowledge about the pattern of tax liabilities they are likely to face, this may induce much larger swings in their investment and financial behavior as they take advantage of intertemporal changes in marginal tax rates. Third, our calculations of the incidence of loss carryforwards may not reflect the steady state to which the economy will move if the post-1981 depreciation schedule had remained in effect. Since the presence of highly accelerated depreciation allowances increases the chance that firms will generate tax losses, there could have been long-term shifts in the fractions of taxable and nontaxable firms.

Data limitations preclude us from considering firms with tax-credit carryforwards. Although many of the loss-carryforward firms in our sample also report either investment or foreign tax-credit carryforwards, there may also be substantial numbers of firms with credit carryforwards but no loss carryforwards. For these firms, the marginal tax rate on additional income may be substantially different from the statutory marginal tax rate. By omitting them, we understate the importance of firms whose marginal tax rates deviate from statutory values. Altshuler and Auerbach (1987) present a more complex model which addresses this issue.

Our effective tax rate calculations embody a number of strong assumptions about the stochastic process determining the tax status of firms. In particular, we maintain the fiction that firms face identical, time-invariant, exogenous probabilities of moving into and out of periods during which tax losses are carried forward. Each of these assumptions is unrealistic and could usefully be relaxed in future work. Perhaps the most intriguing direction for future work concerns the endogeneity of a firm's tax status. There are a wide range of corporate actions that affect marginal tax rates, ranging from the traditional investment and financing choices (see Cooper and Franks [1983] and Auerbach [1986]) to less frequently analyzed accounting choices (see Watts and Zimmerman [1986]). We know relatively little about what firms do in both the real and the financial domains in order to alter their tax status. The potential response of these corporate decisions are fundamental for analyzing the incentive effects of the corporate tax.

The substantial differences across firms in expected future tax-status may provide a useful source of variation that can be used to study how taxes affect financing and investment decisions. If the magnitude of debt tax shields are an important influence on the capital structure of firms, as in DeAngelo and Masulis (1980), then we should observe different borrowing policies from firms with substantial tax-loss carryforwards and those that have large accumulated potential carrybacks and are currently taxable. Firms of the latter kind have a larger tax incentive for borrowing than do those of the former, and this may yield testable predictions of how taxes affect financing choices.

Finally, we can speculate about how the Tax Reform Act of 1986 (passed after the first version of this paper was completed) will affect the incidence and impact of tax losses. The new law changes several provisions affecting firms with tax losses. First, it scales back investment incentives and thereby lowers the chance that high-growth firms undertaking substantial investment programs will experience tax losses. At the same time, firms with tax loss carryforwards will face smaller disincentives to invest in machinery and equipment (relative to structures) because equipment investments will no longer yield substantial amounts of negative taxable income in their early years. These effects imply that inter-firm differentials in investment incentives, as well as inter-asset differentials for firms with losses, are reduced by the new law. These contributions to "levelling the playing field" were not usually recognized in discussions of the new bill.

A final provision in the new law affects the extent to which firms can utilize tax loss carryforwards through merger. Prior to the 1986 Act, tax loss carryforwards from a target firm could, provided certain conditions were met, be utilized immediately. The new law reduces the rate at which the stock of loss carryforwards from the target can be applied to reduce the tax liability of the acquirer: no more than 7% of the transferred stock of losses can be utilized in any year. There are also new restrictions on the preservation of NOL carryforwards when a company is reorganized in a bankruptcy. Although our analysis has not discussed any of these provisions in detail, they all have a common effect in making tax losses less valuable for firms that have them. The new legislation restricts the alternatives available for a firm trying to utilize a stock of losses. It will increase the incentives to undertake investments that will yield taxable cash flows.

Appendix
Computing the Shadow Value of Tax Payments with Carrybacks

This appendix describes our procedure for calculating the shadow value of tax payments, a value that arises from their possible future use in permitting loss carrybacks. A dollar of tax payments is valuable because, according to current law, it may be used to offset a tax loss occurring in the following three years. However, its value is less than the present value of such deductions because there is some probability that the loss that is made deductible in the next three years would have been offset through carryforwards at some future date. Tax losses forgone in future periods also have a shadow value because the associated increase in taxable income will in turn lead to the possibility of eventual carryback.

To compute the value of the carryback option, consider a taxable firm and define v_{TT} as the expected carryback value of a one-dollar tax payment made in the second of a pair of adjacent taxable years. Define v_{LT} in parallel fashion. Let ω_{TL} denote the present value of the future deductions forgone when a loss is realized; it is also the present value of the tax payments which result from a one-dollar increase in taxable income for a firm that was taxable in the previous year but is currently not taxable. This follows from the fact that a carryback is used as soon as possible, which means the first year in which there is insufficient taxable income. The value of v_{TT} is given by:

$$(A.1) \quad v_{TT} = [\beta p_{TTL} + \beta^2 p_{TTT} p_{TTL} + \beta^3 p^2_{TTT} p_{TTL}](1 - \omega_{TL})$$
$$= \beta p_{TTL}[1 + \beta p_{TTT} + \beta^2 p^2_{TTT}](1 - \omega_{TL})$$

where $\beta = (1 - i)/(1 + r)$ denotes the discount factor applied when shifting a tax payment one year into the future. Equation (A.1) denotes the expected present value of the carrybacks associated with a one-dollar tax payment. By the same logic, we can define

$$(A.2) \quad v_{LT} = [\beta p_{LTL} + \beta^2 p_{LTl}p_{TTL} + \beta^3 p_{LTl}p_{TTl}p_{TTL}] (1 - \omega_{TL})$$

for currently taxable firms that were not taxable last year. Each of these expressions depends upon ω_{TL}, which is in turn given by

$$(A.3) \quad \omega_{TL} = p_{TLT}\beta(1 - v_{LT}) + p_{TLL}p_{LLT}\beta^2(1 - v_{LT})$$
$$+ \ldots + p_{TLL}p_{LLL}^{N-2}p_{LLT}\beta^N (1 - v_{LT})$$

where N is the maximum number of periods for which a loss may be carried forward. Solving these three equations for v_{TT}, v_{LT}, and ω_{TL} yields:

$$(A.4) \quad v_{TT} = [\alpha_{TT}(1 - \alpha_{TL})]/(1 - \alpha_{LT}\alpha_{TL})$$

$$(A.5) \quad v_{LT} = [\alpha_{LT}(1 - \alpha_{TL})]/(1 - \alpha_{LT}\alpha_{TL})$$

$$(A.6) \quad \omega_{TL} = [\alpha_{TL}(1 - \alpha_{LT})]/(1 - \alpha_{LT}\alpha_{TL}).$$

where $\alpha_{TT} = \beta p_{TTL}[1 + \beta p_{TTT} + \beta p_{TTT}^2]$, $\alpha_{LT} = \beta p_{LTL} + \beta^2 p_{LTl}p_{TTL}$ $+ \beta^3 p_{LTl}p_{TTl}p_{TTL}$, and $\alpha_{TL} = (1 - v_{LT})[\beta p_{TLT} + \beta^2 p_{TLL}p_{LLT} + \ldots + \beta^N p_{TLL}p_{LLT}p_{LLL}^{N-2}]$.

These shadow values are used in calculating the expected present value of tax liabilities. To account for firms' ability to carry losses back, we multiply each of the expected tax payments generated by the no-carryback analysis by either $(1 - v_{TT})$ or $(1 - v_{LT})$, depending on the firm's tax status. When a firm accrues a tax liability with a distribution of expected payments across many periods, the concurrent value of q_{TT} determines the fraction of the expected tax payment that will be paid immediately in a state following a taxable year. This amount is multiplied by $(1 - v_{TT})$. All of the remaining components associated with this accrued liability are multiplied by $(1 - v_{LT})$, since they occur in states where the firm will have just reentered taxable status. In the notation of section 10.3 this implies

$$(A.7) \quad v_{ts} = \begin{cases} v_{LT} & s > t \\ (q_{TT}^t v_{TT} + q_{LT}^t v_{LT})/(q_{TT}^t + q_{LT}^t) & s = t. \end{cases}$$

This can be substituted into equation (5) to evaluate the internal rate of return, r, and then the effective tax rate.

Notes

1. Cordes and Sheffrin (1983) calculate marginal tax rates using corporate tax-return data but they assume that firms cannot carry back either losses or

credits. This biases their findings toward the result that many firms face tax rates below the statutory maximum.

2. For an excellent summary of the recent debate surrounding average tax rates on large corporations, see the series of essays in *Tax Notes* 9 December 1985. The claim that sizable numbers of large corporations pay no tax is from McIntyre and Folen (1984) and McIntyre and Wilhelm (1986). Their calculations are based on the ratio of current tax payments to earnings, which bears little necessary relation to the firm's marginal tax status.

3. The extent to which firms can claim investment tax credits, foreign tax credits, R and D credits, and a number of other credits depends upon their taxable income. The ITC, for example, is limited to $25,000 + .90*max [0,Tax − 25,000]. Additional taxable earnings for a firm bound by this constraint would raise tax liability by only .10*τ, where τ is the statutory tax rate.

4. Cordes and Sheffrin (1983) were affiliated with the Office of Tax Analysis when they used the Treasury Corporate Tax Model to calculate the distribution of corporate marginal tax rates.

5. We also tried to find examples of loss-carryforward firms that did not appear in the COMPUSTAT sample. For example, we examined the 50 firms with the smallest current tax payments in McIntyre and Folen (1984) and found no cases of firms with loss carryforwards that were not in our sample.

6. Stickney, Weil, and Wolfson (1983) provide a detailed analysis of the accounting by one firm, General Electric, for its financial subsidiary.

7. It is difficult to gauge the importance of omitting the financial subsidiaries of some firms. We studied the published financial statements of several large financial subsidiaries, those of General Motors, Chrysler, General Electric, Ford, and Westinghouse, and in no case did we find evidence of tax-loss carryforwards in the subsidiary; this suggests that the biases from annual reports which exclude these subsidiaries may not be too severe.

8. Although in principle we could model firm heterogeneity and estimate separate transition probabilities for firms with similar characteristics, the sparseness of some off-diagonal cells in our transition matrices suggests that it would be difficult to obtain precise estimates. For example, there are only 14 firms which make the taxable-loss carryforward-taxable transition in 1983–84, and only 20 firms in the loss carryforward-taxable-taxable cell. Another possibility is using a mover-stayer model to describe the data, allowing some firms to be "stayers" in the taxable state. This might be explored in future work.

9. The steady-state probabilities are defined as follows: $q_{LL} = q_{LT}(1 - p_{TLT})/p_{LLT}$, $q_{LT} = q_{TL} = 1/[2 + p_{LTT}/(1 - p_{TTT}) + (1 - p_{TLT})/p_{LLT}]$, and $q_{TT} = q_{TL}p_{LTT}/(1 - p_{TTT})$.

10. The transition probabilities in this table are not directly comparable to those in table 10.5 for two reasons. First, in looking at COMPUSTAT data over a period of many years, we confront the problem of missing values for the tax-loss variables. We assume (very conservatively) that all missing values correspond to taxable years; this substantially overstates the chance of escaping from the tax-loss state. Second, the sample selection problem alluded to in the text with respect to firms which merged or went bankrupt is likely to be much more important in this analysis of transitions over a long time-period than in our previous tabulations, which spanned only four years. The net effect of this bias is unclear.

11. An asset need not have a negative total tax liability for this to occur. Consider a project with negative taxable earnings in its early years, followed

by significant taxable income later in its life. Even if the project's tax payments have a positive net present value, the cost of forgoing tax benefits in the near term may exceed the gain from postponing tax liabilities later in the project.

12. Previous work treating this endogeneity has considered only very simple models; see, for example, Auerbach (1986).

13. The notation L^s refers to s consecutive years of tax-loss carryforwards.

14. By focusing on expected returns, we are implicitly assuming that tax-status risk is entirely nonsystematic. In practice, most firms are more likely to experience tax-loss carryforwards during recessions; this imparts a potentially important systematic component to these tax streams.

15. We also truncate project returns and accrued tax liabilities after forty years. The results are insensitive to these truncations.

16. This overstates the effect of carryforward provisions. When a nontaxable firm incurs a tax liability, there are two possibilities concerning its current income: it may be negative, adding to previous losses, or it may be positive but completely offset by previous losses. In the former case, the additional tax liability (if negative) will add new losses to be carried forward. If the additional tax liability is positive, it will reduce the new losses carried forward. In either case, the tax liability will have a limit of fifteen years during which it can be realized. After that time, the marginal impact on the stock of loss carryforwards disappears. In the case where the firm is currently offsetting some of its previous tax losses, however, the situation is more complicated, since the marginal impact of the accrued tax liabilities will be to increase or decrease the working off of old loss carryforwards. The marginal contribution of a new gain or loss to the tax losses carried forward therefore has fewer than N years to expiration.

17. An additional restriction which has been changed over the years governs the extent to which firms can use investment tax credits to offset taxable income before credits. To model this provision, we would have to modify our analysis to include an intermediate state between taxable and nontaxable, in which a firm pays taxes but has tax credits carried forward. Unfortunately, because our data limitations prevent us from estimating transition probabilities with respect to this state, we must omit it.

18. Ideally, the rate used to discount the components in the carryback shadow price would be the after-tax rate of return for the project. However, this would have required an iteration procedure which seemed inappropriate given the parameter's minor role.

19. This fraction undoubtedly overstates the share of taxable firms in the population as a whole, since we generate smaller estimates of aggregate tax losses than the IRS tabulations suggest.

20. We assume that when structures are purchased they are depreciated only once. Gordon, Hines, and Summers (1987) conclude that "churning" is not profitable for corporations, although it may be attractive to partnerships. We also ignore asset-related differences in leverage capacity. If structures can carry more debt than equipment, as is commonly supposed, then loss-carryforward firms may face greater disincentives to purchasing structures than we have reported.

21. For examples of previous calculations of industry-specific ETRs, see Auerbach (1983), Fullerton (1985), or Fullerton and Henderson (1984).

References

Altshuler, Rosanne, and Alan J. Auerbach. 1987. The significance of tax law asymmetries: An empirical investigation. University of Pennsylvania. Mimeo.

Anderson, Theodore W., and L. A. Goodman. 1957. Statistical inference about Markov chains. *Annals of Mathematical Statistics* 28:89–110.

Auerbach, Alan J. 1983. Corporate taxation in the United States. *Brookings Papers on Economic Activity* 2:451–505.

———. 1986. The dynamic effects of tax law asymmetries. *Review of Economic Studies* 53:205–226.

Cooper, Ian, and Julian Franks. 1983. The interaction of financing and investment decisions when the firm has unused tax credits. Working paper. London: London Business School.

Cordes, Joseph J., and Steven M. Sheffrin. 1983. Estimating the tax advantage of corporate debt. *Journal of Finance* 38:95–105.

DeAngelo, Harold, and Ronald Masulis. 1980. Optimal capital structure under corporate and personal taxation. *Journal of Financial Economics* 8:3–30.

Dworin, Lowell. 1985. On estimating corporate tax liabilities from financial statements. *Tax Notes*, 9 December, pp. 965–70.

Fullerton, Don. 1985. The indexation of interest, depreciation, and capital gains: A model of investment incentives. Working paper no. 1655. Cambridge, Mass.: National Bureau of Economic Research.

Fullerton, Don, and Yolanda Henderson. 1984. Investment effects of taxes on income from capital: Alternative policies in the 1980s. In *The legacy of Reaganomics: Prospects for long-term growth,* edited by Charles R. Hulten and Isabel Sawhill. Washington, D.C.: Urban Institute Press.

Gordon, Roger, James Hines, and Lawrence Summers. 1987. Notes on the tax treatment of structures. Chapter 7 in this volume.

Hulten, Charles R., and Frank C. Wykoff. 1981. The measurement of economic depreciation. In *Depreciation, inflation, and the taxation of income from capital,* edited by Charles R. Hulten. Washington, D.C.: Urban Institute Press.

McIntyre, Robert S., and Robert Folen. 1984. *Corporate income taxes in the Reagan years.* Washington, D.C.: Citizens for Tax Justice.

McIntyre, Robert S., and David Wilhelm. 1986. *Money for nothing: The failure of corporate tax incentives, 1981–1984.* Washington, D.C.: Citizens for Tax Justice.

Majd, Saman, and Stewart Myers. 1985. Valuing the government's tax claim on risky corporate assets. Working paper no. 1553. Cambridge, Mass.: National Bureau of Economic Research.

———. 1987. Tax asymmetries and corporate tax reform. Chapter 11 in this volume.

Mayer, Colin P. 1986. Corporation tax, finance, and the cost of capital. *Review of Economic Studies* 53:93–112.

Mintz, Jack. 1985. An empirical estimate of imperfect loss offsetting and effective tax rates. Forthcoming, *Quarterly Journal of Economics.*

Stickney, Clyde, Roman Weil, and Mark Wolfson. 1983. Income taxes and tax transfer leases: GE's accounting for a Molotov cocktail. *Accounting Review* 58:439–59.

Watts, Ross, and Jerold Zimmerman. 1986. *Positive accounting theory.* Englewood Cliffs: Prentice-Hall.

Comment   David F. Bradford

Economists have often noted the consequences for incentives to invest that follow from the nonrefundability of the corporation income tax. As we usually model it, a firm that shows a current loss on its tax books is unable to take advantage of the deduction of depreciation allowances (or of other deductions, such as interest payments, for that matter)—a disincentive to invest. On the other hand, for a firm that expects to have a tax-loss position in the future, the positive payoff from an incremental project undertaken in the present may be reaped free of tax, giving an extra boost to investment incentives. Examples can readily be constructed of large variation in incentives according to the tax-loss position of the firm.

It is another matter to determine the practical importance of these variations, the project undertaken here by Auerbach and Poterba. As the authors convincingly explain, the task is more daunting than one might have expected. This is partly because data on the occurrence of tax-loss carryforwards are buried in tax returns that are not accessible to the public. It is also because the tax law is complex, as are the options available to the firm to deal with the situation. I shall comment on the approaches Auerbach and Poterba took to both the observational and the analytical difficulties.

A loss in a given year, understood as a negative amount of income calculated according to the usual tax rules, can be carried back and applied against positive levels of the tax base ("income") in the previous three years. For these cases, the tax is, in effect, refundable. To be unable to use currently negative taxable income to save on current taxes, the firm must be in a "tax-loss carryforward" position. In this situation, the firm cannot take an immediate deduction against taxable income but may carry the loss forward to apply it against profits any time in the next fifteen years. The divergence here from refundability derives in part from the possibility that there will be insufficient positive income during the next fifteen years and in part from the time value of money: saving a dollar of taxes in the future is worth less than saving a dollar now.

The major empirical undertaking in this paper is to analyze the experience of actual firms. Since tax-return data, other than on a highly aggregated basis, are not available, the authors have applied their ingenuity to uncovering substitutes. Firms do report some information

David F. Bradford is the associate dean of the Woodrow Wilson School and professor of Economics and Public Affairs at Princeton University, and a research associate of the National Bureau of Economic Research.

about their tax situations in annual reports and 10-K filings with the SEC. Unfortunately, the most readily available collected set of data from corporate accounts, the COMPUSTAT data base, reports tax-loss carryforwards on a different basis than do tax accounts. Actual annual reports and/or 10-K statements include data that come closer than do those reported on the COMPUSTAT tape to providing tax-loss carryforwards according to tax accounting conventions, but the figures must be collected from each firm for each year individually. The authors have therefore organized an army of research assistants to collect figures from these decentralized sources. These data are used both on their own, for the evidence they provide about the significance of tax-loss carryforward status, and as the basis for assessing the reasonableness of results obtained by using COMPUSTAT data as though they were true tax data.

Auerbach and Poterba's principal empirical finding is that loss-carryforward status is rather persistent. Transition probabilities estimated on the basis of individually collected data for 1983 and 1984 suggest that a firm with no loss carryforward in a year has a probability of 97.4% of being in the same position the next year and a firm with a loss carryforward has a probability of 91.3% of carrying a loss forward again in the next year. The second-order transition data indicate that the probability that a firm that has had two "good" years (i.e., has avoided tax-loss carryforward status for two successive years, years that could have had negative taxable income before loss carryback) will at least not have such a bad next year as to drop into tax-loss carryforward status is 97.7%; a firm with two past bad years will have another one (i.e., insufficient positive profit to soak up past loss carryforwards) with a probability of 91.7%. (All these figures are from table 10.4.)

Two problems should be noted about the data supporting Auerbach-Poterba's empirical findings. They may in part explain the finding that the aggregate of loss carryforwards in the authors' sample is substantially below aggregate estimates based on IRS data. One problem they point out themselves: there are divergences between the particular way divisions of firms are consolidated for tax and annual report purposes. They do not attempt to assess the importance of the resulting bias. I do not know how the accounts are kept. It seems implausible that the unit chosen for financial reporting purposes calculates a hypothetical taxable income; rather the tax status of the actual component firms (reflecting the consolidation chosen for tax purposes) is presumably allocated somehow to the financial reporting unit. If so, there may be no bias in the Auerbach-Poterba transition estimates, which are based on equity value weights. If the financial reporting unit does calculate a hypothetical tax position, the use of financial accounts would bias the transition probabilities in the direction of increasing the apparent importance of tax-loss carryforward status, since it will generally be in the interest of firms to choose an aggregation for tax purposes that eliminates carryforwards, whereas carryforwards are of little importance for financial reporting.

A second, and I should think more serious, source of bias in the other direction was pointed out to me by Roger Gordon and has to do with the selection of firms for inclusion in the COMPUSTAT data set. Firms in the COMPUSTAT file have to have survived to the date of observation. Presumably, firms with tax losses are likely candidates for merger with profitable firms, and if it is the profitable firm that carries on there is a potential bias in the data against the appearance of tax-loss carryforwards. Furthermore, because the firms chosen by Auerbach-Poterba for closer examination were those showing tax-loss carryforwards on the COMPUSTAT tape, any such bias would carry over as well to the data they gathered from direct inspection of company reports. This may lead to misstatement of the persistence of loss carryforwards.

To put the empirical findings to use in assessing the effect of the carryforward rules on investment incentives, Auerbach-Poterba make the extreme assumption that carryforward status is an exogenous stochastic event, generated by a second-order Markov process. That means all one needs to know to determine the probability distribution of future carryforward status is the status in the two immediately preceding periods. Even with this rather strong simplification, accounting for the contingent quality of carrying losses backward and forward makes simulating the cash flow consequences at the company level for an equity-financed investment difficult. I find the details of Auerbach-Poterba simulation technique hard to follow, but I believe it can be described as calculating the after-tax consequences of undertaking a typical investment in equipment or structures for each of the possible evolutions of a company's tax-carryforward status, weighting these together by the probabilities generated by the second-order Markov process (as a function of initial conditions) to produce the expected cash flow from each of the two investments. In each case the assumed before-tax rate of return is 6% real, and the "expected effective tax rate" is the difference between 6% and the internal rate of return on the company's expected cash flow.

To me the most interesting "bottom line" results are to be found in table 10.8, which shows the expected effective tax rates under tax laws in effect in 1965, 1975, and 1985 for firms starting from a position of two successive taxable years, two successive loss-carryover years, and for firms that are always taxable (and for which there is therefore a perfect loss offset). The effective tax rates for the first two classes reflect the balance between the disadvantages of reduced value of deductions and increased value of otherwise taxable receipts in loss-carryforward years. Owing to the latter effect, the expected effective tax rates of firms in either initial condition may be lower than those of firms with perfect loss offset, and in every case the currently taxable firm derives an increase in investment incentive from the greater weight on the probability of future receipts that are nontaxable than on deductions that cannot be currently used.

Timing is important to these results and it may be asked whether they give a sufficiently rich picture of the effect of the carryforward provisions. The investment opportunities considered consist simply of current purchase of either equipment or structures (defined by different exponential depreciation rates and by different tax treatments). However, there are other possibilities. For example, if a program of regular annual investment of a dollar per year were substituted for a simple current investment of a dollar in the analysis, the law with immediate loss offset would presumably generate a lower effective tax rate in every case. Another important class of investment possibilities consists of alternative starting dates for projects, especially postponement of investment activity, that might be considered. The incentive effects of the tax-loss carryforward provisions on these choices may be much stronger than those on the simple choice between currently investing or not. There are also many other ways than by adjusting real investment activity that a firm might react to the prospect of being in a tax-loss carryforward position in the future; restructuring financial arrangements (such as by taking more advantage of leasing) and even ownership arrangements (merging with a profitable firm) are examples.

In short, there remains much that might be done to build on the excellent foundation work, both empirical and analytical, that Auerbach and Poterba have accomplished.

11   Tax Asymmetries and Corporate Income Tax Reform

Saman Majd and Stewart C. Myers

11.1   Introduction

Under current (1985) law, corporate income is taxed only when positive. Although losses can be carried back to generate tax refunds up to the amount of taxes paid in the previous three years, losses must be carried forward once these tax refunds are used up. The present value per dollar carried forward is less than the statutory rate for two reasons: the firm may not earn enough to use the carryforwards before they expire, and carryforwards do not earn interest.

In previous work (Majd and Myers 1985), we showed that tax asymmetries can be modeled and valued as contingent claims, using option pricing theory combined with Monte Carlo simulation. Although the asymmetries' effects cannot be expressed in conventional summary measures such as effective tax rates, we did work out impacts on the after-tax net present values (NPVs) of incremental investment outlays. Tax asymmetries can dramatically reduce after-tax NPVs for high-risk investments, although the extent of reduction depends on the tax position of the investing firm. Tax asymmetries are irrelevant at the margin for a firm with sufficient other income that it always pays taxes on a marginal dollar of income or loss. Asymmetries may be the dominant tax effect for "stand-alone" projects, that is, for cases where the project and the firm are the same.

Saman Majd is assistant professor of finance at the Wharton School, University of Pennsylvania. Stewart C. Myers is Gordon Y Billard Professor of Finance at the Sloan School of Management, Massachusetts Institute of Technology, and research associate at the National Bureau of Economic Research.

This chapter develops previous work (Majd and Myers 1985). Comments on that paper from Alan Auerbach, Henry Jacoby, Michael Keen and Colin Mayer have significantly improved this chapter.

Here we focus on the *design* of the corporate income tax. We report the results of a series of numerical experiments comparing current (1985) tax law with a stylized tax "reform" proposal, with tax asymmetries of course emphasized. In doing so we have also improved the methods we used previously, notably by using more realistic and consistent numerical parameters.

We have also included an intelligent, although not fully optimal, project abandonment strategy in the simulations. The abandonment strategy links project life to ex post profitability. We constructed this link because fixing project life ex ante does not make sense under uncertainty, and because the extent to which tax-loss carryforwards can relieve tax asymmetries ought to depend on decisions about project life.

Section 11.2 briefly reviews prior work by others. Section 11.3 describes how option pricing concepts can be applied to value the government's tax claim on risky assets. Since no closed-form option-pricing formulas apply, values must be computed by numerical methods. Section 11.3, backed up by an appendix, also describes our calculations in more detail and presents after-tax values for a reasonably realistic "representative project" under various assumptions about project profitability, risk, and the tax position of the firm owning it. Section 11.4 investigates how the impact of tax asymmetries changes when a stylized, reformed tax system is substituted for the 1985 corporate tax law. Section 11.5 offers some concluding comments.

11.2   Prior Work

Formal analysis of the impacts of asymmetric taxation is just beginning to appear in the finance literature. For example, Cooper and Franks (1983) recognize that the firm's future tax rates are endogenous under asymmetric taxation with carryforward privileges. They use a linear programming framework to analyze the interaction between present and future investment and financing decisions induced by the tax system. They discuss some of the factors that limit financial transactions designed to offset tax losses and conclude that real investment by corporations can be distorted.

Ball and Bowers (1983), Galai (1983), Smith and Stultz (1983), Pitts and Franks (1984), and Green and Talmor (1985) all have noted the analogy between asymmetric taxes and call options. However, none of these papers has introduced realistic elements of the law, such as tax-loss carry provisions, nor have they obtained numerical estimates of the impact of tax asymmetries on asset values.

Building on earlier work in Auerbach (1983), Auerbach and Poterba (this volume) investigate the effects of tax asymmetries on corporate investment incentives. They take the tax position of the firm as exogenous and use estimates of the tax losses carried forward by a sample of corporations to estimate the probability that the firm will pay taxes in the future. They compute effective marginal tax rates on new investment using these "transition probabilities."

The assumption that the future tax position of the firm is exogenous may be reasonable for incremental investment decisions that are small compared with the other assets of the firm. However, this approach cannot handle investment decisions when the project must "stand alone" or when it is a significant part of the assets of the firm. Moreover, as Auerbach and Poterba note, using past data on tax-loss carryforwards will not allow them to analyze proposed changes in tax law, since the change in tax regime will also change the transition probabilities they estimate.

By contrast, we take future pretax cash flows of the firm or project as completely exogenous and thus can allow the future tax position of the firm or project to be completely endogenous. This approach can shed light on effects of proposed changes corporate tax law.

11.3 Taxes as Contingent Claims

In the absence of tax loss carrybacks or carryforwards, the government's tax claim is equivalent to a portfolio of European call options, one on each year's operating cash flow. The heavy line in figure 11.1

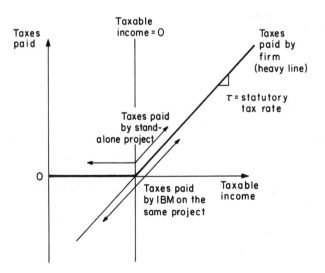

Fig. 11.1   Taxes paid as a function of taxable income.

shows taxes paid as a function of taxable income in a given year and has the same shape as a call option's payoff at exercise.

This option payoff function also describes the taxes paid on the income of a stand-alone project (i.e., taxes paid by a firm undertaking only one project). But in general the taxes paid on a project's income depend on the tax position of the firm owning it. Suppose the project is owned by IBM. It seems safe to say that IBM will not have tax-loss carryforwards at any time in the foreseeable future and will pay taxes at the margin at the full statutory rate. Thus any project losses can be offset against IBM's other income. The tax system *is* symmetrical for IBM when it considers an incremental capital investment project.

We can express these option analogies more formally. Consider a project that is the firm's only asset. Let the pretax operating cash flow and depreciation allowance at time t be y_t and d_t respectively. Ignore for now the investment tax credit (ITC) and assume that the project is all-equity financed. In the absence of tax-loss carryforwards or carrybacks, the project's after-tax cash flow at time t is:

$$c_t = y_t - \tau \max [y_t - d_t, 0].$$

The after-tax cash flow is the difference between the pretax operating cash flow and the government's claim on it. The government's claim is equivalent to τ European call options on the operating cash flow with exercise prices equal to the depreciation allowances.

Since the government taxes the firm's total income, the incremental effect of a new project on the value of the firm depends on the operating cash flows of the firm's existing assets and on their correlation with project cash flows. The after-tax cash flow for the firm and project is:

$$c_t = (y_t + z_t) - \tau \max [(y_t + z_t) - (d_t + d_{zt}), 0],$$

where z_t is the operating cash flow and d_{zt} the depreciation allowance for the firm without the new project. Because the government's claim is an option, the value of the tax claim on the sum of y_t and z_t is not the sum of the values of the tax claims on each taken separately.

Tax-loss carry privileges do not change the shape of the contingent tax payment drawn in figure 11.1. If the firm does not begin paying taxes until that year's taxable income exceeds cumulative tax losses carried forward from previous years, the vertical dividing line shifts to the right. Carrybacks shift the horizontal dividing line down from zero by the sum of taxes paid over the previous three years.

Again we can state this formally. Consider the case of unlimited carryforwards (but without any carrybacks). The tax loss carried forward to time t from the previous period is:

$$\theta_t = \max [\theta_{t-1} + d_{t-1} - y_{t-1}, 0].$$

The carryforward depends on the carryforward in the previous period, which in turn depends on the still-earlier carryforward, and so on. The carryforward at the beginning of the project (time zero) is given. The after-tax cash flow becomes:

$$c_t = y_t - \tau \max [y_t - d_t - \theta_t, 0].$$

Since θ_t depends on all realized incomes before time t, the payoff to the government (i.e., the tax paid) also depends on the realized incomes. It is straightforward to introduce the ITC and carrybacks and to limit the length of time allowed for carryforwards.

The carry privileges do not break the correspondence between the government's tax claims and a series of call options. The government holds a lottery across many possible options on y_t. Which option it ends up with depends on the firm's history of operating cash flow, y_0, $y_1, \ldots, y_{t-1}$. This particular form of path dependency makes it infeasible to use closed-form option-valuation formulas.

Therefore, with carryforwards and carrybacks, developing comparative statics is a numerical rather than an analytical exercise. However, despite the complexity of the government's contingent claim, we have found no instances in which carry privileges reverse the normal properties of call options. For example, we have always found that the present value of the government's tax claim on a stand-alone project increases with project risk, defined as the variance rate at which cash flows evolve, and also with project life. The government is better off if nominal interest rates increase, even if tax depreciation is indexed to inflation. Of course all of these results can be shown analytically, using the Black and Scholes (1973) formula, if carry privileges are ignored and the government's tax claim is modeled as a series of noninteracting calls, one for each year's cash flow.

11.3.1 Valuing the Government's Tax Claim

This section describes the numerical procedure used to calculate the present value (to the corporation) of the taxes paid on a risky project. Our discussion will be restricted to finding the present value of the taxes paid on an operating cash flow in year t, y_t, in the presence of unlimited carryforwards. The present value of the taxes paid on the stream of operating cash flows is simply the sum of the values of the claims on each future year's operating income. Extension of the procedure to include carrybacks and to limit the carryforward period is straightforward.

We exploit a general property of options first explicitly noted by Cox and Ross (1976): if the payoff to the option can be replicated by a portfolio strategy using traded securities, the present value of the option is the expected payoff forecasted under a risk-neutral stochastic process (conditional on the current values of the relevant state variables) and discounted at the risk-free rate. In other words, the option can be valued *as if* both it and the underlying asset are traded in a risk-neutral world.

The reason this risk-neutral valuation principle works is that options are not valued absolutely, but only relative to the underlying asset. For example, the Black and Scholes (1973) formula establishes only the *ratio* of call value to stock price. The stock price is marked down for risk because investors discount forecasted dividends at a risk-adjusted rate. The markdown of the stock to a current, certainty-equivalent value marks down the call value too, but not the ratio of call value to stock price.

The call is in fact riskier than the stock it is written on, and if at any instant investors demand an expected rate of return above the risk-free rate to hold the stock, they will demand a still higher return to hold the call. Suppose the required rate of return on the stock shifts up by enough to reduce the stock price by 1%. Then the call value will fall by more than 1%. However, the change in the stock's required return is not needed to calculate the fall in the call price. The change in stock price is a sufficient statistic.

Of course, the assets and options we are analyzing here are not explicitly traded. That may seem to violate a central assumption of the Black-Scholes model and its progeny. But we have actually taken only a small step away from the standard finance theory of capital investment under uncertainty. That theory assumes the firm maximizes market value, which in turn requires capital markets sufficiently complete that investors can find a security or portfolio of securities to "match" any investment project the firm may embark on. For every real asset, there must be a trading strategy using financial assets that generates a perfect substitute for the project in time pattern and risk characteristics of future cash returns. That assumption is routinely made for publicly traded firms. Incomplete markets are usually treated as a second- or third-order problem in light of the exceedingly rich menu of financial assets and trading strategies.

If investors can replicate real investment projects by trading in financial assets, they can also replicate options written on those projects by trading in the replicating assets and borrowing or lending. The heart of the classic Black and Scholes (1973) paper is the demonstration that a call's payoff can be exactly matched by a strategy of buying the underlying stock on margin, according to a hedging rule for the amount of stock held and the margin amount at each instant. Hedging rules can be written down for more complex or compound options. Thus, if markets are complete enough to support a market value standard for real assets, they are complete enough to support use of option-pricing theory.

There are other ways of justifying option-pricing techniques for options on nontraded assets. For example, the techniques also follow in the traditional capital asset pricing framework provided that asset returns are multivariate normal and there is a representative investor with constant absolute risk aversion (see, e.g., Brennan 1979 and Rubinstein 1976).

11.3.2 Solution Techniques

The path dependencies in our problem rule out closed-form solutions for the value of the government's tax claim. Moreover, these path dependencies would overwhelm the usual numerical option-valuation routines.

Fortunately, the rules for computing taxes are exogenous. Future tax payments are always unknown, but there are no *decisions* to be made about taxes. If the firm has the opportunity to use carrybacks or carryforwards, it does so at the first opportunity.[1] As far as taxes and carry privileges are concerned, the firm faces only an event tree, not a decision tree.

We can therefore employ a Monte Carlo simulation technique to approximate the distribution of the payoff conditional on the prior sequence of operating cash flow.[2] The rule determining the carryback or carryforward at any time (the path-dependent feature in this problem) is specified exogenously and depends only on past realizations of the operating cash flow. The Monte Carlo simulation technique exploits this feature of the problem by simulating the *sequence* of cash flows. Each time a value is generated for the cash flow y_t, the tax liability in t and any carryforward to period $t + 1$ are completely determined.

The simulation must also update the distributions of future cash flows every time a value is generated. Different assumptions about the stochastic process generating the time series of operating cash flow are possible. In our calculations, we break down operating cash flow as: operating cash flow = net revenues − fixed costs, $y_t = x_t − FC_t$, where "net revenues" means revenues less variable costs. We assume that FC_t is known with certainty, and that the stochastic processes generating each year's net revenue are perfectly correlated lognormal diffusions. That is, the forecast error in any one year's net revenue causes the same proportional change in the expectations of all future net revenues and the same proportional change in the present value of each year's future net revenues. If this assumption seems unduly restrictive, note that it is the usual justification for using a single risk-adjusted rate to discount a stream of cash flows. Thus it implicitly underlies standard practice (see Myers and Turnbull 1977 and Fama 1977).

The world of the simulation, however, is risk-neutral. Here is an example of how forecasting and discounting work in that world. Suppose forecasted net revenues grow at a rate $\hat{g}$ and are properly discounted at a rate $r + p$, where r is the risk-free interest rate and p is a risk premium:

$$V_0 = \int_0^H x_0 e^{-(r+p-\hat{g})} \, dt = \frac{x_0}{r + p - \hat{g}} (1 - e^{-(r+p-\hat{g})H}).$$

In the risk-neutral world of the simulation, discounting is at r, but the growth rate is reduced to $g \equiv \hat{g} - p$. Note that this does not change the present value calculated just above: g could be interpreted as a certainty-equivalent growth rate. This rate g would be used in the simulation.

By generating a large number of simulated cash flows, an approximate distribution for the government's tax payment in each year is obtained. The expected value is computed and discounted at the riskless rate to obtain the present value of the payment. The present value of the government's claim on the project is the sum of the present value of the claims on individual cash flows.

11.3.3   Limitations of Monte Carlo Simulation for Tax Analysis

Our method is limited because it cannot capture possible links between the future tax position of the firm and its investment and financing decisions.

Our numerical procedure must take project and firm cash flows as exogenous. We do not consider whether a future tax loss on a project undertaken today will affect future investment decisions. We also rule out cases in which today's project is managed differently, depending on its (or the firm's) tax position. This is undoubtedly unrealistic. For example, an otherwise profitable firm might find it less painful to stick with a losing project in order to establish an immediate tax loss, for the same reason that investors in securities often find it worthwhile to realize capital losses before the end of the tax year.[3]

This is one of several ways a firm can react to tax asymmetries. Four additional examples are: (1) the firm may change its accounting policies to shift taxable income over time; (2) the firm may seek to acquire another firm that has taxable income; (3) the firm may choose to "sell" its tax shields to another firm by a leasing arrangement;[4] (4) the firm may issue equity and buy bonds in order to generate taxable income.[5]

We admit that our results are uninteresting if firms can cash in tax losses at or near face value by these or other transactions. The transactions are not costless, however, and in many cases fall far short of exhausting the entire tax loss. Auerbach and Poterba (this volume) find that the percentages of a large sample of nonfinancial corporations with tax loss carryforwards ranged from about 7 (1981) to 14 (1984). In some industries the percentages were substantially higher. For example, 30% of airline companies had loss carryforwards in 1981 and 40% had them in 1984. They also find that once a firm falls into loss carryforwards, there is less than a 10% chance of climbing out in the following year.[6] If "selling tax losses" was feasible for these firms, the selling price was not attractive for 90% of them.

Our analysis, since it assumes operating cash flows are exogenous, gives a lower bound on after-tax project value and an upper bound on the impact of tax asymmetries.[7] It shows the potential gain from changing financing or investment decisions to shift taxes over time or between firms. Since we do not analyze these tax-shifting decisions specifically, we cannot give point estimates of the effect of tax asymmetries under current law. We can make useful comparisons of corporate tax reform proposals, however. If the *potential* cost of tax asymmetries is reduced under a new tax law, that law is better than the old one, other things equal, because it reduces the real costs firms are willing to incur to sell carryforwards, and because tax asymmetries are less likely to distort real investment decisions.

11.3.4   Example of Numerical Results

Table 11.1 and figure 11.2 show results for the base-case project that is described in detail in the Appendix. The project offers exponentially decaying net revenues, moderate fixed costs, and under certainty would have an economic life of twelve years. Inflation is $i = .06$ and the nominal risk-free rate is $r = .08$. The standard deviations of annual forecast errors for project cash flow are $\sigma_x = .15, .10$, and $.25$. In this section we discuss and plot NPVs only for the base case $\sigma_x = .15$.

Table 11.1   **Project Net Present Value as a Percentage of Initial Investment**

	Reform (indexed)		
ZEROTAX	SYMTAX	ASYMTAX	NOCARRY
−25.03	−17.46	−25.03	−25.03
−19.86	−14.00	−19.86	−19.86
−14.49	−10.45	−14.66	−14.71
−5.32	−5.02	−8.02	−8.79
7.97	3.21	1.05	−0.32
20.54	11.32	9.85	8.19
36.93	22.06	21.10	19.33
60.22	37.45	36.98	35.05

Note: Values are shown for symmetric tax (SYMTAX) and asymmetric tax with and without carry provisions (ASYMTAX and NOCARRY) for a range of pretax profitability (ZEROTAX). The parameters for the calculations correspond to the base case described in the Appendix.

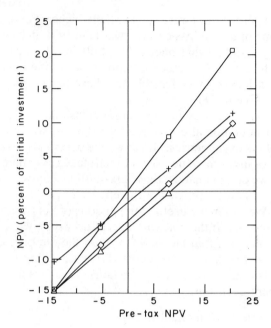

Fig. 11.2   Project NPV as a function of pretax NPV: reform with indexed depreciation. The parameters are for the base case described in the Appendix. Key: □ ZEROTAX   + SYMTAX   ◇ ASYMTAX   △ NOCARRY.

Four sets of numbers are shown in the table and plotted in the figure. These correspond to various extreme assumptions about the firm undertaking the project.

Suppose the project is owned by a firm like Penn Central with such large tax loss carryforwards that we may assume a zero effective tax rate on new projects. We will use ZEROTAX as a label for this extreme case in which pretax and after-tax NPV are the same.

At the other extreme, we can imagine the standard project undertaken by a firm taxed symmetrically on marginal investment because it is sure to pay taxes at the margin at the full statutory rate. We label this case SYMTAX.

The NPVs in table 11.1 are calculated under a stylized tax-reform law, with indexed, exponential tax depreciation to scrap value at the end of the project's or asset's economic life. The tax rate is $\tau = .33$. There is no investment tax credit. The Appendix reviews tax and numerical assumptions in more detail.

The project's values under ZEROTAX and SYMTAX provide two extreme cases. A third extreme case occurs when the firm and the project are the same. Tax asymmetries have their maximum impact for stand-alone projects. Of course, carrybacks and carryforwards mitigate the effects of the asymmetry. We assume three-year carrybacks and fifteen-year carryforwards (i.e., the current [1985] system). Results for stand-alone projects are labeled ASYMTAX. The ASYMTAX NPVs shown under "Reform" in table 11.1 are also plotted in figure 11.2.

The remaining numbers in table 11.1 and figure 11.2, labeled NO-CARRY, show the after-tax NPV of the stand-alone project with no carryforwards or carrybacks of losses allowed. Figure 11.2 shows that the NOCARRY NPVs are, as expected, somewhat worse than the ASYMTAX NPVs. Although carry privileges are valuable, they do not solve the tax asymmetry problem. We will not plot or comment on NOCARRY NPVs in the rest of the chapter.

Stand-alone project NPV (ASYMTAX) is always lower than either pretax NPV or NPV under a symmetric tax. A firm forced to take a negative NPV project would prefer a symmetric tax if it had the choice; second choice is no tax at all. A firm with a strongly positive NPV project would prefer no tax, but second choice is a symmetric tax. At some pretax NPV around zero, the firm is indifferent between no tax and symmetric tax. But the asymmetric tax is always in third place from the firm's point of view. It is furthest behind when pretax NPV is about zero.

In other words, if the firm must have unused tax loss carryforwards, it is better to have a lot of them, so that incremental investments effectively escape tax. The present value of the government's tax claim on a firm or stand-alone project is greatest when it is not known whether the firm or project will have to pay taxes.

Most of the following discussion focuses on experiments where NO-TAX or SYMTAX NPVs are not too far away from zero. Tax law is most likely to affect decisions about breakeven or near-breakeven investments. Investments with high positive or negative NPVs will be taken or rejected regardless of tax.

11.4 Tax Asymmetries and Tax Reform

So far we have confirmed the results of our prior work, that tax asymmetries can have a significant impact on the after-tax value of incremental investment. Now we arrive at the main goal of this chapter, which is to compare the potential impacts of tax asymmetries under current (1985) tax law with their impacts under a reformed law with lower marginal rates, exponential depreciation approximating economic depreciation, and no investment tax credit.

Compare the after-tax NPVs shown under "Reform" in table 11.2 with the after-tax NPVs under current law, shown on the right of the table under "ACRS." The comparisons are easier to grasp in figures

Table 11.2   Project Net Present Value as a Percentage of Initial Investment

	Reform (indexed)			ACRS		
ZEROTAX	SYMTAX	ASYMTAX	DIFF	SYMTAX	ASYMTAX	DIFF
		Base Case ($\sigma = .15$)				
−25.03	−17.46	−25.03	7.57	−9.60	−25.03	15.43
−19.86	−14.00	−19.86	5.86	−6.81	−19.86	13.05
−14.49	−10.45	−14.66	4.21	−4.05	−14.74	10.69
−5.32	−5.02	−8.02	3.00	−0.89	−9.40	8.51
7.97	3.21	1.05	2.16	4.76	−2.17	6.93
20.54	11.32	9.85	1.47	11.01	5.16	5.85
36.93	22.06	21.10	0.96	19.48	14.78	4.70
60.22	37.45	36.98	0.47	31.83	28.46	3.37
		Low Risk ($\sigma = .10$)				
−25.03	−17.46	−25.03	7.57	−9.60	−25.03	15.43
−19.86	−14.00	−19.86	5.86	−6.81	−19.86	13.05
−14.67	−10.53	−14.68	4.15	−4.01	−14.68	10.67
−8.94	−6.93	−9.46	2.53	−1.57	−9.81	8.24
−0.76	−2.31	−3.95	1.64	0.85	−5.82	6.67
9.63	4.07	3.06	1.01	5.27	−0.35	5.62
24.37	13.58	13.09	0.49	12.66	8.12	4.54
46.59	28.22	28.05	0.17	24.39	21.14	3.25
		High Risk ($\sigma = .25$)				
−25.03	−17.46	−25.03	7.57	−9.60	−25.03	15.43
−19.59	−13.87	−19.82	5.95	−6.79	−19.93	13.14
−12.04	−9.25	−14.39	5.14	−3.93	−15.44	11.51
9.26	4.27	0.05	4.22	5.78	−3.74	9.52
30.81	18.35	15.01	3.34	16.73	8.76	7.97
46.17	28.48	25.82	2.66	24.74	18.02	6.72
66.76	42.14	40.05	2.09	35.67	30.11	5.56
93.14	59.67	58.19	1.48	49.74	45.51	4.23

Note: Values are shown for symmetric tax (SYMTAX), asymmetric tax with carry provisions (ASYMTAX), and their difference (DIFF) for a range of pretax profitability (ZEROTAX). Each panel corresponds to a different level of project risk (σ) and compares a stylized tax reform (with indexed depreciation) with current law (ACRS).

11.3, 11.4, and 11.5, which plot after-tax NPVs for SYMTAX and ASYMTAX against pretax project profitability measured by ZEROTAX NPV. Each figure shows NPVs for a different standard deviation of project cash flows.

For a firm facing symmetric taxation on marginal investments, reform reduces after-tax NPV when pretax NPV is negative or moderately positive. This reflects the loss of the investment tax credit and accelerated depreciation. Such a firm is better off when it finds projects with strong positive NPVs, however, because reform lowers the marginal tax rate.

Table 11.3   **Project Net Present Value as a Percentage of Initial Investment**

	Reform (not indexed)			ACRS		
ZEROTAX	SYMTAX	ASYMTAX	DIFF	SYMTAX	ASYMTAX	DIFF
			Base Case (i = .06)			
− 25.03	− 19.32	− 25.03	5.71	− 9.60	− 25.03	15.43
− 19.86	− 15.86	− 19.86	4.00	− 6.81	− 19.86	13.05
− 14.49	− 12.42	− 14.72	2.30	− 4.05	− 14.74	10.69
− 5.32	− 8.47	− 9.30	0.83	− 0.89	− 9.40	8.51
7.97	− 1.60	− 1.93	0.33	4.76	− 2.17	6.93
20.54	5.92	5.76	0.16	11.01	5.16	5.85
36.93	16.23	16.15	0.08	19.48	14.78	4.70
60.22	31.25	31.23	0.02	31.83	28.46	3.37
			No Inflation (i = 0)			
− 25.02	− 17.46	− 25.02	7.56	− 6.79	− 25.02	18.23
− 19.86	− 14.00	− 19.86	5.86	− 4.00	− 19.86	15.86
− 14.49	− 10.46	− 14.67	4.21	− 1.14	− 14.68	13.54
− 5.21	− 5.00	− 8.00	3.00	3.32	− 8.16	11.48
8.72	3.68	1.57	2.11	10.42	0.98	9.44
20.54	11.31	9.85	1.46	16.65	8.97	7.68
36.49	21.76	20.87	0.89	25.17	19.37	5.80
59.88	37.23	36.83	0.40	37.74	34.17	3.57
			High Inflation (i = .12)			
− 25.05	− 21.09	− 25.05	3.96	− 12.26	− 25.05	12.79
− 19.86	− 17.62	− 19.86	2.24	− 9.46	− 19.86	10.40
− 14.54	− 14.27	− 14.92	0.65	− 6.79	− 14.85	8.06
− 5.25	− 10.96	− 11.28	0.32	− 4.34	− 10.57	6.23
9.29	− 4.17	− 4.40	0.23	1.10	− 4.39	5.49
20.90	2.39	2.26	0.13	6.48	1.51	4.97
36.57	11.96	11.91	0.05	14.41	10.16	4.25
60.96	27.53	27.52	0.01	27.18	23.97	3.21

Note: Values are shown for symmetric tax (SYMTAX), asymmetric tax with carry provisions (ASYMTAX), and their difference (DIFF) for a range of pretax profitability (ZEROTAX). Each panel corresponds to a different level of inflation (*i*) and compares a stylized tax reform (without indexed depreciation) with current law (ACRS).

Reform decreases the present value of taxes on stand-alone projects, except at large negative pretax NPVs. In those cases the project is abandoned almost immediately, before any taxes are paid under either current or reformed tax rules. Notice that the ASYMTAX NPVs equal the NOTAX NPVs in the top row of the base-case and low-risk blocks of table 11.2.

SYMTAX and ASYMTAX NPVs are equal at very high pre-tax NPVs, not shown in table 11.2 and off-scale in figures 11.3–11.5. When the stand-alone project is so profitable that it always pays taxes, tax asymmetries are irrelevant.

Table 11.4   **Project Net Present Value as a Percentage of Initial Investment**

	Reform (with interest)			Reform (without interest)		
ZEROTAX	SYMTAX	ASYMTAX	DIFF	SYMTAX	ASYMTAX	DIFF
			Base Case (i = .06)			
−25.03	−17.46	−25.03	7.57	−17.46	−25.03	7.57
−19.86	−14.00	−19.86	5.86	−14.00	−19.86	5.86
−14.49	−10.45	−14.65	4.20	−10.45	−14.66	4.21
−5.32	−5.02	−7.91	2.89	−5.02	−8.02	3.00
7.97	3.21	1.19	2.02	3.21	1.05	2.16
20.54	11.32	9.98	1.34	11.32	9.85	1.47
36.93	22.06	21.19	0.87	22.06	21.10	0.96
60.22	37.45	37.05	0.40	37.45	36.98	0.47
			No Inflation (i = 0)			
−25.02	−17.46	−25.02	7.56	−17.46	−25.02	7.56
−19.86	−14.00	−19.86	5.86	−14.00	−19.86	5.86
−14.49	−10.46	−14.67	4.21	−10.46	−14.67	4.21
−5.21	−5.00	−7.97	2.97	−5.00	−8.00	3.00
8.72	3.68	1.62	2.06	3.68	1.57	2.11
20.54	11.31	9.89	1.42	11.31	9.85	1.46
36.49	21.76	20.90	0.86	21.76	20.87	0.89
59.88	37.23	36.85	0.38	37.23	36.83	0.40
			High Inflation (i = .12)			
−25.05	−17.48	−25.05	7.57	−17.48	−25.05	7.57
−19.86	−14.00	−19.86	5.86	−14.00	−19.86	5.86
−14.54	−10.48	−14.68	4.20	−10.48	−14.68	4.20
−5.25	−4.92	−7.70	2.78	−4.92	−7.86	2.94
9.29	4.12	−2.23	1.89	4.12	2.01	2.11
20.90	11.60	10.26	1.34	11.60	10.07	1.53
36.57	21.84	21.04	0.80	21.84	20.90	0.94
60.96	37.96	37.57	0.39	37.96	37.47	0.49

Note: Values are shown for symmetric tax (SYMTAX), asymmetric tax with carry provisions (ASYMTAX), and their difference (DIFF) for a range of pretax profitability (ZEROTAX). Each panel corresponds to a different level of inflation (*i*) and compares the stylized tax reform (with indexed depreciation) with and without interest in carryforwards.

But in the interesting cases where pretax NPV is moderately positive or negative, stand-alone projects are worth more under reform despite the loss of the investment tax credit and accelerated depreciation. They are worth more *relative to* projects taxed symmetrically or not taxed at all.

These conclusions hold over a range of cash flow standard deviations, as figures 11.3–11.5 illustrate. We have also checked to confirm that they hold for projects with faster and slower tax and economic depreciation, and that they hold when the option to shorten or extend project life is "turned off" and project life is fixed at what it would be under certainty.

Table 11.5   **Effects of Uncertainty and Abandonment Strategy on Pretax and After-Tax NPVs**

σ_x	NOTAX[b]	Reform		ACRS	
		SYMTAX[b]	ASYMTAX	SYMTAX[b]	ASYMTAX
		A. NPVs with Project Life Fixed at Twelve Years			
.0[a]	−0.6	−3.7	−3.7	−1.2	−7.5
.15	0.3	−3.1	−8.6	−0.7	−17.1
.25	1.2	−2.4	−12.5	−0.2	−17.1
		B. NPVs with Option to Abandon before Year 12 or to Extend Life to Year 100			
.0[a]	−0.6	−3.7	−3.7	−1.2	−7.5
.15	26.8	15.4	14.1	14.2	8.8
.25	54.8	34.2	31.7	29.3	23.0

Note: NPV as percentage of project investment. Initial profitability and other project assumptions are given in table 11.A.1.

[a]We actually used $\sigma_x = .001$ in the Monte Carlo simulation. Note that the option to abandon early or extend project life become valueless as $\sigma_x \to 0$. Thus the figures in the first row of each panel are the same.

[b]The results in these columns should in principle be identical in Panel A. Differences reflect numerical errors introduced by the Monte Carlo simulation.

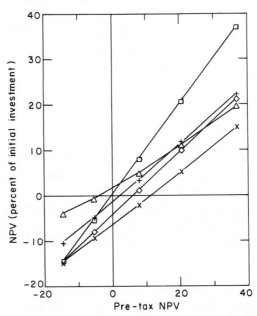

Fig. 11.3   Project NPV as a function of pretax NPV: reform with indexed depreciation versus ACRS. The parameters are for the base case described in the Appendix. Key: □ ZEROTAX + SYMTAX (reform) ◇ ASYMTAX (reform) △ SYMTAX (ACRS) × ASYMTAX (ACRS).

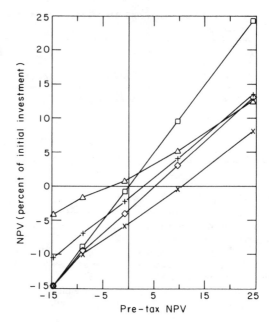

Fig. 11.4   Project NPV as a function of pretax NPV: reform with indexed depreciation versus ACRS, when cash flow volatility
is 10% (other parameters are for the base case described in
the Appendix). Key: □ ZEROTAX   + SYMTAX (reform)   ◇ ASYMTAX (reform)   △ SYMTAX (ACRS)
× ASYMTAX (ACRS).

11.4.1   Indexing Depreciation

Table 11.3 and figures 11.6, 11.7, and 11.8 show NPVs when reform
does not include indexed tax depreciation. (The definitions of indexed
and nonindexed depreciation are reviewed in the Appendix.) The format is identical to that of table 11.2 except that cash flow standard
deviation is held at $\sigma_x = .15$ and the inflation rate is varied from .06
(the base case) to .12 and zero. Note that the "Reform" NPVs calculated under zero inflation match the base case NPVs in table 11.2,
except for minor numerical errors introduced by the Monte Carlo
simulation.

Without indexing higher inflation naturally means lower after-tax
NPVs. Otherwise the patterns we noted in table 11.2 remain in table
11.3. Reform hurts symmetrically taxed projects when pretax NPV is
below or around zero, but helps when pretax NPV is strongly positive.
Stand-alone projects are uniformly helped, both absolutely and relative
to symmetrically taxed projects.

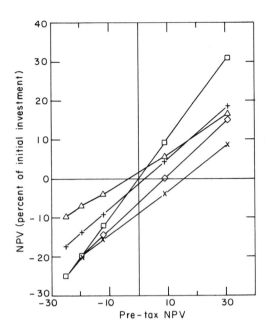

Fig. 11.5   Project NPV as a function of pretax NPV: reform with indexed depreciation versus ACRS, when cash flow volatility
is 25% (other parameters are for the base case described in
the Appendix). Key: □ ZEROTAX   + SYMTAX (reform)   ◇ ASYMTAX (reform)   △ SYMTAX (ACRS)
× ASYMTAX (ACRS).

11.4.2   Paying Interest on Tax-Loss Carryforwards

Paying interest on tax-loss carryforwards is a natural remedy for tax
asymmetries. However, it is not necessarily a complete remedy. Paying
interest on carryforwards works if the firm is sure to pay taxes eventually. If not, the government's option retains value, just as a call option
does if the exercise price increases at the interest rate.

Table 11.4 and figure 11.9 show the extent to which the remedy
works. Even with interest on carryforwards, there is a gap between
ASYMTAX and SYMTAX NPVs. Consider the base-case project at a
profitability level yielding a pretax NPV of 7.97 and an after-tax NPV
under symmetric taxation of 3.21. (See the top block of numbers in
table 11.4.) Allowing interest on carryforwards increases ASYMTAX
NPV from 1.05 to 1.19. This represents an improvement but does not
eliminate the effects of the asymmetry. Allowing interest on carryforwards makes less difference (compared with reform without interest)
when pretax value is very low (ASYMTAX approaches ZEROTAX) or
very high (ASYMTAX approaches SYMTAX).

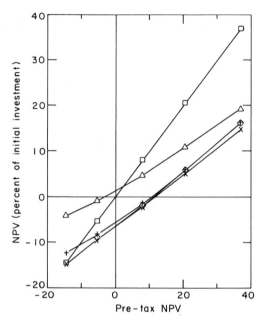

Fig. 11.6   Project NPV as a function of pretax NPV: reform without indexed depreciation versus ACRS. The parameters are for the base case described in the Appendix. Key: ☐ ZERO-TAX   + SYMTAX (reform)   ◇ ASYMTAX (reform)   △ SYMTAX (ACRS)   × ASYMTAX (ACRS).

The other two panels in table 11.4 show the effect of interest on carryforwards when inflation is zero or 12%: allowing interest makes a bigger difference to ASYMTAX NPV when inflation is high, but the effect of the asymmetries remains.

Allowing interest on loss carryforwards completely removes the burden of tax asymmetries only if the stand-alone firm or project is certain to regain tax-paying status sooner or later. But on this point full certainty requires immortality for the firm or project and no limit on the carryforward period. In our simulations the investment project may live to year 100—probably a good approximation of immortality—but it may be abandoned much earlier if its ex post performance is poor. The gap between SYMTAX and ASYMTAX NPVs with interest on carryforwards shows that carryforwards have no value to dead projects. Now if tax law allowed the firm to add a life insurance premium as well as interest to unused loss carryforwards, the potential extra burden of tax asymmetries would be essentially eliminated. The life insurance premium would equal the probability that the firm generating the carryforwards would pass away in the next tax year.

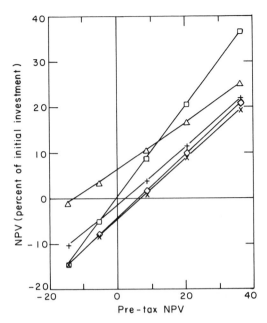

Fig. 11.7   Project NPV as a function of pretax NPV: reform without indexed depreciation versus ACRS, when inflation is 0% (other parameters are for the base case described in the Appendix). Key: □ ZEROTAX   + SYMTAX (reform)   ◇ ASYMTAX (reform)   △ SYMTAX (ACRS)   × ASYMTAX (ACRS).

11.4.3   Uncertainty and Abandonment

We conclude with a brief comment on the role of uncertainty and abandonment strategy in our simulation results.

Figures 11.3–11.5 confirm that the present value of the government's tax claim on a firm or stand-alone project increases with the risk (standard deviation) of the firm's or project's cash flows. But not all of the differences between SYMTAX and ASYMTAX NPVs can be attributed to risk. Some would persist under certainty, simply because the stand-alone project may not be profitable enough, at least in its early years, to use all the tax shields allotted to it.

Panel A of table 11.5 gives NPVs when risk disappears. First read across the row labeled $\sigma_x = 0$. The ZEROTAX NPV is effectively zero. Under Reform tax assumptions, NPV is about -4% of project investment for both a tax-paying firm (SYMTAX) and the stand-alone project. Now read down the columns under "Reform": as risk increases, there is no change in SYMTAX NPVs (the small differences reported are due to numerical errors in the Monte Carlo simulation),

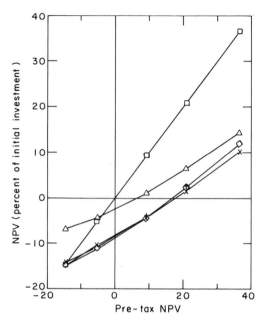

Fig. 11.8   Project NPV as a function of pretax NPV: reform without indexed depreciation versus ACRS, when inflation is 12% (other parameters are for the base case described in the Appendix). Key: □ ZEROTAX   + SYMTAX   (reform) ◇ ASYMTAX   (reform)   △ SYMTAX   (ACS) × ASYMTAX (ACRS).

but a steady decrease in after-tax NPVs for the stand-alone project. At least for projects like those examined in this chapter—projects with smooth downward trends in operating income—tax asymmetries have virtually no effect in the absence of risk. They increase the tax burden on incremental investment in risky assets but not on investment in safe assets.

The results grouped under "ACRS" in panel A tell a different story. The present value of the government's tax claim on the stand-alone project is about −7% of project investment (−7.5 vs. −0.6). The present value of taxes increases further as risk increases, but clearly the largest part of the damage done to the ASYMTAX NPVs can be traced to *deferral* of the stand-alone project's investment tax credit and ACRS write-offs.

The NPVs in panel A of table 11.5 were calculated after "turning off" the option to abandon the project early or to extend its life beyond its optimal life under certainty. We wanted to show how asymmetric taxation and risk interact with project life fixed.

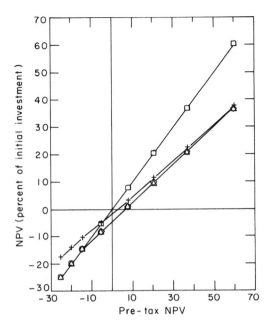

Fig. 11.9   Project NPV as a function of pretax NPV: reform (with indexed depreciation) with and without interest on carryforwards. The parameters are for the base case described in the
Appendix. Key: □ ZEROTAX   + SYMTAX (with interest)   ◇ ASYMTAX (with interest)   △ ASYMTAX (without interest).

Panel B shows what happens when the option is turned on again.
The option sharply increases pretax NPVs as risk increases, because
the firm can bail out of the project, recovering part of the initial capital
outlay, if ex post performance is poor but continue almost indefinitely
if performance is sufficiently good. The option likewise increases after-
tax NPVs, even for the stand-alone project. In other words, additional
risk adds more value to the option to abandon early or extend than it
adds to the government's call options on project cash flows. The government's options still have significant value, however. For example,
when $\sigma_x = .25$, they are worth 3% of project investment under tax
reform (34.2 vs. 31.7) and 6.3% of investment under current law (29.3
vs. 23.0). Note that the latter difference is less than the comparable
difference for $\sigma_x = 0$. Thus, under current law, the option to abandon
or extend may interact with the government's call options to reduce
the value of those options as risk increases. That does not, however,
affect the main results of this chapter, which rest on comparisons of
after-tax NPVs at given risk levels under current tax law and stylized

tax reform. The potential costs and distortions introduced by tax asymmetries depend on the differences between SYMTAX and ASYMTAX NPVs at given levels of investment risk. Under current tax law, these differences are dramatic regardless of risk and regardless of whether the option to abandon or extend project life is "turned on." Under our stylized tax reform the differences are much smaller.

11.4.4   Investment in Intangible Assets

Our tax reform is too pure for real life. Many of the impurities of actual tax reform make the potential costs of tax reform worse. For example, the results presented so far overstate the difference reform might make because most reform proposals continue to allow corporations to expense investment in intangibles. Research and development (R&D) outlays are expensed, for example, as are most startup costs and advertising, which is sometimes intended to generate payoffs in the medium or long term.

Under current law, the present values of tax shields generated by investment in tangible and intangible assets are roughly the same. That is, the present value of ACRS write-offs plus the investment tax credit is roughly equal to the cost of the asset, and therefore roughly equivalent to writing off the asset when it is bought. High-tech companies that invest largely in R&D or other intangibles are not materially disadvantaged compared with smokestack companies that invest in tangible capital assets, providing both types of companies pay taxes year in and year out at the same marginal rate.

For stand-alone projects, however, shifting investment from tangible to intangible assets makes the burden of tax asymmetries worse. Moreover, that burden is carried over to tax reform proposals that allow intangible investments to be expensed.

In other words, tax reform that sets economically sensible tax depreciation schedules only for tangible assets will tend to slant investment toward R&D and other intangibles: high-tech companies will gain *relative to* smokestack companies as long as both types pay taxes regularly. However, the potential burden of tax asymmetries on high-tech projects or companies will remain substantial.

11.5   Summary

In this chapter we combine option-pricing theory with Monte Carlo simulation to derive numerical estimates of the potential effects of tax asymmetries. We confirm earlier results showing that asymmetries *can* have substantial effects on the after-tax NPVs of incremental investment projects. We go on to a more refined and detailed investigation, comparing current (1985) law with a stylized reform that eliminates the investment tax credit and sets tax depreciation approximately equal to economic depreciation. The reformed marginal corporate tax rate is 33%.

This reform would increase the present value of taxes on incremental investments by firms that always pay taxes but *decrease* the present value of taxes on stand-alone projects. Reform dramatically reduces the potential burden of tax asymmetries.

The magnitude of these shifts in tax burden of course depends on numerical assumptions. However, the direction of the effects holds up over all our experiments. The experiments varied risk, the rate of economic depreciation, and the ratio of fixed to variable cost. We also generated results under reform with and without inflation indexing of tax depreciation, and with and without interest on tax-loss carryforwards. Although these measures help, they do not completely eliminate the effects of tax asymmetries.

There is more work to be done. For example, we would like to model uncertain inflation and develop a better understanding of its effects on value under asymmetric taxation. We expect our general conclusions to continue to hold, but this will enable us to make better recommendations regarding inflation indexing and its likely impact on asset values.

Although our methodology allows us to analyze a wide variety of tax codes in considerable detail, it requires that the pretax cash flows of the firm or project not be affected by the tax rules. There are interesting issues regarding the effect of the tax system on the distribution of future cash flows that we have not addressed.

Appendix
Numerical Assumptions and Design of Simulations

Virtually any a priori belief about the magnitude of effects of tax asymmetries might be confirmed by a cleverly constructed numerical example. Many of these examples would have at least one practical analogue somewhere in the corporate sector.

Because our examples are intended to bring out the general effects of tax reform on tax asymmetries, a "representative" investment project is called for. Therefore our numerical examples start with a base-case investment project reflecting the implicit assumptions of the stylized tax reform proposal we concentrate on. We want to avoid results that might be construed as reflecting our choice of an atypical base-case project. Our base project is therefore regular and unexceptional.

Project Life under Certainty

If tax and economic depreciation are exponentially declining, we want project cash flows to decline in the same way. Ignore taxes, and consider a project requiring an investment outlay of 1, with expected nominal cash inflows of $y_t = x_t - FC_t$. FC_t stands for "fixed cost," but for the moment we set $FC_t = 0$.

If both the asset value and "variable" cash flow x_t decay at the expected nominal rate $\hat{\delta}$, project NPV for economic life H[8] is:

$$NPV = -1 + \int_0^H x_0 e^{-(r+p+\hat{\delta})t} dt + e^{-(r+p+\hat{\delta})H},$$

where r is the nominal risk-free interest rate, p a risk premium, $r + p$ is the expected opportunity cost of capital, and $e^{-(r+p+\hat{\delta})H}$ is the present value of the proceeds from sale of assets at $t = H$.

Since our simulations take place in a hypothetical risk-neutral world, we may as well translate immediately to certainty equivalent flows. The decay rate of the certainty equivalents of x_t is $\delta \equiv \hat{\delta} + p$. Discounting at the risk-free rate r:

(A1) $$NPV = -1 + \int_0^H x_0 e^{-(r+\delta)t} dt + e^{-(r+\delta)H},$$

Since this transformation does not affect NPV or decisions about project life H, we assume certainty in the following discussion.

The project summarized by equation (A1) is nicely consistent, because the value of the stream of cash flows x_t does decline at the assumed rate δ. However, project or asset life has only a bit part in the story. Remember that we assume certainty. If NPV > 0, the project would never be voluntarily shut down; H could only be a date of exogenous physical collapse. If NPV = 0, the natural base-case assumption in a competitive economy, then $dNPV/dH = 0$ for any H. In other words, the firm would be just as happy to shut down at $H = 1$ as at $H = 100$.

We can make project life a more interesting variable by introducing fixed costs, FC_t. Varying FC_t will allow us to examine how the tax system interacts with operating leverage. We also give variable cash flow x_t a possibly different decay rate λ.

(A2) $$NPV = -1 + e^{-(r+\delta)H} + \int_0^H x_0 e^{-(r+\lambda)t} dt$$

$$- \int\limits_{0}^{H} FC_0 e^{-(r-i)t} dt,$$

$$= -1 + e^{-(r+\delta)H} + \frac{x_0}{r + \lambda} (1 - e^{-(r+\lambda)H})$$

$$- \frac{FC_0}{r - i} (1 - e^{-(r-i)H}).$$

Note that fixed costs are assumed to increase at the inflation rate i.

Assuming initial NPV > 0 at some life H, project life is determined by:[9]

$$dNPV/dH = -(r + \delta) e^{-(r+\delta)H} + x_0 e^{-(r+\lambda)H} - FC_0 e^{-(r-i)H} = 0.$$

If one multiplies through by e^{rH} and translates to future values x_H and FC_H,

(A3) $$dNPV/dH = x_H - FC_H - (r + \delta)SV_H = 0,$$

where SV_H is asset value at H. In other words, the project continues as long as the cash inflow x_t exceeds the fixed cost FC_t plus the opportunity cost of waiting a little longer for SV_t. The opportunity cost of waiting is the time value of money r plus the continuing depreciation rate δ.

Now imagine a tax czar who models firm's investment decisions as in (A2) and who wishes to assign economically sensible depreciation rates and depreciable lives to various asset classes. Asset lives depend on δ, λ, FC_0, and x_0; x_0 is our index of profitability. The czar would take δ and λ as determined in product and factor markets. Competition would force profitability toward the level x_0, at which NPV $= 0$. Then, given operating leverage (FC_0), asset life would be determined by (A3).[10]

The starting point for each of our numerical experiments is consistent with this story. We pick pairs of δ and depreciable life that roughly correspond to those in the initial Treasury tax reform proposal.[11] For each pair, various initial levels of fixed costs are assumed. For each fixed cost level, the initial level x_0 and decay rate λ of cash inflows are set so that NPV $= 0$ *and* optimal project life H equals the depreciable life originally assumed. A numerical example is given in table 11.6.

These base-case projects are only the starting points for our experiments, which calculate how the present value of the firm's tax liability depends on profitability levels, cash flow variances, the option to end the project early or late, and of course, on the specific tax rules.

Table 11.6   Numerical Example of a Base-Case Project

Variable Definitions

y_t = pretax cash flow = revenue − variable cost − fixed cost
x_t = revenue − variable cost, which decays at the nominal rate λ
FC_t = fixed costs, which increase at the inflation rate i
r = nominal risk-free interest rate
SV_t = asset values; SV_0 = 1, the initial outlay; SV_t decays at the nominal rate δ
σ_x^2 = variance rate of the realized cash flows $\bar{x}_t$
H = optimal project life under certainty

Base-Case Values

x_0	= .259	λ	= .002
FC_0	= .1	δ	= .12
H	= 12	r	= .08
		i	= .06
		σ_x	= .15

Note: in real terms, cash flows decline at $\lambda + i = .062$ per year.

Calculate NPV and Check Project Life

$$(A6) \qquad NPV = -1 + e^{-(r+\delta)H} + \frac{x_0}{r+\lambda}(1 - e^{-(r+\lambda)H})$$

$$- \frac{FC_0}{r-i}(1 - e^{-(r-i)H})$$

$$= -1 + .0907 + 1.9778 - 1.0669 = 0$$

$$dNPV/dH = x_H - FC_H - (r+\delta)SV_H = 0$$

$$= .2529 - .2054 - .0474 = 0$$

Abandonment Value

With σ_x = .15, and $H = \infty$, the NPV of the project with *no* abandonment is −2.84. The value of the abandonment put with last exercise date at $t = 100$, is +3.13. Thus adjusted NPV (APV) is:

$$APV = NPV + \text{abandonment value}$$
$$= -2.84 + 3.13 = .29.$$

NPV without abandonment and $H = 12$ is zero. Thus APV = +.29 is entirely due to the option to end the project beofre $t = 12$ or to extend it to $t = 13, 14, \ldots,$ or 100.

Taxes and Project Life

Suppose the firm always pays taxes at the marginal rate τ. Under stylized tax reform:

$$(A4) \quad NPV = -1 + \int_0^H \tau(\delta + i)e^{-(r+\delta)t}dt + e^{-(r+\delta)H}$$

$$+ \int_0^H (1-\tau)x_0 e^{-(r+\lambda)t}dt - \int_0^H (1-\tau)FC_0 e^{-(r-i)t}dt,$$

where:

$e^{-(r+\delta)H}$ Present value of asset at $t = H$. Since asset values equal tax book value throughout, no tax is paid at the end of project life.

$+ \displaystyle\int_0^H \tau(\delta + i)e^{-(r+\delta)t}\,dt$ The present value of tax depreciation.[12] The depreciation *rate* is expressed in real terms as $(\delta + i)$. Think of this as indexed depreciation: higher inflation would be reflected in a higher r and a *smaller* δ, that is, in slower, possibly negative, decay of nominal asset values. However, higher inflation should not reduce tax depreciation as a fraction of nominal asset value. Thus, we add inflation back to keep the depreciation rate in real terms.

By the way, the present value of *non*indexed depreciation is:

$$\int_0^H \tau(\delta + i)e^{-(r+\delta+i)t}\,dt.$$

In this case tax depreciation charges decline at the real rate $(\delta + i)$ even though inflation is positive and reflected in the nominal discount rate.

The tax rules embodied in equation (A4) describe the "reformed" tax system to be compared with current (1985) law. The only rule not apparent from equation (A4) is the treatment of remaining book value at H; we assume it is written off as a final, lump-sum depreciation allowance.

The NPV formula with taxes (A4) simplifies

$$(A5) \quad NPV = [1 - e^{-(r+\delta)H}][1 - \frac{\tau(\delta + i)}{r + \delta}]$$
$$+ \frac{(1 - \tau)x_0}{r + \lambda}[1 - e^{-(r+\lambda)H}]$$
$$- \frac{(1 - \tau)FC_0}{r - i}[1 - e^{-(r-i)H}].$$

The condition for optimal project life is:

$$(A6) \quad dNPV/dH = x_H - FC_H$$
$$- SV_H(r + \delta)\left[\frac{1 - \tau(\delta + i)/(r + \delta)}{1 - \tau}\right] = 0.$$

In this setup, the "tax term" in brackets tends to shorten project life.[13] However, we do *not* assume that the tax czar takes tax effects such as this into account in setting depreciation rates or asset life classes. For our experiments, we define depreciation rates, asset lives, and so forth, in terms of pretax cash flows.

Optimal Abandonment

When a project description like that given in table 11.A.1 is handed to the Monte Carlo simulation, the assumption of a fixed project life H is left behind. Project life may be cut short if cash flows x_t are sufficiently bad or extended beyond H if they are sufficiently good. The maximum project life is set far beyond H, at $t = 100$.

The option to *choose* project life can be modeled as a long-lived American put, with varying exercise price, written on an asset with a varying dividend yield.[14] The asset is the present value of future project cash flows x_t, *assuming* those cash flows will continue to evolve stochastically out to the far distant future. When the put is exercised, subsequent cash flows are given up in exchange for the exercise price. In our examples, exercise price at t equals SV_t, asset value at t, *plus* the present value at t of subsequent fixed costs, which are avoided by abandoning.

The optimal exercise strategy for the put gives the decision rule for choosing project life, and the value of the put, usually labeled "abandonment value," is incorporated in adjusted project value.[15]

$$\frac{\text{Adjusted}}{\text{NPV}} = \frac{\text{NPV with no}}{\text{abandonment}} + \frac{\text{Abandonment}}{\text{(put) value}} \ .$$

Abandonment value and the optimal abandonment strategy are calculated numerically[16] using *pretax* cash flows. It would be nice to explore how taxation affects the abandonment decision, but the computational problems seem overwhelming once tax-loss carrybacks and carryforwards are introduced. For example, including carry privileges in the put-valuation program would require at least two additional state variables: one for tax paid in the previous three periods and another for tax-loss carryforwards. Some partial analyses of how tax asymmetries interact with project life seem feasible, but we must leave them for further work.

Summary

The procedures used in our numerical experiments may thus be summed up as follows.

1. Choose an asset class described by a depreciation rate δ and a prespecified asset life. Assume an investment outlay of 1.

2. For various levels of operating leverage, measured by initial fixed cost FC_0, pick the initial cash inflow x_0 and its decay rate λ so that project NPV $= 0$ and H, the optimal abandonment date under certainty, matches the prespecified life for the asset class. This step sets the decay rate λ and ensures that there is an initial cash flow level consistent with NPV $= 0$ at the assumed fixed life H.

3. Pick a variance rate $\sigma_{\tilde{x}}^2$ for the cash flow realizations $\tilde{x}_t$ and calculate optimal abandonment strategy and abandonment values. The abandonment strategy does not depend on the initial value x_0, although the abandonment value does.[17]

4. Calculate the after-tax present value of the project for different levels of x_0 under whatever tax rules are being investigated, assuming that project life is terminated by the abandonment strategy calculated in step 3. (For a few runs step 3 was "turned off" to check that our qualitative results stand when project life is fixed.)

Notes

1. Since the value of a call option is convex in the exercise price (see Merton 1973), and no interest is paid on carry-forwards, it is always optimal to use tax losses as soon as possible.

2. Boyle (1977) first used a Monte Carlo simulation technique to value a European call option on a dividend-paying stock.

3. Constantinedes (1983) sets forth the conditions for a tax-paying entity to realize tax losses immediately and to defer gains as long as possible.

4. Tax- loss carryforwards cannot be "sold" at face value via financial leases, for example. A firm with carryforwards can sell tax depreciation deductions to a taxable lessor, but the lessor has to pay taxes on the lease payments received. The net gain to lessee plus lessor occurs only because tax depreciation is accelerated relative to the lease payments. See Myers, Dill, and Bautista (1976). Even if the firm with carryforwards (lessee) captures the full net gain of the lease contract, it cannot capture what the depreciation tax shields would be worth to a taxable corporation.

5. Issuing equity to buy bonds will be effective only under certain assumptions about debt and taxes. See Cooper and Franks (1983) for a discussion of some of the financial transactions designed to exploit the firm's tax losses.

6. The percentages of firms with carryforwards is shown in Auerbach and Poterba's table 10.1 (this volume). The percentages are much smaller when weighted by the market value of equity, since firms with carryforwards tend to be small and poorly performing. The transition probabilities are from their table 10.7.

7. Our simulations of the stand-alone project show the maximum impact for tax asymmetries on incremental projects undertaken by a going concern. That is, the after-tax NPV of the stand-alone project is not reduced, and generally is increased, by adding it to other assets subject to corporate tax. We make this statement based on simulations in Majd and Myers (1985).

8. Interpret H as a precommitted shutdown date. Firms do not precommit, but present value calculations usually assume they do. We relax this assumption in the abandonment analysis described below.

9. Second-order conditions are satisfied in our examples.

10. The story now has some latent inconsistencies. First, as we will show, taxes may affect asset values and lives. Second, we have not shown that secondhand asset values would actually decline at a regular rate δ when $FC_t > 0$. They would do so only if we introduced intangible assets, or at least assets which are not depreciable for tax purposes.

11. U.S. Department of the Treasury (1984, vol. 2, chap. 8.01).

12. Depreciation tax shields should be discounted at $r(1 - \tau)$, the *after-tax* riskless rate, since they are safe nominal flows under symmetric taxation. See Ruback (1986). Thus, we have overstated the burden of a symmetric tax. We accept this bias to ensure comparability with the risk-neutral option valuation framework used in our simulation. The *pretax* risk-free rate is standard in that framework. We are not certain that it should be when a long or short position on an option is held directly by a corporation rather than by investors in its securities. For now, we can only note this as an open issue.

13. We would hardly claim this as a general result. For example, taxes would have no effect on project life providing depreciation is completed before H. (This is common under current law.) The present value of depreciation tax shields is then a "sunk" benefit and does not depend on H; all tax terms cancel out of the derivative.

14. See Myers and Majd (1985). The dividend yield is just project cash flow x_t divided by the present value in t of expected subsequent cash flows x_{t+1}, $x_{t+2}, \ldots$. As in the Myers-Majd paper, the assumption is that yield depends only on time, not on the outcomes $\tilde{x}_0, \tilde{x}_1, \ldots, \tilde{x}_t$.

15. NPV with no abandonment is calculated on an underlying asset that lives to $t = 100$, substantially greater than the optimal life under certainty. Thus NPV with no abandonment is less than NPV from equation (A2). Abandonment value more than makes up for this shortfall, so that adjusted NPV exceeds NPV at the fixed-life H. See table 11.6 for an example.

16. The numerical procedure differs in three ways from that used in Myers and Majd (1985). First, the uncertain cash flows $\tilde{x}_t$ are modeled as a process with monthly ($t/12$) binominal jumps. Second, the present value of remaining fixed costs is rolled into the exercise price. Myers and Majd (1985) ignored fixed costs. Third, abandonment is not allowed before month 13. Accuracy of the abandonment value calculations was checked by comparing present results with results from the method used in Myers and Majd (1985), and by computing abandonment values numerically for special cases for which closed-form solutions are available.

17. The value of the option to extend project life is overstated in our simulations because we have not forced the firm to make replacement investments. The decision to finally bail out is determined solely by the downward trend of "variable" cash flow relative to fixed cost. However, this should not affect the relative sizes of pretax and after-tax NPVs holding initial profitability and risk constant.

References

Auerbach, A. 1983. Corporate taxation in the U.S. *Brookings Papers on Economic Activity* 2:451–505.

Ball, R., and J. Bowers. 1983. Distortions created by taxes which are options on value creation: The Australian resources rent tax proposal. *Australian Journal of Management* 8, no. 2.

Black, F., and M. Scholes. 1973. The pricing of options and corporate liabilities. *Journal of Political Economy* 81:637–59.

Boyle, P. 1977. Options: A Monte Carlo approach. *Journal of Financial Economics* 4:323–38.

Brennan, M. 1979. The pricing of contingent claims in discrete time models. *Journal of Finance* 34:53–68.

Constantinedes, G. 1983. Capital market equilibrium with personal tax. *Econometrica* 51:611–36.

Cooper, I., and J. Franks. 1983. The interaction of financing and investment decisions when the firm has unused tax credits. *Journal of Finance* 38:571–83.

Cordes, J., and S. Sheffrin. 1983. Estimating the tax advantage of corporate debt. *Journal of Finance* 38:95–105.

Cox, J., and S. Ross. 1976. The valuation of options for alternative stochastic processes. *Journal of Financial Economics* 3:145–66.

Cox, J., S. Ross, and M. Rubinstein. 1979. Option pricing: A simplified approach. *Journal of Financial Economics* 7:227–28.

Fama, E. 1977. Risk adjusted discount rates and capital budgeting under uncertainty. *Journal of Financial Economics* 5:3–24.

Galai, D. 1983. Corporate income taxes and the valuation of claims on the corporation. UCLA Working Paper no. 9–83.

Green, R. C., and E. Talmor. 1985. On the structure and incentive effects of tax liabilities. *Journal of Finance* 40:1095–1114.

Majd, S., and S. Myers. 1985. Valuing the government's tax claim on risky corporate assets. NBER Working Paper no. 1553.

Merton, R. C. 1973. Theory of rational option pricing. *Bell Journal of Economics and Management Science* 4:141–83.

Myers, S. C., D. A. Dill, and A. J. Bautista. 1976. Valuation of financial lease contracts. *Journal of Finance* 31:799–819.

Myers, S. C., and S. M. Turnbull. 1977. Capital budgeting and the capital asset pricing model: Good news and bad news. *Journal of Finance* 32:321–32.

Myers, S., and S. Majd. 1985. Calculating abandonment value using option pricing theory. MIT Sloan School of Management Working Paper.

Pitts, C., and J. Franks. 1984. Asymmetric taxes, mergers and risk-taking. Mimeographed, London Business School.

Ruback, R. 1986. Calculating the present value of riskless cash flows. *Journal of Financial Economics* 15:323–39.

Rubinstein, M. 1976. The valuation of uncertain income streams and the pricing of options. *Bell Journal of Economics* 7:407–25.

Smith, C., and R. M. Stulz. 1985. The determinants of firms' hedging policies. *Journal of Financial and Quantitative Analysis* 20:391–405.

U.S. Department of the Treasury, Office of the Secretary. 1984. *Tax reform for fairness, simplicity and economic growth.* Washington, D.C.: Government Printing Office.

Comment   Joseph E. Stiglitz

This is an extremely interesting chapter. I want to make a few comments suggesting some extensions to the authors' analysis and emphasizing certain general implications of their approach.

1. Their analysis makes clear the importance of "options" analysis for an understanding of tax consequences in the presence of uncertainty. There are a variety of circumstances in which the taxpayer has some discretion, for example, about the realization of a gain or a loss; in those circumstances, ignoring uncertainty—that is, looking at the tax consequences of the tax provision assuming there was no uncertainty—can be highly misleading. We encountered another instance of this in the analysis of churning. On average, it may not pay to churn. But there are circumstances in which it does, for example, if there is a large capital gain or if there is a change in the tax status of the owner, so that the tax imposed on the seller is less than the tax write-offs resulting from the step-up in basis for depreciation. (See J. E. Stiglitz, "General Theory of Tax Avoidance," *National Tax Journal,* September 1985.)

It should be emphasized that these options affect the desirability of investing in the given asset; that is, the appropriate way to value the tax consequences of the demand for different investment goods is not on the basis of an ex post analysis of actual taxes paid, but on the basis of an ex ante analysis of the value of the option.

2. The authors' analysis also makes clear the potential importance of disaggregating on the basis of tax status of firms. Earlier discussions have focused on the importance of disaggregation across classes of assets; one may get an inaccurate picture of the effect of the tax system by looking at its effect on an average asset. Similarly, one may get an inaccurate picture of the effect of the tax system by looking at its effect on an average firm.

I should add that the effect of a tax on a firm will depend not only on its tax status (whether it has loss carryforwards), but also on its financial position; that is, whether at the margin it is financing its investment by raising new equity or by borrowing or out of retained earnings.

3. A difficulty we have repeatedly encountered in the analysis of the effects of taxation is that we would like to use a sophisticated max-

Joseph E. Stiglitz is professor of economics at Princeton University and a research associate of the National Bureau of Economic Research.

imization model to describe the firm and the market and to evaluate the effects of a proposed tax change and the responses of the firm (investors). Yet we have considerable evidence that firms (investors) do not act in accordance with our theory. How reliable then are our inferences based on these models?

Here the issue is that there are numerous ways firms can seemingly mitigate the effects of limitations on loss deductibility, for example, through leasing. If these worked perfectly, then the tax status of the firm would make no difference. More generally, the effect of these provisions depends on how well these mechanisms work. These limitations, and how they affect the behavior of the firm, have not been modeled here; accordingly, how these limitations will operate in the presence of a change in the tax law has not been analyzed.

4. How concerned we should be about limitations on the deductibility of losses should also be affected by the extent to which the losses are the result of discretionary actions taken to realize capital losses. Thus, if a firm has an asset that has declined in value and sells that asset, it will record a capital loss. But it could have waited to sell the asset. It chooses to record the loss because of the tax advantages of doing so, just as it chooses not to recognize certain gains.

5. The approach taken here is based on the premise that in valuing risky streams there is a perfect capital market; the values calculated are those that would emerge, if in fact these options could be sold on the stock market. Two caveats are in order. First, the risk attitudes of the government may differ from those in the private sector; thus, these do not represent the value of these risky streams to the government. Second, this approach will have to be modified if a change in tax policy is contemplated that results in flows of funds from the government to firms in states when they have losses (are near bankruptcy). For it is precisely in those circumstances that the standard capital market models, assuming full information, are most inappropriate. For instance, with full loss deductibility the government is often pictured as a full equity partner; alternatively, the government is sometimes said to be lending money to the firm. But these metaphors, while suggestive, are not quite accurate: the government's claims, particularly in the presence of bankruptcy, may be quite different from the claims of another lender or another equity investor.

6. The approach taken here is based on a simulation model, in which an asset with a particular pattern of returns is investigated. The qualitative results that emerge are consistent with standard theory; for example, the greater the risk, the greater the option value. But simulation exercises are of particular use in assessing the quantitative significance of an effect; however, it is difficult to ascertain, on the basis

of this one exercise, how robust the results are. Would they, for instance, be modified if we considered a one-hoss-shay technology, or a technology in which output and labor requirements are fixed but the fixed lifetime of the asset is a result of rising real product wages?

7. Finally, it would be useful if the authors related their results to the Auerbach-Hines results given in chapter 5.

12   The Cash Flow Corporate Income Tax

Mervyn A. King

12.1   Introduction

Two themes have dominated the debate on corporate tax reform in recent years. First, there is a widespread perception that the cumulative effect of piecemeal changes to the tax system has been to produce major distortions in the pattern of savings and investment. The magnitude of these distortions has recently been documented in King and Fullerton (1984). As a result, the goal of "fiscal neutrality" has attracted a good deal of support. Second, there has been growing concern over the steady erosion of revenues accruing to the government from the corporate sector.

The practical expression of these perceptions has been the elimination of many concessions to investment and savings, particularly at the corporate level. This can be seen most clearly in the major overhaul of the corporate tax system that occurred in the United Kingdom in 1984 (the transition to which was completed in April 1986) and in the U.S. Treasury proposals in both their original November 1984 and subsequent May 1985 versions (henceforth Treasury I and Treasury II respectively). Throughout the postwar period, governments of various persuasions have attempted to stimulate capital formation by offering investment incentives of increasing generosity. These have taken the form of cash grants, credits against tax liabilities, or straightforward tax allowances. But the concessions were introduced in an ad hoc fashion, and by the late 1970s the resulting pattern of incentives was difficult to justify in terms of any rational view of the optimal taxation

Mervyn A. King is Professor of Economics at the London School of Economics and research associate at the National Bureau of Economics.

of savings. Effective tax rates on investment projects varied enormously from one type of project to another (King and Fullerton 1984). In response to these problems both, the U.S. and U.K. proposals were an attempt to move toward fiscal neutrality by adopting a tax base that could more accurately be described as a measure of economic income. Many of the concessions to investment were eliminated in return for a cut in the corporate tax rate.

The recent debate on tax reform in the United States and the United Kingdom shows that the attempt to return to a comprehensive income tax raises at least as many questions as it answers. The calculation of economic depreciation of an asset, and the measures that are required to index the corporate tax system for inflation, are very difficult to implement in practice. It is appropriate, therefore, to ask whether there is an alternative way to attain the objective of fiscal neutrality without a significant erosion of the tax base.

In this paper we discuss such an alternative. It is called the *cash flow corporate income tax*. The basic principle behind the idea is that the company is taxed on the net cash flow received from its real business activities. No distinction is made between capital and income in the calculation of a company's tax base. By basing the tax on cash flow the measurement of economic income is removed from the concern of the tax authorities. Such a system achieves fiscal neutrality by harmonizing investment incentives on a common basis, namely immediate expensing of all investment expenditures. The incentive to invest with such a tax is greater than would be the case under either Treasury I or Treasury II plans, and also under the new U.K. corporate tax system. The motivation for the cash flow tax is to apply the principles of a consumption or expenditure tax to the corporate sector. The idea is not new and can be traced back at least as far as Brown (1948); its practical implementation was discussed in King (1975), Kay and King (1978), Meade Committee (1978), and Aaron and Galper (1985).

There are three main parts to this chapter. First, section 12.2 describes the principles of a cash flow corporate income tax and explains how it would work. The second part of the chapter analyzes the effects of the corporate cash flow tax on the firm's choice of financial policy and its debt-equity mix, and also upon the cost of capital facing the company when making investment decisions. Financial policy is analyzed in section 12.3, and section 12.4 discusses the impact of the tax on the cost of capital to a firm and the effective tax rate on an investment project. Attention will be focused on three issues that have received rather little attention in previous discussions. First, the nature of any problems that arise from the interaction between a cash flow tax at the corporate level and an income tax at the personal level. Second, the incidence of the corporate cash flow tax depends upon the marginal source of finance to the representative company, and the identification of the marginal source of funds requires a general equilibrium model of the corporate sector's capital structure. Third, the corporate cash flow tax illustrates vividly the potential for dynamic inconsistency in government fiscal policy.

The final chapter, section 12.5, discusses some of the more practical problems that would arise if the cash flow corporate income tax were to be implemented. These include (i) transitional arrangements, (ii) international considerations, and (iii) the likely revenue consequences of a change in the tax base.

12.2 A Cash Flow Corporate Income Tax

Recent research has shown that the corporate income tax introduces a number of distortions into savings and investment decisions. To eliminate these, one might either move to a more neutral tax base or eliminate the separate tax on corporations altogether. The latter course would have many attractions were it not for the following two considerations. First, a corporate income tax exists already, and to abolish it would be to yield windfall capital gains to the current owners of corporate equity. There is truth in the well-known adage that "an old tax is a good tax." Second, in the absence of a tax on corporate income it may be difficult to tax the capital income received by foreign investors in domestic companies or domestic subsidiaries of foreign corporations.

The cash flow corporate income tax represents an attempt to design a tax that is neutral with respect to both financial and investment decisions, and at the same time continues to yield the government positive revenue from past investments, from profits in excess of the normal rate of return, and also from activities financed by overseas investors. It is attractive for a further reason, namely that the base of the tax requires no adjustment for inflation, and hence that the complicated indexation provisions for depreciation, for example, required under alternative corporate tax systems are unnecessary with a cash flow tax. This is because the tax is based on the sources and uses of funds statement and not on the profit and loss account. The tax eliminates the necessity of calculating "economic profit." Hence there is no need to construct a true measure of depreciation or to make any adjustment for the effects of inflation.

The basic principle of the tax is to levy a charge on the net cash flow to the company resulting from its real economic activities. The tax base can be measured as the difference between the receipts from sales of goods and services and the purchases of all real goods and services required in the production process, including purchases of capital goods. At the same time the tax base would disallow any deduction for the financing of the investment. Hence there would be no deductibility of either interest payments or dividends. The major departures from the present system would be the granting of immediate expensing (100% first-year depreciation allowances) to all forms of investment (but given this there would be no need for an investment tax credit), and interest payments would no longer qualify as a deduction for the purposes of the corporate income tax. Moreover, there would be no room for dividend deduction schemes of the type proposed in the recent Treasury plans. In practice, there would need to be transitional arrangements to prevent both undue hardship and also tax avoidance during the transition from the current system to a new cash flow tax base. These, and other practical questions to which satisfactory answers must be provided before the tax could be implemented, are discussed further in section 12.5 below.

The nature of double-entry bookkeeping means that the total sources of funds to a company are identical to its total uses of funds. An important implication of this identity is that the base of the cash flow tax can be described in either of two ways. The first is the difference between sales and purchases: the net cash flow from real economic activity. The second is the difference between dividends paid to shareholders and issues of new shares.

The former may be described as the corporate cash flow base and the latter as the net equity distributions base. To see the relationship between the two, examine the corporate sources and uses of funds shown in table 12.1. In terms of the notation of table 1, the two tax bases, denoted by TB_1 and TB_2 respectively, are given by the equations

$$(1) \qquad TB_1 = R - I$$

$$(2) \qquad TB_2 = D - S.$$

Table 12.1   Corporate Sources and Uses of Funds

Sources		Uses	
R	Receipts from sales of goods and services less purchases of labour, raw materials and services	I	Investment expenditure (gross investment less receipts from sales of assets)
B	Borrowing (new issues of debt less repayments of old debt)	P	Interest payments (net of interest received)
S	New share issues (less share repurchases), including net sales of shares in other companies.	D	Dividends paid (less dividends received)
		T	Taxes paid.

Accounting Identity $R + B + S \equiv I + P + D + T$

From the flow of funds identity it follows that

(3) $TB_2 + T \equiv TB_1 + (B - P)$.

The two differences between the corporate cash flow and net equity distributions bases can be seen to be the following. First, because taxes paid enter into the sources and uses of funds statement, the corporate cash flow basis is a measure of the tax base on a tax-inclusive basis, whereas the definition in terms of net equity distributions is measured on a tax-exclusive basis. If the tax rate on the corporate cash flow base were 50%, then this would be equivalent to a tax rate of 100% on the net equity distributions base. Second, to the extent that a company earns real profits from transactions in financial assets (other than equities), then the corporate cash flow base would not include those profits. Only if the net equity distributions base were used would such profits be taxed. This is a major consideration for financial institutions, such as banks, which derive their earnings primarily from the provision of financial services for which no direct charge is levied but which are reflected in differences between borrowing and lending rates. The same phenomenon can be observed in the national accounts, in which the real economic profits of the financial sector are recorded as negative. This is because the national accounts use real transactions to measure profits and ignore profits on financial transactions. If no profit is made on such financial transactions, then the present value of interest payments equals the present value of net borrowing, and, over time, given a constant tax rate, the corporate cash flow base and the net equity distributions base are identical. This is likely to be approximately true for major industrial corporations, and as far as nonfinancial activity is concerned the two bases have identical economic effects. It will prove convenient to analyze these effects in terms of the corporate cash flow base because this may more readily be compared with the existing base and with reforms that have been proposed. The two bases could be made identically equal by modifying the corporate cash flow base to include the difference between net new borrowing and net interest payments. In other words, interest deductibility would continue, but new borrowing would constitute a taxable receipt. It is clear from equation (3) that the amended corporate cash flow base must in all circumstances be identical to the net equity distributions base except for the fact that the former is tax-inclusive and the latter tax-exclusive. The tax-exclusive rate, t_2, is related to the tax-inclusive rate, t_1, by the equation

(4) $$t_2 = \frac{t_1}{1 - t_1}.$$

Apart from the treatment of profits on financial transactions, there is a difference between the corporate cash flow base and the net equity distributions base in terms of the transitional problems that might arise in attempting to move from the present system toward a cash flow tax. Some of these practical issues are taken up in section 12.5. But we turn first to an analysis of the long-run effects of the cash flow corporate income tax on the optimal financial and investment policy of a company once the tax is in place, and we contrast these effects with those that would follow from the adoption of alternative tax bases such as those proposed in the recent Treasury plans.

12.3   Financial Policy and the Debt-Equity Mix

It is well known that the current U.S. corporate income tax affords a tax advantage to debt rather than equity, because of the deductibility of interest payments, and discriminates in favor of internal equity finance (retained earnings) and against the issue of new shares. The rationale for this pattern of incentives is unclear. A thriving equity market, particularly for new risk capital, provides one of the main routes by which household savings are channeled into corporate investment. It is perhaps not surprising, therefore, that there have been frequent proposals to relieve the double taxation of dividends inherent in the present system. The most recent were the Treasury I and Treasury II plans, both of which advocated a partial dividend deduction. In this section we contrast the incentives to use debt and equity that are implied by a cash flow tax on the one hand, and alternative reforms, such as the Treasury dividend deduction proposal, on the other.

To do this we first analyze the effects of different taxes on a company's choice of financial policy in general, and then apply the results to particular systems of company taxation. Both personal and corporate taxes are relevant to the choice of debt-equity mix. Two personal tax rates are distinguished here, the marginal income tax rate of investors, denoted by m, and the effective tax rate on accrued capital gains, denoted by z. Differences in tax rates among investors will be discussed below. Because capital gains tax is charged on gains only when they are realized, the effective tax rate on accrued gains is significantly lower than the nominal statutory rate. In addition, it has been argued that the ability to exploit the short-term–long-term gains distinction further erodes the effective rate and may possibly lead to a negative effective tax rate. For our purposes we note solely that the value of z is bounded above by the statutory rate.

Three corporate tax variables are relevant to the analysis. These are the rate of tax on taxable profits that would be paid if no profits were distributed, denoted by τ, the opportunity cost of retained earnings in terms of gross (i.e. pre-income tax) dividends, foregone, denoted by $\hat{\theta}$, and the fraction of interest payments that are tax-deductible, denoted by β. The value of $\hat{\theta}$ measures the rate at which cash in the company's hands may be transformed into cash in the hands of the stockholders (Feldstein 1970; King 1971, 1977). Under the current U.S. tax system a transfer of a dollar from the company to the shareholders produces a gross dividend of one dollar. Hence $\hat{\theta}$ equals unity. With alternative tax systems, such as a dividend deduction scheme or the imputation system employed in most EEC countries, the value of $\hat{\theta}$ generally exceeds unity to reflect the credit given to the shareholders, explicitly or implicitly, for taxes already paid at the corporate level. To evaluate $\hat{\theta}$ under different tax regimes it is helpful to define the total tax liability of the company, denoted by T, as the total taxes paid by the company and stockholders together less the income tax on dividends and capital gains tax paid by the stockholders. From this definition

$$(5) \qquad T = \tau Y + \frac{(1 - \hat{\theta})}{\hat{\theta}} \cdot G$$

where Y is *taxable* corporate income and G is total gross dividends. From the definition of $\hat{\theta}$ the extra taxes (minus the credits) that result from a distribution are $(1 - \hat{\theta})/\hat{\theta}$ per unit of gross dividends.

We may now contrast (5) with the formulas that describe the operation of various tax regimes. Under the current U.S. system the corporate tax liability is simply

$$(6) \qquad T = cY$$

where c is the rate of corporate income tax.

Equating coefficients in (5) and (6) confirms that $\tau = c$ and $\hat{\theta} = 1.0$.

Under the imputation system used widely in Europe, part of the corporate tax liability is credited against the shareholders' income tax liability on dividends. In effect, the company is deemed to have paid income tax on behalf of the shareholders at some rate, which is described as the rate of imputation (denoted by s). Hence

$$(7) \qquad T = cY - sG.$$

This implies that

$$(8) \qquad \tau = c$$

$$\hat{\theta} = \frac{1}{1 - s}.$$

The gross dividend received by the stockholder is equal to the cash dividend payment made by the company grossed up by the rate of imputation.

The Treasury plans proposed that a fraction of dividends be deductible for the purposes of the corporate income tax. Denote the fraction of dividends that are deductible by λ. In Treasury I λ was 0.5, and in Treasury II λ was 0.1. With a dividend deduction the corporate tax liability becomes

$$(9) \qquad T = c(Y - \lambda G).$$

Hence

$$(10) \qquad \tau = c$$

$$\hat{\theta} = \frac{1}{1 - c\lambda}.$$

From this it can be seen that in terms of economic effects the dividend deduction proposed is equivalent to an imputation system with a rate of imputation equal to the product of the corporate tax rate and the fraction of dividends that is deductible. There are two points to note about this. First, a change in the corporate tax rate will automatically change the effective rate of imputation unless a compensating change in λ is made. Second, the effective rate of imputation is very sensitive to the value of λ. For example, in the Treasury I plan, with a corporate tax rate of 33% and $\lambda = 0.5$, the effective imputation rate is 16.5%. Under the Treasury II proposals, with the same corporate tax rate but $\lambda = 0.1$, the effective imputation rate is only 3.3%. Moreover, both values are low when compared with imputation rates in Europe. In the United Kingdom, for example, the rate of imputation is 30% (from April 1986, 29%).

The cash flow tax is a variant of the classical system of corporate income taxation, which is that currently used in the United States. The value of $\hat{\theta}$ in both cases is unity. The major difference between the cash flow tax and the present system lies in the treatment of debt finance. With a cash flow tax, interest payments are not deductible for corporate income tax purposes (or, equivalently, borrowing is a taxable receipt). Debt finance would be less attractive than at present.

The incentive to use different sources of finance can be seen from the following pairwise comparisons between debt finance, retained earnings, and new share issues. In each case we compare the net of tax income that could be distributed out of one unit of corporate profits corresponding to the differing methods of remunerating investors implied by the different sources of finance. The results are simply stated below; derivations may be found in King (1977, 1986). At this stage we ignore indexation of the tax system.

(i) Debt finance is preferred to retained earnings if

$$(11) \qquad (1 - m) > (1 - z)(1 - \beta\tau).$$

(ii) Debt finance is preferred to new share issues if

(12) $$1 > \hat{\theta}\,(1 - \beta\tau).$$

(iii) Retained earnings are preferred to new share issues if

(13) $$(1 - z) > (1 - m)\hat{\theta}.$$

From these equations it is clear that with a cash flow corporate income tax there would be fiscal neutrality between debt finance and new equity issues (from 12). Retained earnings would be the most attractive source of finance for taxable investors, and financial policy would be a matter of complete indifference for tax-exempt investors such as pension funds. Neutrality could be achieved for all investors by either taxing capital gains at income tax rates or adopting a consumption tax treatment of household capital income. Under the current U.S. tax code, debt finance dominates new share issues, and for almost all investors debt finance also dominates retained earnings. With the dividend deduction proposal of the Treasury plans, the condition for debt finance to be more attractive than new equity issues is (from 12)

(14) $$\beta > \lambda.$$

Only if the rate at which dividends may be deducted exceeds the proportion of interest payments that is deductible will new share issues dominate debt finance. The Treasury plan envisaged retaining full deductibility of interest ($\beta = 1$) and values for λ of 0.5 and 0.1 for Treasury I and Treasury II respectively. Under these proposals, debt finance would retain its tax advantage. Moreover, the effective imputation rate would be independent of the tax rate of the investor, and so neutrality between internal and external equity finance would be impossible to achieve.

It has long been argued in the United States that partial integration of the corporate and personal income taxes, as far as dividends are concerned, would alleviate much of the discrimination against equity inherent in the current system. But partial measures of this type do not deal adequately with the substantial spread among marginal investor tax rates. Indeed, the imputation system in Britain has been criticized by the employers' federation (CBI 1985, p. 69) on precisely these grounds.

It is clear that the 1986 system . . . will for a majority of shareholders, provide either a strong bias in favour of distribution or indifference as between distribution and retention . . . the 1986 system will in time produce broadly two types of company:
a) Typical quoted companies with mainly institutional or basic rate taxpayer shareholders, which will make very full dividend payments . . .

b) Companies with largely top rate taxpayer shareholders, making minimal distributions.

The Exchequer will of course lose substantially as a result of this.

The conclusion reached by the CBI's Tax Reform Working Party was that Britain should adopt a cash flow corporation tax.

12.4 The Cost of Capital

The principle aim of the cash flow corporate income tax is to avoid distortion of investment decisions by ensuring that the cost of capital is independent of the particular investment project under consideration. By the cost of capital is meant here the pretax rate of return net of depreciation that is required on a project in order to call forth the funds needed to finance it. It is the financial rather than the user cost of capital (the latter includes also the return necessary to finance depreciation of the asset).

To illustrate the effect of the cash flow tax, and of other possible reforms, on the cost of capital, we consider the simple case in which true economic depreciation occurs at the nonstochastic exponential rate δ. With this assumption a firm's cost of capital, denoted by c, is given by the following expression:

$$(15) \qquad c = \frac{(1 - f_1 A_D - f_2 \tau - f_3 g)}{(1 - \tau)} \{\rho + \delta - \pi\} - \delta$$

where f_1 = proportion of investment expenditure that qualifies for ordinary depreciation allowances.

f_2 = proportion of investment expenditure that receives cash flow tax treatment (i.e. immediate expensing)

f_3 = proportion of investment expenditure that qualifies for a cash grant or investment tax credit.

A_D = present value of tax savings from ordinary depreciation allowances.

g = rate of cash grant or equivalent rate of investment tax credit

ρ = rate at which company discounts net of corporate tax cash flows

δ = exponential rate of true economic depreciation

π = rate of increase of price of investment goods.

Equation (15) states that the required pretax real rate of return on a project, adjusted for depreciation, is equal to the real rate of return that must be offered to the suppliers of finance grossed up by the corporate tax rate and multiplied by the effective price of a new asset. The latter is the market price less the present value of the tax allowances for depreciation and other investment incentives. Indexation of depreciation allowances lowers the effective price of capital goods. For simplicity of exposition, (15) omits corporate wealth taxes and the taxation of the inflationary component of inventory profits. A treatment of these issues may be found in King and Fullerton (1984) and King (1986).

The value of the rate at which the company discounts net of corporate tax cash flows, denoted by ρ, depends upon the source of finance used for the project and upon the identity of the marginal investor. It depends also upon the indexation provisions of the tax code. In a partial equilibrium model in which all investors have identical tax rates, the following are the relevant expressions for the corporate discount rate for each source of finance (see Appendix for the derivations). The nominal interest rate in economy is denoted by i.

(16)   (i) debt finance $\rho = i(1 - \beta\tau) + \beta\tau\pi I_i$

(17)   (ii) new share issues $\rho = i/\hat{\theta} + \left[\dfrac{mI_i - zI_z}{(1 - m)\hat{\theta}}\right]\pi$

(18)   (iii) retained earnings $\rho = i\left[\dfrac{1 - m}{1 - z}\right] + \left[\dfrac{mI_i - zI_z}{1 - z}\right]\pi$

where I_i and I_z are dummy variables that take the value unity when interest payments and capital gains, respectively, are fully indexed for tax purposes and are zero in the absence of indexation.

Partial equilibrium expressions for the cost of capital corresponding to the different sources of finance can be derived by substituting the appropriate values for the corporate discount rate into equation (15). In a general equilibrium model, however, we would expect that the discount rates would be equal for all sources of finance employed by the firm, and the difficulty in constructing convincing general equilibrium models is to imagine plausible mechanisms by which the marginal discount rates are brought into equality. One such model is the Miller equilibrium (Miller 1977), in which investors face constraints on short sales of all assets. In this equilibrium the constraints are binding on all investors except those who are indifferent between equity and debt finance as far as taxes are concerned. The marginal investor is the unconstrained investor, and the company, which itself faces no constraints on its financial policy, is indifferent at the margin between debt and equity finance. For the marginal investor the cost of equity finance is equal to that of debt finance, and the income tax rate of the marginal investor is such that the discount rate given by equations (16) and (18) are equal. Hence from the tax point of view this is equivalent to calculating the cost of capital as if the firm financed marginal projects by debt finance. In such an equilibrium it is easy to evaluate the effects of different tax regimes on the cost of capital and hence on the optimal level of investment. In the case of the cash flow corporate income tax, interest payments are not deductible for tax purposes ($\beta = 0$) and there are no indexation provisions. The corporate discount rate is from (16) simply the nominal interest rate. In addition, all investment expenditure can be immediately expensed ($f_2 = 1, f_1 = f_3 = 0$), and hence from equation (15) the cost of capital is given by the following expression

$$(19) \qquad\qquad c = i - \pi = r$$

In other words, the cost of capital is equal to the real interest rate. The rates of tax, both at the personal and the corporate level, have no effect on the relationship between the market interest rate and the required rate of return on investment projects. The decision rule that a firm uses in the presence of taxes is identical to the rule that it would use in the absence of taxes. The existence of a cash flow corporate income tax does not distort the investment decision.

The reason for this result is clear. With immediate expensing the government is effectively subsidizing investment at exactly the same rate as it taxes profits. The cost of any project is reduced by the same fraction as the future benefits will be reduced when taxes are levied (assuming a constant tax rate). Given that both the benefits and costs of the project are reduced in the same proportion, then, provided the discount rate is unaffected by the tax rate, any project that was accepted in the absence of a tax would be accepted with the tax. This result assumes that there are always sufficient taxable profits for the tax allowances to be used to offset current tax liabilities. Alternatively the tax system must provide for complete loss offset by allowing tax losses to be carried forward marked up by the nominal interest rate. With this tax system the government becomes a partner in the firm, albeit a sleeping partner (see also King 1975). It makes a contribution on new investment at the same rate as it shares in the profits of the enterprise. On new marginal investment projects the system is effectively a zero tax. But on intramarginal projects and on investment made prior to the introduction of the cash flow corporate income tax, the tax acts as a capital levy on the owners of corporate assets.

One of the great advantages of the cash flow tax is that the cost of capital can be seen to be independent of the inflation rate without any need to introduce complicated indexation provisions. The same cannot be said of any tax that attempts to measure "economic profits." The only long-run problem with the cash flow tax is that there is a possible time inconsistency involved in government policy. Given that the tax has no disincentive effects on investment but yields revenue from the intramarginal projects, the government would have an apparent incentive to announce that the tax rate would remain at its present level but in the future to go back on its word and to raise the rate of tax. In this way it would appear to be able to raise additional revenue from lump sum taxes. If this increase in the tax rate were anticipated, then of course the tax would no longer be a lump sum tax and investment decisions would be affected. In practice, the United Kingdom had a very similar tax system in force from 1973 until 1984, and no attempt was in fact made to raise the rate of tax. Moreover, this was a period in which the administration alternated between the two main political parties. It is possible that concern about their reputation led governments to forego the short-run benefits of retrospective taxation.

If we maintain the assumption of a Miller equilibrium and turn to the effects of other possible tax systems, then, with interest deductibility, the only system that is neutral is one that offers no accelerated depreciation but grants ordinary depreciation allowances at rates corresponding to true economic depreciation. These must be fully indexed for inflation. Such was the aim of Treasury I. Since economic depreciation is notoriously difficult to measure, such a system could only be expected to approximate the requirements for neutrality. Moreover, in the discussions that followed the publication of Treasury I, indexation found much less favor with Congress than with the authors of the Treasury plans. This experience appears to support the view of the Meade Committee (1978), which recommended a cash flow corporate income tax over a tax based on comprehensive income partly on the grounds that the calculations required for a measure of "economic profit" were complex and difficult to administer.

If we relax the assumption of a Miller equilibrium, then the discount rate for the company will reflect the tax treatment of dividends and personal tax rates on both dividends and capital gains. There is no really satisfactory general equilibrium model of corporate financial behavior outside of the simple Miller equilibrium, but if one were constructed, the marginal cost of capital would be a weighted average of the costs of capital for the different sources of finance. The difficulty is to identify the weights that would be used. Fewer distortions would be expected from a tax system that discriminated less between the different sources of finance, and, as we saw in section 12.3, the cash flow corporate income tax scored well on this point.

The problem with the simple Miller equilibrium is that it contains a clearly counterfactual prediction, namely that, except for the marginal investor, all other investors would be completely specialized in either debt or equity securities. One simple alternative is to calculate a weighted average cost of capital, using as weights the average proportion of investment financed from different sources. Such calculations were made for the then existing tax system in the comparative study of King and Fullerton (1984). To contrast the effect of a cash flow tax on the cost of capital with that of the Treasury plans, and to compare both possible reforms with the present system, we present below updated estimates of the effective marginal tax rate on capital income as calculated in the King and Fullerton study. To do this, the posttax real rate of return to the investor corresponding to the pretax rate of return on a project (the cost of capital as defined here) is computed for each investor. Denote this posttax rate of return by s. The effective marginal tax rate is now defined as

$$(20) \qquad\qquad t = \frac{c - s}{c}$$

Table 12.2 shows effective marginal tax rates for the United Kingdom and the United States under several alternative tax regimes. For the United Kingdom the figures are shown for the pre-1984 position, the new 1986 regime, and the situation that would result if the 1986 system were converted into a cash flow corporation tax. In the case of the United States, the rates are shown for the 1984 starting point, the two Treasury plans (I and II), and the hypothetical case of Treasury I amended to include a pure cash flow corporate income tax but with all the personal tax changes intact. The inflation rate assumed in the calculations is 5% per annum.

It is clear that even without adopting a consumption tax at the personal level, the cash flow corporate income tax eliminates many of the more extreme distortions that are evident in the current system.

12.5 Problems of Implementation

12.5.1 Transitional Arrangements

Two sets of issues arise when designing a suitable transition to the new tax base. The first consists of the problems that arise from the application of the new tax base. The second is the question of how far the expected consequences of the old base are continued after the introduction of the new tax. The second is the easier to deal with and so is considered first.

On the date when the new base comes into force, companies have a stock of depreciation allowances that they expect to be able to carry forward and deduct (in a predetermined time profile) against future taxable profits. There seems no good reason to deny companies the right to continue to deduct depreciation allowances on past investment. To abolish the existing stock of depreciation allowances would be akin to a windfall profits tax in proportion to past investment—not a happy precedent to set. Nevertheless, the Hall-Rabushka (1983) plan did imply such an effect. Moreover, unless the date on which the tax becomes

Table 12.2 Effective Marginal Tax Rates on Corporate Investment, United Kingdom and United States (percentage)

	United Kingdom			United States			
	pre-1984	1986	Cash Flow Tax	1984	Treasury I	Treasury II	Cash Flow Tax
Asset							
Machinery	−35.6	19.8	12.3	8.0	37.7	24.8	19.5
Buildings	24.2	53.8	47.8	31.0	40.3	34.7	22.6
Inventories	41.7	51.2	12.3	48.2	38.8	36.0	18.9
Finance method							
Debt	−61.1	20.8	46.5	−19.1	29.2	14.0	27.3
New shares	−0.8	22.6	39.4	79.5	46.4	62.5	40.5
Retained earnings	15.2	42.4	17.5	52.8	44.3	41.8	16.1
Overall	−0.1	37.4	24.1	29.9	39.3	31.0	21.1

Assumptions: (a) all projects earn 10% per annum pretax return; (b) inflation is 5% per annum.

effective can be made retrospective, anticipation of the change would lead to a collapse in investment in the period between announcement and the date when the enabling legislation was passed. In the United Kingdom, it is possible for the government to announce that, conditional upon the proposed legislation receiving Parliamentary approval within a certain period, the new tax would be effective from the date of announcement. But in the U.S. context this seems less plausible.

Similar arguments apply to other forms of "losses" that companies had expected to be able to carry forward to offset against future profits. Continuation of such loss carryforwards is straightforward under the real basis, but with the net dividends basis the simplicity of the tax would be reduced because net distributions constitute a tax-exclusive base whereas loss carryforwards are inherited from a tax-inclusive regime. To retain simplicity, the loss carryforwards could be converted into a stock of tax credits (or, more generally, a flow of tax credits over time) on the transition date.

The other set of problems results from the implications of the new base, although their nature differs as between the real and net distributions bases. With the former, the main problem is that debt interest payments are no longer tax-deductible. For new debt finance this raises no problems, but for borrowing incurred before the announcement of the new base there is a retrospective charge on the cost of servicing the debt, which in some, perhaps many, cases could cause acute financial distress for highly geared companies. One solution is simply to phase out interest deductibility by reducing the proportion of interest payments that are deductible (the value of β in section 12.3) gradually over a period of, say 5 to 10 years, from unity to zero. As far as the net distributions basis is concerned there is a more serious transitional problem. Unless the new basis becomes effective on the date of announcement, companies would have a strong incentive to raise their debt-equity ratios by borrowing and paying high dividends before the transition date, and then to issue new equity in order to repay the loans and reduce dividends after the transition date in order to repay the loans and restore their debt-equity ratios to normal levels. Similar incentives existed in the United Kingdom during the major corporate tax reforms of 1965 and 1973, and, although revenue losses occurred, the problem was regarded as manageable. Nevertheless, antiavoidance provisions would be necessary because the scope for avoidance using purely financial transactions is large.

12.5.2 Long-run Administrative Problems

In this section we describe some of the administrative problems that the tax would present on a permanent basis. The first concerns the treatment of borrowing. Under the corporate cash flow basis, only real transactions are taken into account and profits made on financial transactions are exempt from tax. This does not appear to be a satisfactory method of taxing financial institutions. If the cash flow base were adopted, then a separate tax would be required for such institutions. Alternatively, under the net equity distributions basis, which does tax the profits on financial transactions, rules would be required to prevent companies from issuing debt at artificially high interest rates. Such payments would be exempt from corporate tax and would be a method of returning profits to the shareholders free of tax. Of course, this problem exists under the current tax with interest deductibility. Current rules would need to be carried over. Some of the other problems that exist with the current corporate tax system would remain with the new tax. There would still need to be a distinction between corporate and personal expenditure in order to levy the appropriate amounts of personal income tax on benefits provided by the company. Under the net equity distributions basis, new rules would be required to determine the amount of dividends that enter the tax base when some part of the dividend was paid in kind. Shareholder benefits of all types (for example, reductions in the price of the company's products when sold to its shareholders) come under this heading.

A second area of potential problems concerns the phenomenon of tax exhaustion. This is the situation in which the company has no current taxable income and is accumulating tax losses that will be carried forward. A question that arises is how far it is thought to be acceptable for companies to trade such tax losses among themselves. Under the existing tax systems in both the United States and the United Kingdom, trading of tax losses takes place with leasing. The U.S. authorities have taken a much harder line on this than their U.K. counterparts, although it is not easy to see why companies should be prevented from offsetting the unintended effects of an asymmetric tax system. The limiting case would be to create a market in corporate tax losses. Failing that, companies could be allowed to carry forward losses marked up by the market interest rate, which would leave the incentive to invest unaffected by the asymmetric treatment of positive and negative taxable profits. In the absence of such a provision, leasing would be the market solution under the corporate cash flow basis. Under the net equity distributions basis, a rather different set of companies would be tax-exhausted. These would be firms that had made substantial issues of new shares. Such a company could reduce its tax loss by borrowing in order to purchase shares in other resident companies, and in the absence of loss carryforward with interest would have an incentive so to do.

Although these problems are rather different under the two alternative bases, they do not seem to be more serious under one than under the other. The cash flow basis perhaps has a cosmetic advantage in appearing more familiar. But the net equity distributions basis would enable the revenue authorities to adopt a common fiscal year for all companies without the need for companies to change their own accounting periods.

The treatment of overseas investment and profits remitted from abroad also raises some important questions. With a cash flow corporation tax there is no obvious reason to grant credit for foreign taxes paid. This is because the government, as has been argued above, is a partner in the firm's equity. If the foreign corporate tax rate is at least as great as the domestic tax rate, then the government would receive no return on its investment in the firm's activities overseas. But if foreign tax credit is denied, then the firm receives a return on its own share of the investment equal to the net of foreign tax rate return on the investment, i.e. the return to society on this investment overseas. One problem with the denial of foreign tax credit is that it would be difficult to impute that part of foreign taxes attributable to investment made after the introduction of the cash flow tax and that part attributable to investment made before the change in the system. Hence an alternative means of achieving the same objective would be to deny investment relief for overseas investment. Under the cash flow base this would be straightforward in that the investment made overseas would not qualify for immediate expensing. With the net equity distributions base, an additional tax would be levied on overseas investment at the appropriate tax-inclusive rate. Where the foreign tax rate was below the domestic corporate tax rate, then the additional charge (or reduction in allowances for investment) would be scaled down in proportion to the ratio of the two tax rates. It is interesting to note that for 12 years (1972–84) the U.K. government did allow companies both to receive 100% first-year allowances on overseas investment made by branches and also to receive credit for foreign taxes paid. This was effectively a subsidy to overseas investment. Nevertheless, it seems unlikely that this position could be maintained if there were a permanent shift to a cash flow corporation tax.

12.5.3 Revenue Implications of the Cash Flow Tax

At first sight it might appear that a tax which offers such generous investment incentives would require a higher tax rate to raise the same amounts of revenue as under the current corporate tax system. A little reflection, however, demonstrates that this is not the case. The new tax base would imply the abolition of investment tax credits and grants, and also of deductions for interest payments on new loans and for dividends. A full-scale calculation of the tax rate that would be required to raise the same amount of revenue would involve a general equilibrium analysis of the incentive effects of the new tax. This beyond our scope here. Instead we report some partial equilibrium estimates of the rate that will be required assuming no behavioral responses.

In the United Kingdom the Meade Committee (1978) found that over the period 1964–74 the required tax rate would have been 35% under the cash flow base and 34% under the net equity distributions base. These figures compare with the actual tax rate of between 40% and 45% over this period. Subsequently, the 1982 Green Paper on Corporation Tax claimed that the revenue-neutral rate of tax for the net equity distributions basis for the period 1973–81 would have been about 200% on a tax-exclusive basis. But Edwards (1982) showed that this calculation incorrectly attributed Advance Corporation Tax payments to the total corporate tax liability, when it is in fact more appropriately seen as a deduction at source of income tax at the basic rate on dividends. Making this correction, he found that the revenue-neutral rate assuming unchanged behavior was 47% for the net equity distributions base, as compared to the actual rate of 52% that prevailed throughout this period. Using individual company data, Mayer (1982) found that for the period 1965–76 the average rate required for revenue neutrality would have been 52% under the cash flow base and 42% under the net equity distributions base. All of these calculations show that there is no reason to suppose that the tax rate would have to rise if the base were switched to a corporate cash flow base.

Similar calculations for the United States by Aaron and Galper (1985) found that for the net equity distributions base a tax rate of 33% would have raised the same revenue as was in fact raised during the period 1981–83 with a tax rate of 46%. Again there seems reason to suppose that a switch to a cash flow base would lead to problems of revenue loss, provided adequate transitional arrangements were made.

12.6 Conclusions

Recent proposals for tax reform have raised the question of how easy it is to measure economic depreciation for the corporate sector. The effects of any proposed reform on investment will depend upon their impact on the cost of capital, which in turn depends upon how the allowances for depreciation built into the tax code relate to underlying true economic depreciation. The proposals for economic depreciation embodied in Treasury I entailed complete indexation of the corporate tax. It appears that these proposals are unlikely to be implemented. It is worth considering, therefore, whether there is any alternative tax base for which the cost of capital is independent of the inflation rate and which eliminates some of the existing distortions between different types of investment. One possible candidate is the cash flow corporation tax. Two versions of this tax were analyzed in this chapter: the cash flow base on real transactions and the net equity distributions base. From the analysis of their effects on investment incentives, and the administration arrangements that would be required for their implementation, it seems that the cash flow base is worthy of serious consideration in the current debate on reform of corporate taxation.

Appendix

In this appendix we derive expressions for the nominal discount rate that companies will use to compare net of corporate income tax cash flows in different periods. The novel feature is the explicit modeling of indexation of the tax system. The discount rate depends upon the source of finance that the firm uses, and can be thought of as the required net of tax return that the company must earn in order to be able to persuade investors to supply finance to the company. The corporate discount rate is denoted by ρ.

(i) Debt Finance

This is the simplest case in which the nominal discount rate is simply the effective net of tax interest rate at which a company can borrow. This is the market interest rate, i, less the tax savings for interest payments granted at the corporate level. A fraction β of interest payments are deductible against the corporate tax rate, and if such payments are indexed for tax purposes, then the deduction applies only to real interest payments. Hence

$$(A.1) \qquad \rho = i - \beta\tau(i - \pi I_i)$$

$$= i(1 - \beta\tau) + \beta\tau\pi I_i$$

where I_i is an indexation dummy variable that takes the value unity when interest payments are indexed for tax purposes and zero otherwise.

(ii) New Share Issues

Where new share issues are the optimal source of finance, the company will distribute all of its profits as dividends and finance investment by the sale of new equity. The return that the company earns net of corporate tax (the value of ρ) must be such that the net of tax dividend that it can finance is equal to the investor's opportunity cost of funds, which in turn is equal to the net of tax interest rate that the investor can earn on alternative investments. For an investor whose marginal income tax rate is m, this condition implies that

$$(A.2) \qquad i - m(i - \pi I_i) = (1 - m)\hat{\theta}\rho + z\pi I_z$$

where I_z is a dummy variable that takes the value unity when capital gains are indexed for tax purposes and is zero otherwise.

The RHS of (A.2) is the net of tax dividend plus the reduction in capital gains tax resulting from the real capital loss that arises when all profits are distributed as dividends and capital gains tax is indexed for inflation. This tax benefit disappears if either inflation is zero or capital gains tax is unindexed.

Rearranging (A.2) yields

(A.3)
$$\rho = \frac{i}{\hat{\theta}} + \frac{(mI_i - zI_z)\pi}{(1 - m)\hat{\theta}}$$

(iii) Retained Earnings

In the case of retained earnings the nominal return earned by the company, net of the investor's additional capital gains tax liability generated by the return, must equal the investor's opportunity cost of funds. Hence

(A.4)
$$i - m(i - \pi I_i) = \rho - z(\rho - \pi I_z)$$

Rearranging terms gives

(A.5)
$$\rho = i\left[\frac{1 - m}{1 - z}\right] + \left[\frac{mI_i - zI_z}{1 - z}\right]\pi$$

References

Aaron, H. J., and H. Galper. 1985. *Assessing tax reform.* Washington, D.C.: Brookings Institution.

Brown, E. C. 1948. Business-income taxation and investment incentives. In *Income, employment and public policy; Essays in honor of Alvin H. Hansen.* New York: W. W. Norton.

CBI. 1985. *Tax-time for change.* London: Confederation of British Industry.

Edward, J. 1982. The Green Paper on corporation tax: A review article. *Fiscal Studies* 3: 102–13.

Feldstein, M. S. 1970. Corporate taxation and dividend behaviour. *Review of Economic Studies* 37: 57–72.

Hall, R. E. and Rabushka, A. 1983. *Low tax, simple tax, flat tax.* New York: McGraw-Hill.

Kay, J. A., and M. A. King. 1978. *The British tax system.* Oxford: Oxford University Press. (4th edition 1986.)

King, M. A. 1971. Corporate taxation and dividend behaviour—a Comment. *Review of Economic Studies* 38: 377–80.

———. 1975. Current policy problems in business taxation. In *Bedrifts Beskatning.* Bergen: Norwegian School of Economics.

———. 1977. *Public policy and the corporation.* London: Chapman and Hall.

————. 1986. Business taxation, finance and investment. Mimeo, London School of Economics.

King, M. A., and D. Fullerton. 1984. *The taxation of income from capital.* Chicago: University of Chicago Press.

Mayer, C. 1982. The structure of corporation tax in the UK. *Fiscal Studies* 3: 121–41.

Meade Committee. 1978. *The structure and reform of direct taxation.* London: Allen & Unwin.

Miller, M. H. 1977. Debt and taxes. *Journal of Finance* 32: 261–75.

U.S. Treasury. 1984. *Tax reform for fairness, growth and simplicity.* Washington, D.C.: U.S. Government Printing Office.

United States. 1985. *The president's tax proposals for fairness, growth and simplicity.* Washington, D.C.: U.S. Government Printing Office.

Comment   Daniel Feenberg

King's thoughtful and precise analysis shows that a cash flow tax could offer important advantages over the U.S. corporate income tax. A tax on cash flow is inflation-neutral, it allows a required rate of return equal to the interest rate, and it abstracts from the impossible tasks of valuing accrued income and depreciation. While some biases in the valuation of accruals may be attributed to bureaucratic timidity or political interference, the real difficulty of defining income should not be underestimated. A tax levied at a high rate on the difference between two unobserved but highly correlated flows severely strains the tax administration machinery.[1] By removing the unobserved components from the tax base, the cash flow tax reduces the scope for tax avoidance and therefore the need for regulations.

The most difficult and controversial sections of current tax law regulate the treatment of asset transactions. Under the cash flow tax, these are particularly simple. Neither asset valuation nor basis affects (total) tax payments. Revenue authorities could be indifferent among possible characterizations of such transactions as sales, mergers, reorganizations, or acquisitions, because all of them would have identical tax consequence. In contrast, under an income tax the form and substance of a transaction often imply different tax liabilities. There would, however, be a powerful incentive for noncorporate capital to move to the

Daniel Feenberg is a research associate of the National Bureau of Economic Research.

1. There is a large industry devoted to disputing estimates of corporate income and expenses. The local property tax generates a similar government revenue but does relatively little for the legal and accounting professions. The income tax is levied on a very small base (taxable income), and errors in the estimates of gross income and expenses are carried into that base dollar for dollar. Therefore small percentage errors are magnified. Similar percentage errors in a real estate assessment would generate much smaller differences in property tax liability.

corporate sector, because a deduction for the full purchase price would accrue to the corporation, while the individual seller would take as income only the sale price less his basis.[2] Even if cash flow type rules were extended to the personal sector, in the presence of graduated rates there is a prodigious scope for gaming the tax system by the mechanical application of cash flow rules to transactions among tax-payers in different brackets.

In King's proposal the cash flow tax applies approximately current income tax rates to the cash flow minus real investment of the corporation. No deductions for interest or dividends are allowed. Equilibrium in the capital market implies that the present value of the tax on new investment will have an expected value of zero. Discounted at the interest rate, the cash flow generated will just equal the price of capital goods. Since the government takes the same share of gross cash flow as it provides in initial subsidy, the government's share must also have a market value of zero. Nevertheless, the tax does generate revenues from the existing capital in the corporate sector, on which the government takes a share of cash flow but only allows depreciation deductions.

King argues that it is necessary to continue to tax old capital in order to avoid windfall gains to the current owners of corporate equity. This is far from apparent to me. If the investment incentive aspect of the cash flow tax is effective, then enough additional capital will be brought forth to equate the marginal product of capital to the interest rate. Old capital still subject to tax must fall in value relative equally productive capital placed in service under the new and more generous tax regime. This would impose a loss on current owners of capital.

If the cash flow tax were implemented in a small corner of the world, then there would be little effect expected on the aftertax interest rate. The existing equilibrium, which relates the marginal product of capital F_k, the corporate tax rate t and the interest rate p,

$$F_k(1 - t) = p$$

would be disturbed by new investment that is effectively tax-free until

$$F'_k = p.$$

But the present value of capital still subject to the old rules must fall by t to equilibrate the market for old and new capital. The hypothesized windfall gain to the owners of old capital is possible if investment fails to respond to the higher after-tax rate of return. Yet in that case the investment subsidy aspect of the CFT is also ineffective. This may

2. King allows unused depreciation allowances to be carried forward into the new tax regime, but disallows all existing basis. This would be the source of some horizontal inequity.

surprise some readers: if the tax on old capital is not increased, how can the owners have a justified complaint against the government? The answer depends on the constitutional structure of society, and stands apart from the question of the loss itself, which is unambiguous.

Certainly the history of corporate taxes in the United States since 1945 has been one of declining rates on new capital essentially without change in the treatment of existing capital. Therefore the cash flow tax may be the end of a road we are already well along. Current investment may well be inhibited by the expectation that capital placed in service today will be competing with still more lightly taxed capital available to firms tomorrow. In that case failure to adopt the expected incentives will generate windfall gains for owners of existing capital. But there can be no presumption that maintaining current rules only for existing capital will prevent windfall gains and losses. Indeed, in the example above, windfall gains and losses can be avoided only by a commitment to tax all capital under the same rules, even if those rules change through time.

13   The Impact of Fundamental Tax Reform on the Allocation of Resources

Don Fullerton and Yolanda Kodrzycki Henderson

In the fall of 1984, the United States Treasury Department advanced a proposal for fundamental tax reform. The changes in investment incentives were designed to enhance fairness and economic growth. The Treasury Department's plan took large steps toward defining the tax base as economic income, and taxing that base at lower rates. Compared to current law, it was argued that the proposed code would tax more uniformly the returns from alternative assets, sectors, and industries. This more even-handed treatment would produce incentives for a superior mix of investment, which would in turn increase national output. A subsequent proposal by the president and legislation passed by the House of Representatives changed the specific features of tax reform, but they were motivated by the same general principles.[1]

During the continuing debate on fundamental tax reform, several issues have been raised with respect to the treatment of capital income. First, it has been asked whether the rate reduction is enough to offset the more comprehensive base for the tax on corporate income. Higher effective tax rates in the corporate sector might reduce corporate investment and exacerbate misallocations between the corporate sector

Don Fullerton is an associate professor of economics at the University of Virginia. Yolanda Kodrzycki Henderson is an economist at the Federal Reserve Bank of Boston.

Part of the research for this paper was conducted while Fullerton was Deputy Assistant Secretary (Tax Analysis), U.S. Treasury Department, and while Henderson was a visiting scholar at the American Enterprise Institute. We have received helpful comments from Alan Auerbach, J. Gregory Ballentine, and James Poterba. We are grateful to the American Enterprise Institute for financial support, and to Robert Schilit for research assistance. The views expressed in this paper are our own, and should not be attributed to any of the organizations with which we are affiliated. In particular, nothing here should be construed as policy of the Treasury Department.

and the noncorporate sector. Second, there has been concern that tax reform proposals leave largely unchanged the treatment of owner-occupied housing. Under current law, the returns to housing escape federal taxation while mortgage interest payments are deductible. It has been asked whether it is possible to achieve significant reform if we maintain this favorable treatment for housing relative to business capital.

Third, and related to the first two points, the magnitude of the improvements in the allocation of investment within the corporate sector has been questioned. Efficiency might increase from making more equal the tax treatment across different assets such as equipment, structures, inventories, and land. Yet this gain may or may not be enough to offset diminished efficiency from unchanged or worsened disparities across sectors.

Fourth, if tax reform does raise total taxes on income from capital, any gains from a more level playing field might be offset by losses resulting from reduced investment.

Finally, there has been general interest in how tax reform would affect different parts of the economy. Observers would like to know which industries and sectors might be expected to expand or contract.

This paper develops a framework to provide information on all of these important issues. We examine the original Treasury Department proposal and the later proposal submitted to the Congress by the president. We start in section 13.1 by measuring the impact of these plans on capital costs and effective tax rates. Our measures are appropriate for prospective investments, and they take into account the tax treatment of various assets, sectors, and industries. In section 13.2, we describe a general equilibrium simulation model that can evaluate the long-term consequences of tax reform. This model can trace the expected reallocation of resources as well as measure aggregate changes in the economy. Section 13.3 presents our simulation results in detail, and section 13.4 summarizes our conclusions. While this paper contains a comprehensive model of investment incentives, it does not provide information about the effects of tax reform on equity, simplicity, or other criteria essential to final policy judgments.

13.1   Administration Tax Reform Proposals, 1984–85

The Reagan administration has developed two sets of proposals for tax reform. The first was the November 1984 report of the Treasury Department to the president, entitled *Tax Reform for Fairness, Simplicity, and Economic Growth*. It was followed by *The President's Tax Proposals to the Congress for Fairness, Growth, and Simplicity* (May 1985). These will be referred to as the "Treasury plan" and the "president's plan,'' respectively. These proposals include pervasive changes to the tax code, but this paper concentrates on provisions that would affect taxes on income from capital. These include: (1) lower statutory rates, as evidenced in the reduction of the top corporate rate from 46 to 33% and the reduction of personal rates to three brackets of 15, 25, and 35%;[2] (2) revised capital cost recovery provisions, including the repeal of the investment tax credit and indexation of depreciation allowances; and (3) changed treatment of dividends, capital gains, and interest income and expense.

This section measures the investment incentives arising from the changes proposed by the administration, and compares them to incentives under current law. Our model of investment incentives is based on Fullerton (1985). The resulting costs of capital are then used as inputs for the general equilibrium model outlined in section 13.2.

13.1.1   A Model of Investment Incentives

To derive a user-cost-of-capital formula like that of Hall and Jorgenson (1967), consider a perfectly competitive firm contemplating a new investment in a world with no uncertainty. Assume the firm has sufficient tax liability to take associated credits and deductions, and that it does not resell the asset.[3] The acquisition cost is q, but an investment tax credit at rate k reduces the net cost of the asset to $q(1 - k)$. The rental return on this asset starts at level c, increases at the constant inflation rate π, and decreases because of constant exponential depreciation of the asset at rate δ. Local property tax at rate w is paid on the asset's value at any point in time, and the return net of property tax is subject to the corporate income tax at statutory rate u. These net returns are discounted at the firm's nominal after-tax discount rate r. The present value of depreciation allowances per dollar of investment is z, so the present value of savings is uzq.[4] In equilibrium, then, the net outlay must be exactly matched by the present value of net returns:

$$(1) \qquad q(1 - k) = \int_0^\infty (1 - u)(c - wq)e^{(\pi - \delta)t}e^{-rt}dt + uzq$$

This expression can be integrated and solved for the rental rate c/q. Subtraction of δ provides ρ^c, the real social return in the corporate sector, gross of tax but net of depreciation:

$$(2) \qquad \rho^c = \frac{r - \pi + \delta}{1 - u}(1 - k - uz) + w - \delta$$

In calculations below, common values are used for r, π, and u, but each asset has a specific value for δ, k, z, and w.

If u and the corporate discount rate are replaced by the noncorporate entrepreneur's personal marginal tax rate, τ_{nc}, and corresponding discount rate, then (2) gives an analogous expression for ρ^{nc}, the social rate of return in the noncorporate sector. Finally, owner-occupied housing receives no credit or depreciation allowances. A fraction λ of property taxes is deducted at the homeowner's personal marginal tax rate τ_h, and the imputed return is not taxed. Use of the homeowner's discount rate and an equilibrium condition similar to (1) provides ρ^h, the social rate of return to owner-occupied housing:

$$(3) \qquad \rho^h = r - \pi + (1 - \lambda\tau_h)w.$$

To compute the rates of discount in each sector, we first assume that individuals hold debt and equity issued by all three sectors, and that they arbitrage away any differences in net rates of return. Suppose i is the nominal interest rate, τ_d is the debtholder's personal marginal tax rate, and f is the fraction of nominal interest that is taxed (and of nominal interest that is deducted.)[5] Then, under our arbitrage assumption, all assets must provide the real net return that individuals could earn on their debt holdings:

$$(4) \qquad s = i(1 - \tau_d f) - \pi.$$

Here, s represents the net-of-all-tax return in the corporate, noncorporate, and owner-occupied housing sectors. In our computations, we start with an assumption on s and calculate i for all sectors from equation (4) as $(s + \pi)/(1 - \tau_d f)$.

The computation of discount rates then involves examining separately each sector and source of finance—debt, retained earnings, and new share issues. (We assume that the financial decision is exogenous.) The corporation's discount rate for debt is simply the net-of-corporate-income-tax rate of return: $r = i(1 - uf)$. For retained earnings, the individual's nominal net return must match $i(1 - \tau_d f)$. The investment earns a nominal net-of-corporate-tax return r and the resulting share appreciation is taxed at the accrued personal capital gains rate τ_{re}. Also, let $\gamma = 1$ if the system taxes only real capital gains, and $\gamma = 0$ if it taxes nominal gains. Then the return r must be such that $r(1 - \tau_{re}) + \tau_{re}\pi\gamma = i(1 - \tau_d f)$. The solution for r provides the requisite discount rate. For new shares, we assume that each dollar of after-corporate-tax return could instead be distributed as θ dollars of dividends.[6] This dividend is subject to personal taxes at rate τ_{ns}. Thus, new share issues must earn an r such that $r\theta(1 - \tau_{ns}) = i(1 - \tau_d f)$. The corporation's single discount rate is a weighted average of these three discount rates:

$$(5) \qquad c_d\left[i(1 - uf)\right] + c_{re}\left[\frac{i(1 - \tau_d f) - \tau_{re}\pi\gamma}{(1 - \tau_{re})}\right] + c_{ns}\left[\frac{i(1 - \tau_d f)}{\theta(1 - \tau_{ns})}\right],$$

where c_d, c_{re}, and c_{ns} are the proportions of new investment financed by debt, retained earnings, and new shares, respectively.

In the noncorporate sector, recall that τ_{nc} represents the marginal tax rate of entrepreneurs. Then, the noncorporate firm's debt costs $i(1 - \tau_{nc}f)$, and its equity must earn $i(1 - \tau_{df})$ after taxes, because of individual arbitrage. Its overall discount rate is thus:

$$(6) \qquad n_d[i(1 - \tau_{nc}f)] + n_e[i(1 - \tau_{df})],$$

where n_d and n_e represent the shares financed by debt and equity, respectively. For homeowners, τ_h is the marginal tax rate, and a similar logic provides their discount rate:

$$(7) \qquad h_d[i(1 - \tau_h)] + h_e[i(1 - \tau_{df})].$$

All of mortgage interest is deducted, but only f of other interest income is subject to tax. The parameters h_d and h_e are the respective debt and equity shares.[7]

Although investment incentives are properly measured by the marginal product of capital, ρ, we present many of our results in terms of marginal effective total tax rates. These tax rates are the difference between the pre- and post-tax rates of return, as a proportion of the pre-tax rate of return:

$$(8) \qquad t = \frac{\rho - s}{\rho}.$$

Because s is the return net of all taxes, this effective rate reflects the combined impact of corporate taxes, property taxes, and personal taxes. It shows the portion of capital costs attributable to taxes. The reason for looking at effective tax rates is that they are easily interpreted. For example, the effective rate can be compared with the statutory corporate rate, or with the zero rate that would apply in the case of a consumption tax. With s constant throughout the economy, t varies monotonically (but nonlinearly) with ρ: assets or industries or sectors with higher effective tax rates also face higher required gross rates of return for investment.

13.1.2   Alternative Tax Laws

The above framework is useful to sort out the net impact of statutory tax rates, cost recovery provisions, and other rules affecting interest, dividends, and capital gains. This section proceeds to discuss values for the parameters necessary to implement that framework, for current law and for the two Administration proposals.

Statutory tax rates

For current law, we use the top federal statutory rate of .46 for marginal corporate income. The weighted average of states' top-bracket rates has been estimated to be .0655 by King and Fullerton (1984, p. 204). Accounting for the deductibility of state taxes at the federal level, the appropriate value for u is .46 + .0655(1 − .46), which equals 49.5%. The Treasury Department and president's proposals would set a top federal rate of .33 and maintain the deductibility of state corporate taxes. For these reforms, u is thus 37.4%.

Turning to the personal level, we require marginal tax rates for interest income (τ_d), dividend income (τ_{ns}), capital gains (τ_{re}), noncorporate income (τ_{nc}), and interest deductions for owner-occupied housing (τ_h). The marginal investment under consideration is an equiproportionate increase in all capital stocks, with an equiproportionate increase in the holdings of all investors. Additional debt and interest income, for example, would be distributed among debtholders in proportion to their current debt and interest income. The appropriate marginal tax rate is thus the average of all debtholders' marginal rates, weighted by their interest income. We include both federal and state taxes. Furthermore, these rates must reflect the proportions of income received directly by households and the proportions received indirectly through institutions such as nonprofit organizations and life insurance companies.

For households, federal tax rates were calculated by Lawrence Lindsey using the TAXSIM model of the National Bureau of Economic Research.[8] The computed rate for housing interest deductions under current law is 25.0%. The rates for interest recipients (27.8%) and rate for dividend recipients (33.9%) indicate that they are on average in higher brackets than homeowners. The 26.1% capital gains rate reflects the full taxation of realized gains, and the 19.5% noncorporate rate reflects the low brackets of many proprietors and partners with losses for tax purposes. All of these personal tax rates would be reduced by the administration proposals. The TAXSIM calculations are available only for the Treasury plan, but the three brackets for the president's plan are very similar. Since these two plans would reduce the top rate bracket proportionately more than other brackets, they would reduce the weighted average rate on dividends and capital gains proportionately more than the rates on other forms of income. The resulting marginal rates were calculated to be: 21.0% for housing deductions; 21.9% for interest received; 26.2% for dividends; 20.8% for capital gains; and 15.8% for noncorporate income.

In order to include state income taxes, 5 percentage points are added to each federal rate under current law.[9] This percentage reflects the weighted average of the different states' rates, and the deductibility of state taxes at the federal level for those who itemize. Six percentage points are added to the rates for the administration proposals to reflect the repeal of deductibility.

The personal rate on interest is then adjusted to account for the taxation of banks, as described in King and Fullerton (1984, pp. 223–26). The resulting rate for households must then be averaged with a zero rate for the interest income of nonprofit institutions, and a .368 rate for the interest income of life insurance companies. This latter rate reflects their 46% statutory rate and their 20% deduction for reserves under current law. The final estimate for τ_d is 23.1%. The same average under the administration proposals is 20.5%.

The household rate on dividends is similarly raised to account for state taxes and reduced to account for the dividends received by tax-exempt institutions and insurance companies. The resulting value for τ_{ns} is .292 under current law and .242 under the administration proposals. The noncorporate rate is raised by state taxes, but not reduced by any holdings of institutions. It is .245 and .218 under current law and the proposals, respectively. The final rates for capital gains (.052 and .105, respectively) are discussed below.

The weighted average rate for mortgage interest deductions is .25 at the federal level, raised to .30 to account for state taxes. The TAXSIM model indicates that about 70% of household real property taxes are deducted. Thus τ_h and λ are .30 and .7, respectively. The proposals would reduce this personal rate to .27 and eliminate deductibility of property taxes ($\lambda = 0$). The final vectors of personal tax rates are summarized in table 13.1.

Table 13.1   **Personal Tax Rate Parameters**

Type of Income	1985 Law	Administration Plans
Interest Received	.231	.205
Dividends Received	.292	.242
Capital Gains	.052	.105[a]
Noncorporate Income	.245	.218
Housing Deductions	.300	.270

[a]This rate reflects full taxation of real capital gains after deferral.

Capital cost recovery

Potential for nonneutralities arises because different assets depreciate at many different rates, while tax codes tend to simplify by grouping assets into a few categories for depreciation allowances. In order to capture these nonneutralities, it is important to include many diverse assets in the model. Table 13.2 lists the 35 depreciable assets used in this study, including 20 kinds of equipment and 15 types of structures.

Table 13.2   Tax Parameters for Each Asset[a]

	Economic Depreciation Rate[b]	ACRS Tax Lifetime	RCRS Close-out Year	CCRS Close-out Year	Current Law Investment Tax Credit
1 Furniture and Fixtures	.110	5	17	7	.10
2 Fabricated Metal Products	.092	5	17	7	.10
3 Engines and Turbines	.079	5	25	10	.10
4 Tractors	.163	5	12	6	.10
5 Agricultural Machinery	.097	5	17	7	.10
6 Construction Machinery	.172	5	12	6	.10
7 Mining and Oil Field Machinery	.165	5	12	6	.10
8 Metalworking Machinery	.123	5	17	7	.10
9 Special Industry Machinery	.103	5	17	7	.10
10 General Industrial Equipment	.123	5	17	7	.10
11 Office and Computing Machinery	.273	5	8	5	.10
12 Service Industry Machinery	.165	5	12	6	.10
13 Electrical Machinery	.118	5	17	7	.10
14 Trucks, Buses, and Trailers	.254	5	8	5	.10
15 Autos	.333	3	5	4	.06
16 Aircraft	.183	5	12	6	.10

17	Ships and Boats	.075	5	25	10	.10
18	Railroad Equipment	.066	5	25	7	.10
19	Instruments	.150	5	12	6	.10
20	Other Equipment	.150	5	17	7	.10
21	Industrial Buildings	.036	18	63	28	.00
22	Commercial Buildings	.025	18	63	28	.00
23	Religious Buildings	.019	18	63	28	.00
24	Educational Buildings	.019	18	63	28	.00
25	Hospital Buildings	.023	18	63	28	.00
26	Other Nonfarm Buildings	.045	18	63	28	.00
27	Railroads	.018	15	38	10	.10
28	Telephone and Telegraph	.033	15	38	10	.10
29	Electrical Light and Power	.030	15	38	10	.10
30	Gas Facilities	.030	10	38	10	.10
31	Other Public Utilities	.045	10	38	10	.10
32	Farm Structures	.024	18	63	28	.00
33	Mining, Shafts and Wells	.056	5	63	28	.00
34	Other Nonbuilding Facilities	.029	18	63	28	.00
35	Residential Structures	.015	18	63	28	.00

aFor the case of 4% inflation and a 4% net rate of return.

bEconomic depreciation rates come from Hulten and Wykoff (1981), and for assets 27–31, from Jorgenson and Sullivan (1981).

The economic depreciation rates δ are estimated by Hulten and Wykoff (1981) and shown in the first column of table 13.2. These range from a high of .333 for autos to a low of .015 for residential buildings. We also include inventories and land in our study, but these are assumed not to depreciate, and they do not receive any depreciation allowances.

The second column of table 13.2 shows the lifetimes currently available under the accelerated cost recovery system (ACRS). Autos are depreciated over 3 years, other equipment over 5 years, public utility structures over 10 or 15 years, and other structures over 18 years. Allowances over these lifetimes can be read from tables in the law. In effect, equipment and public utilities receive allowances based on 150% of declining balance with a switch at the optimal time to straight line. The depreciation basis is reduced by half the investment tax credit. Other structures receive allowances based on 175% of declining balance with an optimal switch to straight line.

At zero inflation, these allowances are high relative to economic depreciation. They are fixed in nominal terms, however, so that at moderate inflation rates, their real present value may be less than that of economic depreciation. We use a nominal discount rate in calculating z to account for the fact that allowances are based on historical cost. The exact formula is shown in King and Fullerton (1984, p. 211).

The Treasury proposes to set allowances as closely as possible to estimates of economic depreciation (i.e., indexed for inflation). In fact, for their real cost recovery system (RCRS), they use the Hulten-Wykoff estimates to group together similar assets into 7 classes. Each class has an exponential rate for allowances and a "close-out" year in which all remaining basis may be deducted. We use a real discount rate to capture the indexing of allowances. The Treasury's grouping of assets is indicated by the close-out years shown in column 3 of table 13.2 (see *Tax Reform for Fairness, Simplicity, and Economic Growth*, p. 161). These allowances closely match the estimated real rates of depreciation. Since all remaining basis is deducted in the close-out year, however, allowances are slightly accelerated relative to the estimated exponential rates. Moreover, this near neutrality may be misleading to the degree that allowances were designed to reflect these particular estimates of economic depreciation. If δ are mismeasured in some way, then marginal effective tax rates are mismeasured.

The president proposes a capital cost recovery system (CCRS) with 6 asset classes, higher exponential allowances, a switch to straight line at the optimal time, and indexation for inflation. Deductions are not bunched in the close-out year as in RCRS. Our calculations use the formula on page 211 of King and Fullerton (1984), with a real discount rate. The groupings of assets under the president's plan are indicated by the close-out years in column 4 of table 13.2 (see *The President's Tax Proposals to the Congress for Fairness, Growth, and Simplicity,* p. 145).

The other aspect of capital cost recovery is the investment tax credit. Current law provides a 6% credit for automobiles, a 10% credit for other equipment, a 10% credit for public utility structures, and no credit for buildings. These rates are shown in column 5 of table 13.2. Both the Treasury and the president's plan would repeal these credits.

Provisions for capital gains, interest, and dividends

In addition to indexing depreciation allowances, both proposals include provisions to index capital gains. The Treasury plan would further index interest income and expense. This subsection describes these and other innovative features such as the fractional deduction for dividends paid by corporations.

With respect to capital gains, the advantage of deferral cuts the effective rate of tax approximately by half.[10] Current law also excludes 60% of realized long-term gains. Even after adding state taxes, the effective rate on accruals is 6% for households, and it is 5.2% after accounting for tax-exempt institutions and insurance companies. On the other hand, current law taxes nominal capital gains ($\gamma = 0$). The Treasury proposal would lower personal rates and index for inflation, but it would fully tax real gains when realized. After state taxes, halving for deferral, and averaging with institutions, τ_{re} would be .105 (with $\gamma = 1$). The effect of this change can be seen in equation (5). The president's plan taxes 50% of nominal gains at reduced personal rates, so τ_{re} is 5.6%. After 1991, however, the investor can choose indexation in place of the exclusion. For any given inflation rate, our model calculates whether this option would be taken. In particular, if $s = .04$, indexation is preferred to the exclusion if π exceeds .04.

Nominal interest income currently is taxed in the United States, and so f is set to one. In fact, the world has very little experience with attempts to index income, especially interest income. The Treasury recognizes the administrative difficulties of trying to measure real interest income or expense, and so it suggests a more practical procedure that is intended to have approximately the same effect. By knowing the inflation rate π, and assuming a 6% real return at the outset, it can estimate the inflationary portion of the nominal interest as $\pi/(.06 + \pi)$. With 4% inflation, for example, the excluded part is .4, and f is set to .6 in equations (4)–(7). All of mortgage interest is still deductible. The president's plan would not index interest income or expense.

The two administration proposals introduce partial integration of personal and corporate taxes by allowing firms to deduct part of dividends paid. Currently, if the corporation gives up a dollar of retentions, it is able to pay one dollar of dividends gross of personal taxes. Thus θ is one. Suppose instead that a fraction g of dividends is deductible against the corporate tax. The dollar of retentions corresponds to $1/(1 - u)$ dollars of before-tax earnings. If these earnings were paid out in an amount θ of dividends instead of being retained, then corporate tax payments would equal $u[1/(1 - u) - g\theta]$. The after-tax return available for dividends would thus be $\theta = [1/(1 - u)] - u [1/(1 - u) - g\theta]$, simplified as $\theta = 1 + gu\theta$. This equation implies $\theta = 1/(1 - gu)$. With $u = .374$ and half of dividends deductible under the Treasury proposal, θ would be 1.230. With a 10% deduction under the president's plan, θ is 1.039. The effect of such a change is that the firm does not need to earn as much to provide the required after-tax return to the saver (see equation (5)).

Other data

For local property tax rates (w), we use the same parameters under all three tax regimes. Assuming that new investments will pay the same property tax on average as existing investments, data in Fullerton and Henderson (1984) indicate rates of .00768 for equipment and inventories, .01126 for business land and structures, .01550 for public utilities, and .01837 for residential land and structures.

Our initial assumption is that new investments have sources of finance in the same proportions as existing investments. Following King and Fullerton (1984, p. 239), we find that corporations finance 33.7% by debt, 61.4% by retentions, and 4.9% by new shares. Following Fullerton and Henderson (1984), we assume that noncorporate firms and homeowners also finance a third of their investments by debt and two-thirds by equity.

We take the inflation rate, π, and the baseline net-of-all-tax rate of return, s, each to be 4%. Solving equation (4) with these assumptions and $\tau_d = .231$, we find that i for current law equals .104. If s did not change under the Treasury or president's plans, i would be .091 or .101, respectively.

13.1.3 Effective Tax Rate Results

This section first concentrates on the incentives to invest in different assets. We then aggregate assets to reflect investment incentives at the industry and sector levels.

Table 13.3 presents allowances and marginal effective total tax rates for 36 assets in the corporate sector. Under current law, the first 20 assets—types of equipment—have very low tax rates or are even subsidized. These effective tax rates range from -4 percent to $+3$ percent, despite the fact that we are including taxation at both the personal and

Table 13.3   Investment Incentives for Each Asset in the Corporate Sector

		Present Value of Allowances (z)			Marginal Effective Total Tax Rates (t)		
		Current Law	Treasury Plan	President's Plan	Current Law	Treasury Plan	President's Plan
1	Furniture and Fixtures	.812	.769	.891	.019	.416	.280
2	Fabricated Metal Products	.812	.769	.891	.025	.393	.264
3	Engines and Turbines	.812	.685	.855	.029	.429	.286
4	Tractors	.812	.834	.920	.002	.411	.280
5	Agricultural Machinery	.812	.769	.891	.024	.400	.269
6	Construction Machinery	.812	.834	.920	−.001	.418	.286
7	Mining and Oil Field Machinery	.812	.834	.920	.001	.412	.281
8	Metalworking Machinery	.812	.769	.891	.015	.430	.290
9	Special Industry Machinery	.812	.769	.891	.022	.407	.274
10	General Industrial Equipment	.812	.769	.891	.015	.430	.290
11	Office and Computing Machinery	.812	.877	.939	−.036	.435	.302
12	Service Industry Machinery	.812	.834	.920	.001	.412	.281
13	Electrical Machinery	.812	.769	.891	.017	.425	.286
14	Trucks, Buses, and Trailers	.812	.877	.939	−.029	.423	.293
15	Autos	.812	.915	.952	−.021	.401	.292
16	Aircraft	.812	.834	.920	−.005	.428	.293
17	Ships and Boats	.812	.685	.855	.031	.423	.282
18	Railroad Equipment	.812	.685	.891	.033	.409	.241

(continued)

Table 13.3 (continued)

	Present Value of Allowances (z)			Marginal Effective Total Tax Rates (t)		
	Current Law	Treasury Plan	President's Plan	Current Law	Treasury Plan	President's Plan
19 Instruments	.812	.834	.920	.006	.399	.272
20 Other Equipment	.812	.769	.891	.006	.459	.312
21 Industrial Buildings	.607	.436	.617	.458	.480	.398
22 Commercial Buildings	.607	.436	.617	.423	.453	.374
23 Religious Buildings	.607	.436	.617	.404	.438	.360
24 Educational Buildings	.607	.436	.617	.404	.438	.360
25 Hospital Buildings	.607	.436	.617	.419	.450	.371
26 Other Nonfarm Buildings	.607	.436	.617	.483	.501	.417
27 Railroads	.604	.571	.855	.339	.431	.317
28 Telephone and Telegraph	.604	.571	.855	.370	.462	.332
29 Electric Light and Power	.604	.571	.855	.364	.456	.329
30 Gas Facilities	.699	.571	.855	.297	.456	.329
31 Other Public Utilities	.699	.571	.855	.314	.483	.343
32 Farm Structures	.607	.436	.617	.420	.451	.371
33 Mining, Shafts and Wells	.865	.436	.617	.316	.523	.437
34 Other Nonbuilding Facilities	.607	.436	.617	.437	.464	.383
35 Inventories	—	—	—	.481	.442	.418
36 Land	—	—	—	.504	.468	.447

corporate levels.[11] Equipment has these low effective tax rates because of investment tax credits and because of depreciation allowances in excess of economic depreciation. Structures (assets 21–26, 32–34) face considerably higher tax rates, between 32 and 48%, because they are not eligible for the investment tax credit and because of their less generous depreciation allowances. Public utility structures (assets 27–31) have tax rates that are not quite as high as those for most other structures, since they receive a 10% investment tax credit. The highest tax rates are those for inventories (48%) and land (50%). These rates are not reduced by any credits or depreciation deductions.

The Treasury plan eliminates most disparities in tax rates among assets. It rescinds the investment tax credit and provides depreciation allowances that are close to economic depreciation. Any remaining differences are due solely to differential property taxes and to slight variations in depreciation treatment. Effective tax rates in the corporate sector all lie between 39 and 52%. The generally higher level of these rates is due in part to the changes in capital cost recovery provisions, but also to changes in the treatment of interest income and expense. Currently, investments financed by debt are subsidized in that interest payments are deducted by corporations at a 49.5% rate, and included in taxable income of debtholders at an average marginal rate of 23.1%. The difference between 49.5% and 23.1% is a 26.4 percentage-point subsidy that is lowered by the Treasury plan to 16.9 percentage points (interest deductions are made at a 37.4% rate while interest income is taxed at a 20.5% rate). Furthermore, the Treasury plan indexes interest deductions and receipts, so that this subsidy would apply to only the fraction that reflects real interest. The application of the subsidy rate to a lower base is yet another reason for higher effective tax rates on debt-financed investments under the Treasury plan.

The president's plan would reduce the disparities among tax rates for different assets, but not as much as the Treasury plan. The investment tax credit would still be eliminated, but depreciation deductions would be accelerated relative to economic depreciation. These depreciation provisions introduce some disparities in the treatment of assets relative to the Treasury plan. Equipment would be taxed at a lower effective rate than structures. Accelerated depreciation also provides for preferential taxation of depreciable assets relative to inventories and land. As well, the president's plan reduces the number of classes of assets from 10 to 6. It might therefore introduce disparities among effective tax rates of individual assets. Finally, in table 13.3, tax rates are generally lower than those in the Treasury plan because interest is no longer indexed. Compared to current law, effective tax rates rise for equipment but fall for structures. These tax rates range from 24 to 42%. The tax rates for inventories and land remain on the order of 40%.

Next, table 13.4 shows marginal effective tax rates by industry. Tax rates for individual assets were aggregated using estimates of the 1984 stock of each asset used in each industry.[12] Under current law, these industry rates range from 25.5% for utilities and 27.8% for real estate to 42.9% for transportation equipment. The low rate for real estate reflects the favorable treatment of owner-occupied housing, which represents about three-quarters of that industry's capital stock. Utilities make extensive use of investment tax credits. Generally, manufacturing industries face effective tax rates that are higher than average, because they are heavily corporate. For the Treasury plan, real estate remains low at 29.7% because owner-occupied housing retains most aspects of its preferential treatment. Agriculture remains at 35.3% because of the high proportion of noncorporate enterprise. All other industries' rates are between 37 and 46%. Effective rates under the president's plan range from 31.3% (real estate) to 39.6% (transportation equipment). Whereas the Treasury plan had no industry's effective tax rate lower than under current law, the president's plan lowers rates for half the industries in our study. Overall, the president's plan is more successful at narrowing the differences among effective rates across industries, despite the Treasury's relative success at narrowing the effective tax rate across assets.[13] The reason for this apparent contradiction lies in table 13.5.

Table 13.4   **Marginal Effective Total Tax Rates for Each Industry**

Industry	Current Law	Treasury Plan	President's Plan
1 Agriculture, Forestry and Fisheries	.353	.353	.345
2 Mining	.294	.417	.336
3 Crude Petroleum and Gas	.348	.463	.391
4 Construction	.366	.405	.365
5 Food and Tobacco	.397	.442	.383
6 Textiles, Apparel and Leather	.385	.435	.376
7 Paper and Printing	.338	.435	.360
8 Petroleum Refining	.413	.454	.389
9 Chemicals and Rubber	.329	.434	.358
10 Lumber, Furniture, Stone, Clay and Glass	.363	.435	.369
11 Metals and Machinery	.394	.443	.383
12 Transportation Equipment	.429	.445	.396
13 Motor Vehicles	.349	.442	.369
14 Transportation, Communication and Utilities	.255	.431	.318
15 Trade	.410	.410	.378
16 Finance and Insurance	.358	.369	.337
17 Real Estate	.278	.297	.313
18 Services	.244	.382	.314
Total	.331	.372	.342

Table 13.5   Investment Incentives with New View of Dividend Taxes

	Current Law		Treasury Plan			President's Plan		
	ρ	t	ρ	% change	t	ρ	% change	t
Corporate Sector								
Equipment	.040	.010	.069	(+70.5%)	.419	.056	(+37.9%)	.282
Nonresidential Structures	.069	.423	.077	(+10.8%)	.480	.066	(−4.3%)	.398
Public Utility Structures	.061	.348	.074	(+20.1%)	.457	.060	(−2.6%)	.329
Inventories	.077	.481	.072	(−7.0%)	.442	.068	(−10.9%)	.418
Land	.081	.504	.075	(−6.8%)	.468	.072	(−10.4%)	.447
Total	.064	.372	.072	(+12.7%)	.446	.064	(+0.3%)	.374
Noncorporate Business Sector								
Equipment	.034	−.181	.057	(+68.1%)	.298	.052	(+53.4%)	.231
Nonresidential Structures	.059	.322	.062	(+4.7%)	.353	.058	(−1.2%)	.314
Public Utility Structures	.055	.267	.064	(+16.5%)	.371	.058	(+6.2%)	.310
Residential Structures	.065	.386	.067	(+2.5%)	.400	.064	(−1.8%)	.374
Inventories	.060	.334	.059	(−2.5%)	.317	.058	(−2.8%)	.314
Nonresidential Land	.064	.371	.062	(−2.4%)	.356	.062	(−2.8%)	.353
Residential Land	.071	.434	.069	(−2.1%)	.422	.069	(−2.4%)	.420
Total	.061	.347	.062	(+2.0%)	.359	.061	(−0.3%)	.344
Owner-Occupied Housing	.052	.232	.054	(+3.5%)	.257	.056	(+7.9%)	.288
Average Overall Cost of Capital	.060		.064	(+6.8%)		.061	(+1.7%)	
Standard Deviation	.012		.008			.005		
Average Overall Tax Rate	.331		.372			.342		
Interest Rate	.104		.091			.101		

Note: Numbers in parentheses are percentage changes from current law in the cost of capital (ρ).

Table 13.5 presents user costs and effective tax rates for the corporate, noncorporate, and owner-occupied housing sectors. These rates also are presented for several aggregated assets: equipment, residential and nonresidential structures, public utility property, inventories, and residential and nonresidential land.

Under current law, accelerated cost recovery provisions combine with nominal interest deductions to generate a low total tax rate in the corporate sector. Interestingly, the overall effective tax rate in the corporate sector is 37.2%, only 2.5 percentage points higher than the 34.7% effective rate in the noncorporate sector, and 14 points higher than the 23.2% rate on owner-occupied housing (attributable to property taxes). The Treasury Department plan actually increases the spread between the overall tax rate in the corporate sector and the overall rates in the other sectors. Less generous capital cost recovery and interest provisions raise the rate in the corporate sector by 7.4 percentage points. The effect of less generous cost recovery provisions is offset to a large degree in the noncorporate sector by the 3% reduction in the tax rate of proprietors and partners. For housing, the effective tax rate rises by 2.5 points, mainly as a result of the end of deductibility of property taxes. Under the president's plan, by contrast, unchanged corporate sector taxation together with an increase in housing sector taxes produce more equal rates across industries and across sectors.

Our discussion has covered the incentives to invest in different assets, industries, and sectors under each version of the tax code. Before turning to the simulation model, however, we discuss a critical assumption about dividend taxes that affects our evaluation of the administration's tax reform proposals.

13.1.4   Dividend Taxes: "New" vs. "Old" Views

The administration proposals lower the effective tax rate on corporate dividends. Under the Treasury plan, in calculating the base of the corporate tax, firms would be allowed to deduct 50% of dividends paid. Under the president's plan, the deduction would be 10%. Yet these changes have little effect on our results so far. Fullerton (1985) found, for example, that a 50% deduction by itself would lower the effective tax rate in the corporate sector by only 2 percentage points.

The reason for this relatively insignificant effect is that these results concentrate on incentives at the margin. When a firm considers financing a prospective investment by retaining earnings, it necessarily delays a dividend. It may be shown that dividend taxes do not affect the rate of return on such an investment, since they affect symmetrically the dividend foregone initially and the dividend paid out later.[14] In the case of new share issues, on the other hand, there are no foregone dividends when the firm finances a capital investment. The personal tax rate on dividends, τ_{ns}, and the fraction of dividends deducted, g, still affect the later returns to shareholders. Because of this asymmetry, these dividend tax parameters do enter the discount rate for new share issues in equation (5).[15]

Our initial calculations assume that marginal investments are financed in the same way as existing investments. Since new share issues finance only 5% of the capital stock of corporations, changes in the dividend tax have a small impact on the effective taxation of corporate investments.

Our calculations so far are consistent with the "new view" (of Auerbach 1979; Bradford 1981; and King 1977) that dividend taxes do not affect significantly the marginal investment. The competing tradition or "old view" concludes that dividend payout rates affect the cost of capital, and that there is significant double taxation of corporations because profits are taxed once at the firm level and again when distributed as dividends (see McLure 1979). Under this theory, the provisions for a partial deduction of dividend payments would tend significantly to lower the effective tax rate for investments because firms are observed to distribute a sizable fraction of their earnings to shareholders.[16]

It is possible to construct a scenario that is consistent with the findings under the old view, for a payout rate of 50%. Although existing investments are financed 62% by retained earnings, it may not be possible to finance additional new investments entirely from that same source. If corporations have a limited supply of retained earnings and must increase their reliance on new shares to finance marginal investments, then equation (5) may be modified such that equity finance is divided evenly between retained earnings and new shares ($c_{re} = .3315$ and $c_{ns} = .3315$, with c_d still equal to .337). Under this alternative, dividend taxes have a substantial impact on the effective tax rate in the corporate sector.

Table 13.6 indicates the investment incentives consistent with the old view of dividend taxation. Under this alternative assumption, there currently exists a 13-point gap between effective tax rates in the corporate and noncorporate sectors. The two administration plans eliminate about one-third of this gap. Under the old view, both new plans would reduce effective tax rates in the corporate sector and thus reduce intersectoral distortions. The reduction in corporate sector capital taxation also means that the overall effective tax rate in the economy would be virtually unchanged from current law. The rate is 38.2% under current law, 37.6% under the Treasury plan, and 36.9% under the president's plan. This slight overall rate reduction may bring about intertemporal welfare gains under the old view of dividends.[17]

Table 13.6   Investment Incentives with Old View of Dividend Taxes

	Current Law		Treasury Plan			President's Plan		
	ρ	t	ρ	% change	t	ρ	% change	t
Corporate Sector								
Equipment	.051	.211	.069	(+36.9%)	.423	.062	(+22.1%)	.354
Nonresidential Structures	.082	.512	.077	(−5.6%)	.483	.074	(−10.0%)	.458
Public Utility Structures	.073	.448	.074	(+2.2%)	.460	.066	(−9.7%)	.390
Inventories	.093	.570	.072	(−22.4%)	.445	.076	(−18.0%)	.476
Land	.097	.586	.076	(−21.3%)	.472	.080	(−17.4%)	.500
Total	.077	.480	.072	(−5.6%)	.450	.071	(−7.9%)	.435
Noncorporate Business Sector[a]	.061	.347	.062	(+2.0%)	.359	.061	(−0.3%)	.344
Owner-Occupied Housing[a]	.052	.232	.054	(+3.5%)	.257	.056	(+7.9%)	.288
Average Overall Cost of Capital	.065		.064	(−1.1%)		.063	(−2.0%)	
Standard Deviation	.016		.008			.008		
Average Overall Tax Rate	.382		.376			.369		
Interest Rate[a]	.104		.091			.101		

Note: Numbers in parentheses are percentage changes from current law in the cost of capital (ρ).

[a]The choice between the old and new view of dividend taxes does not affect the noncorporate sector, owner-occupied housing, or the overall interest rates.

13.1.5   Summary of Incentives under Tax Reform

Our analysis has emphasized multiple aspects of proposals for fundamental tax reform. When we adopt the assumption that marginal investments are financed in the same manner as existing investments, then our results are consistent with the new view of dividend taxes. We then show that current law and the president's plan provide the highest incentives for investment as a whole. The costs of capital (and equivalently the effective tax rates on income from capital) are similar under these two regimes. The Treasury plan would raise the cost of capital almost 7% from its current level, and it might therefore deter capital formation. On the other hand, both administration plans would tend to allocate capital more efficiently across its uses. The Treasury plan is most effective in narrowing the disparities in the cost of capital across assets (within each sector), while the president's plan is most effective in narrowing these disparities across industries and sectors (but less across assets). Our overall evaluation of the effects of these proposals on the economy will take into account all these distinctions.

When we adopt the alternative assumption that corporations are more limited in using retained earnings to finance marginal investments and must therefore rely more heavily on new share issues, then neither new plan raises the cost of capital. Under this view, both plans also succeed in reducing disparities across assets and across sectors. Therefore, the resulting welfare gains would be expected to be higher than under the new view.

13.2   A General Equilibrium Model with Allocation of Resources among Assets, Sectors, and Industries

The investment incentives measured in the previous section are used as inputs into the general equilibrium model developed in Fullerton and Henderson (1986). This model is capable of simulating the effects of tax reforms on production by different industries, as well as on aggregate output. Furthermore, because of the detail on capital formation, it can trace the flow of capital simultaneously among different assets and sectors.

13.2.1   A Description of the Model

The consumption side of the model is taken directly from the general equilibrium model of Fullerton, Shoven, and Whalley (FSW 1983), as fully described in Ballard, Fullerton, Shoven, and Whalley (1985). Twelve income-differentiated households have initial endowments of labor and capital that can be sold for use in production. As indicated in the top part of figure 13.1, these households each maximize a nested

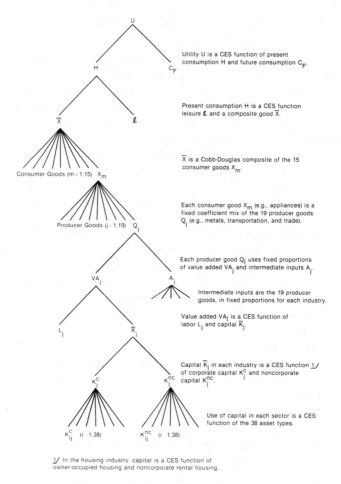

Fig. 13.1   A Diagrammatic Summary of the Model

utility function by making an initial allocation of resources between present consumption and saving. The elasticity of substitution between present and future consumption is based on an exogenously specified aggregate estimate for η, the uncompensated savings elasticity with respect to the net rate of return. We examine alternative savings elasticities.[18]

In evaluating alternative tax reforms, we simulate a sequence of equilibria in which the capital stock increases as a result of saving in the previous period. Domestic saving is the only vehicle by which investment can be affected, since the model is not open to international capital flows. The model is open to balanced trade in commodities, but there is no scope for saving by foreigners to finance domestic capital formation.

With present resources, as indicated in the next level of figure 13.1, a household can choose to buy some of its own labor endowment for leisure. The elasticity of substitution between consumption and leisure is based on an aggregate estimate of 0.15 for the uncompensated labor supply elasticity with respect to the net-of-tax wage. Present consumption expenditures are then divided among 15 consumer goods according to a Cobb-Douglas subutility nest. Each consumer good is a fixed-coefficient combination of outputs of the 18 industries. The model includes the entire spectrum of federal, state, and local taxes. These are typically modeled as *ad valorem* tax rates on purchases of appropriate products or factors.[19]

Our amendments to this model come in the specification of production decisions. We provide a generalized equilibrium model with endogenous allocation of capital across industries, sectors, and assets.

The structure of production is displayed in the bottom half of figure 13.1, where each industry determines its use of factors in a sequence of stages. The first two stages are similar to the FSW model. First, producers have fixed requirements of intermediate inputs and value added per unit of output. Second, they can substitute between labor and capital in a constant elasticity of substitution (CES) value-added function. The elasticity of substitution between labor and capital in each industry is chosen from an average of econometric estimates in the literature. These average elasticity estimates vary from 0.7 to 1.0 across our 18 private industries. In this stage, however, we depart from the FSW model which constructs capital costs from observed tax payments. Instead, we specify that a Hall-Jorgenson (1967) type cost-of-capital formula determines the demand for capital in each of the 18 private industries, emphasizing investment incentives at the margin. We also add two new stages of production decisions, as described in detail in Fullerton and Henderson (1986). In the third production stage of figure 13.1 for each industry, separate cost-of-capital expressions are used to determine the division among the corporate, noncorporate business, and owner-occupied housing sectors. Fourth, within each sector of each industry, individual cost of capital calculations are used to determine demand for up to 38 different asset types. These assets include 20 types of equipment, 15 types of structures, inventories, and land in each sector.

As described in section 13.1.1, the user costs for individual asset types are built up from information on statutory tax rates, credit rates, tax lifetimes, and other statutory specifications. These costs also depend endogenously on the real after-tax rate of return (s) determined in equilibrium. A composite of those costs applies to each sector of a given industry, and an additional composite of the corporate sector and the noncorporate sector applies to the overall cost of capital for that industry. Each industry has a different mix of assets in each sector, as well as a different mix of sectors, all determined endogenously. When the total use of capital equals the total available supply, we have equilibrium in the capital market; when other markets clear as well, we have a general equilibrium.

Our model is not limited to a unitary elasticity of substitution among assets, as implied by the Cobb-Douglas functional form common in previous studies. Instead, capital in the corporate sector or in the noncorporate sector of each industry is a different CES composite of the 38 assets. The elasticity of substitution among assets (ϵ) may be specified exogenously. Capital in each industry is another CES function of composite capital stocks from each sector of that industry. The elasticity of substitution between corporate and noncorporate capital (σ) is also prespecified.

These generalizations are important because the choices of ϵ and σ, as well as of η, have much bearing on the relative size of different distortions and therefore on the relative attractiveness of alternative reforms. If ϵ is high, for example, then changes in the relative tax treatment of different assets would result in a more significant change in the firm's production technology. A high value for ϵ would therefore imply relatively high welfare gains if a reform tends to equalize the tax treatment of different assets. If σ is high, then the sectoral allocation of capital would be quite sensitive to changes in the relative tax treatment of corporations, noncorporate business, and owner-occupied housing. High values of σ would be reflected in high welfare gains from equalizing rates among sectors. Finally, the choice of η, the savings elasticity, matters for aggregate capital accumulation. If η is high, then reduced taxation of the return to income from capital would result in a higher saving response than in the case where η is low. As this assumed elasticity rises, any tax wedge between the gross and net return to saving results in a greater measured efficiency loss. The gain from reducing the overall tax on capital would therefore be larger as η increases.

13.2.2 Simulation and Sensitivity

Before presenting the results themselves, it is necessary to describe our simulations. We simulate a sequence of 6 equilibria that are 10 years apart, so our total simulation interval is 50 years. All our simulations assume an adjustment to lump-sum taxes (positive or negative as appropriate) in order to restore the revenue yield of the baseline. We perform the simulations for each view of dividend taxes under a "standard" set of parameters, and also under several alternatives.

The standard set of parameters include $\epsilon = 1$ and $\sigma = 1$, the Cobb-Douglas case for assets and sectors, plus $\eta = 0.4$, which is consistent with the estimate of Boskin (1978). Our strategy in constructing alternatives is not to show all plausible combinations of ϵ, σ, and η. Instead, we pick combinations that point out the likely range of welfare effects from tax reform. Thus, for each view of dividend taxes, we simulate the effects of one set of parameters that is likely to produce relatively "favorable" effects and one that is likely to produce relatively "unfavorable" effects. As discussed below, these sets of parameters necessarily differ between the new view and old view cases.

We consider values of ϵ and σ between 0.5 and 3, and values of η between 0 and 0.4. As we stressed in our earlier literature review (Fullerton and Henderson, 1986), existing econometric work on substitution elasticities does not consider the number of assets we include in this model. Neither does it attempt specifically to measure a sectoral substitution elasticity. There remains considerable uncertainty about these parameter values. For the savings elasticity, our lower bound of zero is in accord with the estimate of Howrey and Hymans (1978).

Under the case with existing financing shares—or new view—both of the reforms reduce interasset distortions. In addition, the Treasury plan increases intersectoral and intemporal distortions, while the president's plan is approximately neutral in these respects. The welfare gains might therefore be sensitive to the relative importance of these interasset, intersectoral, and intertemporal factors. The two administration proposals could be expected to produce the highest welfare gains in the case where ϵ is high. Low values of σ and η would be expected to raise estimated gains (or reduce losses) from the Treasury plan, but to have minor impact in the evaluation of the president's plan. Therefore a favorable set of parameters for the new view is: $\epsilon = 3$, $\sigma = 0.5$, and $\eta = 0$; and an unfavorable set of parameters for the new view is: $\epsilon = 0.5$, $\sigma = 3$, and $\eta = 0.4$.

We perform a second set of simulations using financing proportions that give results consistent with the old view of dividend taxes. Table 13.6 indicates that, under the old view, both administration plans would lower the differential taxation of assets and of sectors. Thus, these plans would yield higher welfare gains the higher are ϵ and σ. Because they would also slightly lower the overall cost of capital, welfare gains would rise somewhat with η. To analyze the sensitivity of these results, we examine the old view under two alternatives to the standard parameters. The favorable case for the old view is: $\epsilon = 3, \sigma = 3, \eta = .4$;

the relatively unfavorable case for the old view is $\epsilon = .5$, $\sigma = .5$, $\eta = 0$.

13.2.3 Interpretation of Simulations

Simulation analysis such as we perform here can provide highly detailed results. It is always necessary to bear in mind, however, the limitations of such studies. We would like to mention three types of issues: the quantification of tax reform measures; the specification of economic behavior; and the usefulness of our results for policy decisions.

First, although our simulations take into account major elements of the tax reform proposals as they pertain to capital formation, they do not take into account all aspects of fundamental tax reform. For example, both plans introduce substantial proposals for indexing. We capture the effect of indexation on investment incentives at our given inflation rate of 4%, but not on reducing the uncertainties caused by varying inflation. To take another important example, the plans reduce personal marginal income tax rates in ways that might increase participation in the labor force and decrease activity in the underground economy.[20] We do not measure welfare effects from these changes. As well, the proposals introduce new features that could have sizable influences on particular industries. Examples include the changes for energy subsidies and for accounting in the case of multiperiod production. We do not include such policy changes in our measures of capital costs.[21]

Second, any simulation model necessarily simplifies some aspects of economic decisionmaking. One example relevant to our model is the specification of financial choices. The reform plans raise the cost of debt finance for corporations, yet we do not alter firms' debt-equity ratios to reflect this change. Also, we have made specific choices with respect to capital allocation decisions. Our use of the ϵ parameter implies that firms view all assets as substitutes for one another in production; we omit the possibility that some assets are complements. Our use of the σ parameter attempts to capture the impact of capital costs on incorporation decisions, but we do not explicitly model the effect on these decisions of providing limited liability or access to national financial markets.

Finally, it should be emphasized that we do not consider the effects of fundamental tax reform on "fairness" or "simplicity," concepts that are important in both the Treasury's and the president's reports. Any changes in the achievement of these goals would be additional criteria by which to assess tax reform.

In summary, the various results found in section 13.3 must necessarily be interpreted with caution. Any overall evaluation of tax reform should use appropriate additional information and judgment.

13.3   General Equilibrium Results

13.3.1   Welfare, Output, and Capital Formation

Table 13.7 presents the welfare gains or losses as well as the effects on capital formation. First, panel I reflects the new view. As shown there, the tax reform proposals generally cause an increase in economic welfare even if they bring about a decrease in the capital stock. The welfare-reducing effects of the slight 1.7% increase in the cost of capital under the president's plan and even the 6.8% increase under the Treasury plan are generally offset by the welfare-augmenting effect of a better allocation of capital across its uses. It is therefore possible to achieve larger output from a given capital stock, and in fact—as the simulations indicate—to achieve larger output from a slightly smaller capital stock.[22]

In comparing the two reform proposals generally, we find that the president's plan has larger welfare gains and a smaller drop in the capital stock. These results follow from the findings in table 13.5 that the president's plan would achieve greater reduction in the standard deviation of the capital costs and almost no increase in the cost of capital.

Turning specifically to the Treasury plan, efficiency effects are relatively small for any set of parameters. Under the favorable case of a high asset substitution parameter, a low sector substitution parameter, and a low savings elasticity, the present discounted value of welfare gains is $678 billion (1984 dollars). This figure represents an increase of 0.6% over the present value of income and leisure in the baseline. Under the unfavorable set of parameters, there is a welfare loss of $112 billion, or 0.1%. The standard-case parameters yield a slight increase in welfare. The range of estimates for the change in the capital stock is -0.5 to -1.9%.

For the president's plan, the indicated welfare changes are all positive, ranging from $292 billion to $861 billion (or 0.2% to 0.7%). Under the favorable set of parameters, there is no change in the capital stock, indicating that the "price effect" of a slightly raised overall cost of capital is offset by the "income effect" of savings out of the greater output generated by more efficient resource allocation. The other parameter combinations show a 0.2 to 0.3% decline in the capital stock.

We turn next to the old view of dividends, the case where marginal equity investments are half subject to dividend taxation, and half to capital gains treatment. The results in panel II indicate welfare gains that are considerably higher than those in panel I, and changes in the capital stock that are all positive. Under the old view, the proposals reduce interasset distortions, intersectoral distortions, and intertemporal distortions. They therefore produce efficiency gains even in the least favorable case where all relevant elasticities are small ($\epsilon = .5$, $\sigma = .5$, $\eta = 0$).

Table 13.7 Welfare Gains and Capital Formation from Fundamental Tax Reform

	Welfare Gains[a] (billions of 1984 dollars)				Long-Run Change in Capital Stock[b]	
	Treasury Plan		President's Plan		Treasury Plan	President's Plan
I. New View of Dividend Taxes						
A. Standard case: $\epsilon = 1$, $\sigma = 1$, $\eta = .4$	58.8	(0.1)	367.8	(0.3)	-1.9	-0.2
B. Favorable case: $\epsilon = 3$, $\sigma = .5$, $\eta = 0$	678.2	(0.6)	861.3	(0.7)	-0.5	0.0
C. Unfavorable case: $\epsilon = .5$, $\sigma = 3$, $\eta = .4$	-112.1	(-0.1)	291.7	(0.2)	-1.9	-0.3
II. Old View of Dividend Taxes						
A. Standard case: $\epsilon = 1$, $\sigma = 1$, $\eta = .4$	606.4	(0.5)	692.0	(0.6)	+1.0	+1.3
B. Favorable case: $\epsilon = 3$, $\sigma = 3$, $\eta = .4$	1408.0	(1.2)	1419.0	(1.2)	+1.0	+1.0
C. Unfavorable case: $\epsilon = .5$, $\sigma = .5$, $\eta = 0$	329.2	(0.3)	423.6	(0.4)	+0.5	+0.7

[a]Welfare gains are measured as the present discounted value of equivalent variations. The numbers in parentheses express the gains or losses as a percentage of the present discounted value of welfare (consumption plus leisure) in the baseline sequence.

[b]Percent difference from baseline capital stock after fifty years.

Furthermore, the findings for the Treasury and president's plans are similar, as might be anticipated from their similar effects on both the level and the standard deviation of capital costs in table 13.6. For the Treasury plan, the cases shown yield welfare gains between 0.3 and 1.2% and increases in the capital stock between 0.5 and 1.0%. For the president's plan, the welfare gains are estimated between 0.4 and 1.2%, and the capital stock rises between 0.7 and 1.3%. This set of simulations produces larger increases in welfare and capital formation because the partial integration introduced by the administration's proposals is found to lower the cost of capital significantly. The contrast between the new and old views is particularly marked in the simulations of the Treasury plan because firms would deduct half of dividend payments, as opposed to only 10% under the president's plan.

13.3.2   Allocation of Capital among Assets and Sectors

Under current law, investment in equipment is tax-favored as a result of the investment tax credit and very short lifetimes for depreciation. At the other extreme, returns to investments in inventories and land face statutory tax rates.

Both proposed plans narrow the differences in these tax treatments. As a result, firms would alter their relative demands for these assets. Table 13.8 illustrates this reallocation for the corporate sector, for the standard parameters under the new view (where ϵ, the asset substitution elasticity, equals 1). Similar reallocations would take place in the non-corporate business sector.[23] Under our 1984 baseline data, 29.5% of the corporate capital stock is in the form of equipment. This share would drop to 19.7% under the Treasury plan and 21.8% under the president's plan. Inventories currently account for 34.2% of corporate capital stock, but are estimated to account for 41.8% under the Treasury proposal and 39.0% under the president's plan. The use of land in the corporate sector would also increase. Firms would continue to use

Table 13.8   **Eventual Allocation of Corporate Capital Across Asset Types**
(After fifty years, as proportion of total)[a]

	Baseline	Treasury Plan	President's Plan
Equipment	.295	.197	.218
Structures	.149	.155	.160
Public Utility Property	.112	.107	.118
Inventories	.342	.418	.390
Land	.101	.123	.115

[a]Assumes new view of dividends.

about the same share of structures and public utility property, assets that are currently taxed at rates close to the average rate for the corporate sector. In the simulations with a higher value of ϵ (not shown), these reallocations are in the same direction but larger in magnitude. As the asset elasticity parameter increases, corporations change their production processes more sharply in reaction to changes in relative user costs for different assets.

Our simulations also measure the effect of tax reform in redistributing capital among the three sectors of the economy.[24] Under the new view, both proposals would shift capital toward the noncorporate business sector and away from owner-occupied housing. Additionally, in the case of the Treasury plan, the 13% increase in the corporate cost of capital would eventually result in an 8% decrease in the size of capital in the corporate sector (see fig. 13.2). The president's plan would result in essentially no change in the corporate capital stock, given the very slight 0.3% increase in the corporate cost of capital.

The assumption about the effects of dividend taxation is a significant factor in this allocation. When we adopt the conclusion of the old view that the existing taxation of dividends discourages investment, then the administration's proposals would increase capital in the corporate sector. The 50% dividend deduction under the Treasury plan would more than offset the cost-raising effects of less generous depreciation allowances and the removal of the investment tax credit. Relative use of capital would rise in the corporate sector and fall in the noncorporate and housing sectors. These relative flows, together with a 1% increase

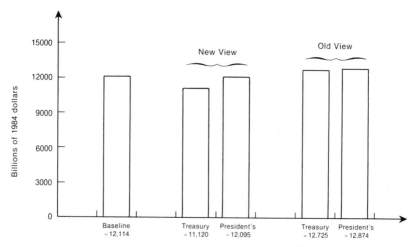

Fig. 13.2   Allocation of Capital in the Corporate Sector after 50 years (standard case parameters)

in total capital, allow the corporate sector capital stock to rise by 5%, as illustrated in figure 13.2. Under the president's plan, the 10% dividend deduction in combination with more generous cost recovery provisions than in the Treasury plan would also yield a 1% increase in total capital, but a 6% increase in corporate capital, and a commensurate decline of 5% in the stock of owner-occupied housing.

13.3.3   Results for Industries

As just indicated, either reform would expand the productive use of land and inventories at the expense of equipment. Also, under our standard parameters ($\epsilon = 1$, $\sigma = 1$, $\eta = 0.4$), and new view of dividends, the noncorporate business sector would grow while the corporate and owner-occupied housing sectors would contract. Since our industry costs of capital are derived from asset- and sector-specific costs of capital, the factors that affect asset and sectoral allocations will also affect industry allocations. In a general equilibrium model such as this one, simulations also indicate changes in demand for the outputs of different industries. This change in the output mix generates changes in the patterns of demand for labor and capital.

Table 13.9 presents the eventual changes in the output and use of capital for 9 private industries.[25] Under the Treasury proposal with the new view, the only industries that experience an increase in output in the long run are agriculture and housing. These industries' capital stocks also increase, as might be expected given their largely noncorporate status and their heavy reliance on land. The capital stock is also projected to rise in the trade industry (because of the high use of inventories) and finance and insurance (because of the low use of equipment).

The industrial pattern under the president's plan is similar, except for the projected decline in real estate.[26] Also, more industries would experience increases in output and capital usage.

Once again the theory of dividend taxation matters for the results, since it affects the attractiveness of doing business under the corporate form. When we adopt the old view (not shown), capital in the real estate industry would decline and capital in the heavily corporate manufacturing industries would increase, under both plans. There would also be large increases in both output and use of capital in the construction and trade industries.

13.4   Conclusions

Recent proposals for fundamental tax reform differ in their relative emphasis on interasset, intersectoral, interindustry, and intertemporal distortions. The model in this paper addresses these multiple issues in the design of taxes on capital incomes. It is capable of measuring the

Table 13.9   Eventual Output and Capital Stock by Industry[a]

Industry	Baseline after Fifty Years (billions of 1984 dollars)		Treasury Plan[b]		President's Plan[b]	
	Output	Capital Stock	% Output	% Capital Stock	% Output	% Capital Stock
1 Agriculture	786.7	6,186.0	+7.4	+7.4	+4.2	+4.0
2 Mining	196.8	1,110.0	−5.8	−12.0	−1.3	−3.7
3 Construction	630.2	699.8	−1.5	−4.1	−0.5	−0.5
4 Manufacturing	4,936.4	4,616.8	−0.2	−5.9	+0.8	+0.1
5 Utilities	1,067.5	3,272.8	−4.8	−19.8	−1.4	−7.5
6 Trade	1,621.9	4,389.5	−0.1	+2.6	+0.9	+5.5
7 Finance and Insurance	588.0	565.7	−0.3	+1.5	+0.3	+4.4
8 Real Estate	1,109.5	10,777.9	+0.2	+0.1	−1.4	−2.1
9 Services	1,685.2	877.2	−0.6	−14.8	−0.0	−8.4
Total	12,622.1	32,495.4	−0.3	−1.9	+0.4	−0.2

[a]Assumes new view of dividends.

[b]Percentage changes from the baseline, after fifty years, in the private sector only.

net effects of changes in statutory rates, credits, depreciation allowances, and other features such as the indexation of interest and capital gains. It can compare costs of capital for individual assets, sectors, and industries, and it weighs these together to evaluate the impact on total investment incentives. In a fully general equilibrium system, it can simulate alternative resource allocations and associated changes in welfare. For the overall evaluation of alternative tax reform proposals, the simultaneous consideration of these multiple effects is crucial.

The model is used to compare current law, the Treasury Department tax reform plan of November 1984, and the president's proposal of May 1985. Under the new view that dividend taxes have a small effect on investment incentives, both reforms would reduce interasset distortions and the president's plan would reduce intersectoral distortions, but the Treasury plan would exacerbate intertemporal distortions. Still, for most parameters, both reforms generate net welfare gains even with slight declines in the capital stock. Under the old view that dividend taxes have a significant effect on investment incentives, both plans reduce corporate taxation through their partial deductions for dividends paid. They thus reduce intersectoral distortions as well as differences among assets. Under this view, the Treasury plan no longer increases intertemporal distortions. Even for the least favorable set of parameters in this case, these reforms raise both the capital stock and the real value of output above their baseline values. Finally, the paper shows alternative allocations of capital among assets, sectors, and industries.

Notes

1. We do not evaluate the House bill here. Charles McLure (1986) provides excellent description and analysis of the revisions in the proposals between fall 1984 and spring 1985.

2. This paper does not consider the effects of these rate cuts on labor income and labor supply. We concentrate exclusively on their effects on capital.

3. The effects of uncertainty and imperfect loss offsets are investigated in Auerbach (1983) and Auerbach and Poterba (1987).

4. For a variety of reasons not captured here, firms may not always minimize their taxes by taking the earliest possible deductions. In order to concentrate on the tax wedge and to insure comparability across tax regimes, however, calculations here assume tax minimizing behavior. Similarly, firms pay unnecessary taxes by using FIFO inventory accounting, but calculations here assume LIFO methods. The effect of FIFO inventory accounting is shown in Henderson (1985).

5. The fraction f is 1.0 under current U.S. law.

6. The parameter θ is the opportunity cost of retentions in terms of forgone dividends (gross of personal taxes). It is 1.0 under current law.

7. One obvious result of our arbitrage assumption is that if individuals earn the same rate of return net of all taxes from debt and equity, then the firm

must earn a higher marginal product on a project financed by equity than on the same project financed by debt. In a context of perfect certainty, this can be justified only if for some reason firms must use a given mix of finance. Here, we do not model the role of uncertainty or institutional restrictions that cause observed financing choices. We take these choices to be exogenous. An alternative assumption might be that firms, rather than individuals, arbitrage between debt and equity. The effects of firm arbitrage on measured tax rates are explored in Fullerton and Henderson (1984), Henderson (1985), and Fullerton (1985). This alternative view would be supported in the perfect certainty framework only if individuals in different income groups specialize in different assets, as in Miller (1977).

8. See Lindsey and Navratil (1985) for further description of this model.

9. See p. 221 of King and Fullerton (1984).

10. See King and Fullerton (1984, pp. 221–22).

11. A subsidy, or negative effective tax rate, means that tax credits and depreciation allowances are so generous that they outweigh the effects of taxes on net income and property values. Under a subsidy, the value of ρ required to earn $s = .04$ after tax is lower than 4%.

12. From the July 1985 *Survey of Current Business*, we obtain 1981 data for corporate equipment, corporate structures, noncorporate equipment, and noncorporate structures. We also obtain data for total depreciable capital stocks by 18 industries. We project each of these 22 capital stock figures to 1984 by using an econometric estimate of the relationship between economic growth and capital formation. We then use an RAS procedure with these 1984 targets to adjust an unpublished 1977 matrix from Dale Jorgenson, showing each of these four types of assets used in each of the 18 industries. Finally, we obtain the finer capital allocations for all 20 types of equipment and 15 types of structures, by using disaggregate proportions in the Jorgenson data. These data also form the basis for our 1984 projections for the values of land and inventories in each of our industries.

13. An important caveat to these statements is that we have assumed identical financing shares for all assets, industries, and sectors.

14. To see this argument, consider a firm that wishes to invest in $1 more of capital by retaining an additional dollar of earnings. To retain an extra dollar, the firm must necessarily reduce dividend payments. As shown in section 13.1.2, the dividends foregone equal $1/(1 - gu)$ gross of personal tax, or $(1 - \tau_{ns})/(1 - gu)$ net of personal tax. (Recall that u is the statutory corporate rate, g the fraction of dividends deductible from corporate income, and τ_{ns} the personal tax rate on dividend income.) In the following period the asset earns a pretax return of r, and the resulting income available for dividend payout is $r(1 - u)/(1 - gu)$, or $(1 - \tau_{ns})r(1 - u)/(1 - gu)$ net of personal tax. The return to shareholders relative to dividends foregone in the first period is thus $r(1 - u)$. This return is independent of the parameters τ_{ns} and g, since these affect identically the numerator and denominator in the calculation of the rate of return.

15. The parameter g enters because $\theta = 1/(1 - gu)$.

16. The new view received empirical support in a study by Auerbach (1984), but the old view was found more compatible with historical evidence in Poterba and Summers (1983, 1985). Poterba and Summers (1985) also explain some conceptual problems associated with each theory.

17. Another finding is that the Treasury plan is neutral with respect to firms' choices between retaining earnings and issuing new shares. That is, the costs of capital in the corporate sector do not differ between Tables 13.5 and 13.6. Although the Treasury plan maintains personal tax rates that are lower for

capital gains than for dividends, the 50% dividend deduction at the corporate level completely offsets this rate differential. We do not attempt to measure potential efficiency gains from any reduced distortions in financial decisions.

18. Our model assumes that households form expectations of the rate of return myopically. Ballard and Goulder (1985) examine the effect of incorporating perfect foresight expectations into the Fullerton-Shoven-Whalley model.

19. The model also requires that government run a balanced budget. Therefore, when our simulations raise (lower) national output and income, we must offset the resulting revenue gains (losses) by cutting (increasing) some other tax. We do this by changing income taxes in a lump-sum manner.

20. These effects are analyzed by Slemrod (1986).

21. The construction of a measure for the cost of capital requires assessments about the degree to which various aspects of taxation affect investment at the margin. Some corporate tax features may affect employment, profits, or other behavior, without affecting investment at the margin. The windfall recapture tax of the president's proposal, for example, would acquire revenue from corporations that received accelerated depreciation on their existing holdings of assets and that would earn income subject to the new lower rate. Other provisions in the proposals would affect the timing of revenue more than they affect the present value of tax on marginal investment. Indeed, it is because tax revenue is often a poor guide to investment incentives that we turn to the concept of the cost of capital. Yet, because the cost of capital cannot account for every feature of the tax code, it may omit important effects on incentives.

22. Although our measure of welfare gain includes changes in the value of leisure time, the simulations affect leisure only slightly. Therefore, output and welfare move in the same direction.

23. The results under standard parameters for the old view are similar. The choice between the old view and the new view primarily affects the relative costs of investment across sectors, not across assets within a sector.

24. Figure 2 again considers the standard parameters, with $\epsilon = 1$, $\sigma = 1$, and $\eta = 0.4$.

25. In Table 13.9, industry 2 combines the two extractive industries in our model, while the manufacturing category combines 9 more detailed industries: food and tobacco; textiles, apparel, and leather; paper and printing; petroleum refining; chemicals and rubber; lumber, furniture, stone, clay, and glass; metals and machinery; transportation equipment; and motor vehicles.

26. The proposals appear to treat owner-occupied housing identically, since both would terminate the deduction for local property taxes and both maintain full deductibility of mortgage interest payments. However, the Treasury proposal indexes interest deductions of businesses and thus reduces the nominal interest rate (see Table 13.5). The Treasury plan therefore lowers the relative cost of housing capital more than does the president's proposal (which has no interest indexing).

References

Auerbach, Alan J. 1979. Wealth maximization and the cost of capital, *Quarterly Journal of Economics* 3:433–46.

Auerbach, Alan J. 1983. Corporate taxation in the United States. *Brookings Papers on Economic Activity* 2:451–513.

Auerbach, Alan J. 1984. Taxes, firm financial policy, and the cost of capital: An empirical analysis. *Journal of Public Economics* 23:27–57.

Auerbach, Alan J., and James M. Poterba. 1987. Tax loss carryforwards and corporate tax incentives. Chapter 10 in this volume.

Ballard, Charles L., and Lawrence H. Goulder. 1985. Consumption taxes, foresight, and welfare: A computable general equilibrium analysis. In John Piggott and John Whalley, eds., *New developments in applied general equilibrium analysis*. New York: Cambridge University Press.

Ballard, Charles L.; Don Fullerton; John B. Shoven; and John Whalley. 1985. *A general equilibrium model for tax policy evaluation*. Chicago: University of Chicago Press.

Boskin, Michael J. 1978. Taxation, saving, and the rate of interest. *Journal of Political Economy* 86:S3–S27.

Bradford, David F. 1981. The incidence and allocation effects of a tax on corporate distributions. *Journal of Public Economics* 15:1–23.

Fullerton, Don. 1985. The indexation of interest, depreciation, and capital gains: A model of investment incentives. NBER Working Paper no. 1655.

Fullerton, Don, and Yolanda Kodrzycki Henderson. 1984. Incentive effects of taxes on income from capital: Alternative policies in the 1980s. In C. R. Hulten and I. V. Sawhill, eds., *The legacy of reaganomics: Prospects for long-term growth*, Washington, D.C.: Urban Institute Press.

Fullerton, Don, and Yolanda Kodrzycki Henderson. 1986. A disaggregate equilibrium model of the tax distortions among assets, sectors, and industries. American Enterprise Institute Occasional Paper no. 7.

Fullerton, Don; John B. Shoven; and John Whalley. 1983. Replacing the U.S. income tax with a progressive consumption tax. *Journal of Public Economics* 20:3–23.

Gorman, John, John Musgrave, Gerald Silverstein, and Kathy Comins. 1985. Fixed private capital in the United States. *Survey of Current Business* 65:36–59.

Gravelle, Jane G. 1982. Effects of the 1981 depreciation revisions on the taxation of income from business capital. *National Tax Journal* 35:1–20.

Hall, Robert, and Dale W. Jorgenson. 1967. Tax policy and investment behavior. *American Economic Review* 57:391–414.

Henderson, Yolanda Kodrzycki. 1985. Does reducing inflation lower the cost of capital? *Proceedings of the Annual Conference of the National Tax Association-Tax Institute of America* (November 1984): 283–92.

Howrey, E. Philip, and Saul H. Hymans. 1978. The measurement and determination of loanable funds saving. *Brookings Papers on Economic Activity* 3:655–85.

Hulten, Charles R., and Frank C. Wykoff. 1981. The measurement of economic depreciation. In C. R. Hulten, ed., *Depreciation, inflation, and the taxation of income from capital*. Washington, D.C.: Urban Institute Press.

Jorgenson, Dale W., and Martin A. Sullivan. 1981. Inflation and corporate capital recovery. In C. R. Hulten, ed., *Depreciation, inflation, and the taxation of income from capital*. Washington, D.C.: Urban Institute Press.

King, Mervyn A. 1977. *Public policy and the corporation*. London: Chapman and Hall.

King, Mervyn A., and Don Fullerton, eds. 1984. *The taxation of income from capital: A comparative study of the U.S., U.K., Sweden, and West Germany*. Chicago: University of Chicago Press.

Lindsey, Lawrence B., and John F. Navratil. 1985. Rate reductions and revenue responses: Evidence from 1982. Harvard University. Mimeo.

McLure, Charles E., Jr. 1979. *Must corporate income be taxed twice?* Washington, D.C.: Brookings Institution.

———. 1986. Rationale underlying the treasury proposals. In *Economic consequences of tax simplification*. Federal Reserve Bank of Boston Conference Series no. 29.

Miller, Merton. 1977. Debt and taxes. *Journal of Finance* 32:261–75.

Poterba, James M., and Lawrence H. Summers. 1983. Dividend taxes, corporate investment, and 'Q.' *Journal of Public Economics* 22:135–67.

———. 1985. The economic effects of dividend taxation. In Edward I. Altman, and Marti G. Subrahmanyam, eds., *Recent advances in corporate finance*. Homewood, Ill.: Richard D. Irwin.

The President's Tax Proposals to the Congress for Fairness, Growth, and Simplicity 1985. Washington: U.S. Government Printing Office.

Slemrod, Joel. 1986. The impact of tax reform on households. In *Economic consequences of tax simplification*. Federal Reserve Bank of Boston Conference Series no. 29.

U.S. Treasury Department. 1984. *Tax reform for fairness, simplicity, and economic growth*. Office of the Secretary, Washington, D.C.

Comment   J. Gregory Ballentine

The Fullerton/Henderson analysis embodies important extensions of previous large scale general equilibrium modeling of tax changes. As such, the analysis is highly valuable. The extensions, however, are far too preliminary and the modeling of tax changes is too limited to provide reliable answers to the questions the paper poses concerning the effect of the Treasury reform proposals on economic efficiency. In particular, the limitations in the modeling of tax changes cause an understatement of the rise in the cost of capital induced by the Treasury proposal that may make the results misleading. This limitation is not unique to the Fullerton/Henderson analysis; it is quite common.

Three specific limitations of the Fullerton/Henderson analysis are presented below. The first, and the one that will be discussed at greatest length, is the incomplete modeling of tax changes. The second is the measurement of certain tax parameters, and the third is the empirical foundation for the modeling of the choice between corporate and noncorporate form.

The Modeling of Tax Law Changes

The Fullerton/Henderson analysis purportedly examines the effect of the two tax reform proposals, Treasury I and II (referred to above as the Treasury plan and the President's plan, respectively), on the

J. Gregory Ballentine is Principal and National Director of Tax Analysis at Peat, Marwick, Mitchell and Co. in Washington, D.C.

interindustry, intersectoral, and intertemporal allocation of capital. Accordingly, the primary focus of the paper is on the effects of the capital income tax changes. The analysis, however, only takes into account some of the tax changes in the Treasury proposals. Specifically, the elimination of the ITC, the new depreciation schedules, indexing, the new tax rates, and the dividend deduction are included; other provisions are omitted.

The table below shows the revenue effect for 1985 and 1990 of the corporate income tax provisions included in the paper compared with the omitted corporate provisions. (The windfall recapture provision and a few other clearly inframarginal provisions are excluded from the table. Indexed FIFO is also excluded since the paper assumes LIFO is used.)

	Treasury I ($ billions)		Treasury II ($ billions)	
	1989	1990	1989	1990
Included Provisions				
Rate Reductions	−51.1	−58.4	−39.7	−42.5
Depreciation	51.8	68.0	8.7	15.4
ITC	29.2	31.7	33.3	37.4
Dividend Deduction	−29.0	−38.2	−7.2	−8.0
Other	−5.2	−4.4	—	—
Subtotal Included	−4.3	−1.3	−4.9	2.3
Excluded Provisions	40.5	43.9	24.3	27.3

This table only includes corporate tax provisions. Also omitted from the paper are various pension changes that, on balance, raise revenues and, presumably, raise the cost of capital. The main point to recognize is that these numbers strongly *suggest* that the Fullerton/Henderson analysis understates the increase in the cost of capital and may, therefore, give a much more favorable impression of the effects of the two reform proposals than is warranted.

The revenue estimates do not prove this conclusion, but only suggest it for at least two reasons. First, revenue estimates include some purely inframarginal effects and, second, they represent some proposals that may improve the interasset allocation of resources.

Broadly speaking, the omitted corporate provisions fall into three categories: those directly affecting certain assets, those affecting financial intermediation, and those affecting international investments. Included in the first category are the changes in multiperiod accounting rules. Consider, for example, work in process inventory investment. Under current law a portion of the cost of such investment is expensed.

That portion includes certain labor costs (mostly pension costs) as well as some interest and capital costs.

Treasury I and II reduce, and perhaps eliminate, the amount that can be expensed. The same changes are proposed for self-constructed assets; under current law part of that investment is expensed and part depreciated using ACRS. Treasury I and II reduce or eliminate that expensing.

With adequate data on inventory investment and investment in self-constructed assets, incorporating the multiperiod accounting changes in the Fullerton/Henderson analysis should be straightforward. That is, fractional expensing fits easily into the Jorgenson cost-of-capital framework that Fullerton/Henderson use. This change alone would be useful. In Treasury II these multiperiod accounting provisions raise $8.3 billion in corporate taxes in 1990. While the revenue estimate overstates the significance of these provisions, since it includes a kind of recapture of past expensing benefits for inventories, an analysis of the impact of the Treasury proposals should not ignore this or similar provisions. (Other omitted provisions that are fairly asset-specific include oil tax changes, mining tax changes, changes for pollution control assets, etc.)

The second category of tax changes deals with financial intermediation. Most of these increase taxes currently paid by banks and insurance companies. Some, including the non-bank bad debt proposal, however, affect other firms in their capacity as lenders that hold accounts receivable. The changes in this area do not fit easily into a Jorgenson cost-of-capital framework. Incorporating them requires modeling the tax treatment of financial intermediaries and its effect on the cost of capital. This is a rather forbidding task and it is unfair to expect Fullerton and Henderson to provide such a new model in an otherwise substantial project. Since, however, virtually all of the financial intermediary changes raise corporate revenues, it is almost certain that they raise the cost of capital. (These financial intermediary changes raise more than $8.8 billion in 1990 under Treasury II.) Thus, due to this omission alone, the Fullerton/Henderson results should be identified as a clear understatement of the increase in the cost of capital caused by the reform proposals.

The last general category of omitted corporate tax increases includes the international tax changes. These involve requiring a per-country foreign tax credit limit instead of a worldwide limit, changing the rules determining whether income is foreign source or U.S. source, and other changes. (In Treasury II the foreign provisions raise corporate taxes by $5.1 billion in 1990.) Incorporating these changes is, presumably, quite difficult since it requires including foreign investment in the model as well as modeling the complex tax changes. As in the case with the financial intermediary changes, all that can be expected of the Fullerton/Henderson analysis is an acknowledgement of the omission and a discussion of the likely bias caused by that omission.

Overall, the omissions make the results of the Fullerton/Henderson study very unreliable. Essentially, Fullerton and Henderson examine two hypothetical tax proposals that appear to involve a net reduction in corporation income taxes. They do not really examine Treasury I and Treasury II; those proposals, particularly Treasury I, involve a significant increase in corporate taxes. Of course, simply looking at the projected revenue changes is not an adequate alternative. Nonetheless, it is disconcerting to have results presented purportedly describing the economic effects of tax reform bills that involve large corporate tax increases balanced by personal tax reductions, whereas, in fact, the results are based on an analysis of corporate tax reductions.

It should be recognized that this problem is not limited to the Fullerton/Henderson analysis. There have been numerous economic studies of the effect of tax reform on the cost of capital, effective tax rates, and the allocation of capital. The Treasury, for example, has confidently asserted that Treasury II lowers the cost of capital. Economists have testified before Congress presenting estimates of the effect various reform proposals have on the cost of capital. Yet all of these studies have the same or more omissions as Fullerton/Henderson. It is unfortunate that economists have spoken with such confidence on the effect of reform proposals that raise corporate taxes 25% to 40% based on conclusions derived from modeling the effects of a corporate tax reduction.

Tax Parameters

The effective tax rates used in the Fullerton/Henderson analysis are the excess of the pre-tax return over the after-tax return divided by the pre-tax return. Using their notation, the rates are given by:

$$\frac{\rho - S}{\rho}$$

With some manipulation, and ignoring property taxes and new share finance, the effective tax rate for the corporate sector is:

$$\frac{\rho - S}{\rho} = \frac{\rho - (r - \pi)}{\rho}$$
$$+ \frac{S + \pi}{\rho} \left(C_d \frac{(1 - u)}{(1 - t_d)} + \frac{C_e}{(1 - t_{re})} - 1 \right).$$

The first term is the effective tax rate at the company level; it depends largely on the investment tax credit, z (the present value of depreciation deductions), and u the corporate tax rate. The second term captures the effects of financial policy and the difference between the corporate tax rate and the tax rate on debt and retained earnings. For many cases, the second term is as important, or more important, than the first in determining the overall tax rate.

An accurate calculation of present law effective tax rates requires accurate values for u, t_d (the tax rate on debt) and t_{re} (the personal tax rate on retained earnings). Comparable tax rates for noncorporate investments require an accurate value for t_{nc}, the personal tax rate on noncorporate investors.

The corporate tax rate, u, is taken to be .46. This would be accurate if, at the margin, all corporations were taxable. However, the computations in the paper indicate large negative effective corporate tax rates. This lends to an apparent contradiction; if corporate rates are generally negative and fairly large in absolute value, then u should be less than .46. If, however, u is less than .46, the effective tax rates are not so negative. The authors should conduct some experiments on hypothetical firms whose growth tracks the overall growth of the modeled economy to see if those firms have a positive tax base, so that u is .46. If they do not have a positive tax base, either u should be lowered or the model should be adjusted to reflect higher taxes.

The issues surrounding the values of t_d and t_{nc} are different. Conceptually, t_d reflects the tax rate on the marginal investors in taxable bonds. It is those marginal investors who determine the taxable interest rate. Similarly, t_{nc} is the tax rate on the marginal investor in noncorporate equity. Calculation of t_d and t_{nc} requires modeling individual portfolio choice assuming progressive tax rates. The Fullerton/Henderson paper does not do this. Instead, in it t_d and t_{nc} are computed as the weighted average tax rate of all those who earn interest or noncorporate profits. This may be consistent with a model of portfolio choice, but no such model is presented or referenced. Instead, the paper asserts that the "marginal investment under consideration is an equiproportionate increase in all capital stocks" (sec. 13.1.2) and from this concludes that additional "debt and interest income, for example, would be distributed among debt holders in proportion to their current debt and interest income" and that the "appropriate marginal tax rate is thus the average of all debt holders' marginal rates, weighted by their interest income."

This reasoning is incorrect. The margin in question does not depend upon some hypothetical proportionate expansion of the capital stock. The margin exists even in a static setting and involves marginal portfolio allocations by individuals. It may be that the computed tax rates are correct, if it is assumed that each individual's portfolio distribution is fixed independent of relative returns or changes in statutory marginal tax rates. This, however, is not so much a model of marginal portfolio choice as it is an *ad hoc* assumption.

To investigate the sensitivity of results to other values of t_d and t_{nc}, Fullerton and Henderson should consider alternatives. For example, they might follow Hendershott's approach in a paper in this volume and infer t_d from the implicit tax on tax exempt bonds. This gives a value of t_d of about .3, higher than that used by Fullerton and Henderson.

The Corporate/Noncorporate Distortion

The authors model most industries as including both corporate and noncorporate firms. The authors do not, however, provide any detailed analysis of the determination of the distribution of corporate and non-corporate firms within any industry. In effect they assume that, absent differences in tax rates on the two business forms, the distribution would be optimal. Tax rate differences cause the distribution to shift, leading to efficiency losses. (They term these losses intersectoral efficiency losses.) The extent of the shift is measured by assuming an elasticity of substitution between the different business forms.

As a conceptual matter, this model of the choice of business form is quite rudimentary. As an empirical tool for estimating the efficiency effect of a realistic tax reform proposal, it is without any grounds. Fullerton and Henderson cannot be criticized for not providing a more substantial empirical basis for their intersectoral efficiency estimates; to do so is a separate and very ambitious research project. The criticism is based on their portrayal of their empirical results as something more than an illustration of their modeling techniques.

In recognition of the lack of empirical evidence on the determinants of business form, Fullerton and Henderson use a range of values for their elasticity from − .5 to 3. When there are different empirical estimates of an elasticity, but the values cover some reasonable range, such sensitivity analysis is often an effective way of dealing with the absence of a fairly precise, agreed upon estimate. In this case, however, there is no real basis for the range used in the sensitivity analysis, nor is there evidence suggesting that any constant elasticity form is appropriate. The sensitivity analysis, if pursued more than is reported in the paper, might show how important changes in business form can be, but unless they are shown to be unimportant over a very wide range of possibilities, the specific results presented by Fullerton and Henderson should not be relied upon in judging realistic tax proposals.

Summary

Overall the Fullerton/Henderson analysis is a significant improvement in the modeling of tax changes. The specific results, however, should not be relied upon for evaluating current reform proposals. They are based on a caricature of the reform proposals. That caricature may be useful, but that is quite unclear and should be investigated, not assumed to be true. Further, crucial tax parameters need to be based on models of portfolio behavior and made consistent with loss limitations under our tax laws. Finally, the distortion in the choice of business form is an interesting issue to include in large scale general equilibrium models, but there is no empirical basis for evaluating its importance.

14 The Value-added Tax: A General Equilibrium Look at Its Efficiency and Incidence

Charles L. Ballard, John Karl Scholz,
and John B. Shoven

14.1 Introduction

The value-added tax (VAT) is among the most widely used tax instruments in the world, and one which is often lauded for its efficiency, simplicity, and ability to raise revenue. It is a very important source of revenue in Europe, and its adoption is being debated in Japan. The VAT has been considered in the United States on a number of occasions, but has not yet been adopted. However, with the increasing pressures of the budget deficit, the value-added tax is likely to be considered once again in the next few years. The purpose of this paper is to examine the likely consequences of adopting a value-added tax.

Textbook taxes almost always look good relative to taxes in the real world, and this may partially account for the good reputation enjoyed by the VAT. In this paper, we seek to learn more about VATs of various sorts, by performing simulations with a computational general equilibrium model of the United States economy and tax system. Among the questions we want to address are the following: (1) How efficient is a flat, textbook-type VAT? (2) How are those efficiency properties affected when a pattern of exemptions and rate differentials similar to those used in Europe are incorporated? (3) How regressive is the text-

Charles L. Ballard is assistant professor of economics at Michigan State University. John Karl Scholz is a graduate student in the Department of Economics, Stanford University. John B. Shoven is professor of economics at Stanford University and research associate of the National Bureau of Economic Research.

This research was supported by the National Science Foundation through a grant to the National Bureau of Economic Research and by the Center for Economic Policy Research at Stanford University. The paper was presented at the NBER Conference on the Effects of Taxation on Capital Formation, Palm Beach, Florida, 14–16 February 1986. We would like to thank Alan Auerbach, Michael Boskin, Harvey Galper, Mervyn King, and Harvey Rosen for helpful suggestions and comments.

book VAT, and how much of that regressivity is alleviated by the exemptions and rate differentials? (4) How much of the efficiency advantage of a consumption-type VAT relative to our current income tax is due to its flat rate structure and how much to its consumption base? (5) What are the efficiency and incidence consequences of using the VAT revenue to replace the corporate income tax rather than the personal income tax? (6) How different are the effects of using different tax instruments to increase tax collections by a given amount? (7) If the answers to the above questions suggest that the replacement of some of our existing taxes with a VAT would be regressive but would also be efficient (in the sense that it would result in a positive sum of equivalent variations), for what types of social welfare functions would the replacement be desirable? And finally, (8) How sensitive are our results to some of the key elasticities and functional form assumptions of our model?

We are going to assume that the reader is familiar with the basic operation of a value-added tax. Those who are not are referred to Lindholm (1976) or Aaron (1981). Also, our general equilibrium model is well documented in Ballard et al. (1985). Therefore, in section 14.2 we provide only a very brief outline of the model. In section 14.3, we provide an equally brief survey of the taxes we examine in this paper. Section 14.4 presents our simulation results by examining the efficiency and incidence effects of replacing a portion of the existing personal income tax with a flat consumption-type VAT, a VAT with a European-style rate structure, and a direct progressive expenditure tax. In section 14.5, we discuss simulations using VAT revenue to replace the corporation income tax. In section 14.6, we consider alternative means of increasing total federal tax receipts. Section 14.7 addresses the change in social welfare resulting from the tax swap, while 14.8 reports on some sensitivity analyses with respect to the structure of the underlying utility function and the elasticity of saving with respect to the real interest rate. We conclude with a brief summary of our results.

14.2   The Model

The model is a medium-scale computational general equilibrium model, calibrated to 1973 data for the United States. We model 19 producer-goods industries that use capital and labor in constant elasticity of substitution (CES) value-added functions. They also use the outputs of other industries through a fixed coefficient input-output matrix. Tax rates on labor and capital income for each industry are taken from payroll, corporate, and property taxes. The 19 producer goods are used indirectly for consumption through a fixed coefficient matrix of transition. This matrix allows the 19 producer goods to be translated into 15 consumer goods which correspond to consumer demands. There are 12 consumer groups, differentiated by income class, each with an initial endowment of capital and labor. These classifications are summarized in table 14.1.

The data for the model are derived from five major sources. These include the July 1976 *Survey of Current Business,* the Bureau of Economic Analysis Input-Output Matrix, unpublished worksheets of the U.S. Commerce Department's National Income Division, the U.S. Labor Department's 1973 Consumer Expenditure Survey, and the U.S. Treasury Department's Merged Tax Files. Adjustments to these data are made to ensure that each source is consistent with the others. All data on industry and government uses of factors are taken to be fixed,

Table 14.1   **Classification of Industries, Consumer Expenditures, and Consumer Groups in the Model**

Industries	Consumer Expenditures
1. Agriculture, forestry, and fisheries	1. Food
2. Mining	2. Alcoholic beverages
3. Crude petroleum and gas	3. Tobacco
4. Contract construction	4. Utilities
5. Food and tobacco	5. Housing
6. Textiles, apparel, and leather products	6. Furnishings
7. Paper and printing	7. Appliances
8. Petroleum refining	8. Clothing and jewelry
9. Chemicals and rubber	9. Transportation
10. Lumber, furniture, stone, clay, and glass	10. Motor vehicles, tires, and auto repair
11. Metals, machinery, miscellaneous manufacturing	11. Services
12. Transportation equipment	12. Financial services
13. Motor vehicles	13. Reading, recreation, miscellaneous
14. Transportation, communications, and utilities	14. Nondurable, nonfood household items
15. Trade	15. Gasoline and other fuels
16. Finance and insurance	
17. Real estate	
18. Services	
19. Government enterprise	

Consumer Groups
(Households classified by $thousands of 1973 gross income)

1. 0–3	5. 6–7	9. 12–15
2. 3–4	6. 7–8	10. 15–20
3. 4–5	7. 8–10	11. 20–25
4. 5–6	8. 10–12	12. 25+

while data on consumers' factor incomes and expenditures are correspondingly adjusted. Tax receipts, transfers, and government endowments are fixed, and government expenditures are scaled to balance the budget. Similar adjustments ensure that supply equals demand for every good and factor.

The fully consistent data set defines a single-period benchmark equilibrium in transactions terms. These observations on values are then separated into prices and quantities by assuming that a physical unit of a good or factor is the amount that sells for one dollar. All benchmark equilibrium prices are thus $1, and the observed values are the benchmark quantities.

The equilibrium conditions of the model are then used to determine the behavioral equation parameters consistent with the benchmark data set. This procedure calibrates the model to the benchmark data, in the sense that the benchmark data can be reproduced as an equilibrium solution to the model before any policy changes are considered. In order to implement this procedure, we specify the elasticities of substitution between capital and labor in each industry on the basis of econometric estimates in the literature. Factor employments by industry are used to derive production function weights, and expenditure data are used to derive utility function weights. This calibration procedure ensures that, given the benchmark data, the various agents' behavior are mutually consistent before we evaluate policy changes.

We use a tâtonnement procedure developed by Kimbell and Harrison (1984) to calculate prices which satisfy the following equilibrium conditions: all profits are zero, and supply equals demand for each good and factor. These conditions hold at each point in time. Single-period equilibria are sequenced through endogenous savings decisions which augment the capital stock of the economy. An exogenous labor force growth rate of 2.89% is assumed.

For the benchmark sequence, we calculate a balanced growth path that begins with our replicated data, has constant prices, and implies quantities that all grow at the labor force growth rate. We then alter tax parameters and calculate a revised sequence of equilibria. For both the base case and revised case sequences, we calculate 21 equilibria spaced 5 years apart. Thus, our calculations cover a span of 100 years. At the end of this period, the economy has approached very close to a new steady state in the revised case. We use the steady-state properties of the model to calculate "termination terms" that measure the welfare changes through infinite time. See Ballard et al. (1985, chap. 7) for details.

In the revised case, we hold real exhaustive government expenditure at the same level in every period as in the corresponding period of the base-case sequence. We also hold transfer payments constant in real terms for each of the consumer groups. (Thus, to the extent that the VAT raises gross consumer prices, we protect consumers by increasing their transfer payments.) This assumption that revenue yields are the same period-by-period is a strong one. We do not consider the use of debt finance to smooth the pattern of taxes over time. (See Goulder 1985 for a general equilibrium model with debt.) Another possibility that we rule out is that society would alter the total amount of government spending over time if it were to become wealthier or poorer.

When a VAT is instituted, it raises revenues. In order to maintain equal tax revenue yield in the manner described above, it is necessary to reduce tax rates elsewhere in the economy. We most often do this by reducing marginal income tax rates. We hold the rest of the tax rates in the economy constant. Thus, we rule out the possibility that the states would respond to a federal VAT by changing the configuration of their own taxes.

The model assumes no involuntary unemployment of factors. Markets are perfectly competitive, with no externalities, quantity constraints, or barriers to factor mobility. Since we compute a complete set of prices and quantities under alternative tax policies, we can estimate the change in national income, the changes in utility or income for each consumer group, and new factor allocations among industries.

At any point in time, each household has a nested CES utility function of the form

(1) $$U = U[H\,(\bar{X},\,L),\,C_F]$$

where H is a CES function determining the allocation of current expenditures between current consumption of goods, $\bar{X}$, and current consumption of leisure, L. The component $\bar{X}$ is itself a composite of the 15 consumer goods, which we shall call the X_i, $i = 1, \ldots, 15$. In earlier applications of the model, purchase decisions on the X_i were determined by a Cobb-Douglas subutility function. In this paper, we make an important change from the standard model by incorporating a Stone-Geary or linear expenditure system of demands. U is another CES function, determining the allocation of income between current expenditures and expected future consumption, C_F. The demand for C_F results in a derived demand for savings.

An important advantage of the structure described here is that the factor supply elasticities can be calibrated exactly to any desired value. The most important of these is the elasticity of savings with respect to the real net rate of return. The savings elasticity is very important in simulating the VAT, because the adoption of a tax on consumption will encourage greater saving. Since some of the largest distortions in the model are those that affect the accumulation and use of capital, a capital-deepening policy change will usually lead to welfare gains. These gains increase as the assumed savings elasticity increases, as we shall see in section 14.8. Thus, it is important to use realistic values for the savings elasticity. We use a value of 0.4 for most of our simulations, and we also consider values of 0.0 and 1.0. Even this range of values may be on the high side. In recent years, real rates of return have been extremely high, and yet savings rates have changed very little. (See Bernheim and Shoven 1985 for a discussion of some of the reasons for the low level of responsiveness.)

It should be noted that there are some limitations with the model structure we have described. Our decisions about intertemporal consumption are governed by equation (1). In each period, our households make a decision which allocates income between the present and the future. There are not any life-cycle aspects incorporated into this decision; in fact, our households are thought to live forever. Households also expect the configuration of prices that exist in any given period to continue throughout time. This assumption of myopic expectations has been relaxed in a paper by Ballard and Goulder (1982). Their paper examines the polar cases of myopic expectations and perfect foresight and intermediate degrees of consumer foresight in a model with a similar structure to that presented here. Ballard and Goulder find the results or policy simulations are quite robust to variations in expectational structure.

In computing the equivalent variation welfare measure with the standard model, we were able to make great use of the homotheticity of the Cobb-Douglas demand function. Here we make similar use of the homotheticity of the Stone-Geary formulation with respect to a "displaced origin." Let γ_i be the ith component of the displaced origin or the minimum required level of consumption for commodity i. Then define

$$(2) \qquad \Gamma = \sum_{i=1}^{15} P_i \gamma_i$$

as the cost of the vector γ. The Stone-Geary demand functions are then

$$(3) \qquad X_i = \gamma_i + \frac{\beta_i(I_x - \Gamma)}{P_i}$$

where β_i is the marginal propensity to consume commodity i out of discretionary income. Given the Stone-Geary utility function

$$(4) \qquad U_x = \prod_{i=1}^{15} (X_i - \gamma_i)^{\beta_i} ; \sum_{i=1}^{15} \beta_i = 1.0$$

we calculate the indirect utility function

(5)
$$V_x = (I_x - \Gamma) \prod_{i=1}^{15} \left(\frac{\beta_i}{P_i}\right)^{\beta_i}$$

and expenditure function

(6)
$$I_x = \frac{V_x}{A} + \Gamma$$

where

(7)
$$A = \prod_{i=1}^{15} \left(\frac{\beta_i}{P_i}\right)^{\beta_i}$$

We exploit the homothetic relationship between discretionary income $(I_x - \Gamma)$ and the indirect utility from consumption in excess of the requirement. We use

(8)
$$P_{xD} = \prod_{i=1}^{15} \left(\frac{P_i}{\beta_i}\right)^{\beta_i}$$

as the price for the composite of discretionary consumption in the next higher stage of the maximization process. In order to evaluate welfare, we first compare discretionary H in the base case with discretionary H in the revised case. We then compare the base case Γs and revised case Γs.[1]

14.3 Modeling of Taxes

In this paper, our simulations focus on three types of consumption-based taxes. The first is an ideal flat consumption VAT, where the tax base is the value of current period production less investment. All expenditures/goods (other than leisure) are taxed at a uniform rate.

Against this idealized VAT, we model a more politically realistic "stylized European VAT." The primary distinguishing characteristics of the European VATs are the consumption base, the destination basis,[2] and differentiated rate structure. Based on the discussion of rate structures of the European VATs in Aaron (1981) and Cnossen (1982), we model a destination-based, consumption-type VAT with rates ranging from 0 to 15%. The rate differentiation is believed to be caused by a number of political and practical considerations. Food and housing are lightly taxed in an attempt to reduce the regressive nature of the VAT. Services, particularly financial services, are believed to be particularly difficult to tax. In all, as is illustrated in table 14.2, the average European

Table 14.2   Rates of Value-added Tax for the "Stylized European VAT"

Commodity Group	Percentage Rate	Commodity Group	Percentage Rate
Food	5	Motor vehicles, tires, and auto repair	15
Alcoholic beverages	15		
Tobacco	15	Services	0
Utilities	5	Financial services	0
Housing	0	Reading, recreation and miscellaneous	10
Furnishings	15		
Appliances	15	Nondurable, nonfood household items	10
Clothing and jewelry	15		
Transportation	5	Gasoline and other fuels	15

rate structure is far from the flat tax on consumption of an idealized VAT. By comparing the flat VAT with the differentiated VAT, we can determine the magnitude of the distortions in consumption decisions caused by a differentiated rate structure. We can also determine the effect that rate differentiation has on the gains or losses of the various consumer groups.

Our model has a fairly high degree of disaggregation. Nevertheless, at the 19-industry level of disaggregation, we are not able to capture all of the intricacies of the VATs that exist in Europe. The tables presented in Scott and Davis (1985) show the enormously detailed tax structures used in some of the European nations. For example, our model does not distinguish between small firms and large firms in an industry, even though it is often the case that firms of different sizes are treated differently under the European VATs.

The third type of tax we examine is a progressive expenditure tax. In order to compare this tax with a differentiated VAT, we assign the tax rates in such a way that they will collect the same commodity-tax revenue from consumers in the first period. This is achieved by imposing a progressive tax on consumers of consumption goods. Tax rates range from 0.3% for the consumer group with the lowest income to 11.6% for the highest-income group. Under the differentiated VAT, each consumer group faces the same rate schedule, with variation in tax rates by consumption good. Under the progressive expenditure tax, rates differ among the consumer groups, but for each consumer group, tax rates are equal on all consumption goods.

14.4 The Consequences of Rate Differentials

We begin by reporting on the efficiency and equity effects of rate differentiation with a VAT. We also compare the flat VAT with a progressive expenditure tax which has the same first-period yield. Table 14.3 shows the sum of equivalent variations for our 12 household groups for the different policies. In all cases, it is the personal income tax which is scaled back to preserve revenue neutrality relative to the base case tax system. However, we look at two patterns of scaling the personal income tax rates down—a multiplicative one and an additive one. With the multiplicative scaling, each household's marginal tax rate is multiplied by a constant less than unity so that revenue neutrality is achieved. In the additive case, a common number of percentage points is subtracted from each household's marginal tax rate.

The model has the capability of solving for these equal yield adjustment amounts. It also computes the flat VAT rate that is necessary to generate the same first-period commodity tax revenue yield as the differentiated rate structure shown earlier in table 14.2. This rate turns out to be 6.52%. Since the same amount of extra commodity-tax revenue is raised in each case, the amount of reduction in income tax revenue is also the same. The pattern of changes in revenues is almost identical after the first period, as well. In order to save computational cost, we only hold first-period commodity-tax revenue exactly constant. We do preserve overall revenue neutrality, however. If, in ad-

Table 14.3   **Efficiency Gains for Progressive Expenditure Tax, Differentiated VAT, and Flat VAT, for Model with Stone-Geary Commodity Demands**

Type of Tax[a]	Type of Replacement for Equal Yield	
	Additive	Multiplicative
Differentiated rate VAT	0.286%	0.558%
	($142.2)	($277.2)
Flat rate VAT (6.52%)	0.490%	0.759%
	(243.4)	($377.3)
Progressive expenditure tax	0.285%	0.574%
	($141.5)	($285.2)

Note: Figures are percentages of the total present value of welfare. Numbers in parentheses are in billions of 1973 dollars.

[a]All taxes raise the same amount of first-period commodity tax revenue from consumers. Personal income tax rates are scaled back so that the pattern of total tax revenue is the same in both the base case and revised case.

dition to overall revenue neutrality, we had held the additional commodity-tax revenue exactly constant in every period, we would have generated nearly identical results.

Our interpretation of the results in table 14.3 is that the potential efficiency gains from introducing a VAT or a progressive expenditure tax are rather large. The gain from a flat 6.52% consumption type VAT is 0.76% of the present value of economic welfare when multiplicative replacement is used. Using a 4% real discount rate, the present discounted value of future consumption plus leisure is $49 trillion, which is definitionally equivalent to the total value of wealth, physical and human, in the economy. Another way to assess the efficiency consequences of the multiplicative replacement with a flat 6.52% VAT is to note that the present value gain of $377 billion is equivalent to 29% of GNP for 1973, the base data year. It should be emphasized that this is a true efficiency gain, with the government having the same resources available to it after the tax switch. Further, this efficiency gain is roughly equivalent to the previously computed gain from integrating the corporate and personal income taxes, and amounts to about two-thirds the gain from completely switching to a progressive expenditure tax (see Ballard et al. 1985, chap. 9).

The multiplicative rate adjustment, emphasized so far, results in larger efficiency improvements than the additive adjustment because it lowers the marginal tax rates for higher-income, higher-tax-rate households more. The households with higher rates have already had the allocation of their resources and labor supply distorted more, and because these distortions increase approximately with the square of the tax rate, their situations improve more per dollar of rate relief than do the situations of those with lower initial tax rates. In fact, table 14.3 indicates that a 6.52% flat VAT would improve efficiency by slightly less than one-half of 1% of the present value of welfare if the personal income tax were scaled back additively (that is, with the same number of percentage points of relief in marginal tax rates for all households). This is just under two-thirds as large as with the multiplicative rate adjustment.

Differentiation also is costly in terms of economic efficiency. In comparing the first two rows of table 14.3, one can see that the present value of the cost of differentiation is just over $100 billion, which amounts to 8% of 1973's GNP and 0.2% of the present value of future welfare. The gain from a differentiated VAT with additive replacement is only about half as great as the gain from a flat VAT with additive replacement, and only about one-third as great as with a flat VAT with multiplicative rate relief.

As we have modeled it, the progressive expenditure tax shares the intersectoral neutrality of a flat VAT, but has a progressive rate structure similar to the current personal income tax. Table 14.3 indicates that a progressive expenditure tax with the same first period revenue as the other two taxes would offer an increase in efficiency of roughly the same magnitude as the differentiated rate VAT. One interpretation of these results, then, is that rate progressivity and rate differentiation cost roughly the same amount in terms of efficiency sacrifice relative to a flat VAT. All of these results use the linear expenditure system to allocate expenditures on commodities, and incorporate our base assumptions of a saving elasticity with respect to the real interest rate of 0.4 and a labor supply elasticity of 0.15. In section 14.8, we examine the sensitivity of some of our results to the saving elasticity and to the LES functional form.

In interpreting the succeeding tables that deal with tax incidence, several factors should be taken into account. Our dynamic model is calibrated with cross-sectional data where households are differentiated only by income. Because of the model structure and the fact that households are not distinguished by age, we are unable to address life-cycle or lifetime tax incidence questions. Rather, our incidence calculations address the long-run gains and losses falling on households in the various income classes. Households clearly move up and down the income scale over the life cycle, so these calculations should not be interpreted as gains or losses which fall on an individual household. It has been suggested that, over the lifetime, our calculations overstate the regressivity of taxes on consumption. This can most easily be seen by noting there is considerably greater variation in the average propensity to consume in a cross-section data set than over consumers' lifetimes. Since saving is more concentrated in higher-income classes, consumption is more concentrated in lower-income classes, and this results in the overstatement of the regressivity of consumption taxes. Furthermore, since age is not an explicit dimension of our model, we are not able to look into problems raised by Auerbach and Kotlikoff (1983) which surround the transition from income-based to consumption-based taxes.

It should be clear, however, that life-cycle or lifetime tax incidence is not without problems of its own. Despite evidence of a great deal of income fluidity among people who fall in and out of poverty, a general consensus has emerged in support of transfer programs such as food stamps and unemployment insurance. Similarly, the fact that low-income people will receive higher earnings at other times in their career should not mitigate the fact that the burden of consumption-based taxes falls on individuals at times when they are least able to afford them, namely when they are young and when they are old. This consideration would obviously be less important if perfect capital markets existed, but until we have capital market perfection we argue that lifetime *and* shorter time horizon (i.e., annual) tax incidence analysis is important for policy makers.

These caveats should be kept in mind when interpreting the following tables on tax incidence. Table 14.4 displays the personal incidence of the six tax replacement policies discussed in table 14.3. The results of table 14.4 show that there is an unpleasant tradeoff between efficiency and equity with a VAT. In addition, the stringency of the tradeoff depends a great deal on the method of personal income-tax rate adjustments for revenue neutrality. The flat VAT is slightly more regressive than the differentiated one. However, for the flat VAT, the multiplicative replacement is significantly more regressive than the additive one. One interpretation of this would be that the design of the rate adjustments in the personal income tax is more crucial in terms of equity than is the exemption of products that are deemed to be necessities. An example of this is to look at two plans that are fairly close in terms of economic efficiency. The flat VAT with additive rate adjustments is much less regressive than the differentiated VAT with a multiplicative method of rate adjustments.

The expenditure tax with a progressive rate structure illustrates many of the same points. Recall that the efficiency gain from introducing a revenue-neutral progressive expenditure tax is about the same as the gain resulting from the differentiated VAT. However, the expenditure tax has a much more progressive incidence. In fact, the progressive expenditure tax with multiplicative relief from the existing income tax yields a Pareto improvement in the sense that all our 12 household classes are better off. As with the VAT introduction, the incidence is very sensitive to the pattern of rate relief.

Table 14.5 shows the efficiency gains of flat VATs with different rate levels. It displays the result that the gain from trading the existing personal income tax for a flat consumption-type VAT exhibits a modest degree of decreasing returns. The improvement from a 15% VAT is somewhat less than three times the gain from a 5% VAT. Table 14.6 finds a similar pattern for the revenue-neutral introduction of a progressive expenditure tax.

14.5 Using the VAT Revenues to Lower the Corporate Income Tax

Despite the fact that economists have not reached a consensus regarding the nature of the corporate income tax, it is fair to say that it is widely criticized. The criticisms are based on several grounds. First, there is the double taxation of the return to capital, where net income generated within the corporate sector is subject to tax at the corporate level and then again at the personal level, either as a tax on dividends or as a tax on capital gains.[3] In addition, the corporate income tax has

Table 14.4   **Welfare Effects of Value-added Taxes and Progressive Expenditure Tax, By Consumer Income Class, for Model with Stone-Geary Commodity Demands**

Household Income (in Thousands of 1973 Dollars)	Differentiated VAT Additive Replacement (%)	Flat VAT Additive Replacement (%)	Progressive Expenditure Tax Additive Replacement (%)[a]	Differentiated VAT Multiplicative Replacement (%)	Flat VAT Multiplicative Replacement (%)	Progressive Expenditure Tax Multiplicative Replacement (%)[a]
0–3	0.009	−0.408	2.759	−2.007	−2.485	0.602
3–4	−0.016	−0.208	2.212	−1.745	−1.928	0.432
4–5	0.081	−0.072	1.806	−1.350	−1.496	0.343
5–6	0.083	−0.003	1.601	−1.174	−1.253	0.324
6–7	−0.052	0.041	1.479	−1.201	−1.101	0.317
7–8	−0.081	0.126	1.239	−1.010	−0.797	0.310
8–10	−0.028	0.219	0.964	−0.683	−0.431	0.321
10–12	−0.070	0.320	0.677	−0.414	−0.021	0.355
12–15	−0.020	0.368	0.526	−0.195	0.194	0.378
15–20	0.119	0.529	0.125	0.443	0.850	0.483
20–25	0.306	0.642	−0.148	0.997	1.328	0.582
25+	1.226	1.136	−1.277	3.682	3.576	1.199

Note: The figures are percentages of the total present value of welfare.

[a]This tax raises from consumers the same amount of first-period commodity tax revenue as the differentiated VAT and the flat 6.52 percent VAT.

Table 14.5   **Efficiency Gains from the Substitution of a Destination-Based Consumption-Type Flat VAT for Some of the Personal Income Tax Revenue (equal yield), for Model with Stone-Geary Commodity Demands**

VAT Rate	Type of Income Tax Scaling	
	Additive	Multiplicative
5%	0.383%	0.596%
	($190.3)	($296.2)
10%	0.719%	1.105%
	($357.4)	($549.2)
15%	1.016%	1.544%
	($505.1)	($767.4)

Note: Figures are percentages of the total present value of welfare. Numbers in parentheses are in billions of 1973 dollars.

Table 14.6   **Efficiency Gains from the Substitution of a Progressive Expenditure Tax for Some of the Personal Income Tax Revenue (equal yield), for Model with Stone-Geary Commodity Demands**

Analog of VAT Rate[a]	Type of Income Tax Scaling	
	Additive[b]	Multiplicative[b]
5%	0.225%	0.415%
	($111.6)	($223.9)
10%	0.410%	0.835%
	($203.8)	($414.7)
15%	0.564%	1.164%
	($280.2)	($578.3)

[a]The progressive expenditure tax raises the same amount of first-period commodity tax revenue as a consumption-type flat VAT of 5, 10, or 15 percent.

[b]Figures are percentages of the total present value of welfare. Numbers in parentheses are in billions of 1973 dollars.

been held to reduce overall rates of return and hence inhibit capital accumulation. Perhaps of greatest concern to the public finance economist is the nonneutrality of the CIT. The CIT obviously discriminates against the corporate sector, as the noncorporate sector is free of this form of taxation. Further nonneutralities are introduced by special provisions in the corporate tax law. Finally, the corporate tax has a bias toward debt finance, since only equity returns are subject to it.

Because of the problems with the CIT, various schemes of integrating the corporate and personal tax system have been considered in the past few years.[4] In this section, we examine the welfare effects of replacing

the corporate income tax with three different taxes: a flat-rate VAT, a differentiated-rate VAT, and a progressive expenditure tax. One of the first groups to advocate replacing the CIT with a VAT was a business group, the Committee for Economic Development, in 1966. More than a decade later, an extensive partial equilibrium analysis of the CIT-VAT substitution was made by Dresch, Lin, and Stout (1977). Their analysis explicitly concentrates on first-round, or impact, effects of the CIT-VAT switch. Our analysis, being a general equilibrium analysis, takes a somewhat different focus. We calculate the long-run, dynamic welfare effects by consumer group, for three types of corporate tax replacement. Despite the different focus, we are nevertheless able to examine several of the issues raised by Dresch, Lin, and Stout. In particular, they find that multiple-rate VATs do not mitigate the underlying regressivity of the VAT. In fact, they claim that the allocative distortions generated by differentiation eliminate many of the beneficial effects of the CIT-VAT substitution. Finally, they suggest that the substitution of a progessive expenditure tax for the CIT would be worth examination. The progressive expenditure tax would preserve many of the desirable characteristics of the VAT that relate to investment and trade.

In our model, personal taxes combine with corporate taxes to raise effective tax rates in industries that are highly incorporated. Similarly, taxes are reduced to the extent that each industry makes use of credits, deductions, and allowances. It is important to note that, while our model considers intertemporal and intersectoral distortions in the allocation of capital, it does not include endogenous financial decisions regarding debt/equity ratios or dividend payout ratios.

The policy program we investigate involves eliminating the corporate income tax while modifying the personal income tax to tax total shareholder earnings, rather than simply dividends. The increase in the revenue raised by the personal income tax is not sufficient to compensate for the elimination of the CIT. The amount of government revenue is maintained by implementing a flat VAT, a differentiated-rate VAT, and a progressive expenditure tax.

In tables 14.7 and 14.8, we present the efficiency gains in aggregate and by consumer group for the different types of corporate tax replacement. The numbers found in table 14.7 are larger than the previously published estimates for corporate income tax integration where the lost revenue was made up by raising the marginal rates of the personal income tax. This is simply another demonstration that the three tax replacements computed in table 14.7 are more efficient than an incremental increase in the current income tax.

We find that a flat VAT is the most efficient replacement scheme and that the progressive expenditure tax is the least efficient. However, the

Table 14.7   Efficiency Gains from Replacing the Corporate Income Tax with Different Types of Value-added Taxes (equal yield), for Model with Stone-Geary Commodity Demands

Type of Replacement	Efficiency Gain
Flat VAT	1.074%
	($533.8)
Differentiated VAT	1.021%
	($507.6)
Progressive expenditure tax	0.965%
	($479.4)

Note: Figures are percentages of the total present value of welfare. Numbers in parentheses are in billions of 1973 dollars.

Table 14.8   Welfare Effects of Replacing the Corporate Income Tax with a Flat VAT, Differentiated VAT, or Progressive Expenditure Tax, by Consumer Group, for Model with Stone-Geary Commodity Demands

Household Income (in thousands of 1973 dollars)	Type of Replacement		
	Flat VAT (%)	Differentiated VAT (%)	Progressive Expenditure Tax (%)
0–3	2.399	2.754	4.291
3–4	1.634	1.840	3.058
4–5	1.120	1.296	2.212
5–6	1.025	1.156	1.954
6–7	0.895	0.919	1.724
7–8	0.705	0.662	1.343
8–10	0.422	0.348	0.848
10–12	0.438	0.280	0.644
12–15	0.182	0.016	0.275
15–20	0.201	0.021	−0.019
20–25	0.529	0.385	0.092
25+	3.394	3.510	2.012

The figures are percentages of the total present value of welfare.

differences in efficiency are relatively small. From table 14.8, we see that there are modest distributional differences between the three methods of replacement. It is immediately apparent in all the plans that there is a pronounced U-shape to the welfare results. The reason for the U-shape lies on the sources side of the consumer's budget. The distributional impact of the policy change is driven by the fact that the capital/labor ratio of income is U-shaped across our twelve consumer groups (see table 14.9). Since we eliminate the corporate income tax,

Table 14.9   Ratio of Capital Income to Labor Income by Consumer Group

Household Income (in thousands of 1973 dollars)	$\left(\dfrac{\text{Capital Income}}{\text{Labor Income}}\right)$ in Base Case	Household Income (in thousands of 1973 dollars)	$\left(\dfrac{\text{Capital Income}}{\text{Labor Income}}\right)$ in Base Case
0–3	.547	8–10	.123
3–4	.337	10–12	.123
4–5	.227	12–15	.106
5–6	.203	15–20	.111
6–7	.178	20–25	.139
7–8	.149	25 +	.424

Reproduced from table 8.5 of Ballard et al. (1985).

the net return to capital rises sharply. Capital is also allocated more efficiently, which pushes net returns up even further. The higher return to capital naturally leads to U-shaped gains by consumer groups.

Removal of the CIT also has differing incidence effects arising from the uses side of the consumer's budget. Low-income consumers tend to spend a larger proportion of their income on consumer goods that are produced by lightly taxed, capital-intensive industries, such as agriculture and real estate. For example, the poorest consumer group spends 42% of its income on food and housing, while the wealthiest group spends 27%. Thus, removal of the CIT has a regressive impact on the income distribution when viewed from the uses side of the budget.

Differentiation of the VAT rates generates slightly higher welfare gains for the bottom four income groups (38% of the population) and the highest income group (5% of the population), although it is clear from table 14.8 that the various consumer groups neither gain nor lose much from differentiation. It should also be noted that we have a Pareto improvement under both the VAT and differentiated VAT replacement schemes.

The results for the distribution of welfare under the progressive expenditure tax are quite different. Despite having a smaller total welfare gain than the two VAT replacement schemes, the progressive expenditure tax yields welfare improvements for the first 9 consumer groups (78% of the population) which significantly exceed the gains from the VAT replacement schemes. This is a consequence of the progressive nature of the expenditure tax rate schedule, under which the lowest consumer group faces a marginal tax rate of 0.3%, while the highest consumer group faces a rate of 11.6%. While significantly altering the distribution of welfare results, the progressive expenditure tax yields an aggregate welfare gain that is 0.1 percentage point smaller than the gain that results from the flat VAT.

14.6   The Costs of Using Alternative Taxes to Increase Government Revenues

Even the comparisons we have been presenting regarding the relative efficiency and incidence of alternative forms of consumption-based taxes and the use of the revenues may leave some readers without a good impression of how important these differences are. Another presentation in table 14.10 may clarify the relative magnitudes. What is presented is the private cost of increasing government receipts by 10%. Thus, we have abandoned the revenue neutrality assumption that has prevailed in all the previous results. Rather, the scale of government expenditures and receipts is increased. What we examine is the welfare

Table 14.10   **Welfare Effects of Increases in Spending with Different Types of Replacement**

	Additive Income Tax Increases	Multiplicative Income Tax Increases	Flat VAT	Differentiated VAT
10% increase in G & T	−5.051% ($2510.1)	−5.587% (−$2776.4)	−4.132% (−$2053.4)	−4.391% (−$2182.0)
10% increase in G	−4.563% ($2267.2)	−4.957% (−$2463.3)	−3.874% (−$1924.8)	−4.054% (−$2015.4)
10 increase in T	−0.384% (−$190.9)	−0.476% (−$236.6)	−0.219% (−$108.7)	−0.259% (−$128.7)

Note: G = exhaustive government expenditure
    T = government transfers

costs of the additional taxes, for different tax instruments. Exhaustive government expenditures do not directly enter the utility functions of our consumers, so consumer welfare is reduced by the higher taxes but not increased due to the additional public goods. Since the extra public goods are the same in the four cases examined, the relative loss in welfare reflects the relative efficiency of the tax instruments. When transfers are increased, the increased revenue is returned to the households. In this model, transfers are treated as lump-sum payments. So, in the case of the third row of table 14.10, what is shown is the true efficiency or resource cost of collecting the revenue.

What strikes us is the magnitude of the differences in the efficiency numbers in table 14.10. The first row shows the figures for a 10% increase in both transfers and exhaustive expenditures. With all four incremental tax measures, the resulting revenue is the same. However, a flat VAT "hurts" more than 25% less than a multiplicative increase in the present income tax. In present-value dollar terms, the cost of the permanent 10% expansion of the government ranges from $2,053 billion to $2,776 billion, depending on the design of the tax increase. This strikes us as a nontrivial choice. The real resource cost of a 10% increase in lump-sum transfers would range between $109 billion and $237 billion, depending on the efficiency of the tax instrument used to finance the increment. So, in this case, there is more than a two-for-one difference. These results accord with the results from the paper by Ballard, Shoven, and Whalley (1985), which used a very similar version of this model to show that marginal excess burdens are fairly large, and that the marginal excess burdens can differ fairly widely among different tax instruments.

Table 14.11 displays the incidence of the cost of government expansion for the four possible incremental taxes of table 14.10. The inci-

Table 14.11   Welfare Effects of 10% Increases in Government and Transfers
                   with Different Types of Financing

Household Income (in thousands of 1973 dollars)	Additive Income Tax Increase (%)	Multiplicative Income Tax Increase (%)	Flat VAT (%)	Differentiated VAT (%)
0–3	−0.577	2.286	−1.039	−0.376
3–4	−1.497	0.895	−1.654	−1.313
4–5	−2.605	−0.616	−2.545	−2.251
5–6	−3.345	−1.601	−3.177	−2.985
6–7	−3.759	−2.170	−3.514	−3.586
7–8	−4.370	−3.095	−3.983	−4.219
8–10	−4.689	−3.808	−4.166	−4.470
10–12	−4.996	−4.570	−4.311	−4.829
12–15	−5.219	−5.040	−4.475	−5.006
15–20	−5.460	−6.024	−4.475	−5.039
20–25	−5.615	−6.736	−4.476	−4.949
25+	−6.262	−10.183	−4.386	−4.234

dence of a flat VAT is not dramatically different from that of an additive surcharge to the income tax (as would be expected), despite the much greater efficiency of the VAT. In this case, all households with incomes greater than $4,000 (in 1973 dollars) would be better off with a flat VAT. A differentiated VAT dominates an additive surcharge, in that all income classes lose less in financing the expanded government.

14.7 Would the Substitution of a VAT Increase Social Welfare?

So far, we have measured the change in economic efficiency by calculating the change in the sum of equivalent variations. The implicit social welfare function is Benthamite, and the measure is in the tradition of cost-benefit analysis. The linearity of the social welfare function means that the social value of a dollar is the same for all households. Of course, the social welfare function may display curvature. Following Atkinson (1970), we look at the family of social welfare functions

$$(9) \qquad SW = \frac{\sum_{i=1}^{12} V_i^{1-\rho}}{1 - \rho}$$

where V_i is the indirect utility of household i. We can compute social welfare for both the revised and base distributions of V_i for any particular value of ρ. The form is quite general, in that the limit as ρ goes to infinity is the Rawlsian social welfare function where only the welfare of the poorest household matters. For $\rho = 0$, the social welfare function is Benthamite and therefore corresponds to the measure of economic efficiency that we have been using so far. For $\rho < 0$, the social value of a dollar is higher for those who are richer. Therefore, the range $0 \leq \rho < \infty$ probably includes all values for reasonable social welfare functions.

To examine the social welfare functions for which the tax swap is desirable, we calculate the critical value of ρ for which the change in social welfare is zero. The change in social welfare is given by

$$(10) \qquad \Delta SW = \frac{\sum_{i=1}^{12} {}^r V_i^{1-\rho}}{1 - \rho} - \frac{\sum_{i=1}^{12} {}^b V_i^{1-\rho}}{1 - \rho}$$

where ${}^r V_i$ is the value of indirect utility with the revised tax plan and ${}^b V_i$ is the value in the base case. The tax cases examined are the 6 on which we initially reported in tables 14.3 and 14.4. The results are shown in table 14.12. Two of the 6 cases result in an increase in social welfare for all values of ρ. They are the differentiated VAT with an additive adjustment in the personal income tax rates and the progressive

Table 14.12   **Values of ρ for which the Tax Swap Increases Social Welfare**

	LES Inner Nest	
Type of VAT	Additive	Multiplicative
Differentiated rates	All values	$\rho < .59932$
Flat rate (6.52)	$\rho < 1.9146$	$\rho < .73045$
Progressive expenditure tax	$\rho > -.65095$	All values

expenditure tax with a multiplicative adjustment. The flat VAT with an additive adjustment results in an increase in social welfare if ρ is less than 1.915. Despite its greater efficiency (gain in social welfare when $\rho = 0$), the flat VAT with a multiplicative adjustment results in an increase in social welfare only in the more limited range of $\rho < 0.73$. The revenue-neutral introduction of a differentiated VAT with a multiplicative replacement not only results in a smaller gain in economic efficiency than a flat VAT with a multiplicative replacement, but it also increases social welfare for a more limited range of social welfare functions. In the case of a differentiated VAT with a multiplicative adjustment, social welfare increases if social welfare is of the form (9) and if ρ is less than 0.60. The progressive expenditure tax, which is unambiguously an improvement with a multiplicative adjustment, also improves social welfare for all reasonable values of ρ in the case of an additive adjustment (for all values exceeding -0.65). Our interpretation of these results is that a progressive expenditure tax would certainly increase social welfare. A value-added tax with additive adjustments in income tax rates would increase social welfare for a large range of social welfare functions. The only exception would be in the case of a flat VAT and a social welfare function that displays rapidly decreasing social valuation of a dollar with increasing wealth. The introduction of a VAT with multiplicative replacements, which offers considerable gains in economic efficiency, may or may not increase social welfare depending on the value of ρ.

14.8 Sensitivity Analysis

Up to this point, all of the results presented in this paper have been based upon the model with Stone-Geary commodity demands. In addition, we have assumed that the elasticity of saving with respect to the real net rate of return is 0.4. In this section, we perform sensitivity analysis with respect to these assumptions.

First, as an alternative to the Stone-Geary specification, we present results based on a Cobb-Douglas model of commodity demands. (This Cobb-Douglas formulation was the standard formulation for earlier applications of our model.) In table 14.13, we present the overall efficiency effects of the differentiated VAT, flat VAT, and progressive expenditure tax in the Cobb-Douglas case. Table 14.13 can be compared with table 14.3. For the flat VAT and the progressive expenditure tax, the overall welfare gains with the Cobb-Douglas formulation are only slightly less than the overall welfare gains in the Stone-Geary case. This is not surprising, since these tax replacements have their greatest effects on intertemporal consumption choices rather than on the allocation of consumption among goods within any period. However, when

Table 14.13   **Efficiency Gains for Progressive Expenditure Tax, Differentiated VAT, and Flat VAT, for Model with Cobb-Douglas Commodity Demands**

Type of Tax[a]	Type of Income Tax Scaling	
	Additive	Multiplicative
Differentiated-rate VAT	0.011%	0.267%
	($5.4)	($132.6)
Flat-rate VAT (6.242%)	0.477%	0.740%
	($236.9)	($367.7)
Progressive expenditure tax	0.280%	0.564%
	($139.2)	($280.3)

Note: Figures are percentages of the total present value of welfare. Numbers in parentheses are in billions of 1973 dollars.

[a]All taxes raise the same amount of first-period commodity tax revenue from consumers.

we consider the VAT with differentiated rates, the choice of model makes a more significant difference. This is because the Cobb-Douglas formulation implies that consumers have more elastic choices among goods than would be implied by the Stone-Geary formulation. Therefore, the rate differentiation causes more damage under the Cobb-Douglas model. With additive replacement for equal yield, the differentiated VAT generates almost no welfare gain in the Cobb-Douglas case, versus a gain of $142 billion, or 0.28%, of welfare in the Stone-Geary case. With multiplicative replacement, the differentiated VAT does generate modest welfare gains in the Cobb-Douglas case, but these are only about half as great as the gains in the Stone-Geary case.

In table 14.14, we present the distributional results of the simulations presented in table 14.13. Table 14.14 can be compared with table 14.4. Again, the results from the Cobb-Douglas model are very close to those from the Stone-Geary model for the flat VAT and the progressive expenditure tax. In most cases, the welfare effect is slightly less favorable under the Cobb-Douglas model. When we consider the differentiated VAT, however, the differences are somewhat larger for every group, due to the greater elasticity of the Cobb-Douglas form.

Next, we return to the Stone-Geary formulation but incorporate savings elasticities of 0.0 and 1.0. The aggregate welfare effects are shown in tables 14.15 and 14.17, and the effects for the various consumer groups are shown in tables 14.16 and 14.18. As may be expected, the welfare gains are always greater when the responsiveness of savings is greater. For the range of parameter values considered here, the results are moderately sensitive to the savings elasticity. For the flat VAT and the progressive expenditure tax, the welfare gains are in the neighborhood of 15% lower for the zero elasticity than for the elasticity of 0.4, and about 15–20% higher for the elasticity of 1.0 than for the elasticity of 0.4. In the case of the differentiated VAT, the relative differences are somewhat larger, in the vicinity of 25–40%.

Earlier in this paper, we emphasized the point that the method of tax replacement for equal yield is often more important than the tax change experiment itself. This point emerges forcefully once again in tables 14.13, 14.15, and 14.17. In every case we have a substantially greater aggregate improvement in welfare with multiplicative replacement, since this involves relatively larger reductions in the highest personal income tax rates.

The disaggregated results in tables 14.16 and 14.18 are fairly similar to those from table 14.4. Nearly all of the groups do better under these tax policy changes when the elasticity of savings is higher. The difficult equity-efficiency tradeoff that we saw when looking at the VATs in table 14.4 is still very much present in tables 14.16 and 14.18. Once again, even though multiplicative replacement for equal revenue yield leads

Table 14.14   Welfare Effects of Value-added Taxes and Progressive Expenditure Tax, By Consumer Income Class, for Model with Cobb-Douglas Commodity Demands

Household Income (in Thousands of 1973 Dollars)	Differentiated VAT Additive Replacement (%)	Flat VAT Additive Replacement (%)	Progressive Expenditure Tax Additive Replacement (%)[a]	Differentiated VAT Multiplicative Replacement (%)	Flat VAT Multiplicative Replacement (%)	Progressive Expenditure Tax Multiplicative Replacement (%)[a]
0–3	-0.132	-0.405	2.719	-2.076	-2.422	0.573
3–4	-0.186	-0.208	2.179	-1.806	-1.896	0.410
4–5	-0.118	-0.073	1.771	-1.460	-1.472	0.325
5–6	-0.136	-0.006	1.571	-1.317	-1.239	0.307
6–7	-0.282	0.037	1.450	-1.358	-1.089	0.302
7–8	-0.324	0.121	1.213	-1.191	-0.788	0.297
8–10	-0.280	0.214	0.943	-0.891	-0.428	0.309
10–12	-0.336	0.313	0.661	-0.656	-0.025	0.345
12–15	-0.291	0.360	0.513	-0.452	0.188	0.368
15–20	-0.165	0.516	0.119	0.138	0.831	0.475
20–25	0.008	0.624	-0.146	0.653	1.296	0.573
25+	0.894	1.106	-1.241	3.198	3.500	1.195

Note: The figures are percentages of the total present value of welfare.

[a]This tax raises from consumers the same amount of first period commodity tax revenue as the differentiated VAT and the flat 6.242 percent VAT.

Table 14.15   **Efficiency Gains for Value-added Taxes and Progressive Expenditure Tax, for the Model with Stone-Geary Commodity Demands, for Savings Elasticity of Zero.**

Type of tax[a]	Replacement	
	Additive	Multiplicative
Differentiated-rate VAT	0.184%	0.426%
	($91.6)	($211.7)
Flat-rate VAT (6.53%)	0.422%	0.663%
	($209.8)	($329.7)
Progressive expenditure tax	0.230%	0.491%
	($114.3)	($243.9)

Note: Figures are percentages of the total present value of welfare. Numbers in parentheses are in billions of 1973 dollars.

[a] All taxes raise the same amount of first-period commodity tax revenue from consumers.

to higher aggregate welfare gains than does additive replacement, it does so at the expense of even greater inequality. In addition, we see once again that the progressive expenditure tax is distinctly more progressive than are the VATs.

14.9   Summary and Conclusion

In the introduction to this paper, we posed a series of eight questions which this paper addresses. In this final section, we return to these questions. We find that the adoption of a flat, textbook-type VAT leads to modest welfare gains in the aggregate when equal revenue yield is preserved by reductions in personal income tax rates. For our central case simulations, the aggregate welfare gains are approximately one-half of 1% of the total present value of welfare when additive reductions in marginal income tax rates are used. When multiplicative replacement is used to scale back income tax rates the gains are larger, approximately three-fourths of 1% of the total present value of welfare. This illustrates a recurring theme of the paper, that the method of tax replacement can be just as important as the tax policy change itself.

For political and administrative reasons, the VATs adopted in Europe have differentiated rates. We find that rate differentiation leads to substantial reductions (on the order of 25–40%) in the welfare gains from adoption of a VAT. European governments have instituted differentiated rate schedules for their VATs with the thought that differentiated rates may reduce the regressive effects of the VAT. We find that rate differentiation does indeed produce a less regressive distribution of welfare gains and losses than those of a flat VAT. However, for three of the

Table 14.16   Welfare Effects of Value-added Taxes and Progressive Expenditure Tax, by Consumer Income Class, for the Model with Stone-Geary Commodity Demands, for Savings Elasticity of Zero

Household Income (in Thousands of 1973 Dollars)	Differentiated VAT Additive Replacement (%)	Flat VAT Additive Replacement (%)	Progressive Expenditure Tax Additive Replacement (%)[a]	Differentiated VAT Multiplicative Replacement (%)	Flat VAT Multiplicative Replacement (%)	Progressive Expenditure Tax Multiplicative Replacement (%)[a]
0–3	−0.176	−0.537	2.665	−2.279	−2.645	0.468
3–4	−0.198	−0.336	2.126	−1.966	−2.107	0.287
4–5	−0.101	−0.199	1.721	−1.582	−1.684	0.191
5–6	−0.096	−0.130	1.520	−1.416	−1.452	0.164
6–7	−0.226	−0.083	1.403	−1.446	−1.304	0.155
7–8	−0.251	0.006	1.165	−1.256	−1.000	0.147
8–10	−0.189	0.105	0.894	−0.926	−0.633	0.159
10–12	−0.221	0.214	0.611	−0.652	−0.217	0.197
12–15	−0.155	0.272	0.468	−0.419	0.008	0.227
15–20	−0.001	0.446	0.067	0.245	0.691	0.351
20–25	0.199	0.570	−0.205	0.826	1.196	0.468
25+	1.287	1.197	−1.288	3.897	3.810	1.366

Note: The figures are percentages of the total present value of welfare.

[a]This tax raises from consumers the same amount of first-period commodity tax revenue as the differentiated VAT and the flat 6.53% VAT.

Table 14.17   **Efficiency Gains for Value-added Taxes and Progressive Expenditure Tax, for the Model with Stone-Geary Commodity Demands for Savings Elasticity of 1.0**

Type of Tax[a]	Replacement	
	Additive	Multiplicative
Differentiated-rate VAT	0.408%	0.714%
	($202.6)	($354.6)
Flat-rate VAT (6.52%)	0.571%	0.874%
	($283.8)	($434.1)
Progressive expenditure tax	0.351%	0.672%
	($174.3)	($333.9)

Note: Figures are percentages of the total present value of welfare. Numbers in parentheses are in billions of 1973 dollars.
[a]All taxes raise the same amount of first-period commodity tax revenue from consumers.

four VAT simulations, the VAT is still a regressive tax-policy change.[5] In addition, rate differentiation leads to a variety of problems in administration and compliance. These problems are discussed at length in Aaron (1981).

A progressive expenditure tax also leads to aggregate welfare gains that are somewhat lower than those associated with a flat VAT. Comparison of these two tax policies suggests that roughly 60% of the efficiency of a consumption-type flat VAT relative to our current income tax is due to its consumption base. We also note that the progressive expenditure tax yields a much more progressive distribution of gains and losses than those generated by either type of VAT. In fact, with multiplicative replacement, all income groups gain under the progressive expenditure tax.

In section 14.5, we considered integrating the corporate and personal income taxes, and replacing the lost revenue with either a flat VAT, a differentiated VAT, or a progressive expenditure tax. This reform reduces both the distortions of the intersectoral allocation of capital and the distortions of capital accumulation over time. We find that this reform produces fairly substantial welfare gains regardless of the type of replacement for equal revenue yield. These gains, in all cases, take a U-shape. Under the flat and differentiated VAT, all groups gain.

When we remove the revenue neutrality assumption and allow the level of government expenditures and receipts to increase, we find large differences in the efficiency of the various tax policies. For example, the cost to households of funding a 10% increase in transfers and exhaustive government expenditures is 25% less if a flat VAT is used rather than a multiplicative income tax surcharge.

Table 14.18   Welfare Effects of Value-added Taxes and Progressive Expenditure Tax, by Consumer Income Class, For Model with Stone-Geary Commodity Demands, for Savings Elasticity of 1.0

Household Income (in Thousands of 1973 Dollars)	Differentiated VAT Additive Replacement (%)	Flat VAT Additive Replacement (%)	Progressive Expenditure Tax Additive Replacement (%)[a]	Differentiated VAT Multiplicative Replacement (%)	Flat VAT Multiplicative Replacement (%)	Progressive Expenditure Tax Multiplicative Replacement (%)[a]
0–3	0.236	−0.249	2.872	−1.720	−2.283	0.771
3–4	0.209	−0.050	2.314	−1.458	−1.697	0.620
4–5	0.303	0.085	1.905	−1.049	−1.251	0.541
5–6	0.303	0.154	1.694	−0.854	−0.990	0.533
6–7	0.162	0.195	1.567	−0.876	−0.830	0.523
7–8	0.128	0.276	1.324	−0.683	−0.524	0.526
8–10	0.171	0.362	1.045	−0.359	−0.161	0.534
10–12	0.116	0.454	0.755	−0.098	0.243	0.565
12–15	0.146	0.489	0.595	0.107	0.450	0.581
15–20	0.265	0.632	0.194	0.701	1.062	0.657
20–25	0.433	0.730	−0.079	1.213	1.498	0.726
25+	1.137	1.046	−1.256	3.310	3.195	0.921

Note: The figures are percentages of the total present value of welfare.

[a]This tax raises from consumers the same amount of first-period commodity tax revenue as the differentiated VAT and the flat 6.52% VAT.

The attractiveness of the policies we examine ultimately depends on the social welfare function one uses to evaluate the policies. We find that a Benthamite would favor any of the policies summarized in tables 14.3 and 14.4, while a Rawlsian would advocate a differentiated VAT with additive replacement or the progressive expenditure tax with either additive or multiplicative replacement. Within this spectrum, it appears that a flat VAT with additive replacement has a more progressive distribution than the differentiated or flat VAT with multiplicative replacement.

We performed sensitivity analyses with respect to the specification of commodity demands and with respect to the savings elasticity. The Cobb-Douglas formulation is the more elastic of our two formulations. Thus, we find the welfare cost of rate differentiation is higher than when we assume a Stone-Geary formulation. We also find that, for each of the tax substitution policies we consider, increases in the savings elasticity lead to modest increases in the welfare gains.

Notes

1. For a more detailed discussion of these derivations, see Ballard and Shoven (1985).
2. See Goulder, Shoven, and Whalley (1983) for a discussion of the equivalence between origin-based and destination-based taxes.
3. We reject the argument that the corporate tax is simply a form of risk sharing by the government (Gordon 1981), because it does not share proportionately in the capitalization risk. Our position is consistent with the analysis of Bulow and Summers (1984).
4. For an extensive discussion, see McLure (1979). Corporate tax integration has also been simulated using an earlier version of the simulation model used here. See Fullerton et al. (1981).
5. The differentiated VAT with additive replacement has a U-shaped welfare distribution and the smallest aggregate welfare gain.

References

Aaron, Henry J., ed. 1981. *The value-added tax: Lessons from Europe*. Washington, D.C.: Brookings Institution.

Atkinson, Anthony B. 1970. On the measurement of inequality. *Journal of Economic Theory* 2:244–63.

Auerbach, Alan J., and Laurence J. Kotlikoff. 1983. National savings, economic welfare, and the structure of taxation. In Martin Feldstein, ed., *Behavioral Simulation Methods in Tax Policy Analysis*. Chicago: University of Chicago Press.

Ballard, Charles L., Don Fullerton, John B. Shoven, and John Whalley. 1985. *A general equilibrium model for tax policy evaluation.* Chicago: University of Chicago Press.

Ballard, Charles L., and Lawrence H. Goulder. 1982. Expectations in numerical general equilibrium models. Research Paper no. 31, Stanford Workshop, The Microeconomics of Factor Markets, Department of Economics, Stanford University.

Ballard, Charles L., and John B. Shoven. 1985. The value-added tax: The efficiency cost of achieving progressivity by using exemptions. Mimeo (October). Stanford University.

Ballard, Charles L., John B. Shoven, and John Whalley. 1985. General equilibrium computations of the marginal welfare costs of taxes in the United States *American Economic Review* 75, Number 1 (March): 128–38.

Bernheim, B. Douglas, and John B. Shoven. 1985. Pension funding and saving. NBER Working Paper no. 1622 (May).

Bulow, Jeremy I., and Lawrence H. Summers. 1984. The taxation of risky assets. *Journal of Political Economy* 92 (February): 20–39.

Cnossen, Sijbren. 1982. What rate structure for a value-added tax? *National Tax Journal* 35, no. 2 (June): 205–14.

Dresch, Stephen P., An-loh Lin, and David K. Stout. 1977. *Substituting a value-added tax for the corporate income tax: First round analysis.* Cambridge, Mass.: Ballenger.

Fullerton, Don, A. Thomas King, John B. Shoven, and John Whalley. 1981. Corporate tax integration in the United States: A general equilibrium approach. *American Economic Review* 71 (September): 677–91.

Gordon, Roger H. 1981. Taxation of corporate capital income: Tax revenue versus tax distortions. NBER Working Paper no. 687.

Goulder, Lawrence H. 1985. Intergenerational and efficiency effects of tax- and bond-financed changes in government spending. Mimeo, Harvard University (November).

Goulder, Lawrence H., John B. Shoven, and John Whalley. 1983. Domestic tax policy and the foreign sector: The importance of alternative foreign sector formulations to results from a general equilibrium tax analysis model. In Martin Feldstein, ed., *Behavioral Simulation Methods in Tax Policy Analysis.* Chicago: University of Chicago Press.

Kimbell, Larry J., and Glenn W. Harrison. 1984. General equilibrium analysis of regional fiscal incidence. In Herbert E. Scarf and John B. Shoven, eds., *Applied General Equilibrium Analysis.* New York: Cambridge University Press.

Lindholm, Richard. 1976. *Value-added tax and other tax reforms.* Chicago: Nelson-Hall.

McLure, Charles E., Jr. 1979. *Must corporate income be taxed twice?* Washington, D.C.: Brookings Institution.

Scott, Claudia, and Howard Davis. 1985. *The gist of GST: A briefing on the goods and services tax.* Wellington, New Zealand: Victoria University Press for the Institute of Policy Studies.

United States Department of the Treasury. 1984. *Tax reform for fairness, simplicity, and economic growth,* vol. 3: *Value-Added Tax.* Report Submitted to the President (November).

Comment   Harvey Galper

The Ballard-Scholz-Shoven paper is very much what we have come to expect from the general equilibrium (GE) modeling work of John Shoven and his colleagues: a useful and clearly presented application of an impressive GE model containing simulation results of a range of policy options, alternative ways of using whatever revenue is gained from these options (maintaining revenue neutrality in today's jargon), sensitivity of the results to alternative specifications of the model, and along the way useful insights into what one learns from the general equilibrium framework that might not otherwise be apparent. All this and more are in this current paper, an examination of the efficiency and incidence effects of various forms of value-added or consumption taxes.

Since the publication of Ballard et al. (1985), the model is now accessible to everyone in full detail. The only significant change in the version used in this paper is that a Stone-Geary linear expenditure system has replaced the Cobb-Douglas commodity demand specification for households (but even here sensitivity analysis of these alternatives has been performed).

Three kinds of consumption taxes are considered in this paper as partial replacements for the current individual income tax: (1) a European-type value-added tax where substantial variations exist in the rate of tax among commodities; (2) a flat-rate VAT designed to raise the same revenue as in (1) at a rate of 6.52%; and (3) a progressive expenditure tax with marginal rates increasing from 0.3% at the lowest consumption level to 11.6% at the top. The main efficiency findings are not surprising.

First, the efficiency gains of these structural tax changes are not trivial, ranging from 0.3% to 0.8% of the total present value of welfare (itself equal to $49 trillion in this model). Second, the flat rate yields the highest efficiency gain with the differentiated rate VAT and the personal expenditure tax of lesser but about equal efficiency. Third, actually one of the insights from GE modeling, how the revenue from a VAT is used to reduce other taxes is as important as the particular kind of consumption tax that raises the revenue in the first place. A proportionate reduction in all income tax rates (multiplicative change) yields greater efficiency gains than a constant absolute rate reduction (additive change) because the very highest and most distorting marginal tax rates are reduced more.[1]

Harvey Galper is a senior fellow at the Brookings Institution.

1. Differential effects depending upon how the government uses the new revenue (or makes up the lost revenue in the case of tax cuts) were also emphasized in GE simulations performed by Fullerton and Gordon (1983).

Up to this point, the results are not dissimilar to those derived from this model earlier—e.g., chapter 9 of Ballard et al. (1985). The new wrinkle here is that with these current simulations the model is used to address directly the efficiency-equity tradeoff of various forms of consumption taxes. Specifically, the simulations display for each alternative tax regime the change in tax incidence for each of the twelve consumer groups in the model. The authors are correct to focus on the equity issue. From a policy perspective, it is *the* critical issue in the consumption tax debate. And yet I feel that the approach adopted here is something of a disservice to the cause of consumption taxes, despite the fact that my own particular favorite—the progressive expenditure tax—seems to score highest on equity grounds.

I will explore in more detail my reasons for this view, but in any event the model makes clear the direct tradeoff between efficiency and equity. Despite overall efficiency gains, the simulations show that a VAT, in general, makes the lowest-income classes worse off and the higher-income classes better off. Only the progressive expenditure tax reverses this pattern, with one variant actually yielding a Pareto-superior outcome that improves the welfare of all income classes.

Other simulations show the efficiency and equity effects of integrating personal and corporate income taxes and making up the revenue lost from this proposal with either the flat or differentiated VAT or a progressive expenditure tax. These changes generally yield efficiency gains approximating 1% of the present value of welfare. On the equity side, gains are realized for all consumer groups, but the key finding is the U-shaped pattern of welfare gains by income class. This reflects the underlying U-shaped distribution of the capital income-labor income ratio, another indication of the problem introduced by the incidence measures used in this paper.

I will make two comments on this work. First, the particular simulations presented here lead me to want to see one more experiment simulated with this model. This is what might be called the European compromise: raising taxes by means of a more regressive tax such as the VAT in order to support more redistributive social spending. Specifically, the simulation I have in mind is to use the proceeds from the VAT to both (1) compensate by direct transfers the lower-income groups who lose from the VAT and (2) reduce income tax rates multiplicatively across the board. One could then show that the redistributive effects shown in the paper are not inevitable; or, even more pointedly, that a specifically redistributive use of the proceeds must accompany any VAT to counteract the tendency to welfare losses among lower-income groups. But even this experiment does not address a fundamental problem of the incidence calculations, my second and more substantive comment.

As Harberger (1978) noted in discussing an earlier version of this model, all models are partial equilibrium models in the sense that they cannot, in fact should not, fully replicate all elements of the economy. The "partial equilibrium" elements of this model have often been alluded to by the authors here and in other work and include the failure to incorporate firm financing decisions, household portfolio choices, and potentially significant international capital flows. Perhaps most important for the current application, however, and indeed the particular point about which Harberger was most concerned, is whether this model tells us anything useful about issues of income distribution. This question is important because the application presented here is the first use of the GE model that attempts to examine specifically the equity-efficiency tradeoff. All earlier applications concentrated on efficiency gains or revenue considerations, and kept equity concerns deep in the background (Ballard et al. 1985, chaps. 8–11).

But with the incidence of alternative tax regimes brought so much to the fore, it is logical to ask whether the distributional measures used are adequate to the task. My answer to this question must be in the negative. The reason for this assessment is that the paper employs a measure of the distribution of income at a single point in time, the year 1973, as the benchmark for determining how particular consumer groups in the economy will fare over a period of sequenced equilibria extending 100 years into the future. In other words a *one-year snapshot* of the income distribution is the standard for determining long-term tax incidence. According to this model, as the economy expands over time due to productivity growth and capital accumulation (forget pure population growth), each taxpayer group simply expands its labor and capital income along the base-case balanced growth path. Neither the ratio of capital to labor income (with an exception to be noted below), nor consumption relative to income exhibit any life-cycle tendencies for the 12 consumer groups. Each income class observed in 1973 is assumed to be in long-run life-cycle equilibrium.

None of this is, of course, true, nor is it news to the authors. They not only recognize this snapshot problem but, in fact, have informed me that they correct for at least one of the most obvious manifestations of it, namely the negative saving of the lowest-income class. If this class were simply continued forward through time for 100 years, it would soon exhaust its capital assets and not be able to continue consumption. To forestall this result, the authors allocate each period's capital accumulation among income classes, not according to each class's *own* saving, but according to its stock of capital. That is, aggregate capital accumulation is equal to the sum of the saving of each income class, but the *distribution* of this new capital is proportional to the distribution of existing capital. The rationale for this assumption is that there is some movement of individuals among income classes so that the 1973 snapshot cannot really represent a long-term income distribution. Despite this ad hoc assumption to deal with one specific aspect of the snapshot problem, the fundamental issue is not addressed.

Basing incidence on a one-year pretax income distribution misses two separate effects: first, an initial cohort or transition effect emphasized by Auerbach and Kotlikoff (1983); second, the long-term incidence of the new tax rules once these rules have been in effect for the entire lifetime of each taxpayer. Even assuming that the two effects can be separated, and the Auerbach-Kotlikoff work does not provide great grounds for optimism here, this model is clearly in the spirit of long-term incidence rather than short-term adjustments. In general, transition issues have not been the focus of the Shoven-Whalley GE work.

The questions then become: how closely does the 1973 income distribution represent lifetime income distributions and how closely does one-year tax incidence represent lifetime tax incidence? There is much evidence suggesting considerable bias in the incidence results and, perhaps more important, bias that makes consumption-based taxes appear much more regressive than they actually are. For this reason, it is particularly important that in the policy debate we move away from one-year incidence measures to lifetime incidence measures, while still recognizing that initial cohort or transitional effects must be carefully considered in any regime change.

The first piece of evidence on the snapshot problem comes from the data used in this model itself. The U-shaped capital-to-labor income share, as noted, and the low and negative saving of the lowest-income classes reflect a mixture of cohort (that is life-cycle) effects and distributional effects within cohorts. Capital income is a relatively high share at the low end of the income scale because these classes are made up in substantial part of retired people with little labor income who are drawing down capital assets to sustain their consumption and hence have low saving. At the top of the income distribution are, those at the peak of their earning years who have also accumulated many financial assets preparatory to retiring a few years hence. In the middle are younger households just starting to accumulate assets.

A few observations from the March 1985 CPS data on 1984 incomes give similar results a decade later. When households are arrayed by 11 income classes by age of head, the following conclusions emerge: (1) For the three lowest-income classes ($0–$5,000, $5,000–$10,000, $10,000–$15,000), the modal age group is 65 and over (with 34%, 43%, and 31%, respectively, of all households in the class). (2) For the next four income classes ($10–$15,000, $15–$20,000, $20–$25,000, and $25–

Table 14.19

Age of Household	Median Household Income (dollars)
15–24	$14,028
25–34	23,735
35–44	. 29,784
45–54	31,516
55–64	24,094
65 and over	12,799

Source: U.S. Bureau of the Census, Current Population Reports, Series P-60, No. 149, *Money Income and Poverty Status of Families and Persons in the United States: 1984 (Advance Data from the March 1985 Current Population survey),* (Washington, D.C. USGPO, 1985), table 13, p. 19.

$30,000) the 25–34 age head is the modal class. (3) In contrast, for the top income class ($75,000 and over) the modal age group is 45–54, and for the next two highest-income classes ($40–$50,000 and $50–$75,000) the modal age group is 35–44. (4) Furthermore, for ages up to the age group 45–54, median household income increases substantially before declining for the age groups 55–64 and 65 and over (see table 14.19).

A recent article by Davies, St-Hilaire, and Whalley (1984) makes this same point regarding the contrast between cross-section and life-cycle income distributions in Canada, and the resulting effects on the incidence of consumption-based taxes. They find that income is much more evenly distributed on a lifetime basis than on an annual basis, and the distribution of components of income change markedly as well. For example, the distribution of transfers is much more concentrated in lower-income groups in annual data than in lifetime data, comprising over 44% of income for the lowest two deciles for annual data, but never more than 15% of income for any decile for lifetime data. Similarly, consumption of income is much more evenly distributed on a lifetime than on an annual basis. These results imply, therefore, that the incidence of consumption taxes is much less regressive on a lifetime basis.

What is the solution to this problem for the current model? I am not sure I have a good answer here. In my work with Eric Toder on household portfolio choice (1984), we have much the same problem if we wish to examine distributional effects. Observed portfolio holdings reflect both cohort effects and distributional effects within each cohort. For analytical purposes these two effects must be distinguished.

The most conceptually satisfying procedure is a full overlapping generations model, but, even short of such a major restructuring, some changes are needed if equity-efficiency tradeoffs are to be adequately examined. One possible solution may be to separate out age cohorts, perhaps by the 6 age categories used in the CPS table (14.1), for each household income class. Distributional data can then be displayed separately for each cohort.

In the context of the current GE model, this would still require some care in interpreting the simulations. One would certainly *not* want to interpret the results as representing what a household currently headed by a 25-year old would look like in 100 years when the head is 125. Instead, the results may be taken to represent the taxes a household of age 25 head would pay 100 years from now if regime 2 rather than 1 had been in effect over this entire period. Also, with the results for each age cohort displayed separately, one could either use a particular cohort, such as the 35–45 age group, as the basis for making distributional judgments, or else use a social welfare function that weights each age cohort as well as each income class within an age cohort. In any event, by distinguishing across-cohort and within-cohort distribution effects, incidence measures would be more comprehensive and useful than those presented in this paper.

References

Auerbach, Alan J., and Laurence J. Kotlikoff. 1983. National savings, economic welfare, and the structure of taxation. In Martin Feldstein, ed., *Behavioral Simulation Methods in Tax Policy Analysis*. Chicago: University of Chicago Press.

Ballard, Charles L., et al. 1985. *A general equilibrium model for tax policy evaluation*. Chicago: University of Chicago Press.

Davies, James, France St-Hilaire, and John Whalley. 1984. Some calculations of lifetime incidence. *American Economic Review,* September, pp. 633–49.

Fullerton, Don, and Roger H. Gordon. 1983. A reexamination of tax distortions in general equilibrium models. In Martin Feldstein, ed., *Behavioral simulation methods in tax policy analysis,* Chicago: University of Chicago Press.

Galper, Harvey, and Eric Toder. 1984. Transfer elements in the taxation of income from capital. In Marilyn Moon, ed., *Economic transfers in the United States*. Chicago: University of Chicago Press.

Harberger, Arnold C. 1978. Comment, in U.S. Treasury Department, Office of Tax Analysis, *1978 Compendium of Tax Research.*

Contributors

Andrew B. Abel
Department of Economics
Littauer Center 111
Harvard University
Cambridge, MA 02138

Alan J. Auerbach
Department of Economics
University of Pennsylvania
3817 Locust Walk/CR
Philadelphia, PA 19104

Charles L. Ballard
Department of Economics
Michigan State University
East Lansing, MI 48824

J. Gregory Ballentine
Peat, Marwick, Mitchell & Co.
1990 K Street NW
Washington, DC 20006

Michael J. Boskin
National Bureau of Economic
   Research
204 Junipero Serra Boulevard
Stanford, CA 94305

David F. Bradford
Woodrow Wilson School
Princeton University
Princeton, NJ 08544

Angus Deaton
Woodrow Wilson School
Princeton University
Princeton, NJ 08544

Daniel Feenberg
National Bureau of Economic
   Research
1050 Massachusetts Avenue
Cambridge, MA 02138

Martin Feldstein
National Bureau of Economic
   Research
1050 Massachusetts Avenue
Cambridge, MA 02138

Don Fullerton
Department of Economics
114 Rouss Hall
University of Virginia
Charlottesville, VA 22901

William G. Gale
Department of Economics
Stanford University
Stanford, CA 94305

Harvey Galper
Senior Fellow
Brookings Institution
1775 Massachusetts Avenue, NW
Washington, DC 20036

Roger H. Gordon
Department of Economics
University of Michigan
Ann Arbor, MI 48109

David G. Hartman
Data Resources, Inc.
24 Hartwell Avenue
Lexington, MA 02173

Patric H. Hendershott
Department of Finance
Ohio State University
Hagerty Hall
1775 South College Road
Columbus, OH 43210

Yolanda Kodrzycki Henderson
Research Department T–28
Federal Reserve Bank of Boston
600 Atlantic Avenue
Boston, MA 02106

James R. Hines, Jr.
Woodrow Wilson School
Princeton University
Princeton, NJ 08544

Joosung Jun
Department of Economics
Littauer Center
Harvard University
Cambridge, MA 02138

Mervyn A. King
London School of Economics
Lionel Robbins Building, R404
Houghton Street
London WC2A 2AE
ENGLAND

Laurence J. Kotlikoff
Department of Economics
Boston University
Boston, MA 02115

Lawrence B. Lindsey
Department of Economics
Littauer Center 231
Harvard University
Cambridge, MA 02138

Saman Majd
Finance Department
The Wharton School
University of Pennsylvania
2300 Steinberg-Dietrich Hall
Philadelphia, PA 19104

John H. Makin
American Enterprise Institute
1150 Seventeenth Street, NW
Washington, DC 20016

N. Gregory Mankiw
Department of Economics
Littauer Center
Harvard University
Cambridge, MA 02138

Stewart C. Myers
Sloan School of Management, E52–243F
Massachusetts Institute of Technology
50 Memorial Drive
Cambridge, MA 02139

James M. Poterba
Department of Economics
Massachusetts Institute of Technology
50 Memorial Drive
Cambridge, MA 02139

Harvey S. Rosen
Department of Economics
Dickinson Hall
Princeton University
Princeton, NJ 08544

John Karl Scholz
Department of Economics
Stanford University
Stanford, CA 94305

John B. Shoven
Department of Economics
Stanford University
Encina Hall, 4th Floor
Stanford, CA 94305

Joseph E. Stiglitz
Department of Economics
Dickinson Hall
Princeton University
Princeton, NJ 08544

Lawrence H. Summers
Department of Economics
Littauer Center 229
Harvard University
Cambridge, MA 02138

Emil M. Sunley
Deloitte Haskins and Sells
Metropolitan Square, Suite 700
655 15th Street, NW
Washington, DC 20005

Steven F. Venti
Department of Economics
Dartmouth College
Hanover, NH 03755

David A. Wise
John F. Kennedy School of
    Government
Harvard University
79 John F. Kennedy Street
Cambridge, MA 02138

Author Index

Subject Index